Marketing for Hospitality and Tourism

Philip Kotler

John Bowen

James Makens

PRENTICE HALL, Upper Saddle River, NJ 07458

Library of Congress Cataloging-in-Publication Data

Kotler, Philip
  Marketing for hospitality and tourism / Philip Kotler, John Bowen,
James Makens.
    p.   cm.
  Includes bibliographical references and index.
  ISBN 0-13-395625-3 (cloth)
  1. Hospitality industry—Marketing. 2. Tourist trade—Marketing.
I. Bowen, John (John T.).   II. Makens, James C.
III. Title.
TX911.3.M3K68 1996   95-40868
647.94'068'8—dc20   CIP

Executive editor: *Robin Baliszewski*
Managing editor: *Mary Carnis*
Editorial/production supervision, page layout,
  and electronic composition: *Julie Boddorf*
Interior design: *Lorraine Mullaney*
Cover design: *Amy Rosen*
Art production: *Mark LaSalle/North Market Street Graphics*
Director of production and manufacturing: *Bruce Johnson*
Production coordinator: *Ed O'Dougherty*
Supplements editor: *Judith Casillo*
Marketing manager: *Frank Mortimer, Jr.*
Editorial assistant: *Rose Mary Florio*

Cover photography courtesy of Best Western International, Inc.,
Cunard Line, Egyptian Tourist Authority, Hilton Hotels Corporation,
The Jamaica Tourist Board, and United Airlines.

© 1996 by Prentice-Hall, Inc.
A Simon & Schuster Company
Upper Saddle River, NJ 07458

Printed in the United States of America
10 9 8 7 6 5 4 3 2 1

ISBN 0-13-395625-3

PRENTICE-HALL INTERNATIONAL (UK) LIMITED, *London*
PRENTICE-HALL OF AUSTRALIA PTY. LIMITED, *Sydney*
PRENTICE-HALL CANADA INC., *Toronto*
PRENTICE-HALL HISPANOAMERICANA, S.A., *Mexico*
PRENTICE-HALL OF INDIA PRIVATE LIMITED, *New Delhi*
PRENTICE-HALL OF JAPAN, INC., *Tokyo*
SIMON & SCHUSTER ASIA PTE. LTD., *Singapore*
EDITORA PRENTICE-HALL DO BRASIL, LTDA., *Rio de Janeiro*

Chapter opening photo credits
Chapter 1: The Hard Rock Hotel and
Casino, Las Vegas; Chapters 2 and 11:
The Jamaica Tourist Board; Chapters 3
and 15: System One; Chapters 4 and 21:
Hilton Hotels Corporation; Chapter 5:
Juneau Conventions and Visitors Bureau,
John Erben, photographer; Chapter 6:
Marriott International; Chapter 7: The
French Government Tourist Office;
Chapters 8 and 18: Marriott International,
Dan Ham, photographer; Chapter 9:
Carnival Cruise Lines; Chapter 10: The
Old Spaghetti Factory; Chapters 12 and
16: Mirage Resorts, Inc.; Chapter 13:
Royal Caribbean Cruises, Ltd.; Chapter
14: The Bermuda Department of
Tourism; Chapter 17: Cunard Cruise
Lines; Chapter 19: Best Western
International, Inc.; and Chapter 20: The
Greater Milwaukee Convention and
Tourist Bureau.

Contents

21 Next Year's Marketing Plan 659

Preface

Persons employed in hospitality and tourism-related businesses have to be customer oriented; they are part of the product their company is selling. How they answer the phone, greet customers, and solve customers' problems can make the difference between satisfied customers and dissatisfied customers. Marketing calls upon everyone in the company to "think customer" and do all that they can to help create and deliver superior customer value and satisfaction. As Professor Stephen Burnett of Northwestern puts it, "In a truly great marketing organization, you can't tell who's in the marketing department. Everyone in the organization has to make decisions based on the impact on the customer." Everyone has to embrace marketing as a business philosophy.

Marketing for Hospitality and Tourism is a new book. Each chapter was carefully researched and constructed, using sound marketing concepts, and illustrates these concepts with examples from the hospitality and tourism industry. The result is a book that provides a rich depth of practical examples and applications, showing the major decisions that hospitality and travel managers face in their efforts to balance the organization's objectives and resources against varying customer needs and opportunities in the global marketplace.

The book is written with the hospitality and tourism student in mind. The working manuscripts of the book were classroom tested and comments from both students and instructors were incorporated into the book. All of us have extensive experience working with hospitality and tourism businesses around the globe. Our understanding of the hospitality and tourism business ensured that the end result was a book that clearly explains marketing concepts and then shows how they apply to real life situations.

Chapter Opening Cases and Boxed Marketing Highlights

Each chapter opens with a mini-case describing an actual company situation. These cases show the students how the material in the chapter relates to actual business situations. Boxed marketing highlights, short examples, and color illustrations highlighted with high-interest stories, ideas, and marketing strategies make this an interesting book for the reader. In fact, one student wrote, "I enjoyed reading this book—it didn't seem like I was reading a textbook."

Key Terms

Key terms are found at the back of each chapter.

Chapter Review

Each chapter ends with a review of the chapter in outline form. This learning aid was suggested by a student and recommended by reviewers as the preferred way to summarize the chapter.

Review Questions

Each chapter contains a set of questions that covers the chapter's main points and can be used to develop classroom discussions.

Full Color

This is the first hospitality and tourism textbook in a full-color format. It is not done in full color to *create* a lively textbook but rather to *maintain* the lively style of the material. *Marketing for Hospitality and Tourism* tells the stories that reveal the drama of modern marketing: Carnival Cruise Lines' rise to the largest cruise line company in the world; Domino's Pizza's initial positioning strategy against Pizza Hut; the failure of Wendy's breakfast in the 1980s; the success of Hampton Inns' service guarantee; Disney's marketing of positive customer attitudes to its employees; the brilliantly staged publicity stunt of the Mirage Corporation that reached an international audience of hundreds of millions; the building of Ruth Fertel's Ruth's Chris Steak House chain; KKR's repositioning of Motel 6; and Marriott's use of corporate intelligence in building Fairfield Inns. These and hundreds of other examples and illustrations throughout the book reinforce key concepts and bring hospitality and travel marketing to life.

Video Cases

We have found the use of video cases to provide an excellent bridge between marketing theory and reality. The video cases take only a few minutes of class time, but can lead into excellent discussions on the application of marketing concepts. This is just another way *Marketing for Hospitality and Tourism* will increase classroom learning and interest.

Class Outlines

The book contains some chapters and features not found in most hospitality and tourism marketing texts. For example, there is a complete chapter on internal marketing. Hospitality and tourism companies must get their employees enthused about their products if the employees are in turn going to get their customers enthused. This chapter discusses such topics as establishing a service culture, developing a marketing approach to human resource management, communicating with employees, and developing a reward and recognition system. Chapter 12, "Building Customer Satisfaction Through Quality," focuses on how to use relationship marketing to improve customer satisfaction. This chapter includes a discussion of the popular service quality models and applies them to hospitality and tourism marketing. Chapter 14, "Managing Capacity and Demand," discusses techniques for measuring demand, managing demand, and managing capacity. We have also added a full chapter on public relations that shows students how to use this powerful promotional set of tools.

We believe that these additional chapters cover important topics. These additional chapters enable the book to reach a larger market. Thus, we are able to provide you with the flexibility of a 21-chapter text at the same price of a 16-chapter text with a smaller market. And while most instructors welcome these new additions, some instructors may not have time to cover all the information presented in the book. Therefore, in the Instructor's Manual we have developed several course outlines, from a basic course using 16 chapters to an outline which incorporates all 21 chapters. The Instructor's Manual also contains an overview of each chapter with teaching suggestions and chapter objectives. The support material also includes a test bank and color transparencies.

Marketing for Hospitality and Tourism gives the marketing student a comprehensive, innovative, managerial, and practical introduction to marketing. Its style and extensive use of examples and illustrations make the book easy to read and enjoyable.

Acknowledgments

This book is the result of the efforts of many individuals. We owe special thanks to a number of people, including Michael Gallo for his research efforts, Karen Kephart for her editorial work,

Ming (Michael) Liang for suggesting the chapter review format, and Christa Myers for her help in managing the project and writing the Instructor's Manual.

Many thanks also to those who reviewed the manuscript: Jennifer A. Aldrich, Johnson & Wales University, Providence, RI; James A. Bardi, Penn State Berks Campus, Reading, PA; Jonathan Barsky, McLaren School of Business, University of San Francisco; David C. Bojanic, University of Massachusetts; Tim H. Dodd, Texas Tech University, Lubbock, TX; Rich Howey, Northern Arizona University; C. Gus Katsigris, El Centro College, Dallas, TX; Ed Knudson, Linn-Benton Community College, Albany, Oregon; Allen Z. Reich, University of Houston; Howard E. Reichbart, Northern Virginia Community College; and Anna Graf Williams, Johnson & Wales University, Providence, RI.

We appreciate the support and enthusiasm of the companies that provided advertisements and illustrations for the book. These companies and organizations put forth a great deal of effort in finding and providing the materials we requested; working with them was one of the most rewarding parts of the project. The names of these companies are listed on the copyright page for those who provided cover and chapter opening photos and next to the respective photos and advertisements for other illustrations throughout the text.

We would also like to thank Robin Baliszewski, Julie Boddorf, Mary Carnis, and Judy Casillo at Prentice Hall for their help and advice throughout the project.

Finally, we thank our families for all their support and encouragement.

Philip Kotler
John Bowen
James Makens

Introduction: Marketing for Hospitality and Tourism

*M*ichael Leven, one of the world's best hotel marketers, was hired *from Americana Hotels to become the CEO of Days Inn.[1] During his tenure at Days Inn, the number of hotels and hotel rooms more than doubled. One of the keys to Leven's success was introducing a program showing Day's Inn management and employees the importance of having a customer orientation. Under Leven's management, employees were rewarded—never penalized—for taking the initiative to help a customer. According to Leven, "Service falls short when employees are always trying to please their immediate boss. You end up putting layers between yourself and the customer."[2]*

Leven's concern for the customer went back 30 years when he started as a sales rep at the Hotel Roosevelt in New York City. One day, he received a call from a meeting planner wishing to book a banquet for 60 people, requiring ten tables of six. After confirming the arrangements with the meeting planner, he proudly sent the function sheet to the banquet department. To his surprise, the function sheet was returned with a big red mark saying "No Way! We can't do tables of six." The banquet department went on to say that the union required banquet tables to be set for either eight or ten people. Leven then called the client. Years later he stated that the meeting planner's reply was never forgotten. "I don't care what the union con-

tract says, I'm the customer. I'll go somewhere where my needs can be met," said the client before banging the phone down.

Instead of giving up, this future CEO returned to the banquet department and learned that waiters had to be paid a minimum of eight gratuities per table. This knowledge led to a creative solution. Leven phoned the meeting planner, explained the contract restrictions, and got the client to agree to pay for two extra gratuities at each table. The booking was salvaged by finding a way to meet the customer's needs.[3]

We start the chapter by explaining that marketing is a business philosophy. Marketing is not a function that is only carried out by the marketing department. **Marketing is a way of doing business that is focused on the customer**. This customer orientation must permeate the organization.

Next we discuss how **customer satisfaction** leading to profits is the central goal of hospitality marketing. It is wise to assess the customer's long-term value and take appropriate actions to ensure a customer's long-term support.

Finally, we introduce the **marketing mix**: promotion, product, price, and distribution. Marketing also includes research, information systems, and planning. If marketers do a good job of identifying consumer needs, developing a good product, and pricing, distributing, and promoting it effectively, the result will be attractive products and satisfied customers.

As a manager, you will need to become familiar with marketing. Today the customer is king. Satisfying the customer is a priority in most businesses. Managers must realize they cannot satisfy all customers; they have to choose their customers carefully. They must select those customers that will enable the company to meet its objectives. To compete effectively for their chosen customers, companies must create a marketing mix that gives their target markets more value than their competitor's marketing mix.

The cruise industry provides an illustration of the importance of marketing. Imagine for a moment a beautiful new 100,000-ton cruise liner capable of holding 2600 passengers and built at a cost of $300 million. Now picture that same ship sitting forlorn, forgotten, and rusting at some second-rate dock.

Many experts, including *Forbes Magazine*, predicted that dismal factor for cruise lines. Why? Because cruise lines were keeping their old ships while building megaliners that could easily have flooded the market with overcapacity and floating "white elephants." The experts goofed! They hadn't counted on cruise lines developing sophisticated marketing. They hadn't counted on the power of modern marketing. Marketing won and the experts lost.

If you don't believe it, check out these results. Between 1990 and 1993 the cruise line industry added 10,000 new berths each year, while the United States and Canada (world's major cruise markets) endured an economic recession. Instead of sending industry shivers from the bow to the poop deck, cruise lines got busy and added 300,000 to 400,000 new passengers each year while maintaining an 87% average occupancy.[4] Just as marketing was the key to the cruise lines' success during this period, marketing is your key to success.

Today's marketing isn't simply a business function. It's a philosophy, a way of thinking and a way of structuring your business and your mind.

New cruise ships, such as Royal Caribbean's Nordic Empress, *create strong competition for resorts. Photo courtesy of Royal Caribbean Cruises Ltd.*

Marketing is not a new ad campaign or this month's promotion. Marketing is part of everyone's job from the receptionist to the board of directors.[5] The task of marketing is never to fool the customer or endanger the company's image. Marketing's task is to design a product/service combination that provides real value to targeted customers, motivates purchase, and fulfills genuine consumer needs.

Whether you want to be a restaurant manager, executive housekeeper, or any other career choice, marketing will directly affect your personal and professional life. This book will start you on a journey that will cause your customers to embrace you and make marketing your management philosophy.

The purpose of a business is to create and maintain profitable customers.[6] Customers are attracted and retained when their needs are met. Not only do they return to the same cruise line, hotel, rental car firm, and restaurant, but they also talk favorably to others about their satisfaction. Customer satisfaction leading to profit is the central goal of hospitality marketing.

"What about profits?" Hospitality managers sometimes act as if today's profits are primary, and customer satisfaction is secondary. This attitude eventually sinks a firm as it finds fewer repeat customers and faces increasingly negative word of mouth. Successful managers understand that profits are best seen as the result of running a business well, rather than as its sole purpose. When a business satisfies its customers, the customers will pay a fair price for the product. A fair price includes a profit for the firm.

Managers who forever try to maximize short-run profits are short-selling both the customer and the company. Consider the following episode:

> A customer arrived at a restaurant before closing time and was greeted with "What do you want?" Somewhat surprised, the customer replied that he would like to get a bite to eat. A surly voice informed the customer that the restaurant was closed. At this point, the customer pointed to a sign on the door stating that the restaurant was open until nine. "Yeah, but by the time I clean up and put the food away it'll be nine, so we're closed." The customer left and went to another restaurant a block away.

Let's speculate for a moment. Why was the customer treated in such a shabby manner? Perhaps:

- The employee wanted to leave early.
- The employee suffered from a headache.
- The employee had personal or family problems.
- The employee was just following a company policy that said, "no overtime allowed, we close promptly at nine."

Consider these reasons and others. How many are really valid? All of us have aches and pains, family problems, and places to go. So does the customer, and as long as we depend on customers for our livelihood, their needs come first. Midas Muffler Shops spends millions in advertising to let the customer know that if she arrives five minutes before closing she will be treated like the queen she is and her problem will become a Midas problem. Midas didn't accidentally select a woman to play the role of the troubled motorist. Midas understood the genuine fears of that customer segment, the size of that market, and the potential rewards in solving that customer's problems.

What really happened in the restaurant episode is that this employee once served a customer right before closing time, resulting in the employee

CUSTOMER
ORIENTATION

working until ten thirty. Instead of the corporate office thanking her for serving the customer and staying late, it reprimanded her for putting in extra time. The corporate office wanted to keep down overtime expenses. The employee's response was to close the business by nine whatever the cost. Now the corporate office is happy. But they don't realize they are losing customers and hundreds of dollars of future business. Much of the behavior of employees toward their customers is the result of management philosophy.

The alternative management approach is to put the customer first and reward employees for serving the customer well. Roger Dow, Marriott's vice-president of sales and marketing services, states that "we used to reward restaurant managers for things that were important to us, such as food costs. When have you heard a customer ask for the restaurant's food costs? You have to reward for what customers want from your business."[7] Consider the following episode:

> A hotel guest received a notice that the hotel could not honor a reservation made and confirmed the previous day. The hotel could honor the $62 single rate quoted for two nights, but due to an oversight on the third night, the guest would have to be moved to a suite. The rack rate of the suite was $145 a night, but because the hotel made a mistake, the charge for the third night would be reduced to $95. This was the lowest rate the front-office manager could offer, as the general manager gave explicit instructions that no one would stay in a suite for less than $95. The front-desk manager felt the guest had been extended a great favor.

> The guest felt otherwise and was furious. The guest wanted to know why the hotel didn't offer the suite at the $62 rate since it was their mistake. Furthermore, the guest did not want to change rooms in the middle of his stay. The guest felt he should be offered the suite for all three nights at $62!

Let's examine this little drama.

- Why did the customer and the front-desk manager both clearly see the problem, yet arrive at opposite conclusions? Was the customer trying to "rip off" the hotel?
- What would you estimate the marginal cost of a suite might be? Forget allocated fixed costs for that room. What would be the additional variable costs? Now, could the hotel have sold that room for $62 to their special customer? Suppose that you said, yes, it could sell the room for $62. Should the hotel sell all suites to all customers for $62?
- As a manager, what kind of a policy might you design to protect both the hotel and the guest?

It is wise to assess the customer's long-term value and take appropriate actions to ensure a customer's long-term support. Two recent studies document this. The Forum Company found that the cost of retaining a loyal customer is just 20% of the cost of attracting a new one.[8] Another study found that an increase of five percentage points in customer retention rates yielded a profit increase of 25% to 125%. Accordingly, a hotel that can increase its repeat customers from 35% to 40%, should gain at least an additional 25% in profits.[9] Jan Carlzon, president of Scandinavian Airlines, summed up the importance of a satisfied customer:

> Look at our balance sheet. On the asset side, you can still see so-and-so many aircraft worth so-and-so many billions. But it's wrong; we are fooling ourselves. What we should put on the asset side is that last year SAS carried so-and-so many happy passengers. Because that's the only asset we've got—people who are happy with our service and willing to come back and pay for it once again.[10]

Nothing validates Carlzon's point more than driving down Las Vegas Boulevard past McCarran International Airport. One can see rows of mothballed commercial aircraft that have been brought to the desert because lack of moisture helps preserve the aircraft. These aircraft were once worth hundreds of millions of dollars and listed on balance sheets for their full value less depreciation. Today they are worth a fraction of their former balance sheet value. Why? Because the airlines whose planes are sitting on the desert are either bankrupt or were forced to cut back on their schedules because of an insufficient customer base. Precisely the point that Carlzon was making! Without customers our assets have little value. Without customers a new multimillion dollar restaurant will close and without customers a $20 million hotel will go into receivership, with the receivers selling the hotel at a fraction of its book value. Marketing will enable you to create and maintain customers that will increase the value of your business.

WHAT IS HOSPITALITY AND TOURISM MARKETING?

In the hotel industry, marketing and sales are often thought to be the same, and no wonder. The sales department is one of the most visible in the hotel. Sales managers provide prospective clients with tours and entertain them in the hotel's food and beverage outlets. Thus the sales function is highly visible, while most of the nonpromotional areas of the marketing function take place behind closed doors. In the restaurant industry, many people confuse marketing with advertising and sales promotion. It is not uncommon to hear restaurant managers say that they "do not believe in marketing," when they actually mean that they are disappointed with the impact of their advertising. In reality, selling and advertising are only two marketing functions, and often not the most important. Advertising and sales are components of the promotional element of the marketing mix. Other marketing mix elements include product, price, and distribution. Marketing also includes research, information systems, and planning.

If marketers do a good job of identifying consumer needs, developing a good product, and pricing, distributing, and promoting it effectively, the result will be attractive products and satisfied customers. Marriott developed its Courtyard concept, General Mills designed its first Olive Garden, Mrs. Fields introduced her cookies, and they were swamped with customers. They designed differentiated products—ones offering new consumer benefits. Marketing means "hitting the mark." Peter Drucker, a leading management thinker put it this way:

The aim of marketing is to make selling superfluous. The aim is to know and understand customers so well that the product or service fits them and sells itself.[11]

This does not mean that selling and promotion are unimportant, but rather that they are part of a larger *marketing mix,* a set of marketing tools that work together to produce satisfied customers. The only way selling and promoting will be effective is if we first define customer targets and needs and then prepare an easily accessible and available value package.

Here is our definition of marketing:

Marketing is a social and managerial process by which individuals and groups obtain what they need and want through creating and exchanging products and value with others.

This definition will be discussed further in Chapter 2.

MARKETING IN THE HOSPITALITY INDUSTRY

Importance of Marketing

The hospitality industry is one of the world's major industries. In the United States, it is the second largest employer, providing jobs for approximately 10 million people. In more than half the 50 states, it is the largest industry. Total sales for the hospitality industry now exceed $400 billion per year.

Marketing has assumed an increasingly important role in the restaurant sector of the hospitality industry. The industry's bright future has attracted giants from the packaged-foods industries who operate restaurant systems, such as Pizza Hut (Pepsico), Kentucky Fried Chicken (Pepsico), and Olive Garden (General Mills). These companies operate in a highly competitive environment where aggressive marketing skills are needed to win shelf space and supermarket dollars. They have transferred marketing skills to their restaurant properties, increasing the sophistication of marketing.

Companies such as Pizza Hut have brought strong marketing skills to the restaurant industry. Courtesy of Pizza Hut.

The entrance of corporate giants into the hospitality market transformed it from a mom-and-pop industry, where individually owned restaurants and hotels were the norm, into an industry dominated by chains. Twenty-five companies now account for about one-third of all food service sales (see Table 1-1).

Hotels have followed a similar trend, with seven U.S. chains (Holiday Inn, Sheraton, Marriott, Hilton, Hyatt, Ramada, and Quality) reporting more than $1 billion in sales. Analysts predict that the hotel industry will consolidate in much

Table 1-1
Billion Dollar Food Service Companies

COMPANY	1994 SALES IN BILLIONS
McDonald's	25.99
Burger King	7.50
Kentucky Fried Chicken (KFC)	7.10
Pizza Hut	4.80
Taco Bell	4.50
Wendy's	4.20
Hardee's	3.67
ARAMARK	3.20
7-Eleven	2.90
Subway Sandwiches & Salads	2.70
Marriott Management Services	2.66
Domino's Pizza	2.50
Dairy Queen	2.45
Little Caesars	2.00
Red Lobster	1.92
Gardner Merchant Food Services	1.90
Arby's	1.80
Sodexho	1.80
Dunkin' Donuts	1.61
ITT Sheraton	1.57
Denny's	1.55
Holiday Inn Hotels	1.33
Hilton Hotels	1.33
Shoney's	1.32
The Olive Garden	1.25
Marriott Lodging Group	1.20
Canteen Corporation	1.10
Baskin-Robbins	1.10
Jack In the Box	1.05
U.S. Army Center of Excellence, Subsistence	1.03
Caterair International	1.00
Chili's Grill & Bar	1.00

Source: Restaurants and Institutions, July 1, 1995, p. 62.

the same way as the airline industry, with five or six major chains. Such a consolidation will create a market that is highly competitive (see Table 1-2).

In response to growing competitive pressures, hotel chains are relying more on the expertise of the marketing director. The position of food and beverage manager or rooms division manager is no longer the only career path leading to the general manager's position. In many chains, the position of marketing director is emerging as an alternative career path to general manager. Some hotel chains have created a structure in which the marketing director reports to a corporate manager, thus elevating the hotel's chief marketer to the same level as the general manager. Marketing is a philosophy needed by all managers. While the marketing director is a full-time marketer, everyone else must be part-time marketers.

Tourism Marketing

The two main industries that comprise the activities we call tourism are the hospitality and travel industries. Thus, throughout this text we will be referring to the hospitality and travel industries. Successful hospitality marketing

Table 1-2
Largest Hotel Chains

BRAND	NUMBER OF ROOMS	NUMBER OF PROPERTIES
Holiday Inn Worldwide	327,886	1686
Best Western International	268,046	3199
Choice Hotels International	240,668	2695
Days Inn of America	142,810	1413
ITT Sheraton Corporation	128,228	409
Ramada Franchise Systems	105,427	659
Hilton Hotels Corporation	95,844	247
Marriott Hotels, Resorts & Suites	94,005	212
Motel 6 L.P.	86,934	769
SRS Hotels	69,316	329
Super 8 Motels	63,438	1040
Howard Johnson Franchise Systems	60,786	563
Radisson Hotels International	59,015	230
Hyatt Hotels	54,118	103
Hilton International	52,581	162
Forte PLC	50,901	436
Hampton Inns	46,895	407
Inter-Continental Hotels Group	41,671	104
Richfield Hotel Management	41,517	189
Renaissance Hotels & Resorts	41,054	136

Few industries are as interdependent as travel/hospitality. This joint advertisement of the Australia Tourist Commission and Qantas will attract customers for hotels, restaurants, and tourist attractions. Photo courtesy of the Australia Tourist Commission.

is highly dependent on the entire travel industry. For example, many resort or hotel guests purchase travel/hospitality packages assembled by wholesalers offered through travel agents. By agreeing to participate in packages arranged by wholesalers, hotels effectively eliminate competitors. Similarly, hotels and rental car companies have developed cooperative relationships with airlines who offer frequent-flyer plans.

The success of cruise lines is really the result of coordinated marketing by many travel industry members. For example, the Port of Boston wanted to attract more cruise line business. Massport (the port authority) aggressively marketed Boston to cruise lines. Having convinced them to come, they then promoted Boston to key travel agents. This was critical because travel agents account for 95% of all cruise line business.

The result: Boston doubled the number of port calls by cruise lines and added $17.3 million to the local economy through this combined marketing effort.

That's only the beginning of travel industry marketing cooperation to promote cruise lines. Airlines, auto rental firms, and passenger railways cooperatively develop packages with cruise lines. This requires coordination in pricing, promotion and delivery of those packages.

Like Massport, government or quasi government agencies play an important role through legislation aimed at enhancing the industry and through promotion of regions, states, and nations.[12]

Few industries are as interdependent as travel/hospitality. This interdependence will increase in complexity. The travel industry will require marketing professionals who understand the Big Picture and can respond to changing consumer needs through creative strategies based on solid marketing knowledge.

Marketing's Future

As competition becomes more intense, companies will be forced to focus on satisfying their customers. The future will be short for those companies that do not. Robert Keith wrote about marketing's future more than 30 years ago in his classic article, "The Marketing Revolution."

> Soon it will be true that every activity of the corporation—from finance to sales production—is aimed at satisfying the needs and desires of the consumer. When that stage of development is reached, the marketing revolution will be complete.[13]

Today, for many successful firms, the marketing revolution is moving to completion. All departments are becoming involved in satisfying the customer. For example, accounting has to develop bills that the meeting planner can understand, maintenance people should be able to answer a guest's basic questions, such as where the hotel's restaurants are located, and all employees should have a genuine concern about the customer's well being.

Peter Drucker wrote, "It [marketing] encompasses the entire business. It is the whole business seen from the point of view of the final result, that is, from the customer's point of view."[14] This book is not just for students who desire a successful career in marketing; it is for students who desire a successful career. Marketing with its customer orientation has become the job of everyone.

Although marketing is relatively new to the hospitality industry, a common characteristic among many of the great hospitality industry leaders is their successful application of basic marketing principles. These principles include focusing on guests to satisfy their wants (external marketing) and satisfying employees who serve the guests (internal marketing). Here are sketches of four outstanding hospitality industry marketers. These early industry leaders of the past are all white males. But today's hospitality leaders are a diverse group, with representatives from different racial groups, ethnic backgrounds, and both genders. We can learn from these past leaders, but the future is yours.

Ellsworth Statler (1863—1928)

Ellsworth Statler was an innovator whose ideas still play a vital role in today's lodging industry. Statler constantly sought innovations that would make the guest's experience more comfortable and pleasant. In 1908, he opened the Buffalo Statler, the most innovative hotel of its time. It was the first middleclass hotel to have a bath in every room, rather than the large public baths common at that time. His architect tried to dissuade him, arguing that it would be impossible to recapture the investment required to provide this convenience at the rates that Statler planned to charge. Statler then explained that the baths would be constructed back to back, with common plumbing shafts. These plumbing shafts would also carry electrical conduit, and hot water for the heating system.

Statler added other conveniences. The Buffalo Statler was one of the first hotels to have a phone in every room. Statler felt this innovation would be paid for by increased room-service sales, and with many hotel guests eating in their rooms, the hotel restaurant could be made more attractive to local diners.[15]

Internal marketing, or marketing to the employees, was also a part of Statler's marketing efforts. Statler understood that, by taking good care of his employees and fostering a sense of pride in where they worked, his employees would be more sensitive to customer needs. As part of his internal marketing program, he developed an employee publication called the *Statler Salesman*. He also developed a profit-sharing plan for all employees, a radical policy at the time.

Statler's attitude toward his guests is summarized in the Statler Service Code.

Statler Service Code

It is the business of a good hotel to cater to the public. It is the avowed business of the Hotel Statler to please the public better than any other hotel in the world.

Have everyone feel that for his money we want to give him more sincere service than he ever before received at any hotel.

Never be perky, pungent or fresh. The guest pays your salary as well as mine. He is your immediate benefactor.

Hotel service, that is, Hotel Statler service, means the limit of courteous, efficient attention from each particular employee to each particular guest. It is the object of the Hotel Statler to sell its guest the best service in the world.

No employee of this hotel is allowed the privilege of arguing any point with a guest. He must adjust the matter at once to the guest's satisfaction or call his superior to adjust it. Wrangling has no place in Hotel Statler.

In all minor discussions between Statler employees and guests the employee is dead wrong, from the guest's point of view and from ours.

Any Statler employee who is wise and discrete enough to merit tips is wise and discrete enough to render like service whether he is tipped or not.

Any Statler employee who fails to give service or who fails to thank the guest who gives him something falls short of Statler standards.[16]

Ralph Hitz (1891–1940)

Ralph Hitz headed the largest hotel organization in the United States during the 1930s, called the National Hotel Company. His company was paid to manage hotels owned by real estate investors. Hitz had great personal involvement in each of his hotels until his death in 1940.

Hitz came to the United States from Vienna in 1906. Three days after his family arrived in New York, he ran away from home. During the next 9 years he supported himself by taking assorted jobs in the hospitality industry. In 1915 he married, putting an end to his transient life-style. After holding a number of secondary management positions, he became manager of the Gibson Hotel in Cincinnati in 1927. Here he more than tripled the hotel's profits over the next 2 years. In 1929, Hitz became manager of the 2,500-room New Yorker, a position that moved him into national prominence.

Hitz was a marketing genius, creating innovations that today are industry standards. He was first to develop a customer database. This guest history file was used to order hometown newspapers for guests. Imagine the feeling of guests when their hometown newspapers were delivered to their rooms.

Hitz also developed a history file of 3000 active conventions. From these data, weekly bulletins on convention prospects were sent to each of his hotels. Hitz staffed three national sales offices and had two national salespeople. In the cities in which he had hotels, he networked with the local chapters of the major trade associations and helped them lobby to have regional or national conventions in their hometown, also the location of Hitz's hotel.

Hitz was a master at merchandising hotel services. He used an in-house radio system much the same way today's hotels use in-house television channels to advertise their products. He scheduled radio promotions in the mornings, afternoons, and evenings describing the hotel's breakfast, lunch, and evening entertainment offerings. He created the position of "Tony" in the dining rooms. The Tony's job was created to merchandise cafe diablo and crepes suzettes. By standardizing the production process and dedicating one person to the task, he was able to sell these two items for 50 cents, making them affordable to the average guest. Guests perceived these treats as a real value, while Hitz made a handsome profit through volume sales. This exemplified his philosophy—give the customer value and you will get volume sales in return.

Hitz, like Statler, recognized the critical importance of having satisfied employees. He paid more than competitive wages. He sent gifts to all employees on the birth of their children and developed extensive training programs for his staff. Hitz developed a special club for employees with 5 or more years of service. Members of the 5-year club had an automatic appeal to the general manager before they could be fired.[17]

J. Willard Marriott (1900–1985)

J. Willard Marriott also recognized the importance of his employees and treated them like family members. He visited them when they were sick, helped them when they were in trouble, and listened to them when they wanted to talk. Marriott spent much of his personal time letting his employees know that he cared about them. He often visited restaurants and shook hands with all the employees. He knew the importance of the employee/customer relationship and tried to make sure his employees felt comfortable in their jobs. J. W. Marriott, Jr., current president of Marriott, recalls that, at one time, his father employed a person whose sole responsibility was to make sure that the restaurant employees enjoyed their work and were fairly treated.[18] It has been said that J. Willard Marriott treated line employees better than management.

Marriott valued good locations. He often located his restaurants adjacent to bridges, citing his belief that they might reroute highways, but they would not remove bridges. Marriott was also expert at analyzing the environment and picking up trends. He recognized the importance of the automobile in the 1920s and geared his first restaurant toward automobile traffic. In the late 1930s, he had the foresight to see the airplane as the future commercial transportation mode and was one of the first to enter the airline catering business.

Marriott was an innovative marketer. His Hot Shoppes had the famous curb-cut, which allowed cars to come onto the lot. He used the first drive-in trays. He ran gala grand openings for his Hot Shoppes that included bands and entertainment and had his employees promote the restaurant by handing out coupons to cars stopped at traffic lights.

Today the Marriott corporation has sales of more than $7.5 billion annually, operating a broad range of food and lodging facilities. Its lodging chains include Marriott Hotels and Resorts, Marriott Suites, Residence Inns, Courtyard Hotels, and Fairfield Inns. Its food service operations emphasize contract feeding, such as dining rooms in office buildings, employee cafeterias, and college and school feeding.

Ray Kroc (1902–1984)

Ray Kroc is considered the father of the fast-food industry. He started franchising McDonald's in 1955 to create a demand for the multimixer. Kroc was the exclusive distributor of this machine, which could mix up to five milkshakes at once. His largest single user was a hamburger restaurant in

California called McDonald's.[19] Kroc made a deal with the McDonald brothers to expand this restaurant concept, which would create a larger demand for his mixers. The success of the restaurants soon changed his focus from mixers to hamburgers.

Kroc had great marketing skills. He managed to develop a restaurant concept that appealed to younger families—quick service, clean surroundings, and inexpensive food. He offered value by keeping the menu simple and developing an excellent service delivery system. His formula, QSC&V (Quality, Service, Cleanliness, and Value), was the key to his restaurants' success. He maintained consistency throughout the chain by insisting that all the franchisees adhere to strict product specifications, keep the stores clean, and provide good value through his pricing structure. To maintain a family atmosphere and discourage teen-agers from hanging out, he would not allow telephones or juke boxes in the restaurants.

Kroc was one of the first restauranteurs to understand the value of public relations and include it in McDonald's strategic plans. He hired the public relations firm of Cooper, Burns, and Golin in 1957, knowing that a favorable article in the paper was much more valuable than an advertisement. McDonald's quickly gained national publicity through media such as *Time* and Associated Press. Cooper, Burns, and Golin also developed kits for the franchisees to use in their local markets. These kits explained how to support the community through involvement in local charities and events and how to get media coverage from such activities.[20] Some chains are just now starting to emulate the form of local store marketing that McDonald's began using more than 30 years ago.

Ronald McDonald House is one of McDonald's national charities. A study[21] found that customers had a preference for McDonald's because of their perceived community involvement through Ronald McDonald House. Kroc realized that image is not only important for a company's customers, but that it has an impact on stockholders, franchisees, prospective employees, and communities in which the company locates its stores.

Through Kroc's leadership McDonald's became the largest restaurant company in the world, as measured by gross sales. Today it is an international organization with more than 14,000 stores. More than 2000 people apply for a McDonald's franchise every year.

None of these hospitality industry leaders took a formal marketing course before entering business, as marketing was not taught in most colleges until the 1960s. Yet the concepts that have been formalized into the discipline of marketing were the keys to the success of these past leaders.

Chapter Review

I.   Introduction: Marketing in the Hospitality Industry

Customer orientation: The purpose of a business is to create and maintain profitable customers. Customer satisfaction leading to profit is the central goal of hospitality marketing.

II.   What Is Hospitality Marketing? Marketing is a social and managerial process by which individuals and groups obtain what they need and want through creating and exchanging products and value with others.

III.   Importance of Marketing

1) The entrance of corporate giants into the hospitality market and the marketing skills these companies have brought to the industry have increased the importance of marketing within the industry.

2) Analysts predict that the hotel industry will consolidate in much same way as the airline industry has, with five or six major chains dominating the market. Such consolidation will create a market that is highly competitive. The firms that survive this consolidation will be the ones that understand their customers.

3) In response to growing competitive pressures, hotel chains are relying on the expertise of the marketing director.

IV.   Travel Industry Marketing

1) Successful hospitality marketing is highly dependent on the entire travel industry.

2) Government or quasi government agencies play an important role in travel industry marketing through legislation aimed at enhancing the industry and through promotion of regions, states, and nations.

3) Few industries are as interdependent as the travel and hospitality industries.

V.   Great Leaders in the Hospitality Industry

1) Although marketing is a relatively new discipline, marketing principles were practiced by the great corporate leaders of the past.

2) The marketing oriented hospitality leaders of the past include Statler, Hitz, Marriott, and Kroc.

DISCUSSION QUESTIONS

1. Many managers view the purpose of business as making a profit, while some view the purpose as being to create and maintain a customer. Explain how these alternative viewpoints could affect a company's interactions with its customers. If a manager views the purpose as being to create and maintain a customer, does this mean the that manager is not concerned with profits?

2. A guest in your hotel complains that the air conditioning in his room did not work and because of this he did not get a good night's sleep. What would you do?

3. Find and describe how an international firm has affected the hospitality industry in your area.

4. Describe a situation when you purchased a restaurant meal or stayed in a hotel that was not customer oriented.

5. Give a specific example of two firms in different areas of the travel and tourism industry joining forces to create a competitive advantage.

6. Give an example of one of today's hospitality leaders that is marketing oriented. Provide examples of their customer orientation to support your choice.

KEY TERMS

Create and maintain a customer The purpose of a business.

Hospitality industry The hospitality industry is made up of those businesses that do one or more of the following: provide accommodation for the traveler, prepared food and beverage service, and entertainment for the traveler.

Internal marketing Marketing directed toward the employees within the organization.

Marketing Marketing is a social and managerial process by which individuals and groups obtain what they need and want through creating and exchanging products and value with others.

Marketing mix The marketing mix elements include product, price, promotion, and distribution. Sometimes distribution is called place and the marketing mix is referred to as the 4 P's.

QSC&V Quality, Service, Cleanliness, and Value. Kroc insisted that all McDonald's possess these attributes.

Travel and tourism The travel industry is made up of industries that provide or facilitate temporary transportation for business or pleasure.

REFERENCES

1. ANTHONY E. HEFFERNAN, "Franchises Are the Customers at Days Inn," *Franchising World* (January/February 1988), p. 52–54.

2. *"Lodging Hospitality, Our People–Our Strength,"* Advertising Supplement II, *Lodging Hospitality*, 22, no. 1 (1988), pp. 12–13.

3. MICHAEL LEVEN, "What Does the H in Hospitality Mean?" in *The Practice of Hospitality Management II*, ROBERT C. LEWIS ET AL., EDS. (Westport, Conn.: AVI, 1986).

4. "The New Wave: The Ships of 1993," *Tour-and-Travel News* (March 29, 1993), p. 56.

5. REGIS MCKENNA, *Relationship Marketing* (Reading, Mass.: Addison-Wesley Publishing Co.)

6. THEODORE LEVITT, *Marketing Imagination* (New York: Free Press, 1986).

7. CHRISTIAN GRONROOS, *Service Management and Marketing* (Lexington, Mass.: Lexington Books, 1990).

8. PATRICIA SELLERS, "Getting Customers to Love You," *Fortune* (March 13, 1989), pp. 38–49.

9. JAMES L. HESKETT, JR., W. EARLE SASSER, AND W. L. HART CHRISTOPHER, *Service Breakthroughs* (New York: Free Press, 1990).

10. KARL ALBRECHT, *At America's Service* (Homewood, IL: Dow Jones–Irwin 1988), p. 23.

11. PETER F. DRUCKER, *Management: Tasks, Responsibility, Practices* (New York: Harper & Row, 1973), pp. 64–65.

12. "Cruise Forum," *Travel Agent* (May 2, 1994), sec. B, p. 2.

13. ROBERT J. KEITH, "The Marketing Revolution," *Journal of Marketing*, 20 (January 1960), pp. 35–38.

14. *Business Week*, (June 24, 1950), pp. 30–36.

15. FLOYD MILLER, *Statler America's Extraordinary Hotelman* (New York: The Statler Foundation, 1968).

16. IBID, p. 140.

17. *Fortune* (1937), "Hitz Hotels," 15, no. 5 (May), pp. 139–154.

18. WILLARD J. MARRIOTT, JR., Interview at Marriott Headquarters with Karl Conrad and Bill Heaton of the Conrad N. Hilton College, on April 8, 1986.

19. CHARLES MORITZ, *Current Biography Yearbook* (New York: H.W. Wilson Company, 1972).

20. JOHN F. LOVE, *McDonald's, Behind The Golden Arches* (New York: Bantam Books, 1986).

21. JOHN T. BOWEN, "Advertising to Children: Restaurants Should Proceed with Caution," *Consultant*, 18, no. 1 (1985), pp. 45–46.

22. LISA BERTAGNOLI, "McDonald's Company of the Quarter Century," *Restaurants and Institutions*, 98, no. 18 (1989), pp. 32–44+.

Social Foundations of Marketing: Meeting Human Needs

*A*s the guest's taxi pulled away, Roy Dyment, a doorman at Toronto's Four Seasons, noticed the guest's briefcase still sitting near the entrance to the hotel. Dyment phoned the guest at Washington, D.C., to let him know that he had found the briefcase. He learned that the briefcase contained key documents for an important meeting in the morning. Dyment knew one sure way of getting the briefcase to Washington before the morning meeting—take it himself. He caught a plane and delivered the briefcase. His first concern was taking care of the guest. He didn't worry about getting his boss's approval. Upon his return, instead of getting remanded or terminated, he was made employee of the year.[1]

Four Season's is one of the world's great hotel chains that practices the marketing concept. Isadore Sharp, CEO of Four Seasons, states that the company's top priority is a satisfied guest. Concern for the customer starts with top management and flows through the operation. The Four Season's corporate culture encourages employees to go that extra mile and respond with concern and dedication to customer needs. Employees are never penalized for trying to serve the customer. [2]

According to a study by Peat Marwick Mclintock, Four Seasons is an oddity, because most hotel firms place profitability or growth as their number one goal. This, in part, explains why this small hotel company has won

an international reputation for customer service. Four Season's exemplary customer service is highlighted in such books such as In Search of Excellence, The Service Edge, Service Breakthroughs, *and* Total Customer Service. *Four Seasons has also shown that putting the customer first leads to profits with above-average financial performance and profit percentages that many hotel chains only dream about.*

Chapter 2 introduces the fundamental concepts of marketing.

First, we explain our definition of marketing. This is accomplished by explaining the **core concepts of marketing.** These concepts are needs, wants, and demands; products; value and satisfaction; exchange, transactions, and relationships; and market.

Next we discuss five alternative **marketing management philosophies**— the production, product, selling, marketing, and societal marketing concepts—which influence the way competitors approach their customers.

In Chapter 1, we defined marketing as follows:

> Marketing is a social and managerial process by which individuals and groups obtain what they need and want through creating and exchanging products and value with others.

To explain this definition, we will look at the following terms: needs, wants, demands; products; exchange, transactions, and relationships; and markets (see Figure 2-1).

MARKETING

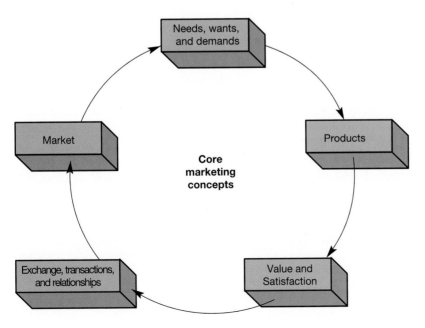

Figure 2-1
Core marketing concepts.

Needs, Wants, and Demands

Needs. The most basic concept underlying marketing is that of human needs. A **human need** is a state of felt deprivation.

Human beings have many complex needs. These include basic physical needs for food, clothing, warmth, and safety; social needs for belonging, affection, fun, and relaxation; esteem needs for prestige, recognition, and fame; and individual needs for knowledge and self-expression. These needs are not created by Madison Avenue, but are part of the human makeup.

When a need is not satisfied, a void exists. An unsatisfied person will do one of two things—look for an object that will satisfy the need or try to reduce the need. People in industrial societies try to find or develop objects that will satisfy their desires. People in poor societies try to reduce desires to what is available.

Some restaurants have built a business aimed at satisfying the esteem needs for prestige and recognition. Tony's is one of the finer and more expensive restaurants in Houston. Dining at Tony's, particularly on a regular basis, is a sign that one is financially successful. Some patrons ask to be seated at a center table where others will be sure to notice them and they can satisfy their need for recognition.

Other restaurants such as Bennigan's have built a business by satisfying social needs: the need to be with other people and the need to have fun and relax.[3] The restaurant chain creates a casual, relaxed atmosphere, and the open bar area encourages customers to use the restaurant as a neighborhood gathering place.

Wants. The second basic concept to marketing is that of **human wants**—the form taken by human needs as they are shaped by culture and individual personality. Wants are how people communicate their needs. A hungry aboriginal wants witchetty grubs, lizard eggs, and bush onions. A hungry person in the United States may want a hamburger, French fries, and a Coke. Wants are described in terms of objects that will satisfy needs. As a society evolves, the wants of its members expand. As people are exposed to more objects that arouse their interest and desire, producers try to provide more want-satisfying products and services. Restaurants were once able to serve generic white wine by the glass. Today customers are more sophisticated; restaurants now serve chardonnay, sauvignon blanc, and riesling by the glass. Today's restaurant customers appreciate and expect good wine.

Many sellers often confuse wants with needs. A manufacturer of drill bits may think that customers need a drill bit, but what the customer really needs is a hole. These sellers suffer from "marketing myopia."[4] They are so taken with their products that they focus only on existing wants and lose sight of underlying customer needs. They forget that a physical product is only a tool to solve a consumer problem. These sellers get into trouble if a new product comes along that serves the need better or cheaper. The customer will then have the same need but want a new product.

Demands. People have almost unlimited wants, but limited resources. They chose products that produce the most satisfaction for their money. When backed by buying power, wants become **demand.**

Listing demands in a society at a given time is easy. In a single year, 230 million Americans might purchase 45 billion meals, 675 million hotel rooms, and over 1133 billion domestic passenger airline miles. These and other hospitality and travel products make up just part of the economy.

Consumers view products as **bundles of benefits** and choose those that give them the best bundle for their money. Thus Motel 6 means basic accommodations, a low price, and convenience. The Four Seasons means comfort, luxury, and status. People choose the product whose benefits add up to the most satisfaction, given their wants and resources.

Products

Human needs, wants, and demands suggest that products are available to satisfy them. A **product** is anything that can be offered to a market for attention, acquisition, use, or consumption and that might satisfy a need or want.

Suppose that an executive feels the need to reduce the stress of the job in a highly competitive industry. We will call all the products that can satisfy this need the *product choice set*. They may include a concert, dining at a restaurant, a four-day Caribbean vacation, and exercise classes. These products are not all equally desirable. The more available and less expensive products, such as a concert and dining at a restaurant, are likely to be purchased first and more often. The closer the product matches the consumer's want, the more successful the producer will be. Thus producers must know what consumers want and provide products that come as close as possible to satisfying those wants.

The concept of product is not limited to physical objects. Anything capable of satisfying a need can be called a product. In addition to physical products and service products, this includes *persons, places, organizations, activities, and ideas*. A consumer decides which restaurants to go to, places to vacation, airlines to fly, organizations to contribute to, and ideas to support. To the consumer, these are all products. If at times the term *product* does not seem to fit, we could substitute such terms as *satisfier, resource,* or *offer*. All describe something of value to someone.

Value, Cost, and Satisfaction

Jane Burr wants to go from New York to Washington, D.C. She could take an airplane, bus, or train or rent a car. These alternatives constitute the traveler's *product choice set*. Assume that the traveler has the following needs: safety, economy, speed and relaxation. We call these her *need set*. Now each product has the ability to satisfy her need set. The airplane will offer the fastest travel, while the bus will offer the cheapest travel. The car may provide the most relaxing travel for Jane. Somehow Jane Burr needs to decide which product delivers the most satisfaction.

The guiding concept is value. Jane Burr will form an estimate of the value of each product in satisfying her needs. She might rank the products from the most need satisfying to the least need satisfying. **Value** is the consumer's estimate of the product's overall capacity to satisfy his or her needs.

We can ask Jane to imagine the characteristics of an ideal product. She might state that the ideal product would get her to Washington on the ground, slowing down on scenic sections of the route and speeding through the rest of the route. It would be completely safe and cost nothing.

Then the value of each actual product would depend on how close it came to this ideal product. Value is the consumer's estimate of the overall capacity to satisfy his or her needs.

Suppose that Jane's primary concern is speed. The airplane would get her there faster than any of the other methods; however, it will cost more than the other methods of transportation. Since the product involves a **cost**, she will not necessarily take the plane. The airplane costs substantially more than the bus. Costs not only involve money, but everything one gives up to gain the product. A business person may associate a dollar value to the time given up in a transaction or as the result of purchasing a product. Thus a business person will pay more for hospitality and travel products that save time. Jane will have to consider the product's value and costs before making a choice. She will choose the product that will produce the most benefit for the dollar—the greatest **value**.

Satisfaction with a product is determined by how well the product meets the customer's expectations for that product. If Jane's expectations are met, the product will be satisfactory. If her expectations about the product are not met, the product will be judged as unsatisfactory.[5] For example, if she chooses a plane because she wants to save time and the plane is delayed for four hours due to maintenance problems, she will not be satisfied with the experience.

Today's consumer behaviorists have gone beyond narrow economic assumptions of how consumers form value in their minds and make product choices. We will look at the modern theories of consumer-choice behavior in Chapter 7. These theories are important to marketers because the whole marketing plan rests on assumptions about how consumers make choices. Therefore, concepts of value, cost, and satisfaction are crucial to the discipline of marketing.

Exchange, Transactions, and Relationships

Exchange marketing occurs when people decide to satisfy needs and wants through exchange. **Exchange** is the act of obtaining a desired object from someone by offering something in return. Exchange is only one of several ways people can obtain a desired object. For example, hungry people can find food by hunting, fishing, or gathering fruit. They could beg for food or take it from someone else. Or they can resort to exchange. They could offer money, another good, or a service in return for food.

As a means of satisfying needs, exchange has much in its favor. People do not have to prey on others or depend on charity. Nor do they need the skills to produce every necessity for themselves. They can concentrate on making the things that they are good at making and trade them for needed items made by others. Through a division of labor and specification, the people in a society produce much more than with any alternative system.

Exchange is the core concept of marketing.[6] For an exchange to take place, several conditions must be satisfied. There must be at least two parties, and each must have something valued by the other. Each party must want to deal with the other. Each must be free to accept or reject the other's offer. Finally, each party must be able to communicate and deliver.

These conditions make exchange possible. Whether exchange actually takes place depends on the parties' coming to an agreement. If they agree, we conclude that the act of exchange leaves them all better off (or at least not worse off) because each was free to reject or accept the offer. In this sense, just as production creates value, exchange creates value. It gives people more consumption possibilities.

Transaction. A transaction is marketing's unit of measurement. A transaction consists of a trade of values between two parties. We must be able to say A gives X to B and gets Y in return at a certain time and place and with certain understood conditions. IBM gives $200 to Hilton and obtains the use of a meeting room. This is a classic monetary transaction. Not all transactions involve money. In a barter transaction, The Anchorage Restaurant might provide free meals to WBUC radio station in return for free advertising on that station. A transaction involves at least two things of value, conditions that are agreed to, a time of agreement, and a place of agreement.

In the broadest sense, the marketer tries to bring about a response to some offer. And the response may be more than buying or trading goods and services in the narrow sense. A political candidate wants a response called "votes." A church wants "joining," a social action group wants "adopting the idea." Marketing consists of actions taken to obtain a desired response from a target audience toward some product, service, idea, or other object.

Transaction marketing is part of the larger idea of **relationship marketing**. Smart marketers work at building relationships with valued customers, distributors, dealers, and suppliers. They build strong economic relationships with social ties by promising and consistently delivering high-quality products, good service, and fair prices. Increasingly, marketing is shifting from trying to maximize the profit on each individual transaction to maximizing mutually beneficial relationships with consumers and other parties. The operating assumption is the following: *Build good relationships and profitable transactions will follow.*

Relationship marketing is most appropriate with customers who can most affect the company's future. For many companies, a small proportion of customers account for a large share of the company's sales. Salespeople working with these key customers must do more than just call when they think a customer might be ready to place an order. They should monitor each key account, know its problems, and be ready to serve in a number of ways. They should call or visit frequently, make useful suggestions about how to improve the customer's business, take the customer out for a meal or entertainment event, and take an interest in the customer as a person.

The importance of relationship marketing will no doubt increase in the future. Most companies are finding that they earn a higher return from resources invested in getting repeat sales from current customers than from money spent to attract new customers. They realize the benefits gained from cross-selling opportunities with current customers. More companies are forming strategic partnerships, making skilled relationship marketing essential. And for customers who buy large, complex products—such as facilities for conventions and large meetings—the sale is only the beginning of the relationship. Thus, although it is not appropriate in all situations, relationship marketing continues to grow in importance.

Relationship marketing within the hospitality industry is particularly important in the following areas:

- Between retailers of travel/hospitality services such as hotels or airlines and marketing intermediaries, such as tour wholesalers, incentive houses, and travel agency conglomerates.
- Between retailers of travel/hospitality services and key customers such as large corporations and government agencies.
- Between retailers of food service such as ARA or McDonald's and organizations such as universities, bus terminals, and large corporations in which this food chain is one of a handful of providers.
- Between retailers of one type of travel/hospitality service such as a motel chain and a restaurant chain. Both are mutually interdependent. The Iron Skillet Restaurant chain is dependent on selected truck stops.
- Between retailers of travel/hospitality services and key suppliers.
- Between hospitality organizations and their employees.
- Between hospitality organizations and their marketing agencies, banks, and law firms.

Marketing

The concept of transactions leads to the concept of a market. A **market** is a set of actual and potential buyers who might transact with a seller. The size of a market depends on the number of persons who exhibit a common need, have the money or other resources that interest others, and are willing to offer these resources in exchange for what they want.

Originally, the term market stood for a physical location where buyers and sellers gathered to exchange goods, such as a village square. In third-world countries, this definition still applies. Sellers constitute the industry and buyers constitute the market. Sellers and buyers are connected by four flows. Sellers provide **products** for the market and also supply the market with **information** about these products. In return the market provides sellers with **money** and **information**. The fact is that modern economies operate on the principle of the division of labor by which each person specializes in the production of something, receives payment, and buys needed things with money. Thus modern economies abound in markets.

Markets

The concept of markets finally brings us full circle to the concept of marketing. **Marketing** means working with markets to bring about exchanges for satisfying human needs and wants. Thus we return to our definition of marketing as human activity directed at satisfying needs and wants through exchange processes.

Exchange processes involve work. Sellers have to search for buyers, identify their needs, design attractive products, promote them, deliver them, and set prices. Such activities as product development, research, communication, distribution, pricing, and service are core marketing activities.

Although we normally think of marketing as being carried on by sellers, buyers also carry on marketing activities. Consumers do marketing when they search for the goods that they need at prices they can afford. Meeting planners do marketing when they track down hotel sales managers and bargain for good terms. A seller's market is one in which sellers have more power and buyers have to be the more active marketers. In a buyer's market, buyers have more power and sellers have to be more active marketers.

During the early 1950s, the supply of goods began to grow faster than the demand. Marketing became identified with sellers trying to find buyers. This book primarily examines the marketing problems of sellers in a buyers market.

Those who engage in exchange activities learn over time how to do it better. We define marketing management as follows:

MARKETING MANAGEMENT

Marketing management is the analysis, planning, implementation, and control of programs designed to create, build, and maintain beneficial exchanges with target buyers for the purpose of achieving organizational objectives.

Most people think of a marketing manager as someone who finds enough customers to buy the company's current output. But this is too limited a view. The marketing manager is interested in shaping the level, time, and composition of demand for the company's products and services. At any time, there may be no demand, adequate demand, irregular demand, or too much demand. For example, a hotel with a 75% occupancy rate would be considered to be doing reasonably well. However, the 75% occupancy may be achieved by running in the nineties during mid-week and in the thirties on weekends. Many restaurants are empty at 11:30 A.M., have a waiting line at 12:30 P.M., and are empty again at 2:00 P.M. In the hospitality industry, there are incredible peaks and valleys. This is why we have devoted a chapter later in the book to managing capacity and demand.

Thus marketing managers are concerned not only with finding and increasing demand, but also at times with changing or even reducing it.[7] Simply put, marketing management is *demand management*. By marketing managers, we mean company people who are involved in marketing analysis, planning, implementation, or control activities. They include general managers, sales managers and salespeople, advertising executives, sales promotion people, marketing researchers, public relations people, and consultants. We will say more about these marketing jobs in succeeding chapters.

MARKETING MANAGEMENT PHILOSOPHIES

We have described marketing management as carrying out tasks to achieve desired exchanges with target markets. What philosophy should guide these marketing efforts? What weight should be given to the varying and sometimes competing interests of the organization, customers, and society? Clearly, marketing activities should be carried out under some philosophy.

There are five competing concepts under which organizations conduct their marketing activity: the production, product, selling, marketing, and societal marketing concepts.

Production Concept

The production concept is one of the oldest philosophies guiding sellers. The production concept holds that consumers will favor products that are available and highly affordable, and therefore management should focus on production and distribution efficiency. The problem with the production concept is that management may become so focused on production systems that they forget the customer.

> A tourist was staying at a hotel in the Swiss Alps with a beautiful view of Lake Geneva. The dining room had an outdoor balcony that allowed one to fully experience the beauty of the surroundings. Enjoying breakfast on the balcony was a perfect way to start a summer day. To the guest, the balcony was a great benefit; to the hotel, it was a nuisance. The balcony was at the edge of the dining room and thus the farthest spot from the kitchen. There were no service stations near the balcony, so all supplies had to come from the dining room. There was only one entrance to the balcony, making access difficult. Simply put, serving customers on the balcony was not efficient.
>
> The hotel discouraged customers from eating on the balcony by not setting up the tables. If one asked to eat on the balcony, they received a pained expression from the service person. Then they had to wait for 15 minutes for the table to be set. Once the food was served, the service person disappeared, never to be seen again. This was their way of reminding the guest that one should not eat on the balcony. Yet, the hotel should have viewed the balcony as providing a competitive advantage. This point of difference creates customers and positive comments from those customers.

Every reader has surely experienced a common production-oriented restaurant after normal dining hours. The restaurant may be one-third filled, yet all customers are forced to cluster in one section of the restaurant, thus creating unnecessary density and customer dissatisfaction. This is usually done to facilitate cleaning or to enable the wait staff to provide service with a minimum of walking.

Unionization of service staff is another reason for a production mentality. As in many other nations, the passenger train crews in New Zealand are unionized. The train between the capital city Wellington and the largest city Auckland serves breakfast until 50 or 60 kilometers from Auckland. The kitchen then shuts down and passengers are no longer able to acquire as much as a cup of coffee. For the next hour, the kitchen crew may be seen sitting together talking, smoking and enjoying the train ride. A market- or customer-driven operation would keep the kitchen open until the train reaches Auckland. Crews would be expected to clean up and take inventory after the journey, not an hour before.

The New Zealand public is well aware of this unhelpful situation. The New Zealand travel industry realizes that it is a negative factor in attracting more travelers, but the unionized train crew is above reproach. A similar situation exists on many of the world's airlines and probably accounts for much of the decline in services and the inability of airlines to provide a truly differentiated product.

Product Concept

The product concept, like the production concept, has an inward focus. The product concept holds that consumers prefer existing products and product forms, and the job of management is to develop good versions of these products. This misses the point that consumers are trying to satisfy needs and might turn to entirely different products to better satisfy their needs, such as motels instead of hotels or fast-food outlets in student centers instead of cafeterias.

Victoria Station was a restaurant chain that specialized in excellent prime rib. They were very successful and quickly expanded into over 50 units. Management focused on how to make their product better and at a lower cost. They came up with the right number of days to age their beef. The rib roasts were slow cooked to maintain the juices and avoid shrinkage. They had an excellent product. But their customers no longer wanted red meat every time they went out. They wanted chicken, seafood, and pasta. Victoria Station developed a system that produced a great prime rib dinner, but their target market no longer wanted prime rib. Victoria Station had a product orientation when they should have had a market orientation.

Many full-service hotels have been slow to recognize guest dining needs despite the fact that dissatisfaction with the traditional sit-down, over-priced, lack-of-taste hotel restaurant has been evident since the late 1950s. Countless consultants and writers have advised these hotels to count the hamburger wrappers and pizza boxes found in the trash cans in guest rooms to determine guest preferences.

Full-service airlines in the United States are facing a serious threat from short-haul, limited-service carriers such as Southwest, Kiwi, and Spirit Airlines. The fact is that North American air passengers view all air travel under 2 hours as a commodity.

Selling Concept

The selling concept holds that consumers will not buy enough of the organization's products unless the organization undertakes a large selling and promotion effort. The aim of a selling focus is to get every possible sale, and not to worry about satisfaction after the sale or the revenue contribution of the sale.

The selling concept does not establish a long-term relationship with the customer, since the focus is on getting rid of what one has, rather than creating a product to meet the needs of the market. Restaurants often advertise when sales start to drop, without first analyzing why sales are dropping. They do not try to change their product to fit the changing market. They sell harder, pushing their products on the customer through increased advertising and couponing. Eventually, they will go out of business because their product no longer satisfies the needs of the marketplace.

The selling concept is endemic within the hospitality industry. A major contributing factor is chronic overcapacity. Virtually every major sector of this industry has suffered, is currently plagued by, or will soon experience overcapacity.

When owners and top management face overcapacity, the tendency is to sell–sell–sell. Why do major sectors such as hotels, resorts, airlines, cruise lines, and even restaurants continuously face overcapacity?

- Pride in being the biggest, having the most capacity.
- A false belief that economies of scale will occur as size increases.
- Tax laws that encourage real estate developers to overbuild properties because of the generous tax write-offs.
- New technology, such as new products from aircraft manufacturers that offer higher productivity through larger seating capacity in spite of adequate existing capacity.
- Failure to merge revenue management with sales/marketing management.
- Economic incentives by governments to build a larger tourism/hospitality infrastructure to create economic growth.
- Poor or nonexistent forecasting and planning by owners, consultants, financial organizations, and governments.
- A myth that the travel industry faces almost unlimited future demand.
- The myth that a burgeoning population, a breakdown of international barriers, and increasing disposable income will correct temporary overcapacity problems.

Marketing Concept

The marketing concept is a more recent business philosophy and one that is being rapidly adopted in the hospitality industry.[8] Many companies have adopted the marketing concept. We know that Four Seasons Hotels, Marriott, and McDonald's follow this concept fully (see Marketing Highlight 2-1 on page 34). The marketing concept holds that achieving organizational goals depends on determining the needs and wants of target markets and delivering the desired satisfaction more effectively and efficiently than competitors.

The marketing concept has been stated in colorful ways, such as "Find a need and fill it;" "Make what you can sell instead of trying to sell what you can make;" "Have it your way (Burger King);" and "You're the boss" (United Airlines).

The marketing concept is frequently confused with the selling concept. Figure 2-2 compares the two. The selling concept takes an inside-out perspective. It starts with the company's existing products and calls for heavy selling and promoting to achieve profitable sales. The marketing concept starts with the needs and wants of the company's target customers. By contrast, the marketing concept takes an outside-in perspective. It starts with a well-defined market, focusing on customer needs. Second, marketing activities must be coordinated through the organization. Third, the marketing activities must work toward achieving the goals and objectives of the organization. The marketing concept is summarized in the following statement: **The company coordinates all the activities that will affect customer satisfaction and makes its profits by creating and maintaining customer satisfaction**.

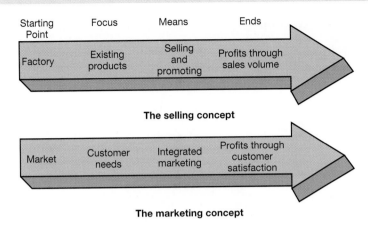

The selling concept

The marketing concept

Figure 2-2
The selling and marketing
concepts contrasted.

Societal Marketing Concept

The societal marketing concept is the newest marketing concept. The societal marketing concept holds that the organization should determine the needs, wants, and interests of target markets and deliver the desired satisfactions more effectively and efficiently than competitors in a way that maintains or improves the consumer's and society's well-being.

The societal marketing concept questions whether the marketing concept is adequate in an age of environmental problems, resource shortages, rapid population growth, worldwide inflation, and neglected social services.[9] It asks if the firm that senses, serves, and satisfies individual wants is always doing what's best for consumers and society in the long run. The pure marketing concept ignores possible conflicts between short-run consumer wants and long-run societal needs.

Advocates of the societal marketing concept would like public-interest groups to guide corporations toward decisions that will benefit society over the long term. Societal pressures are already manifest in the marketing of cigarettes and liquor. Hotel chains have established no smoking floors and no smoking sections in their restaurants. Delta Airlines made all its international flights smoke free at the beginning of 1995. MADD and other antidrunk driving groups have brought about stiffer drunk driving laws, laws against happy hour promotions, and laws that increase restaurant liability for serving excessive alcoholic beverages to guests. Restaurants and their state associations have developed training programs on how to responsibly serve alcohol. The cocktail reception is a thing of the past; today at most receptions a variety of mineral waters, fruit juices, and soft drinks is served. Today, managers and employees must be aware of how to prevent customers from becoming intoxicated and how to handle customers that are intoxicated.

Fast-food restaurants that practice the societal marketing concept will pursue more environmentally sound packaging and produce foods with more nutritional value. Smart restauranteurs will do this before they are forced into it by public outcry or laws. Resort developers must consider the impact on the environment not only of their initial construction, but also of the disposal of waste products and their use of water. The denigration of Earth's environment will make it necessary for marketers to become more socially responsible.

Marketing Highlight 2-1

McDonald's Applies the Marketing Concept

Twenty million customers pass through the famous golden arches each day, and an astounding 96% of all Americans eat at McDonald's each year. McDonald's now serves 145 hamburgers per second. Credit for this performance belongs to a strong marketing orientation: McDonald's knows how to serve people and adapt to changing consumer wants.

McDonald's has mastered the art of serving consumers, and it carefully teaches the basics to its franchisees and employees, all of whom take training courses at McDonald's "Hamburger University" in Oakbrook, Illinois. They emerge with a degree in "Hamburgerology." McDonald's monitors product and service quality through continuous customer surveys and puts great energy into improving hamburger production methods in order to simplify operations, bring down costs, speed up service, and bring greater value to customers. Beyond these efforts, each McDonald's restaurant works to become a part of its neighborhood through community involvement and service projects.

In 4700 restaurants outside the United States, McDonald's carefully customizes its menu and service to local tastes and customs. It serves teriyaki burgers in Japan, pasta salads in Rome, and wine with its McNuggets® in Paris. When McDonald's opened its first restaurant in Moscow, it quickly won the hearts of Soviet consumers. However, the company had to overcome some monstrous hurdles in order to meet its high standards for consumer satisfaction in this new market. It had to educate suppliers, employees, and even consumers about the time-tested, McDonald's way of doing things. Technical experts with special strains of disease-resistant seed were brought in from Canada to teach Soviet farmers how to grow russet Burbank

potatoes for French fries, and the company built its own pasteurizing plant to ensure a plentiful supply of fresh milk. It trained Soviet managers at Hamburger University and subjected each of 630 new employees (most of whom didn't know a Chicken McNugget® from an Egg McMuffin®) to 16 to 20 hours of training on such essentials as cooking meat patties, assembling Filet-O-Fish sandwiches, and giving service with a smile. McDonald's had to train consumers—most Muscovites had never seen a fast-food restaurant. Customers waiting in line were shown videos telling them everything from how to order and pay at the counter to how to handle a Big Mac®. And in its usual way, McDonald's began immediately to build community involvement. On opening day, it held a kick-off party for 700 Muscovite orphans, and it donated all opening-day proceeds to the Moscow Children's Fund. As a result, the new Moscow restaurant got off to a very successful start. About 50,000 customers swarmed the restaurant during its first day of business.

McDonald's focus on consumers has made it the world's largest food-service organization. It now captures about 20% of America's fast-food business. The company's huge success has also been reflected in the increased value of its stock over the years: 250 shares of McDonald's stock purchased for less than $6000 in 1965 would be worth more than a million dollars today!

Sources: Penny Moser, "The McDonald's Mystique," *Fortune*, July 4, 1988; Scott Hume, "McDonald's Fred Turner: Making All the Right Moves," *Advertising Age*, January 1, 1990, pp. 6, 17; Gail McKnight, "Here Comes Bolshoi Mac," *USA Today Weekend*, January 26–28, 1990, pp. 4–5; and Rosemarie Boyle, "McDonald's Gives Soviets Something Worth Waiting For," *Advertising Age*, March 19, 1990, p. 61. Photo courtesy of McDonald's Corporation.

The hotel industry has been advised of many eco-friendly steps that can be taken. Among these are removing waste products such as plastics, glass, and metal from the trash; reducing chemical use; and extending the life of products such as machinery and even linen by using them as rags.[10] Energy conservation, landscaping, preventive maintenance, and water-saving plumbing fixtures are other popular recommendations. The area of green marketing has evolved from the public's concern about the environment. The Boston Park Plaza Hotel & Towers developed a total of 65 environmental initiatives. These initiatives included every thing from soap dispensers that reduced packaging and used less soap to a guideline for meeting planners on how to conduct green meetings. The publicity received from these initiatives attracted additional convention business from groups sympathetic to the environmental movement.[11] Quaker Oats of Canada changed from polystyrene cups to reusable cups in its staff cafeteria for environmental reasons. At the end of the year they were surprised to find that in addition to creating less solid waste they also had saved $6000.[12] Thus, being environmentally conscious can produce positive publicity and reduce costs, in addition to helping the environment.

Green Suites of Los Angeles has developed an "environmentally friendly" hotel room. Green Suites uses all natural, biodegradable, and cruelty-free soaps, shampoos, and body lotions. The room's air is filtered to remove dust and pollen. Filtered water is used in the lavatories and in the shower. The paper goods are produced from recycled paper. They also offer the following options: furniture made from new-growth forest, organic bedding and linens, nontoxic floor and wall coverings, energy-efficient lighting, and environmentally safe cleaning supplies. Green Suites claims that the investment in their suites provides a good return because guests are willing to pay a premium for their suites.

Gambling is another societal issue with significant ramifications for the hospitality industry. Gambling and gambling casinos are spreading rapidly throughout North America and many other nations. Legislators have generally viewed gambling as an attractive source of revenue. Responsible casinos ban players known to have compulsive gambling behavior and provide financial support for organizations that help compulsive gamblers break their habit. They realize that they must be socially responsible if they are to gain community acceptance and future licenses in new communities.

A broader issue facing the hospitality and travel industries is expansion that has a positive impact on local residents. Poorly planned tourism developments have the potential of creating great damage to an area. This damage can be caused by the disposal of solid waste, lack of proper sewage treatment facilities resulting in the contamination of groundwater, congested roads as the result of poor infrastructure support, increased rents as the result of attracting employees to the area but not providing additional housing, and damage to the area's flora and fauna.

The hospitality and travel industries cannot insulate themselves from the continuing need for societal approval. Few industries have a greater need to recognize and proactively adopt the societal marketing concept.

Responsible casinos ban players known to have compulsive gambling behavior. Courtesy of Hilton Hotels Corporation.

MARKETING CHALLENGES

Marketing operates within a dynamic global environment. Every decade calls on marketing managers to think freshly about their marketing objectives and practices. Rapid changes can quickly make yesterday's winning strategies out of date. As management thought-leader Peter Drucker once observed, a company's winning formula for the last decade will probably be its undoing in the next decade.

Two of the current challenges facing today's companies are increased global competition and an increased call for companies to take social responsibility.

Rapid Globalization

The world economy has undergone radical change during the past two decades. Geographical and cultural distances have shrunk with the advent of jet planes, fax machines, global computer networks, international telephone hookups, world satellite broadcasts, global distribution systems, and other technical advances. This has allowed companies to greatly expand their geographical market coverage, purchasing, and manufacturing. The result is a vastly more complex marketing environment for both companies and consumers.

Domestic companies are expanding overseas, while their home markets are being invaded by international companies. Business markets have become internationalized. Independents such as the Seoul Plaza Hotel need worldwide connections; domestic business alone is not enough to fill their rooms. Many companies are forming strategic alliances with foreign partners, enabling them to access foreign markets. For example, most major airlines have developed international alliances.

United Airlines has developed land packages with international travel partners.
Courtesy of Leo Burnett USA and United Airlines.

The Call for More Ethics and Social Responsibility

Conscientious marketers face many moral dilemmas. The best thing to do is often unclear. Because not all managers have fine moral sensitivity, companies need to develop **corporate marketing ethics policies**—broad guidelines that everyone in the organization must follow. These polices should cover distributor relations, advertising standards, customer service, pricing, product development, and general ethical standards.

The finest guidelines cannot resolve all the difficult ethical situations that the marketer faces. Consider the following situations.

You have just hired a sales manager from a competitive hotel. He suggests that he could provide you with a copy of their marketing plan and copies of some of their client files. What do you do?

You know that prohibiting smoking in your restaurant will create a healthier atmosphere for your employees and customers. But research has told you sales will drop by 10% if you ban smoking. What do you do?

You know that you should rekey a lock when a guest does not return all the keys they were issued. But you also know some guests unknowingly pack their extra keys or lose them. Since your hotel does not put the room number on keys, lost keys are not much of a threat. It costs $50 to rekey a lock, and one out of eight guests does not return all keys issued to them. Would you rekey locks each time a key was missing?

There is an opening at one of your hotels for a general manager. The most qualified candidate that you have is a woman. You also know that the owner would strongly prefer a man. The owner has plans for three new hotels; you would like to get the management contract on the new hotels. What do you do?

The answers to these questions are difficult. Managers need to develop a set of principles that will help them figure out the moral importance of each situation and decide how far they can go in good conscience. Companies and managers need to apply high standards of ethics and morality when making corporate decisions, regardless of "what the situation allows." History provides many examples of company actions that were legal and allowed, but were highly irresponsible. Consider the following example:

Prior to the Pure Food and Drug Act, the advertising for a diet pill promised that a person taking this pill could eat virtually anything at any time and still lose weight. Too good to be true? Actually, the claim was quite true; the product lived up to its billing with frightening efficiency. It seems that the primary active ingredient in this "diet supplement" was tapeworm larvae. These larvae would develop in the intestinal tract and, of course, be well fed: the pill taker would in time quite literally starve to death.[13]

Each company and manager must work out a philosophy of socially responsible and ethical behavior. Under the societal marketing concept, each manager must look beyond what is legal and allowed and develop standards based on personal integrity, corporate conscience, and long-run consumer welfare. A clear and responsible philosophy will help the marketing manager deal with the many knotty questions posed by marketing and other human activities.

Chapter Review

I.   Understanding marketing. Marketing is a social and managerial process by which individuals and groups obtain what they need and want through creating and exchanging products and value with others.

To understand the definition, we must understand the following terms: needs, wants, and demands; products; value, cost, and satisfaction; exchange, transactions, and relationships; and markets.

1) Needs, wants, and demands. Human beings have many complex **needs**. These include basic physical needs for food, clothing, warmth, and safety; social needs for belonging, affection, fun, and relaxation; esteem needs for prestige, recognition, and fame; and individual needs for knowledge and self-expression.

Wants: Wants are how people communicate their needs.

Demands: People have almost unlimited wants, but limited resources. They chose products that produce the most satisfaction for their money. When backed by buying power, wants become demand.

2) Products. A product is anything that can be offered to a market for attention, acquisition, use, or consumption and that might satisfy a need or want.

3) Value, cost, and satisfaction. Value is the consumer's estimate of the product's overall capacity to satisfy his or her needs. Today's consumer behaviorists have gone beyond narrow economic assumptions of how consumers form value in their mind and make product choices. Modern theories of consumer-choice behavior are important to marketers because the whole marketing plan rests on assumptions about how consumers make choices. Therefore, concepts of value, cost, and satisfaction are crucial to the discipline of marketing.

Costs: Costs not only involve money, but everything one gives up to gain the product.

Satisfaction: Satisfaction with a product is determined by how well the product meets the customer's expectations for that product.

4) Exchange, transactions, and relationships. Exchange is the act of obtaining a desired object from someone by offering something in return.

Transactions: A transaction is marketing's unit of measurement. A transaction consists of a trade of values between two parties.

Relationship marketing focuses on building a relationship with a company's profitable customers. Most companies are finding that they earn a higher return from resources invested in getting repeat sales from current customers than from money spent to attract new customers.

5) Markets. A market is a set of actual and potential buyers who might transact with a seller.

II.   Marketing Management. Marketing management is the analysis, planning, implementation, and control of programs designed to create, build, and maintain beneficial exchanges with target buyers for the purpose of achieving organizational objectives.

III. Five Marketing Management Philosophies

1) Production concept. The production concept holds that customers will favor products that are available and highly affordable, and therefore management should focus on production and distribution efficiency.

2) Product concept. The product concept holds that customers prefer existing products and product forms, and the job of management is to develop good versions of these products.

3) Selling concept. The selling concept holds that consumers will not buy enough of the organization's products unless the organization undertakes a large selling and promotion effort.

4) Marketing concept. The marketing concept holds that achieving organizational goals depends on determining the needs and wants of target markets and delivering the desired satisfaction more effectively and efficiently than competitors.

5) Societal marketing concept. The societal marketing concept holds that the organization should determine the needs, wants, and interests of target markets and deliver the desired satisfactions more effectively and efficiently than competitors in a way that maintains or improves the consumer's and society's well-being.

DISCUSSION QUESTIONS

1. If you went into a restaurant as a customer, how could you tell if the restaurant had embraced the marketing concept?

2. A restaurant has a great reputation as the result of providing consistent food for over 10 years. The restaurant is full every weekend and has above-average business during the week. The manager claims that they do not practice marketing because they do not need marketing; they have more than enough business now. Is it true that this restaurant does not practice marketing?

3. Explain the difference between marketing and sales.

4. Is another fast-food restaurant (Burger King, Wendy's, etc.), as market oriented as McDonalds? Why or why not?

5. Contrast the marketing management philosophies of the production concept and the marketing concept with respect to the firm's attitude toward the customer and product offering, the role of marketing research, the importance of profit, and the role of the sales force.

6. Delta Airlines decided to make all its international flights smoke free on January 1, 1995. This decision will result in the loss of some passengers that smoke. Do you think the smoking ban was a good decision on Delta's part?

KEY TERMS

Demands   Human wants that are backed by buying power.

Exchange   The act of obtaining a desired object from someone by offering something in return.

Hospitality industry   The food service and lodging industries, along with their support groups.

Human need   A state of felt deprivation in a person.

Human want   The form that a human need takes when shaped by culture and individual personality.

Market   The set of actual and potential buyers of a product.

Marketing   Human activity directed at satisfying needs and wants through the exchange process.

Marketing concept   The marketing management

philosophy that holds that achieving organizational goals depends on determining the needs and wants of target markets and delivering desired satisfactions more effectively and efficiently than competitors.

Marketing management The analysis, planning, implementation, and control of programs designed to create, build, and maintain beneficial exchanges with target buyers for the purpose of achieving organizational objectives.

Marketing manager A person who is involved in marketing analysis, planning, implementation, and control activities.

Product Anything that can be offered to a market for attention, acquisition, use, or consumption.

Product concept The idea that consumers will favor products that offer the most quality, performance, and features, and therefore the organization should devote its energy to making continuous product improvements.

Production concept The philosophy that consumers will favor products that are available and highly affordable, and therefore management should focus on improving production and distribution efficiency.

Selling concept The idea that consumers will not buy enough of the organization's products unless the organization undertakes a large selling and promotion effort.

Societal marketing concept The idea that the organization should determine the needs, wants, and interests of target markets and deliver the desired satisfactions more effectively and efficiently than competitors in a way that maintains or improves the consumer's and society's well-being.

Transaction A trade between two parties that involves at least two things of value, agreed upon conditions, a time of agreement, and a place of agreement.

REFERENCES

1. PATRICIA SELLERS, "Getting Customers to Love You," *Fortune* (March 3, 1989), pp. 38–44+.

2. ISADORE SHARP, "Quality for All Seasons," *Canadian Business Review*, 17, no. 1 (Spring 1990), pp. 21–23.

3. HENRY A. MURRAY, *Explorations in Personality* (New York: Oxford University Press, 1938).

4. THEODORE LEVITT, "Marketing Myopia," *Harvard Business Review* (July–August 1960), pp. 45–56.

5. LEONARD L. BERRY, VALARIE A. ZEITHAML, AND A. PARASURAMAN, "Quality Counts in Services, Too," *Business Horizons*, 28 (May–June 1985), pp. 44–52.

6. PHILIP KOTLER, "A Generic Concept of Marketing," *Journal of Marketing* (April 1972), pp. 46–54.

7. PHILIP KOTLER, "The Major Tasks of Marketing Management," *Journal of Marketing* (October 1973), pp. 41–49.

8. For more on the marketing concept, see THEODORE LEVITT, "Marketing and Its Discontents," *Across the Board* (February 1984), pp. 42–48; and FRANKLIN S. HOUSTON, "The Marketing Concept: What It Is and What It Is Not," *Journal of Marketing* (April 1986), pp. 81–87.

9. LAWRENCE P. FIELDMAN, "Societal Adaptation: A New Challenge for Marketing," *Journal of Marketing* (July 1971), pp. 54–60; and MARTIN L. BELL AND C. WILLIAM EMERY, "The Faltering Marketing Concept," *Journal of Marketing* (October 1971), pp. 37–42.

10. KIRK IWANOWSKI AND CINDY RUSHMORE, "Introducing the Eco-friendly Hotel," *Cornell Hotel & Restaurant Administration Quarterly*, 35, no. 1 (February 1994), pp. 34–38.

11. LESLEE JAQUETTE, "Hoteliers Are Seeing Green with Ecology Efforts," *Hotel and Motel Management* 207, no. 13 (July 27, 1992), pp. 19–20.

12. PATRICK CARSON AND JULIA MOULDEN, *Green is Gold* (Toronto: Harper Collins Publishers, 1991), p. 58.

13. DAN R. DALTON AND RICHARD A. COSIER, "The Four Faces of Social Responsibility," *Business Horizons* (May–June 1982), pp. 19–27.

The Role of Marketing in Strategic Planning

3

*S*omehow, the customer was forgotten at Greyhound. Instead of customer-focused strategic planning, management concentrated on unproven technology, several cutbacks, and management perks.[1]

Greyhound had been troubled for years by increased automobile ownership and discount airlines that reduced the bus industry's share of interstate travel to 6% in 1994 from 30% in 1960. Greyhound somehow survived a leveraged buyout from Dial Corporation. However, two violent strikes plunged Greyhound into bankruptcy.

Finally, in October 1991, Greyhound reemerged from federal bankruptcy in the hands of Frank Schmieder, a merchant banker, and Michael Doyle, who had come from a finance position at Philips Petroleum Company.

Instead of developing a badly needed customer-focused strategic plan, management created a reorganization plan that called for relentless cutting of workers, routes, and services, reducing the fleet from 3700 to 2400 buses.

At first, Wall Street cheered and the newly issued stock soared. They also cheered the planned development of a sophisticated reservation system known as Trips.

In the glory of this praise, Schmieder's salary rose 57% to $526,000 and Doyle's nearly 65% to $264,000. There was money for a $50,000 dona-

tion to the Dallas Museum of Art and season tickets at the Dallas Cowboys, Texas Rangers, and Washington Redskins.

A new corporate travel policy issued by Doyle ordered employees to use efficient and economical travel while he and other executives took limousines to airports, flew first class, and stayed at the Ritz Carlton.

There was also money for consultants such as Meridian Institute of Crested Butte Colorado, who charged $560,000 for a pair of "breakthrough" corporate communication seminars in Los Angeles and Atlanta.

Meanwhile, things weren't going so well on the line. At some terminals, employee turnover was nearly 100%. Virtually all customer surveys showed that customers were displeased. In fact, some complained that bus terminal workers made fun of them. Baggage piled up in corners and disappeared or arrived late.

Finally, the much touted Trips reservation system arrived to save the day. Unfortunately, it was introduced at the busiest time of the year and then failed to work. Reservation clerks were forced to go back to writing tickets by hand and checking old timetables for information.

When ridership fell still further, the company promoted a plan to go anywhere on the system for $68 with a three-day advance purchase. Customers responded in hordes. But buses and drivers were in such short supply that there simply wasn't room. Some terminals were so crowded that they stopped selling tickets. In the meantime, Greyhound's regional competitors were aggressively courting the market and increased their revenues.

The result was a net loss of $61.4 million for Greyhound. The honeymoon with Wall Street ended and Greyhound's stock plummeted, but not before Schmieder could exercise stock options for a reported profit of $155,000.

First, we discuss the four major organizational levels of strategic planning; the corporate level, the division level, the business level, and the product level.

Then we discuss **defining the company mission, setting goals** and **objectives,** and designing a **business portfolio** to meet the **mission, goals,** and **objectives.**

Next we discuss **strategic options** for new businesses; **intensive growth** opportunities, **integrative growth** opportunities, and **diversification growth** opportunities. Finally we present the **strategic planning process,** discussing each of its steps.

In previous chapters, we discussed the need to continuously satisfy changing consumer needs. Companies who view this as fundamental to success practice the art of market-oriented strategic planning.

Market-oriented strategic planning is the managerial process of developing and maintaining a viable fit between the organization's objectives, skills, and resources and its changing market opportunities.

The aim of strategic planning is to help a company select and organize its businesses in a way that keeps the company healthy in spite of unexpected upsets occurring in any of its specific businesses or product lines.

Three key ideas define strategic planning. The first calls for managing a company's businesses as an investment portfolio, for which it will be decided which business entities deserve to be built, maintained, phased down (harvested, milked), or terminated.

The second key idea is to assess accurately the future profit potential of each business by considering the market's growth rate and the company's position and fit. It is not sufficient to use current sales or profits as a guide. For example, if Hyatt, Marriott, and Holiday Inns had used only current profits as a guide to investment opportunities, they would have continued to invest primarily or solely in commercial hotels in downtown and airport locations and, in the case of Holiday Inns, solely in family motels. Instead, Marriott offers a diverse portfolio of brand name lodging such as Marriott Marquis, Courtyard, Fairfield Inn, and so on, for different market segments. Hyatt has been very active in resort development and is a recognized leader in programs for children and teen-agers with Camp Hyatt and Rock Hyatt. Holiday Inn has a diversified portfolio of hospitality products, including casino hotels and Holiday Inn Express.

The third key idea underlying strategic planning is that of strategy.[2] For each business, the company must develop a game plan for achieving its

The Big Red Boat positions itself as a family cruise ship. Courtesy of Robinson, Yesawich & Pepperdine, Inc.

long-run objectives. Furthermore, no one strategy is optimal for all competitors in that business. Each company must determine what makes the most sense in the light of its industry position and its objectives, opportunities, skills, and resources. Thus, in the airline industry American Airlines is pressing for cost reduction as a full-service airline and a strong global market share. Southwest continues to strive for low-cost, limited domestic service while acquiring other carriers such as Markair with similar strategies. The future of the airline industry remains uncertain, but it is possible that the strategies of both carriers could prove to be correct.

Marketing and strategic planning should be viewed as partnerships contributing to the long-run success of a hospitality firm. Prior to 1986, Motel 6 did virtually no consumer research or planning. The chain was then purchased by Kohlberg Kravis Roberts & Company (KKR), leveraged buy-out specialists. The new owner, wanting to expand the chain and enhance its investment value, initiated a process of strategic planning.

Those responsible for marketing planning at Motel 6 knew that, "Even a brilliant marketing plan or creative concept will misfire if it is lost in competitive advertising clutter. Likewise, a highly visible effort will be ineffective if it is not based on sound relevant strategy."[3]

The Tom Bodett Motel 6 advertising campaign proved to be a winner. This advertising was not a random, chance occurrence but was instead the result of carefully studying the needs of target consumers and responding to them. For instance, the choice of radio as the media was based on listening habits of this group, not simply media cost. "The lesson of the Motel 6 campaign is not necessarily to use radio, a witty spokesperson, or even to appeal to consumers' desire to make a smart choice. The lesson of this campaign is to use a disciplined process that begins with research to learn about consumers' behavior, responds unwaveringly to those insights, and then follows through with consistent creativity and measurement."[4]

Lessons can also be learned outside the hospitality industry.

Marketing plays a critical role in General Electric's strategic-planning process. According to a strategic-planning manager at General Electric:

> the marketing manager is the most significant functional contributor to the strategic-planning process, with leadership roles in defining the business mission; analysis of the environmental, competitive, and business situations; developing objectives, goals, and strategies; and defining product, market, distribution, and quality plans to implement the business's strategies. This involvement extends to the development of programs and operating plans that are fully linked with the strategic plan.[5]

To understand strategic planning, we need to recognize that most large companies consist of four organizational levels: the corporate, division, business, and product levels. In recent years, hospitality companies such as Marriott or Disney have taken on the organizational appearance of multilevels. Corporate headquarters is responsible for designing a corporate strategic plan to guide the whole enterprise into a profitable future; it makes decisions on how much resource support to allocate to each division as well as which businesses to start or eliminate. Each division establishes a division plan covering the allocation of funds to each business unit within that division. Each business unit in turn develops a business unit strategic plan to carry that business unit into a profitable future. Finally, each product level (product line, brand) within a business unit develops a marketing plan for achieving its objectives in its product market. These plans are then implemented at the various levels of the organization, results are monitored and evaluated, and corrective actions are taken. The whole planning, implementation, and control cycle is shown in Figure 3-1.

In this chapter, we will first examine three questions:

1. What are the characteristics of a high-performance business?

2. How is strategic planning carried out at the corporate level?

3. How do individual business units carry out strategic planning?

NATURE OF HIGH-PERFORMANCE BUSINESS

The major challenge facing today's hospitality companies is how to build and maintain viable businesses in the face of the rapidly changing marketplace and environment. The consulting firm of Arthur D. Little proposed a model of the characteristics of a high-performance business.[6] They pointed to the four factors shown in Figure 3-2. We will review these factors here.

Stakeholders

The starting point for any business is to define the stakeholders and their needs. Traditionally, most businesses primarily nourished their stockholders. Today's businesses increasingly recognize that unless other stakeholders—customers, employees, suppliers, distributors—are nourished the business may never earn sufficient profits for the stockholders. Thus, if British Airways employees, customers, dealers, and suppliers are unhappy, profits will not be achieved. This leads to the principle that a business must at least strive to satisfy the minimum expectations of each stakeholder group.

It has been suggested that an employee stakeholder group that may be of increased importance to hospitality firms is that of women with small

Figure 3-1
The relationship between analysis, planning, implementation, and control.

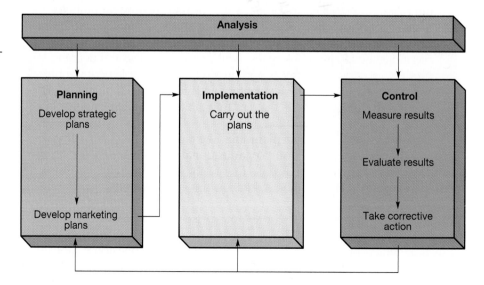

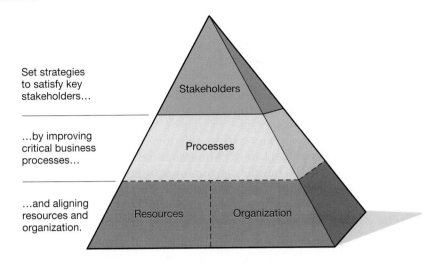

Set strategies to satisfy key stakeholders...

...by improving critical business processes...

...and aligning resources and organization.

Figure 3-2
The high-performance business. *Source:* Excerpted from The First Quarter 1992 issue *Prism,* the quarterly journal for senior managers, published by Arthur D. Little, Inc.

children who do not wish to work full time. Many do not want to entirely leave the workplace but are forced to do so since their employers do not permit flexible scheduling and reduced work hours. Many of these individuals could provide valuable contributions, but find this impossible under the current organizational structure and policy.[7]

A dynamic relationship connects the stakeholder groups. This is shown in Figure 3-3. The progressive company creates a high level of employee satisfaction which leads employees to work on continuous improvements as well as breakthrough innovations. The result is higher-quality products and services, which create high customer and stakeholder satisfaction.

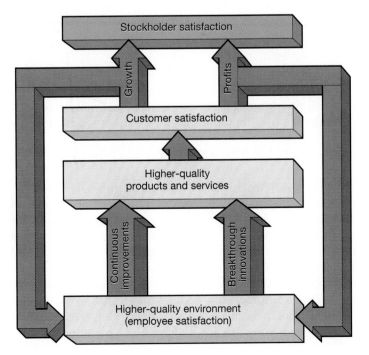

Figure 3-3
Dynamic relationships among stakeholder groups in a high-performance business. *Source:* Excerpted from The Fourth Quarter 1992 issue *Prism,* the quarterly journal for senior managers, published by Arthur D. Little, Inc.

Processes

Company work is traditionally carried on by departments. But departmental organization poses some problems. Departments typically operate to maximize their own objectives, not necessarily the company's. Walls come up between departments and there is usually less than ideal cooperation. Work is slowed down and plans often are altered as they pass though departments.

Companies are increasingly refocusing their attention on the need to manage processes even more than departments. They are studying how tasks pass from department to department and the impediments to effective output. They are now building cross-functional teams that manage core business processes.

The Las Vegas Hilton was concerned with the profit contribution from different market segments and how to deal with this issue. The result was a radically different approach to hotel accounting called *market segment accounting*. This new approach incorporated marketing and strategic planning into accounting, rather than viewing them as separate stand-alone areas and philosophies.[8]

The Las Vegas Hilton decided that "It is important to determine the optimal mix of the major market segments before deciding the strategic direction of the property." This demanded an interdepartment analysis, since different guests may have widely varying impacts on the profit implications for various departments.

This hotel wanted answers to the following questions:

1. What is the relative profitability of the gaming guest? The premium-gaming guest? The tour and travel guest?
2. How many room nights can each segment fill a year?
3. How much money should be spent to attract each segment?
4. How should rooms be priced for each segment?
5. How should these rooms be allocated to the segments during critical periods of the year?

Interdepartmental teams were formed representing finance, marketing, and information services. Eventually, the heads of all the hotel's major departments contributed to the new market segment accounting model.

Resources

To carry out processes, a company needs resources such as human resources, materials, machines, and information. Traditionally, companies sought to own and control most of the resources that entered the business. Now that is changing. Companies are finding that some resources under their control are not performing as well as those that they could obtain from outside. More companies today have decided to outsource less critical resources. On the other hand, they appreciate the need to own and nurture those core resources and competencies that make up the essence of their business. Smart companies are identifying their core competencies and using them as the basis for their strategic planning.

Organization

The organizational side of a company consists of its structure, policies, and culture, all of which tend to become dysfunctional in a rapidly changing company. While structure and policies can be changed, the company's culture is the hardest to change. Companies must work hard to align their organization's structure, policies, and culture to the changing requirements of business strategy.

The corporate culture at Rockresorts worked for 30 years, but in the late 1980s it became an obstacle to meeting customer needs. Rockresorts was founded by Laurence A. Rockefeller in the 1950s. The original market for Rockresorts was the CEO who could delegate business so that his vacation wouldn't be disturbed. At that time, decisions could wait until the CEO returned.

Policies at Rockresorts were sacrosanct and involved no phones in the guest rooms, no television, adherence to a mandatory meal plan (the modified American plan) and small, nonostentatious guest rooms. The corporate culture had been product driven. A change in corporate culture is now occurring at Rockresorts. Michael Glennie, president and CEO of Rockresorts said, "We have to listen to what the customer wants and cater to that without compromising the philosophy and ideals of our founder."

This meant, among other changes, pampering guests with more amenities, larger bathrooms, and placing telephones in the room. "I believe that the mission for Rockresorts is to take a company with a wonderful tradition and build on that to meet the expectations of today's guests" said Glennie.[9]

CORPORATE
STRATEGIC
PLANNING

Corporate headquarters has the responsibility for setting into motion the whole planning process. Some corporations give a lot of freedom to their business units but let them develop their own strategies. Others set the goals and get heavily involved in the strategies of the individual business units.

The hospitality industry faces the need for greater empowerment of employees, particularly at middle management levels. It has been suggested that many of the traditions within the hospitality industry have experienced little change. "Most of its managers for instance, were trained in the classical management style." That system ensured that "formal rules and regulations guide decision making and ensure organizational stability. Work is done by the book . . . one's rank in the hierarchical structure determines authority and decision making tends to be centralized, coming primarily from the top."[10] Increasingly, hospitality industry executives and researchers view this traditional approach as needing change.

We will now examine four planning activities that all corporate headquarters must undertake:

- Defining the corporate mission
- Establishing strategic business units (SBUs)
- Assigning resources to each SBU
- Planning new businesses

Defining the Corporate Mission

A hospitality organization exists to accomplish something: to entertain, provide a night's lodging, and so on. Its specific mission or purpose is usually clear at the beginning. Over time some managers may lose interest in the mission, or the mission may lose its relevance in light of changed market conditions.

When management senses that the organization is drifting, it must renew its search for purpose. According to Peter Drucker, it is time to ask some fundamental questions.[11] What is our business? Who is the customer? What is value to the customer? What will our business be? What should our business be? These simple-sounding questions are among the most difficult the company will ever have to answer. Successful companies continuously raise these questions and answer them thoughtfully and thoroughly.

The company's mission is shaped by history. Every company has a history of aims, policies, and achievements. The organization must not depart too radically from its past history. It would not make sense for Denny's Restaurant to begin to manufacture glass bottles. Current preferences of the owners and management also affect a company's mission. Laurence Rockefeller clearly had a preference for his resorts, but several years later Glennie set a new vision for these resorts.

The organization's resources determine which missions are possible. Singapore Airlines would be deluding itself if it adopted the mission to become the world's largest airline. Finally, the organization should base its mission on its distinctive competencies. McDonald's could probably enter the solar energy business, but that would not use its core competence—providing low-cost food and fast service to large groups of customers.

Organizations develop mission statements in order to share them with their managers, employees, and, in many cases, customers and other publics. A well worked-out mission statement provides company employees with a shared sense of purpose, direction, and opportunity. Writing a formal mission statement is not easy. Some organizations spend a year or two trying to prepare a satisfactory statement about their company's purpose.

Good mission statements embody a number of characteristics. They should focus on a limited number of goals. The mission statement should define the major competitive scopes within which the company will operate.

- **Industry scope.** The range of industries that the company will consider. Some companies will operate in only one industry, some in only a set of related industries, some in only hotels, some in airlines, and some in any industry.

- **Products and applications scope.** The range of products and applications in which the company will participate. American Airlines has demonstrated a willingness to diversify into technology that drives the airline industry such as Sabre Reservations Systems and Yield Management Systems, but has indicated no desire to construct airports and runways.

- **Competencies scope.** The range of technological and other core competencies that the company will master and leverage.

- **Market-segment scope.** The type of market or customers the company will serve. Some companies will serve only the upscale market. For example, Four Seasons Hotels and Resorts has shown no inclination to enter the budget roadside motel sector.

- **Vertical scope.** The number of channel levels from raw materials to final product and distribution in which the company will engage. At one extreme are companies with a large vertical scope. Many individuals have dreamed of a huge travel corporation that vertically ties together an airline, a hotel chain, and a chain of travel agents. Thus far, attempts in this area in the United States have been unsuccessful. At the other extreme are corporations with low or no vertical integration, such as the "hollow corporation" or "pure marketing company," which consists of a person with a phone, fax, computer, and desk who contracts outside for every service, including design, manufacture, marketing, and physical distribution.[12] Some tour operators may be viewed as hollow corporations. They tie together airline travel, ground transportation, sightseeing, restaurant meals, club entertainment, hotel lodging, and even travel gifts to send home without owning any of the enterprises. Eventually, many tour operators begin to acquire one or more of these enterprises and may eventually become a vertically integrated company.

- **Geographical scope.** The range of regions, countries, or country groups where the corporation will operate. At one extreme are companies that operate in a specific city or state, such as the fast-food chain Biscuitville in North Carolina. At the other extreme are large multinationals like Sheraton or Hilton Hotels and smaller multinationals that may operate in only a few countries, like Canada's Delta Hotels, which operates in Canada, the United States, and Thailand, or the Camino Real Hotel chain in Latin America. Choice Hotels International clearly has decided to become a major multinational chain. Choice has set a goal of having 300 hotels in Europe alone by 1997.[13]

The company's mission statement should be motivating. Employees need to feel that their work is significant and contributes to people's lives. Missions are at their best when they are guided by a vision, an almost "impossible dream." Thomas Monaghan wanted to deliver hot pizza to any home within 30 minutes and he created Domino's Pizza. Bob Burns wanted to develop world-class luxury hotels throughout Asia and he created Regent International Hotels. Ruth Fertel wanted to provide customers with the finest steak dinners available and she created Ruth's Chris Steak Houses.

The corporate mission statement should stress major policies that the company wants to honor. Policies define how employees should deal with customers, suppliers, distributors, competitors, and other important groups.

The company's mission statement should provide a vision and direction for the company for the next 10 to 20 years. Missions are not revised every few years in response to every new turn in the economy. On the

FOR VOYAGES THAT CAPTURE THE IMAGINATION

You've never seen anything like it, because there's never been anything like it before. It's a visionary cruise liner offering the unrestricted choices and open-sea freedoms of a private yacht. And it's an incentive ship that's a technological masterwork.

ON THIS SHIP, YOU CONTROL TIME AND SPACE.

Traditionally, the substantial restrictions and inflexibilities associated with cruise ships have disqualified them from consideration by group planners.

When the Diamond is launched in May 1992, it will demolish these feasibility barriers.

First, the Diamond specializes in "plan your own" four-, five- and seven-day cruises. Sailing schedules and ports of call are arranged to suit each group's specific needs, providing maximum flexibility in itineraries.

Second, the Diamond promises parity in accommodations. In every facet of quality and usable space, our ship's 177 staterooms are equivalent—and each offers the same high standard of luxury.

Third, the Diamond physically expands cruise ship hospitality even further than other cruise ships. By featuring unconditional availability of group dining accommodations and by arranging theme parties and social affairs that take over the whole ship. Plus, the ship's unique twin-hull design allows decks and staterooms

significantly more spacious—and a cruise significantly steadier—than previously possible.

ON A 21ST CENTURY CRUISE, EXPECT THE EXCEPTIONAL.

Not only will the Diamond feature plenty of flexible meeting space, an unequaled variety of activities and amusements (including the added water sports attractions of our retractable floating marina), a comprehensive spa, a full casino and the widest range of faultlessly prepared food—it will offer some very special extras. Like a shipboard TV studio for video conferencing and an in-house shipboard publishing center. And, for each passenger,

computerized personal daily agendas.

Perhaps you're beginning to realize that this is a ship with some amazing new points of departure. Because the voyages that capture their imaginations begin with the first ship that frees their dreams.

The SSC Radisson Diamond.

SSC RADISSON DIAMOND

For information focused toward your specific group needs, please contact your incentive travel expert or call (305) 932-3388.
Fax: (305) 935-5440.

Radisson has defined its business broadly enough to include cruise ships as well as hotels. This ad positions the cruise ship against upscale resorts in the incentive travel market. Courtesy Radisson Hospitality Worldwide.

other hand, a company must redefine its mission if that mission no longer defines an optimal course for the company.[14]

The Ruby Tuesday group of restaurants was developed as being fully consistent with the mission statement of its parent, Morrison Hospitality Group, the oldest food-service company on the New York Stock Exchange. This mission statement is that "our mission is to be a great restaurant company that provides the highest quality and greatest value to every guest, every team member, and every shareholder we serve."[15]

Establishing Strategic Business Units

Most companies operate several businesses. However, they often fail to define them carefully. Companies too often define their businesses in terms of products. They are in the "hotel business" or the "cruise line business." But market definitions of a business are superior to product definitions.[16] A business must be viewed as a customer-satisfying process, not a goods-producing process. Companies should define their business in terms of customer needs, not products.

Las Vegas has dramatically changed from a city primarily based on adult casinos to an entertainment complex for the entire family. Contrast Las Vegas to Reno, where the emphasis is still basically on casinos, lodging, food and beverage, and adult entertainment, with the exception of Circus Circus Hotel. Ski resorts are no longer content to sell only ski tickets. Today major ski resorts offer children's programs, summer mountain biking, and rock concerts.

Management, of course, should avoid a market definition that is too narrow or too broad. Holiday Inns, Inc., the world's largest hotel chain with over 300,000 rooms, fell into this trap. Some years ago it broadened its business definition from the "hotel business" to the "travel industry." It acquired Trailways, Inc., then the nation's second largest bus company, and Delta Steamship Lines, Inc. But Holiday Inns did not manage these companies well and later divested the properties. Holiday Inns decided to "stick close to its knitting" and concentrate on the "hospitality industry."[17]

Companies have to identify those of its businesses that they must manage strategically. These businesses are called strategic business units (SBUs). An SBU has three characteristics:

1. It is a single business or collection of related businesses that can be planned for separately from the rest of the company.
2. It has its own set of competitors.
3. It has a manager who is responsible for strategic planning and profit performance and who controls most of the factors affecting profits.

Assigning Resources to Each SBU

The purpose of identifying the company's strategic business units is to assign to these units strategic-planning goals and appropriate funding. These units send their plans to company headquarters, which approves them or sends them back for revision. Headquarters reviews these plans in order to decide which of its SBUs to build, maintain, harvest, and divest. Management cannot rely just on impressions. Analytical tools are needed for classifying businesses by profit potential. Two of the best known business portfolio evaluation models are the Boston Consulting Group model and the General Electric model.[18]

Boston Consulting Group Approach

The Boston Consulting Group (BCG), a leading management consulting firm, developed the growth/share matrix shown in Figure 3-4. The 10 circles represent the current sizes and positions of businesses making up a hypothetical company. The dollar-volume size of each business is proportional to the circle's area. The location of each business indicates its market growth rate and relative market share.

Specifically, the market growth rate on the vertical axis indicates the annual growth rate of the market in which the business operates. In the figure, it ranges from 0% to 20%, although a larger range could be shown. A market growth rate above 10% is considered high.

The horizontal axis, relative market share, refers to the SBU's market share relative to that of the largest competitor. It serves as a measure of the company's strength in the relevant market. A relative market share of 0.1 means that the company's sales volume is only 10% of the leader's sales volume, and 10 means that the company's SBU is the leader and has 10 times the sales of the next strongest company in that market. Relative market share is divided into high and low share, using 1.0 as the dividing line.

The growth/share matrix is divided into four cells, each indicating a different type of business.

Figure 3-4
The BCG growth/share matrix.

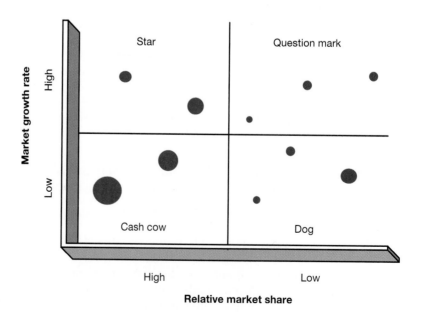

- **Question marks.** Question marks are company businesses that operate in high-growth markets but have low relative market shares. Most businesses start off as a question mark. A question mark requires a lot of cash. The term question mark is well chosen because the company has to think hard about whether to keep pouring money into this business. The company in Figure 3-4 operates three question-mark businesses, and this may be too many.

- **Stars.** If the question-mark business is successful, it becomes a star. A star is the market leader in a high-growth market. This does not necessarily mean that the star produces a positive cash flow for the company. The company must spend substantial funds to keep up with the high market growth and fight off competitor's attacks. Stars are usually profitable and become the company's future cash cows. In the illustration, the company has two stars.

- **Cash cows.** When a market's annual growth rate falls to less than 10%, the star becomes a cash cow if it still has the largest relative market share. A cash cow produces a lot of cash for the company. Since the business is the market leader, it enjoys economies of scale and higher profit margins. The company uses its cash-cow businesses to pay its bills and support the stars, question marks, and dogs, which tend to be cash hungry. In the illustration, the company has two cash-cow businesses.

- **Dogs.** Dogs describe company businesses that have weak market shares in low-growth markets. They typically generate low profits or losses, although they may throw off some cash. The company in the illustration manages three dog businesses. Dog businesses often consume more management time than they are worth.

Having plotted its various businesses in the growth/share matrix, the company then determines whether its business portfolio is healthy. An unbalanced portfolio would have too many dogs or question marks and/or too few stars and cash cows.

The company's next task is to determine what objective, strategy, and budget to assign to each SBU. Four alternative objectives can be pursued.

- **Build.** Here the objective is to increase the SBU's market share, even foregoing short-term earnings to achieve this objective. Building is appropriate for question marks whose shares have to grow to become stars.

- **Hold.** Here the objective is to preserve the SBU's market share. This objective is appropriate for strong cash cows if they are to continue to yield a large positive cash flow.

- **Harvest.** Here the objective is to increase the SBU's short-term cash flow regardless of the long-term effect. This strategy is appropriate for weak cash cows whose future is dim and from whom more cash flow is needed. Harvesting can also be used with question marks and dogs.

- **Divest.** Here the objective is to sell or liquidate the business because resources can be better used elsewhere.

As time passes, SBUs change their position in the growth/share matrix. Successful SBUs have a life cycle. They start as question marks, become stars, then cash cows, and finally dogs toward the end of their life cycle. For this reason, companies should examine not only the current positions of their businesses in the growth/share matrix, but also their moving positions.

Although the portfolio in Figure 3-4 is basically healthy, wrong objectives or strategies could be assigned. The worst mistake would be to require all the SBUs to aim for the same growth rate or return level. The very point of SBU analysis is that each business has a different potential and requires its own objective. Additional mistakes would include the following:

1. Leaving cash-cow businesses with too little in retained funds, in which case they grow weak, or leaving them with too much in retained funds, in which case the company fails to invest enough in new growth businesses.
2. Making major investments in dogs hoping to turn them around, but failing each time.
3. Maintaining too many question marks and underinvesting in each. Question marks should either receive enough support to achieve segment dominance or be dropped.

General Electric Approach

The appropriate objective to assign to an SBU cannot be determined solely on the basis of its position in the growth/share matrix. If additional factors are introduced, the growth/share matrix can be seen as a special case of the multifactor portfolio matrix that General Electric (GE) pioneered; see Figure 3-5.

Each business is rated in terms of two major dimensions, market attractiveness and business strengths. These two factors make excellent marketing sense for rating a business. Companies will be successful to the extent that they go into attractive markets and possess the required business strengths to succeed in those markets.

The real issue is to measure these two dimensions. To do so, the strategic planners must identify the factors underlying each dimension and find a way to

Figure 3-5
General Electric's strategic business-planning grid. *Source:* Slightly modified and adapted with permission from *Analysis for Strategic Marketing Decisions* by George S. Day (St. Paul, MN: West Publishing, 1986), pp. 202 and 204.

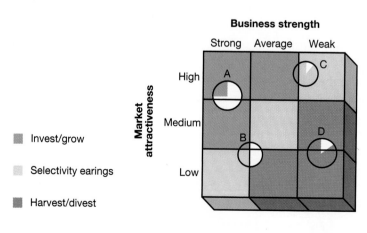

measure them and combine them into an index. Market attractiveness varies with the market's size, annual market growth rate, historical profit margins, and so on. Competitive position varies with the company's market share, share growth, and product quality. The GE model leads strategic planners to look at more factors in evaluating an equal or potential business than the BCG model.

The GE matrix is divided into nine cells, which in turn fall into three zones. The three cells at the upper left indicate strong SBUs in which the company should invest/grow. The diagonal cells stretching from the lower left to the upper right indicate SBUs that are medium in overall attractiveness. The three cells at the lower right indicate SBUs that are low in overall attractiveness. Consider a full-service downtown hotel business that represents an SBU with a small market share in a fair-sized, unattractive market and in which the company has a weak competitive position. It is a fit candidate for harvest/divest.

Management should also forecast the expected position of each SBU in the next 3 to 5 years given the current strategy. This involves analyzing where each product is in its product life cycle.

The final step is for management to decide what it wants to do with each business. Table 3-1 outlines plausible strategy options for businesses in each cell. The strategy for each business has to be discussed and debated. Marketing managers will discover that their objective is not always to build sales in each SBU. Their job might be to maintain existing demand with fewer marketing dollars or to take cash out of the business. Thus the task of marketing management is to manage demand or revenue to the target level negotiated with corporate management. Marketing contributes to assessing each SBU's sales and profit potential, but once the SBU's objective and budget are set, marketing's job is to carry out the plan efficiently and profitably.

Critique of Portfolio Models

The use of portfolio models has produced a number of benefits. The models have helped managers to think more strategically and to better understand the economics of their businesses.

On the other hand, portfolio models must be used cautiously. They may lead the company to place too much emphasis on market-share growth and entry into high-growth businesses, to the neglect of managing the current businesses well. The results are sensitive to the ratings and weights and can be manipulated to produce a desired location in the matrix. A lot of businesses will end up in the middle of the matrix owing to compromises in ratings, and this makes it hard to know what the appropriate strategy should be. Finally, the models fail to delineate the synergies between two or more businesses, which means that making decisions for one business at a time might be risky. There is a danger of terminating a losing business unit that actually provides an essential core competence needed by several other business units.

Planning New Businesses

The company's plans for its existing businesses will allow it to project total sales and profits. Often, however, this will be less than what corporate management wants to achieve. After all, the portfolio plan will include divesting some businesses. If there is a gap between future desired sales and project-

Table 3-1
Business Strength

MARKET ATTRACTIVENESS		(STRONG)	(MEDIUM)	(WEAK)
	HIGH	PROTECT POSITION	INVEST TO BUILD	BUILD SELECTIVELY
		Invest to grow at maximum digestible rate. Build selectively on strengths. Concentrate effort on maintaining strength. areas.	Challenge for leadership. Seeks ways to overcome Reinforce vulnerable Withdraw if indications of sustaining growth are lacking.	Specialize around limited strengths. weaknesses.
	MEDIUM	BUILD SELECTIVELY	SELECTIVITY/MANAGE FOR EARNINGS	LIMITED EXPANSION/ HARVEST
		Invest heavily in most attractive segments. Concentrate investments Build up ability to counter competition. risks are relatively low. Emphasize profitability by raising productivity.	Protect existing program. minimize investment and in segments where profitability is good and	Look for ways to expand without high risk; otherwise, rationalize operations.
	LOW	MANAGE FOR PROTECT AND REFOCUS	EARNINGS	DIVEST
		Manage for current earnings. segments. Concentrate on attractive segments. Defend strengths.	Protect position in most profitable Upgrade product line. Minimize investment.	Sell at time that will maximize cash value. Cut fixed costs and avoid investment meanwhile.

ed sales, corporate management will have to develop or acquire new businesses to fill this strategic planning gap.

Figure 3-6 illustrates the strategic planning gap for a major restaurant company with several types of theme restaurants. The lowest curve projects the expected sales over the next 10 years from the company's current portfolio of businesses. The highest curve describes the corporation's desired sales over the next 10 years. Evidently, the company wants to grow much faster than its current businesses will permit. In fact, it wants to double its size in 10 years. How can it fill the strategic-planning gap?

A company can fill the gap in three ways. The first is to identify further opportunities to achieve growth within the company's current businesses (intensive growth opportunities). The second is to identify opportunities to build or acquire businesses that are related to the company's current businesses (integrative growth opportunities). The third is to identify opportunities to add attractive businesses that are unrelated to the compa-

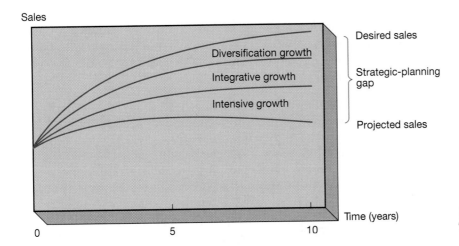

Figure 3-6
The strategic planning gap.

ny's current businesses (diversification growth opportunities). The specific opportunities within each broad class are listed and discussed next.

Intensive Growth

Corporate management should first review whether there are any further opportunities for improving the performance of its existing businesses. Ansoff has proposed a useful framework for detecting new intensive growth opportunities. Called a product/market expansion grid, it is shown in Figure 3-7.[19] Management first considers whether it could gain more market share with its current products in their current markets (market penetration strategy). Next it considers whether it can find or develop new markets for its current products (market development strategy). Then it considers whether it can develop new products of potential interest to its current markets (product-development strategy). Later it will also review opportunities to develop new products for new markets—diversification strategy. Let us examine the three major intensive growth strategies further.

Market Penetration Strategy. Here management looks for ways to increase the market share of its current products in their current markets. There are three major approaches.

1. Encourage current customers to buy more. This could work if customers are infrequent buyers, such as once per month customers of Wendy's.

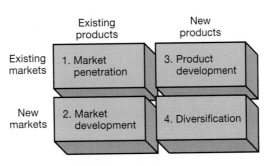

Figure 3-7
Market opportunity identification through the product/market expansion grid.

2. Attract McDonalds competitors' customers to switch to Wendy's.

3. Try to convince nonusers of fast food to start eating at the restaurant. This could work if there are still many people who do not eat at fast-food restaurants. This is particularly applicable in some foreign markets.

Market-Development Strategy. Management should also look for new markets whose needs might be met by its current products. First, try to identify potential user groups in the current sales areas whose interest in the product might be stimulated. Second, the company might seek additional distribution channels in its present locations. McDonalds has set a long-term strategy of being wherever the customer is, according to Ed Resi, president of McDonalds, USA. McDonalds serves more than 30 million customers in a day in the United States and opens a new restaurant every 8 hours. McDonalds plans to open restaurants in schools, trains, gas stations, and supermarkets. "The more locations you can have close to your customers, the more business you'll get," said Jack Greenberg, vice chairman and CFO for McDonalds.[20] Third, the company might consider selling in new locations here or abroad. This clearly is a strategy for many U.S. fast-food companies and hotel chains.

Product Development Strategy. Next, management should consider new product possibilities. Again, McDonalds has pursued this strategy. While continuing to concentrate on core hamburgers, fries, and drink products, McDonalds offers breakfast items such as sausage gravy biscuits and specialty items for select markets such as Saimin for the Hawaiian market.

By examining these three intensive growth strategies, management will hopefully discover several ways to grow. Still, that may not be enough, in which case management must also examine integrative growth opportunities.

Integrative Growth

Often a business's sales and profits can be increased through integrating backward, forward, or horizontally within that business's industry. The travel industry is unique since a basic supplier (hotel) will sell through wholesalers such as tour operators, through travel agents, or directly to the customer. The manufacturing sector seldom sells directly to the customer but instead goes through intermediaries.

A hotel company could select backward integration by acquiring one of its suppliers such as a food distributor. Or it could acquire tour wholesalers or travel agents (forward integration). Finally, the hotel company might acquire one or more competitors, provided the government does not bar the move (horizontal integration).

Marriott developed a restaurant supply distribution system known as Marriott Distribution Systems. This grew out of Marriotts' Fairfield Farms Commissary operation. The commissary operation was shut down and the business was refocused on distribution. Marriott opened six of these distribution centers to service concentrations of Marriott Hotels. With this guaranteed core business, each distribution center then aggressively markets to other restaurants in the area.[21]

Through investigating possible integration moves such as those by Marriott, a company may discover additional sources of sales volume increases over the next 10 years. These new sources may still not deliver the desired sales volume. In that case, the company may consider diversification moves.

Diversification Growth

Diversification growth makes sense when good opportunities can be found outside the present businesses. A good opportunity is one where the industry is highly attractive and the company has the mix of business strengths to be successful. Three types of diversification can be considered. The company could seek new products that have technological and/or marketing synergies with existing product lines, even though the products may appeal to a new class of customers (concentric diversification strategy). Second, the company might search for new products that could appeal to its current customers, though technologically unrelated to its current product line (horizontal diversification strategy). Hotels, restaurants, cruise lines, and airlines all pursue this strategy when they sell gift items such as T-shirts, perfume, and luggage. Many restaurants such as Hard Rock Cafes have found that the sale of restaurant-logo clothing in their restaurants is highly profitable and that clothing serves as an excellent advertising media.

Finally, the company might seek new businesses that have no relationship to the company's current technology, products, or markets (conglomerate diversification strategy). Some hotel chains have entered markets such as retirement homes. Hyatt operates a retirement division known as Classic Residence: Senior Living by Hyatt.

Thus we see that a company can systematically identify new business opportunities by using a marketing systems framework, first looking at ways to intensify its position in current product markets, then considering ways to integrate backward, forward, or horizontally in relation to its current businesses, and finally searching for profitable opportunities outside of its current businesses.

Having examined the strategic planning tasks of company management, we can now examine the strategic planning tasks facing business unit managers. The business unit strategic planning process consists of eight steps. We shall examine these steps.

BUSINESS STRATEGY PLANNING

Business Mission

Each business unit needs to define its specific mission within the broader company mission. Thus an SBU must define its various scopes more specifically: its products and applications, competence, market segments, vertical positioning, and geography. It must also define its specific goals and policies as a separate business.

External Environment Analysis (Opportunity and Threat Analysis)

The business manager now knows the parts of the environment to monitor if the business is to achieve its goals. In general, a business unit has to monitor key macroenvironment forces (demographic/economic, technological, political/legal, and social/cultural) and significant microenvironment factors (customers, competitors, distribution channels, suppliers) that will affect its ability to earn profits in this marketplace. The business unit should set up a marketing intelligence system to track trends and important developments. For each trend or development, management needs to identify the implied opportunities and threats.

Jonathan Tisch, president and CEO of Loews Hotels, predicted that the resort industry would see a decline in mega resorts due to intense competition. Tisch believed that mid-sized resorts capable of handling a group of 250 would be well positioned to meet current and future market needs.[22]

A trend of bringing one's spouse on a business trip was observed at many golf resorts, particularly those in Seattle, San Francisco, San Diego, Chicago, and Washington, D.C. Golf resort developers and managers need to assess whether this is a trend that might offer opportunities to competitively position one's resort in an increasingly crowded market.[23]

Opportunities

A major purpose of environmental scanning is to discern new opportunities. We define a marketing opportunity as follows: *A marketing opportunity is an area of need in which a company can perform profitably.*

Opportunities can be listed and classified according to their attractiveness and the success probability. The company's success probability depends on whether its business strengths not only match the key success requirements for operating in the target market but also exceed those of its competitors. The best performing company will be the one that can generate the greatest customer value and sustain it over time.

The concept of incorporating recreation clubs into resorts might be an opportunity for some resorts. Such programs are aimed at local markets allowing members to enjoy the resort facilities and sometimes even stay in the rooms. Membership programs offer opportunities for increased revenue, but there is also a negative side if they are not well managed. Resort guests who pay full rack rates may not appreciate the competition for tennis or golf times from local residents.[24]

Threats

Some developments in the external environment represent threats. We define an environmental threat as follows: *An environmental threat is a challenge posed by unfavorable trends or developments that would lead, in the absence of defensive marketing action, to sales or profit deterioration.* Threats should be classified according to their seriousness and probability of occurrence.

By assembling a picture of the major threats and opportunities facing a specific business unit, it is possible to characterize its overall attractiveness. Four outcomes are possible. An ideal business is high in major opportunities and low in major threats. A speculative business is high in both major opportunities and threats. A major business is low in major opportunities and threats. Finally, a troubled business is low in opportunities and high in threats.

Traditional institutional food-service providers to hospitals, schools, government offices, and office buildings face the threat of competition from quick-service restaurants (QSR). Many QSRs such as Pizza Hut, Dunkin Donuts, Burger King and others, have entered this market. Traditional institutional food-service firms such as ARAMARK cannot ignore this threat.[25]

Internal Environment Analysis (Strengths/Weaknesses Analysis)

It is one thing to discern attractive opportunities in the environment; it is another to have the necessary competencies to succeed in these opportunities. Each business needs to evaluate its strengths and weaknesses periodically. This can be done by using a form such as shown in Figure 3-8. Management or an outside consultant reviews the business's marketing,

Figure 3-8
Strengths/weaknesses analysis.

	Performance					Importance		
	Major Strength	Minor Strength	Neutral	Minor Weakness	Major Weakness	Hi	Med	Low
Marketing								
1. Company reputation	—	—	—	—	—	—	—	—
2. Market share	—	—	—	—	—	—	—	—
3. Product quality	—	—	—	—	—	—	—	—
4. Service quality	—	—	—	—	—	—	—	—
5. Pricing effectiveness	—	—	—	—	—	—	—	—
6. Distribution effectiveness	—	—	—	—	—	—	—	—
7. Promotion effectiveness	—	—	—	—	—	—	—	—
8. Salesforce effectiveness	—	—	—	—	—	—	—	—
9. Innovation effectiveness	—	—	—	—	—	—	—	—
10. Geographical coverage	—	—	—	—	—	—	—	—
Finance								
11. Cost/availability of capital								
12. Cash flow	—	—	—	—	—	—	—	—
13. Financial stability	—	—	—	—	—	—	—	—
Manufacturing								
14. Facilities	—	—	—	—	—	—	—	—
15. Economies of scale	—	—	—	—	—	—	—	—
16. Capacity	—	—	—	—	—	—	—	—
17. Able dedicated workforce	—	—	—	—	—	—	—	—
18. Ability to produce on time	—	—	—	—	—	—	—	—
19. Technical manufacturing skill	—	—	—	—	—	—	—	—
Organization								
20. Visionary capable leadership	—	—	—	—	—	—	—	—
21. Dedicated employees	—	—	—	—	—	—	—	—
22. Entrepreneurial orientation	—	—	—	—	—	—	—	—
23. Flexible/responsive	—	—	—	—	—	—	—	—

financial, manufacturing, and organizational competencies. Each factor is rated as to whether it is a major strength, minor strength, neutral factor, minor weakness, or major weakness. A company with strong marketing capability would show up with the 10 marketing factors all rated as major strengths.

In examining its pattern of strengths and weaknesses, clearly the business does not have to correct all its weaknesses nor gloat about all its strengths. The big question is whether the business should limit itself to those opportunities for which it now possesses the required strengths or should consider better opportunities.

Many hospitality industry specialists believe that to compete effectively, companies such as hotels, resorts, and cruise lines will need "seamless connectivity" within their computer reservation systems (CRS), including a global distribution system (GDS). If a hotel company wishes to increase its international business and its reservations through travel agents, the existence or development of such a system would surely be viewed as a strength.[26]

Sometimes a business does poorly not because its department lacks the required strengths, but because they do not work together as a team. In some hospitality companies salespeople are viewed as overpaid, good-time playboys/playgirls who produce business by practically giving it away to customers. In turn, salespeople often view those in operations as incompetent dolts who consistently foul up their orders and provide poor customer service. It is therefore critically important to assess interdepartmental working relationships as part of the internal environmental audit.

Every company must manage some basic processes, such as new-product development, raw materials to finished products, sales leads to orders, customer orders to cash payment, and so on. Each process creates value and each process requires interdepartmental teamwork. Although each department may possess a core competence, the challenge is to develop superior competitive capability in managing these processes.

Goal Formulation

After the business unit has defined its mission and examined its strengths/weaknesses/opportunities/threats (called SWOT analysis), it can proceed to develop specific objectives and goals for the planning period. This stage is called goal formulation.

Very few businesses pursue only one objective. Most business units pursue a mix of objectives, including profitability, sales growth, market-share improvement, risk containment, innovativeness, reputation, and so on. The business unit sets these objectives and manages by objectives.

The business unit should strive to arrange its objectives hierarchically, from the most to the least important. Where possible, objectives should be stated quantitatively. The objective "increase the return on investment (ROI)" is not as satisfactory as "increase ROI to 15%" or, even better, "increase ROI to 15% within 2 years." Managers use the term goals to describe objectives that are specific with respect to magnitude and time. Turning objectives into measurable goals facilitates management planning, implementation, and control. A business should set realistic goals. The levels should arise from an analysis of the business unit's opportunities and strengths, not from wishful thinking.

Finally, the company's objectives need to be consistent. Objectives are sometimes in a trade-off relationship. Here are some important trade-offs:

- High profit margins versus high market share
- Deep penetration of existing markets versus developing new markets
- Profit goals versus nonprofit goals
- High growth versus low risk

Strategy Formulation

Goals indicate what a business unit wants to achieve; strategy answers how to get there. Every business must tailor a strategy for achieving its goals. Although we can list many types of strategies, Michael Porter has con-

Lufthansa and United Airlines have formed a strategic alliance. Courtesy of Leo Barnett, United Airlines, and Lufthansa Airlines.

A world of experience.
Times two.

Two renowned airlines. One global alliance. From over 250 cities throughout North America to over 170 cities around the world.

Newly expanded opportunities to earn and redeem miles with access to our combined global route networks under two different frequent flyer programs.

For reservations, contact your Travel Professional. Or call United at 1-800-538-2929 or Lufthansa at 1-800-645-3880 today.

United and Lufthansa. A world of experience. Times two.

United's service to 250 cities includes United Express.

Lufthansa / UNITED AIRLINES

densed them into three generic types that provide a good starting point for strategic thinking.[27]

- **Overall cost leadership.** Here the business works hard to achieve the lowest costs. The problem with this strategy is that other firms will usually emerge with still lower costs. The real key is for the firm to achieve the lowest costs among those competitors adopting a similar differentiation or focus strategy.
- **Differentiation.** Here the business concentrates on achieving superior performance in an important customer benefit area valued by a large part of the market.
- **Focus.** Here the business focuses on one or more narrow market segments, rather than going after a large market. The firm gets to know the needs of these segments and pursues either cost leadership or a form of differentiation within the target segments.

According to Porter, those firms pursuing the same strategy directed to the same market or market segment constitute a strategic group. Porter suggests that firms that do not pursue a clear strategy—middle-of-the-roaders—do the worst. Middle-of-the-roaders try to be good on all strategic dimensions, but these firms end up being not particularly excellent at anything.

Program Formulation

Once the business unit has developed its principal strategies, it must work out supporting programs. Thus, if an upscale hotel has decided to attain service leadership, it must run recruiting programs to attract the right employees, conduct training programs, develop leading-edge products and amenities, motivate the sales force, develop ads to communicate its service leadership, and so on.

Implementation

Even a clear strategy and well-thought-out supporting programs may not be enough. The firm may fail at implementation. Employees in a company share a common way of behaving and thinking. They must understand and believe in the company's strategy. The company must communicate its strategy to the employees and make them understand their part in carrying out the strategy. To implement a strategy the firm must have the required resources including employees with the skills needed to carry out the company's strategy.

Feedback and Control

As it implements its strategy, the firm needs to track results and monitor new developments in the environment. Some environments are fairly stable from year to year. Others evolve slowly in a fairly predictable way. Still other environments change rapidly. The company can count on one thing:

that the environment will change. And, when it does, the company will need to review and revise its implementation, programs, strategies, or even objectives. Peter Drucker pointed out that it is more important to do the right thing (being effective) than to do things right (being efficient). Excellent companies excel at both.

Once an organization starts losing its market position through failure to respond to a changed environment, it becomes increasingly harder to retrieve leadership.

Organizations, especially large ones, have much inertia. Yet organizations can be changed through leadership, one hopes in advance of a crisis but certainly in the midst of a crisis. The key to organizational health is the organization's willingness to examine the changing environment and to adopt appropriate new goals and behaviors. Adaptable organizations continuously monitor the environment and attempt through flexible strategic planning to maintain a viable fit with the evolving environment.

The Emperor Hotel, a 3-star property in Singapore, caters primarily to independent and corporate travelers, many in the oil industry. Due to a recession in Singapore, corporate income fell from $2.2 million to a loss of nearly $300,000.

Problem areas were the following:

- A 45% drop in food and beverage revenue
- Declining hotel occupancy from 92% to 57%
- Intensive competition
- Rising fixed costs
- Shrinking market niche (oil industry people fewer in numbers)
- Autocratic management style

The owner conducted a strategic analysis of the hotel and determined critical strengths and weaknesses.

STRENGTHS	WEAKNESSES
Image	Need for face lift
Location	Slow management response
Financial support	Weak market niche
Service orientation	Pool cultural orientation
	Intensified competition

As a result of the strategic analysis, the Emperor Hotel decided to "shrink selectively," particularly in the food and beverage area. Food and beverage operations were contracted out. This strategy was selected because it was felt that if a hotel boom occurred the hotel would be in a good position to take advantage of the good times. If not, the hotel would be attractive to a prospective buyer and could be sold on short notice.[28]

UNIQUE CHALLENGES OF THE HOTEL INDUSTRY

The hotel/resort industry faces unique challenges in strategic planning. Most other members of the hospitality industry, such as airlines, cruise lines, and major restaurant chains, may approach strategic planning in much the same manner as a manufacturing company. These organizations have highly centralized management operations in which major strategic decisions are made.

The hotel/resort industry is characterized by a unique management and ownership structure that complicates the process of strategic planning.

- Major chains commonly do not own all the properties that they manage. Some hotel chains may in fact own no individual properties.

- Owners of hotels/resorts often show surprisingly little interest or knowledge of their properties. Hotels throughout the world have commonly been acquired because of tax benefits, perceived real estate appreciation, or as an ego fulfilling device, particularly in the case of upscale showcase properties.

- Occasionally, owners complain that hotel management companies are nonresponsive, have little expertise in planning, and do not work closely with owners or their representatives. In Asia, there reportedly exists an association of hotel owners who have grouped together in an effort to place pressure on hotel management companies.

- Hotel management companies that are generally unknown or invisible to the general public may own or manage many diverse properties, such as Ramada, Holiday Inn, and Days Inn hotels.

- Professional managers of individual properties have commonly been educated and trained to manage properties with concern for areas such as maintenance and front-desk operations, but with little or no training in strategic planning. Many feel this is the responsibility of the owner, yet if the owner has little interest in this function, strategic planning at the property level is overlooked.

- Hotel management companies often have little real power to force owners to make necessary investments or strategic changes deemed essential. In many cases, the only alternative has been to drop the property from the chain.

- Hotels may or may not own or manage secondary properties within the hotel, such as restaurants, retail stores, health and fitness centers, and nightclubs. This creates added complexity in strategic planning.

- Strategic alliances between hotel chains on a global basis may further complicate the planning process.

Marketing has a definite role to play in strategic planning. This department must maintain close and continuous ties with customers. Marketing is responsible for identifying and studying consumer needs and, as such, has a level of expertise in this area that is invaluable in strategic planning.

Chapter Review

I.   The Aim of Strategic Planning. It helps a company select and organize its business in a way that keeps the company healthy in spite of unexpected upsets occurring in any of its specific business or product lines.

II.   Three Ideas Define Strategic Planning

1)   Managing a company's business as an investment portfolio, for which it will be decided which business entities deserve to be built, maintained, phased down, or terminated.

2)   Assessing accurately the future profit potential of each business by considering the market's growth rate and the company's position and fit.

3)   Underlying strategic planning is that of strategy and developing a game plan for achieving its long-run objective.

III.   Four Major Organizational Levels

1)   Corporate Level. The corporate level is responsible for designing a corporate strategic plan to guide the whole enterprise. It makes decisions on how much resource support to allocate to each division, as well as which businesses to start or eliminate.

2)   Division Level. Each division establishes a division plan covering the allocation of funds to each business unit's strategic plan to carry that business unit within that division.

3)   Business Level. Each business unit in turn develops its business unit's strategic plan to carry that business unit into a profitable future.

4)   Product Level. Each product level within a business unit develops a marketing plan for achieving its objectives in its product market.

IV.   Four Natures of High-performance Business

1)   Stakeholder. The principle that a business must at least strive to satisfy the minimum expectations of each stakeholder group.

2)   Processes. Companies build cross-functional teams that manage core business processes to be superior competitors.

3)   Resources. Companies decide to outsource less critical resources. They identify their core competencies and use them as the basis for their strategic planning.

4)   Organization. Companies align their organization's structure, policies, and culture to the changing requirements of business strategy.

V.   Four Elements of Defining the Corporate Mission. A mission statement provides company employees with a shared sense of purpose, direction, and opportunity. The company mission statement guides geographically dispersed employees to work independently and yet collectively toward realizing the organization's goal.

1)   History: Every company has a history of aims, policies and achievements, and the organization must not depart too radically from its past history.

2)   Consideration of the current preferences of the owner and management.

3)   The organization's resources determine which missions are possible.

4)   The organization should base its mission on its distinctive competencies.

VI. Mission Statement's Characteristic and Focused Goals

1) Industry scope. The range of industries that the company will consider.

2) Products and application scope. The range of products and applications in which the company will participate.

3) Competencies scope. The range of technological and other core competencies that the company will master and leverage.

4) Market-segment scope. The types of market or customers that the company will serve.

5) Vertical scope. The number of channel levels from raw materials to final products and distribution in which the company will engage.

6) Geographical scope. The range of regions or countries where the corporation will operate.

VII. Establishing Strategic Business Units. Three dimensions in defining a business: customer groups, customer needs, and technology.

VIII. Strategic Business Units (SBUs). An SBU is a single business or collection of related businesses that can be planned for separately from the rest of the company. It has its own set of competitors and a manager who is responsible for strategic planning and profit performance.

IX. Boston Consulting Group Model

1) Question mark. Company businesses that operate in high-growth markets but have relatively low market shares.

2) Stars. The market leader in a high-growth market. This does not necessarily mean that the star produces a positive cash flow for the company.

3) Cash cows. When a star's annual growth rate falls to less than 10%, it becomes a cash cow. A cash cow produces a lot of cash for the company and enjoys economies of scale and higher profit margins.

4) Dogs. Dogs describe company businesses that have weak market shares in low-growth markets. They typically generate low profits or losses.

X. Planning New Businesses

Strategic planning gap: The gap between future desired sales and projected sales. Three ways to fill the gap:

1) Intensive growth opportunities. To identify further opportunities to achieve growth within the company's current business.

2) Integrative growth opportunities. To identify opportunities to build or acquire businesses that are related to the company's current business.

a) **Backward integration:** A hotel company acquiring one of its suppliers.

b) **Forward integration:** A hotel company acquiring a tour wholesaler or travel agents.

c) **Horizontal integration:** A hotel company acquiring one or more competitors, provided the government does not bar the move.

3) Diversification growth opportunities. To identify opportunities to add attractive businesses that are unrelated to the company's current businesses.

a) **Concentric diversification strategy:** Company seeks new products that have technological and/or marketing synergies with existing product line, even though the product may appeal to a new class of customers.

b) Horizontal diversification strategy: Company searches for new products that could appeal to its current customers though technologically unrelated to its current product line.

c) Conglomerate diversification strategy: Company seeks new businesses that have no relationship to the company's current technology, product, or market.

XI. **Business Strategy Planning**

1) **Business Mission**. SBU defines its various scopes: its products and applications, competence, market segments, vertical positioning, and geography. It must also define its specific goals and policies as a separate business.

2) **External environment analysis**

   a) Macroenvironment forces: Demographic/economic, technological, political/legal, competition, and social/cultural.

   b) Microenvironment factors: Customers, competitors, distribution channels, suppliers.

   c) Opportunities: A marketing opportunity is an area of need in which a company can perform profitably. Opportunities can be listed and classified according to their attractiveness and the success probability.

   d) Threats: An environmental threat is a challenge posed by unfavorable trends or developments that would lead, in the absence of defensive marketing action, to sales or profit deterioration. Threats can be classified according to their seriousness and probability of occurrence.

3) **Internal environment analysis (strengths analysis and weaknesses analysis):** Company reviews the business's marketing, financial, manufacturing, and organizational competencies. Each factor is rated as to whether it is a major strength, minor strength, neutral factor, or minor weakness.

4) **Goal formulation** (*What do we want?*)

Four characteristics of SBU's objectives:

   a) Hierarchical: The business unit should strive to arrange its objectives hierarchically, from the most to the least important.

   b) Quantitative: Managers use the term goals to describe objectives that are specific with respect to magnitude and time.

   c) Realistic: The levels should arise from an analysis of the business unit's opportunities and strengths, not from wishful thinking.

   d) Consistent: Long-run market-share growth and high current profits, for example.

5) **Strategy formulation** (*How do we get there?*)

Michael Porter's three generic types of strategy:

   a) Overall cost leadership: The real key is for a firm to achieve the lowest costs among those competitors adopting a similar differentiation or focus strategy.

   b) Differentiation: The firm cultivates strengths that will give it a competitive advantage in one or more benefits.

   c) Focus: The firm gets to know the needs of these segments and pursues either cost leadership or a form of differentiation within the target segments.

6) Program formulation. Supporting programs, such as running recruiting programs to attract the right employee, conducting training programs, developing leading-edge products and amenities, motivating the sales force, developing advertisements to communicate its service leadership.

7) Implementation. To implement a strategy the firm must have the required resources including employees with the skills needed to carry out the company's strategy.

8) Feedback and control. The firm needs to track results and monitor new developments in the environment. The company will need to review and revise its implementation, programs, strategies, or even objectives.

DISCUSSION QUESTIONS

1. What is meant by strategic planning?
2. Is strategic planning the same thing as marketing planning, sales planning, and restructuring?
3. Give examples of how strategic planning might benefit the following:
   (a) An individual hotel
   (b) A regional hotel firm
   (c) A national hotel firm
4. What is the significance of an SBU?
5. What forms of vertical integration do you feel are likely to occur in the travel industry during the next 10 years?

KEY TERMS

Ansoff product/market expansion grid A model that assists management to plan product line growth.

Backward integration A growth strategy by which companies acquire businesses that supply them with products or services, such as a restaurant chain purchasing a bakery.

Concentric diversification strategy A growth strategy whereby a company seeks new products that have technological or marketing synergies with existing product lines.

Conglomerate diversification strategy A product growth strategy in which a company seeks new businesses that have no relationship to the company's current product line or markets.

Corporate mission statement A guide to provide all the publics of a company with a shared sense of purpose, direction, and opportunity that allows all to work independently yet collectively toward the organization's goals.

Corporate strategic planning Long-run planning that incorporates defining the mission statement, establishing strategic business units, assigning resources to each SBU, planning new business.

Forward integration A growth strategy by which companies acquire businesses that are closer to the ultimate consumer, such as a hotel acquiring a chain of travel agents.

General Electric multifactor portfolio matrix A model developed by General Electric to assist managers to plan business portfolios.

Growth/share matrix A model developed by the Boston Consulting Group to assist managers to plan business portfolios.

Horizontal diversification strategy A product growth strategy whereby a company looks for new products that could appeal to current customers, which are technologically unrelated to its current line.

Horizontal integration A growth strategy by which companies acquire competitors.

Internal environmental analysis A periodic evaluation of a company's strengths and weaknesses.

Macroenvironmental forces Demographic, economic, technological, political, legal, social, and cultural factors.

Market-oriented strategic planning The managerial process of developing and maintaining a viable fit between the organization's objectives, skills, and resources and its changing market opportunities.

Marketing opportunities   An area of need in which a company can perform profitably.

Marketing threats   A challenge posed by unfavorable trends or developments that would lead, in the absence of defensive marketing action, to sales or profit deterioration.

Microenvironmental forces   Customers, competitors, distribution channels, suppliers.

Seamless connectivity   The ability to make direct reservations electronically without interfacing with another party.

Strategic alliances   Relationships between independent parties that agree to cooperate but still retain separate identities.

Strategic business units (SBUs)   A single business or collection of related businesses that can be planned separately from the rest of the company.

REFERENCES

1. ROBERT TOMSHO, "Real Dog: How Greyhound Lines Re-engineered Itself Right into a Deep Hole," *Wall Street Journal*, (October 30, 1994), pp. 1 and A6.

2. See FRANCIS BUTTLE, "The Marketing Strategy Worksheet: A Practical Tool," *Cornell Hotel and Restaurant Administration Quarterly*, 33, no. 3 (June 1992), pp. 55–67.

3. MARK W. CUNNINGHAM AND DEV S. CHEKITAN, "Strategic Marketing: A Lodging End Run," *Cornell Hotel and Restaurant Administration Quarterly*, 33, no. 4 (August 1992), p. 43.

4. Ibid.

5. STEVE HARRELL, in a speech at the plenary session of the American Marketing Association's Educator's Meeting, Chicago, August 5, 1980.

6. See TAMARA J. ERICKSON AND C. EVERETT SHOREY, "Business Strategy: New Thinking for the 90's," *Prism*, Fourth Quarter (1992), pp. 19–35.

7. CATHY A. ENZ, "Organizational Architectures for the 21st Century: The Redesign for Hospitality Firms," *Hospitality Research Journal*, 17, no. 1 (1993), p. 108.

8. CHRISTOPHER W. NORDLING AND SHARON K. WHEELER, "Building a Market-segment Accounting Model to Improve Profits," *Cornell Hotel and Restaurant Administration Quarterly*, 33, no. 3 (June 1992), pp. 29–36.

9. AL GLANZBERG AND GLENN WITHIAM, "Culture at the Crossroads: Boca Raton and Rockresort," *Cornell Hotel and Restaurant Administration Quarterly*, 32, no. 1 (May 1991), p. 39.

10. BRUCE J. TRACEY AND TIMOTHY R. HINKIN, "Transformational Leaders in the Hospitality Industry," *Cornell Hotel and Restaurant Administration Quarterly*, 35, no. 2 (April 1994), p. 18.

11. See PETER DRUCKER, *Management: Tasks, Responsibilities, and Practices* (New York: Harper & Row, 1973), Chapter 7.

12. See "The Hollow Corporation," *Business Week* (March 3, 1986), pp. 57–59.

13. SUSAN EARDLEY, "Momentum Builds for Choice's Europe Growth," *Hotel & Motel Management*, 208, no. 6 (April 5, 1993), pp. 1, 38.

14. For more discussion, see Laura Nash, "Mission Statements—Mirrors and Windows," *Harvard Business Review* (March–April 1988), pp. 155–156. See also: TOM FELTENSTEIN, "Strategic Planning for the 1990's: Exploiting the Inevitable," *Cornell Hotel and Restaurant Administration Quarterly*, 33, no. 3 (June 1992), pp. 50–54.

15. ROBERT H. WOODS, "Strategic Planning: A Look at Ruby Tuesday," *Cornell Hotel and Restaurant Administration Quarterly*, 35, no. 3 (June 1994), p. 45.

16. THEODORE LEVITT, "Marketing Myopia," *Harvard Business Review* (July–August 1960), pp. 45–56.

17. See "Holiday Inns: Refining Its Focus to Food, Lodging, and More Casinos," *Business Week* (July 21, 1980), pp. 100–104.

18. See ROGER A. KERIN, VIJAY MAHAJAN, AND P. RAJAN VARADARAJAN, *Contemporary Perspectives on Strategic Planning* (Boston: Allyn & Bacon, 1990).

19. IGOR H. ANSOFF, "Strategies for Diversification," *Harvard Business Review* (September–October 1957), pp. 113–124.

20. CLIFF EDWARDS, "McDonalds Goal: Restaurants on Every Block, Plane, Train," *Denver Post* (April 26, 1994), p. 2D

21. GREGORY X. NORKUS AND ELLIOTT MERBERG, "Food Distribution in the 1990's," *Cornell Hotel and Restaurant Administration Quarterly*, 35, no. 3 (June 1994), pp. 60–61.

22. SARAH MORSE AND PAMELA LANIER, "Golf Resorts—Driving into the 90's," *Cornell Hotel and Restaurant Administration Quarterly*, 33, no. 4 (August 1992), p. 45.

23. Ibid.

24. MICHAEL P. SIM AND CHASE M. BURRITT, "Enhancing Resort Profitability with Membership Programs," *Cornell Hotel and Restaurant Administration*

Quarterly, 34, no. 4 (August 1993), pp. 59–63.

25. H. G. PARSA AND MAHMOOD A. KHAN, "Quick Service Restaurants of the 21st Century: An Analytical Review of Macro Factors," *Hospitality Research Journal*, 17, no. 1 (1993), p. 164.

26. RITA M. EMMER, CHUCK TAUCK, SCOTT WILKINSON, AND RICHARD G. MOORE, "Marketing Hotels Using Global Distribution Systems," *Cornell Hotel and Restaurant Administration Quarterly*, 34, No. 6 (December 1993), pp. 80–89.

27. See MICHAEL E. PORTER, *Competitive Strategy: Techniques for Analyzing Industries and Competitors* (New York: Free Press, 1980), Chapter 2.

28. KEE LEE WENG AND B. C. GHOSH, "Strategies for Hotels in Singapore," *Cornell Hotel and Restaurant Administration Quarterly*, 31, no. 1 (May 1990), pp. 78–79.

Service
Characteristics
of Hospitality and
Tourism Marketing

The Victoria House is a small Caribbean Island resort hotel located on an island off the shore of Belize. There is one phone, no television, and no newsstand. Looking at the ocean from the Victoria House's beach, guests can see waves breaking over the barrier reef renowned for its fishing and diving. Victoria House offers North American executives a chance to escape stress and relax in a tropical paradise. Victoria House's brochures communicate this message well, showing thatched villas, palm trees, and the Caribbean Sea.

But when guests arrived at the resort, the initial impression was much different than that created by the brochure. The resort consists of a main lodge (guest rooms upstairs and the reception, dining room and bar downstairs), employee quarters, and 12 thatched roof guest cottages. The van delivering guests to the hotel drops them off between the main lodge and the employee quarters. Instead of enjoying a beautiful ocean view, guests see the kitchen, the employee quarters, their laundry hanging out to dry, and a car being repaired with its motor hanging from a tree.

Victoria House did not create a positive first impression. Guests stepping out of the van wonder if they made a terrible mistake. The management of Victoria House grew up on the island and accept the breathtaking ocean views as common and uninspiring. The entrance was designed for

efficiency to allow delivery trucks to drop their goods near store rooms and to drop the guests off at a convenient entrance to the lodge.

The management of Victoria House failed to consider that many guests had never been to the island and were expecting Shangri La. The New York executive who purchased a Victoria House vacation had only the promise of stress-free relaxation, an air ticket, and a hotel voucher before the trip. Management should have made certain that guest's impressions upon arriving at the resort matched those created by the brochure. In hospitality marketing, this is called "managing the tangible evidence."

When management finally recognized this error, they built a separate driveway allowing guests to be delivered to the front of the resort. The view now included beautifully landscaped grounds with native flowers, palm trees, and a breathtaking view of the ocean. This provided immediate positive guest reinforcement.

Chapter Preview

We start the chapter by discussing four distinguishing characteristics of services: intangibility, inseparability, variability, and perishability.

Next we discuss several things management of service firms can do to increase the effectiveness of their business. These **service management strategies** include **tangiblizing the product, managing employees, managing perceived risk, managing capacity and demand,** and **managing consistency.**

Marketing developed initially in connection with selling physical products such as toothpaste, cars, steel, and equipment. But, today, one of the major trends in many parts of the world is the phenomenal growth of services, or products with little or no physical content. Services account for 95% of the new U.S. jobs created since 1969 and over 75% of GNP.[1] The hospitality and travel industries are part of this growing service sector. Other service industries include banking, health care, entertainment, legal aid, and transportation. As a result of increasing affluence and leisure time, most western countries now are service economies. The growth of service industries has created a demand for research into their operation and marketing. This book will include the results of recent research into services marketing issues.

In this chapter, we will examine the characteristics of firms in the hospitality industry. These characteristics will be referred to throughout the remainder of the book.

Some managers think of their operations only in terms of tangible goods. Thus managers of fast-food restaurants who think they sell only hamburgers often have "slow, surly service personnel, dirty unattractive facilities, and few return customers."[2] One of the most important tasks of a hospitality business is to develop the service side of the business, to develop a strong service culture.

This culture focuses on serving and satisfying the customer. The service culture has to start with top management and flow down. Isadore Sharp drives the service culture in Four Seasons Hotels through employee communications, company policies, and personal actions. This belief that the customer comes first at Four Seasons is reinforced for all Four Seasons

THE SERVICE CULTURE

employees when employees who go to extraordinary efforts to satisfy the customer are made Employee of the Year.

A service culture empowers employees to solve customer problems. It is supported by a reward system based on customer satisfaction. Humans generally do what is rewarded. If an organization wants to deliver a quality product, then the organization's culture must support and reward customer need attention.[3] In Chapter 11, we will discuss service culture in more detail.

CHARACTERISTICS OF SERVICE MARKETING

Service marketers must be concerned with four characteristics of services: intangibility, inseparability, variability, and perishability.

Intangibility

Unlike physical products, services cannot be seen, tasted, felt, heard, or smelled before they are purchased. Prior to boarding an airplane, airline passengers have nothing but an airline ticket and the promise of safe delivery to their destination. Members of a hotel sales-force cannot take a hotel room with them on a sales call. In fact, they do not sell a room; instead they sell the right to use a room for a specific period of time. When hotel guests leave, they have nothing to show for the purchase but a receipt. Robert Lewis has observed that someone who purchases a service may go away empty handed, but they do not go away empty headed.[4] They have memories that can be shared with others.

To reduce uncertainty caused by intangibility, buyers look for tangible evidence that will provide information and confidence about the service. The exterior of a restaurant is the first thing that an arriving guest sees. The condition of the grounds and the overall cleanliness of the restaurant provide cues as to how well the restaurant is run. Various tangibles provide signals as to the quality of the intangible service. The Regent Hotel in Hong Kong makes sure that all its uniformed and nonuniformed employees reinforce the Hotel's image of elegance and professionalism. The appearance of the employees is part of the Regent's tangible evidence. This hotel also purposely parks luxury automobiles such as a Rolls Royce in front to instantly deliver a message of quality and upscale service.

As a niche segment of the hospitality/lodging industry, conference centers face a continuous need to make their products tangible. They must differentiate themselves from resorts and hotels. Product features that conference centers use to differentiate themselves include the following:

- *Dedicated meeting rooms*, that cannot be used for other purposes as in most hotels.
- *Twenty-four-hour use*, which offers security and personalization for clients. Computers, briefcases, and the like, can be left in the room.
- *Continuous coffee*, not just coffee breaks.
- *All inclusive pricing*, a set price per day per meeting attendee.

The International Association of Conference Centers offers an on-line database for travel planners. This important customer segment can access a great amount of information about conference centers, such as size of property, location, availability, and pricing. To help tangibilize the product, the system allows meeting planners to see a layout of a potential property's meeting space on the display screen. Clients can get a concrete idea of the mix of general session, breakout, boardroom, and amphitheater spaces to match with their needs.[5]

Inseparability

In most hospitality services, both the service provider and the customer must be present for the transaction to occur. Customer-contact employees are part of the product. The food in a restaurant may be outstanding, but if the service person has a poor attitude or provides inattentive service, customers will downrate the overall restaurant experience. They will not be satisfied with their experience.

Inseparability also means that customers are part of the product. A couple may have chosen a restaurant because it is quiet and romantic, but if a group of loud and boisterous conventioneers is seated in the same room, the couple will be disappointed. Managers must manage their customers so that they do not create dissatisfaction for other customers.

Another implication of inseparability is that customers and employees must understand the service delivery system. The Holiday Inn—Newark is popular with international tourists who have just arrived from overseas. Many of these guests pay in cash or with travelers checks, as they do not use credit cards. On more than one occasion the front-desk clerk has been observed answering the phone of an upset guest who claims their movie system does not work. The clerk must explain that they did not establish credit, since they paid only for the room and therefore would have to come to the front desk and pay for the movie before it could be activated. Guests obviously become upset upon receiving this information. The hotel could avoid this problem and improve customer relations by asking guests if they would like to make a deposit for anything they might charge, such as in-room movies. The characteristic of inseparability requires hospitality managers to manage both their employees and their customers.

Variability

Services are highly variable. Their quality depends on who provides them and when and where they are provided. There are several causes of variability. Services are produced and consumed simultaneously, which limits quality control. Fluctuating demand makes it difficult to deliver consistent products during periods of peak demand. The high degree of contact between the service provider and the guest means that product consistency depends on the service provider's skills and performance at the time of the exchange. A guest can receive excellent service one day and mediocre service from the same person the next day. In the case of mediocre service, the service person may not have felt well or perhaps experienced an emotional problem. Variability or lack of consistency in the product is a major cause of customer disappointment in the hospitality industry.

This advertisement for the Acapulco Princess helps tangibalize the stress-free environment of a seaside resort. Courtesy of DDB Needham Worldwide and Princess Hotels.

Perishability

Services cannot be stored. A 100-room hotel that only sells 60 rooms on a particular night cannot sell 140 the next. Revenue lost from not selling the remaining 40 rooms is gone forever. Because of perishability, some hotels charge guests holding guaranteed reservations even when they fail to check into the hotel. Restaurants are also starting to charge a fee to customers who do not show up for a reservation. They, too, realize that if someone does not show for a reservation the opportunity to sell that seat may be lost. If services are to maximize revenue, they must manage capacity and demand since they cannot carry forward unsold inventory.

Service marketers can do several things to increase service effectiveness in the face of intrinsic service characteristics.

Tangibilizing the Product

Service marketers should take steps to provide their prospective customers with evidence that will help tangibilize the service.[6] Promotional material, employees' appearance, and the service firm's physical environment all help tangibilize service. A hotel's promotional material might include a meeting planner's packet containing photographs of the hotel's public area, guest rooms, and meeting space. The packet would also contain floor plans of the meeting space, including room capacities for the different types of setups to help the meeting planner visualize the meeting space.

A banquet salesperson for a fine restaurant can tangibilize the product by taking pastry samples on morning sales calls. This creates goodwill and provides the prospective client with a tangible clue about the restaurant's food quality. The salesperson might also bring a photo album showing photographs of banquet setups, plate presentations for different entrees, and testimonial letters from past clients.

The salesperson may be the prospective customer's first contact with that business. A salesperson who is well-groomed and dressed appropriately and who answers questions in a prompt professional manner can do a great deal to help the customer develop a positive image of the hotel.

Despite her problems, Leona Helmsley served as an excellent salesperson for her chain of hotels. She made her hotels tangible in advertisements by showing a large oversize towel; one could almost feel the quality and body-hugging appeal of this towel.

Physical evidence comes in many forms. The wrappers put on drinking glasses in the guest rooms serve the purpose of letting the guest know that the glasses have been cleaned. The fold in the toilet paper in the bathroom lets the guest know that the bathroom has been tidied.

Everything about a hospitality company communicates something. Red and white awnings, the outside patio, the blue and white striped building displaying T.G.I. Friday's sign in large letters, all are signs to indicate this restaurant offers informality and fun. A couple looking for an elegant, intimate restaurant would be disappointed at Friday's. Similarly, Hampton Inn's exterior appearance suggests to travelers that it will provide clean, comfortable, and safe lodging at a moderate price. When guests arrive, they find no door or bell clerks, concierge desk, or other features of an upscale hotel. They instead find an attentive desk clerk in an appropriate uniform and a small lobby with comfortable, but moderate furnishings.

Trade Dress. Hospitality companies have become very sensitive to protecting the distinctive nature of their total visual image and overall appearance known as trade dress. McDonald's and Holiday Inn have brought suit against competitors who dared to copy any form of the golden arches or Holiday Inn sign.

Friday's exterior provides evidence that Friday's is a casual restaurant. Courtesy of TGI Friday's, Inc.

A U.S. court has found that the decor, menu, layout and style of service of a restaurant was protectable trade dress.[7] The restaurant Taco Cabana sued Two Pesos, Inc., for trade dress infringement under the Lanham Act. Taco Cabana complained that the interior of Two Pesos was too close to that of Taco Cabana. Likewise, Prufrock Ltd. sued Dixie House Restaurants, claiming that this competitor had copied its concept of a full-service restaurant serving down-home country cooking in a relaxed and informal atmosphere with a full service bar using booth seating, small print wallpaper, antique drop-leaf tables, an exposed kitchen area, antique light fixtures, an antique bar and country style wall decor.[8]

Experts in this field have concluded that, "It's not a simple matter to know when an operation's total visual image and overall product presentation can be considered exclusive to a particular chain or company." To compete effectively in today's marketplace, an entrepreneur, operator or owner must design an effective trade dress while taking care not to imitate too closely that of a competitor.[9]

Members of the hospitality industry should not be misled by thinking that protection of trade dress is a worldwide concept. One only has to visit other nations, particularly those in the third world, to observe that local entrepreneurs commonly copy successful trade dress from other nations. In some cases this makes it impossible for a company to use its own name or trade dress in a foreign nation. Burger King cannot use this name in Australia and instead calls its restaurants Hungry Jack.

Physical Surroundings

Physical evidence that is not managed properly can hurt a business. Negative messages communicated by poorly managed physical evidence include signs that continue to advertise a holiday special two weeks after the holiday has passed, signs with missing letters or burned out lights, parking lots and grounds that are unkempt and full of trash, and employees in dirty uniforms at messy work stations. Such signs send negative messages to customers.

Physical surroundings should be designed to reinforce the product's position in the customer's mind. The front-desk staff in a luxury hotel should dress in professional apparel—wool or wool blend conservative clothes. The front-desk staff at a tropical resort might wear tropical, Hawaiian-style shirts. The counter staff at a fast-food restaurant might wear a simple polyester uniform.

A firm's communications should also reinforce their positioning. Ronald McDonald is great for McDonald's, but a clown would not be appropriate for a Four Season's Hotel. All said, a service organization should review every piece of tangible evidence to make sure that each delivers the desired image to target customers.[10]

Stress Advantages of Nonownership

In a service the customer does not have ownership of the product. Lack of ownership, sometimes cited as a major characteristic of a service, can be stressed as a benefit.[11] For example, rather than own corporate lodging and provide a staff to maintain the lodging, corporations are usually better off negotiating a rate with a hotel. The advantages of nonownership in this case include only paying for the rooms when they are used, not having to maintain apartments, having access to capital that is not tied up in the ownership of the lodging facilities, and the extra services provided by the hotel (food and beverage, meeting rooms, and shops).

"Greening" of the Hospitality Industry

In recent years the use of outside natural landscaping and inside use of light and plants has become a widely used and popular method of creating differentiation and tangibilizing the product. The term "fern bars" became associated with yuppies and the types of restaurants they prefer. But it is not just yuppies who are positively influenced by landscaping and the interior use of plants.

In some communities such as Lake Tahoe, the government sets strict visual guidelines that hospitality companies must observe. The developers of the Embassy Suites Resort in Lake Tahoe had to undertake a complex and lengthy planning process. The design of this hotel was 70% dictated by governing agencies, including the style of the hotel, scenic thresholds, and the selection of exterior colors.[12]

Managing Employees

In the hospitality industry, employees are a critical part of the product and marketing mix. This means that the human resources and marketing departments must work closely together. In restaurants without a human resources department, the restaurant manager serves as the human resource manager. The manager must hire friendly and capable employees and for-mulate polices that support positive relations between employees and guests. Even minor details related to personnel policy can have a significant effect on the product's quality.[13] One fast-food restaurant had a policy that all employees must be off the clock by 10:15 P.M. To implement the policy, employees had to shut down the restaurant starting at 9:40 P.M., even though it advertised that it was open until 10 P.M.

In a well-run hospitality organization, there are two customers, the paying customers and the employees.[14] The task of training and motivating employees to provide good customer service is called **internal marketing**. In the hospitality industry, it is not enough to have a marketing department focused on **traditional marketing** to a targeted external market. The job of the marketing department includes encouraging everyone in the organi-zation to practice customer-oriented thinking[15] (see Chapter 11). The follow-ing excerpt from **In Search of Excellence** illustrates the importance of well-trained employees in a hospitality operation:

> We had decided, after dinner, to spend a second night in Washington. Our business day had taken us beyond the last convenient flight out. We had no reservations, but were near the new Four Seasons, had stayed there once before, and liked it. As we walked through the lobby won-dering how best to plead our case for a room, we braced for the usual chilly shoulder accorded to latecomers. To our astonishment, the concierge looked up, smiled, called us by name, and asked how we were. She remembered our names! We knew in a flash why in the space of a brief year the Four Seasons had become the "place to stay" in the District and was a rare first-year holder of the venerated four-star rating.[16]

Managing Perceived Risk

Customers who buy hospitality products experience some anxiety because they cannot experience the product beforehand.[17] Consider a salesperson who is asked by her sales manager to set up a regional sales meeting. Suppose that the salesperson has never set up a meeting or worked with hotels. The sales-person is obviously nervous. If the meeting goes well, the sales manager will be favorably impressed; if it goes badly, the salesperson may be blamed.

In arranging for the meeting place, the salesperson has to trust the hotel's salesperson. Good hotel salespeople will alleviate client fears by let-ting them know that they have arranged hundreds of successful meetings. The salesperson's claims to professionalism can be tangibilized through let-ters of praise from former clients and a tour of the hotel's facilities. A sales-person must reduce client fear and gain the client's confidence.

One way of combating concern is to encourage the client to try the hotel or restaurant in a low-risk situation. Hotels and resorts offer familiar-ization (or FAM) trips to meeting planners and travel agents. Airlines often offer complimentary flight tickets because they are also interested in creat-ing business. Hotels provide rooms, food, beverage and entertainment at no cost to the prospective client in hope that this exposure will encourage them to recommend the hotel. FAM trips reduce a product's intangibility by letting the intermediary customer experience the hotel beforehand.

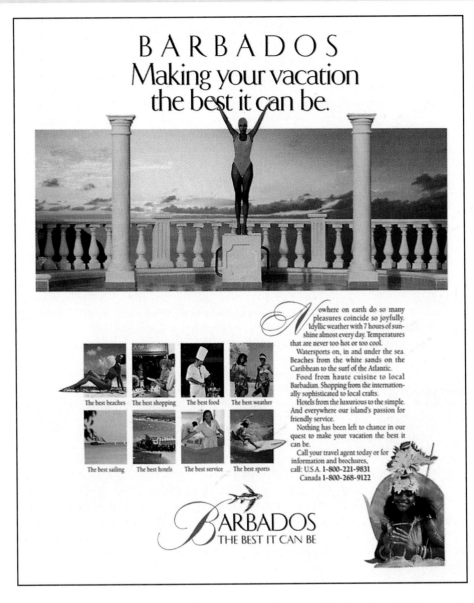

This advertisement for Barbados reduces a potential customer's perceived risk by stressing the consistency of its weather, the variety of activities available, good food, and the friendly characteristics of its people. Pictures in the advertisement provide tangible evidence of these features. Courtesy of Barbados Tourism Authority and D'Arcy, Masius, Benton, & Bowles.

The high risk that people perceive when purchasing hospitality products increases loyalty to companies that have provided them with a consistent product in the past. Crowne Plaza attracted their competitor's loyal customers by using the following tactic: Guests were billed at the regular room rate. However, they were free to pay less if they felt the accommodations and service were not worth the price. The promotion was highly successful, attracting a number of new guests, almost all of whom paid the full rate.

Managing Capacity and Demand

Since services are perishable, managing capacity and demand is a key function of hospitality marketing. For example, Mother's Day is traditionally a restaurant's busiest day of the year, with the peak time at brunch from 11 A.M. to 2 P.M. This 3-hour period presents restauranteurs with one of the greatest sales opportunities during the year. To take full advantage of this opportunity, restaurant managers must accomplish two things. First, they must adjust their operating systems to enable the business to operate at maximum capacity. Second, they must remember that their goal is to create satisfied customers.

Many restaurants feature buffets on Mother's Day to increase capacity. An attractive buffet creates a festive atmosphere, provides an impression of variety and value, and expedites service by eliminating the need to prepare food to order. Customers provide their own service, with the service staff providing the beverage and check, which frees the staff to wait on more customers. Buffets eliminate the time required for order taking and preparing the order. Food is available when customers arrive, allowing them to start eating almost immediately. This increases turnover of tables, further increasing the restaurant's capacity. The buffet also allows the restaurant to create a buffer inventory. Although 3 hours' worth of food cannot be kept on a steam table without a reduction in quality and attractiveness, the food can be cooked in batches that will last 20 to 30 minutes.

A few restaurants, such as Boomerangs of Steamboat Springs, expect guests to prepare their own entrees. Guests select a cut of meat and grill it over a charcoal grill. They also help themselves to the salad bar.

Good cafeterias such as K&W of North Carolina remain successful and popular because they manage inventory very well. Food is moderately priced, fresh, and selected to meet ordinary food preferences, such as roast beef and chicken pot pie, not specialty interests such as Indian curry.

How can a hotel prepare for an expected low-occupancy period? Suppose that the hotel projects a 2-week period of low occupancy 6 months from now. One system is to reduce staff and other expenses when the period arrives, including arranging for the staff to take its holidays during the period. This, however, creates service problems. A more proactive move is to book extra corporate business during this period. Corporate group meetings are generally booked 1 to 6 months in advance, while national associations may book 1 to 6 years prior to the event. The sales manager may reassign a salesperson from association groups to corporate groups, thus putting more emphasis on a market with a high probability of producing business during the predicted soft spot. Hotels can also use this period for FAM trips and public relations in which members of the press, such as travel writers and food section reporters, can be invited to the hotel.

When hotels operate near capacity or restaurants are hit with a sudden influx of guests, problems are likely to occur. Research has shown that customer complaints increase when service firms operate above 80% of their capacity.[18] A restaurant may seat more customers than its service staff and kitchen can handle, which results in a negative guest experience. Guests may not return and may spread bad word of mouth to potential customers. Balancing demand and capacity is critical to success in the hospitality business (see Chapter 14).

Managing Consistency

Consistency is one of the key factors in the success of a service business.[19] Consistency means that customers will receive the expected product without unwanted surprises. In the hotel industry, this means that a wake-up call requested for 7 A.M. will occur as planned and that coffee ordered for a 3 P.M. meeting break will be ready and waiting. In the restaurant business, consistency means that the shrimp scampi will taste the same way it tasted 2 weeks ago, towels will always be available in the bathrooms, and the brand of vodka specified last week will be in stock next month.

Consistency seems like a logical and simple task to accomplish, but in reality it is elusive. Many factors work against consistency. The company's policy may not be clear. For example, one employee of an American plan hotel may credit a guest for a missed meal, while another refuses to do so on the grounds that the guest purchased a package and there are no refunds for unused parts of the package.

Company policies and procedures often unintentionally create service inconsistency. The purchasing manager may order a new brand of vodka or switch seafood suppliers to reduce costs. The effect of such a change on the shrimp scampi or guest satisfaction in the cocktail lounge may be immediate and negate the savings on the purchase order.

A corporate customer of a Sheraton Hotel in Dallas booked a successful conference for over 100 people, appreciated the hotel's service, and called 2 years later to rebook the same conference. The client had paid all bills promptly and expected the hotel's sales staff to respond accordingly. Instead, the client was told that a strict financial and room numbers guarantee was essential. The client explained that such a guarantee was not required 2 years ago and that conference participants always made their own room bookings, so the client could not assume responsibility for "no shows," but would assume responsibility as before for banquets and coffee breaks. In response, the client was told that a new sales manager was now in charge and required adherence to corporate policies. Sheraton lost that account! A competitive hotel was willing to bend corporate policy for the business after calling the Sheraton in Dallas to check on the credit worthiness of the client and being told that the client had an excellent rating.

Fluctuating demand can affect consistency. If a busload of high school students arrives at a fast-food restaurant 2 minutes before a family of three, no matter how well the restaurant is managed, employees will not be able to deliver good service to the family. While it is impossible to completely eliminate variability, managers should strive to develop as consistent a product as possible. Today's customers are knowledgeable and have come to expect and demand consistency.

Points-of-Encounter

Efforts to control consistency in the hospitality industry are sometimes unsuccessful since concentration is not placed on the right areas. In the book, *You Can't Lose If the Customer Wins*, Ron Nykiel, a former senior vice-president, marketing, for Stouffer Hotels discusses the importance of points-of-encounter.[20]

A **point-of-encounter** is any point at which an employee encounters the customer. This seems simple enough, but let's take an imaginary journey in which we will be staying at the fictitious King's Crown Hotel.

Our flight has landed and we are now standing near the carousels waiting for our luggage. Suddenly, one of us gets the idea to call the hotel on those free phones you find in airports. The purpose of this call is to inform the hotel that we are here and arrange for a pickup in their free airport van.

Encounter Point 1: The Voice on the Phone. Unfortunately, the free phone must have been surplus World War II equipment as a constant squeal resounds in one's ear. The phone is ringing and ringing and ringing. After what seems like a number of rings equal to the national debt, a voice answer. Hello! We wonder is this the hotel or perhaps Tony's pool hall. Sure enough, after asking, the voice confirms it is the King's Crown Hotel. Before we can say more, that voice says, "Please hold," and bingo the voice is gone. The squeal is now accompanied by elevator music.

When the voice returns, we state our name and ask if a van can be sent to pick us up. Just a moment says the voice and we now hear the phone ringing elsewhere. A voice from reservations now answers and asks why we called. We repeat our message and give our name. We have you booked for tomorrow, are you sure you're here?

We reply we are very much here and in fact the only ones left at the carousel as the baggage arrived sometime during the previous decade. After considerable discussion, we are told that we can have a room, but all the nonsmoking ones are gone. Fortunately, there is one available smoking room since the previous guest just died of emphysema, leaving available space.

We are then instructed to proceed to Section 32E across the street from Terminal 2 and through an unlit alley to the van loading area. Fortunately, no one is mugged as we backpack our way to this area and proceed to *wait*. By this time there is a constant cold drizzle and the van waiting area is free of anything that resembles a roof.

Encounter Point 2: Our Delightful Driver. Twenty-nine and one-half minutes later the van arrives. A nonuniformed individual of questionable gender informs us that someone forgot to tell (him/her?) that passengers were waiting until just now so (he/she) cannot be blamed for being late. Mr. or Ms. driver threw a bad disc out of joint yesterday so we place our own bags in the van. Upon arriving at the hotel we also unload the bags, but find our driver waiting with palm up.

Encounter Point 3: The Invisible Bell Cap. Thirty centimeters before dragging ourselves to the front desk, a uniformed bell cap emerges from thin air and attempts to "de-bag" us. Having dragged tonnage this far, we reject the offer only to be given that look of "miserable low-class skinflints".

Encounter Point 4: The Front Desk. The bell cap is not the only person to suddenly emerge as now a Convention of Royal Muskrats of Muskeyon races in front of us to the only desk clerk on duty. Forty-seven and six-tenths minutes later it is our turn.

You guessed it; reservation somehow did not relay the message that we were coming and the body still has not been removed from that single remaining smoke-filled room. Suddenly, the desk clerk asks if we don't love the appearance of the lobby, which was just renovated with pure gold at a cost of $365 million. One or both of us is now being escorted to police headquarters for attempted strangulation of a desk clerk.

Contrast this to the experience Ron Nykiel claims is commonly accorded to top management and owners. "Picture the hotel executive being met at the airport and whisked off in the hotel's limo, bypassing vans and cabs. He then bypasses the front desk by being taken to his room by a member of the hotel's management team. I could go on to describe the prompt room service and the superb gourmet meal, all the way to bypassing the infamous check-out counter."[21]

Members of management do not purposely neglect points-of-encounter; they simply do not see them. Points-of-encounter are so familiar they become invisible. In far too many cases, management and owners are concerned with features such as the lobby. The owners of a Singapore hotel reportedly spent over $1 million dollars on a staircase railing leading to the mezzanine.

Elegant features are nice but do not rank in guest importance to encounter points. Encounter point service can be improved only if such points are recognized and experienced by management or their representatives, such as "mystery guests."

Figure 4-1 shows the different variables of a service delivery that we have been discussing. Consider customer A entering a restaurant. Customer A sees others seated at tables. Their dress and facial expressions influence customer A. If everyone looks happy and seems to be enjoying the restau-

Figure 4-1

Elements in a service encounter. Adapted from P. Eiglier and E. Langeard, "A Conceptual Approach of the Service Offering," in *Proceedings of the EAARMX Annual Conference,* eds. H. Hartvig Larsen and S. Heede, Copenhagen School of Economics and Business, 1981.

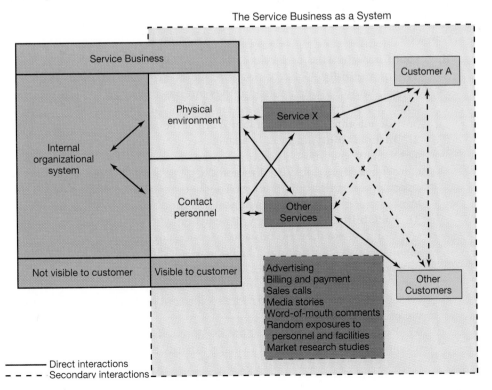

rant, customer A will feel relaxed. On the other hand, if everyone is looking at his watch and trying to gain the attention of the service staff, customer A will immediately experience apprehension. The physical environment and the restaurant's employees will also be visible to customer A. The kitchen may not be visible unless the restaurant has an exhibition kitchen. One of the choices in developing a service system is to decide what the customer should see. Some restaurants are designed so that the customer's first view upon entering is not the cash register. Customers realize the importance of this work station, but appreciate a friendlier entrance. Instead of a cash register as the immediate focal point, many restaurants offer a large pot of free coffee in case a waiting period is necessary. Others feature an attractive gift shop, photos of specialty menu items, and even entertainment such as cartoons. It is difficult to enter the restaurant in a poor frame of mind despite a short wait if the entrance was designed to create a positive and welcoming impression. If a restaurant decides to use an exhibition kitchen, it is critical that the kitchen and the employees be meticulously clean and professional in appearance. This is often very difficult to continuously maintain. Many chefs refuse to work in such an atmosphere. They view themselves as professionals, not actors on a stage. Thus the service outcome is influenced by a host of highly variable elements.

Chapter Review

I.   **The Service Culture**. The service culture focuses on serving and satisfying the customer. The service culture has to start with top management and flow down.

II.   **Four Characteristics of Services**

    1) Intangibility. Unlike physical products, services cannot be seen, tasted, felt, heard, or smelled before they are purchased. To reduce uncertainty caused by intangibility, buyers look for tangible evidence that will provide information and confidence about the service.

    2) Inseparability. In most hospitality services, both the service provider and the customer must be present for the transaction to occur. Customer-contact employees are part of the product. Inseparability also means that customers are part of the product. The third implication of inseparability is that customers and employees must understand the service delivery system.

    3) Variability. Service quality depends on who provides service and when and where they are provided. Services are produced and consumed simultaneously. Fluctuating demand makes it difficult to deliver consistent products during periods of peak demand. The high degree of contact between the service provider and the guest means that product consistency depends on the service provider's skills and performance at the time of the exchange.

    4) Perishability. Services cannot be stored. If service providers are to maximize revenue, they must manage capacity and demand since they cannot carry forward unsold inventory.

III. **Management Strategies for Service Businesses**

1) **Tangibilizing the Service Product**. Promotional material, employees' appearance, and the service firm's physical environment all help tangibilize service.

Trade dress: Trade dress is the distinctive nature of a hospitality industry's total visual image and overall appearance. To compete effectively, an entrepreneur, operator, or owner must design an effective trade dress while taking care not to imitate too closely that of a competitor.

Employee uniform and costumes: Uniforms and costumes are common to the hospitality industry. These have a legitimate and useful role in differentiating one hospitality firm from another and for instilling pride in the employees.

Physical surroundings: Physical surroundings should be designed to reinforce the product's position in the customer's mind. A firm's communications should also reinforce their positioning.

"Greening" of the hospitality industry: The use of outside natural landscaping and inside use of light and plants have become a widely used and popular method of creating differentiation and tangibilizing the product.

2) **Managing Employees**. In the hospitality industry, employees are a critical part of the product and marketing mix. The human resource and marketing department must work closely together.

Internal marketing: The task of marketing to employees is called internal marketing. Internal marketing involves the effective training and motivation of customer-contact employees and supporting service personnel.

3) **Managing Perceived Risk**. The high risk that people perceive when purchasing hospitality products increases loyalty to companies that have provided them with a consistent product in the past.

4) **Managing Capacity and Demand**. Since services are perishable, managing capacity and demand is a key function of hospitality marketing. First, services must adjust their operating systems to enable the business to operate at maximum capacity. Second, they must remember that their goal is to create satisfied customers. Research has shown that customer complaints increase when service firms operate above 80% of their capacity.

5) **Managing Consistency**. Consistency means that customers will receive the expected product without unwanted surprises.

DISCUSSION QUESTIONS

1. Relate the four characteristics of the hospitality industry to the purchase of a meal at a fine restaurant.

2. Why are hotel rooms considered perishable?

3. Identify the physical evidence provided by a restaurant and a hotel in your community to help tangibilize their products.

4. Discuss how the service person in a restaurant is part of the product the customer receives when purchasing a meal.

5. A company applying the marketing concept integrates all activities that will affect customer satisfaction. Explain why this is particularly important in the hospitality industry.

6. How can a reservation forecast for a hotel be used as a tool in managing demand?

7. What are some common management practices that restaurants use to provide a consistent product?

KEY TERMS

Inseparable   A service cannot exist separately from its providers.

Intangible   Something without physical properties, incapable of being seen, tasted, felt, heard, or smelled. A service is intangible.

Interactive marketing   Marketing by a service firm that recognizes that perceived service quality depends heavily on the quality of buyer/seller interaction.

Internal marketing   Marketing by a service firm to effectively train and motivate its customer-contact employees and all the supporting service people to work as a team to provide customer satisfaction.

Organization image   The way an individual or a group sees an organization.

Physical evidence   Tangible clues such as promotional material, employees of the firm, and the physical environment of the firm. Physical evidence is used by a service firm to make its product more tangible to the customer.

Service   Any activity, benefit, or satisfaction that is offered for sale. It is essentially intangible and does not result in the ownership of anything. Its production may or may not be tied to a physical product.

Service culture   A system of values and beliefs in an organization that reinforces the idea that providing the customer with quality service is the number one concern of the business.

Service inseparability   A major characteristic of services; they are produced and consumed at the same time and cannot be separated from their providers, whether the providers are people or machines.

Service intangibility   A major characteristic of services; they cannot be seen, tasted, felt, heard, or smelled before they are bought.

Service perishability   A major characteristic of services; they cannot be stored for later sale or use.

Service variability   A major characteristic of services; their quality may vary greatly, depending on who provides them and when, where, and how they are provided.

REFERENCES

1. JAMES COOK, "You Mean We've Been Speaking Prose All These Years?" *Forbes* (April 11, 1983), pp. 142–149. Also see NORMAN JONAS, "The Hollow Corporation," *Business Week* (March 3, 1986), pp. 57–59.

2. EARL W. SASSER, R. PAUL OLSEN, AND DARYL WYCOFF, *Management of Service Operations* (Boston: Allyn and Bacon, 1978).

3. See KARL ALBRECHT, *At America's Service* (Homewood, Ill.: Dow Jones–Irwin, 1988). Also see KARL ALBRECHT AND RON ZEMKE, *Service America!* (Homewood, Ill.: Dow Jones–Irwin, 1985).

4. ROBERT C. LEWIS AND RICHARD E. CHAMBERS, *Marketing Leadership in Hospitality* (New York: Van Nostrand Reinhold, 1989).

5. BRUCE SERLEN, "Call Conference Centers Up On Your Computer," *Business Travel Management*, 5, no. 6 (June 1993), pp. 42–44.

6. G. LYNN SHOSTACK, "Breaking Free from Product Marketing," *Journal of Marketing* (April 1977), pp. 73–80.

7. JEANNA ABBOTT AND JOSEPH LANZA, "Trade Dress: Legal Interpretations of What Constitutes Distinctive Appearance," *Cornell Hotel and Restaurant Administration Quarterly*, 35, no. 1 (Feb. 1994), p. 54.

8. Ibid., p. 56.

9. Ibid., p. 58.

10. BERNARD H. BOOMS AND MARY J. BITNER, "Marketing Services by Managing the Environment", *Cornell Hotel and Restaurant Administration Quarterly*, 23, no. 1 (May 1982), pp. 35–39.

11. DONALD W. COWELL, *The Marketing of Services* (London: William Heinemann, 1984).

12. MEGAN ROWE, Greening For Dollars, 48, no. 12, *Lodging Hospitality* (December 1992), pp. 76–78.

13. RICHARD NORMANN, *Service Management: Strategy and Leadership in Service Businesses* (John Wiley & Sons: New York, 1984).

14. See KARL ALBRECHT, *At America's Service* (Homewood, Ill., Dow Jones–Irwin, 1988).

15. See LEONARD BERRY, "Big Ideas in Services Marketing," in *Creativity in Services Marketing*, M. Venkatesan et al., eds. (Chicago: American Marketing Association, 1986), pp. 6–8.

16. THOMAS J. PETERS AND ROBERT H. WATERMAN, JR., *In Search of Excellence* (New York: Warner Books, 1922), p. xv.

17. See VALARIE A. ZEITHAML, "How Consumer Evaluation Processes Differ between Goods and Services," in *Marketing of Services*, James H. Donnelly and William George, eds. (Chicago: American Marketing Association, 1981), pp. 186–190.

18. MARY J. BITNER, JODY D. NYQUIST, AND BERNARD H.

BOOMS, "The Critical Incident as a Technique for Analyzing the Service Encounter," in *Services Marketing in a Changing Environment*, Thomas M. Bloch et al., eds. (Chicago: American Marketing Association, 1985), pp. 48–51. ROBERT C. LEWIS AND SUSAN V. MORRIS, "The Positive Side of Guest Complaints," *Cornell Hotel and Restaurant Quarterly*, 27, no. 4 (February 1987), pp. 13–15.

19. DIANE SCHANLENSEE, KENNETH L. BERNHARDT AND NANCY GUST, "Keys to Successful Services Marketing: Customer Orientation, Creed, Consistency," in *Services Marketing in a Changing Environment*, THOMAS BLOCH et al., eds. (Chicago: American Marketing Association, 1985), pp. 15–18.

20. RONALD A. NYKIEL, *You Can't Lose If the Customer Wins*, Long Meadow Press, 201 High Ridge Rd., Stanford, CT 06904, 1990.

21. Ibid., p. 19.

The Marketing Environment

*D*omino's is the leader today in the home-delivery pizza business and the number two pizza maker in the country. The chain was started by Tom Monaghan and his brother in 1960 in Ypsilanti, Michigan, based on the concept of delivering pizzas to homes within 30 minutes. Their first week's sales averaged less than $15 a day. After eight months, Tom's brother decided to leave the pizza business. Monaghan's ambitious expansion program brought with it a large debt, a debt the company could not support. After working with the chain for nearly a decade, Monaghan was forced to give the chain up to his creditors. The creditors soon discovered that managing a restaurant chain was a difficult task. They brought Monaghan back to manage the company in exchange for equity. Tom Monaghan managed to revive the chain and build it into a chain of 290 restaurants by 1980. Domino's sales skyrocketed in the 1980s, and it presently has more than 5000 units and sales of more than $2.2 billion.

Several environmental factors during the 1980s propelled Domino's growth. An increase in the number of two-income families caused Americans to place increasing value on their time. Growth in the number of one- and two-person households with high discretionary incomes led people to buy prepared food more often. Childless, middle-aged, singles and couples are responsible for the highest consumption of restaurant-prepared

*meals eaten at home. Domino's success can be attributed to sound manage-
ment and its development of a marketing mix aimed at the rapidly growing
home-delivery segment of the market.*

*Domino's maintained its competitive lead with the use of technology.
Domino's was the first pizza maker to use a VCM (vertical chopper mixer).
They were the first to deliver their product in a corrugated box, which
retained heat much better than single-layer boxes. Another Domino's innovation was airtight fiber-glass boxes to hold dough, which eliminated the
need to brush dough balls with oil. Domino's was one of the first chains to
use Ferris-wheel-type ovens. Today they use a more advanced technology,
conveyor ovens.*

*Success does not go unnoticed. Arthur Gunther, chairman of Pizza
Hut, announced in 1985 that they would aggressively pursue the delivery
market. Yet Monaghan welcomes competition. As he states in his book
Pizza Tiger, "Competition makes us sharper, keeps us looking for answers,
and prevents us from getting complacent and thinking we know it all".*

*Every business is bound to face some environmental backlashes.
Domino's delivery of more than a million pizzas by 80,000 drivers
inevitably resulted in accidents. In 1988, Domino's drivers were involved in
accidents that resulted in 20 fatalities. This fact was publicized on NBC's
"First Edition" news magazine, on CBS news, in the New York Times, and
in local papers. Some groups claimed that the accidents were a direct result
of Domino's 30-minutes or less delivery promise. Domino's responded with
a campaign stating that safety had always been a major company concern.
Domino's instituted a toll-free number that people can call if they witness
traffic violations by Domino's drivers.*

*Tom Monaghan is committed to his beliefs. Not all his beliefs are pop-
ular with all groups. As a national figure, he has come under fire from the
National Organization for Women (NOW) for opposition to abortion, resulting in NOW's boycott of Domino's. His stores were also picketed because he
supported anticommunist forces in Central America.*

*In 1989, Monaghan announced that he was considering selling the
chain to devote more time to religious and philanthropic concerns. This
made the franchisees, suppliers, and competitors wonder who would purchase the chain and how the new owner might change the organization.
Pizza Hut begin to eat into Domino's share of the home-delivery market.
Domino's, which at one time owned the home-delivery market with a 90%
market share, was down to 46% in 1991, while Pizza Hut was up to 24%.
Little Caesar's also started to erode Domino's sales and is currently in a
battle with Domino's for the number two spot. As a result of these setbacks,
Monaghan turned his attention back to Domino's.*

*Domino's provides an excellent example of how a business interacts
with external forces. The pizza home-delivery concept grew because it was
presented at a time when the whole home-delivered food concept was grow-*

ing. The company used technology to gain a competitive advantage. As Domino's became more successful, other pizza chains entered the home-delivery market more aggressively. When Domino's drivers had accidents, it suffered adverse publicity from those who claimed the accidents resulted from company pressure on drivers to deliver within 30 minutes. Social groups who opposed Monaghan's beliefs demonstrated against the chain. When Monaghan turned his attention away from the company, it began to suffer. Domino's, like all other companies, must maintain alertness in a rapidly changing environment.[1]

Victoria Station provides an example of a hospitality firm so concerned with doing things right that it ended up doing the wrong things extremely well. Victoria Station was a successful restaurant concept in the early 1970s. The unique feature of Victoria Station was railroad boxcars and cabooses incorporated into the building. Railroad memorabilia in the restaurant's interior reinforced the rail dining room feeling. The menu listed red meat items and featured prime rib. The restaurant aimed at couples who wanted good food, a casual atmosphere, and moderate prices. Victoria Station grew very quickly from its formation in 1969 to 46 restaurants in 1976. As the chain grew, the benefits of building a more efficient system also grew. Every point drop in food cost would bring several hundred thousand dollars to the chain's bottom line. Management developed cooking procedures to reduce shrinkage, cost control systems to maximize profits, site location procedures to ensure good customer counts, and improved building construction methods.[2]

Victoria Station's focus was on internal efficiency. But they failed to note the changing environment. Meat prices started to rise in the mid-1970s. Victoria Station either had to absorb these increases or raise its menu prices. People's tastes were changing from red meat to chicken and pasta. The uniqueness of the railroad cars was wearing out. Victoria Station had built the most efficient systems for preparing and serving prime rib, but now their customers wanted something else. Victoria Station management did not react to these trends until they affected the profit and loss statements, further evidence of their internal focus. Victoria Station was not able to change the image of its restaurants, and by the late 1980s the chain had been through bankruptcy with only a few restaurants in the northeast surviving. Victoria Station provides an example of what can happen when a firm becomes internally oriented and does not have an effective environmental scanning program.

Domino's provides an example of an externally oriented company that took advantage of new opportunities created by the environment. Victoria Station illustrates an internally focused company whose marketing mix failed to evolve to meet the changing desires of consumers whose wants were influenced by the environment.

Chapter 5 describes the marketing environments in which companies operate, and shows the influence of external forces on marketing decisions.

Initially, we define a company's **microenvironment** as the forces close to the company that affect its ability to serve customers. The microenvironment includes the **company** itself, **suppliers, marketing channel firms, customers**, and **publics**.

Next we put the microenvironment into a larger context: the **macroenvironment** of larger societal influences such as **competitive, demographic, economic, natural, technological, political** and **cultural environments**. We discuss how these forces can affect marketing decisions.

Each of these environments is discussed, and the **major trends** in the macroenvironment of the United States are set forth.

We conclude with thoughts on **responding to the marketing environment**. Two alternative philosophies for dealing with these external forces are the typical passive response and adaption and the aggressive **environmental management perspective**.

Chapter Preview

A company's **marketing environment** consists of the outside actors and forces that affect a company's ability to develop and maintain successful transactions with its target customers. The marketing environment is made up of a microenvironment and a macroenvironment. The **microenvironment** consists of actors and forces close to the company that can affect its ability to serve its customers—the company itself, marketing channel firms, customer markets, and a broad range of publics. The **macroenvironment** consists of the larger societal forces that affect the whole microenvironment—demographic, economic, natural, technological, political, competitor, and cultural forces. We first examine the company's microenvironment and then its macroenvironment.

THE COMPANY'S MICRO-ENVIRONMENT

Marketing management's task is to create attractive offers for target markets. Its degree of success will be affected by various actors in its microenvironment. These actors are shown in Figure 5-1. They include the company, suppliers, market intermediaries, customers, and publics.

The Company

Marketing managers don't operate in a vacuum. They must work closely with top management and the various company departments. The finance department is concerned with finding and using funds required to carry out the marketing plan. The accounting department has to measure revenues and costs to help marketing know how well it is achieving its objectives. Product development is responsible for creating new products to fit the needs of the changing marketplace. Housekeeping is responsible for delivering clean rooms sold by the sales department. All company departments will have some impact on the success of marketing plans.

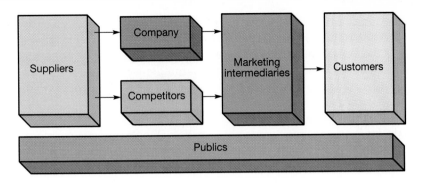

Figure 5-1
Major actors in the company's microenvironment.

Suppliers

Suppliers are firms and individuals that provide the resources needed by the company to produce its goods and services. Trends and developments affecting suppliers can seriously affect a company's marketing plan. Suppose that a restaurant manager decides to run a live lobster special for the weekend. The seafood supplier is called, who promises to supply 200 lobsters for the weekend promotion. Friday morning the supplier calls and reports that lobsters were shorted on the shipment from Boston, and they will not be delivered until Saturday morning. The manager must now find an alternative source or disappoint guests who have reservations for Friday night.

In another case, Steak and Ale wanted to add a new scallop seafood dish to its menu. The corporate offices spent six months perfecting the scallop dish. During the development period, the price of scallops doubled. The restaurant would now have to charge a price higher than customers would pay. The project was scrapped. Marketing management must pay attention to changes in supply availability (as affected by shortages and strikes) and supply costs.

Marketing Intermediaries

Marketing Intermediaries are firms that help the company promote, sell, and distribute its goods to the final buyers. Intermediaries are business firms that help hospitality companies find customers or make sales. Distribution channel firms are business firms that help hospitality companies find customers or make sales. They include travel agents, wholesale tour operators, and hotel representatives. For example, a wholesaler creates leisure packages that include air transportation, ground transportation, and hotel accommodations. These packages are promoted through newspaper advertising and travel agents. Through volume purchasing, the wholesaler receives reduced prices, which enable the wholesaler to pay the travel agent a commission for selling the product, give the customer a good price, and produce a profit. In choosing wholesalers, hotels must select reputable firms that will deliver the promised product to the customer and pay the hotel for their services.

In manufacturing industries, **transportation systems** move the product from the factory to the customer. The firm makes contractual arrangements with transportation companies to perform this service for them or has their own transportation system. Like manufacturing firms, some hospitality firms have central commissaries and depend on transportation systems to move the product to their restaurants. Red Lobster, for example, has a large food processing plant in Orlando, Florida. The hospitality industry also uses transportation systems to bring customers to the business. In this case the hospitality often has less control over the transportation provider, since there is usually no contractual arrangement between the firm and the provider; most guests make their own reservations when traveling for business or pleasure. This gives the hospitality company less control over the transportation system. As airline fares increase, both companies and individuals cut back on travel. An airline strike or bankruptcy can limit the number of persons to whom remote resort destinations and secondary city destinations are accessible. Air fare increases can significantly depress profits in the hotel and travel industries. For example, 60% of Sheraton's guests arrive by airline, while 70% of car rental customers arrive by air; both industries will be adversely affected by a rise in air fares.[3]

Some companies that are heavily dependent on their guests being delivered by air travel have started their own airlines. The passengers taking Carnival cruises come from all over North America. Carnival started its own airline to keep transportation costs down and ensure a consistent capacity from key cities in North America.

Airline crashes or terrorist events can make tourists reluctant to fly. For example, in December 1985, terrorists opened fire in the Rome and Vienna airports killing 22 people and causing a 60% drop in U.S. tourism to Italy.[4] As an example of one response, the Sheraton EUR of Rome changed marketing strategies. Instead of viewing American tourists as their target market, the Sheraton went after airline flight crews and captured a significant share. This market segment did not produce revenue equal to American tourists, but it allowed the hotel to survive a crisis. Upscale businesses, rental car companies, resorts, and convention centers are dependent on air travel to bring their guests. These organization must work with local and state tourist bureaus to ensure that there are enough airline flights serving their region.

Marketing services agencies include marketing research firms, advertising agencies, media firms, and marketing consulting firms that help companies target and promote their products to the right markets. These firms can vary in creativity, quality, service, and price. The company should regularly review their performance and replace those that no longer perform well.

Financial intermediaries include banks, credit companies, insurance companies, and other firms that help hospitality companies finance their transactions or insure risks associated with the buying and selling of goods and services. Rising insurance costs, and in particular liquor liability insurance, has forced some hospitality firms out of business. Because a company's marketing performance can be seriously affected by rising credit costs, limited credit, or both, the company has to develop strong relationships with important financial institutions.

The Company's Macroenvironment

The company and its suppliers, marketing intermediaries, customers, and publics all operate in a larger macroenvironment that shapes opportunities and poses threats. The company must watch and respond to these uncontrollable forces. The macroenvironment consists of the seven major forces shown in Figure 5-2. The remaining sections of this chapter will examine these forces and show how they can affect marketing plans.

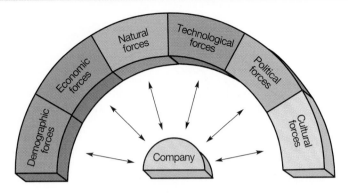

Figure 5-2
Major forces in the company's macroenvironment.

Competitors

Every company faces a broad range of competitors. The marketing concept states that to be successful a company must satisfy the needs and wants of consumers better than its competitors do. Marketers must do more than adapt to the needs of target customers. They must also adapt to the strategies of other companies serving the same target markets. Companies must gain strategic advantage by strongly positioning their product in the minds of consumers.

No single competitive marketing strategy is best for all companies. Each firm must consider its size and industry position in relation to its competitors. Large firms with dominant positions in an industry can use certain strategies that smaller firms cannot afford. But small firms can also choose strategies that give them certain advantages. For example, a large restaurant chain can use its buying power to purchase national advertising, spreading the cost among hundreds or thousands of operations. But small individually owned restaurants are able to adjust quickly to local trends and can offer more menu variety since they do not have to worry about standardizing menu items across thousands of restaurants. Both large and small firms must find marketing strategies that give them specific advantages over competitors operating in their markets.

Managers often fail to correctly identify their competitors. The manager of Houston Seafood Restaurant said that his restaurant had no competition because there were no other seafood restaurants within several miles. Several months later the restaurant was out of business. Customers decided to spend their money at competitors, either by driving farther to other seafood restaurants or dining at other nearby nonseafood restaurants.

Every company faces four levels of competitors (see Figure 5-3):

1. A company can view its competitors as other companies that offer similar products and services to the same customers at a similar price. At this level, McDonald's will view its competition as Burger King, Wendy's, and Hardee's.
2. A company can see its competitors as all companies making the same product or class of products. Here McDonald's may see its competition as all fast-food restaurants, including Boston Chicken, Kentucky Fried Chicken, Taco Bell, and Arby's.

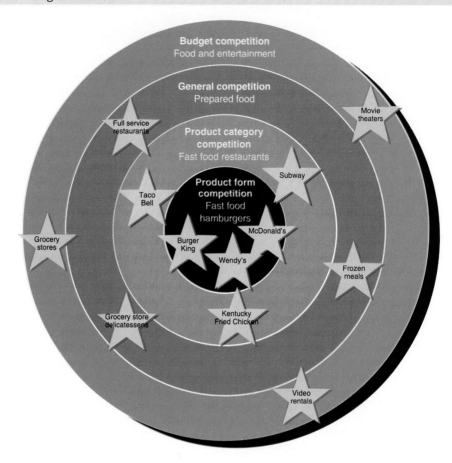

Figure 5-3
Levels of competition.
Adapted from *Analysis for Marketing Planning,* Donald R. Lehmann and Russell S. Winer, p. 22, ©1994 by Richard D. Irwin.

3. A company can see its competitors more broadly as all companies supplying the same service. Here McDonald's would see itself competing with all restaurants and other suppliers of prepared food, such as the deli section of a supermarket.

4. A company can see its competition even more broadly as all companies that compete for the same consumer dollars. Here McDonald's would see itself competing with grocery stores and the self-provision of the meal by the consumer.[5]

McDonald's "You Deserve a Break Today" advertising campaign was aimed at the fourth level of competition, telling the homemaker to give herself a break from cooking. Carnival Cruise Lines viewed its competition at the third level, that is, as other vacation destinations, such as Hawaii.

Budget Motels correctly identified potential competitors as fast-food restaurants such as Bob Evans or Dennys had they decided to offer food and beverage operations in connection with their motels. Owners of these motel chains decided against competing on this scale and instead decided to compete against convenience stores for the sale of microwave popcorn, snacks, sodas and even a limited line of frozen entrees such as pizza.

Barriers to Entry, Exit and Competition

Two forces that affect the competition are the ability of companies to enter and exit markets.[6] Entry barriers prevent firms from getting into a business, while barriers to exit prevent them from getting out. The restaurant industry is characterized by **low barriers to entry**. It takes a relatively small amount of capital to get started in the restaurant business. Some restaurateurs who open without direct competition soon find themselves with four or five competitors in a year's time. This points out the importance of anticipating competition and operating on the premise that one always has competition. Always assume that customer satisfaction is important, because the customer can always go somewhere else.

Hotels find themselves with a different problem, **high barriers of exit** from the industry. The large capital investment required to build a hotel becomes a sunk cost. As a result, hotels that cannot meet all their debt payments, taxes, and other fixed costs, but can produce enough gross profit to partially offset their fixed costs, may operate at a loss rather than close their doors completely. Thus, when hotel demand plummets, room supply remains the same, resulting in intensified competition for customers.

The hotel's competitive environment is affected by another factor—most hotels are planned during upswings in the business cycle when there is not enough supply to meet demand. But it can take 4 years or more from the planning stages to the opening of a hotel. By that time, the economic cycle may have turned down. Sadly, new hotels often open their doors during a recessionary period.

There appears to be a herd mentality in the development of hotels. A total of 50 new hotel brands or concepts were introduced during one 18-month period. These included Renaissance, Emerald, Royce, Courtyards, Marquis, Crown Plazas, Embassy Suites, Residence Inns, Park Suites, Quality Inns, and others.[7]

Demographic Environment

Demography is the study of human populations in terms of size, density, location, age, sex, race, occupation, and other statistics. The demographic environment is of major interest to marketers because markets are made up of people. The most important demographic trends are described here.

Changing Age Structure of the Population

The single most important demographic trend in the United States today is the aging of its population. A falling birthrate has meant fewer young people. At the same time, life expectancy is increasing, which raises the population's average age.

The U.S. population stood at 260 million in 1995 and is expected to reach 300 million by the year 2030. During the **baby boom** that began after World War II and lasted until the early 1960s, the annual birthrate reached an all-time high. The baby boom was followed by a "birth dearth"; by the mid-1970s the birth rate had fallen sharply, due to the desire of many couples to improve their personal living standards, an increase in the number of working women, and improved birth control. Although family sizes are expected to remain smaller, the birthrate climbed again through the end of the 1980s as the baby-boom generation moved through the child-bearing years and created a second, but smaller, baby boom. The birthrate is expected to decline in the 1990s. The baby boom created a large bulge in the U.S. age distribution, and as the baby boom generation ages, it pulls the average up.[8]

The second factor in the general aging of the population is increased life expectancy. Current average life expectancy is 75 years (71.5 for males and 78 for females), a 26-year increase since 1900. The U.S. median age is now 31 and is expected to reach 36 by the year 2000. By 2050, the median age will be 42.[9]

The changing age structure of the population will result in different growth rates for various age groups during the decade, and these differences will strongly affect marketers' targeting strategies. The growth trends for six groups are summarized here.[10]

Children. The number of preschoolers will taper off slightly through the 1990s as the baby boomers move out of the childbearing years. As this century closes, fast-food restaurants will have to find a replacement for this market. One market they have already targeted is the senior's market.[11]

Youths. The number of 10- to 19-year-olds will drop through the early 1990s and then begin to increase at the end of the century. This is a prime market for fast-food restaurants in terms of customers and employees (older teen-agers). Both the youth group and the children's group will affect the demand for school feeding.

Young adults. This 20- to 34-year-age-group will decline during the 1990s as the "birth dearth" generation moves in. The group is important to casual restaurants such as Bennigan's and Friday's. It is also a prime group for the night club and bar market.

Early middle age. The baby-boom generation will continue to move into the 35-to-49 age group, creating huge increases. For example, the number of 40- to 44-year-olds will increase by 50%. This group will have more sophisticated tastes in food and beverage and appreciate the more upscale hotels.

Late middle age. The 50-to-64 age group will continue to shrink until the end of the century. The wage earners in this group are at the top of their career. This group is a major market for eating out, entertainment, and travel.

Retirees. The over-65 age group will increase by over one-third between 1980 and 2000. By the year 2000 there will be twice as many elderly as there are teen-agers. This group has a demand for retirement communities, quieter forms of recreation, and travel. They can also be a market for moderately priced restaurants that provide nutritious meals, such as cafeterias.[12]

Figure 5-4 shows that the projected increase in persons over 65 as a percentage of the population in the world and selected countries. The aging population creates many opportunities for the hospitality and travel industries. People over age 55 account for more than 75% of the dollars spent on leisure travel. Bus tours, which are now a major business, are expected to

Age 65 and over population as a percentage of total percentage change 1990–2025

	1950	1970	1990	1995	2000	2010	2025	% change
World	5.1	5.4	6.2	6.5	6.8	7.3	8.7	+56.5
More developed regions	7.6	9.6	12.0	12.9	13.5	14.4	18.3	+52.5
Britain	10.7	12.9	15.7	15.6	15.4	15.8	19.4	+23.6
Germany	9.7	13.7	14.6	14.8	15.5	18.4	20.5	+40.4
France	11.4	12.9	14.0	14.9	15.6	16.0	21.2	+51.4
Italy	8.3	10.9	14.1	15.6	17.0	18.9	22.3	+58.2
U.S.	8.1	9.8	12.6	12.6	12.3	12.8	18.5	+46.8
Canada	7.7	7.9	11.5	12.0	12.4	13.3	18.6	+61.7
Japan	4.9	7.1	11.7	13.9	16.2	20.1	24.4	+208.5

Figure 5-4
Retirees' swelling ranks.
Source: International Herald Tribune, Money Report, September 24/25, 1994.

become even more popular. Restaurants catering to the elderly will need good lighting, easy-to-read menus, and waiters who provide leisurely service.

The Changing American Family

The American ideal of the two-child, two-car suburban family has been losing its luster.[13] Couples are marrying later and having fewer children. Although 96% of all Americans marry, the average age of first-time marriage has been increasing. Couples with no children under 18 now make up almost half of all families. Of those families that have children, the average number of children is less than 2, down from 3.5 in 1955.

The number of working mothers has also increased. The percentage of mothers with children under age 18 who hold a job has more than doubled since 1960, to over 67%. Seventy-nine percent of the women with no children under 18 work, whereas only 74% of the men in this group work. Women's wages account for 40% of the household's income and allow the purchase of more and higher-quality goods and services. This trend has resulted in shorter but more frequent vacations. With both members working, it is difficult for both to be away from their work for long periods of time.

Parents facing time pressures now plan to take children with them on vacations such as ski, tennis, and golf vacations. Formerly, many parents considered these to be adult-only times. Some business travelers also take children with them on business trips; this has created new challenges and opportunities for hotels and resorts previously unaccustomed to serving children. Responsive hotels have been creating day-care services and children activities to respond to family vacations.

The average vacation has dropped from 6.0 days in 1983 to 4.8 days in 1988, and is presently at 4.3 days. Weekend vacations were a fast growing segment in the 1980s and they continue to grow in the 1990s.[14] Also, the two-income family has increased the demand for home delivery of restaurant meals, take-out food, and fast-food meals because there is limited time to prepare meals, and there is more income to purchase them.

These trends offer opportunity and threat to the hospitality industry. For example, modern society has produced new levels and forms of stress. The world depression stress of the 1930s with near starvation, has been replaced with stress induced by time pressures, materialism, crime, and many other societal causes.

The average age when someone gets married for the first time is increasing, as a result many couples are well into their careers when they have their first child. These couples are used to traveling and eating out. When their children arrive they continue this pattern of traveling and dining out, creating a need for restaurants, hotels, and resorts to provide activities for their children.

Marketing Highlight 5-1

Days Inn Targets Senior Employees

In 1985, Days Inn of America decided to actively seek workers over 65 for its reservation center. At the time its reservation center had a turnover of 100%, and it was difficult to find replacements for the current job openings. The older workers seemed to be a perfect solution to this problem. People were living longer and retiring earlier. According to the *New York Times* most American men now leave the work force before they are 63. Some retire, looking forward to a life of leisure; others are forced or enticed into early retirement. In 1930, two of every three men over 60 was in the work force; by the year 2000 this is projected to drop to one in four. Additionally, the number of people over 65 is increasing. One study found that 25% of retirees are unhappy with their situation. They are bored and would like to work. This group represents several million potential employees, an employee pool that Days Inn wanted to tap.

The initial results by Days Inn were unsuccessful. There was no response to their ads. After doing some initial research, Days Inn found that most seniors had been turned down in applying for other jobs because of their age. They had given up. They shifted their campaign to talking in person to seniors and using residence bulletin boards. This proved to be successful, and now over one-third of those working at reservation centers are older workers. The turnover rate has been reduced, and tardiness and absenteeism are virtually nonexistent.

Days Inn is so pleased with the senior labor force that they started a job fair for senior citizens held at Days Inns across the country. These job fairs were not just for Days Inn, but were open to any prospective employer. In addition, the individual hotels now use seniors as front-desk clerks, van drivers, service persons, night auditors, housekeepers, sales representatives, and general managers. The environment made it difficult for Days Inn to find employees from conventional sources to staff their national reservation system, a key part of the chains distribution system. Days Inn discovered a new source of employees, the older worker.

Source: Days Inn Public Relations Releases.

Members of the hospitality industry sometimes unwittingly increase or induce stress in their guests. This jeopardizes repeat business. "Unfortunately, not many restaurant owners are aware of the stress-inducing potential of their operations and even fewer are able to convert those stressful experiences into positive results so that they can develop loyal customers."[15] Over 60 cultural and psychometric variables have been found to induce stress in a restaurant.[16]

Many proactive steps can be taken by a restaurant to reduce stress in today's environment. For example:[17]

- People in western cultures often require more personal space than in Asian cultures.
- *Table size:* A study in England showed that when a restaurant offered only tables with four chairs, customers left rather than ask to sit at a table occupied by one patron.[18] The author observed this same phenomenon in a study of the company cafeteria for the Electric Company of Costa Rica, where patrons complained of crowding, slow service, and stress. The answer in hotel cases was to offer more tables for two persons only. Customers still refused to ask a lone patron to sit with them, but table turn was improved.

- *Noise:* In an era of heavy environmental noise pollution, this is one of the first factors that must be improved.

- *Color and lighting:* Color and lighting are critical factors in any hospitality operation, not simply restaurants. Dark wood paneling that used to be considered perfect for a predominantly male market have been found to be less appealing to women guests. It has been suggested that some fast-food chains select colors that cause customers to remain less time, thus increasing table turn.[19]

- Hampton Inns uses an unconditional service guarantee to reduce guest stress. Hampton Inns employees are empowered to take immediate action to satisfy guests.

Finally, the number of nonfamily households is on the rise. Many young adults leave home and move into apartments; others choose to remain single. Still others are divorced or widowed and living alone. By the year 2000, 47% of all households will be single-person or single-parent households. They are the fastest growing category of households. This group has its own special needs. For example, single-person households have more discretionary income to spend on entertainment and dining out, and they will also be higher users of take-out food. The National Restaurant Association reports that solo diners spend more than half of their food budget on restaurants compared to 37% for married couples.[20]

Geographic Shifts in Population

Movement to Sunbelt States. During the 1980s, the western and Sunbelt states grew at a much faster pace than the rest of the country. This trend is expected to continue, with population increases of more than 20% projected in Arizona, Florida, Nevada, and New Mexico between 1990 and 2000[21] (see Figure 5-5 on page 114).

Movement from Rural to Urban Areas. Except for a short period during the early 1970s, Americans have been moving from rural to metropolitan areas for a century. The metropolitan areas show a faster pace of living, more commuting, higher incomes, and greater variety of goods and services than can be found in the small towns and rural areas that dot the United States.

Movement from the City to the Suburb. In the 1950s, Americans made a massive exit from the cities to the suburbs. Big cities became surrounded by even bigger suburbs. Today, the migration continues. The U.S. Census Bureau calls sprawling urban areas MSAs (Metropolitan Statistical Areas).[22] Restaurant companies will look at the demographics of MSAs to determine new cities to target. They will look for a match between their current customers and the demographics of other MSAs. Chains usually like to go into an MSA with multiple stores to make promotion and regional administration more efficient.

Better-educated and More White-collar Population

In 1950, only half of all U.S. adults had progressed beyond the ninth grade. By 1980, 70% of Americans over age 24 had completed high school. In 1992, more than 20% of Americans over age 24 had completed college.[23]

Marketing Highlight 5-2

The Baby Boomers

The postwar baby boom, which began in 1946 and ran through 1964, produced 75 million babies. Since then, the baby boomers have become one of the biggest forces shaping the marketing environment. The boomers have presented a moving target, creating new markets as they grew through infancy to preadolescent, teen-age, young-adult, and now middle-age years. They created markets for baby products and toys in the 1950s; jeans, records, and cosmetics in the 1960s; fun and informal fashions in the 1970s; premium foods and performance cars in the 1980s; and fitness, new homes, and child care in the 1990s.

Today, the baby boomers are starting to gray at the temples and spread at the waist. And they are reaching their peak earning and spending years—the boomers account for a third of the population but make up 40% of the work force and earn over half of all personal income. They are moving to the suburbs, settling into home ownership, raising families, and maturing into the most affluent generation in history. Thus, they constitute a lucrative market for housing, furniture and appliances, children's products, low-calorie foods and beverages, physical fitness products, high-priced cars, convenience products, and financial services.

Baby boomers cut across all walks of life. But marketers typically have paid the most attention to the small upper crust of the boomer generation—its more educated, mobile, and wealthy segments. These segments have gone by many names. In the early mid-1980s, they were called "yuppies" (young urban professionals); "yumpies" (young upwardly mobile professionals); "bumpies" (black upwardly mobile professionals); and "yummies" (young upwardly mobile mommies). These groups were replaced by the "DINKs"—dual-income, no-kids couples.

The rising number of educated Americans will increase the demand for higher-quality products. Customers will also become more sophisticated in their purchasing habits, demanding finer wines and more nutritious foods.

Globally, people are becoming better educated. As countries become industrialized their citizens usually become better educated. The following are

In 1990s, however, yuppies and DINKs have given way to a new breed, with names such as DEWKs (dual earners with kids); MOBYs (mother older, baby younger); WOOFs (well-off older folks); or just plain GRUMPIES (just what the name suggests). The older boomers are now well into their forties; the youngest are in their thirties. Thus, the boomers are evolving from the "youthquake generation" to the "backache generation." They are slowing up, having children, and settling down. They are experiencing the pangs of midlife and rethinking the purpose and value of their work, responsibilities, and relationships.

The maturing boomers are approaching life with a new stability and reasonableness in the way they live, think, eat, and spend. Baby boomers now head up 44% of the nation's households, and 60% of all boomer households include children under 18 years old. Thus, they have shifted their focus from the outside world to the inside world. Staying home with the family is becoming their favorite way to spend an evening. Community and family values have become more important. The upscale boomers still exert their affluence, but they indulge themselves in more subtle and sensible ways. They spend heavily on convenience and high-quality products, but they have less of a taste for lavish or conspicuous buying.

Some marketers think that focusing on the boomers has caused companies to overlook other important segments. For example, one advertising executive suggests that marketers are in danger of losing touch with younger consumers, especially those now 18 to 29 years old, labeled by some as "Generation X":

> [Our fortunes] have been directly tied to the fortunes of the baby boomer generation for so long that we may have begun to lose our per-spective. ... Until now, Generation X has lived in the shadow of the baby boomers. But by the year 2000, Generation X will have grown to 62 million strong and, 10 years later, will have overtaken the boomers as the primary target for virtually every product category—for beauty, for fashion and fragrance, for packaged goods, travel and home furnishings. The Xers [have] open minds and still to be realized earning potential—not [like] the boomers [who will be] sitting on the edge of retirement, with established product preferences. The Xers will represent the market of opportunity for blue jeans and new cars and laundry soap from 1995 on into the next decade.

Still, for the present, the boomers continue to dominate the marketing scene. Some marketers think that upscale boomers are tiring of all the attention. They are using subtler approaches that avoid stereotyping these consumers or tagging them as yuppies, or DEWKs, or something else. But whatever you call them, you can't ignore them. The baby boomers have been the most potent market force for the past 40 years, and they will continue to be for some time yet to come.

Sources: The quote is from Karen Ritchie, "Get Ready for 'Geneeration X,'" *Advertising Age,* November 9, 1992, p. 21. Also see Jon Berry, "It's Hip, It's Intense—The Midlife Crisis," *Adweek,* June 25, 1990, pp. 54–55; Cheryl Russell, "On the Babyboom Bandwagon," *American Demographics,* May 1991, pp. 25–31; Susan B. Garland, "Those Aging Boomers," *Business Week,* May 20, 1991, pp. 106–12; Margaret L. Usdansky, "Older, Younger Boomers Split by Time, Values," *USA Today,* February 11, 1992, p. 6A; and Scott Donaton, "The Media Wakes up to Generation X," *Advertising Age,* February 1, 1993, pp. 16–17.

the percentages of people aged 25 to 34 who have graduated from college in the following countries: Canada, 16.1%; France, 7.6%; Germany, 11.8%; Great Britain, 11.2%; Italy, 6.7%; Japan, 22.9%; and the United States, 24.2%.[24] Some of these differences also reflect cultural differences. In some countries there is an emphasis on technical training, which accounts for some of these differences.

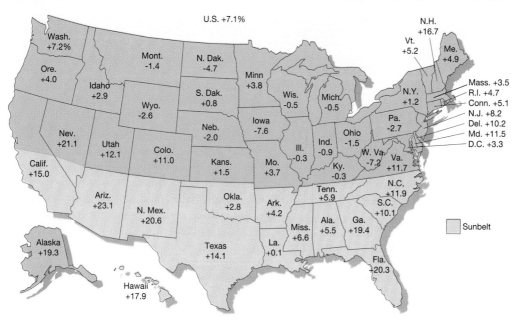

Figure 5-5
Projected population growth rates: 1990 to 2000. *Source:* U.S. Department of
Commerce, Bureau of Census.

The work force is becoming more white collar. Between 1950 and 1985, the proportion of white-collar workers rose from 41% to 54% and that of blue-collar workers declined from 47% to 33%.[25] Firms such as Marriott Foodservice and ARAMARK have benefited from these trends by providing food service in the office buildings of companies employing white-collar workers.

Increasing Ethnic and Racial Diversity

The United States has often been called a melting pot in which diverse groups from many nations and cultures have melted into a single, more homogeneous whole. But there are increasing signs that such melting did not occur. Rather, the United States seems to have become more of a "salad bowl" in which various groups have mixed together but have maintained their diversity by retaining and valuing important ethnic and cultural differences.

The U.S. population is 84% white, with blacks making up another 12%. The Hispanic population has grown rapidly and now stands at over 22 million people. The U.S. Asian population has also grown rapidly in recent years. During the 1980s, some 500,000 immigrants a year accounted for one-fifth of all U.S. population growth. Mexicans, Filipinos, Chinese, Koreans, and Vietnamese were the most common new arrivals. Each group has specific wants and buying habits.[26] Many hospitality marketers have developed products and promotional campaigns to target one or more of these groups.

Economic Environment

The **economic environment** consists of factors that affect consumer purchasing power and spending patterns. Markets require buying power as well as people. Because total purchasing power depends on current income, prices, savings, and credit, marketers must be aware of major economic trends in income and changing consumer spending patterns.

Changes in Income

Real income per capita declined during the 1970s and early 1980s, as inflation, high unemployment, and increased taxes reduced the amount of money people had to spend. As a result, many Americans became cautious buyers. Hotel firms introduced economy chains, and the restaurant industry responded with rapid growth of lower-priced fast-food chains.

In recent years, however, economic conditions have improved, and current projections suggest real income will rise due to rising income in certain important segments.[27] The baby-boom generation will move into its prime wage-earning years, and the number of small families headed by dual-career couples will increase substantially. About half of all families have two incomes. These more affluent groups will demand higher quality and buy more time-saving products, more travel and entertainment, more physical fitness products, more cultural activities, and more continuing education. However, the 1990s will also be the decade of the "squeezed customer." Along with rising incomes will come increased financial burdens: repaying debts acquired during the spending splurges of the 1980s, facing declining home values and increased taxes, and saving ahead for college tuition payments and retirement. Thus, despite their higher incomes, financially squeezed customers will probably continue to spend more slowly and carefully than in the previous decade. And they will continue to seek greater value in the products and services that they buy.

Marketers should pay more attention to *income distribution* as well as average income. Income distribution in the United states is still very skewed. At the top are *upper-class* consumers, whose spending patterns are not affected by current economic events and who are a major market for luxury goods. There is a comfortable *middle class* that is somewhat careful about its spending but can still afford the good life some of the time. The *working class* must stick close to the basics of food, clothing, and shelter and must try hard to save. Finally, the *underclass* (persons on welfare and many retirees) must count their pennies when making the most basic purchases.

Changing Consumer Spending Patterns

Changes in major economic variables such as income, cost of living, interest rates, and savings and borrowing patterns have a large impact on the marketplace. Companies use economic forecasting to anticipate changes in these variables. With adequate warning, businesses can reduce their costs and adjust their marketing mix to ride out the economic storm. Restaurants, for example, can vary their menus and offer a number of lower-priced entrees during a recession.

People have different spending patterns as their income increases. For example, people earning $20,000 to $30,000 spend 15.8% of their income on food, while people making $50,000 and over only spend 12.8% of their income on food. The amount spent on entertainment jumps from 4.7% for the $20,000 to $30,000 group to 6.1% for the $50,000 and over group.[28] Ernst Engel found that as family income increases the percentage spent on food declines, the percentage spent on housing remains almost constant, and the percentage spent on other categories increases. Studies have generally supported **Engel's laws**.

Natural Environment

The **natural environment** consists of natural resources required by marketers or affected by marketing activities. During the 1960s, the public grew concerned that the natural environment was being damaged by modern industrial activities. Popular books warned about shortages of natural resources and about the damage to water, earth, and air caused by industrial activity. Watchdog groups such as the Sierra Club and Friends of the Earth sprang up, and legislators proposed measures to protect the environment.

Conservation of Resources

In Texas, watchdog groups gathered sufficient support to have redfish and sea trout banned from commercial fishing, forcing restaurants to import these popular fish from other states or eliminate them from the menu altogether. Some areas have a ban on the use of charbroilers because of the smoke that they emit. In the Southwest, water is becoming a scarce resource. In choosing markets and marketing mixes, marketers should be aware of environmental concerns.

The Florida Solid Waste Act of 1988 required resorts to reduce their waste stream by 30% by 1994. At the time of the law's passage Disney already had a number of programs designed to eliminate or recycle waste. Disney simply continued its aggressive program against waste to meet the 1994 requirements. These efforts included purchasing food in large containers to eliminate waste. For example, purchasing tomato paste in 55-gallon drums, instead of number 10 cans, saved 86,000 cans a year. Disney shreds its paper products and sends the shredded paper to the gift shops to use as packing material, and torn linens are made into rags, reducing the need for paper towels. A 25% reduction in the size of its napkins reduced paper waste by over 130 tons. Disney World uses "gray water," treated waste water, to water its golf courses, lawns, and gardens. Robert Penn, director of environmental affairs of Disney's municipal arm, Ready Creek improvement district, states that using gray water can help operators of many lodging facilities. Gray water is not only less expensive than municipal water; it is an environmentally sound method of watering large gardens and golf courses.

Disney waste management has eliminated tons of waste and its recycling program handles 30 tons of waste a day. Disney receives anywhere from $10 a ton for newspaper to $650 a ton for aluminum cans. Even with this income, Disney's waste reduction is not a money maker. The efforts continue because management feels its the right thing to do, and they are following the wishes of the company's founder. Walt Disney said, "Our forests, waters, grasslands, and wildlife must be wisely protected and used. I urge all citizens to join the effort to save America's natural beauty."[29]

Here are some examples of other ecologically minded hospitality marketers. Kim Richards is the president of a resort development firm that works with the environment. When developing the Ventana Canyon Resort,

FantastiQue, EconomiQue.

US·CAN **38%** Save thanks to the exchange rate!

* Exchange rate quoted as of June 3, 1994. Subject to change. Call for current rate.

"The hills, the snow, the thrills, the view, the people…that's the MagiQue of skiing in Québec, your ski heaven right next door!"

For information
**Call toll free
1 800 363-7777**
Ask for operator 226
(9 am to 5 pm, 7 days a week)
or call your travel agent.

Ski conditions available toll free at 1 800 463-9777 from mid-November 1994 to mid-March 1995.
For your free brochure and Winter Holiday Guide, call the number below.

Québec
It Feels So Different.

Tourisme Québec   *Bonjour!*

One aspect of the economic environment that is increasing in importance with the growth of international travel is the currency exchange rate. Quebec uses Canada's favorable exchange rate to attract skiers from the United States. Courtesy of Tourisme Quebec and Cossette Communication–Marketing.

he designed a golf course that used 40% less turf than a conventional design. This reduced the amount of water needed to maintain the course, as well as helping to preserve the natural habitat. Rather than bulldoze trees on the resort site, he transplanted them.

When Hyatt developed the Hyatt Regency Waikoloa, they wanted to avoid destroying the micro-organic marine life that lived in pools on the property. The developer created new locations where this marine life could live and flourish. Sheraton asks guests at its African and Indian Ocean properties to agree to the addition of a dollar to their bill to be used for conservation projects.[30] Inter-Continental Hotels publishes "The Daily Planet," a newsletter describing what its hotels are doing to reduce pollution and waste. For example, a recent newsletter featured the Hotel Inter-Continental Wien's purchase of new laundry equipment that significantly reduced toxic chemical emissions and was also more energy efficient than the equipment it was replacing.

Solid Waste Disposal

Hospitality companies will need to be proactive in their efforts to conserve the environment. Industry will invariably affect the quality of the natural environment. One major concern is solid waste disposal. The gross annual discard of municipal solid waste is expected to grow from 157.2 million tons in 1986 to 192.7 million tons in the year 2000. At the current rate, several states, including Ohio, Pennsylvania, New Jersey, Kentucky, and Virginia, will have exhausted their landfill capacity by the late 1990s, and half of the states will have used up their land space by the year 2000. Restaurants are often singled out as a major cause of this landfill exhaustion:

- Plastic disposable containers consume an inordinate volume of landfill space because they do not degrade.
- Disposable plastic is not recyclable.
- Expanded plastic foams may damage the atmospheric ozone by the release of chlorofluorocarbons.

As a consequence, the food-service industry, especially the fast-food segment, has received negative publicity. Public concern has lead some cities and counties to ban disposable food packaging, institute mandatory recycling programs, and tax packaging materials based on their recyclability and degradability. The facts, however, are as follows: Only about one-third of one percent of landfills is taken up by fast-food packaging materials. Chlorofluorocarbons were used in the production of only 3% of all expanded foam products, and they now have been completely eliminated.[31]

As a result of activist group pressure, governmental units are drawn into environmental protection. Businesses need to regulate themselves to avoid overly strict government regulation. The food-service industry has started programs to reduce waste materials, encourage recycling, and dispose of waste products through combustion. In addition, they must encourage joint business/community efforts to educate the public about the landfill problem and possible solutions.

Increased Cost

One nonrenewable resource, oil, has created the most serious problem for future economic growth. The major industrial economies of the world depend heavily on oil, and until economical energy substitutes can be developed, oil will continue to dominate the world political and economic picture. Large increases in the price of oil during the 1970s and dramatic events like the 1991 Persian Gulf War that affect oil availability have spurred the search for alternative forms of energy. Coal is again popular; and many companies are searching for practical ways to harness solar, nuclear, wind, and other forms of energy. In fact, hundreds of firms already are offering products that use solar energy for heating homes and other uses.

Technological Environment

The most dramatic force shaping our destiny is technology. Technology has given us penicillin, open-heart surgery, and the birth-control pill. It has also released such horrors as the hydrogen bomb, nerve gas, and chemical warfare. It has also produced products with mixed blessings, such as television and the automobile.

Technological change is occurring at an ever increasing rate.[32] Many products that are taken for granted today either were uncommon or did not exist, 30 years ago—electronic calculators, copier machines, fast-food chains, personal computers, jet airplanes, all-suite hotels, fax machines, and VCRs to name a few. Scientists are also speculating on products for the future, such as flying cars, personal rocket belts, and voyages to space that include a stay at a space hotel.

Technology has affected the hospitality industry in many ways: Robots are used to deliver hospital food trays to stations throughout the hospital. Machines cook food automatically, eliminating human error. Computerized video check-in and check-out services are now common practice in many hotels. Fax machines now receive orders at restaurants. Computerized yield management systems are helping hotels to optimize their profits through pricing to demand. These and other technological advances will help companies to be more effective in the marketplace. Firms that adopt useful technological advances will gain a competitive advantage.

Taco Bell has a program called K-minus, which means minus the kitchen. As part of its value orientation started in the mid-1980s, Taco Bell has been working to reduce and eventually eliminate its kitchen. One reason for this is that they found that the kitchen tasks were least preferred by their employees. Another reason is that a smaller, kitchenless Taco Bell will be able to fit in more places, such as malls, supermarkets, airports, and movie theaters. Taco Bell is working with robotics to develop production processes for its food products. It has a Taco Flex-Station that can produce 900 tacos per hour. Taco Bell sees technology as the way to enable it to retain service-oriented employees and gain access to thousands of points of distribution that would not be available through its conventional stores.[33]

The Australian Airline, Qantas Airways, provides an example of technological thinking. Qantas has developed "The PC Capable Chair" for their first-class passengers. Realizing that many executives now travel with notebook computers, Qantas developed a way to provide them with a power source. The internal power source on notebook computers at the time when Qantas made its decision lasted about 3 hours. This is

System One was the first computer reservation system (CRS) to have electronic ticket delivery through an electronic ticket delivery network. Hyatt Hotels has used similar technology to develop a computerized check-in system. Courtesy of System One Corporation.

adequate for most domestic flights, but hardly adequate for a 13-hour flight over the Pacific. Qantas hopes the provision of an external power source will be perceived as a benefit by a significant number of first-class travelers.[34]

Today you can make airline, car rental, and hotel reservations over the airline's computer. Some airlines have eliminated the need for a paper ticket and are using an "electric ticket." For these airlines, the record of a passenger's reservation and credit card payment in their computer serves as the ticket. At some Hyatt Hotels, guests can check in at a video kiosk using multimedia technology, avoiding the front desk. Guests can then check out using their television. Fax machines have become a standard feature on executive floors and are available on call at most upscale business hotels. Business travelers are also expecting two phone lines in the room, one for their phone and one for a fax machine or computer modem. In the future a "smart card" will serve as the traveler's ticket. The smart card looks like a credit card and contains a computer chip. Reservation information will be downloaded from a computer. The guest will swipe their card through an airline gate instead of handing a ticket to an agent; they will also be able to receive their rental car and hotel room through a computer. As technology managers will have to realize, there will always be high-touch guests. Frequent travelers will enjoy the time savings of the technology, but many less frequent travelers will still want to receive their products through a human. The use of technology will be able to reduce waiting time, but it will not completely replace conventional check-in procedures in the near future.[35]

Technological change faces opposition from those who see it as threatening nature, privacy, simplicity, and even the human race. Various groups have opposed the construction of restaurants in suburban and historical areas and high-rise hotels, airports, and recreational facilities in national parks. Marketers must understand and anticipate changes in the technological environment and utilize technologies that serve human needs. They must be sensitive to aspects of any innovation that might harm users and bring about opposition.

Political Environment

Marketing decisions are strongly affected by developments in the political environment. The **political environment** is made up of laws, government agencies, and pressure groups that influence and limit the activities of various organizations and individuals in society. We will cite some current political trends and their implications for marketing management.

Increased Legislation and Regulation Affecting Business

As products become more complex, public concern about their safety increases. Governmental agencies have become involved in the investigation and regulation of everything from fire codes to food-handling practices. Employment and employee practices fall under government regulation, as do sales of liquor, which vary from state to state and sometimes from precinct to precinct in the same county. Travelers are also seen as good sources of revenue by politicians, since they cannot vote at their destinations. Hotel taxes and restaurant taxes have become popular sources of revenue for local governments. In many cases, hotel taxes are supposed to be used to support tourism; however the spending of this money has been subject to liberal interpretation, such as for statues for suburban parks. Hotel managers must make sure that those taxes designated to promote tourism are used effectively. Managers must also work with hotel and restaurant associations to make sure that the taxes do not become oppressive. New York City hiked its hotel tax to over 21.25% for rooms over $100 in 1990. Many meeting and convention planners avoided New York because of the unfriendly tax; they simply took their business elsewhere. Convention business plunged by 37% during the next 3 years, and overall tax revenue declined despite the increase in the tax. The real loser was New York City's hospitality industry. New York has since reduced its hotel tax in line with other cities (see Figure 5-6).[36]

Legislation and regulation affecting business has been enacted for three reasons. First, it protects companies from each other. While most businesses praise competition, they try to neutralize it when it affects them. In the United States it is the job of the Federal Trade Commission and the Antitrust Division of the Justice Department to define and prevent unfair competition. Cases often emerge in which one company lodges a complaint that another is guilty of an unfair practice, such as deceptive pricing or deceptive advertising, thereby injuring its business.

Second, government legislation and regulation also aim at protecting consumers from unfair business practices. If unregulated, firms might make unsafe or low-quality products, be untruthful in their advertising, or deceive through packaging and pricing. Various government units define unfair consumer practices and offer remedies. Businesses, of course, can minimize government intervention through active self-regulation. Such associations as the American Motel and Hotel Association and the National Restaurant Association define and encourage good trade practices. These associations

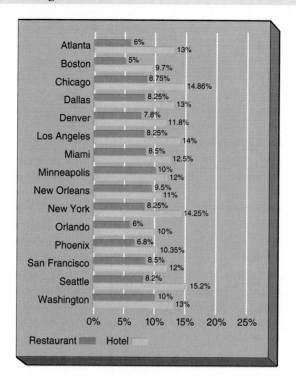

Figure 5-6
Restaurant and hotel taxes in major cities. Copyright 1994, USA TODAY. Reprinted with permission.

have developed guidelines for truth in menu presentation, alcoholic beverage service, and sanitation.

Third, government regulation also aims to protect society's interests against unrestrained business behavior. Profitable business activity does not always improve the quality of life. Thus regulations are passed to discourage smoking, littering, polluting, overcongestion of facilities, and the like, all in the name of protecting society's interests. Regulation aims to make firms responsible for the social as well as private costs of their production and distribution activities.

Government regulation and enforcement are likely to increase in the future. Business executives must know the major laws protecting competition, consumers, and society when planning their products and marketing programs.

Changing Government Agency Enforcement

To enforce laws, Congress has established several federal regulatory agencies: the Federal Trade Commission, the Food and Drug Administration, the Interstate Commerce Commission, the Federal Communications Commission, the Federal Power Commission, the Civil Aeronautics Board, the Consumer Products Safety Commission, the Environmental Protection Agency, and the Office of Consumer Affairs. These agencies can have a major impact on a company's marketing performance. Government agencies have some discretion in enforcing the laws and, from time to time, they appear to be overly eager. The agencies frequently are dominated by lawyers and economists, who often lack a practical sense of marketing and other business principles.

In recent years, the Federal Trade Commission has added marketing experts to its staff to gain a better understanding of these complex issues.

The power of government is so great that government can often dramatically affect a hospitality business without ever enforcing a law. An example is the case of a strike by American Airlines flight attendants in 1993. President Clinton intervened by calling Robert Crandal, CEO of American Airlines, and urging him to resolve the problem. The power and prestige of a head of state is so large that American Airlines settled in favor of the flight attendants. An airline is subject to many federal agencies, and the management at American Airlines obviously was intimidated.

Another example is offered by the proposed sale of the Tarrytown Hilton in Westchester County, New York. The property's owners, Prudential Insurance and Hilton, put the hotel up for sale. Normally, hotel sales are concluded in private and without publicity. In this case, the chairman of Westchester's County Board publicly announced that the county was considering purchasing the hotel as a temporary shelter for the homeless. This caused public outcry and forced the owner to cancel the sale of the hotel. The public thought the property was going to become a homeless shelter and canceled reservations for parties, meetings, and banquets. Management of the Tarrytown Hilton estimated the loss of revenue at $800,000 and a 45% reduction in market share for some of its services.[37]

Growth of Public-interest Groups

The number of public-interest groups has increased during the past two decades as has their clout in the political arena. MADD (Mothers Against Drunk Driving) has had a major impact on the hospitality industry by demanding that restaurants be more responsible in their serving of alcohol. Hundreds of consumer, environmental, minority, and other interest groups, both private and governmental, operate at the national, state, and local levels. Alert members of the hospitality industry have recognized that many of these groups represent excellent marketing opportunities for seminars, conferences, meetings, and social gatherings; for instance, there is a national association of black skiers that is aggressively courted by ski resorts.

Increased Emphasis on Ethics and Socially Responsible Actions

Written regulations cannot possibly cover all potential marketing abuses, and existing laws are often difficult to enforce. However, beyond written laws and regulations, business is also governed by social codes and rules of professional ethics. Enlightened companies encourage their managers to look beyond what the regulatory system allows and to simply "do the right thing." These socially responsible firms actively seek out ways to protect the long-run interests of their consumers and the environment.

The recent rash of business scandals and increased concerns about the environment have created fresh interest in the issues of ethics and social responsibility. Almost every aspect of marketing involves such issues. Unfortunately, because these issues usually involve conflicting interests, well-meaning people can disagree honestly about the right course of action in a particular situation. Thus, many industrial and professional trade associations

Marketing Highlight 5-3

Popcorn's Ten Cultural Trends

Futurist Faith Popcorn runs BrainReserve, a marketing consulting firm that monitors cultural trends and advises companies such as AT&T, Citibank, Black & Decker, Hoffman-La Roche, Nissan, Rubbermaid, and many others on how these trends will affect their marketing and other business decisions. Using its trend predictions, BrainReserve offers several services: BrainJam generates new product ideas for clients, and BrainRenewal attempts to breathe new life into fading brands. FutureFocus develops marketing strategies and concepts that create long-term competitive advantage. Another service, TrendBank, is a database containing culture monitoring and consumer interview information. Popcorn and her associates have identified ten major cultural trends affecting U.S. consumers:

1. *Cashing out:* the urge to change one's life to a slower but more rewarding pace. An executive suddenly quits his or her career, escapes the hassles of big city life, and turns up in Vermont or Montana running a small newspaper, managing a bed-and-breakfast establishment, or starting a band. People cash out because they don't think the stress is worth it. They nostalgically try to return to small town values, seeking clean air, safe schools, and plain-speaking neighbors.

2. *Cocooning:* the impulse to stay inside when the outside gets too tough and scary. Many people are turning their homes into nests: redecorating their houses, becoming "couch potatoes," watching TV movies, ordering from catalogs, and using answering machines to filter out the outside world. In reaction to increases in crime and other social problems, cocooners are burrowing in and building bunkers. Self-preservation is the underlying theme. Another breed is Wandering Cocoons, people who eat in their cars and communicate through their car phones. Socialized Cocooners form a small group of friends who frequently get together for conversation or for "salooning."

3. *Down-aging:* the tendency to act and feel younger than one's age. Today's sex symbols include Cher (over 45), Paul Newman (over 65), and Elizabeth Taylor (over 60). Older people spend more on youthful clothes, hair coloring, and facial plastic surgery. They engage in more playful behavior and act in ways previously thought not to be appropriate for their age group. They buy adult toys, attend adult camps, and sign up for adventure vacations.

4. *Egonomics:* the desire to develop individuality in order to be seen and treated as different from others. This is not an ego trip, but simply the wish to individualize oneself through possessions and experiences. People increasingly subscribe to narrow-interest magazines; join small groups with narrow missions; and buy customized clothing, cars, and cosmetics. Egonomics gives marketers an opportunity to succeed by offering customized goods, services, and experiences.

5. *Fantasy adventure:* the need to find emotional escapes to offset one's daily routines. People might seek vacations, eat exotic foods, go to Disneyland and other fantasy parks, or redeco-

have suggested codes of ethics, and many companies are now developing policies and guidelines to deal with complex social responsibility issues.

Cultural Environment

The cultural environment includes institutions and other forces that affect society's basic values, perceptions, preferences, and behaviors. As a collective entity, a society shapes the basic beliefs and values of its members.

rate their homes with a Santa Fe look. For marketers, this is an opportunity to create new fantasy products and services, or to add fantasy touches to their current products and services.

6. *99 lives:* the desperate state of people who must juggle many roles and responsibilities. An example is the "SuperMom" who must handle a full-time career while also managing her home and children. People today feel time-poor. They attempt to relieve time pressures by using fax machines and car phones, eating at fast food restaurants, and through other means. Marketers can meet this need by creating *cluster marketing* enterprises—all-in-one service stops, such as Video Town Launderette which, in addition to its laundry facilities, includes a tanning room, an exercise bike, copying and fax machines, and 6,000 video titles for rent.

7. *S.O.S. (Save Our Society):* the drive on the part of a growing number of people to make society more socially responsible with respect to education, ethics, and the environment. People join groups to promote more social responsibility on the part of companies and other citizens. The best response for marketers is to urge their own companies to practice more socially responsible marketing.

8. *Small indulgences*: the need on the part of stressed-out consumers for occasional emotional fixes. A consumer might not be able to afford a two-week trip to Europe but might spend a weekend in New Orleans instead. He or she might eat healthily all week, then splurge with a pint of superpremium Haagen-Dazs ice cream over the weekend. Marketers should be aware of the ways in which consumers feel deprived and look for opportunities to offer small indulgences that provide an emotional lift.

9. *Staying alive:* the drive to live longer and better lives. People now know that their life-styles can kill them—eating the wrong foods, smoking, breathing bad air, abusing drugs. They are increasingly taking responsibility for their own health and choosing better foods, exercising more regularly, and relaxing more often. Marketers can meet these needs by designing healthier products and services for consumers.

10. *The vigilante consumer:* Vigilante consumers are those who will no longer tolerate shoddy products and poor service. They want companies to be more aware and responsive. They want auto companies to take back "lemons" and fully refund their money. They subscribe to the *National Boycott News* and *Consumer Reports*, join MADD (Mothers Against Drunk Driving), buy "green products," and look for lists of good companies and bad companies. Marketers must serve as the consciences of their companies to bring these consumers better, more responsible products and services.

Source: From *The Popcorn Report* by Faith Popcorn. ©1991 by Faith Popcorn. Used by permission of Bantam Doubleday Dell Publishing Group.

They absorb a world view that defines their relationship with themselves and others. The following cultural characteristics can affect marketing decision making.

Persistence of Cultural Values

People in any society hold certain persisting core beliefs and values. For example, most Americans believe in working, getting married, giving to charity, and being honest, beliefs that shape the more specific attitudes and behaviors found in everyday life. Core beliefs and values are passed on from parents to children and are reinforced by schools, churches, business, and government. Secondary beliefs and values, however, are more open to change. Believing in marriage is a core belief; believing that people should get married early is a secondary belief. Family planning marketers, for instance, could argue more effectively that people should get married later rather than that they should not get married at all. Marketers have some chance of changing secondary values, but little chance of changing core values.

Throughout much of the Western World, cultural values concerning certain personal habits such as drinking and smoking have changed. The United States has witnessed wide swings in cultural values concerning the drinking of alcoholic beverages. The Frontier witnessed a relatively relaxed attitude toward the use of alcohol. Prohibition in the United States attempted to completely eliminate alcoholic beverages. Today, society approves the use of alcohol, but has called for increased responsibility on the part of those who drink and those who sell and serve alcoholic beverages. The alcoholic beverage industry has responded with its leading companies encouraging responsible drinking. The hospitality industry has responded with employee training and rules regulating the sale of alcohol. The industry has also been urged to assume proactive marketing. "In place of pushing alcoholic beverages, the operator can stress the social side of the tavern experience, or offer food as a happy hour business stimulant. The current popularity of menu items designed for "grazing" can be the basis for promotions. For example, the Westwater Inn in Olympia, Washington, uses table tents to sell absorbers: meatballs, chicken wings, stuffed mushrooms, and deep-fried snacks."[38]

The hospitality industry is worldwide. Chances are very good that many readers of this book will find themselves serving in a foreign setting sometime during their careers. Cultural norms and cultural prohibitions may affect their managerial roles in ways quite different from in the United States and Canada. For example, hoteliers in Israel are expected to understand and observe the rules of kashruth, or keeping kosher. These are complicated and require constant supervision. Hotels in Israel must have two kitchen setups, one for meat and one for dairy products. Because kosher meat is expensive in Israel, hotel food costs are higher.[39]

Subcultures

Each society contains subcultures, groups of people with shared value systems based on common life experiences or situations. Episcopalians, teenagers, and working women all represent separate subcultures whose members share common beliefs, preferences, and behaviors. To the extent that subcultural groups have specific wants and buying behavior, marketers can choose subcultures as their target markets.

RESPONDING TO THE MARKETING ENVIRONMENT

Many companies view the marketing environment as an "uncontrollable" element to which they must adapt. They passively accept the marketing environment and do not try to change it. They analyze environmental forces and design strategies that will help the company avoid the threats and take advantage of the opportunities that the environment provides.

Table 5-1
Example of an Environmental Scanning System for a Restaurant

ENVIRONMENTAL FACTOR	SOURCE OF INFORMATION	PERSON RESPONSIBLE	FREQUENCY
Customers	Customers	Service staff	Daily
	Employees	Management	Daily
	Customer counts	Accountant	Daily
	Tourist/convention bureau	Management	Monthly
Social/cultural	Trade magazines	Management	Weekly or
		Bartender	monthly
		Service staff	
		Secretarial staff	
		Accounting	
	Consumer magazines	Management	Weekly or
		Host/hostess	monthly
		Secretarial staff	
	Newspaper	Management	Daily
Competition	Customers	Management	Daily
		Service staff	
	Newspaper	Management	Daily
	Visits	Management, chef	Weekly
Economic	Newspaper	Management	Daily
	Average check	Accountant	Daily
		Sales	
	Economic newsletters	Management	Weekly or monthly
	Chamber of commerce	Management	Monthly
Legal	Trade magazines	Management association	Monthly
	Newsletters		
	Trade magazines	Management	Weekly or monthly
Technology	Trade magazines	Management	Weekly or
		Chef	monthly
		Accountant	
	Trade shows	Management	Yearly
		Chef	
		Accountant	

This table provides an example of a scanning system. Each restaurant or hotel should determine its own needs and develop a specific model to fit its needs.

Other companies take an **environmental management perspective.**[40] Rather than simply watching and reacting, these firms take aggressive action to affect the publics and forces in their marketing environment. These companies hire lobbyists to influence legislation affecting their industries and stage media events to gain favorable press coverage. They run "advertorials" (ads expressing editorial points of view) to shape public opinion. They press lawsuits and file complaints with regulators to keep competitors in line. And they form contractual agreements to better control their distribution channels.

Marketing management cannot always affect environmental forces; in many cases, it must settle for simply watching and reacting to the environment. For example, a company would have little success trying to influence geographic population shifts, the economic environment, or major cultural values. But, whenever possible, smart marketing managers take a proactive rather than reactive approach to the publics and forces in their marketing environment.

Environmental scanning.   The use of an environmental scanning plan has proved beneficial to many hospitality companies. The following steps are involved: (1) determine the environmental areas that need to be monitored; (2) determine how the information will be collected, including information sources, the information frequency, and who will be responsible; (3) implement the data collection plan; and (4) analyze the data and use them in the market planning process.

One of the most important tasks, especially in a small business such as a restaurant, is to assign responsibilities for the collection of data. Bob Southwell, former manager of the Houston Country Club, urged his secretarial staff to scan magazines for new menu ideas. Bar managers can look for lounge promotions. Dining room managers can study serving and promotional ideas. The staff feeds ideas to the manager. Table 5-1 (on page 127) provides an example of an environmental scanning plan.

Using Information about the Marketing Environment.   It is never sufficient to simply collect data about the environment. Information must be reliable and timely and used in decision making. William S. Watson, senior vice-president of Best Western Worldwide Marketing offered advice on this subject.

> As marketers, we are willing to make some intuitive leaps because of the creative aspects of our characters. Nevertheless, we need enough information to make reasonable decisions, enough good data so that we can let our judgment move beyond the obvious, traditional interpretations we have learned as professionals. Researchers must put less emphasis on data and more on the interpretation of those data. They must work toward turning data into useful information. Collecting data for its own value is like collecting stamps. It is a nice hobby but it does not deliver the mail.[41]

Chapter Review

I.   Microenvironment. The **microenvironment** consists of actors and forces close to the company that can affect its ability to serve its customers. The actors in the microenvironment include the company, suppliers, market intermediaries, customers, and publics.

1) **The Company.** Marketing managers work closely with top management and the various company departments.

2) **Suppliers.** Firms and individuals that provide the resources needed by the company to produce its goods and services.

3) **Marketing Intermediaries.** Firms that help the company promote, sell, and distribute its goods to the final buyers.

4) **Transportation System.** The system moves the product from the factory to the customer. The hospitality industry depends on transportation systems to move supplies and customers to their businesses.

5) **Marketing Services Agencies.** Marketing research firms, advertising agencies, media firms, and marketing consulting firms help companies to target and promote their products to the right market.

6) **Financial Intermediaries.** Includes banks, credit companies, insurance companies, and other firms that help hospitality companies to finance their transactions or insure risks associated with the buying and selling of goods and services.

II.   Macroenvironment. The macroenvironment consists of the larger societal forces that affect the whole microenvironment demographic, economic, natural, technological, political, competitor, and cultural forces. These are the seven major forces in a company's macroenvironment:

1) **Competitive Environment.** Each firm must consider its size and industry position in relation to its competitors. A company must satisfy the needs and wants of consumers better than its competitors do in order to survive.

2) **Demographic Environment. Demography** is the study of human populations in terms of size, density, location, age, sex, race, occupation, and other statistics. The demographic environment is of major interest to marketers because markets are made up of people.

3) **Economic Environment.** The economic environment consists of factors that affect consumer purchasing power and spending patterns. Markets require both power as well as people. Purchasing power depends on current income, price, saving, and credit; marketers must be aware of major economic trends in income and changing consumer spending patterns.

4) **Natural Environment.** the natural environment consists of natural resources required by marketers or affected by marketing activities.

5) **Technological Environment.** The most dramatic force shaping our destiny is technology.

6) **Political Environment.** The political environment is made up of laws, government agencies, and pressure groups that influence and limit various organizations and individuals in society.

7) **Cultural Environment.** The cultural environment includes institutions and other forces that affect society's basic values, perceptions, preferences, and behaviors.

III.   Responding To The Marketing Environment. Many companies view the marketing environment as an "uncontrollable" element to which they must adapt. Other companies take an environmental management perspective. Rather than simply watching and reacting, these firms take aggressive actions to affect the publics and forces in their marketing environment. These companies use environmental scanning to monitor the environment.

DISCUSSION QUESTIONS

1. How has McDonald's concept changed since the 1960s? What environmental forces were behind these changes? How will the McDonald's concept change in the next decade, given the new forces operating in the environment?

2. What environmental trends will affect the success of Hyatt hotels through the 1990s? If you were corporate director of marketing for Hyatt, what plans would you make to deal with these trends?

3. Identify the key competitors for Pizza Hut, or a restaurant in your town.

4. How have environmental trends affected the design of hotels?

5. Explain how environmental trends have affected the food and beverage offerings of a Sheraton hotel.

6. If we have little control over the macroenvironment, why should we be concerned with it?

7. Give an example of a trend of each element of the macroenvironment and explain how that trend will affect a hospitality firm of your choice.

KEY TERMS

Consumerism An organized movement of citizens and government to strengthen the rights and power of buyers in relation to sellers.

Cultural environment Institutions and other forces that affect society's basic values, perceptions, preferences, and behaviors.

Demography The study of human populations in terms of size, density, location, age, sex, race, occupation, and other statistics.

Economic environment Factors that affect consumer buying power and spending patterns.

Engel's laws Differences noted more than a century ago by Ernst Engel regarding family spending patterns in response to increased income; categories studied included food, housing, transportation, health care, and other foods and services.

Environmental management perspective A management perspective in which the firm takes aggressive actions to affect the publics and forces in its marketing environment, rather than simply watching and reacting to it.

Financial intermediaries Banks, credit companies, insurance companies, and other businesses that help finance transactions or insure against the risks associated with the buying and selling of goods.

Macroenvironment The larger societal forces that affect the whole microenvironment: competitive, demographic, economic, natural, technological, political, and cultural forces.

Marketing environment The actors and forces outside marketing that affect marketing management's ability to develop and maintain successful transactions with its target customers.

Marketing intermediaries Firms that help the company to promote, sell, and distribute its goods to final buyers; they include middlemen, physical distribution firms, marketing-service agencies, and financial intermediaries.

Marketing services agencies Marketing research firms, advertising agencies, media firms, marketing consulting firms, and other service providers that help a company to target and promote its products to the right markets.

Microenvironment The forces close to the company that affect its ability to serve its customers: the company, market channel firms, customer markets, competitors, and publics.

Middlemen Distribution channel firms that help the company find customers or make sales to them.

Natural environment Natural resources that are needed as inputs by marketers or are affected by marketing activities.

Physical distribution firms Warehouse, transportation, and other firms that help a company stock and move goods from their points of origin to their destinations.

Political environment Laws, government agencies, and pressure groups that influence and limit various organizations and individuals in a given society.

Public Any group that has an actual or potential interest in or impact on an organization's ability to achieve its objectives.

Suppliers Firms and individuals that provide the resources needed by the company and its competitors to produce goods and services.

Technological environment Forces that create new technologies, in turn creating new product and market opportunities.

REFERENCES

1. TOM MONAGHAN, *Pizza Tiger* (New York: Random House, 1986); "Domino's Launches Safety Ads," *Nation's Restaurant News* (August 14, 1986), pp. 1+; "Domino's Truck Kills 2 en Route to Delivery," *Nation's Restaurant News* (August 29, 1988), p. 4; "Domino's May Go to the Block," *Houston Chronicle* (September 12, 1989), p. 46; "Fight on Quick Pizza Delivery Grows," *New York Times* (August 29, 1989), sec. D, pp. 1+; "Policy on Driver's at Domino's Pizza," *New York Times* (June 23, 1989), sec. D, p. 4; "Domino's Pizza: How It Became the No. 2 Chain," *Business Week* (August 15, 1983), p. 114; "Tom Monaghan: The Fun-loving Prince of Pizza," *Business Week* (February 8, 1988), pp. 90, 93; Ron Simpson, "Can Monaghan Deliver," *Restaurant Business* (April 10, 1992), pp. 78–88.

2. "A Fast Food Formula Helps Sell Dining Out," *Business Week* (August 9, 1976), pp. 30–31; "Spooning Profits from a Bowl of Soup," *Business Week* (September 21, 1974); ROBERT C. LEWIS, "The Dwindling Boxcars," *Cases in Hospitality Marketing and Management* (New York: John Wiley & Sons, 1989).

3. JONATHAN DAHL, "Car-rental Firms and Hotels Hit Hard by High Air Fares," *Wall Street Journal* (May 16, 1989), sec. B, p. 1.

4. JOHN A. HURLEY, "The Hotels of Rome: Meeting the Marketing Challenge of Terrorism," *Cornell Hotel and Restaurant Administration Quarterly*, 29, no. 1 (May 1988), p. 74.

5. PHILIP KOTLER, *Marketing Management* (Englewood Cliffs, N.J.: Prentice Hall, 1988); DONALD R. LEHMANN AND RUSSEL S. WINER, *Analysis for Marketing Planning* (Plano, Texas: Business Publications, Inc., 1988).

6. MICHAEL PORTER, *Competitive Strategy* (New York: Free Press, 1980).

7. MELINDA BUSH, "The Critical Need to Know," *Cornell Hotel and Restaurant Administration Quarterly*, 26, no. 3 (November 1985), p. 1.

8. See "The Mommy Boom," *Sales & Marketing Management* (October 27, 1986), pp. 8–29.

9. RICHARD KERN, "USA 2000," *Sales and Marketing Management* (October 27, 1986), pp. 8–29.

10. RICHARD KERN, "The Year 2000: A Demographic Profile of Consumer Market," *Marketing News* (May 25, 1984), sec. 1, pp. 8–10 and KERN, "USA 2000," pp. 10–12.

11. PAUL BROWN, PETE ENGARDIO, STEVE KLINKERMAN, AND KIRVEN RINGE, "Bringing up Baby: A New Kind of Marketing Boom," *Business Week* (April 22, 1985), pp. 58–65; AMY DUNKIN AND JONATHAN B. LEVINE, "Toddlers in $90 Suits? You Gotta Be Kidding," *Business Week* (September 21, 1987), pp. 52–54; HORST H. STIPP, "Children as Consumers," *American Demographics* (February 1988), pp. 27–32.

12. TAMAR LEWIN, "Too Much Retirement Time? A Move Is Afoot to Change It," *New York Times*, (April 22, 1990), pp. 1+; LUCIA MOUAT, "Demographics Prompt Labor Shift," *Christian Science Monitor* (March 21, 1990), p. 8; "Days Recruits Older Workers" and "Senior Power National Job Fair," *press releases by Days Inn*.

13. PAUL GLICK, "How American Families Are Changing," *American Demographics* (January 1984), pp. 21–25; FABIAN LINDEN, "In the Rearview Mirror," *American Demographics* (April 1987), pp. 4–5; KERN, "USA 2000", pp. 16–17; and JUDITH WALDROP, "America's Households," *American Demographics* (March 1989), pp. 20–32.

14. "Weekend Pleasure Travel," *Restaurants USA*, 9, no. 5, 1989, p. 40; PATRICIA ABURDENE AND JOHN NAISBITT, *Megatrends 2000* (New York: William Morrow, 1990), pp. 216–240.

15. PETER JONES AND PETER A. JONES, "Stress: Are You Serving It up to Your Restaurant Patrons?" *Cornell Hotel and Restaurant Administration Quarterly*, 31, no. 3 (November 1990), pp. 38–43.

16. SMITH G. CAMPBELL, *Marketing the Meal Experience* (Guildford, England: University of Surrey, 1967).

17. JONES, "Stress," pp. 38–43.

18. PETER JONES, *Food Service Operations* (London: Cassell, 1989).

19. JONES, "Stress," p. 43.

20. GARY M. STERN, "Tables for One," *Restaurants USA* (March 1990), pp. 15–16.

21. JUDITH WALDROP, "2010," *American Demographics*, 11, no. 2 (February 1989), pp. 18–21.

22. See RICHARD KERN, "You Say Potato and I say ADIMSADMAPMSA," *Sales & Marketing Management*, (December 1988), p. 8.

23. KERN, "The Year 2000," sec. 1, p. 10.

24. Organization for Economic Cooperation and Development data, as reported in *The Condition of*

Education 1992 (Washington, D.C.: U.S. Department of Education, 1992), p. 94, as reported in JOEL EVANS AND BARRY BERMAN, *Principles of Marketing* (Prentice Hall: Englewood Cliffs, N.J.), p. 174.

25. FABIAN LINDEN, "In the Review Mirror," *American Demographics* (April 1984), p. 5 and BRYANT ROBEY AND CHERYL RUSSELL, "A portrait of the American Worker," *American Demographics* (March 1984), pp. 17–21.

26. JUDITH WALDROP AND THOMAS EXTER, "What the 1990 Census Will Show," *American Demographics* (January 1990), p. 25; *American Diversity*, American Demographic Desk Reference Series, No. 1 (July 1991); BRIAN BREMNER, "A Spicier Stew in the Melting Pot," *Business Week* (December 21, 1992), pp. 29–30; and "New Projections Show Faster Growth, More Diversity," *American Demographics*, (February 1993), pp. 9, 59.

27. "Consumer Expenditure Survey," U.S. Department of Labor, Bureau of Labor Statistics, *Bulletin 2383* (August 1991), pp. 15–17.

28. THOMAS EXTER, "Where the Money Is," *American Demographics* (March 1987), pp. 26–32; WILLIAM LAZER, "How Rising Affluence Will Reshape Markets," *American Demographics* (February 1984), pp. 17–20; KERN, "USA 2000," p. 19; and BICKLEY TOWNSEND, "Dollars and Dreams," *American Demographics* (December 1987), pp. 10, 55.

29. PHILIP HAYWARD, "Disney Does the Environment," *Lodging*, 19, no. 7 (March 1994), pp. 46–51+.

30. JULIE BAKER, "The Natural Resort," *Successful Meetings*, 39, no. 1 (January 1990), pp. 32–34.

31. See *The Solid Waste Program* (Washington, D.C.: The National Restaurant Association).

32. LEONARD D. GOODSTEIN, TIMOTHY M. NOLAN, AND J. WILLIAM PFEIFFER, *Shaping Strategic Planning* (Glenview, Ill.: Scott, Foresman, and Co., 1989), pp. 3–4.

33. DON NICHOLS, "Taco Machine Proves a Big Hit in Its Test Run," *Restaurant Business*, 92, no. 4 (March 1, 1993), p. 16.

34. See "PCs Hit Wild Blue Yonder," *Business Travel News* (July 24, 1989), p. 33.

35. JULIE SCHMIT, "The Ticket to Ride: Smart Cards," *USA Today*, (January 11, 1994), sec. B, pp. 1–2.

36. GENE SLOAN, "Restaurant Taxes Gain Weight in Cash-strapped Cities," *USA Today, International Edition* (Asia) (September 28, 1994), sec. B, p. 7.

37. GLENN WITHIAM, "The Strange Death and Energetic Rebirth of the Tarrytown Hilton Inn," *Cornell Hotel and Restaurant Administration Quarterly*, 30, no. 3 (November 1989), p. 46.

38. DENNEY G. RUTHERFORD, "Managing Guest Intoxication: A Policy to Limit Third-party Liability," *Cornell Hotel and Restaurant Administration Quarterly*, 26, no. 3, (1985), p. 67.

39. KENNETH J. GRUBER, "The Hotels of Israel: Pressure and Promise," *Cornell Hotel and Restaurant Administration Quarterly*, 28, no. 4, (February 1988), p. 42.

40. CARL P. ZEITHAML AND VALARIE ZEITHAML, "Environmental Management: Revising the Marketing Perspective," *Journal of Marketing* (Spring 1984), pp. 46–53.

41. WILLIAM S. WATSON, Letters, The New Research Responsibility," *Cornell Hotel and Restaurant Administration Quarterly*, 34, no. 5, (October 1993), p. 7.

Marketing Research and Information Systems

*O*ne Sunday morning in the summer of 1986, six Marriott employees checked into an inexpensive hotel outside the Atlanta airport. Once they were inside their $30-a-night room, decorated with red shag rugs and purple velour curtains, the team went into their routine. One called from the front desk saying that his shoelace had broken—could someone get him a new one? Another carefully noted the brands of soap, shampoo, and towels. A third took off his suit jacket, laid it down on the bed, and began moaning and writhing and knocking the headboard against the wall, while a colleague in the next room listened for the muffled cries of feigned ecstasy and calmly noted that the room wasn't soundproof.

For 6 months, Marriott's intelligence team traveled the country gathering information on the players in the economy hotel business, a market Marriott strongly wished to enter. Armed with detailed data about potential rivals' strengths and weaknesses, Marriott budgeted $500 million for a new hotel chain that would beat the competition in every respect, from soap to service to soundproof rooms.

Marriott also hired an executive placement firm to interview 15 regional managers of the five leading economy chains. From these managers, they learned about the needs and expectations of the unit managers that they were supervising. They gained knowledge on the managers'

career expectations, training, and salary ranges. They gained insights into the cultures of each chain—their values, beliefs, and ideals. Lee Pillsbury, formerly a Marriott executive, defended the ethics of this competitive intelligence campaign by stating that the Marriott employees identified themselves as Marriott employees upon checking into the hotels. The recruitment firm told the regional managers that there were no immediate openings, but there may be some positions in the future. In fact, Marriott hired five of the regional managers from among the interviewees.[1]

Marriott named its entry into the economy hotel business Fairfield Inns. Inspecting competitors' products was just one way Marriott gained information that aided in the development of its new chain. They also hired a headhunting team to interview their competitors' district and regional managers. Through talking with employees and making their own observations, Marriott discovered their competitors' weaknesses and developed a superior product. Marriott continues to collect marketing information after opening each Fairfield Inn hotel. The company conducts extensive marketing research, including phone and mail surveys, to track its standing in the marketplace and investigate client perceptions of its services.[2] Marriott managers understand the value of marketing information, both for special projects such as developing its Fairfield Inn concept and for introducing further improvements. The attention Marriott's managers pay to collecting, interpreting, and using information has contributed greatly to the company's growth.

Chapter 6 explains the underlying concepts of marketing research and details the importance of information to the company.

In the beginning of the chapter, we describe the **marketing information system**, an integrated collection of people, equipment, and procedures used to gather, evaluate, and distribute relevant information to marketing decision makers.

We continue with a discussion of the four key steps in the marketing research process: **defining the problem and objectives, developing a research plan, implementing the plan, and interpreting and reporting the findings**.

Next, we describe possible sources of information, including primary and secondary data, and approaches that can be used to collect such knowledge, including observational, survey, and experimental research.

We conclude with a discussion of ways to **distribute information** to the right managers at the right time.

In carrying out marketing analysis, planning, implementation, and control, marketing managers need information at almost every turn. They need information about customers, competitors, suppliers, and other forces in the marketplace. One marketing executive put it this way: "To manage a business well is to manage its future; and to manage the future is to manage information."[3]

During the past century, most hotels and restaurants were independently owned or a part of a small regional chain. Managers obtained information by being around people, observing them, and asking questions. During this century, many factors have increased the need for more and better information. As companies become national or international in scope, they need information on larger, more distant markets. As companies become more selective, they need better information about how buyers respond to different products and appeals. As companies use more complex marketing approaches and face intensified competition, they need information on the effectiveness of their marketing tools. Finally, in today's rapidly changing environments, managers need up-to-date information to make timely decisions.

The supply of information has also increased greatly. John Naisbitt suggests that the United States is undergoing a "megashift" from an industrial to an information-based economy.[4] He found that more than 65% of the U.S. work force is now employed in producing or processing information, compared to only 17% in 1950. Using improved computer systems and other technologies, companies can provide information in great quantities. In fact, today's managers sometimes receive too much information. For example, one study found that, with many companies offering data and information available through supermarket scanners, a packaged-goods brand manager is bombarded with 1 million to 1 billion new numbers each week.[5] As Naisbitt points out, "Running out of information is not a problem, but drowning in it is".[6]

Yet managers frequently complain that they lack enough information of the right kind and accumulate too much of the wrong kind. They also complain that marketing information is so widely spread throughout the company that it takes great effort to locate even simple facts. Subordinates may withhold information that they believe will reflect badly on their performance. Important information often arrives too late to be useful or is not accurate. Marketing managers need precise and timely information. Many companies are now studying their managers' information needs and designing systems to meet those needs.

THE MARKETING INFORMATION SYSTEM

A marketing information system (MIS) consists of people, equipment, and procedures to gather, sort, analyze, evaluate, and distribute needed, timely, and accurate information to marketing decision makers. The marketing information system concept is illustrated in Figure 6-1. The MIS begins and ends with marketing managers, but managers throughout the organization should be involved in the MIS. First, it interacts with managers to assess their information needs. Next, it develops needed information from internal company records, marketing intelligence activities, and the marketing research process. Information analysts process information to make it more useful. Finally, the MIS distributes information to managers in the right form and at the right time to help in marketing planning, implementation, and control.

We will now take a closer look at the functions of a company's marketing information system.

Figure 6-1
The marketing information system.

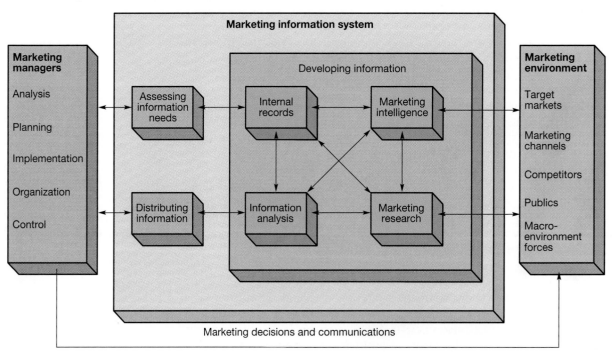

A good marketing information system balances information that managers would like to have against that which they really need and is feasible to obtain. A company begins by interviewing managers to determine their information needs. For example, Mrs. Fields' Cookies provides their managers with sales forecasts with updates each hour. When sales are falling behind, the computer suggests merchandising techniques such as sampling in the mall to pick up sales.[7]

Some managers will ask for whatever information they can get without thinking carefully about its cost or usefulness. Too much information can be as harmful as too little. Other busy managers may fail to ask for things they need to know. Or managers may not ask for some types of information that they should have.

For example, managers need to anticipate new competitive product offerings. However, competitors withhold information to prevent their competition from knowing about the product. During Kentucky Fried Chicken's development of their "Chicken Little" sandwich, only a few corporate managers knew of the project. Kentucky Fried Chicken had developed ingredient specifications for the making of the sandwich, and its suppliers had to sign secrecy agreements. Kentucky Fried Chicken did not want competitors to learn about the new product offering before its test marketing. Yet a competitor with a good MIS system might have picked up clues in advance about KFC's plans. They may have heard a bread supplier commenting about KFC's orders for small hamburger-style buns. They may have heard an executive stating how KFC would be strengthening its lunch business. Even with secret agreements, news inadvertently leaks out, and managers that keep their eyes and ears open can pick up on competitive moves.

The company must estimate the value of having an item of information against the costs of obtaining it. The value depends on how it will be used and this judgment is highly subjective. Similarly, estimating the cost of obtaining a specific item of information may be difficult.

The costs of obtaining, processing, storing, and delivering information can add up quickly. Sometimes additional information will contribute little to improving a manager's decision. Its cost may exceed its benefit. Suppose that a restaurant manager estimates that launching a new menu item without any further information will yield a lifetime profit of $500,000. The manager believes that additional information will improve the marketing mix and increase the company's profit to $525,000. It would be foolish to pay $30,000 or more to obtain the additional information.

ASSESSING INFORMATION NEEDS

Information needed by marketing managers can be obtained from internal company records, marketing intelligence, and marketing research. The information analysis system processes this information and presents it in a form that is useful to managers.

DEVELOPING INFORMATION

Internal Records

Most marketing managers use internal records and reports regularly for making day-to-day planning, implementation, and control decisions. **Internal records information** consists of information gathered from sources within the company to evaluate marketing performance and to detect marketing problems and opportunities. The company's accounting department develops financial statements and keeps detailed records of sales, costs, and cash flows. Daily reports from restaurants can include total sales, sales by service person, sales by menu item, guest counts, and average check. Hotel daily reports can include occupancy, number of guests, total revenue, average daily rate, no-shows, and groups in the house. The answers to the questions in Table 6-1 will help managers assess their marketing information needs.

Useful marketing information is contained in kitchen production schedules and sales reports, front-desk reports, sales call reports, and functions. Managers can use information gathered from these and other sources to evaluate performance and detect problems and opportunities. Here are some examples of how companies use internal records to make marketing decisions.

> Hotel managers use reservations records and registration information to aid in timing their advertising and sales calls. If most vacationers book February reservations in November, advertising in December will be too late.
>
> Reservation records also provide information concerning the hotel's top-producing travel agents. Hotel representatives can phone, fax, or visit travel agents to inform them of hotel-sponsored promotional activities in an effort to generate a higher volume of room sales.[8]

Guest History Information

The single most important element in any hospitality marketing information system is to have a process for capturing and using information concerning guests. Guest information is vital to improving service, creating effective advertising and sales promotion programs, developing new products,

Table 6-1

Questions for Assessing Marketing Information Needs

1. What types of decisions do you make regularly?
2. What types of information do you need in order to make these decisions?
3. What types of useful information do you get regularly?
4. What types of information would you like to get that you are not getting now?
5. What types of information do you get now that you don't really need?
6. What information would you want daily? Weekly? Monthly? Yearly?
7. What topics would you like to be kept informed about?
8. What databases would be useful to you?
9. What types of information analysis programs would you like to have?
10. What would be the four most helpful improvements that could be made in the present information system?

improving existing products, and developing marketing and sales plans and to the development and use of an effective revenue management program. Unfortunately, far too many hospitality firms have only a vague idea of who their guests are.

Specific guest information needs may include any or all of the information shown in Table 6-2.

At first appearance this list undoubtedly seems overbearing and unduly inquisitive. The fact is that hospitality companies increasingly collect and use this type of information. Obviously, a hotel, resort, cruise line, or other hospitality company must be very careful not to infringe on the privacy rights of guests or to disturb them. An amazing amount of this information is available from internal records. This requires interfacing with other departments, such as reservations and accounting.

Table 6-2

Specific Guest Information That Might Be Collected

Personal Guest Information	Type of primary product/service purchased
Name	Examples for a hotel
Address	Regular sleeping room
Postal Code	Suite
Fax no.: Home	Deluxe suite
Fax no.: Business	*Other Purchases (cross purchases)*
Phone numbers	Examples for a hotel
Home	Long-distance phone
Work	Laundry
Auto	Room service
Number in Party	Mini bar
Reason for Trip	Other food and beverage
Business	Health club
Pleasure	Recreational facilities
Emergency	Retail products charged to bill
Person who made reservation	*Length of stay*
Self	*Days stayed*
Employer	*Specific dates as guest*
Travel agent	*Method of arrival*
Name of employer	Personal auto
Address of employer	Rental auto
Title/position	Tour bus
Method of payment	Train
Credit Card	Taxi or Limo
Which?	*Member of frequent guest programs*
Cash	This hotel (number)
Check	Others presented for credit
Bill to company	Airline (number)
	Company (number)

Guest Information Trends

Information concerning guest trends is vital to planning and revenue/yield management. Types of guest trend information used by hotels, airlines, cruise lines, and auto rental companies include the following:

Booking patterns
Cancellations
Conversion percentages (% inquiries to reservations)
Overbooking patterns
Historical trends on occupancy for prime, shoulder, and low seasons
Yield patterns by season

Gathering this vital information requires careful planning by a management information system. It is seldom if ever sufficient to try to retrieve and use data from a company's files if prior consideration was not given to the form in which it would be needed.

Guest history records enable hotel marketers to identify repeat guests and their individual needs and preferences. If a guest requests a particular newspaper delivered during one stay, a notation entered into the guest's file will ensure that the newspaper is received during all future visits. If a luxury hotel upgrades its guests to a better room on their fifth visit, its managers are increasing guest satisfaction. Frequent guests appreciate the free upgrade, and many request the higher-priced room on the next visit.

Guest Information Management

Acquisition of this critical information cannot be left to chance or the whims of department managers. A system for obtaining guest information may include any or all of the following techniques:

Handwritten Journals and Card Files from Guest Registrations and Personal Observations. This system has disappeared from use except for B&B's, fishing lodges, small hotels, country inns, and farm/ranch guest homes. Despite its apparent nineteenth-century style, this technique is often adequate for small hospitality enterprises.

Guest Comment Cards. Guest comment cards are often found on dining room tables and in guest rooms or are handed to departing customers. They provide useful information and can provide insights into problem areas. For example, several negative comments on food would indicate a potential problem for a restaurant. If corrective action is taken and fewer negative comments are registered, then the correction has been successful.[9]

A problem with guest comment cards is that they may not reflect the opinions of the majority of guests. Commonly, only individuals who are very angry or well pleased take the time to complete a card. Thus comment cards can be useful in spotting problem areas, but they are not a good indication of overall guest satisfaction.

Guest Registration and Reservation Cards Transferred to PCs. This time-consuming technique is practical only for small enterprises, but does permit retrieval of data in an orderly manner.

Automated Systems.   "The decreasing cost and increasing capacity of automated guest history systems will allow hotels to create close relationships with their customers once again."[10]

Obviously, any hotel property or hospitality company, such as a large cruise line, must utilize an automated system. A variety of systems are available and should be carefully examined and tried before purchasing. Remember that an automated guest information system is part of broader systems such as database marketing and yield/revenue management.

An automated guest history system can be of great benefit to the sales force. Salespeople can pull guest histories by a specific geographic area, such as a city. This information can greatly assist in a sales blitz by identifying frequent guests who can receive top priority in the blitz. The guest history can also identify former frequent guests who are no longer using the hotel. Salespeople will want to call on these former clients to see if they can regain their business.

An automated guest history system offers a real competitive advantage to a chain, particularly a smaller chain. "By means of a centralized system or network a group of hotels could share guest information. Imagine how impressed a guest would be if he or she requested a suite, champagne, and a hypoallergenic pillow when staying at a hotel in Boston, then received the same services at a chain affiliate in Maui without even having to ask."[11]

Disguised Shoppers.   Hospitality companies often hire disguised or mystery shoppers to pose as customers and report back on their experience. The managers of Ruby's, a chain of restaurants based in California, uses shoppers to alert managers and employees to pay attention to important areas of the operation. Employees realize that they may be "shopped." The management of Ruby's hopes to catch employees doing the right things and doing them well. When employees score well on the shopper's report, Ruby's scores well.[12]

A mystery shopper works best if there is a possibility for recognition and reward for good job performance. This is the concept of positive reinforcement. If employees feel that the only purpose of a disguised shopper program is to report poor service and reprimand them, the program will not fulfill its full potential.

Company Records.   One of the most misused sources of information is company records. Marketing managers should take advantage of the information that is currently being generated by various departments. Likewise guest history and client history on potential corporate clients is also useful information.

Point of Sale Information.   For restaurants, the point-of-sale (POS) register will undoubtedly offer opportunities to compile and distribute, through a computer, information that is currently manually entered into reports. A POS system could collect information about individual restaurant patrons where credit cards are used.

Some observers of the fast-food industry believe that future POS systems will use expert systems that employ computers using artificial intelligence. One possible scenario is the "computaburger." Data concerning customer preference, order size, and volume will be taken from a POS machine and provided to an expert system. The expert system will then predict and possibly even order a volume of hamburger and the accompanying condiments for specific times in each day.[13]

The casino industry has displayed a high interest in POS systems and their increasing sophistication. Some slot machines are now capable of recording the numbers of play and the win/loss record of frequent players who activate the machines through the use of a magnetic card. The player receives points based on the amount of play, and the casino is able to track the playing habits of players using the slot club cards.

Systems are also in place in most casinos to track players who are brought to the casino by junket reps. Tracking of these players is the responsibility of the pit boss in each gaming area, such as blackjack.

The Las Vegas Hilton provides an example of an internal system that can provide needed marketing information,[14] which includes the following:

- A front-desk tracking system that can classify each room night sold into the proper market segment.
- A casino player tracking system that can identify players by market segments, that is, gaming rate versus slot tournament.
- A database of all customers staying at the Hilton to identify their spending patterns by market segment.
- Market research detailing guests' demographic characteristics, visitor frequency, and spending habits by customer segment.

Corporate Customer and Marketing Intermediary Information

A database of internally generated and external customers/prospects is of great value to a professional sales force. The sales force of Benchmark Hospitality Conference Resorts is trained to go beyond demographic studies and to target prospects by geography and industry segment. Benchmark's salespeople monitor the health of specific industries and qualify prospects. Before arranging a sales meeting with any corporate meeting planner, the salesperson obtains marketing information concerning the prospect, such as the following:

- The industry standing and strategic outlook for growth.
- Profit and loss statements from annual reports.
- Debt to equity ratios.
- Corporate culture information.
- Data concerning how this company uses meetings.

This information can be obtained from annual reports, financial analyses of public companies, and articles on the company and by talking with employees of the company. In addition to detailed information concerning prospects, Benchmark expects sales force members to regularly read the business press, such as the *Wall Street Journal* and the *New York Times*.[15]

Marketing Intelligence

Marketing intelligence includes everyday information about developments in the marketing environment that helps managers prepare and adjust marketing plans and short-run tactics. Marketing intelligence systems determine the needed intelligence, and collect and deliver it in a useful format to marketing managers.

Internal Sources of Marketing Intelligence

Marketing intelligence can be gathered by a company's executives, front-desk staff, service staff, purchasing agents, and sales force. Employees, unfortunately, are often too busy to pass on important information. The company must sell them on their role as intelligence gatherers and train them to spot and report new developments. Managers should debrief contact personnel on a regular basis.

Hotel owners and managers are essential parts of a marketing intelligence system. John F. Power, the general manager of the New York Hilton and Towers, served in this role on a trip to Japan. "I realized how different a Japanese breakfast is from our own," said Power, "and while most people like to sample the cuisine of the country they are visiting, everyone prefers to eat familiar food for breakfast."

As a result of marketing intelligence gathered on Power's trip, the New York Hilton now serves miso soup, nori (dried seaweed), yakizanaka (grilled fish), raw eggs, natto (fermented beans), oshiako (pickled vegetables), and rice as an authentic Japanese breakfast buffet.[16]

External Sources of Marketing Information

A hospitality company must encourage suppliers, convention and tourist bureaus, and travel agencies to pass along important intelligence. There are three types of external marketing information: (1) macro market information, (2) competitive information, and (3) new innovation and trends. The three types and their sources are shown in Table 6-3. It is worthwhile for a hospitality company to encourage the gathering of this information by treating vendors, salespeople, and potential employees in a friendly and receptive manner. Members of management should be encouraged to join community and professional organizations where they are likely to obtain essential marketing information.

Hotel and restaurant managers are in a particularly good position to acquire excellent information by entertaining key information sources in their properties. Sales-force members are excellent conduits of information.

Sources of Competitive Information

Competitive intelligence is available from competitor's annual reports, trade magazine articles, speeches, press releases, brochures, and advertisements. Hotel and restaurant managers should also visit their competitor's premises periodically.

A major consideration in any competitive information system is clearly defining the competition. Apparently obvious conclusions are often erroneous. An airport hotel might regard competitors as other hotels near the same airport. In fact, these are probably only a portion of the competitors. Downtown and suburban hotels might be competitors for certain groups. Airport hotels at other airports might also be competitors. The president of an association was overheard stating that the next conference should be at

Table 6-3

External Marketing Information Needs and Concerns for the Hospitality Industry

TYPES OF INFORMATION	EXTERNAL SOURCES OF INFORMATION
Visitor Marketing Information	
Profile of visitors to area	Visitors bureau (local, state, federal)
Visitor trends	Chambers of Commerce
Visitor expenditures	Colleges/universities
Visitation days	Public utility companies
Purpose of visit	Ski resorts
Recreational facilities desired/used	Publications (newspapers, magazines)
Lodging accommodation desired/used	Public parks, national forests, Bureau of
Food and beverage accommodation desired/used	Land Management
Retail shopping desired/used	Airlines, cruise lines
	Associations (hotel, restaurant, airline,
	cruise line, casinos)
	Environmental groups
	Historic restorations and museums
	Private companies offering plant tours
	Banks and other financial institutions
Competitive Information	
Pricing strategy	Suppliers/vendors
Product mix	Consultants
Planned expansion, renovation	Travel agencies
Product line extensions	Tour operators
Customer mix	Airlines, cruise lines, bus and rail companies
Strategic direction	Publications of competitors
Advertising/promotional thrust	Trade publications
Employee dissatisfaction/satisfaction	Association publications
Occupancy rates, discounts	Meetings/conventions
	Employees of competitors
	Trade association representatives
New Innovations and Trends	
Technological improvements in products/ services	Same list as those who provide competitive information
Pricing technology, such as yield management	
Technological advances in equipment	

a midwestern airport hotel, but the exact location depended on price, availability, and willingness to work with the association. Cruise lines who are competitors for destination resorts and resort hotels in Cancun, Mexico, may also be competitors to those in Hawaii. Colonial Williamsburg in Virginia came to the realization that its major competitor was not other historic restorations, but was instead Disney World. Managers must start by defining their competition. Once they have done this, they can then collect information on their competitors.

Commercial Sources of Marketing Information

Companies can also purchase information from outside suppliers. One such source of information is a system called Dialogue that provides access to over 350 databases. While sitting at a computer, managers can retrieve information on new products and locations, industry trends and projections, press releases, and the detailed finances of public and privately held businesses.[17] Today there are over 3000 on-line databases of information services. For example, Adtrack on-line database tracks all the advertisements of a quarter-page or larger from 150 major consumer and business publications. Companies can use these data to assess advertising strategies and styles, shares of advertising space, media usage, and ad budgets. The Donnelly Demographics database provides demographic data from the U.S. census plus demographic projections by state, city, or zip code. Companies can use it to measure markets and develop segmentation strategies. The Electronic Yellow Pages, containing listings from nearly all the nation's 4800 phone books, is the largest directory of American companies available. A firm such as Burger King might use this database to count McDonald's restaurants in different geographic locations. A readily available on-line database exists to fill almost any marketing information need.[18]

Associations sometimes collect data from member companies, compile it, and make it available to members for a reasonable fee. Information of this nature can often be misleading, since member companies frequently provide incorrect data or may refuse to contribute any statistics if they have a dominant market share.

Marketing Research

Managers cannot always wait for information to arrive in bits and pieces from the marketing intelligence system. They often require formal studies of specific situations. When McDonald's decided to add salads to its menu, its planners needed to research customers' preferences for types of vegetables and dressings.

Ben's Steakhouse, in Palm Beach, Florida, would like to know what percentage of its target market has heard of Ben's, how they heard about Ben's, what they know, and how they feel about the steakhouse. This would enable Ben's Steakhouse to know how effective their marketing communications have been. Casual marketing intelligence cannot answer these questions. Managers sometimes need to commission formal marketing research.

Marketing research is a process that identifies and defines marketing opportunities and problems, monitors and evaluates marketing actions and performance and communicates the findings and implications to management.[19]

Marketing researchers engage in a wide variety of activities. Their 10 most common activities are measurement of market potentials, market-share analysis, the determination of market characteristics, sales analysis, studies of business trends, short-range forecasting, competitive product studies, long-range forecasting, marketing information systems studies, and testing of existing products.

The Cantonese Opera is a tourist attraction of Hong Kong. Tourist authorities such as the Hong Kong Tourist Association use research to determine who comes to their cities and what tourist attractions create value for them. Courtesy of the Hong Kong Tourist Association.

A company can conduct marketing research by employing its own researchers or hiring outside researchers. Most large companies, in fact, more than 73% have their own marketing research departments. But even companies with their own departments hire outside firms to do fieldwork and special tasks.

Frank Camacho, a former vice-president of corporate marketing services for Marriott, listed Marriott's research priorities as follows:

- Market segmentation and sizing
- Concept development and product testing
- Price sensitivity assessment
- Advertising and promotions assessment
- Market tracking
- Customer satisfaction[20]

Small hotels or restaurants can obtain research help from nearby universities or colleges with business or hospitality programs. College marketing classes can be used to do exploratory research, find information about perspective customers, and conduct customer surveys. Instructors often arrange for their classes to gain marketing research experience in this way.

Marketing Research Process

The marketing research process consists of four steps (Figure 6-2): defining the problem and research objectives, developing the research plan, implementing the research plan, and interpreting and presenting the findings.

Defining the Problem and Research Objectives

Managers must work closely with marketing researchers to define the problem and the research objectives. While the manager best understands the problem or decision for which information is needed, it is the researcher who best understands marketing research and how to obtain information.

Managers must know enough about marketing research to interpret the findings carefully. If they know little about marketing research, they may accept the wrong information, draw the wrong conclusions, or request much more information than they need. Marketing researchers can help the manager define the problem and use the findings correctly.

In one case, a restaurant manager hired a researcher to determine the restaurant's level of awareness among the target market. The manager felt that lack of awareness explained low patronage. The researcher found, to the contrary, that many people were aware of the restaurant, but thought of it as a special-occasion rather than an everyday restaurant. The manager had misdefined the problem and the research objective.

Assuming that the problem is well defined, the manager and researcher must set research objectives. A marketing research project can have one of three types of objectives: **exploratory**, to gather preliminary information that will help define the problem and suggest hypotheses; **descriptive**, to describe the size and composition of the market; and **causal**, to test hypotheses about cause-and-effect relationships. Managers often start with exploratory research and later follow with descriptive and/or causal research.

A sad example of the need for marketing research was a self-help project initiated on U.S. Indian reservations. A total of 52 hotels were built as a result of promoting and anticipating tourism. Only two survived due to poorly conceived plans. In several cases, hotels were built in seldom visited remote areas. Marketing research could have provided valuable information such as visitor trends to the areas, identification of possible market segments, plus their size and travel preferences.[21]

Developing the Research Plan

The second marketing research step calls for determining the needed information and developing a data collection plan.

Figure 6-2
The marketing research process.

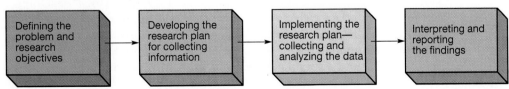

| Defining the problem and research objectives | Developing the research plan for collecting information | Implementing the research plan—collecting and analyzing the data | Interpreting and reporting the findings |

Determining Specific Information Needs.   Research objectives must be translated into specific information needs. When Marriott decided to research a new, lower-priced hotel system, it had two goals: to pull travelers away from competitors and to minimize cannibalization of its own existing hotels. This research might call for the following specific information:

- What features should the hotel offer? (See Table 6-4 on pages 152 and 153.)[22]
- How should the new hotels be priced?
- Where should the hotels be located? And can they safely be located near existing Marriott hotels without incurring cannibalization?
- What are the probable sales and profits?

Surveys of Secondary Information.   To meet a manager's information needs, researchers can gather secondary data, primary data, or both. **Secondary data** consist of information already in existence somewhere, having been collected for another purpose. **Primary data** consist of information collected for the specific purpose at hand.

Researchers usually start by gathering secondary data. Secondary data are usually obtained more quickly and at a lower cost than primary data. Table 6-5 (on pages 154 and 155) shows many secondary sources, both internal and external.

For example, *Restaurants USA*, published by the National Restaurant Association, provides a yearly projection of sales for food-service establishments, presenting the projections by state and by industry segment. A company has the options of paying a research firm to develop this information or of joining the National Restaurant Association and receiving this information through its publication. The latter is more cost effective.

Basing decisions on secondary data, however, can also present problems. The required information may not exist. Even when it exists, it might not be very relevant, accurate, current, and impartial. For example, a trade magazine wanted to identify the best hotel chains in the minds of corporate travel managers and travel agents. It distributed its survey as inserts in its magazine. The response rate was less than 0.05 percent. Yet the magazine issued a ranking based on this totally unreliable response rate.[23]

Secondary data provide a good starting point for marketing research. However, when secondary sources cannot provide all the needed information, the company must collect primary data.

Planning Primary Data Collection

Some managers collect primary data by developing a few questions and finding people to interview. But casually collected data can be useless or, even worse, misleading. Table 6-6 (on page 156) shows that designing a plan for primary data collection calls for decisions about research approaches, contact methods, a sampling plan, and research instruments.

Research Approaches.   Three basic research approaches are observations, surveys, and experiments. **Observational research** is the gathering of primary data by observing relevant people, actions, and situations. For example, a multiunit food-service operator sends researchers into competing restaurants to learn menu item prices, check portion sizes and consistency, and observe point-of-purchase merchandising. Another restaurant evaluates possible new locations by checking the locations of competing restaurants, traffic patterns, and neighborhood conditions. A hotel chain sends observers posing as guests into its coffee shops to check on cleanliness and customer service.

Observational research can yield information that people are normally unwilling or unable to provide. Observing numerous plates containing uneaten portions of the same menu item indicates that the food is not satisfactory. On the other hand, feelings, beliefs, and attitudes that motivate buying behavior cannot be observed. Long-run or infrequent behavior is also difficult to observe. Because of these limitations, researchers often supplement observation with survey research.

Survey research is the approach best suited to gathering descriptive information. Survey research can be **structured** or **unstructured**. Structured surveys use formal lists of questions asked of all respondents in the same way. Unstructured surveys let the interviewer probe respondents and guide the interview according to their answers.

Survey research may be **direct** or **indirect**. In the direct approach, the researcher asks direct questions about behavior or thoughts, for example, "Why don't you eat at Arby's?" Using the indirect approach, the researcher might ask, "What kinds of people eat at Arby's?" From the response, the researcher may be able to discover why the consumer avoids Arby's. In fact, it may suggest factors of which the consumer is not consciously aware.

The major advantage of survey research is its flexibility. It can be used to obtain many different kinds of information in many different marketing situations. Depending on the survey design, it may also provide information more quickly and at lower cost than observational or experimental research.

Survey research also has some limitations. Sometimes people are unable to answer survey questions because they cannot remember or never thought about what they do and why. Or they may be reluctant to answer questions asked by unknown interviewers about things that they consider private. Busy people may not want to take the time. Respondents may answer survey questions even when they do not know the answer in order to appear smart or well informed. Or they may try to help the interviewer by giving pleasing answers. Careful survey design can help minimize these problems.

In the early 1980s, Hardee's fast-food restaurant chain knew it was not effectively responding to consumer needs. Extensive consumer perception surveys were conducted. The results showed that consumers were confused about what kind of a chain Hardee's was. Research results also showed that the chain needed to improve its service and ambiance. Hardee's responded with a new positioning statement, upgraded equipment, and improved decor and committed the company to a total redesign of the hamburger manufacturing process.

While observation is best suited for exploratory research and surveys for descriptive research, **experimental research** is best suited for gathering causal information. Experiments involve selecting matched groups of

Table 6-4
Hotel Features with Choices for Levels of Each Feature

EXTERNAL FACTORS
Building Shape
L-shaped w/landscape
Outdoor courtyard
Landscaping
Minimal
Moderate
Elaborate
Pool type
No pool
Rectangular shape
Free form shape
Indoor/outdoor
Pool location
In courtyard
Not in courtyard
Corridor/View
Outside access/restricted view
Enclosed access/Unrestricted view/Balcony or window
Hotel size
Small (125 rooms, 2 stories)
Large (600 rooms, 12 stories)

ROOMS
Entertainment
Color TV
Color TV w/movies at $5
Color TV w/30 channel cable
Color TV w/HBO, movies, etc.
Color TV w/free movies
Entertainment/Rental

Sink location
In bath only
In separate area
In bath and separate
Bathroom Features
None
Shower Massage
Whirlpool (Jacuzzi)
Steam bath
Amenities
Small bar soap
Large soap/shampoo/shoeshine
Large soap/bath gel/shower cap/sewing kit
Above items + toothpaste, deodorant, mouthwash

FOOD
Restaurant in hotel
None (coffee shop next door)
Restaurant/lounge combo,
Coffee shop, full menu
Full-service restaurant, full menu
Coffee shop/full menu and good restaurant
Restaurant nearby
None
Coffee shop
Fast food
Fast food or coffee shop and moderate restaurant
Fast food or coffee shop and good restaurant

Type of people
Hotel guests and friends only
Open to public—general appeal
Open to public—many singles
Lounge nearby
None
Lounge/bar nearby
Lounge/bar w/ entertainment nearby

SERVICES
Reservations
Call hotel directly
800 reservation number
Check-in
Standard
Pre-credit clearance
Machine in lobby
Check-out
At front desk
Bill under door/leave key
Key to front desk/bill by mail
Machine in lobby
Limo to airport
None
Yes
Bellman
None
Yes
Message service
Note at front desk
Light on phone
Light on phone and message under door

Car rental/Airline reservations
None
Car rental facility
Airline reservations
Car rental and airline reservations

LEISURE
Sauna
None
Yes
Whirlpool/jacuzzi
None
Outdoor
Indoor
Exercise room
None
Basic facility w/weights
Facility w/Nautilus equipment
Racquet ball courts
None
Yes
Tennis courts
None
Yes
Game room/Entertainment
None
Electric games/pinball
Electric games/pinball, ping pong
Above + movie theater, bowling
Children's playroom/playground
None
Playground only

None
Rental Cassettes/in-room Atari
Rental Cassettes/stereo cassette playing in room
Rental Movies/in-room BetaMax
Size
Small (standard)
Slightly larger (1 foot)
Much larger (2 1/2 feet)
Small suite (2 rooms)
Large suite (2 rooms)
Quality of Decor (in standard room)
Budget motel decor
Old Holiday Inn decor
New Holiday Inn decor
New Hilton decor
New Hyatt decor
Heating and Cooling
Wall unit/full control
Wall unit/soundproof/full control
Central H or C (seasonal)
Central H or C/full control
Size of Bath
Standard bath
Slightly larger/sink separate
Much larger bath w/ larger tub
Very large/tub for 2

Free continental
None
Continental included in room rate
Room service
None
Phone-in order/guest to pick up
Room service, limited menu
Room service, full menu
Store
No food in store
Snack items
Snacks, refrigerated items, wine, beer, liquor
Above items and gourmet food items
Vending service
None
Soft drink machine only
Soft drink and snack machines
Soft drink, snack, and sandwich machines
Above and microwave available
In room kitchen facilities
None
Coffee maker only
Coffee maker and refrigerator
Cooking facilities in room
LOUNGE
Atmosphere
Quiet bar/lounge
Lively, popular bar/lounge

Recorded message
Cleanliness/upkeep/management skill
Budget motor level
Holiday Inn level
Nonconvention Hyatt level
Convention Hyatt level
Fine hotel level
Laundry/Valet
None
Client drop off and pick up
Self-service
Valet pick up and drop off
Special Services (concierge)
None
Information on restaurants, theaters, etc.
Arrangements and reservations
Travel problem resolution
Secretarial services
None
Xerox machine
Xerox machine and typist
Car maintenance
None
Take car to service
Gas on premises/bill to room

Playroom only
Playground and playroom
Pool extras
None
Pool w/slides
Pool w/slides and equipment
Pool w/slides, waterfall, equipment
SECURITY
Security guard
None
11 a.m. to 7 p.m.
7 p.m. to 7 a.m.
24 hours
Smoke detector
None
In rooms and throughout hotel
Sprinkler system
None
Lobby and hallways only
Lobby/hallways/rooms
24-hour video camera
None
Parking/hallway/public areas
Alarm button
None
Button in room, rings desk

Source: Jerry Wind et al. *Interfaces*, January 1, 1989.

Table 6-5

Sources of Secondary Data

A. Internal Sources

Internal sources include company profit and loss statements, balance sheets, guest checks, sales figures, sales call reports, invoices, inventory records, daily reports, prior research reports, registration cards, and reservation information.

B. Government Publications

Statistical Abstract of the U.S., updated annually, provides summary data on demographic, economic, social, and other aspects of the U.S. economy and society.

County and City Data Book, updated every 3 years, presents statistical information for counties, cities, and other geographical units on population, education, employment, aggregate and median income, housing, bank deposits, retail sales, and so on.

U.S. Industrial Outlook provides projections of industrial activity by industry and includes data on production, sales, shipments, employment, and the like. *Marketing Information Guide* provides a monthly annotated bibliography of marketing information. Other government publications include the *Annual Survey of Manufacturers; Business Statistics; Census of Manufacturers; Census of Population; Census of Retail Trade, Wholesale Trade, and Selected Service Industries; Census of Transportation; Federal Reserve Bulletin; Monthly Labor Review; Survey of Current Business;* and *Vital Statistics Report.*

C. Periodicals and Books

Business Periodicals Index, a monthly, lists business articles appearing in a wide variety of business publications.

Standard and Poor's Industry Surveys provide updated statistics and analyses of industries.

Moody's Manuals provide financial data and names of executives in major companies.

Encyclopedia of Associations provides information on every major U.S. trade and professional association.

Marketing journals include the *Journal of Marketing, Journal of Restaurant and Foodservice Marketing, Journal of Services Marketing,* and *HSMAI Marketing Review.*

Useful trade magazines include *Advertising Age, Business Travel News, The Consultant, Food Management, Lodging, Lodging Hospitality, Nation's Restaurant News, Restaurant Business, Restaurant Hospitality, Restaurants and Institutions, Restaurants USA,* and *Travel Weekly.*

Useful general business magazines include *Business Week, Cornell Hotel and Restaurant Administration Quarterly, Fortune, Forbes,* and *Harvard Business Review.*

D. Commercial Data

A. C. Nielsen Company provides data on products and brands sold through retail outlets (Retail Index Services), data on television audiences (Media Research Services), magazine circulation data (Neodata Services, Inc.), and more.

Market Research Corporation of America provides data on weekly family purchases of consumer products (National Consumer Panel), data on home food consumption (National Menu Census), and data on 6000 retail, drug, and discount retailers in various geographical areas (Metro Trade Audits).

Selling Areas—Marketing, Inc., provides reports on warehouse withdrawals to food stores in selected market areas (SAMI reports).

Simmons Market Research Bureau provides annual reports covering television markets, sporting goods, proprietary drugs, and others, giving demographic data by sex, income, age, and brand preferences (selective markets and the media reaching them).

Table 6-5
Continued

Other commercial research houses selling data to subscribers include the Audit Bureau of Circulation, Audits and Surveys, Dun and Broadstreet, National Family Opinion, Standard Rate and Data Service, and Starch.

E. Electronic Databases

ABI/Inform references 800 publications in business and related fields.

Asia–Pacific covers the business activity of the Pacific Rim. It contains information from business journals, as well as information on companies operating in this area.

Company Intelligence contains financial and marketing information on 100,000 U.S. private and public companies.

Food Science and Technology Abstracts provides access to research and new development literature in areas related to food science and technology. It indexes more than 1200 journals.

D&B—Dun's Electronic Yellow Pages provides listings for 8.2 million businesses and professionals. The listing includes phone numbers, address, and number of employees.

D&B—Dun's European Market Identifier's presents detailed information on over 1.5 million companies located in 36 European countries.

Investext provides sales and earning forecasts, market share projections, research and development expenditures, and related data on 8000 U.S. firms and 1500 international firms.

Mergers contains information on all merger and acquisition documents released by the U.S. Securities and Exchange Commission since 1985.

OAG Electronic Edition provides not only worldwide flight information, but also contains files on several travel publications.

Source: Dialogue Database Catalog, Dialogue: Palo Alto, CA, 1990.

subjects, giving them different treatments, controlling unrelated factors, and checking for differences in group responses.

Researchers at Arby's might use experiments before adding a new sandwich to the menu to answer such questions as the following:

- How much will the new sandwich increase Arby's sales?
- How will the new sandwich affect the sales of other menu items?
- Which advertising approach would have the greater effect on sales of the sandwich?
- How would different prices affect the sales of the product?
- Should the new item be targeted toward adults, children, or both?

For example, to test the effects of two different prices, Arby's might set up the following simple experiment. The company could introduce the new sandwich at one price in its restaurants in one city and at another price in restaurants in a similar city. If the cities are very similar and if all other marketing efforts for the sandwich are identical, differences in sales volume

Table 6-6

Planning Primary Data Collection

RESEARCH APPROACHES	CONTACT METHODS	SAMPLING PLAN	RESEARCH INSTRUMENTS
Observation	Mail	Sampling unit	Questionnaire
Survey	Telephone	Sample size	Mechanical instruments
Experiment	Personal	Sampling procedure	

between the two cities should be related to the price charged. More complex experiments can be designed to include other variables and other locations.

Contact Methods.   Information can be collected by mail, telephone, or personal interview. Table 6-7 shows the strengths and weaknesses of each contact method.

Mail questionnaires have many advantages. They can be used to collect large amounts of information at a low cost per respondent. Respondents may give more honest answers to personal questions on a mail questionnaire than they would to an unknown interviewer in person or over the phone. No interviewer is involved to bias the respondent's answers. Mail questionnaires are convenient for respondents, who can answer the survey when they have time. It is also a good way to reach people who often travel, such as meeting planners.

Mail questionnaires also have some disadvantages. They are not very flexible, they require simple and clearly worded questions, all respondents answer the same questions in a fixed order, and the researcher cannot adapt the questionnaire based on earlier answers. Mail surveys usually take

Table 6-7

Strengths and Weaknesses of the Three Contact Methods

	MAIL	TELEPHONE	PERSONAL
Flexibility	Poor	Good	Excellent
Quantity of data that can be collected	Good	Fair	Excellent
Control of interviewer effects	Excellent	Fair	Poor
Control of sample	Fair	Excellent	Fair
Speed of data collection	Poor	Excellent	Good
Response rate	Poor	Good	Good
Cost	Good	Fair	Poor

Source: Adapted with permission of Macmillan Publishing Company from *Marketing Research Measurement and Method,* 6th ed., by Donald S. Tull and Del I. Hawkins, ©1993 by Macmillan Publishing Company.

longer to complete than telephone or personal surveys, and the response rate (the number of people returning completed questionnaires) is often very low. When the response rate is low, respondents may not be typical of the population being sampled. Also, the researcher has little control over who answers the questionnaire in the household or office.

Telephone interviewing provides a method for gathering information quickly. It also offers greater flexibility than mail questionnaires. Interviewers can explain questions that are not understood; they can skip some questions and probe more on others, depending on the respondent's answers. Telephone interviewing allows greater sample control. Interviewers can ask to speak to respondents who have the desired characteristics or can even request someone by name, and response rates tend to be higher than with mail questionnaires.

Telephone interviewing also has drawbacks. The cost per respondent is higher than with mail questionnaires, and some people may not want to discuss personal questions with an interviewer. Using an interviewer increases flexibility, but also introduces interviewer bias. The interviewer's manner of speaking, small differences in the way interviewers ask questions, and other personal factors may affect respondents' answers. Different interviewers may interpret and record responses in a variety of ways; and under time pressures, there is the possibility that some interviewers may record answers without actually asking the questions.

Unfortunately, the general public has become increasingly reluctant to participate in telephone surveys. Many unethical companies have misled respondents into believing that legitimate research is being conducted when in fact this was a ruse for a sales call. Thieves have also used this approach to find out when homeowners are likely to be away and even to determine the contents of the house.

Personal interviewing takes two forms: individual (intercept) and group interviewing. Intercept interviewing involves talking with people in their homes, offices, on the street, or in shopping malls. The interviewer must gain the interviewee's cooperation, and the time involved can range from a few minutes to several hours. For longer surveys, a small payment is sometimes offered to respondents in return for their time.

Intercept interviews are widely used in tourism research. For instance, Steamboat Springs, Colorado, used this technique to interview 600 summer visitors to the city. Intercept interviews allow the research sponsor to reach known visitors in a short period of time. There may be few or no alternative methods of reaching visitors whose names and addresses are unknown. Intercept interviews generally involve the use of *judgmental sampling*. The interviewer may be given guidelines as to whom to "intercept," such as 20% under age 20 and 40% over age 60. This always leaves room for error and bias on the part of the interviewer, who may not be able to correctly judge age, race, and even sex from appearances. Interviewers may also be uncomfortable talking to certain ethnic or age groups.

Focus group interviewing is usually conducted by inviting six to ten people to gather for a few hours with a trained moderator to talk about a product, service, or organization. The moderator needs objectivity, knowledge of the subject and industry, and some understanding of group and consumer behavior. Participants normally receive a small sum or gift certificates for attending. The meeting is held in a pleasant place, and refreshments are served to create a relaxed environment. The moderator starts with broad questions before moving to more specific issues, encouraging open and easy discussion to foster group dynamics that will bring out true feelings and thoughts. At the same time, the interviewer focuses the discussion; hence the name **focus group interviewing**. Comments are recorded through note taking or on videotape and studied later to understand the consumers' buying process. In many cases a two-way mirror separates respondents from observers, who commonly include individuals from the ad agency and the client.

Focus group interviewing is rapidly becoming one of the major marketing research tools for gaining insight into consumers' thoughts and feelings. This method is especially suited for use by managers of hotels and restaurants, who have easy access to their customers. For example, some hotel managers often invite a group of hotel guests from a particular market segment to have a free breakfast with them. During the breakfast the manager gets a chance to meet the guests and discuss what they like about the hotel and what the hotel could do to make their stay more enjoyable and comfortable. The guests appreciate this recognition, and the manager gains valuable information. Restaurant managers use the same approach by holding discussion meetings with guests at lunch or dinner.

Here are examples of how restaurants have used group interviews.

A steak house suffering from declining sales went to its customers to gain insight into the causes of its problem. Two focus groups were conducted, one composed of customers who indicated they would return and another composed of those who said they would not. From these sessions the owners learned that patrons considered the restaurant a fun place, but thought the food was boring. The problem was solved by expanding and upgrading the menu. [24]

Focus groups provided critical information to Andy Reis of Cafe Provincial in Evanston, Illinois. He found that his clientele wanted valet parking. Reis had assumed, because there was on street parking and a nearby parking garage, that parking was not a problem. He also found that his diners felt uncomfortable in the restaurant's Terrace Room. This was a casual dining room with glass tables and porch furniture. Apparently, it was too casual for his diners. The Terrace room was remodeled and valet parking was added. Now people request to sit in the Terrace Room. Reis states that focus groups are worthwhile if you listen and listen carefully. [25]

Personal interviewing is very flexible and can be used to collect large amounts of information. Trained interviewers can hold the respondent's attention for long periods of time and are available to clarify difficult questions. They can guide interviews, explore issues, and probe as the situation requires. Personal interviews can be used with any type of questionnaire. Interviewers can show subjects actual products, advertisements, or packages and observe and record their reactions and behavior. Personal interviews usually can be conducted fairly quickly.

The main drawbacks to personal interviews are cost and sampling. Personal interviews may cost three to four times as much as telephone interviews. Because group interview studies usually use small sample sizes to keep time and costs down, it may be hard to generalize from the results. And since interviewers have more freedom in personal interviews, interview bias is a greater problem.

The contact method that is most effective depends on the information the researcher wants and on the number and types of respondents to be contacted. Advances in computers and communications have had an impact on methods of obtaining information. Some research firms now use computer-aided interviewing (CAI). The interviewer reads a set of questions from a video screen and types the respondent's answers directly into the computer, eliminating data editing and coding, reducing errors, and saving time. This type of interview is particularly useful for guests checking into or out of a hotel. The computer can be placed in the lobby, making it easily accessible to the hotel's guests. The high visibility of the computer also promotes an image that the hotel is concerned about their guest's opinions.

Sampling Plan.   Marketing researchers usually draw conclusions about large consumer groups by taking a sample. A **sample** is a segment of the population selected to represent the population as a whole. Ideally, the sample should be representative and allow the researcher to make accurate estimates of the thoughts and behaviors of the larger population.

Designing the sample calls for three decisions. First, **who** will be surveyed? This is not always obvious. For example, to study the decision-making process for a family vacation, should the researcher interview the husband, wife, other family members, travel agent, or all of these? The researcher must determine what type of information is needed and who is most likely to have it.

Second, **how many people should be surveyed?** Large samples give more reliable results than small samples. However, it is not necessary to sample the entire target market or even a large portion to obtain reliable results. If well chosen, samples of less than 1% of a population can give good reliability.

Third, **how should the sample be chosen?** Sample members might be chosen at random from the entire population (a probability sample), or the researcher might select people who are easiest to obtain information from (a convenience sample). Or the researcher might choose a specified number of participants from each of several demographic groups (a quota sample). These and other ways of drawing samples have different costs and time limitations and varying accuracy and statistical properties. The needs of the research project will determine which method is most effective. Table 6-8 describes the different kinds of samples.

Research Instruments.   In collecting primary data, marketing researchers have a choice of primary research instruments: the interview (structured and unstructured), mechanical devices, and structured models such as a test market. Structured interviews employ the use of a questionnaire.

Table 6-8
Types of Samples

Probability sample	
Sample random sample	Every member of the population has a known and equal chance of selection.
Stratified random sample	The population is divided into mutually exclusive groups (such as age groups), and random samples are drawn from each group.
Cluster (area) sample	The population is divided into mutually exclusive groups (such as blocks), and the researcher draws a sample of the groups to interview.
Nonprobability sample	
Convenience sample	The researcher selects the easiest population members from which to obtain information.
Judgment sample	The researcher uses his or her judgment to select population members who are good prospects for accurate information.
Quota sample	The researcher finds and interviews a prescribed number of people in each of several categories.

The *questionnaire* is by far the most common survey instrument. A questionnaire consists of a set of questions presented to a respondent for answers. Because there are many ways to ask questions, the questionnaire is very flexible. Questionnaires should be carefully developed and tested before being used on a large scale. You can usually spot several errors in a carelessly prepared questionnaire (see Marketing Highlight 6-1).

In preparing a questionnaire, the marketing researcher must decide what questions to ask, what form the questions should take, and how to word and sequence the questions. Questionnaires too often leave out questions that should be answered and include questions that cannot, will not, or need not be answered. *Each question should be examined to ensure that it contributes to the research objectives.* Questions that are merely interesting should be dropped.

The form of the question can influence the response. Marketing researchers distinguish between closed-end and open-end questions. Closed-end questions include all possible answers, and subjects are asked to choose among them. Examples include multiple-choice and scale questions. Open-end questions allow respondents to answer in their own words. In a survey of airline users, Delta might ask, "What is your opinion of Delta Airlines?" Or it might ask people to complete this sentence: "When I choose an airline, the most important consideration is …." These and other kinds of open-end questions often reveal more because respondents are not limited in their answers. Open-end questions are especially useful in exploratory research where the researcher is trying to find out how people think, rather than measure how many people think in a certain way. Closed-end questions, on the other hand, provide answers that are easier to interpret and tabulate.

Care should be taken in the phrasing of questions. The researcher should use simple, direct, unbiased wording. The questions should be

Marketing Highlight 6-1

A "Questionable" Questionnaire

Suppose that the following questionnaire has been prepared by a restaurant manager to build a profile of his potential market. How do you as a consumer feel about each question?

1. What is your income to the nearest hundred dollars?

   People don't necessarily know their income to the nearest hundred dollars nor do they want to reveal their income that closely. Furthermore, a questionnaire should never open with such a personal question.

2. How often do you go out to eat?

   The question is very ambiguous. It does not specify the meal or the type of restaurant. For a descriptive survey, it would be useful to add appropriate response categories.

3. During the business week how often do you eat breakfast?

   1 ____   2 ____   3 ____   4 ____   5 ____

   The responses are not collectively exhaustive. That is, they do not provide all the possible responses. What if a person never eats breakfast? The addition of a sixth response, 0 ____ , would solve the problem.

4. On average, how much do you spend for lunch?

   ____ 0 to $2.00   ____ $2.00 to 4.00
   ____ $4.00 to 6.00   ____ $6.00 to 8.00

The choices are overlapping. If someone spent, $2.00, $4.00, or $6.00, they could mark their response in one of two spots. Also, the response choices are not collectively exhaustive. If someone spends more than eight dollars, there is nowhere to mark this response.

5. Would you like (name of restaurant) to have live bands on Friday and Saturday night? Yes ( ) No ( )

   The word "like" does not indicate purchase behavior. Many respondents would answer yes, because it offers them an entertainment option, but they would not come out on a regular basis. Also, many times there is a cost to adding an extra feature. If the respondent is going to pay for the cost through a cover charge or higher drink prices, that should be addressed. Finally, the question does not specify the type of band. Someone who wants a country and western band may answer yes and then be disappointed when the manager puts in a heavy metal band.

6. Did you receive more restaurant coupons this April or last April?

   Who can remember this?

7. What are the most salient and determinant attributes in your evaluation of restaurants?

   What are "salient and determinant attributes"? Don't use big words that the respondent may not understand.

pretested before they are widely used, and care should also be taken in the ordering of questions. The first question should create interest. Questions should follow in a logical order, with difficult or personal questions asked last so that respondents do not become defensive. Table 6-9 provides an overview of common formats for closed-end and open-end questions.

Researchers in the hospitality industry must be extremely careful in developing questions and selecting the sample not to unwittingly offend respondents. This problem is less pervasive with many products, such as building tile or brass fittings. A classic example of a marketing research mistake was made by a U.S. airline. This company offered a special companion

Table 6-9
Types of Questions

A. CLOSED-END QUESTIONS

NAME	DESCRIPTION	EXAMPLE
Dichotomous	A question offering two answer choices.	"In arranging this trip, did you personally phone Delta?" Yes □ No □
Multiple choice	A question offering three or more answer choices.	"With whom are you traveling on this flight?" No one □ Children only □ Spouse □ Business associates/friends/relatives □ Spouse and children □ An organized tour group □
Likert scale	A statement with which the respondent shows the amount of agreement or disagreement.	"Small airlines generally give better service than large ones." Strongly disagree 1□ Disagree 2□ Neither agree nor disagree 3□ Agree 4□ Strongly agree 5□
Semantic differential	A scale is inscribed between two bipolar words, and the respondent selects the point that represents the direction and intensity of his or her feelings.	*Delta Airlines* Large X :___:___:___:___:___: Small Experienced ___:___:___:___: X :___: Inexperienced Modern ___:___:___: X :___:___: Old-fashioned
Importance scale	A scale that rates the importance of some attribute from "not at all important" to "extremely important"	"Airline food service to me is" Extremely Important 1___ Very important 2___ Somewhat important 3___ Not very important 4___ Not at all important 5___
Rating scale	A scale that rates some attribute from "poor" to "excellent."	"Delta's food service is" Excellent 1___ Very good 2___ Good 3___ Fair 4___ Poor 5___
Intention-to-buy scale	A scale that describes the respondent's intentions to buy.	"If in-flight telephone service were available on a long flight, I would" Definitely buy 1___ Probably buy 2___ Not certain 3___ Probably not buy 4___ Definitely not buy 5___

B. OPEN-END QUESTIONS

NAME	DESCRIPTION	EXAMPLE
Completely unstructured	A question that respondents can answer in an almost unlimited number of ways.	"What is your opinion of Delta Airlines?"
Word association	Words are presented, one at a time, and respondents mention the first word that comes to mind.	"What is the first word that comes to your mind when you hear the following?" Airline _____ Delta _____ Travel _____
Sentence completion	Incomplete sentences are presented, one at a time, and respondents complete the sentence.	"When I choose an airline, the most important consideration in my decision is _____"
Story completion	An incomplete story is presented, and respondents are asked to complete it.	"I flew Delta a few days ago. I noticed that the exterior and interior of the plane had very bright colors. This aroused in me the following thoughts and feelings." *Now complete the story.*
Picture completion	A picture of two characters is presented, with one making a statement. Respondents are asked to identify with the other and fill in the empty balloon.	 Fill in the empty balloon.
Thematic Aapperception Tests (TAT)	A picture is presented, and respondents are asked to make up a story about what they think is happening or may happen in the picture.	 Make up a story about what you see.

price for business travelers with the idea that the companion would be the executive's spouse. Following the promotion, questionnaires were sent to the spouse not the executive. These innocently asked, "How did you like the recent companion trip?" In several cases the answer was, "What trip? I didn't go!" The airline received angry calls and threats of suits for invasion of privacy or contribution to the breakup of a marriage.

The Observation City Resort Hotel in Perth, Australia, offers an example of a hotel that used marketing information and research to produce enviable results.[26] This hotel had reached a plateau and wished to emerge from this static position into one of greater success. The hotel's manager collected government statistical abstracts to establish a profile of guests to the area. From this they realized that the hotel needed more than leisure travelers to be more successful. Managers also analyzed competition in Perth. From this, occupancy trend differences were discovered between hotels.

Competitive analysis convinced management that the hotel needed and could attract away from competitors a piece of the weekday corporate market. Management of the Observation City Resort knew that the hotel would have to develop a plan to obtain corporate business and that the staff would have to be heavily involved.

A marketing research study was conducted to provide information essential to developing a marketing plan.

- A business-consumer survey was conducted at Perth's central business district and the airport.
- Questionnaires were given to travel managers and executives in charge of travel.
- Observations were made of high-profile properties known for their corporate-client service.
- The hotel's Human Resources Department trained hotel staff members to collect primary data. Survey teams were then placed in Perth and its suburbs to administer questionnaires.

The results were excellent. The program produced a percentage increase in corporate room-nights from 8% before the research to 40% four years later. A further advantage was that the management and staff of the hotel learned the market, became close to the customer, and found ways to satisfy their needs.

Presenting the Research Plan. At this stage, the marketing researcher should summarize the plan in a written proposal. A written proposal is especially important when the research project will be large and complex or when an outside firm will be engaged to carry out the research. The proposal should cover the management problems addressed and research objectives, information to be obtained, sources of secondary information or methods for collecting primary data, and how the results will aid in management decision making. The proposal should also include research costs. A written research plan or proposal ensures that the marketing manager and researchers have considered all the important aspects of the research and that they agree on why and how the research will be done. The manager should review the proposal carefully before approving the project.

Implementing the Research Plan

The researcher puts the marketing research plan into action by collecting, processing, and analyzing the information. Data collection can be done by the company's marketing research staff, which affords the company greater control of the collection process and data quality or by outside firms. Outside firms that specialize in data collection can often do the job more quickly at lower cost.

The data-collection phase of the marketing research process is generally the most expensive and the most subject to error. The researcher should watch the fieldwork closely to ensure that the plan is correctly implemented and to guard against problems with contacting respondents, respondents who refuse to cooperate or who give biased or dishonest answers, and interviewers who make mistakes or take shortcuts.

The collected data must be processed and analyzed to pull out important information and findings. Data from questionnaires are checked for accuracy and completeness and coded for computer analysis. The researcher applies standard computer programs to prepare tabulations of results and to compute averages and other measures for the major variables.

Advertisers conduct research to help direct and test their advertising. Courtesy of Pizza Hut, Inc.

Interpreting and Reporting the Findings

The researcher must now interpret the findings, draw conclusions, and report them to management. The researcher should avoid overwhelming managers with numbers and complex statistical techniques and focus. Instead, management desires major findings that will be useful in decision making.

Interpretation should not be left entirely to the researcher. Findings can be interpreted in different ways, and discussions between researchers and managers will help point to the best interpretations. The manager should also confirm that the research project was properly executed. After reviewing the findings, the manager may raise additional questions that can be answered with research data. Researchers should make the data available to marketing managers so that they can perform new analyses and test relationships on their own.

Interpretation is an important phase of the marketing process. The best research is meaningless if a manager blindly accepts wrong interpretations. Similarly, managers may have biased interpretations. They sometimes accept research results that show what they expected and reject those that did not provide expected or hoped for answers. Thus managers and researchers must work closely together when interpreting research results. Both share responsibility for the research process and resulting decisions.

Interpreting and reporting findings is the last step of the four step research process. It is important for managers to remember that research is a process and that the researcher must proceed through all steps of the process. Marketing highlight 6-2 explains some of the problems that can occur during a research project.

Information Analysis

Information gathered by the company's marketing intelligence and marketing research systems can often benefit from additional analysis. This might

Marketing Highlight 6-2

Research Problem Areas

1. Making assumptions.

A restaurant was considering adding a piano bar. Researchers developed a customer survey. One question asked customers if they would like entertainment in the lounge without mentioning the type of entertainment. The customers could answer this question positively, thinking of a dance band. The manager, seeing the positive responses, would put in the piano bar and then wonder why so many customers did not respond to the piano bar. Luckily, this question was modified during a pretest of the survey.

A country club asked its members if they felt the club needed a renovation. Most members said yes. The club then paid consultants to draw up designs for the renovations. When these, along with the proposed dues increase, were presented, the members expressed outrage at the higher dues. If the original survey had addressed the costs associated with the renovation, it could have saved thousands of dollars in consulting fees.

2. Lack of qualitative information.

Most surveys reported in trade magazines provide descriptive information. For example, a study done by Procter and Gamble found that the most important attribute in the frequent travelers' decision to return to a hotel was a clean appearance. To use this information, management needs to know how their guests judge clean appearance. Through focus groups, managers can learn what guests look for to determine whether the room is clean, what irritants there are concerning cleanliness, and other more specific information.

3. Failing to look at segments within a sample.

Survey results should be analyzed to determine differences between customer groups. Often the arithmetic means (averages) for each question are calculated and the survey is analyzed based on this information, which can mask important differences between segments. For example, a club surveyed its membership on how satisfied they were with the lunches purchased in the dining room. The average of all responses was 2.0, with 1 being very satisfied, 3 being satisfied, and 5 being not satisfied. However, when the total sample was divided into membership classes, it was found that one class had a high level of satisfaction, 1.5, while another class

include advanced statistical analysis to learn more about the relationships within a set of data. Such analysis allows managers to go beyond means and standard deviations in the data and answer such questions as the following:

- What are the major variables affecting sales and how important is each?

- If the price is raised 10% and advertising is increased 20%, what will happen to sales?

- What are the best predictors of who are likely to come to my hotel versus my competitor's hotel?

- What are the best variables for segmenting my market, and how many segments exist?

Mathematical models might also help marketers to make better decisions. Each model represents a real system, process, or outcome. These models can help answer the questions "what if" and "which is best." In the past 20 years, marketing scientists have developed a great number of mod-

gave an average rating of 2.7. This information is more useful to management than the overall mean of 2.0. Management now had to decide whether to build satisfaction for the members who gave the room a lower rating or promote its food and beverage room to the satisfied segment.

4. Improper use of sophisticated statistical analysis.
One researcher reported that faculty size explained a remarkable 96% of the enrollment in hospitality management programs housed in business schools. He then presented a formula for projecting student enrollment based on the number of faculty, implying that if a school had three faculty members they would have 251 students, but if two more faculty were hired, they would have 426 students. Schools who base decisions on this formula might be disappointed.

The above factors can contribute to disappointment with survey research results. It may appear that customers fail to act as they indicated they would in the survey, when in fact research results were skewed or misinterpreted because of mistakes made in these problem areas.

5. Failure to have the sample representative of the population.

A sample is a segment of the population selected to represent the population as a whole. Ideally, the sample should be representative so that the researcher can make accurate estimates of the thoughts and behaviors of the larger population. It is common for hotel managers to receive a bonus based on a customer satisfaction score. Sometimes segments of the population will give ratings that are lower than other segments, even though they seem satisfied with the service. For example, in one customer satisfaction survey respondents aged between 26 and 35 years rated the service attributes of the company lower than other segments. However, they also rated the competition lower, making the company's relative satisfaction compared to the competition the same as other segments. This segment did not appear to be displeased with the service; they just tended to rate lower on the scale. When segments like this are present in the population, they can skew the results of the survey if they are over- or underrepresented. If they are underrepresented, the overall satisfaction will increase; if they are overrepresented, the overall satisfaction score will decrease.

els to help marketing managers make better marketing-mix decisions, design sales territories and sales call plans, select sites for retail outlets, develop optimal advertising mixes, and forecast new-product sales.[27]

Distributing Information

Marketing information has no value until managers use it to make better decisions. The gathered information must reach the appropriate marketing managers at the right time. Large companies have centralized marketing information systems that provide managers with regular performance reports, intelligence updates, and reports on the results of studies. Managers need these routine reports for making regular planning, implementation, and control decisions. But marketing managers also need non-routine information for special situations and on-the-spot decisions. For example, a sales manager having trouble with an important customer needs a summary of the account's sales during the past year. Or a restaurant manager whose restaurant has stocked-out of a best-selling menu item needs to know the current inventory levels in the chain's other restaurants. In companies with centralized information systems, these managers must request the information from the MIS staff and wait. Often the information arrives too late to be useful.

Recent developments in information handling have led to a revolution in information distribution. With recent advances in microcomputers, software, and communications, many companies are decentralizing their marketing information systems and giving managers direct access to information stored in the systems. In some companies, marketing managers can use a desk terminal to tie into the company's information network. Without leaving their desks, they can obtain information from internal records or outside information services, analyze the information, prepare reports on a word processor, and communicate with others in the network through telecommunications (see Marketing Highlight 6-3).

Such systems offer exciting prospects. They allow managers to obtain needed information directly and quickly and tailor it to their needs. As more managers become skilled in using these systems and as improvements in technology make them more economical, hospitality companies will increasingly use decentralized marketing information systems.

International Marketing Research

International marketing researchers follow the same steps as domestic researchers, from defining the research problem and developing a research plan to interpreting and reporting the results. However, these researchers often face more and different problems. Whereas domestic researchers deal with fairly homogeneous markets within a single country, international researchers deal with markets in many different countries. These different markets often vary dramatically in their levels of economic development, cultures and customs, and buying patterns.

In many foreign markets, the international researcher has a difficult time finding good *secondary data*. Whereas U.S. marketing researchers can obtain reliable secondary data from any of dozens of domestic research services, many countries have almost no research services at all. Even the largest international research services operate in only a relative handful of countries. For example, A. C. Nielsen, the world's largest marketing research company, has offices in only 28 countries outside the United States.[28] Thus, even when secondary information is available, it usually must be obtained from many different sources on a country-by-country basis, making the information difficult to combine or compare.

Because of the scarcity of good secondary data, international researchers often must collect their own primary data. Here researchers face problems not encountered domestically. For example, they may find it difficult simply to develop appropriate samples. Whereas U.S. researchers can use current telephone directories, census tract data, and any of several sources of socioeconomic data to construct samples, such information is largely lacking in many countries. Once the sample is drawn, the U.S. researcher usually can reach most respondents easily by telephone or mail or in person. Reaching respondents is often not so easy in other parts of the world. In some countries, few people have phones— there are only four phones per thousand people in Egypt, six in Turkey,

Marketing Highlight 6-3

Information Networks: Decentralizing the Marketing Information System

The last decade's centralized information systems are giving way to systems that take information management out of the hands of staff specialists and put it into the hands of managers. Many companies are developing information networks that link separate technologies such as word processing, data processing, and image processing into a single system.

Envision the working day of a future hotel manager. On arriving at work, the manager turns to a desk-top computer and reads the daily report. Next she flips to the incident report from security to see what happened during the night. Then she prints out her daily schedule. The manager turns to the function schedule and notices that a key group is having a coffee break at 10:30. She would like to be visible to the key people during their break. She sets the computer to ring at 10:25 to let her know that it's time to go downstairs.

After walking through the hotel, she returns to her computer. She pulls an environmental scan of hotel-related articles in the local papers and the *Wall Street Journal*. She selects those that she wants to skim. She thinks some articles should be sent to her co-managers and instructs the computer to route copies to them on their computers.

In the afternoon, she will meet Frank Crossan, one of the hotel's key corporate clients. She pulls up information on Crossan and his company. This will help her personalize her meeting and provide information about his company's use of the hotel.

That evening she takes home her notebook computer. After dinner see travels through the Internet, accessing several special-interest groups. One of the groups is for travelers interested in Miami, the city where she lives and works. She learns what these tourists like and dislike about her city, including their comments on the city's hotels, restaurants, and tours.

It is rumored that SARA of Sweden is going to purchase a hotel in Miami. Her general manager has asked her to develop a report on SARA. In the morning she accesses CompuServe and gets several corporate profiles of SARA through CompuServe's business databases. She then goes into the business reference databases and finds several business journal and newspaper articles about SARA. She downloads full copies of these articles onto her hard drive.

The next morning is her day off. She prints out the articles on SARA and writes her report. She retrieves the hotel's daily report and sends messages to the department heads. Now it's time to relax at the beach.

and thirty-two in Argentina. In other countries, the postal system is notoriously unreliable. In Brazil, for instance, an estimated 30% of the mail is never delivered. In many developing countries, poor roads and transportation systems make certain areas hard to reach, making personal interviews difficult and expensive.[29]

Differences in cultures from country to country cause additional problems for international researchers. Language is the most obvious culprit. For example, questionnaires must be prepared in one language and then translated into the languages of each country researched. Responses then must be translated back into the original language for analysis and interpretation. This adds to research costs and increases the risks of error.

Marketing Highlight 6-4

Marketing Research in Small Business

Managers of small businesses often believe that marketing research can be done only by experts in large companies with large research budgets. But many marketing research techniques can be used by smaller organizations and at little or no expense.

Managers of small businesses can obtain good marketing information by observing what occurs around them. Thus restauranteurs can evaluate their customer mix by recording the number and type of customers in the restaurant at different times during the day. Competitor advertising can be monitored by collecting advertisements from local media.

Managers can conduct informal surveys using small convenience samples. The manager of a travel agency can learn what customers like and dislike about travel agencies by conducting informal focus groups, such as inviting small groups to lunch. Restaurant managers can talk with customers; hospital food service managers can interview patients. Restaurant managers can make random phone calls during slack hours to interview consumers about where they eat out and what they think of various restaurants in the area. Managers can also conduct simple experiments. By changing the design in regular direct mailings and watching results, a manager can learn which marketing tactics work best. By varying newspaper advertisements, a manager can observe the effects of ad size and position, price coupons, and media used.

Small organizations can obtain secondary data. Many associations, local media, chambers of commerce, and government agencies provide special help to small organizations. The U.S. Small Business Administration offers dozens of free publications giving advice on topics ranging from planning advertising to ordering business signs. Local newspapers often provide information on local shoppers and their buying patterns.

Sometimes volunteers and colleges will carry out research. Many colleges are seeking small businesses to serve as cases for projects in marketing research classes. Sales management classes are eager to do sales blitzes for hotels.

Thus secondary data collection, observation, surveys, and experiments can be used effectively by small organizations with small budgets. Although informal research is less complex and costly, it must still be done carefully. Managers must carefully think through the objectives of the research, formulate questions in advance, and recognize the biases systematically. If carefully planned and implemented, low-cost research can provide reliable information for improving marketing decision making.

Translating a questionnaire from one language to another is far from easy…. Many points are [lost], because many idioms, phrases, and statements mean different things in different cultures. A Danish executive observed, "Check this out by having a different translator put back into English what you've translated from the English. You'll get the shock of your life. I remember [an example in which] "out of sight, out of mind" had become "invisible things are insane".[30]

Buying roles and consumer decision processes vary greatly from country to country, further complicating international marketing research. Consumers in different countries also vary in their attitudes toward marketing research. People in one country may be very willing to respond; in other countries, nonresponse can be a major problem. For example, customs in some Islamic countries prohibit people from talking with strangers—a researcher simply may not be allowed to speak by phone with women about brand attitudes or buying behavior. High functional illiteracy rates in many countries make it impossible to use a written survey for some segments. And middle-class people in developing countries often make false claims in order to appear well off. For example, in a study of tea consumption in India, over 70% of middle-income respondents claimed that they used one of several national brands. However, the researchers had good reason to doubt these results; more than 60% of the tea sold in India is unbranded generic tea.

Despite these problems, the recent growth of international marketing has resulted in a rapid increase in the use of international marketing research. Global companies have little choice but to conduct such research. Although the costs and problems associated with international research may be high, the costs of not doing it—in terms of missed opportunities and mistakes—might be even higher. Once recognized, many of the problems associated with international marketing research can be overcome or avoided.

Marketing Research in Smaller Organizations

So far in this section, we have looked at the marketing research process—from defining research objectives to interpreting and reporting results—as a lengthy, formal process carried out by large marketing companies. But many small businesses and nonprofit organizations also use marketing research. Almost any organization can find informal, low-cost alternatives to the formal and complex marketing research techniques used by research experts in large firms (see Marketing Highlight 6-4).

Chapter Review

The Marketing Information System (MIS). A MIS consists of people, equipment, and procedures to gather, sort, analyze, evaluate, and distribute needed, timely, and accurate information to marketing decision makers.

The MIS begins and ends with marketing managers, but managers throughout the organization should be involved in the MIS. First, the MIS interacts with managers to assess their information needs. Next, it develops needed information from internal company records, marketing intelligence activities, and the marketing research process. Information analysts process information to make it more useful. Finally, the MIS distributes information to managers in the right form and at the right time to help in marketing planning, implementation, and control.

I.   Assessing Information Needs. A good marketing information system balances information that managers would like to have against that which they really need and is feasible to obtain.

II.   Developing Information. Information needed by marketing managers can be obtained from internal company records, marketing intelligence, and marketing research. The information analysis system processes this information and presents it in a form that is useful to managers.

1) Internal Records. Internal records information consists of information gathered from sources within the company to evaluate marketing performance and to detect marketing problems and opportunities.

2) Marketing Intelligence. Marketing intelligence includes everyday information about developments in the marketing environment that help managers to prepare and adjust marketing plans and short-run tactics. Marketing intelligence can come from internal sources or external sources.

   a) Internal sources include the company's executives, owners, and employees.

   b) External sources include competitors, government agencies, suppliers, trade magazines, newspapers, business magazines, trade association newsletters and meetings, and databases available on the internet.

   ***c)* Marketing Research.** Marketing research is a process that identifies and defines marketing opportunities and problems, monitors and evaluates marketing actions and performance, and communicates the findings and implication to management. Marketing research is project oriented and has a beginning and an ending. It feeds information into the marketing information system that is ongoing. The marketing research process consists of four steps: defining the problem and research objectives, developing the research plan, implementing the research plan, and interpreting and presenting the findings.

   ***i)* Defining the problem and research objectives:**
   There are three types of objectives for a marketing research project:

   a)   Exploratory. To gather preliminary information that will help define the problem and suggest hypotheses.

   b)   Descriptive. To describe the size and composition of the market.

   c)   Causal. To test hypotheses about cause-and-effect relationships.

   ***ii)*Developing the research plan for collecting information:**

   a)   Determining specific information needs. Research objectives must be translated into specific information needs. To meet a manager's information needs, researchers can gather secondary data, primary data, or both. **Secondary data** consist of information already in existence somewhere, having been collected for another purpose. **Primary data** consists of information collected for the specific purpose at hand.

   b)   Research approaches. Three basic research approaches are observations, surveys, and experiments.

      i)   Observational research. Gathering of primary data by observing relevant people, action, and situations.

      ii) Survey research (structured/unstructured, direct/indirect). Best suited to gathering descriptive information.

      iii) Experimental research. Best suited to gathering causal information.

c) Contact methods. Information can be collected by mail, telephone, or personal interview.

d) Sampling plan. Marketing researchers usually draw conclusions about large consumer groups by taking a sample. A **sample** is a segment of the population selected to represent the population as a whole. Designing the sample calls for three decisions.

   i)   Who will be surveyed?
   ii) How many people should be surveyed?
   iii) How should the sample be chosen?

e) Research instruments. In collecting primary data, marketing researchers have a choice of primary research instruments: the interview (structured and unstructured), mechanical devices, and structured models such as a test market. Structured interviews employ the use of a questionnaire.

f) Presenting the research plan. At this stage, the marketing researcher should summarize the plan in a written proposal.

iii) Implementing the research plan: The researcher puts the marketing research plan into action by collecting, processing, and analyzing the information.

iv) Interpreting and reporting the findings: The researcher must now interpret the findings, draw conclusions, and report them to management.

d) Information Analysis. Information gathered by the company's marketing intelligence and marketing research systems can often benefit from additional analysis. This additional analysis helps to answer the questions "what if" and "which is best."

III. Distributing Information. Marketing information has no value until managers use it to make better decisions. The gathered information must reach the appropriate marketing managers at the right time.

DISCUSSION QUESTIONS

1. What role should marketing research play in helping a firm to implement the marketing concept?

2. How does a marketing information system differ from a marketing intelligence system?

3. Identify and discuss the major steps in the marketing research process.

4. List some research tasks for the following areas: distribution decisions, product decisions, advertising decisions, personal selling decisions, pricing decisions.

5. Explain why defining the problem and research objective is often the hardest step in the research process.

6. Researchers usually start the data-gathering process by examining secondary data. What secondary data sources would be available to the manager of a full-service restaurant that wanted to research consumer trends?

7. Discuss the advantages and disadvantages of using guest comment cards in a restaurant.

8. Which type of research would be the most appropriate in the following situations and why? (a) McDonald's wants to investigate the effect that children have on the actual purchase of its products. (b) Hilton wants to gather some preliminary information on how business travelers feel about the menu variety, food, and

service in its restaurants. (c) Bennigan's is considering locating a new outlet in a fast-growing suburb. (d) Arby's wants to test the effect of two new advertising themes for its roast beef sandwich sales in two cities. (e) The director of tourism for your state wants to know how to effectively use her promotion dollars.

9. Focus groups have become one of the most common research techniques in the hospitality industry. What are the advantages and disadvantages of focus groups?

KEY TERMS

Causal research Marketing research to test hypotheses about cause-and-effect relationships.

Closed-end questions Questions that include all the possible answers and allow subjects to make choices among them.

Descriptive research Marketing research to better describe marketing problems, situations, or markets, such as the market potential for a product or the demographics and attitudes of consumers.

Experimental research The gathering of primary data by selecting matched groups of subjects, giving them different treatments, controlling related factors, and checking for differences in group responses.

Exploratory research Marketing research to gather preliminary information that will help to better define problems and suggest hypotheses.

Focus group interviewing Personal interviewing that consists of inviting six to ten people to gather for a few hours with a trained interviewer to talk about a product, service, or organization. The interviewer focuses the group discussion on important issues.

Internal records information Information gathered from sources within the company to evaluate marketing performance and to detect marketing problems and opportunities.

Marketing information system (MIS) A structure of people, equipment, and procedures to gather, sort, analyze, evaluate, and distribute needed, timely, and accurate information to marketing decision makers.

Marketing intelligence Everyday information about developments in the marketing environment that helps managers to prepare and adjust marketing plans.

Marketing research The systematic design, collection, analysis, and reporting of data and findings relevant to a specific marketing situation facing the company.

Observational research The gathering of primary data by observing relevant people, actions, and situations.

Open-end questions Questions that allow respondents to answer in their own words.

Primary data Information collected for the specific purpose at hand.

Sample A segment of the population selected for marketing research to represent the population as a whole.

Secondary data Information that already exists somewhere, having been collected for another purpose.

Shoppers Person paid to experience the hotel or restaurant and report back to management on their experience.

Survey research The gathering of primary data by asking people questions about their knowledge, attitudes, preferences, and buying behavior.

REFERENCES

1. BRIAN DUMAINE, "Corporate Spies Snoop to Conquer," *Fortune* (November 1988), pp. 68–76.

2. KATE BERTRAND, "With Customers, the Closer the Better," *Business Marketing* (July 1989), pp. 68–69.

3. MARION HARPER, JR., "A New Profession to Aid Management," *Journal of Marketing* (January 1961), p. 1.

4. JOHN NAISBITT, *Megatrends: Ten New Directions Transforming Our Lives* (New York: Warner Books, 1984).

5. "Harnessing the Data Explosion," *Sales and Marketing Management* (January 1987), p. 31.

6. NAISBITT, *Megatrends*, p. 16.

7. TOM RICHMAN, "Mrs. Field's Secret Ingredient," *Inc. Magazine*, (October 1987) as cited in *Managing Services* by Christopher Lovelock, Englewood Cliffs: Prentice Hall, 1992, pp. 365–372.

8. JOHN BOWEN, "Computerized Guest History: A Valuable Marketing Tool," *The Practice of Hospitality Management II*, Robert C. Lewis et al., eds. (Westport, Conn.: AVI).

9. DAVID MENZIES, "Comment Cards," *Foodservice and Hospitality*, 21, no. 5 (July/August 1988), p. 14; and ROBERT C. LEWIS AND ABRAHAM PIZAM, "Guest Surveys: A Missed Opportunity," in *Strategic Marketing and Planning in the Hospitality Industry*, Robert L. Bloomstrom ed. (East Lansing, Mich.: Educational Institute of the AH&MA).

10. CHEKITAN S. DEV AND BERNARD O. ELLIS, "Guest Histories: An Untapped Service Resource," *Cornell Hotel and Restaurant Administration Quarterly*, 32, no. 2, (August 1991), p. 31.

11. TAMMY P. BIEBER, "Guest History Systems: Maximizing the Benefits," *Cornell Hotel and Restaurant Administration Quarterly*, 30, no. 3 (November 1989), p. 22.

12. PAUL B. BROWN, "Who Was that Masked Shopper," *INC.*, 11, no. 10 (October 1989), pp. 135–136.

13. JOSEPH F. DUROCHER AND NEIL B. NEIMAN, "Technology: Antidote to the Shakeout," *Cornell Hotel and Restaurant Administration Quarterly*, 31, no. 1 (May 1990), p. 35.

14. CHRISTOPHER W. NORDLING AND SHARON K. WHEELER, "Building a Market-segment Accounting Model to Improve Profits," *Cornell Hotel and Restaurant Administration Quarterly*, 33, no. 3 (June 1992), p. 32.

15. BURT CABANAS, "A Marketing Strategy for Resort Conference Centers," *Cornell Hotel and Restaurant Administration Quarterly*, 33, no. 3 (June 1992), p. 47.

16. ANONYMOUS, "Making Them Feel at Home," *Cornell Hotel and Restaurant Administration Quarterly*, 30, no. 3 (November 1989), p. 4.

17. JOHN BOWEN, "Scanning the Environment: Electronically," *Hospitality Education and Research Journal*, 14, no. 2 (1991); and "Business Is Turning Data into a Potent Strategic Weapon," *Business Week* (August 22, 1987), p. 92.

18. TIM MILLER, "Focus: Competitive Intelligence," *Online Access Guide* (March/April 1987), pp. 43–57.

19. *American Marketing Association*, officially adopted definition in 1987.

20. FRANK E. CAMACHO AND D. MATTHEW KNAIN, "Listening to Customers: The Market Research Function at Marriott Corporation," *Marketing Research* (March 1989), pp. 5–14.

21. ANONYMOUS, "The Entrepreneurial Approach to Indian Affairs," *Cornell Hotel and Restaurant Administration Quarterly*, 29, no. 2 (August 1988), p. 5.

22. JERRY WIND, PAUL E. GREEN, DOUGLAS SHIFFLET, AND MARSHA SCARBROUGH, "Courtyard by Marriott: Designing a Hotel Facility with Consumer-based Marketing," *Interfaces*, 19, no. 1 (January–February 1989), pp. 25–47.

23. ROBERT C. LEWIS AND RICHARD E. CHAMBERS, *Marketing Leadership in Hospitality Foundations and Practices* (New York: Van Nostrand Reinhold, 1989), p. 518.

24. JOE L. WELCH, "Focus Groups for Restaurant Research," *Cornell Hotel and Restaurant Administration Quarterly*, 26, no. 2 (August 1985), pp. 78–85.

25. DOROTHY DEE, "Focus Groups," *Restaurants USA*, 10, no. 7 (August 1990), pp. 30–34.

26. DAVID H. SOGAR AND MICHAEL H. JONES, "Attracting Business Travelers to a Resort," *Cornell Hotel and Restaurant Administration Quarterly*, 34, no. 5 (October 1993), pp. 43–47.

27. For further reading, see GARY L. LILIEN, PHILIP KOTLER, AND K. SRIDHAR MOORTHY, *Marketing Models*, Englewood Cliffs, N.J.: Prentice Hall, 1992.

28. JACK HONOMICHL, "Top Marketing/Ad/Opinion Research Firms Profiled," *Marketing News* (June 2, 1992), p. H2.

29. Many of the examples in this section, along with others, are found in SUBHASH C. JAIN, *International Marketing Management*, 3rd ed. (Boston: PWS-Kent Publishing Company, 1990), pp. 334–339. See also VERN TERPSTRA AND RAVI SARATHY, *International Marketing* (Chicago: Dryden Press, 1991), pp. 208–213.

30. JAIN, *International Marketing Management*, p. 338.

Consumer Markets and Consumer Buying Behavior

In 1988 Working Woman *magazine surpassed all other North American business magazines in circulation, including* Fortune, Forbes, *and* Business Week. *Two-thirds of all women and 79% of women with no children under the age of 18 work outside the home. A higher percentage of women without children under the age of 18 work than men. John Naisbitt and Patricia Aburdene state that the 1990s will be the decade of women in leadership.[1] These trend forecasters state that women have now reached a critical mass in virtually all the white-collar professions; they hold almost 40% of the executive, administrative, and managerial positions.*

The growth of women in management positions created a new consumer for hotels, the female business traveler. In 1970 women accounted for less than 1% of all business travelers. They currently account for about 40% of all business trips and by the year 2000 they will account for 50%. In the late 1970s, hotel managers started to realize the importance of this new group of consumers. But they were not sure how they should attract them. Should they develop special floors for women only? Should they designate certain rooms for women travelers, placing extra lights around the mirrors, hair dryers, and skirt hangers in these rooms? Should they develop a special program for women travelers and put "Lady" in front of their brand name as the name for this program? Hotel chains did all this and more. Some conducted research asking women how they wanted to be treated dif-

ferently from their male counterparts. This provided little insight, as most women had not traveled as males, so they did not know how their male counterparts were treated. Second, they wanted to be treated as business travelers; they didn't want to be differentiated as a unique type of business traveler.

Many of the early programs aimed at the woman business traveler were unsuccessful. The male management of the hotel chains did not understand the behavior of this new segment. Women did not want to be patronized, or singled out as a special group, but they did have special needs. James Evans, a senior vice president with Hyatt, pointed out some of these needs. He stated that security is more important for the female traveler. Extended room service hours, make-up mirrors, well-lit bathrooms, light food entrees, and open-air lounges were other features mentioned by Evans.

Hotels reacted by lighting parking lots, changing menus, adding full-length mirrors in the rooms, decorating the rooms in lighter colors, increasing the selection of bathroom amenities, providing hair dryers in the rooms, and putting skirt hangers in the closets. With the exception of skirt hangers, most of these changes would be viewed positively by the male business traveler. In the security area, training at the front desk was increased so that room numbers of guests were not announced to bellmen, allowing them to be overheard by others. New hotels installed electronic locking devices and lowered the height of peep holes in doors so that women would not have to stand on stools to see who was at the door. The other major change that can be attributed to women is the increased construction of concierge and club floors. These floors require a key to gain access. They have a special lounge area where cocktails and continental breakfasts are served. Women prefer these floors because they can meet clients in the lounge area rather than their room, and they can relax in the concierge floor lounge, instead of going to the hotel's public lounge.

Hotels spent a great deal of effort and resources to please the female business traveler, a segment for which they projected rapid growth, but that they did not understand. Hotels that gained an understanding of this segment were able to attract more than their fair share of the market. As marketers it is important that we gain an understanding of how our consumers behave.[2]

Chapter 7 develops the concepts of consumer behavior and applies them to the actual buying decision.

At the beginning of the chapter we introduce a **model of buyer behavior.** Then we show how consumer purchases are strongly influenced by **cultural, social, personal,** and **psychological** characteristics.

Next we summarize the **consumer buying roles** that people might play: **initiator, influencer, decider, buyer,** and **user.**

We conclude with a discussion of the **buyer decision process.** The stages of this process are defined as **need recognition, information search, evaluation of alternatives, purchase decision,** and **postpurchase behavior.**

Marketers must exercise care in analyzing consumer behavior. Consumers often turn down what appears to be a winning offer. As soon as managers believe that they understand their customers, buyer decisions are made that appear to be irrational. But what looks like irrational behavior to a manager is completely rational to the consumer. Buying behavior is never simple. It is affected by many different factors, and yet understanding it is the essential task of marketing management.

Chambers, Chacko, and Lewis have summarized the basic beliefs about consumer behavior into five premises. These premises provide a good basis on which to start a discussion of consumer behavior.

Premise 1: Consumer behavior is purposeful and goal oriented. As we mentioned in the introduction, what looks like irrational behavior to a manager is completely rational to the consumer.

Premise 2: The consumer has free choice. Consumers do not have to pay attention to your marketing communications. Messages are processed selectively. In most cases the consumer has several products from which to choose.

Premise 3: Consumer behavior is a process. Marketers need to understand the process.

Premise 4: Consumer behavior can be influenced. By understanding the purchase decision process and the influences on this process, marketers can influence how consumers behave.

Premise 5: There is a need for consumer education. Consumers may act against their own interests because of a lack of knowledge. For example, some people think they can handle their alcohol and drive safely after excessive drinking. Marketers have a social responsibility to educate consumers.[3]

This chapter explores the dynamics of consumer buying behavior and the consumer market. **Consumer buying behavior** refers to the buying behavior of final customers—individuals and households who buy goods and services for personal consumption. The **consumer market** consists of all the individuals and households who buy or acquire goods and services for personal consumption. The U.S. consumer market includes over 255 million persons who consume more than $2 trillion of goods and services—almost $9000 worth for every man, woman, and child. Each year this market grows by several million persons and more than $100 billion, making it one of the most attractive consumer markets in the world.

Consumers vary tremendously in age, income, education level, and tastes. And they buy an incredible variety of goods and services. We will now look at how consumers make their choices among these products.

A MODEL OF CONSUMER BEHAVIOR

Today's marketplace has become very competitive. During the last 30 years, hundreds of multiunit restaurant and hotel companies have been formed, resulting in the development of thousands of hotels and restaurants. In addition, during recent years the hospitality and travel industries have undergone globalization. Hotel companies headquartered in nations as diverse as Germany, the United States, and Hong Kong compete aggressively in markets such as Singapore and Japan. The result is a fiercely competitive international market with companies fighting for their share of consumers. To win this battle they invest in research that will reveal what customers want to buy, which locations they prefer, which amenities are important to them, how they buy, and why they buy.

The central question is this: How do consumers respond to the various marketing stimuli that a company might use? The company that really understands how consumers will respond to different product features, prices, and advertising appeals has a great advantage over its competitors. As a result, researchers from companies and universities have heavily studied the relationship between marketing stimuli and consumer response. Their starting point is the model of buyer behavior shown in Figure 7-1. This figure shows that marketing and other stimuli enter the consumer's "black box" and produce certain responses. Marketers must determine what is in the buyer's black box.

On the left, marketing stimuli consist of the four P's—product, price, place, and promotion. Other stimuli include major forces and events in the buyer's environment—economic, technological, political, and cultural. All

Figure 7-1
Model of buyer behavior.

Marketing stimuli	Other stimuli		Buyer's black box			Buyer's responses
Product	Economic		Buyer characteristics	Buyer decision process		Product choice
Price	Technological					Brand choice
Place	Political					Dealer choice
Promotion	Cultural					Purchase timing
						Purchase amount

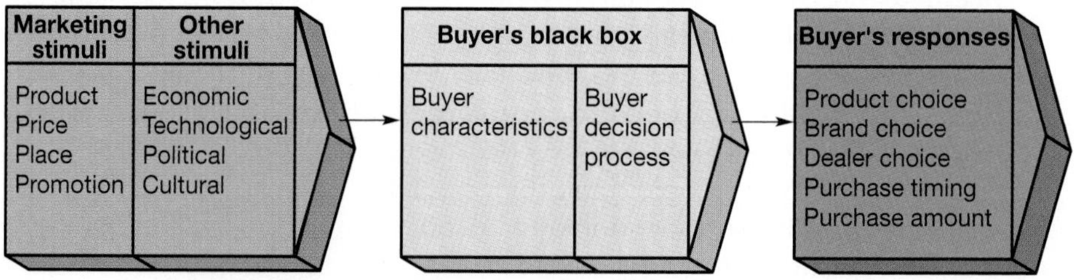

these stimuli enter the buyer's black box, where they are turned into the set of observable buyer responses shown on the right—product choice, brand choice, dealer choice, purchase timing, and purchase amount.

Marketers must understand how the stimuli are changed into responses inside the consumer's black box. The black box has two parts. First, a buyer's characteristics influence how he or she perceives and reacts to the stimuli. Second, the buyer's decision process itself affects outcomes. This chapter looks first at buyer characteristics that affect buying behavior and then examines the buyer decision process.

Consumer purchases are strongly influenced by cultural, social, personal, and psychological characteristics. These factors are shown in Figure 7-2. For the most part, they cannot be controlled by the marketer, but they must be taken into account.

PERSONAL CHARACTERISTICS AFFECTING CONSUMER BEHAVIOR

Cultural Factors

Cultural factors exert the broadest and deepest influence on consumer behavior. We will examine the role played by the buyer's culture, subculture, and social class.

Culture

Culture is the most basic determinant of a person's wants and behavior. It comprises the basic values, perceptions, wants, and behaviors that an individual continuously learns in a society. Today, most societies are in a state of flux. Determinants of culture learned as a child are changing in societies from Chile to California. Culture is expressed through tangible items such as food, buildings, clothing, and art. Culture is an integral part of the hospitality and travel business. It determines what we eat, how we travel, where we travel, and where we stay. Culture is dynamic, adapting to the environment.

Figure 7-2
Factors influencing behavior.

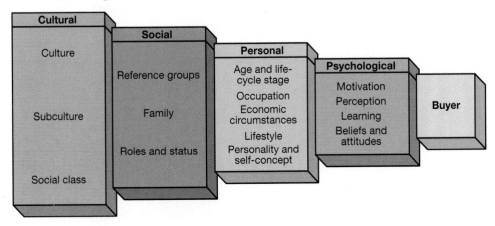

Marketers continuously try to identify cultural shifts in order to devise new products and services that might find a receptive market. For example, the cultural shift toward greater concern about health and fitness has resulted in many hotels adding exercise rooms or health clubs or developing an agreement with a local health club so that their guests can have access to it. The shift toward lighter and more natural food has resulted in menu changes in restaurants. The shift toward lighter-colored and simpler home furnishings is reflected in new restaurant designs.

At the same time a significant number of consumers seem to be rebelling against foods that are good for them and are saying give me good taste. Restaurants face a consumer who orders broiled flounder and a light salad only to top it off with high-butter fat ice cream for dessert.

Consumer Behavior across International Cultures

Understanding consumer behavior is difficult enough for companies marketing within the borders of a single country. For companies operating in many countries, however, understanding and serving the needs of consumers can be daunting. Although consumers in different countries may have some things in common, their values, attitudes, and behaviors often vary dramatically. International marketers must understand such differences and adjust their products and marketing programs accordingly. Consider the following examples:

- Shaking your head from side to side means "no" in most countries but "yes" in Bulgaria and Sri Lanka.
- In South America, Southern Europe, and many Arab countries, touching another person is a sign of warmth and friendship. In the Orient, it is considered an invasion of privacy.
- In Norway or Malaysia, it's rude to leave something on your plate when eating; in Egypt, it's rude *not* to leave something on your plate.[4]

Failing to understand such differences in customs and behaviors from one country to another can spell disaster for a company's international products and programs.

Marketers must decide on the degree to which they will adapt their products and marketing programs to meet the unique needs of consumers in various markets. On the one hand, they want to standardize their offerings in order to simplify operations and take advantage of cost economies. On the other hand, adapting marketing efforts within each country results in products and programs that better satisfy the needs of local consumers. The question of whether to adapt or standardize the marketing mix across international markets has created a lively debate in recent years.

Subculture

Each culture contains smaller **subcultures**, or groups of people with shared value systems based on common experiences and situations. Nationality groups such as the Irish, Polish, Italians, and Puerto Ricans are found within large communities and have distinct ethnic tastes and interests. Religious groups such as Roman Catholics, Mormons, Protestants, Muslims, and Jews are subcultures with their own preferences and taboos. Racial groups such as African Americans and Asians have distinctive cultural styles and attitudes. Geographical areas such as the Deep South, California, and New England are distinct subcultures with characteristic life-styles.

The following examples illustrate how consumer behavior is affected by culture. The first example was provided by a student working in a city club in Corpus Christi. She stated that the club had added dry-aged prime beef to its menu. Aging is referred to as natural tenderization because the enzymes already present in the meat break down the myofibrillar and connective proteins.[5] Aging can also impart a distinctive flavor, which many people enjoy. However, dry aging is an expensive process. The meat shrinks due to moisture loss, valuable refrigeration space is required, and inventory is tied up. Thus dry-aged beef is more expensive to purchase. In some areas of the country, it is viewed as a delicacy. Many consumers are willing to pay a premium for the flavor and tenderness of dry-aged beef. In south Texas this flavor was neither recognized as something special nor appreciated. Many of those who ordered the prime rib sent it back because the meat had a "funny" taste to it. What was a delicacy in many areas was sent back as spoiled meat in Corpus Christi.

Accordingly, some fast-food chains realize that people in different areas of the country like different foods; thus they have established regional differences in their menus. For this reason, restaurant concepts that thrive in one area of the country, die quick deaths when introduced into other regions. Alcoholic beverages are considered a part of the dining experience in some areas and are forbidden in others, particularly the Bible Belt areas of the South.

It is important to recognize that the products of subcultures sometimes become popular national and even international favorites. For example, Mexican food restaurants are now appearing in London, Montreal, Auckland, and Singapore. In each case the restauranteurs have "localized" the dishes to fit the tastes of their patrons. Travelers from Santa Fe, New Mexico, are likely to be disappointed by the Mexican food served in Auckland. These Mexican restaurants have developed profitable businesses by taking the food of one culture and adapting it to fit the tastes of another culture.

Marketers must understand cultural influences and track changes over time. Many subcultures make up important market segments, and marketers often design products and marketing programs tailored to the needs of these segments.

Social Class

Almost every society has some form of social class structure. **Social classes** are relatively permanent and ordered divisions in a society whose members share similar values, interests, and behaviors. Social scientists have identified the seven American social classes shown in Table 7-1.

Social class in newer nations such as the United States, Canada, Australia, and New Zealand is not indicated by a single factor such as income, but is measured as a combination of occupation, source of income, education, wealth, and other variables. In many older nations, social class is

Table 7-1

Characteristics of Seven Major American Social Classes

Upper uppers (less than 1%)
Upper uppers are the social elite who live on inherited wealth and have well-known family backgrounds. They give large sums to charity, run debutante balls, own more than one home, and send their children to the finest schools. They are a market for jewelry, antiques, homes, and vacations. They often buy and dress conservatively rather than showing off their wealth. While small in number, upper uppers serve as a reference group for others to the extent that their consumption decisions trickle down and are imitated by the other social classes.

Lower uppers (about 2%)
Lower uppers have earned high income or wealth through exceptional ability in the professions or business. They usually begin in the middle class. They tend to be active in social and civic affairs and buy for themselves and their children the symbols of status, such as expensive homes, schools, yachts, swimming pools, and automobiles. They include the new rich who consume conspicuously to impress those below them. They want to be accepted in the upper-upper stratum, a status more likely to be achieved by their children than by themselves.

Upper middles (12%)
Upper middles possess neither family status nor unusual wealth. They are primarily concerned with "career." They have attained positions as professionals, independent businesspersons, and corporate managers. They believe in education and want their children to develop professional or administrative skills so that they will not drop into a lower stratum. Members of this class like to deal in ideas and "high culture." They are joiners and highly civic minded. They are the quality market for good homes, clothes, furniture, and appliances. They seek to run a gracious home, entertaining friends and clients.

Middle class (32%)
The middle class is made up of average-pay white- and blue-collar workers who live on "the better side of town" and try to "do the proper things." To keep up with the trends, they often buy products that are popular. Twenty-five percent own imported cars, and most are concerned with fashion, seeking the better brand names. Better living means owning a nice home in a nice neighborhood with good schools. The middle class believes in spending more money on worthwhile experiences for their children and aiming them toward a college education.

Working class (38%)
The working class consists of average-pay blue-collar workers and those who lead a "working class life-style," whatever their income, school background, or job. The working class depends heavily on relatives for economic and emotional support, for tips on job opportunities, for advice on purchases, and for assistance in times of trouble. The working class maintains sharper sex role divisions and stereotyping. Car preferences include standard size and larger cars, rejecting domestic and foreign compacts.

Upper lowers (9%)
Upper lowers are working (are not on welfare), although their living standard is just above poverty. They perform unskilled work for very poor pay although they strive toward a high class. Often, upper lowers are educationally deficient. Although they fall near the poverty line financially, they manage to "present a picture of self-discipline" and "maintain some effort at cleanliness."

Lower lowers (7%)
Lower lowers are on welfare, visibly poverty stricken, and usually out of work or have "the dirtiest jobs." Often they are not interested in finding a job and are permanently dependent on public aid or charity for income. Their homes, clothes, and possessions are "dirty," "raggedy," and "broken-down."

Source: See Richard P. Coleman, "The Continuing Significance of Social Class to Marketing." *Journal of Consumer Research*, December 1983, pp. 265–80, © Journal of Consumer Research, Inc., 1983: and Richard P. Coleman and Lee P. Rainwater, *Social Standing in America: New Dimension of Class* (New York: Basic Books, 1978).

something to which one is born. Bloodlines often mean more than income or education in such societies. Marketers are interested in social class because people within a given class tend to exhibit similar behavior, including buying behavior. Social classes show distinct product and brand preferences in such areas as food, travel, and leisure activity. Some marketers focus on only one social class. The Four Seasons restaurant in upper Manhattan targets upper-class patrons, while Joe's Coffee Shop in lower Manhattan focuses on lower-class patrons. Because magazines such as *Town and Country* or *Family Circle* often target a certain social class, it is important to advertise in media that reach the targeted social class. There are also language differences between social classes, which means advertisers must compose copy and dialogue that ring true to the targeted social class.

Carnival Cruise Lines became the largest cruise line through targeting lower-middle and upper-lower classes. Previously, cruise lines had not targeted the lower social classes. Conversely, Cunard's Sea Goddess Line is designed to emulate a large private yacht. The Sea Goddess brochure promotes the enjoyment of meeting other sophisticated and discriminating travelers. "The privilege of having at your fingertips around the clock the best cuisine, the finest wines, and plushest creature comforts." Sea Goddess addresses the upper class, and the upper-middle class. Each product is well designed for its chosen market.

Social Factors

Consumer behavior is also influenced by social factors, including the consumers' reference groups, family, social roles, and status. Because social factors can strongly affect consumer responses, companies must take them into account when designing marketing strategies.

Groups

An individual's attitudes and behavior are influenced by many small groups. Those to which the individual belongs that have a direct influence are called **membership groups**. They include *primary groups*, such as family, friends, neighbors, and co-workers, specifically, those with whom there is regular but informal interaction. *Secondary groups* are more formal and have less regular interaction; they include religious groups, professional associations, and trade unions. In some societies, secondary groups may be membership groups. Members of the Mormon faith for example are greatly influenced by their religious affiliation. For example, Mormons do not drink alcoholic beverages; therefore, they are a less attractive group for fine restaurants serving wine and other alcoholic beverages.

Reference groups serve as direct (face-to-face) or indirect points of comparison or reference in the forming of a person's attitudes and behavior. People can also be influenced by **aspirational groups** to which they do not belong but would like to. For example, a college freshman may aspire to be part of Hyatt's management team and may identify with this group even though not a member.

Marketers try to identify the reference groups of their target market. Reference groups influence consumers in at least three ways: (1) They expose the person to new behaviors and life-styles. (2) They influence the person's attitudes and self-concept. (3) They create pressures to conform that may affect the person's product, brand, and vendor choices.

The importance of group influence varies by product and brand. It tends to be strongest when the product is visible to others whom the buyer respects. Purchases of products that are used privately are not greatly affected by group influence. Certain night clubs can be associated with reference groups attracting individuals who belong or wish to belong to the groups who frequent the night clubs. Country clubs and city clubs tend to attract members who want to affiliate with their type of members.

Groups commonly have **opinion leaders**. These are people within a reference group who, because of special skills, knowledge, personality, or other characteristics, exert influences over others. Opinion leaders are found in all strata of society, and one person may be an opinion leader in one product area and a follower in another. A business should identify the opinion leaders in their community and make sure that they are invited to important events. For example, the guest list for the grand opening of a restaurant or the first anniversary of a hotel should include opinion leaders.

Family

Family members have a strong influence on buyer behavior. The family remains the most important consumer buying organization in American society and has been extensively researched. Marketers have examined the role and influence of the husband, wife, and children on the purchase of different products and services. Children, for instance, exert a large influence on decisions involving fast-food restaurants. Thus McDonald's aims fast-food advertising directly at children. The chain's advertisements appear during Saturday morning cartoon shows and regularly offer new toys with its "happy meals," giving children an incentive to return to McDonald's.

Roles and Status

A person belongs to many groups—family, clubs, and organizations. An individual's position in each group can be defined in terms of role and status. A **role** consists of the activities a person is expected to perform according to the persons around him or her. Common roles include son or daughter, wife or husband, and manager or worker.

Each role influences buying behavior. For example, college students dining with their parents may act differently than when they are dining with peers. A person purchasing a banquet for his church men's club may be more price conscious than usual if he believes church activities call for frugality. The same person might be more interested in detail and quality than in price when purchasing a banquet for his company. Thus a person's role at that time significantly affects his or her purchasing behavior.

Our roles are also influenced by the surroundings. People dining at an elegant restaurant behave differently than when they dine at a fast-food restaurant. They also have expectations about the roles that employees in different establishments should play. Failure to meet these *role expectations* creates dissatisfaction.[6] For example, diners at an elegant restaurant might expect waiters to hold their chairs during seating. The same diners would be surprised and possibly offended if a person cleaning tables at a White Castle hamburger restaurant assisted with seating.

Each role carries a *status* reflecting the general esteem given to it by society. People often choose products that show their status in society. For example, a business traveler became upset when all first-class seats were sold on a desired flight. The traveler was forced to fly economy class. When questioned about his concern over flying economy class, the traveler's main concern was what someone he knew might think if they saw him sitting in the economy section. He did not seem to be concerned over the lower level of service or the smaller seating space provided by the economy section.

Role and status are not constant social variables. Many marketing and sales professionals have made serious judgmental errors relative to the role and status of prospective customers. The role and status of individuals may change remarkably as they enter the Elks Lodge, Knights of Columbus, Rotary, League of Women Voters, and many other organizations. Here they may become the grand knight, president, or national secretary or reach other positions of authority and recognition. People in these positions may have considerable influence in selecting locations, airlines, hotels and auto rental firms to be used by hundreds or thousands of delegates to the next convention or national conference.

Personal Factors

A buyer's decisions are also influenced by personal characteristics such as age and life-cycle stage, occupation, economic situation, life-style, personality, and self-concept.

Age and Life-cycle Stage

The types of goods and services people buy change during their lifetimes. For example, diet is limited to baby food in the early years, expands to include most foods in the growing and mature years, and is often restricted to special diets in later years. Preferences for leisure activities, travel destinations, and entertainment are also age related.

Important age-related factors are often overlooked by marketers. This is probably due to wide differences in age between those who determine marketing strategies and those who purchase the product/service. A study of mature travelers showed that this segment places great importance on grab bars in bathrooms, night lights, legible, visible signs in hallways, extra blankets, and large printing on menus. Despite the logical importance of the factors the researchers found that this information "is not usually included in advertising and information listings."[7]

Successful marketing to various age segments may require specialized and targeted strategies. This will almost certainly require segmented target publications and database marketing. It may also require a marketing staff and advertising agency with individuals of varying ages and cultural backgrounds.

Buying behavior is also shaped by the **family life-cycle** stages listed in Table 7-2, along with the financial situation and typical product interests of each group. Marketers often define their target markets in life-cycle terms and develop appropriate products and marketing plans.

Many restaurants have been successful operating in neighborhoods with singles and married couples without children. These restaurants have sometimes sought new locations and have been attracted to affluent suburbs, where household incomes approach six figures. In several cases the results have been disastrous. One such restauranteur moved to the suburbs to target "people who don't have to worry about mortgage payments." Six months later the restaurant was closed. It was discovered that suburbanites have mortgages, multiple car payments, and heavy expenses in raising a family, which includes paying a baby sitter when eating out. The amount of discretionary income in a household is greatly affected by the family life-cycle stage.

Occupation

A person's occupation affects the goods and services bought. For example construction workers often buy their lunches from industrial catering trucks that come out to the job site. Business executives purchase meals from a full-service restaurant, while clerical employees may bring their lunch or purchase lunch from a nearby quick-service restaurant. Employees of some consulting firms are not allowed to eat in fast-food restaurants. The management of these companies do not think it creates a proper image to have their client see consultants they have just been billed by for $200 an hour eating in a fast-food restaurant. Marketers try to identify occupational groups that have above-average interest in their products.

Table 7-2
Family Life-cycle Stages

YOUNG	MIDDLE-AGED	OLDER
Single	Single	Older married
Married without children	Married without children	Older unmarried
Married with children	Married with children	
Infant children	Young children	
Young children	Adolescent children	
Adolescent children	Married without dependent	
Divorced with children	children	
	Divorced without children	
	Divorced with children	
	Young children	
	Adolescent children	
	Divorced without	
	dependent children	

Sources: Adapted from Patrick E. Murphy and William A. Staples, "A Modernized Family Life Cycle," *Journal of Consumer Research,* June 1979, p. 16; ©Journal of Consumer Research, Inc., 1979. Also see Janet Wagner and Sherman Hanna, "The Effectiveness of Family Life Cycle Variables in Consumer Expenditure Research," *Journal of Consumer Research,* December 1983, pp. 281–91.

Marketing Highlight 7-1

Senior Consumers

As the U.S. population ages, seniors (people 55 and older) are becoming a very attractive market. They currently make up a market of over 55 million people. In 1996, when the baby boomers start reaching the age of 50, over 4 million people will start turning 50 and this phenomena will continue for the next 20 years. Those 55 and over control almost half of the discretionary income in the United States, $600 billion dollars. Those in the 55 to 64 age group have the highest discretionary income of any group. They have some special health care needs, but most are healthy and active, with many of the same needs and wants as younger consumers. Because seniors have more time and money, they are ideal customers for travel, entertainment, dining out, and other leisure activities. Marketers must also recognize that the seniors market consists of many segments with varied demographics and life-styles. As the seniors' segment grows in size and buying power and as the stereotype of seniors as impoverished shut-ins fades, more marketers will develop special strategies for this important market.

Those hotels marketing to this group should understand the time and money factor mentioned above. Members of this segment have plenty of time. Some hotels have targeted this market without training their staff on the wants of the group. Service personnel catering to business clientele provide quick efficient service. But seniors might interpret quick service to indicate that the server does not want them in the dining room. Seniors want leisurely service. Many senior couples may prefer rooms with two beds due to back problems and other physical problems. This does not mean the romance in the relationship is gone. Seniors will often purchase candlelight meals in the hotel's upscale restaurant. Many have the income to pay for luxury and convenience. They may prefer a suite with an oversized spa bathtub, remote control TV, and good lighting.

Source: Margaret Rose Caro, "The Mature Market: Destroying the Myths," *Lodging* (June 1989), pp. 27–30; and Stowe Shoemaker, "Marketing to Older Travelers," *Cornell Hotel and Restaurant Administration Quarterly* (August 1984), pp. 84–91.

Economic Situation

A person's economic situation greatly affects product choice and the decision to purchase a particular product. Consumers cut back on restaurant meals, entertainment, and vacations during recessions. They trade down in their choice of restaurants and/or menu items and eat out less frequently, looking for a coupon or deal when they do go out. Marketers need to watch trends in personal income, savings, and interest rates. If economic indicators point to a recession, they can redesign, reposition, and reprice their products. Restaurants may need to add lower-priced menu items that will still appeal to their target markets.

Conversely, periods of economic prosperity create opportunities. Consumers are more inclined to buy expensive wines and imported beers, menus can be upgraded, and air travel and leisure expenditures increase. Companies must take advantage of opportunities caused by economic upturns and take defensive steps when facing an economic downturn. Managers sometimes react too slowly to changing economic conditions. It pays to remain continuously aware of the macro environment facing customers. Regular reading of publications such as the *Wall Street Journal*, the business section of the local press, and regional economic reports by local and regional banks helps to keep managers informed.

Life-style

People from the same subculture, social class, and even occupation may have quite different **life-styles**. Life-style studies capture something more than the consumer's social class or personality. They profile the person's whole pattern of acting and interacting in the world.

The technique of measuring life-styles is known as psychographics. It involves measuring the major dimensions shown in Table 7-3.[8] The first three are known as AIO dimensions (activities, interests, opinions). Several research firms have developed life-style classifications. The most widely used is the SRI Values and Lifestyle (VALS) typology. The original VALS typology, introduced in 1978, classifies consumers into nine life-style groups according to whether they were inner directed (for example, "experientials"), outer directed ("achievers," "belongers") or need driven ("survivors").[9]

The more recent version, VALS 2, classifies people according to their consumption tendencies—by how they spend their time and money. It divides consumers into eight groups based on two major dimensions: self-oriented and resources (see Table 7-4). The *self-orientation* dimension captures three different buying approaches: Principle-oriented consumers buy based on their views of how the world is or should be; status-oriented buyers base their purchases on the actions and opinions of others; and action-oriented buyers are driven by their desire for activity, variety, and risk taking. Consumers within each orientation are further classified into one of two *resource* segments depending on whether they have high or low levels of income, education, health, self-confidence, energy, and other factors. Consumers with either very high or low levels of resources are classified into separate groups without regard to their self-orientations (actualizers,

Table 7-3
Lifestyle Dimensions

ACTIVITIES	INTERESTS	OPINIONS	DEMOGRAPHICS
Work	Family	Themselves	Age
Hobbies	Home	Social issues	Education
Social events	Job	Politics	Income
Vacation	Community	Business	Occupation
Entertainment	Recreation	Economics	Family size
Club membership	Fashion	Education	Dwelling
Community	Food	Products	Geography
Shopping	Media	Future	City Size
Sports	Achievements	Culture	Stage in life cycle

Source: Joseph T. Plummer, "The Concept and Application of Life-Style Segmentation," *Journal of Marketing*, January 1974, p. 34.

Table 7-4
VALS 2: Eight American Lifestyles

SELF-ORIENTATION

Principle Oriented

Fulfilleds

Mature, responsible, well-educated professionals. Their leisure activities center on their homes, but they are well informed about what goes on in the world, and they are open to new ideas and social change. They have high incomes, but they are practical, value-oriented consumers.

Believers

Principle-oriented consumers with more modest incomes. They are conservative and predictable consumers who favor American products and established brands. Their lives are centered on family, church, community, and nation.

Status Oriented

Achievers

Successful, work-oriented people who get their satisfaction from their jobs and their families. They are politically conservative and respect authority and the status quo. They favor established products and services that show off their success.

Strivers

People with values similar to those of achievers, but fewer economic, social, and psychological resources. Style is extremely important to them as they strive to emulate consumers in other, more resourceful groups.

Action Oriented

Experiencers

People who like to affect their environment in tangible ways. They are the youngest of all groups. They have a lot of energy, which they pour into physical exercise and social activities. They are avid consumers, spending heavily on clothing, fast food, music, and other youthful favorites. They especially like new things.

Makers

People who like to affect their environment, but in more practical ways. They value self-sufficiency. They are focused on the familiar—family, work, and physical recreation—and have little interest in the broader world. As consumers, they are unimpressed by material possessions other than those with a practical or functional purpose.

RESOURCES

Actualizers

People with the highest incomes and so many resources that they can indulge in any or all self-orientations. Image is important to them, not as evidence of status or power, but as an expression of their taste, independence, and character. Because of their wide range of interests and openness to change, they tend to buy "the finer things in life."

Strugglers

People with the lowest incomes and too few resources to be included in any consumer orientation. With their limited means, they tend to be brand-loyal consumers.

Source: See Martha Farnsworth Riche, "Psychographics for the 1990's," *American Demographics*, July 1989, pp. 25–31, ©1989, with permission.

Robinson, Yesawich, and Pepperdine created this advertisement to position Crystal Palace as the best vacation destination for high energy "achievers." Courtesy of Robinson, Yesawich, and Pepperdine.

strugglers). The eight VALS 2 life-style groups are described in Table 7-4. A person may progress through several of these life-styles over the course of a lifetime. People's life-styles affect their buying behavior.[10]

Life-style classifications are by no means universal; they can vary significantly from country to country. McCann-Erickson London, for example, found the following British life-styles: avant guardians (interested in change); pontificators (traditionalists); very British; chameleons (follow the crowd); and sleepwalkers (contented underachievers).

The life-style concept, when used carefully, can help the marketer understand changing consumer values and how they affect buying behavior.[11] For example, a female corporate executive can choose to live the role of a career woman or a free spirit—or all three of these. She plays several roles, and the way she blends them expresses her life-style.

Prizm, developed by Jonathan Robbin, groups the nation's population into life-style clusters and provides information on the products and brands these clusters purchase, the media they watch, the channels they shop, and their concentration in different geographic areas. For example, the largest users of fast-food restaurants are Blue-Chip Blues and Blue-Collar Nursery. The largest users of scheduled airlines are Urban Gold Coast, Blue Blood Estates, and Money and Brains (see Table 7-5), all using airlines at least twice as often as the national average.[12] Prizm, the brand name of one of these geodemographic systems, allows researchers to know the mix or density of life-style groups in each of the nation's 36,000 zip code areas. Thus 48236, the zip code for Grosse Pointe, Michigan, has a disproportionately high percentage of money and brains residents. Therefore, Grosse Point, Michigan, would be a good location for selling books, computers, and other products and services sought by professional people. This information enables hospitality and travel marketers to make better decisions on locations, areas for direct mail, and telemarketing promotions.

Personality and Self-concept

Each person's personality influences his or her buying behavior. By **personality**, we mean distinguishing psychological characteristics that disclose a person's relatively individualized, consistent, and enduring responses to the environment.[13]

Personality can be useful in analyzing consumer behavior for some product or brand choices. For example, a beer company may discover that heavy beer drinkers tend to rank high in sociability and aggressiveness. This information can be used to establish a brand image for the beer and to suggest the type of people to show in an advertisement.

Stanley Paskie, the 72-year-old head bartender at the Drake Hotel in Chicago's Gold Coast, says, "It's imperative that a bartender possess the human touch. Unfortunately human relations isn't a required course at the nation's bartending schools where most bartenders now learn the craft.... I've had conversations with customers in which I never said a word. I remember one customer who, as he was leaving, said thanks for listening to me fella."[14] Paskie believes that a good bartender is part father, philosopher, confessor, and devil's advocate. These traits are undoubtedly important in many areas of hospitality and travel marketing.

Table 7-5

The Clustering of America

LARGEST USERS OF FAST FOOD

Blue Chip Blues (6% of U.S. households): The nation's most affluent blue-collar households are concentrated in Blue-Chip Blues, composed of postwar suburban subdivisions in major metropolitan areas. Here lives a blue-collar version of the American dream: the majority of adults have high-school educations, earn between $25,000 and $50,000 annually, and own comfortable, middle-class homes. Boasting one of the highest concentrations of married couples with children, Blue-Chip Blues is the type of neighborhood with fast-food restaurants attached to every shopping center, baseball diamonds in the parks, and motorboats in the driveways.

Sample Neighborhoods: Coon Rapids, Minnesota 55433, South Whittier, California 90605, Mesquite, Texas 75149, Ronkonkoma, New York 11779, St. Charles, Missouri 63301, Taylor, Michigan 48180

Blue-collar Nursery (2.2% of U.S. households): They are America's starter family neighborhoods, places where the baby bust never occurred. In Blue-collar Nursery, young, middle-class families first settle down in a landscape of recently built subdivisions and overcrowded schools. Often located on the fringes of midwestern cities, these communities of modest ramblers and split-levels are home to union men employed as skilled laborers and machine operators, homemakers and working women who serve as nurses and secretaries, and their elementary-school-age children. More traditional families (married couples with children) live in Blue-collar Nursery than any other type of neighborhood.

Sample Neighborhoods: West Jordan, Utah 84084, Maryville, South Carolina 29440, Princeton, Texas 75044, Richmond, Michigan 48062, Haysville, Kansas 67060

LARGEST USERS OF SCHEDULED AIRLINES

Urban Gold Coast (0.5% of U.S. households): Composed of upscale high-rise neighborhoods in only a handful of big cities, Urban Gold Coast tops many demographic lists: most densely populated, most employed, most white collar, most renters, most childless, and most New York based. Almost two-thirds live in residences worth more than $200,000, decorating their rooms according to *Metropolitan Home*, buying clothes at Brooks Brothers, frequenting the same hand-starch Chinese laundries. In Urban Gold Coast, residents have the lowest incidence of auto ownership in the nation; these cliff-dwellers get around by taxi and rental car. Residents usually eat out for dinner and lunch.

Sample Neighborhoods: Manhattan, New York, Upper East and Upper West Sides, 10021, 10024, West End, Washington, D.C. 20037, Fort Dearborn, Illinois 60611, Rincon East (San Francisco), California 94111

Money and Brains (0.9% of U.S. households): The nation's cluster of exclusive in-town neighborhoods characterized by swank townhouses, renovated condos, and elegant apartments. Frequently located near prestigious city colleges, Money and Brains ranks second among clusters in both educational achievement and affluence. These are the neighborhoods that attract the nation's well-off intelligentsia, the leaders of science, academia, and management. These are the Americans who value conspicuous consumption of tasteful goods.

Sample Neighborhoods: Georgetown, Washington, D.C. 20007, Grosse Pointe, Michigan 48236, Palo Alto, California 94301, Princeton, N.J. 08450, Park Cities (Dallas), Texas 75205, Coral Gables, Florida 33146

©1988 by Michael J. Weiss. Reprinted by permission of HarperCollins Publishers, Inc.

Many marketers use a concept related to personality—a person's **self-concept** (also called self-image). Each of us has a complex mental self-picture, and our behavior tends to be consistent with that self-image.[15] Individuals who perceive themselves as outgoing and active will be unlikely to purchase a cruise vacation if their perception of cruises is one of elderly persons lying on lounge chairs. These individuals would be more likely to select a scuba-diving or skiing vacation. The cruise line industry has been quite successful in changing its "geriatric" image and now attracts outgoing and active consumers.[16]

The role of self-concept obviously has a strong bearing on the selection of recreational pursuits, including golf, sailing (with sails), dirt bike riding, fishing, and hunting. Anyone who enjoys boating will testify to the difference in boaters who use sails and engines. Yachters/sailboaters refer to those who use engines as "stink potters." Stink potters think of the sailing crowd as stuffy, pretentious, and generally not much fun.

Psychological Factors

A person's buying choices are also influenced by four major psychological factors: motivation, perception, learning, and beliefs and attitudes.

Motivation

A person has many needs at any given time. Some are biological, arising from hunger, thirst, and discomfort. Others are psychological, arising from states of tension, such as the need for recognition, esteem, or belonging. Most of these needs are not strong enough to motivate a person to act at a given point in time. A need becomes a **motive** when it is aroused to a sufficient level of intensity. Creating a tension state causes the person to act to release the tension. Psychologists have developed theories of human motivation. Two of the most popular, the theories of Sigmund Freud and Abraham Maslow, have quite different meanings for consumer analysis and marketing.

Freud's Theory of Motivation.   Freud assumes that people are largely unconscious about the real psychological forces shaping their behavior. He sees the person as growing up and repressing many urges. These urges are never eliminated or under perfect control; they emerge in dreams, in slips of the tongue, in neurotic and obsessive behavior, or ultimately in psychoses.

Motivation researchers collect in-depth information from small samples of consumers to uncover the deeper motives for their product choices. They use nondirective depth interviews and various *projective techniques* to throw the ego off guard—techniques such as word association, sentence completion, picture interpretation, and role playing. Motivation researchers have reached some interesting and sometimes odd conclusions about what may be in the buyer's mind regarding certain purchases. For example, one classic study concluded that consumers resist prunes because they are wrinkled looking and remind people of sickness and old age. Despite its sometimes unusual conclusions, motivation research remains a useful tool for marketers seeking a deeper understanding of consumer behavior.[17]

Maslow's Theory of Motivation.   Abraham Maslow sought to explain why people are driven by particular needs at particular times.[18] Why does one person spend much time and energy on personal safety and another on gaining the esteem of others? Maslow's answer is that human needs are arranged in a hierarchy, from the most pressing to the least pressing. Maslow's hierarchy of needs in order of importance are physiological needs, safety needs, social needs, esteem needs, and self-actualization needs. A person tries to satisfy the most important need first. When that important need is satisfied, it will stop being a motivator, and the person will then try to satisfy the next most important need. For example, a starving man (need 1) will not take an interest in the latest happenings in the art world (need 5), or in how he is seen or esteemed by others (need 3 or 4), or even in whether he is breathing clean air (need 2). But as each important need is satisfied, the next most important need will come into play.

Normally, needs are prioritized. For example, a college student with $500 to pay for incidental and recreational expenses during the term is unlikely to spend $400 on a trip to Florida over spring break. Instead, the money will probably be spent on smaller purchases of entertainment throughout the semester. If the student unexpectedly receives $2000, there might be a strong temptation to satisfy a higher-order need.

Perception

A motivated person is ready to act. How that person acts is influenced by his or her *perception* of the situation. In the same situation, two people with the same motivation may act quite differently based on how they perceive conditions. One person may perceive the waiters at Friday's as casual and unsophisticated, while another person may view them as spontaneous with a cheerful personality. Friday's is targeting those in the second group.

Why do people have different perceptions of the same situation? All of us experience a stimulus by the flow of information through our five senses: sight, hearing, smell, touch, and taste. However, each of us receives, organizes, and interprets this sensory information in an individual way. Perception is the process by which an individual selects, organizes, and interprets information to create a meaningful picture of the world.[19]

People form different perceptions of the same stimulus because of three perceptual processes: selective exposure, selective distortion, and selective retention.

Selective Exposure.   People are exposed to a great number of stimuli every day. The average person may see more than 1500 ads on a given day. Because it is impossible to pay attention to all these stimuli, most will be screened out. Selective exposure means that marketers have to work especially hard to attract the consumer's attention. Their message will be lost on most people who are not in the market for the product, and even people who are in the market may not notice the message unless it stands out from the surrounding ocean of ads.

This is the basis for *positioning*. Consumers can recall about four to seven brand names within a product class. To test this, ask your friends to suddenly recall within 30 seconds the names of auto rental agencies or ski resorts or upscale hotel chains. Chances are that Hertz, Avis, and Budget will be mentioned for auto rental companies, but not any more. How can this occur when there are many competitors in each product group? These brands have managed to position themselves in our minds so that they are quickly and repeatedly recalled. The quality, quantity, message, and media make the difference in how well a brand is positioned and remembered.

Selective Distortion. Even stimuli that consumers notice are not always perceived in the intended way. Each person tries to fit incoming information into his or her existing mind-set. Selective distortion describes the tendency of people to adapt information to personal meanings. If a person reads a poor restaurant review on their favorite Thai restaurant, they may distort the data to rationalize their positive view of the restaurant. For example, they may decide that the reviewer did not like Thai seasonings and prefers localized Thai food to authentic Thai cuisine. People tend to interpret information in a way that will support what they already believe.

Selective Retention. People forget much of what they learn. They tend to retain information that supports their attitudes and beliefs. Because of selective retention, the consumer who prefers to stay at Sheraton Hotels will remember a write-up in a business magazine praising Sheraton Hotels. Someone who prefers Hilton is not likely to remember the article. People retain information that supports their beliefs.

These three perceptual factors—selective exposure, distortion, and retention—mean that marketers have to work harder to get their messages through, which explains why drama and repetition are favored in sending messages to markets.

Learning

When people act, they learn. **Learning** describes changes in an individual's behavior arising from experience. Most human behavior is learned. Learning theorists say that learning occurs through the interplay of drives, stimuli, cues, responses, and reinforcement.

When consumers experience a product, they learn about it. Members of the site-selection committee for a convention often sample the services of competing hotels. They eat in the restaurants, note the friendliness and professionalism of the staff, and examine the hotel's features. Based on what they have learned, a hotel is selected to host the convention. During the convention, they experience the hotel once again. Based on their experience and those of the attending conventioneers, they will either be satisfied or dissatisfied with the hotel.

Hotels should help guests to learn about the quality of their facilities and services. Luxury hotels give tours to first-time guests and apprise them of the services offered. Repeat guests should be updated on the hotels services by employees and by letters and literature.

Beliefs and Attitudes

Through acting and learning, people acquire beliefs and attitudes, which, in turn, influence their buying behavior.

A **belief** is a descriptive thought a person holds about something. A customer may believe that Adam's Mark Hotels have the best facilities and most professional staff of any hotel in the price range. These beliefs may be based on real knowledge, opinion, or faith. They may or may not carry an emotional charge.

Marketers are interested in the beliefs people have about specific products and services. Beliefs reinforce product and brand images. People act on beliefs. If unfounded consumer beliefs deter purchases, marketers will want to launch a campaign to change them.

Unfounded consumer beliefs can severely affect the revenue and even the life of hospitality and travel companies. Among these beliefs might be the following:

- A particular hamburger chain served ground kangaroo meat.
- A particular hotel served as Mafia headquarters.
- A particular resort was for gays only.
- A particular motel was really the original "roach motel."
- A particular airline has poor maintenance.
- A particular country has unhealthy food handling standards.

People have attitudes about almost everything: religion, politics, clothes, music, and food. An **attitude** describes a person's relatively consistent evaluations, feelings, and tendencies toward an object or an idea. Attitudes put people into a frame of mind for liking or disliking things and moving toward or away from them. For example, many people who have developed the attitude that eating healthy food is important perceive chicken as a healthy alternative to beef and pork. As a result, the per capita consumption of chicken has increased during recent years, leading the American Beef Council and National Pork Producers Council to try to change consumer attitudes that beef and pork are unhealthy. The National Pork Producers Council promotes pork as "the other white meat," trying to associate pork with chicken. Companies can benefit by researching attitudes toward their products. Understanding attitudes and beliefs is the first step toward changing or reinforcing them.

Attitudes are very difficult to change. An individual's attitudes fit into a pattern, and changing one attitude may require making many difficult adjustments. It is easier for a company to create products that are compatible with existing attitudes than to change the attitudes toward their products. There are exceptions, of course, where the high cost of trying to change attitudes may pay off.

There is a saying among restauranteurs that a restaurant is only as good as the last meal served. Attitudes explain in part why this is true. A customer who has returned to a restaurant several times and on one visit receives a bad meal may begin to believe that it is impossible to count on having a good meal at that restaurant. The customer's attitudes toward the restaurant begin to change. If this customer again receives a bad meal, negative attitudes may be permanently fixed and prevent a future return. Serving a poor meal to first-time customers can be disastrous. Customers develop an immediate negative attitude that prevents them from returning.

The National Pork Producers Council is trying to direct people's attitudes toward pork, a healthier and more versatile meat, and away from fatty, unhealthy meats. Courtesy of The National Pork Producers Council.

Attitudes developed as children often influence purchases as adults. Children may retain negative attitudes toward certain vegetables, people, and possibly places. Chances are equally good that they may retain very positive images toward McDonald's and Disneyland. Hospitality and travel companies are particularly subject to life-long consumer attitudes that result from positive or negative childhood experiences. Harsh words from the manager of a miniature golf course or air sickness on a commercial flight in which the flight attendant showed little sympathy are negative attitude building experiences.

Disney and McDonald's both view children as life-long customers. They want children to return as teenagers, parents, and grandparents and treat them in a manner to ensure future business. Many hospitality and travel companies have still not learned from McDonald's and Disney.

Ski, golf, and ocean resorts have taken heed and have developed special programs, menus, and activities for kids. In many cases, hospitality and travel companies have discovered there is good profit potential in kids' programs, as well as future patron building potential. Steamboat Springs Ski Resort offers a professionally run children's program for kids from 6 months to 15 years of age. Emphasis is on safety and fun at Steamboat. Other examples of top-notch kids' programs may be found at Smuggler's Notch in Vermont and the Omni Sagamore in New York. Hyatt Hotels is a leader in the field with its Camp Hyatt. Hyatt has proved that a hotel can be upscale and child directed.

Once negative attitudes are developed, they are hard to change. New restaurant owners often want quick cash flow and sometimes start without excellent quality. A new restauranteur complained that customers are fickle. When his restaurant first opened, there were lines of people waiting for a seat. A few months later, he had plenty of empty seats every night. Obviously, he had not satisfied his first guests. Even though he may have subsequently corrected his early mistakes, his original customers had been disappointed, were not returning, and probably were reporting negative comments to their friends.

We can now appreciate the many individual characteristics and forces influencing consumer behavior. Consumer choice is the result of a complex interplay of cultural, social, personal, and psychological factors. Many of these cannot be influenced by the marketer; however, they help the marketer to better understand customers' reactions and behavior.

CONSUMER INVOLVEMENT IN THE BUYING DECISION

A marketer needs to know which people are involved in the buying decision and what role each person plays. Identifying the decision maker in many transactions is fairly easy. Business people usually choose the hotel or at least brand or type of hotel that they will stay in on a business trip and have their secretary make the reservation. Children often select the fast-food restaurant for the family's dinner with the parent's approval. The choice of the destination for the family vacation may be a group decision. The suggestion to go on a vacation might come from the oldest child. A friend who just took her family to the MGM Grand in Las Vegas might recommend Las Vegas as a vacation spot. The husband might want to go to the mountains in Utah, while the wife wants to go to the beach in Southern California. The husband and wife might then make the final decision jointly.

Figure 7-3 shows that people might play any of several roles in a buying decision:

- **Initiator:** the person who first suggests or thinks of the idea of buying a particular product or service. For example, the spouse may say, "Let's go out to eat tonight."
- **Influencer:** a person whose views or advice carries some weight in making the final buying decision. For example, the children like the children's buffet section at the Sizzler and suggest going to the Sizzler.

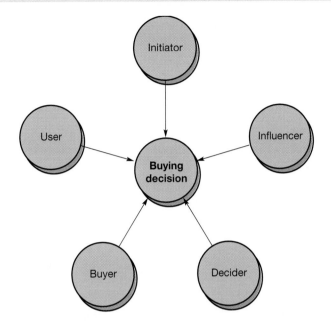

Figure 7-3
Consumer buying roles.

- **Decider:** the person who ultimately makes a buying decision or any part of it—whether to buy, what to buy, how to buy, or where to buy. The spouse says that she does not want to go to a buffet and decides that the family will go to Garcia's.
- **Buyer:** the person who makes an actual purchase. The husband charges the meal on his American Express card.
- **User:** the person who consumes or uses a product or service. The satisfaction of the different family members will influence if and how soon the family comes back to Garcia's.

A company needs to identify these roles because they affect product design and advertising. A resort for scuba divers on the island of Roatan off the coast of Honduras might be aware that males age 25 to 40 are the predominant decision makers concerning selection of a dive destination. They might also find that companions in the group exert a disproportionate influence concerning the selection of a resort hotel on the island. Resort hotels catering to the dive market could not exclude either party in advertisements since both occupy positions as decision makers. Knowing the main participants and the roles that they play helps the marketer to fine-tune the marketing program.

Southwest Airlines clearly understood the importance of a forgotten decision maker or influencer, the corporate secretary. When Southwest opened for business in Dallas, it developed a program for secretaries that included lunch, promotions, and even a glass bowl of candy kisses "from the Airline that loves you and the only one with departures and arrivals at Love Field in Dallas." Secretaries loved Southwest and responded by keeping the glass bowl on their desks even when the candy was gone. The bowl was printed with the reservation number for Southwest, and Dallas secretaries called that number thousands of times.

THE BUYER DECISION PROCESS

We are now ready to look at how consumers make buying decisions. Figure 7-4 shows that the buyer decision process consists of five stages: need recognition, information search, evaluation of alternatives, purchase decision, and postpurchase behavior. This model emphasizes that the buying process starts long before and continues long after the actual purchase. It encourages the marketer to focus on the entire buying process, rather than just the purchase decision.

The model appears to imply that consumers pass through all five stages with every purchase they make. But in more routine purchases, consumers skip or reverse some of these stages. A customer in a bar purchasing a glass of beer may go right to the purchase decision, skipping information search and evaluation. This is referred to as an automatic response loop.[20] The dream of every marketer is to have customers develop an automatic response to purchase their products. However, this does not typically happen. The model in Figure 7-4 shows the considerations that arise when a consumer faces a new and complex purchase situation.

To illustrate this model, we will follow Rosemary Martinez, a college student. She has just remembered that next Saturday is her boyfriend's birthday. We will follow her as she passes through the different stages.

Need Recognition

The buying process starts when the buyer recognizes a problem or need. The buyer senses a difference between his or her actual state and a desired state. The need can be triggered by internal stimuli. From previous experience, the person has learned how to cope with this need and is motivated toward objects that he or she knows will satisfy it.

Needs can also be triggered by external stimuli. Rosemary passes a restaurant, and the aroma of freshly baked bread stimulates her hunger; she has lunch with a friend who just came back from Bali and raves about her trip; or she watches a television commercial for a Hyatt resort. All these stimuli can lead her to recognize a problem or need.

At this stage, marketers must determine the factors and situations that trigger consumer problem recognition. They should research consumers to find out what kinds of needs or problems led them to purchase an item, what brought these needs about, and how they led consumers to choose this particular product.

Rosemary might have mentioned that she passed a card shop and noticed birthday cards, which reminded her that her boyfriend's birthday was approaching. She knew he liked German food, so she decided to take him to a German restaurant.

By gathering such information, marketers can identify stimuli that most often trigger interest in the product and develop marketing pro-

Figure 7-4
Buyer decision process.

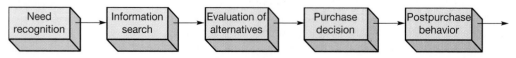

grams that involve these stimuli. Marketers can also show how their product is a solution to a problem. For example, TGI Friday's advertised its gift certificates as a solution to Christmas shopping. Friday's food and atmosphere attracts a broad range of people, the gift certificates are easy to buy, avoiding the need to go to crowded shopping centers, and they can be bought in denominations that fit with planned expenditures. TGI Friday's promoted gift certificates as a solution to a common problem experienced before Christmas.

Information Search

An aroused consumer may or may not search for more information. If the consumer's drive is strong and a satisfying product is near at hand, the consumer is likely to buy it at that moment. If not, the consumer may simply store the need in memory and search for relevant information.

How much searching a consumer does will depend on the strength of the drive, the amount of initial information, the ease of obtaining more information, the value placed on additional information, and the satisfaction one gets from searching.

Rosemary asked several of her friends if they knew of a good German restaurant. Then she scanned a city magazine's restaurant listings. Finally, she looked in the yellow pages to see if she could find additional German restaurants. As a result of her search, Rosemary identified three German restaurants.

The consumer can obtain information from several sources. These include:

- *Personal sources:* family, friends, neighbors, acquaintances.
- *Commercial sources:* advertising, salespeople, dealers, packaging, displays.
- *Public sources:* restaurant reviews, editorials in the travel section, consumer-rating organizations.

The relative influence of information sources varies with the product and the buyer. Generally, consumers receive the most information about a product from commercial sources, those dominated by the marketer. The most influential sources, however, tend to be personal. Commercial sources normally inform the buyer, but personal sources legitimize or evaluate products for her. For example, people may hear of a restaurant through advertising, but ask their friends about the restaurant before they try it. Responses from personal sources have more impact than advertising because they are perceived to be more credible.

By gathering information, consumers increase their awareness and knowledge of available choices and product features. A company must design its marketing mix to make prospects aware of and knowledgeable about the features and benefits of its products or brands. If it fails to do this, it has lost its opportunity to sell the customer. A company must also gather information about competitors and plan a differentiated appeal.

Marketers should carefully identify consumers' sources of information and the importance of each source. Consumers should be asked how they first heard about the brand, what information they received, and the importance they place on different information sources. This information is helpful in preparing effective communication.

Evaluation of Alternatives

We have seen how the consumer uses information to arrive at a set of final brand choices. But how does the consumer choose among the alternatives? How does the consumer mentally sort and process information to arrive at brand choices? Unfortunately, there is no simple and single evaluation process used by all consumers or even by one consumer in all buying situations. There are several evaluation processes.

Rosemary Martinez preferred a restaurant with good food and service. However, she believed that all the restaurants under consideration offered these attributes. She also wanted to patronize a restaurant with entertainment and a romantic atmosphere. Finally, she had a limited amount of money, so price was important. If several restaurants met her criteria, she would choose the one with the most convenient location.

Certain basic concepts will help explain consumer evaluation processes. First, we assume that each consumer sees a product as a bundle of product attributes. For restaurants, these attributes include food quality, menu selection, quality of service, atmosphere, location, and price. Consumers vary as to which of these attributes they consider relevant. The most attention is paid to attributes connected with their needs.

Second, the consumer attaches different degrees of importance to each attribute. That is, each consumer attaches importance to each attribute according to his or her unique needs and wants. Third, the consumer is likely to develop a set of beliefs about where each brand stands on each attribute. The set of beliefs held about a particular brand is known as the **brand image**. The consumer's beliefs may vary from true attributes because of the consumer's experience and the effects of selective perception, selective distortion, and selective retention. Fourth, the consumer is assumed to have a utility function for each attribute. A utility function shows how the consumer expects total product satisfaction to vary with different levels of different attributes. Fifth, the consumer arrives at attitudes toward the different brands through some evaluation procedure. One or more of several evaluation procedures are used, depending on the consumer and the buying decision.

Purchase Decision

In the evaluation stage, the consumer ranks brands in the choice set and forms purchase intentions. Generally, the consumer will buy the most preferred brand, but two factors can come between the purchase intention and the purchase decision. These factors are shown in Figure 7-5.

Attitudes of others represent the first. Rosemary Martinez selected a German restaurant since her boyfriend liked German food. Rosemary's choice depended on the strength of another person's attitudes toward her buying decision and on her motivation to comply with those wishes. The more intense the other person's attitude and the closer that person is to the decision maker, the more influence the other person will have. Nowhere is

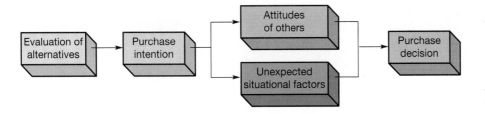

Figure 7-5
Steps between evaluation of alternatives and a purchase decision.

this better identified than in the case of children. Children do not hide their desires and parents and grandparents are intensely affected.

Purchase intention is also influenced by unexpected situations. The consumer forms a purchase intention based on factors such as expected family income, expected price, and expected benefits from the product. When the consumer is about to act, unexpected situations may arise to change the purchase intention. Rosemary Martinez may have an unexpected car problem that will cost $200 for repairs. This may cause her to cancel dinner reservations and select a less expensive gift.

Postpurchase Behavior

The marketer's job does not end when the customer buys a product. Following a purchase, the consumer will be satisfied or dissatisfied and will engage in postpurchase actions of significant interest to the marketer. What determines postpurchase satisfaction or dissatisfaction with a purchase? The answer lies in the relationship between *consumer expectations* and *perceived product performance*.[21] If the product matches expectations, the consumer will be satisfied. If it falls short, the consumer will experience dissatisfaction.

Consumers base expectations on past experiences and on messages they receive from sellers, friends, and other information sources. If a seller exaggerates the product's likely performance, the consumer will be disappointed. The larger the gap between expectations and performance, the greater the consumer's dissatisfaction. This suggests that sellers must faithfully represent the product's performance so that buyers are satisfied. For example, Bermuda enticed tourists to enjoy the island during the off season at a lower price. They called this period "Rendezvous Time" and advertised that all the island's amenities would be available. When tourists arrived, they found that many facilities and attractions were closed. Hotels had shut down many of their food and beverage facilities, leaving tourists disappointed. Advertising claims initially brought tourists, but the truth got out and hotel occupancy dropped by almost 50% over a period of 6 years.[22]

In May 1994, Continental Airlines announced a "save now, eat later" program. The purpose was to save money by eliminating food service in coach class. Unfortunately, many passengers were not notified of this change until they reached the airport and even then were notified only through a few signs on seats in the waiting area or in the seat pockets on the plane.

Passengers who had paid full coach fare and had expected a light meal were furious. Many read the notice and then immediately complained to the flight attendant. Continental failed to meet postpurchase expectations

Marketing Highlight 7-2

Unique Aspects of Hospitality and Travel Consumers

Valarie Zeithaml, a marketing consultant, published a classic article describing how the consumer evaluation process differs between goods and services. Persons purchasing hospitality and travel services rely more on information from personal sources. When looking for a good restaurant, people will ask friends or people familiar with the town, such as front-desk employees or the concierge. Restaurants should attempt to positively affect those persons who potential customers may contact. In larger cities there is a concierge association. Smart restauranteurs seek to host this club, letting their members experience the restaurants.

Postpurchase evaluation of services is important. The intangibility of services makes it difficult to judge the service beforehand. Consumers may seek advice from friends, but will use the information they receive from actually purchasing service to evaluate it. The first-time customer is on a trial basis. If the hotel or restaurant satisfies the customers, they will come back.

When purchasing hospitality and travel products, customers often use price as an indication of quality. A business executive who has been under a lot of pressure decides to take a three-day vacation now that the project is complete. She wants luxury accommodations and good food and service. She is prepared to pay $175 a night for the room. She calls a hotel that offers a special rate of $85. This hotel may be able to satisfy her needs and has simply dropped its rate to encourage business. In this case, the hotel has dropped its rate too low to attract this customer. Since she has never visited the hotel, she will perceive that the hotel is below her standard. Likewise, a person who enjoys fresh seafood and

sees grilled red snapper on the menu for $7.99 will assume that it must be a low-quality frozen product, because fresh domestic fish usually costs at least twice as much. When using price to create demand, care must be taken to ensure that one does not create the wrong consumer perceptions about the product's quality.

When customers purchase hospitality and travel products, they often perceive some risk in the purchase. If customers want to impress friends or business associates, they will usually take them to a restaurant they have visited previously. Customers tend to be loyal to restaurants and hotels that have met their needs. A meeting planner is reluctant to change hotels if the hotel has been doing a good job.

Customers of hospitality and travel products often blame themselves when dissatisfied. A person who orders scampi may be disappointed with the dish but not complain because he blames himself for the bad choice. He loves the way his favorite restaurant fixes scampi, but he should have known that this restaurant would not be able to prepare it the same way. When the waiter asks how everything is, he replies it was okay. Employees must be aware that dissatisfied customers may not complain. They should try to seek out sources of guest dissatisfaction and resolve them. A waiter noticing someone not eating their food may ask if they could replace it with an alternative dish and suggest some items that could be brought out very quickly.

Source: Valarie Zeithaml, "How Consumer Evaluation Processes Differ between Goods and Services," in *Marketing of Services*, James Donnelly and William R. George eds. (Chicago: American Marketing Association, 1981), pp. 186–190.

and compounded the problem by communication that was perceived as haughty and noncustomer oriented. The message was perceived as completely in favor of the airline. Harassed flight attendants, who had not participated in the decision, were left to accept blame. In some cases they responded by saying, "Your travel agent should have notified you of the change," thus attempting to shift blame and only making matters worse.

Almost all major purchases result in **cognitive dissonance**, or discomfort caused by postpurchase conflict. *Every purchase involves compromise!* Consumers feel uneasy about acquiring the drawbacks of the chosen brand and losing the benefits of the rejected brands. Thus, consumers feel some postpurchase dissonance with many purchases. And they often take steps after the purchase to reduce dissonance.[23]

Dissatisfied consumers may take any of several actions. They may return the product or complain to the company and ask for a refund or exchange. They may initiate a lawsuit or complain to an organization or group that can help them get satisfaction. Buyers may also simply stop purchasing the product and discourage purchases by family and friends. In each of these cases, the seller loses.

Marketers can take steps to reduce consumer postpurchase dissatisfaction and help customers to feel good about their purchases. Hotels can send a letter to meeting planners congratulating them on having selected their hotel for their next meeting. They can place adds featuring testimonials of satisfied meeting planners in trade magazines. They can encourage customers to suggest improvements.

Understanding the consumer's needs and buying process is the foundation of successful marketing. By understanding how buyers proceed through problem recognition, information search, evaluation of alternatives, the purchase decision, and postpurchase behavior, marketers can acquire many clues as to how to better meet buyer needs. By understanding the various participants in the buying process and major influences on buying behavior, marketers can develop a more effective marketing program.

THE BUYER DECISION PROCESS FOR NEW PRODUCTS

We have looked at the stages buyers go through in trying to satisfy a need. Buyers may pass quickly or slowly through these stages, and some of the stages may even be reversed. Much depends on the nature of the buyer, the product, and the buying situation.

We now look at how buyers approach the purchase of new products. A **new product** is a good, service, or idea that is perceived by some potential customers as new. It may have been around for a while, but our interest is in how consumers learn about products for the first time and make decisions on whether to adopt them. We define the **adoption process** as "the mental process through which an individual passes from first learning about an innovation to final adoption"[24] and **adoption** as the decision by an individual to become a regular user of the product.

Stages in the Adoption Process

Consumers go through five stages in the process of adopting a new product:

1. *Awareness.* The consumer becomes aware of the new product, but lacks information about it.
2. *Interest.* The consumer seeks information about the new product.
3. *Evaluation.* The consumer considers whether trying the new product makes sense.
4. *Trial.* The consumer tries the new product on a small scale to improve his or her estimate of its value.

5. *Adoption.* The consumer decides to make full and regular use of the new product.

This model suggests that the new product marketer should think about how to help consumers move through these stages. For example, a company building a new hotel will often bring in the general manager and sales manager a year before the hotel opens. The sales manager will try to create awareness of the product during the preopening period. Interest in the project will be generated through press releases and tours. The management team will often host target markets for hard-hat tours and receptions in the hotel while it is under construction. During this period the hotel will communicate its benefits to their target markets to try to create a favorable evaluation of the hotel by these markets. After the hotel opens, potential key customers will be given complimentary meals and rooms at the hotel to try the new product. There will often be an introductory rate, reducing the risk for customers who might want to try the hotel. During this trial period the hotel must perform well to get the potential customers to adopt the hotel. Many hotels and restaurants open without proper staffing levels or well-trained staff. This results in a low conversion rate from customers trying the product to those who adopt the product and become repeat customers.

Individual Differences in Innovativeness

People differ greatly in their readiness to try new products. In each product area, there are "consumption pioneers" and early adopters. Other individuals adopt new products much later. This has led to a classification of people into the adopter categories shown in Figure 7-6.

After a slow start, an increasing number of people adopt the new product. The number of adopters reaches a peak and then drops off as fewer nonadopters remain. Innovators are defined as the first 2.5% of the buyers to adopt a new idea (those beyond 2 standard deviations from mean adoption time); the early adopters are the next 13.5% (between 1 and 2 standard deviations); and so forth.

The five adopter groups have differing values. *Innovators* are venturesome—they try new ideas at some risk. *Early adopters* are guided by respect—they are opinion leaders in their community and adopt new ideas

Figure 7-6
Adopter categorization on the basis of relative time of adoption of innovations. *Source:* Redrawn from Everett M. Rogers, *Diffusion of Innovations*, 3rd. ed. (New York: 1983), p. 247. Adapted with permission of Macmillan Publishing Company, Inc. Copyright © 1962, 1971, 1983 by the Free Press.

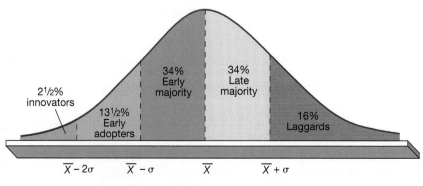

Time of adoption of innovations

early but carefully. Companies developing new restaurant concepts should research the characteristics of innovators and early adopters. Direct-mail campaigns can then be targeted to these groups. The *early majority* are deliberate—although they rarely are leaders, they adopt new ideas before the average person. The *late majority* are skeptical—they adopt an innovation only after a majority of people have tried it. Finally, *laggards* are tradition bound—they are suspicious of changes and adopt the innovation only when it has become something of a tradition itself.

Chapter Review

I.   Model of Consumer Behavior. The company that really understands how consumers will respond to different product features, prices, and advertising appeals has a great advantage over its competitors. As a result, researchers from companies and universities have heavily studied the relationship between marketing stimuli and consumer response. The marketing stimuli consist of the four P's—product, price, place, and promotion. Other stimuli include major forces and events in the buyer's environment—economic, technological, political, and cultural. All these stimuli enter the buyer's "black box," where they are turned into a set of observable buyer responses: product choice, brand choice, dealer choice, purchase timing, and purchase amount.

II.   Personal Characteristics Affecting Consumer Behavior

  1)   Cultural Factors

   a) **Culture:** Culture is the most basic determinant of a person's wants and behavior. It compromises the basic values, perceptions, wants, and behaviors that an individual continuously learns in a society.

   b) **Subculture:** Each culture contains smaller subcultures, or groups of people with shared value systems based on common experiences and situations.

   c) **Social classes** are relatively permanent and ordered divisions in a society whose members share similar values, interests, and behaviors. Social class in newer nations such as the United States, Canada, Australia, and New Zealand is not indicated by a single factor such as income, but is measured as a combination of occupation, source of income, education, wealth, and other variables.

  2)   Social Factors

   a) **Reference groups** serve as direct (face-to-face) or direct point of comparison or reference in the forming of a person's attitude and behavior.

   b) **Family:** Family members have a strong influence on buyer behavior. The family remains the most important consumer-buying organization in American society.

   c) **Roles and status:** A **role** consists of the activities a person is expected to perform according to the persons around him or her. Each role carries a **status** reflecting the general esteem given to it by society. People often choose products that show their status in society.

    3) Personal Factors

      a) **Age and life-cycle stage:** The types of goods and services people buy change during their lifetimes. As people grow older and mature, the products they desire change. The makeup of the family also affects purchasing behavior. For example, families with young children dine out at fast-food restaurants.

      b) **Occupation:** A person's occupation affects the goods and services bought.

      c) **Economic Situation:** A person's economic situation greatly affects product choice and the decision to purchase a particular product.

      d) **Life-style:** Life-styles profile the person's whole pattern of acting and interacting in the world. The life-style concept, when used carefully, can help the marketer understand changing consumer values and how they affect buying behavior.

      e) **Personality and self-concept:** Each person's personality influences his or her buying behavior. By **personality**, we mean distinguishing psychological characteristics that disclose a person's relatively individualized, consistent and enduring responses to the environment. Many marketers use a concept related to personality—a person's **self-concept** (also called self-image). Each of us has a complex mental self-picture, and our behavior tends to be consistent with that self-image.

    4) Psychological Factors

      a) **Motivation:** A need becomes a **motive** when it is aroused to a sufficient level of intensity. Creating a tension state causes the person to act to release the tension.

      b) **Perception:** Perception is the process by which an individual selects, organizes, and interprets information to create a meaningful picture of the world.

      c) **Learning:** describes changes in an individual's behavior arising from experience.

      d) **Beliefs and attitudes:** A belief is a descriptive thought that a person holds about something. An attitude describes a person's relatively consistent evaluations, feelings, and tendencies toward an object or an idea.

III.   **Consumer Involvement in the Buying Decision.** A marketer needs to know which people are involved in the buying decision and what role each person plays. Identifying the decision maker in many transactions is fairly easy. People might play any of several roles in a buying decision:

    1) Initiator. The person who first suggests or thinks of the idea of buying a particular product or service.

    2) Influencer. A person whose views or advice carries some weight in making the final buying decision.

    3) Decider. The person who ultimately makes a buying decision or any part of it.

    4) Buyer. The person who makes an actual purchase.

    5) User. The person who consumes or uses a product or service.

IV.   **Purchasing Decision Process**

    1) Problem Recognition. The buying process starts when the buyer recognizes a problem or need.

    2) Information Search. An aroused consumer may or may not search for more information. How much searching a consumer does will depend on the strength of the drive, the amount of initial information, the ease of obtaining more information, the value placed on additional information, and the satisfaction one gets from searching.

3) Evaluation of Alternatives. Unfortunately, there is no simple and single evaluation process used by all consumers or even by one consumer in all buying situations. There are several evaluation processes.

4) Purchase Decision. In the evaluation stage, the consumer ranks brands in the choice set and forms purchase intentions. Generally, the consumer will buy the most preferred brand.

5) Postpurchase Behavior. The marketer's job does not end when the customer buys a product. Following a purchase, the consumer will be satisfied or dissatisfied and will engage in postpurchase actions of significant interest to the marketer.

V.   Stages in the Adoption Process. Consumers go through five stages in the process of adopting a new product:

1) Awareness. The consumer becomes aware of the new product, but lacks information about it.

2) Interest. The consumer seeks information about the new product.

3) Evaluation. The consumer considers whether trying the new product makes sense.

4) Trial. The consumer tries the new product on a small scale to improve his or her estimate of its value.

5) Adoption. The consumer decides to make full and regular use of the new product.

DISCUSSION QUESTIONS

1. Discuss the importance of the black box component in the model of buyer behavior.

2. Choose a restaurant concept that you would like to take overseas. How will the factors shown in Figure 7-2 work for or against the success of this restaurant?

3. Discuss when the family can be a strong influence on buying behavior regarding the choice of restaurants.

4. Apply the five stages in the decision process to your selection of a destination for your next vacation.

5. Why is the postpurchase behavior stage included in the model of the buying process?

6. Why is customer satisfaction so important in the restaurant business?

KEY TERMS

Adoption   The decision by an individual to become a regular user of the product.

Adoption process   The mental process through which an individual passes from first hearing about an innovation to final adoption.

Alternative evaluation   The stage of the buyer deci-

sion process in which the consumer uses information to evaluate alternative brands in the choice set.

Aspirational group   A group to which an individual wishes to belong.

Attitude   A person's enduring favorable or unfavorable cognitive evaluations, emotional feelings, and action tendencies toward some object or idea.

Belief   A descriptive thought that a person holds about something.

Brand image   The set of beliefs consumers hold about a particular brand.

Buyer   The person who makes an actual purchase.

Cognitive dissonance   Buyer discomfort caused by postpurchase conflict.

Consumer market   All the individuals and households who buy or acquire goods and services for personal consumption.

Culture   The set of basic values, perceptions, wants, and behaviors learned by a member of society from family and other important institutions.

Decider   The person who ultimately makes a buying decision or any part of it—whether to buy, what to buy, how to buy, or where to buy.

Extensive problem solving   Buyer behavior in cases in which buyers face complex buying decisions for more expensive, less frequently purchased products in an unfamiliar product class. Buyers engage in extensive information search and evaluation.

Family life cycle   The stages through which families might pass as they mature.

Influencer   A person whose views or advice carries some weight in making a final buying decision.

Information search   The stage of the buyer decision process in which the consumer is aroused to search for more information; the consumer may simply have heightened attention or may go into active information search.

Initiator   The person who first suggests or thinks of the idea of buying a particular product or service.

Learning   Changes in an individual's behavior arising from experience.

Life-style   A person's pattern of living as expressed in his or her activities, interests, and opinions.

Limited problem solving   Buying behavior in cases in which buyers are aware of the product class but not familiar with all the brands and their features. Buyers engage in limited information search and evaluation.

Membership groups   Groups that have a direct influence on a person's behavior and to which a person belongs.

Motive (or drive)   A need that is sufficiently pressing to direct the person to seek satisfaction of that need.

New product   A good, service, or idea that is perceived by some potential customers as new.

Opinion leaders   People within a reference group who, because of special skills, knowledge, personality, or other characteristics, exert influence on others.

Perception   The process by which an individual selects, organizes, and interprets information inputs to create a meaningful picture of the world.

Personal influence   The effect of statements made by one person on another's attitude or probability of purchase.

Personality   A person's distinguishing psychological characteristics that lead to relatively consistent and lasting responses to his or her environment.

Postpurchase behavior   The stage of the buyer decision process in which consumers take further action after the purchase based on their satisfaction or dissatisfaction.

Problem recognition   The first stage of the buyer decision process in which the consumer recognizes a problem or need.

Psychographic   The technique of measuring life-styles and developing life-style classifications; it involves measuring the major AIO dimensions (activities, interests, and opinions).

Purchase decision   The stage of the buyer decision process in which the consumer actually buys the product.

Reference groups   Groups that have a direct (face-to-face) or indirect influence on the person's attitude or behavior.

Role   The activities a person is expected to perform according to the persons around him or her.

Routine response behavior   Buying behavior in cases in which buyers face simple buying decisions for low-cost, low-involvement, frequently purchased items in familiar product classes. Buyers do not give much thought, search, or time to the purchase.

Selective distortion   The tendency of people to adapt information to personal meanings.

Self-concept   Self-image, or the complex mental pictures people have of themselves.

Social classes   Relatively permanent and ordered

divisions in a society whose members share similar values, interests, and behaviors.

Status   The general esteem given to a role by society.

Subculture   A group of people with shared value systems based on common life experiences and situations.

User   The person who consumes or uses a product or service.

REFERENCES

1. JOHN NAISBITT AND PATRICIA ABURDENE, *Megatrends 2000* (New York: William Morrow and Co., 1990).

2. See REGINA MCGEE,"What Do Women Travelers Really Want?," *Successful Meetings*, 37, no. 9 (August 1988), pp. 54–56; "The Woman Traveler, A Special Report," *Lodging Hospitality* (December 1985), pp. 32–48; MICHELE MANGES, "Hotels Change Pitch to Businesswomen," *Wall Street Journal* (October 14, 1988), sec. B, p. 1.

3. RICHARD CHAMBERS, HARSHA CHACKO, AND ROBERT LEWIS, *Marketing Leadership in Hospitality* (New York: Van Nostrand Reinhold, 1995), p. 199.

4. For these and other examples, see MICHAEL J. ETZEL, WILLIAM J. STANTON, AND BRUCE J. WALKER, *Fundamentals of Marketing* (New York: McGraw-Hill, 1991), p. 536.

5. See STEPHEN MUTKOSKI, *Meat and Fish Management* (Belmont, Calif.: Wadsworth, 1981), p. 53; HAROLD MCGEE, *On Food and Cooking* (New York: Charles Scribner and Sons, 1984); and JOHN M. STEFANELLI, *Purchasing: Selection and Procurement for the Hospitality Industry* (New York: John Wiley & Sons, 1985).

6. JOHN E. G. BATESON, *Managing Services Marketing* (New York: Dryden, 1989), pp. 291–300.

7. RICHARD M. HOWEY, ANANTH MANGALA, FREDERICK J. DE MICCO, AND PATRICK J. MOREO, "Marketplace Needs of Mature Travelers," *Cornell Hotel and Restaurant Administration Quarterly*, 33, no. 4 (August 1992), pp. 19–20.

8. KIM FOLTZ, "Wizards of Marketing," *Newsweek* (July 22, 1985), p. 44.

9. Ibid.

10. For more on VALS and on psychographics in general, see WILLIAM D. WELLS, "Psychographics: A Critical Review," *Journal of Marketing Research* (May 1975), pp. 196–213; ARNOLD MITCHELL, *The Nine American Lifestyles* (New York: Macmillan, 1983); REBECCA PIIRTO, "Measuring Minds in the 1990s," *American Demographics* (December 1990), pp. 35–39; and REBECCA PIIRTO, "VALS the Second Time," *American Demographics* (July 1991), p. 6.

11. This and other examples of companies using VALS 2 can be found in PIIRTO, "VALS the Second Time."

12. For more reading on the pros and cons of using VALS and other life-style approaches, see LYNN R. KAHLE, SHARON E. BEATTY, AND PAMELA HOMER, "Alternative Approaches to Consumer Values: The List of Values (LOV) and Values and Lifestyles (VALS)," *Journal of Consumer Research* (December, 1986), pp. 405–9; and "Lifestyle Roulette," *American Demographics* (April 1987), pp. 24–25.

13. MICHAEL J. WEISS, *The Clustering of America* (New York: Harper & Row, 1988).

14. EDMUND O. LAWLER, "50 Years behind the Bar," *F&B Magazine*, 2, no. 1 (March/April 1994), p. 44.

15. JAMES U. MCNEAL, *Consumer Behavior, an Integrative Approach* (Boston: Little, Brown and Company, 1982), pp. 83–90.

16. CARL R. ROGERS, *Client-centered Therapy* (Boston: Houghton Mifflin, 1951), p. 507.

17. See ANNETTA MILLER AND DODY TSIANTAR, "Psyching out Consumers," *Newsweek* (February 27, 1989), pp. 46–47; and REBECCA PIIRTO, "Words That Sell," *American Demographics* (January 1992), p. 6.

18. ABRAHAM H. MASLOW, *Motivation and Personality*, 2nd ed. (New York: Harper & Row, 1970), pp. 80–106.

19. M. JOSEPH SIRGY, "Self-concept in Consumer Behavior: A Critical Review," *Journal of Consumer Research* (December 1982), pp. 287–300.

20. MCNEAL, *Consumer Behavior, an Integrative Approach*, p. 77.

21. PRISCILLA A. LABARBARA AND DAVID MAZURSKY, "A Longitudinal Assessment of Consumer Satisfaction/Dissatisfaction: The Dynamic Aspect of the Cognitive Process," *Journal of Marketing Research* (November 1983), pp. 393–404.

22. THOMAS BEGGS AND ROBERT C. LEWIS, "Selling Bermuda in the Off Season," in *The Complete Travel Marketing Handbook* (Lincolnwood, Ill.: NTC Business Books, 1988).

23. LEON FESTINGER, *A Theory of Cognitive Dissonance* (Stanford, Calif.: Stanford University Press, 1957), and LEON G. SCHIFFMAN AND LESLIE LAZAR KANUK, *Consumer Behavior*, (Englewood Cliffs, N.J.: Prentice-Hall, 1991), pp. 304–305.

24. The following discussion draws heavily on EVERETT M. ROGERS, *Diffusion of Innovations*, 3rd ed. (New York: Free Press, 1983). Also see HUBERT GATIGNON AND THOMAS S. ROBERTSON, "A Propositional Inventory for New Diffusion Research," *Journal of Consumer Research* (March 1985), pp. 849–67.

Organizational Buyer Behavior of Group Markets

*D*on Walter was a 1994 inductee of the Convention Liaison Council's Hall of Leaders. He received this honor because of his contribution to the meetings and convention business over the last 30 years. During his career, Don Walter has purchased or influenced the purchase of close to a $100 million worth of hospitality and travel products. When asked what is the important factor in negotiating with a hotel, he replied honest, straightforward negotiations. He states if both the meeting planner and the hotel sales manager are up front with each other, it saves hours of unnecessary negotiation for each party.

Walter does not buy on price alone and avoids properties that appear desperate for his business. He claims that often these hotels have financial problems, which result in staff turnover and understaffing. In this type of hotel you may have to deal with several people because of the turnover problem. When the meeting is held, the service is poor, meals that should take an hour end up taking an hour and a half because of understaffing, and changes in setups are difficult to accomplish. When people do show up to change the meeting room for you, they are often irritated and let the meeting planner know it. Walter goes on to say that this type of poor service can ruin a meeting. If the meeting does not go off well, the savings in cost seems trivial in comparison to the damage done to the sponsoring association's reputation.

Thus, when negotiating, Walter looks for a fair deal. He expects the hotel to make money, but he also expects good service and overall value. He observes the employees during a site visit to get a good idea of the type of service he can expect for his meeting. When he sees an employee bend over and pick up a gum wrapper, this is an indication to him that the employees have pride in their hotel. He likes to go back to a hotel where he sees the same faces he saw last year. Low turnover and promotion from within give him a good feeling about a hotel. Similarly, when an employee greets him by name as he enters the hotel, this shows that the hotel has gone to the effort of getting the employees to recognize him—a sign of attention to detail and caring.

After signing a contract with a hotel, he likes to deal with one person. By the way, Walter brings his own contract; he does not use the hotel's contract. Sometimes it is necessary to make changes to the room layouts he provided to the hotel. When he needs to make changes, he expects them to be done promptly and cheerfully.

When discussing things that have affected the meeting business, Walter said that requirements because of the Americans with Disabilities Act (ADA) should be a concern to both hotels and meeting planners. First, compliance ensures that everyone wanting to attend the meeting has access to the meeting. Second, failure to comply could result in lawsuits from attendees against both the meeting sponsor and hotel.

Don Walter provides an example of the tremendous purchasing power of an organizational buyer. He also provides some insights into what is important to meeting planners and association executives. They want good service at a fair price. They do not want any surprises, and when they need to make some changes during the event, they expect the hotel or convention hall to be supportive.

In most hotels and many food-service operations, organizations account for a large percentage of sales. In some ways, business markets are similar to consumer markets. For example, both involve people who assume buying roles and make purchase decisions to satisfy needs. However, business markets differ in many ways from consumer markets.[1] The differences are in market structure and demand, the nature of the buying unit, and the types of decisions and the decision process involved.

Chapter 8 places the concepts of individual buyer behavior into a business market context.

We explain the **key differences** between markets and consumer markets, including market structure and demand, the nature of the **buying unit**, and the **types of decisions** and the **decision process**.

Next we look at the **participants** in the organizational buying process and **major influences** on organizational buyers.

We close with a look at the group market segments and the corporate travel market.

Market Structure and Demand

The American Marketing Association holds more than 20 conferences annually. Hyatt and Marriott share the majority of the AMA's conference business, with Marriott's share close to 3000 room nights a year. When food and beverage sales are included, the value of this account approaches a half million dollars. A national corporate contract with a major company such as General Motors could bring in even more revenue. Each organizational customer can deliver thousands of dollars worth of business.

Organizational demand is derived demand; it comes ultimately from the demand for consumer goods or services. The American Marketing Association plans and hosts conferences because its members, who are marketing managers, suppliers, and educators, have attended past conferences on these topics. If a particular conference receives poor attendance, the AMA drops it from future schedules. Ultimately, the demand for the AMA member's products determines the demand for AMA products. For example, if class enrollments are low, universities typically cut travel budgets. If car sales fall, GM will cut its travel costs. Both events will cause attendance at AMA conferences to fall.

Nature of the Buying Unit

Compared with consumer purchases, a business purchase usually involves *more buyers* and a *more professional purchasing effort*. Corporations that frequently use hotels for meetings may hire their own meeting planners. Professional meeting planners receive training in negotiating skills. They belong to associations such as Meeting Planners International, which educates its members in the latest negotiating techniques. A corporate travel agent's job is to find the best airfares, rental car rates, and hotel rates. Therefore, hotels must have well-trained salespeople to deal with well-trained buyers.

Types of Decisions and the Decision Process

Organizational buyers usually face more complex buying decisions than consumer buyers. Their purchases often involve large sums of money, complex technical features (room sizes, room setups, break-out rooms, audio-visual equipment, and the like), economic considerations, and interactions among many people at all levels of the organization. The organizational buying process tends to be *more formalized* than the consumer process and a more *professional purchasing effort*. The more complex the purchase, the more likely it is that several people will participate in the decision-making process. The total bill for a one-day sales meeting for 20 people can be several thousands of dollars. If IBM is having a series of sales meetings around the country, it will be worthwhile for the company to get quotations from several hotel chains and spend time analyzing the bids.

Finally, in the organizational buying process, buyer and seller are often very dependent on each other. Sales has become a consultative process. The hotel staff develops interesting and creative menus, theme parties, and coffee breaks. The hotel's convention service staff works with meeting planners to solve problems. In short, the hotel's staff members roll up their sleeves and work closely with their corporate and association customers to find customized solutions to customer needs. When management at the Sands Exposition Center in Las Vegas discovered that there was insufficient floor space to accommodate a major automobile parts trade show, the Sands rented a temporary 40,000-square-foot pavilion. To help attract attendees to the pavilion, the Sands positioned a restaurant at the back of the facility. In the end, hotels and catering firms retain customers by meeting their current needs and thinking ahead to meet the customer's future needs.

PARTICIPANTS IN THE ORGANIZATIONAL BUYING PROCESS

The decision-making unit of a buying organization, sometimes called the *buying center*, is defined as "all those individuals and groups who participate in the purchasing decision-making process, who share common goals and the risks arising from the decisions."[2]

The buying center includes all members of the organization who play any of six roles in the purchase decision process.[3]

1. **Users.** Users are those who will use the product or service. They often initiate the buying proposal and help define product specifications. If attendees of a sales meeting have a poor experience, they will usually be able to influence the company against using that hotel in the future.

2. **Influencers.** Influencers directly influence the buying decision, but do not themselves make the final decision. They often help define specifications and provide information for evaluating alternatives. Past presidents of trade associations may exert influence in the choice of a meeting location. Executive secretaries, a spouse, regional managers, and many others can and do exert considerable influence in the selection of sites for meetings, seminars, conferences, and other group gatherings.

3. **Deciders.** Deciders select product requirements and suppliers. For example, a company's sales manager for the Denver area will select the hotel and negotiate the arrangements when the regional sales meeting is held in that area.

4. **Approvers.** Approvers authorize the proposed actions of deciders or buyers. Although the Denver sales manager arranges the meeting, the contracts may need to be submitted to the corporate vice-president of marketing for formal approval.

5. **Buyers.** Buyers have formal authority for selecting suppliers and arranging the terms of purchase. Buyers may help shape product specifications and play a major role in selecting vendors and negotiating.

6. **Gatekeepers.** Gatekeepers have the power to prevent sellers or information from reaching members of the buying center. For example, a hotel salesperson calling on a meeting planner may have to go through a secretary. This secretary can easily block the salesperson from seeing the meeting planner. This can be accomplished by failing to forward messages, telling the salesperson the meeting planner is not available, or simply telling the meeting planner not to deal with the salesperson.

Buying centers vary by number and type of participants. Salespersons calling on organizational customers must determine the following:

- Who are the major decision participants?
- What decisions do they influence?
- What is their level of influence?
- What evaluation criteria does each participant use?

When a buying center includes multiple participants, the seller may not have the time or resources to reach all of them. Smaller sellers concentrate on reaching the *key buying influencers and deciders*. It is important not to go over the decider's head. Most deciders like to feel in control of the purchasing decision; going over the deciders head and working with the boss will be resented. In most cases the boss will leave the decision up to the decider, and the ill-will created by not dealing with the decider directly will result in him or her choosing another company. Larger sellers utilize *multilevel, in-depth selling* to reach as many buying participants as possible. Their salespeople virtually "live" with their high-volume customers.

MAJOR INFLUENCES ON ORGANIZATIONAL BUYERS

Organizational buyers are subject to many influences as they make their buying decisions. Some vendors assume that the most important influences are economic. They see buyers as favoring the supplier who offers the lowest price, best product, or most service. This view suggests that hospitality marketers should concentrate on price and cost variables.

Others believe that buyers respond to personal factors such as favors, attention, or risk avoidance. A study of buyers in 10 large companies concluded that emotions and feelings play a part in the decision process of corporate decision makers. They respond to "image," buy from known companies, and favor suppliers who show them respect and personal consideration. They "overreact" to real or imagined slights, tending to reject companies that fail to respond or delay in submitting bids.[4]

In reality, organizational buyers commonly respond to both economic and personal factors. Where there is substantial similarity in supplier offers, price becomes an important determinant. When competing products differ substantially, buyers are faced with many decision variables other than price comparisons.

The various influences on organizational buyers may be classified into four main groups: environmental, organizational, interpersonal, and individual.[5] Figure 8-1 illustrates these groups.

Environmental Factors

Organizational buyers are heavily influenced by the current and expected economic environment. Factors such as the level of primary demand, the economic outlook, and the cost of money are important. In a recession, companies cut their travel budgets, while in good times travel budgets are usually increased.

Organizational Factors

Each organization has specific objectives, policies, procedures, organizational structures, and systems related to buying. The hospitality marketer has to be as familiar with them as possible and will want to know the following: How many people are involved in the buying decision? Who are they? What are the evaluation criteria? What are the company's policies and constraints on the buyers?

Figure 8-1

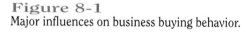
Major influences on business buying behavior.

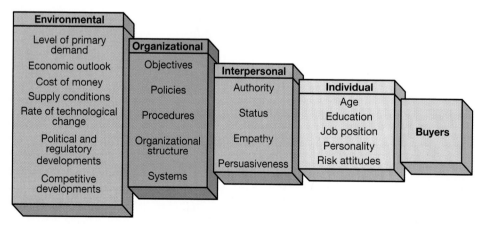

Interpersonal Factors

The buying center usually includes several participants with differing levels of interest, authority, and persuasiveness. Hospitality marketers are unlikely to know the group dynamics that take place during the buying decision process. However, salespeople commonly learn the personalities and interpersonal factors that shape the organizational environment and provide useful insight into group dynamics.

Individual Factors

Each participant in the buying decision process has personal motivations, perceptions, and preferences. The participant's age, income, education, professional identification, personality, and attitudes toward risk all influence the participants in the buying process. Buyers definitely exhibit different buying styles. Hospitality marketers must know their customers and adapt their tactics to known environmental, organizational, interpersonal, and individual influences.

Organizational buyers do not buy goods and services for personal consumption. They buy hospitality products to provide training, to reward employees and distributors, and to provide lodging for their employees. Eight stages of the organizational buying process have been identified and are called *buyphases*.[6] This model is called the *buygrid* framework. The eight steps for the typical new-task buying situation follow.

ORGANIZATIONAL BUYING DECISIONS

1. Problem Recognition

The buying process begins when someone in the company recognizes a problem or need that can be met by acquiring a good or a service. Problem recognition can occur because of internal or external stimuli. Internally, a new product may create the need for a series of meetings to explain the product to the sales force. A human resource manager may notice a need for employee training and set up a training meeting. A CEO may feel that the executive team would benefit from a weekend retreat to reformulate the firm's strategy. Externally, the buyer sees an ad or receives a call from a hotel sales representative who offers a favorable corporate program. Marketers can stimulate problem recognition by developing ads and calling on prospects.

2. General Need Description

Having recognized a need, the buyer goes on to determine the requirements of the product. For a training meeting, this would include food and beverage, meeting space, audiovisual equipment, coffee break, and sleeping room requirements. The corporate meeting planner will work with others—the director of human resources, the training manager, and potential participants—to gain insight into the requirements of the meeting. Together, they determine the importance of the price, meeting space, sleeping rooms, food and beverage, and other factors.

The hotel marketer can render assistance to the buyer in this phase. Often, the buyer is unaware of the benefits of various product features. Alert marketers can help buyers define their companies' needs and show how their hotel can satisfy them.

3. Product Specification

Once the general requirements have been determined, the specific requirements for the meeting can be developed. For example, a meeting might require 20 sleeping rooms, a meeting room for 25 set up classroom style with a whiteboard and overhead projector, and a separate room for lunch. For larger meetings with an exhibit area, the information need becomes more complex. Information often requested includes availability of water, ceiling heights, door widths, security, and procedures for receiving and storing materials prior to the event. A salesperson must be prepared to answer their prospective client's questions about their hotel's capabilities.

4. Supplier Search

The buyer now tries to identify the most appropriate hotels. The buyer can examine trade directories, do a computer search, or phone familiar hotels. Hotels that qualify may receive a site visit from the meeting planner, who eventually will develop a short list of qualified suppliers.

5. Proposal Solution

Once the meeting planner has drawn up a short list of suppliers, qualified hotels will be invited to submit proposals. Thus hotel marketers must be skilled in researching, writing, and presenting proposals. These should be marketing oriented, not simply technical documents. They should position their company's capabilities and resources so that they stand out from the competition. Many hotels have developed videos for this purpose.

6. Supplier Selection

In this stage, members of the buying center review the proposals and move toward selection. They conduct an analysis of the hotel, considering physical facilities, the hotel's ability to deliver service, and the professionalism of its employees. Frequently, the buying center specifies desired supplier attributes and suggests their relative importance. In general, meeting planners consider the following attributes in making their selection of a location:

- Sleeping rooms
- Meeting rooms
- Food and beverage
- Billing procedures
- Check-in/check-out
- Staff

The buying center may attempt to negotiate with preferred suppliers for better prices and terms before making the final selection. There are several ways the hotel marketer can counter the request for a lower price. For example, the dates can be moved from a high demand period to a need period for the hotel or menus can be changed. The marketer can cite the value of the services the buyer now receives, especially where services are superior to competitors.

7. Order-routine Specification

The buyer now writes the final order with the chosen hotels, listing the technical specifications of the meeting. The hotel will respond by offering the buyer a formal contract. The contract will specify cutoff dates for room blocks, the date when the hotel will release the room block for sale to other guests, and minimum guarantees for food and beverage functions. Many hotels and restaurants have turned what should have been a profitable banquet into a loss by not having or enforcing minimum guarantees.

8. Performance Review

The buyer does postpurchase evaluation of the product. During this phase the buyer will determine if the product meets the buyer's specifications and if the buyer will purchase from the company again. It is important for hotels to have at least daily meetings with a meeting planner to make sure everything is going well and to correct those things that did not go well. This manages the buyer's perceived service and helps to avoid a negative postpurchase evaluation by the buyer.

GROUP BUSINESS MARKETS

One of the most important types of organizational business is group business. It is important for marketing managers to understand the differences between a group market and a consumer market. The group business market is often more sophisticated and requires more technical information than the consumer market. Many group markets book more than a year in advance. During this time, cognitive dissonance can develop; thus marketers must keep in contact with the buyer to assure them that they made the right decision in choosing the seller's hotel.

There are four main categories of group business: conventions, association meetings, corporate meetings, and the SMERF (social, military, educational, religious, and fraternal organizations) groups. Figure 8-2 shows the attendance at three types of functions, while Figure 8-3 gives the number of functions held. From these figures, we can see that conventions attract large numbers, but that meetings occur much more frequently than conventions. There are about 100 meetings held for each convention. Nine hundred people attend the average convention, 70 people attend the average corporate meeting, and 90 people attend the average association meeting. When choosing a hotel, an important consideration for a meeting planner is whether the hotel can house the participants. Most hotels have the potential of attracting hundreds of small meetings, while larger hotels can attract conventions. Group business is a very important segment for most hotels. Successful hotels know which groups to

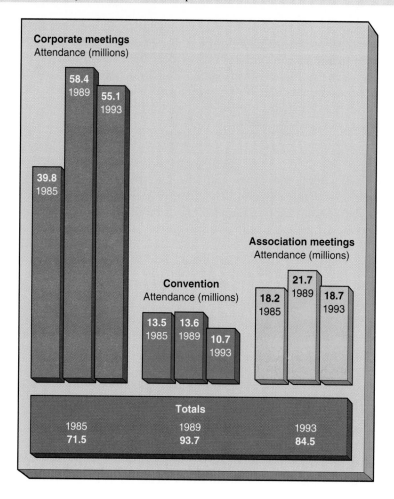

Figure 8-2
Meeting attendance.

attract, how to use group business to fill need dates, and how to sell groups on the hotel's benefits, rather than just price.

Conventions

Conventions are a specialty market requiring extensive meeting facilities. They are usually the annual meeting of an association and include general sessions, committee meetings, and special-interest sessions. A trade show is often an important part of an annual convention. Hotels with convention facilities, such as the Chicago Hyatt or the Atlanta Marriott Marquis, can house small and mid-sized conventions. Conventions that use a major facility, such as the Jacob Javitts Convention Center in New York, often have tens of thousands of delegates. They are called citywide conventions, because hotels throughout the city house their delegates.

Associations usually select convention sites 2 to 5 years in advance, with some large conventions planned 10 to 15 years before the event. June is the most popular month for conventions, followed by May, March, April, July, and August.[7] Some associations prefer to have their conventions in the same city year after year, while others prefer to move to a different area of the country each year.

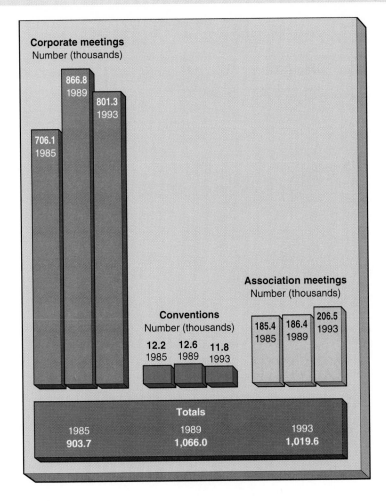

Figure 8-3
Number of meetings.

A convention can be a major source of income for the sponsoring organization. Registration fees and sales of exhibition space are major sources of revenue. The price that can be charged for exhibition space is related to the number of attendees. When choosing a convention location, an association looks for sites that will be both accessible and attractive to members. Balancing the annual budget depends on a good turnout.

Convention planners listed the following as the most important factors in choosing a destination: availability of hotels and facilities, ease of transportation, transportation costs, distance from attendees, climate, recreation, and sights and cultural activities. The most important attributes of the hotel are meeting rooms, rates, food quality, sleeping rooms, support services, billing procedures, check-in/check-out, staff assignment, exhibit space, and previous experience.[8] Note that food quality is very important to the convention planner. Exceptional banquets, out-of-the-ordinary cocktail receptions, and unique coffee breaks can be a point of differentiation at a convention, something the attendees will discuss with colleagues. On the other hand, poor food and poor service can generate negative feelings about the convention among the participants. Support services must be available when needed. A nonfunctioning VCR must be repaired or replaced quickly

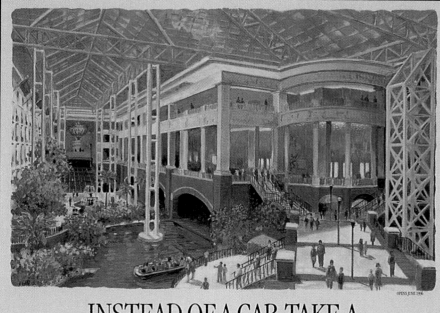

INSTEAD OF A CAB, TAKE A RIVERBOAT TO YOUR NEXT MEETING.

Imagine traveling a winding river by flatboat in our 4.5-acre atrium, with a 600,000-square-foot convention center just a stone's throw away. Now imagine it all, and more, under one roof.

Introducing The Delta at Opryland Hotel Convention Center-- a spectacular glass-domed environment soaring 15 stories in the air, offering everything from meeting and exhibit space to restaurants and shops. With The Delta's completion, in the summer of 1996, Opryland Hotel

will offer the meeting and trade show industry 600,000 square feet of dedicated exhibit and meeting facilities, five ballrooms, over 85 breakout rooms and 2,870 guest rooms and suites. It will be the world's largest convention center in a hotel, yet one that can still bring versatility, convenience and accessibility to groups of any size. You see, creating a dedicated meeting environment was, and still is, our main goal.

Few destinations can meet the demands of the meeting and trade

show industry, much less exceed them. We're proud to say we do both.

For more information, and to receive our convention brochure, write or call Jerry Wayne, Vice President of Marketing, or Kent Wasmuth, Vice President of Sales, at 2800 Opryland Drive, Nashville, Tennessee 37214, (615) 871-5824, FAX (615) 871-5843.

OPRYLAND HOTEL CONVENTION CENTER

A GAYLORD ENTERTAINMENT COMPANY

THE DELTA FEATURES A 55,465-SQ.-FT. BALLROOM AND OVER 300,000 SQ. FT. IN DEDICATED EXHIBIT FACILITIES.

The most important attribute of a hotel for a convention planner is meeting space. This advertisement introduces planners to Opryland's new addition. The copy focuses on meeting space. Courtesy of Opryland Hotel Convention Center, A Gaylord Entertainment Company.

to ensure that the presenter's flow is not interrupted. The author once attended a convention at which two advertising executives had been flown in to give a presentation. When they turned on the slide projector, it would not work. The hotel was unable to resolve the problem, and after about 20 minutes the presentation was canceled.

Many hotels now contract with independent audiovisual (AV) companies to supply and maintain this equipment. In large hotels AV companies will have an office in the hotel to store equipment and house technicians.

For large meetings, AV companies will have on-site technicians to remain with the group during the meeting to correct problems as they occur, thus ensuring that speaker presentations proceed as planned.

Billing procedures are also important to convention planners. Billing can create problems for hotels who take it for granted and do not have a customer-oriented accounting department. Professional meeting planners want a bill that is understandable, accurate, and delivered in a timely manner. Without these characteristics, the bill can be a nightmare. Important attributes for a convention planner other than facilities and rates are food quality, billing procedures, and the professionalism and attention of the hotel's staff.

Convention Bureaus. Convention bureaus are nonprofit marketing organizations that help hotels sign conventions and meetings. These organizations are often supported by a hotel or sales tax and are run by Chambers of Commerce, Visitor Bureaus, or city and county governments. They are often one of the first sources of information for a convention or meeting planner. A hotel relying on meeting business for a significant portion of its occupancy should have a good working relationship with the convention bureau, which includes active membership in the organization.

Association Meetings

Associations sponsor many types of meetings, including regional, special interest, educational, and board meetings. For example, the American Marketing Association has chapters in many large cities. These chapters gather once a month, usually at a luncheon or dinner meeting. The American Marketing Association sponsors or cosponsors educational meetings. The AMA also has special-interest meetings, such as the marketing educators meeting held every August and February. Every major association schedules scores of meetings held throughout the year in various locations.

The most important attributes of a location for an association meeting planner are availability of hotel and facilities, ease of transportation, distance from attendees, and transportation costs. Climate, recreation, and cultural activities are not as important as they are to the convention market, because the meeting itself is the major draw. In selecting a hotel, the association meeting planner looks for food quality, rates, meeting rooms, billing procedures, and attributes similar to the convention planner except for exhibition space.[9] Notice that for the association meeting planner, food and beverage are the most important attributes.

Membership in the American Society of Association Executives (ASAE) is beneficial for hotels actively pursuing association business. It provides an opportunity to network with association executives and is a source of information on national and local associations. Many of the hotel's corporate clients are also members of trade associations. These customers can become ambassadors for the hotel at their trade association meetings.

Members voluntarily attend association meetings. The hotel should work with meeting planners to make the destination seem as attractive as possible. Making sure the meeting planner is aware of local attractions, offering suggestions for spousal activities, and assisting in the development of after-convention activities can be useful to the hotel and the meeting planner. It is important to market both the destination and the hotel.

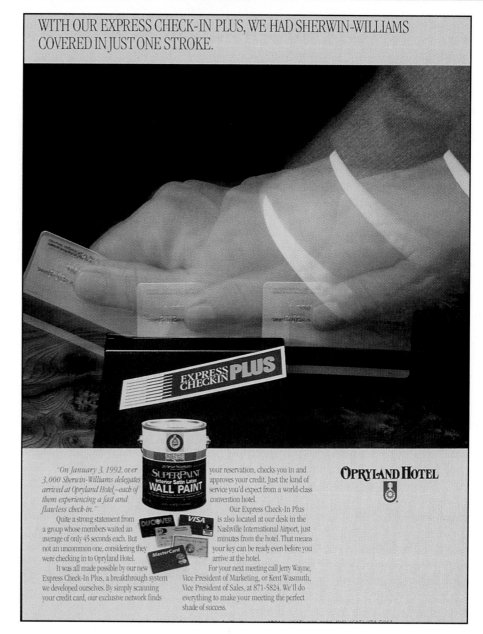

Opryland developed a system to avoid the long check-in lines often associated with meetings. Courtesy of Opryland Hotel Convention Center, A Gaylord Entertainment Company.

Corporate Meetings

For employees of a company, a corporate meeting is a command performance. They are directed to attend the meeting without choice. One implication of required attendance is a short lead time. Because corporations do not have to develop and implement a marketing plan to gain attendees, they often plan meetings with a few weeks lead time.

The corporation's major concern is that the meeting be productive and accomplish the company's objectives. Types of corporate meetings include training, management, and planning. Another type of corporate meeting is the incentive meeting, which will be discussed later.

To a corporate meeting planner, the most important attributes in the choice of a site are the availability of hotels, ease of transportation, transportation costs, and distance from the attendees. The most important factors in the choice of a hotel are food quality, meeting rooms, rates, sleeping rooms, support service, and billing procedures. Corporate meeting planners want to ensure that meetings are productive and that the corporation gets good value for the money it spends. Their success depends on planning smooth-running meetings. Hotels interested in capturing and retaining corporate meeting business must make sure that meeting rooms are adequate and properly set up. Because meeting planners want attendees to be comfortable, sleeping rooms are important to them. They are also concerned about the quality of food. Recreation facilities may also be important. In a multiday technical meeting, the interaction of the participants outside the formal meetings is valuable. Golf or tennis can be used to encourage participants to interact on a social basis and break up the monotony of the classroom sessions. Likewise, an evening outing to an area restaurant or sporting or cultural event can serve as an enjoyable break for participants.

Corporate culture also plays an important part in the choice of a hotel. Hotel salespeople must develop an understanding of the client's corporate culture to gain insight into benefits the hotel can offer. Some companies feel meetings should be austere, rather than lavish. Such companies may feel that they are setting an example for their employees, encouraging them by example to spend money wisely. Others view meetings as a time for employees to relax and enjoy themselves, a well-deserved break. Companies that believe meetings should both educate and rejuvenate employees and build their enthusiasm toward the company are willing to spend more money on food and beverage, entertainment, and deluxe hotel facilities.

Incentive Travel. Incentive travel, a unique subset of corporate group business, is a reward participants receive for achieving or exceeding a goal. Companies give awards for both individual and team performance. For instance, the employees of the best performing region might be recognized. Since travel serves as the reward, participants must perceive the destination and the hotel as something special. The Caribbean, Hawaii, Europe, and resort destinations within the continental United States are common incentive travel destinations. Incentive trips are longer than meetings and often last from 5 to 7 days. Winners of incentive trips sometimes receive a cash deposit to their account that can be used for charges to their account or services provided through the hotel, such as rental cars. For example, participants in an incentive trip sponsored by Revlon for the best regional sales performance received a $500 credit on their hotel bill that could be spent as they wished. In such cases, the participants spend freely in the hotel's restaurants and bars, often supplementing the credit with their own money. Thus incentive travel can be very profitable for a hotel.

Incentive travel planners usually determine the budget on a per person basis. It is important for hotel salespeople to recognize that incentive meeting planners work on a per person cost, since certain costs may not be proportional. For example, a meeting room may cost $7.50 per person for 50 people, but the cost can be reduced to $4.00 per person for 100 people. Likewise, the entertainment for a gala banquet may cost $2000. If 100 people attend, this is $20 per person. If 200 attend, the cost is reduced to $10 per person. When the meeting planner is thinking in per person costs, the hotel salesperson must also think in per person costs.[10]

Incentive travel is handled in house or by incentive houses, travel agencies, consultants, and travel fulfillment firms that handle only the travel arrangements. The trend is moving away from in-house planners to incentive houses, fulfillment houses, and travel agencies.[11] One reason for the shift is that outside organizations specializing in incentive travel often buy blocks of airline seats and hotel rooms. As a result, they can put together packages more efficiently than in-house planners. Incentive houses usually provide a choice of several locations to the company, so the ultimate choice of location is made by the company, even when it uses an incentive house. The hotel must work with both the incentive house and the decision makers within the company.

SMERF

SMERF stands for social, military, educational, religious, and fraternal organizations. This group of specialty markets has a common price-sensitive thread. The majority of the functions sponsored by these organizations are paid for by the individual, and sometimes the fees are not tax deductible. As a result, participants are usually price conscious. They want a low room rate and often find the food and beverage within the hotel too expensive, preferring to eat elsewhere or purchase food and eat in their room. Many groups within this category do not make use of the hotel beverage outlets.

On the positive side, SMERFs are willing to be flexible to ensure a lower room rate. They are willing to meet during off season or weekends. Weekends are often preferred, because most participants attend meetings during their free time. Thus SMERFS provide good filler business during off-peak times.

Segmentation of Group Markets by Purpose of the Meeting

Besides dividing group markets into convention, association, corporate, and SMERF, they also can be broken into the purpose of the meeting. Four major purposes are conventions and conferences typically held by associations and seminars and meetings held by both associations and corporations. A matrix describing some of the critical sales decision variables for these types of gatherings is given in Table 8-1. A discussion of major sale segments of the group market now follows.

DEALING WITH MEETING PLANNERS

When negotiating with meeting planners, it is important to try to develop a win/win relationship. Meeting planners like to return to the same property. Jim Jones, president of James E. Jones Associates, states, "For me, prior successful experience is the number-one factor in choosing a site. Knowing the property takes away most of the anxiety. I know what the hotel can and cannot do, and I know that they're familiar with the idiosyncrasies of my client... I never book a hotel if I plan to use it once."[12]

Not all meetings are large. There are thousands of meetings held with less than 20 attendees. Courtesy of Best Western International, Inc.

Discussions over price can drive the meeting planner and the hotel sales executive apart or it can bring them together. One successful technique for negotiating with a meeting planner is to determine the group's requirements in detail and work out a package based on needs and budget. Some meeting planners try to negotiate every item separately, starting with

Table 8-1

Decision Variable Matrix—Group Markets

SALES DECISION VARIABLES	CONVENTIONS	CONFERENCES	SEMINARS	MEETINGS
Decision makers	Many: committees, chapter presidents, high-ranking officers	Conference organizer meeting planner	Seminar organizer The boss Secretary	Boss, secretary, regional manager, meeting planner
Decision influencers	Many	Limited	Limited	Few
Degree of politicalization	Highly political	Somewhat political	Personal	Highly personal
Decision time	Years	One year or less	Months	Short time, sometimes tomorrow
Customer price sensitivity	Very	Somewhat	Somewhat	Not highly price sensitive
Personal service sensitivity	Low	Moderate	High	Extreme
Opportunity for upsell	Low	Moderate	Moderate	High
Team selling opportunity	Yes, definitely	Sometimes	Probably not	no
Special advertising promotion	Yes, definitely	Usually no	No	No
International versus local	International, yes definitely	International, possible	International, probably not	Usually not but opportunities exist (Board of Directors)
Repeat sales opportunity	Long time, poor	Moderate time	Yes	Definitely
Need for personal sales call (Travel)	Probably yes	Probably no	Probably no	Yes and no

This matrix reflects the general nature of sales decision variables within the group market. Exceptions can and do exist.

the room rate. Then they choose a $35 banquet and try to negotiate the price to $25. In this scenario, every line item becomes a point of contention between the meeting planner and the hotel salesperson.

Taking a consultative approach is much more effective. If the hotel knows that the meeting planner wants to spend $25 for dinner, the chef can develop alternatives within this price range, suggesting something the attendees will enjoy, and the hotel can produce at a profit and sell for $25. The hotel gains a profitable meeting and the meeting stays within the planner's budget.

The hotel salesperson must remember that most group rates are noncommissionable. Meeting planners sometimes turn meetings over to travel agents, who book about 5% of all corporate meetings. If the meeting planner does so without understanding that the rate is noncommissionable, problems can arise when the travel agent tries to collect a commission. If the rates are to be commissionable, it should be determined during the negotiation process. It is also common for hotels to give one complimentary room night for every 50 room nights that the group produces, another point of negotiation. Suites are usually counted as two rooms. Thus a suite for three nights would be the equivalent of six room nights. When a hotel has a smaller meeting room that it will not be able to sell during a proposed meeting, it can be used in the negotiation process as a boardroom or a space for the meeting manager to work. The hotel salesperson must look for items that will create value for the meeting planner without creating costs or sacrificing revenue for the hotel.

Many associations have a president, elected from the membership, and a professional executive, often called the executive vice-president. In such case, the executive vice-president usually sets up the meeting or supervises a meeting planner. In larger associations there may be a paid executive director, a convention manager, and one or more meeting managers who handle the association's meetings. In some associations the elected officers like to get involved in the selection of sites and hotels for meetings or conventions. To make matters worse, last year's president usually becomes the chairman of the association's board of directors. The chairman of the board can hold great power in the association, as can other past presidents. It is important for the salesperson to find out who is involved in the decision-making process, both officially and unofficially. Gatekeepers can give useful insights into the decision-making process within the organization.

A major shift in food and beverage is toward lighter, healthier meals, particularly at lunch. Salad and cold-cut buffets make a nice lunch break. Pasta was once an indicator of a low budget. Today, it is considered a healthy and enjoyable meal. Breaks now include flavored mineral water, yogurt, and fruit, instead of, or in addition to, cookies and brownies. Health clubs have become more important as meeting attendees become more health conscious.

Meeting planners may be divided into three levels of professionalism.[13] The *facilitator* makes up 50% to 60% of meeting planners. This category includes the secretary who calls the hotel to reserve rooms and the salesperson who is given responsibility for setting up the regional sales meeting. The facilitator usually has other responsibilities, in addition to setting meetings. The *meeting manager* is a professional meeting planner. Meeting managers make up about 25% of the meeting planners. The *meeting administrator* is a highly qualified meeting planner. Most have advanced degrees and years of experience. Meeting administrators often earn more than $100,000 per year. As you can see, there is a great deal of difference in the level of expertise of those who plan meetings.

When the vice-president of sales asks a junior salesperson to organize a sales meeting, the salesperson is usually unsure of how to proceed with newly assigned and unfamiliar tasks. On the other hand, meeting administrators often know the business as well as the hotel salesperson. Salespeople should listen to the meeting administrator to understand their requirements. Sometimes they will know exactly what they want and simply desire a quote for the meeting according to their specifications. If this is the case, a salesperson trying to arbitrarily alter their specifications can appear unprofessional and lose the meeting administrator's business. For example, a hotel salesperson altered the meeting administrator's menu and developed a quotation based on the altered menus. The meeting administrator was planning a series of training sessions to be presented at various locations throughout the United States and had developed menus to meet group needs. This uninvited intrusion by the hotel salesperson infuriated the meeting administrator, who then proceeded to a competitive hotel.

Most meeting planners maintain a history of the group for the purpose of planning future meetings. This includes past dates, locations, and attendance figures. They also have evaluations of past meetings. A salesperson can gain valuable information by asking questions about past conferences. These questions can provide insight into room pickups, attendance at banquets, past problems with a hotel, and what their members have enjoyed. In addition to information volunteered by the meeting planner, the salesperson should interview hotels that hosted the conference in past years.

Consider the following expectations of meeting planners.[14] Meeting planners want their calls returned the same day they are received. When they ask about the availability of meeting space, they expect a response the same day and a complete proposal in 5 days. They want check-in and check-out to last no more than 4 minutes. Most meeting planners want their bill within 1 week of the event, while 25% want it within two days. Planners feel that hotel management should empower the convention service manager to solve their problems. They do not want to wait while the convention service manager checks with a superior to find out how to handle a problem. The top four amenities desired by meeting planners are nonsmoking rooms, 24-hour room service, a gift shop, and a fitness center.

Ultimately, when dealing with group business, the hotel has to please both the meeting planner and the meeting planner's clients. These clients include those attending the conference, association executives, and the president or senior officer of a corporation. Jonathan Tisch, president and CEO of Loews Hotel states, "What we're looking to do is to create a win/win situation. If the senior officer is happy, then the planner's happy, and if the planner's happy, we've done our job."[15]

A nongroup form of organizational business is the individual business traveler. Most hotels offer a corporate rate, which is intended to provide an incentive for corporations to use the hotel. Because of competitive pressures, most hotels have dropped the qualification requirements for their basic corporate rate, offering it now to any business person who requests the corporate rate. To provide an incentive system for heavy users, hotels developed a second set of corporate rates. The basic corporate rate is about 10% to 20% below the hotel's rack rate, while the contract is a negotiated rate, usually 10% to 40% below the hotel's rack rate. It often includes other benefits besides a discounted rate. The following are examples of corporate rate programs:

Days Inn

Inn-Credible Card Club
No minimum requirement
10% to 30% off rack rates, free coffee and paper

Corpo Rate
Total travel budget must exceed $1 million a year.
Rate negotiated on an individual basis, based on the amount of business Days Inn will receive.

Ritz-Carlton

Executive Reservation Service
Must provide 48 reservations per year.
Discount of 10% to 20% off rack rates, room upgrades, free stay for companions, newspaper, shoe shine, fitness center, priority room availability.

Sheraton

Suresaver Business
No minimum
Up to 30% off rack rates

SET (Sheraton Executive Traveler)
Must book 100 room nights per year
Up to a 30% discount off rack rates

Global Preference
Must be a multinational corporation providing Sheraton Hotels in multiple nations with a volume of 5000 room nights.
Up to a 40% discount off rack rates, enrollment in Sheraton Club International (provides free upgrades, newspaper, 4 P.M. check out, and hotel points toward free stays at Sheraton hotels).[16]

The corporate business traveler is a sought-after segment. Although the corporate contract rate is a discounted rate, it is higher than group rates. In addition to paying a good rate, the business traveler is also on an expense account and makes use of the hotel's restaurants, health club, laundry, and business center facilities.

The competition for business travelers, once limited to mid-class and luxury hotels, has spread to limited-service hotels. Budget and economy hotels now have a 34.5% market share of rooms generated by the business traveler. The strong showing of economy hotels in this segment can be attributed to the upgrading of amenities found in economy hotels and businesses needing to cut costs to remain competitive. Companies, who a few years ago would have not thought of putting their people in an economy brand, are now using economy brands such as Red Rood Inns. These companies realize they can save thousands of dollars by purchasing less expensive accommodations.

The Corporate Travel Manager

Larger companies have corporate traveler management programs run by the company or in-house branches of a travel agency. In larger companies the travel managers set per diem rates, specifying the amount a company traveler can spend on food and beverage. Often these rates are set at different levels, with the per diem amount increasing as one moves up in the corporation. It is important to find out what a company's per diem rates are to determine whether the hotel is in the company's price range and what level of manager the hotel can expect to attract. The hotel can use this information to determine the volume the company will give them. For example, if the per diem for a company's salespeople is in the hotel's rate range, the hotel can expect more volume than it could expect if only the executive management falls within the price range.

In-house travel agencies, or in-plants, offer the company the advantage of negotiating leverage. A business represented through an in-plant may have only 100 room nights a year in New York, but the travel agency the in-plant represents may service 10 companies with a total of 1500 room nights in New York. The travel agency can negotiate a rate based on the 1500 room nights and pass this rate along to the individual companies. The hotel compensates in-plants by either straight commissions, monthly fees, or a combination of a fee and commission.[17]

Chapter Review

I.   The Nature of Organizational Buyers. Their purchases often involve large sums of money, complex technical, economic considerations, and interactions among many people at all levels of the organization. Buyer and seller are often very dependent on each other.

II.   Participants in the Organizational Buying Process.
    1) Users. Users are those who will use the product or service.
    2) Influencers. Influencers directly influence the buying decision but do not themselves make the final decision.
    3) Deciders. Deciders select product requirements and suppliers.
    4) Approvers. Approvers authorize the proposed actions of deciders or buyers.

5) Buyers. Buyers have formal authority for selecting suppliers and arranging the terms of purchase.

6) Gatekeepers. Gatekeepers have the power to prevent sellers or information from reaching members of the buying center.

III. **Major Influences on Organizational Buyers**

    1) Environmental Factors. Organizational buyers are heavily influenced by the current and expected economic environment.

    2) Organizational Factors. Each organization has specific objectives, policies, procedures, organizational structures, and systems related to buying.

    3) Interpersonal Factors. The buying center usually includes several participants with differing levels of interest, authority, and persuasiveness.

    4) Individual Factors. Each participant in the buying decision process has personal motivations, perceptions, and preferences. The participant's age, income, education, professional identification, personality, and attitudes toward risk all influence the participants in the buying process.

IV. **The Organizational Buying Process**

    1) Problem Recognition. The buying process begins when someone in the company recognizes a problem or need that can be met by acquiring a good or a service.

    2) General Need Description. The buyer goes on to determine the requirements of the product.

    3) Product Specifications. Once the general requirements have been determined, the specific requirements for the product can be developed.

    4) Supplier Search. The buyer now tries to identify the most appropriate suppliers.

    5) Proposal Solicitation. Qualified suppliers will be invited to submit proposals. Skilled research, writing, and presentation are required.

    6) Supplier Selection. Once the meeting planner has drawn up a short list of suppliers, qualified hotels will be invited to submit proposals.

    7) Order-routine Specification. The buyer writes the final order, listing the technical specification. The supplier responds by offering the buyer a formal contract.

    8) Performance Review. The buyer does postpurchase evaluation of the product. During this phase the buyer will determine if the product meets the buyer's specifications and if the buyer will purchase from the company again.

V. **The Group Markets Segments**

    1) Conventions. Conventions are usually the annual meeting of an association and include general sessions, committee meetings, and special-interest sessions. A trade show is often an important part of an annual convention.

    2) Association Meetings. Associations sponsor many types of meetings, including regional, special-interest, educational, and board meetings.

    3) Corporate Meetings. A corporate meeting is a command performance for employees of a company. The corporation's major concern is that the meeting be productive and accomplish the company's objectives.

    4) Incentive Travel. Incentive travel, a unique subset of corporate group business, is a reward participants receive for achieving or exceeding a goal.

5) SMERF Groups. SMERF stands for social, military, educational, religious and fraternal organizations. This group of specialty markets has a common price sensitive thread.

VI. Dealing with Meeting Planners. When negotiating with meeting planners, it is important to try to develop a win/win relationship. Meeting planners like to return to the same property.

VII. The Corporate Account and Travel Manager. A nongroup form of organizational business is the individual business traveler. Most hotels offer a corporate rate, which is intended to provide an incentive for corporations to use the hotel.

DISCUSSION QUESTIONS

1. What is derived demand? Why is it important for marketers to understand this concept?

2. The buying center consists of six roles. Why is it important for marketers to understand these roles?

3. Discuss the major environmental influences that affect the purchase meeting space by IBM for its sales meetings.

4. How does organizational buying differ from buying by a consumer?

5. How can a hotel sales representative identify who is responsible for purchasing meeting space, banquets, and rooms for corporate travelers in the corporate headquarters of an insurance company?

KEY TERMS

Approvers Approvers authorize the proposed actions of deciders or buyers.

Buyers Buyers have formal authority for selecting suppliers and arranging the terms of purchase.

Buying center All those individuals and groups who participate in the purchasing and decision-making process, who share common goals and the risks arising from the decisions.

Convention A convention is a specialty market requiring extensive meeting facilities. It is usually the annual meeting of an association and includes general sessions, committee meetings, and special-interest sessions.

Convention bureau A convention bureau is a non-profit marketing organization that promotes a city or region to the conventions and meetings market.

Corporate meeting A meeting held by a corporation for its employees.

Decider Deciders select product requirements and suppliers.

Derived demand Organizational demand that ultimately comes from (derives from) the demand for consumer goods.

Gatekeepers Gatekeepers have the power to prevent sellers or information from reaching members of the buying center.

General need description The stage in the industrial buying process in which the company describes the general characteristics and quantity of a needed item.

Incentive travel Incentive travel is a reward participants receive for achieving or exceeding a goal.

Influencers Influencers directly influence the buying decision but do not themselves make the final decision.

Order-routine specification The stage of the industrial buying process in which the buyer writes the final order with the chosen supplier(s), listing the technical specifications, quantity needed, expected time of delivery, return policies, warranties, and so on.

Organizational buying The decision-making

process by which formal organizations establish the need for purchased products and services and identify, evaluate, and choose among alternative brands and suppliers.

Performance review The stage of the industrial buying process in which the buyer rates its satisfaction with suppliers, deciding whether to continue, modify, or drop the relationship.

Problem recognition The stage of the industrial buying process in which someone in the company recognizes a problem or need that can be met by acquiring a good or a service.

Product specification The stage of the industrial buying process in which the buying organization decides on and specifies the best technical product characteristics for a needed item.

SMERF SMERF stands for social, military, educational, religious, and fraternal organizations. This group of specialty markets has a common price-sensitive thread.

Supplier search The stage of the industrial buying process in which the buyer tries to find the best vendors.

Supplier selection The stage of the industrial buying process in which the buyer receives proposals and selects a supplier or suppliers.

Users Those who will use the product or service.

REFERENCES

1. For discussions of similarities and differences in consumer and business marketing, see EDWARD F. FERN AND JAMES R. BROWN, "The Industrial/Consumer Marketing Dichotomy: A Case of Insufficient Justification," *Journal of Marketing* (Fall 1984), pp. 68–77; AND RON J. KORNAKOVICH, "Consumer Methods Work for Business Marketing: Yes; No," *Marketing News* (November 21, 1988), pp. 4, 13–14.

2. FEDERICK E. WEBSTER JR. AND YORAM WIND, *Organizational Buying Behavior*, Englewood Cliffs, NJ: Prentice Hall, 1972, pp. 33–37.

3. Ibid., pp. 78–80.

4. See MURRAY HARDING, "Who Really Makes the Purchasing Decision?" *Industrial Marketing* (September 1966), p. 76. This point of view is further developed in ERNEST DICHTER, "Industrial Buying Is Based on Same 'Only Human' Emotional Factors That Motivate Consumer Market's Housewife," *Industrial Marketing* (February 1973), pp. 14–16.

5. WEBSTER AND WIND, *Organizational Buying Behavior*, pp. 33–37.

6. PATRICK J. ROBINSON, CHARLES W. FARIS, AND YORAM WIND, *Industrial Buying Behavior and Creative Marketing* (Boston: Allyn & Bacon, 1967), p. 14.

7. PENNY C. DOTSON, *Introduction to Meeting Management* (Birmingham, Ala.: Professional Convention Management Association, 1988), p. 17.

8. LARRY LETICH, "Let's Make a Deal," *Meeting and Conventions—Meeting Market Report* (March 1, 1992), p. 123.

9. Ibid.

10. MARGARET SHAW, *The Group Market: What It Is and How to Sell It* (Washington, D.C.: The Foundation of the Hotel Sales and Marketing Association, 1986), pp. 45–49.

11. PENNY C. DOTSON, *Introduction to Meeting Management* (Professional Convention Management Association: Birmingham, Alabama, 1988).

12. LETICH, "Let's Make a Deal," p. 127.

13. RICHARD A. HILDRETH, *The Essentials of Meeting Management* (Prentice Hall: Englewood Cliffs, N.J., 1990).

14. HOWARD FEIERTAG, "New Survey Reveals Meeting Planners' Priorities," *Hotel and Motel Management* (November 23, 1992), p. 11.

15. JAMES P. ABBEY, *Hospitality Sales and Advertising* (East Lansing, Mich.: Educational Institute of the American Hotel & Motel Association, 1993), page 569.

16. LISA CASEY WEISS, "How Different Hotel Rate Programs Stack Up," *Business Travel News* (July 26, 1993), pp. 9–16.

17. ROBERT C. LEWIS, RICHARD E. CHAMBERS, AND HARSHA E. CHACKO, *Marketing Leadership in Hospitality* (New York: Van Nostrand Reinhold, 1995), p. 259.

Market Segmentation, Targeting, and Positioning

*I*n 1972 the Mardi Gras, *an old transatlantic cruise ship, went on its maiden voyage for Carnival Cruise Lines. Carnival was hosting 300 travel agents on the* Mardi Gras, *hoping to set up a distribution network that would fill up its cruises in the coming years. The* Mardi Gras *ran aground, sinking the hopes of its owners. It was not until 1975 that the ship sailed again. Ted Arison, a founder of Norwegian Cruise Lines, purchased Carnival for $1, assumed the company's debt, and quickly turned it into a profitable venture.*

The tired Mardi Gras *could not compete directly with the luxury cruise liners of Royal Viking, Holland America, Princess, Sitmar, Royal Caribbean, and Norwegian Caribbean Lines. The* Mardi Gras *was older and less efficient than its competition. To reduce fuel consumption, the ship had to operate at slower speeds, making fewer port calls than liners owned by competitors. Arison was able to convert this obstacle into a new approach for marketing cruises. Instead of promoting exotic ports of call, his company created the idea of the "fun ship" and promoted it. The fun ship had night clubs, a casino, shows, 24-hour room service, and enough activities to keep passengers busy. The ship itself became the destination. Carnival also went after less sophisticated first-time cruise passengers, forging a new market segment that included families with household incomes of $25,000 to $35,000. While other cruise lines competed for the older, more sophisti-*

cated market, with incomes of $50,000 plus, Carnival brought cruising to the blue-collar market. Its 3- and 4-day cruises allowed the first-time passenger to try cruising without spending a great deal of time or money.

Carnival had identified a new market for cruises. Recognizing that only 5% of the population had at that time taken a cruise, Carnival went after the segment that the other cruise lines were ignoring—the middle and lower-middle class. Carnival positioned itself as a destination vacation, competing against other vacation spots, such as Disneyland or Hawaii, rather than other cruise lines. Carnival defined its market as the 150 million people who take vacations, rather than the 10 million people who take cruises. By identifying a market opportunity and targeting a segment that the competition had neglected, Carnival was able to grow into the largest cruise line in the world.[1]

Chapter 9 shows different approaches that companies can take to a market in order to best serve customer and company needs.

We begin with an overview of three approaches that companies can take toward a market: **mass marketing, product-variety marketing**, and **target marketing**.

A fuller discussion of target marketing details **market segmentation:** dividing a market into groups that are **measurable, accessible, substantial,** and **actionable.** This can be done in different ways by using **geographic, demographic, psychographic, behavioral,** or other variables.

Next, we explain the process of **market targeting** and the different approaches a company can take, including **undifferentiated, differentiated,** and **concentrated marketing.** We finish the chapter with a discussion of **market positioning strategy** and how companies can position their products for the best **competitive advantage.**

MARKETS

The term market has acquired many meanings over the years. In its original meaning, a market was a physical place where buyers and sellers gathered to exchange goods and services. To an economist, a market is all the buyers and sellers who transact for a good or service. Thus the fast-food market consists of many sellers, such as Burger King, McDonald's, and Kentucky Fried Chicken, and all the consumers who buy fast-food meals. To a marketer, a **market** is the set of all actual and potential buyers of a product.

Organizations that sell to consumers and industrial markets recognize that they cannot appeal to all buyers in those markets, or at least not to all buyers in the same way. Buyers are too numerous, widely scattered, and varied in their needs and buying practices.

Sellers have not always practiced this philosophy. Their thinking passed through three stages:

1. **Mass marketing.** In mass marketing, the seller mass produces, mass distributes, and mass promotes one product to all buyers. At one time McDonald's produced only one size of hamburger for the whole market, hoping it would appeal to everyone. The argument for mass marketing is that it should lead to the lowest costs and prices and create the largest potential market.

2. **Product-variety marketing.** Here the seller produces two or more products that have different features, styles, quality, sizes, and so on. Today, McDonald's offers regular hamburgers, Big Macs, and quarter pounders. The product line is designed to offer variety to buyers, rather than to appeal to different market segments. The argument for product-variety marketing is that consumers have different tastes that vary over time. Consumers seek variety and change.

3. Target marketing. Here the seller identifies market segments, selects one or more, and develops products and marketing mixes tailored to each selected segment. For example, McDonald's developed its salad line to meet the needs of diet-conscious diners.

Today, many companies are moving away from mass marketing and product-variety marketing toward target marketing. Target marketing helps sellers to find better marketing opportunities and allows companies to develop the right product for each target market. Companies can adjust their process, distribution channels, and advertising to reach each market efficiently. Instead of scattering their marketing efforts (the "shotgun" approach), they can focus on buyers who have the greatest purchase interest (the "rifle" approach).

As a result of increasing fragmentation of U.S. mass markets into hundreds of micromarkets, each with different needs and life-styles, target marketing is increasingly taking the form of **micromarketing**. Using micromarketing, companies tailor their marketing programs to the needs and wants of narrowly defined geographic, demographic, psychographic, or behavior segments. The ultimate form of target marketing is **customized marketing** in which the company adapts its offers to the needs of specific customers or buying organizations.

Figure 9-1 shows the three major steps in target marketing. The first is **market segmentation**, dividing a market into distinct groups of buyers who might require separate products and/or marketing mixes. The company identifies different ways to segment the market and develops profiles of the resulting market segments. The second step is **market targeting**, evaluating each segment's attractiveness and selecting one or more of the market segments. The third step is **market positioning**, developing a competitive positioning for the product and an appropriate marketing mix. This chapter will describe the principles of market segmentation, market targeting, and market positioning.

MARKET SEGMENTATION

Markets consist of buyers, and buyers differ in one or more ways. They may differ in their wants, resources, locations, buying attitudes, and buying practices. Any of these variables can be used to segment a market.

Figure 9-1
Steps in segmentation, targeting, and positioning.

Market segmentation	Market targeting	Market positioning
1. Identify bases for segmenting the market 2. Develop profiles of resulting segments	3. Develop measures of segment attractiveness 4. Select the target segment(s)	5. Develop positioning for each target segment 6. Develop marketing mix for each target segment

Segmenting a Market

Figure 9-2 shows a market of six buyers. Each buyer is potentially a separate market with unique needs and wants. Ideally, a seller might design a separate marketing program for each buyer, as illustrated in Figure 9-2b. For example, a small meeting planner company may have only a few major clients and treat them as separate markets. Each client accounts for a significant portion of the company's business; some small meeting planners can survive with as few as 10 good corporate clients. The planner works with each client, developing a unique program for that client.

Most sellers will not find it worthwhile to customize their product for each specific buyer. Instead, the seller looks for broad classes of buyers who differ in their product needs and buying responses. For example, a wholesale tour operator segmenting the pleasure traveler market might find that income groups differ in their wants. In Figure 9-2c, a number (1,2,3) is used to identify each buyer's income class. Segmentation by income results in three segments, the most numerous being income class 1.

On the other hand, the wholesaler may find that younger and older vacationers have different needs. In Figure 9-2d, A and B are used to represent the buyers' age groups. Segmentation by age class results in two segments, each with three buyers.

The wholesaler may prefer to segment the market by both age and income, as in Figure 9-2e, resulting in five segments. As a market is segmented using more characteristics, the seller achieves finer precision, but at the price of multiplying the number of segments and thinning out the populations within each segment.

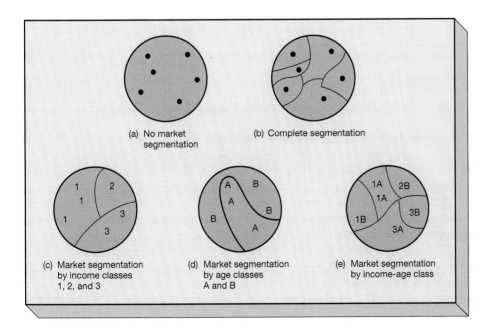

Figure 9-2
Different segmentations in a market.

Bases for Segmenting Consumer Markets

There is no single way to segment a market. A marketer has to try different segmentation variables, alone and in combination, hoping to find the best way to view the market structure. Table 9-1 outlines major variables that might be used in segmenting consumer markets. Here we will look at the major geographic, demographic, psychographic, and behavioristic variables used in segmenting consumer markets.

The restaurant industry offers many examples of segmentation by a variety of variables. "Because each customer group in an eating-out market will want a different product, a restaurant cannot reach out to all customers with equal effectiveness. The restaurant must distinguish the easily accessible consumer groups from those that are hard to reach and the responsive segments from the unresponsive ones. To gain an edge over its competition, a restaurant must examine market segments by identifying one or more subsets of customers within the total market and concentrating its efforts on meeting their needs."[2]

Geographic Segmentation

Geographic segmentation calls for dividing the market into different geographic units, such as nations, states, regions, counties, cities, or neighborhoods. A company decides to operate in one or a few geographical areas or to operate in all, paying attention to geographical differences in needs and wants. For example, General Foods' Maxwell House ground coffee is sold nationally but is flavored regionally. People in the West want stronger coffee than people in the East. Fast-food companies often vary their menus to take regional tastes into account. For example, McDonald's introduced a Texas Burger, a large burger with lettuce, tomato, and the condiments of choice for many Texans—pickles and mustard. One local Texas chain, Whataburger, had been successfully providing Texans with a good pickle and mustard burger. Recognizing the importance of this regional variation, McDonald's developed and introduced a new product for this market.

Within the United States, national fast-food chains such as Burger King, Taco Bell, Wendy's, and McDonald's exist. Despite this powerful competition, a rich variety of regional or local chains continues to thrive, such as Biscuitville, Bojangles, Uncle John Tacos, and The Waffle House. Some may have the potential for national expansion, but others serving regional tastes may find it difficult to reach a national market.

Lodging companies also begin as local or regional firms but seem to have greater flexibility in national expansion. Holiday Inn began as a regional motel company out of Memphis, Tennessee. Motel 8 began in Aberdeen, South Dakota, with original appeal to a midwestern and western market, but expanded well beyond regional boundaries. Others such as La Quinta have not moved into the national market.

Hyatt Hotels recognized the need to modify its product line to meet regional needs. In 1992, Hyatt initiated a program to offer 70% national staples in its menus and the remainder in local dishes. The Four Seasons Hotel in Washington, D.C., become so concerned about offering local cuisine that it contracted with nearby farmers to ensure a supply of local products that were not always available from traditional wholesale vendors.[3]

Table 9-1

**Major Segmentation Variables
for Consumer Markets**

VARIABLE	TYPICAL BREAKDOWN
GEOGRAPHIC	
Region	Pacific, Mountain, West North Central, West South Central, East North Central, East South Central, South Atlantic, Middle Atlantic, New England
City or Metro size	Under 5,000; 5,000–20,000; 20,000–50,000; 50,000–100,000; 100,000–250,000; 250,000–500,000; 500,000–1,000,000; 1,000,000–4,000,000; 4,000,000 or over
Density	Urban, suburban, rural
Climate	Northern, southern
DEMOGRAPHIC	
Age	Under 6, 6–11, 12–19, 20–34, 35–49, 50–64, 65+
Gender	Male, female
Family size	1–2, 3–4, 5+
Family life cycle	Young, single; young, married, no children; young, married, youngest child under 6; young, married, youngest child 6 or over; older, married, with children; older, married, no children under 18; older, single; other
Income	Under $10,000; $10,000–$15,000; $15,000–$20,000; $20,000–$30,000; $30,000–$50,000; $50,000–$100,000; $100,000 and over
Occupation	Professional and technical; managers, officials, and proprietors; clerical, sales; craftspeople, foremen; operatives; farmers; retired; students; housewives; unemployed
Education	Grade school or less; some high school; high school graduate; some college; college graduate
Religion	Catholic, Protestant, Jewish, Muslim, Hindu, other
Race	White, black, Asian
Nationality	American, British, French, German, Italian, Japanese
PSYCHOGRAPHIC	
Social class	Lower lowers, upper lowers, working class, middle class, upper middles, lower uppers, upper uppers
Lifestyle	Straights, swingers, longhairs
Personality	Compulsive, gregarious, authoritarian, ambitious
BEHAVIORAL	
Occasions	Regular occasion, special occasion

(continued)

Table 9-1
Continued

Benefits	Quality, service, economy, speed
User status	Nonuser, ex-user, potential user, first-time user, regular user
Usage rate	Light user, medium user, heavy user
Loyalty status	None, medium, strong, absolute
Readiness stage	Unaware, aware, informed, interested, desirous, intending to buy
Attitude toward product	Enthusiastic, positive, indifferent, negative, hostile

Demographic Segmentation

Demographic segmentation consists of dividing the market into groups based on demographic variables such as age, gender, family life cycle, income, occupation, education, religion, race, and nationality. Demographic factors are the most popular bases for segmenting customer groups. One reason is that consumer needs, wants, and usage rates often vary closely with demographic variables. Another is that demographic variables are easier to measure than most other types of variables. Even when market segments are first defined using other bases, such as personality or behavior, demographic characteristics must be known in order to assess the size of the target market and to reach it efficiently.

Here we will show how certain demographic factors have been used in market segmentation.

Age and Life-cycle Stage.   Consumer needs and wants change with age. Some companies offer different products or marketing strategies to penetrate various age and life-cycle segments. For example, McDonald's offers happy meals that include toys, aimed at young children. These toys are often part of a series, encouraging children to return until they have collected the entire set. The chain has added salads to attract the health-conscious adult market. Appeals to the senior-citizen market have employed advertisements with elderly actors.[4]

American Express focuses much of its marketing attention on the "mature" market since individuals in this age segment account for 70% of the tour industry's bookings. Historic restorations such as Williamsburg and Old Salem receive a large percentage of elderly bus tours. The entire museum and historic sites industry depends heavily on this market segment.

Age and life-cycle variables can be misleading. For example, the Ford Motor Company used buyers' age in developing the target market for its initial Mustang automobile. But when Ford found that the car was being purchased by all age groups, it realized that its target market was not the physiologically young but the psychologically young. Likewise, Southwest Airlines realized that many senior citizens are psychologically young. Their advertisements for senior fares show active older people enjoying themselves.

Gender.   **Gender segmentation** has long been used in marketing clothing, hairdressing, cosmetics, and magazines. It is just beginning to be used in the hotel industry. In 1970, women accounted for less than 1% of all business travelers. Currently, that figure stands at about 40%.[5] Hotel corporations are now taking women into consideration in designing their hotel rooms. Other design changes include lobby bars, fitness facilities, hair dryers, and rooms decorated in lighter colors. While these changes are attractive to women, many are also attractive to men. Hotel corporations are also subtly including more women executives in their advertisements.[6]

Researchers from the University of Guelph discovered that a single woman living in a large Canadian city is more likely than her male counterparts or her married friends to increase her spending in restaurants as a result of a pay increase.[7]

Income.   Income segmentation has long been used by marketers of products and services such as automobiles, boats, clothing, cosmetics, and travel. Other industries have also recognized its possibilities. For example, Suntory, the Japanese liquor company, introduced a scotch selling for $75 to attract high-income drinkers who want the very best. Country clubs often use income to identify potential members for their direct-mail campaigns.

Income does not always predict which customers will buy a given product or service. Some upscale urban restauranteurs opened branches in upper-middle-class suburbs. They were attracted by high suburban house-

The U.S. military gets a daily travel allowance called a per diem. The amount of per diem not spent on lodging can be spent on food and entertainment or saved. Hotels targeting this market offer special military rates. Courtesy of Best Western International, Inc.

BEST WAY TO REPAY THE TROOPS.

Here's a benefit your recruiter didn't tell you about. Best Western gives special rates and packages to military personnel. That means you can get a great night's sleep without surrendering your entire per diem. And you'll find all our locations will pass your inspection. We've spent more than a billion dollars upgrading properties and our tough new standards keep them shipshape.

There are more than 3,400 Best Westerns from the halls of Montezuma to just outside the base. YOUR BEST BET IS A BEST WESTERN.

CALL 1-800-528-1234 FOR RESERVATIONS OR A FREE BEST WESTERN GOVERNMENT RATE DIRECTORY.

© 1994 Best Western International, Inc.

hold incomes. But many had to close their doors. Why? Urban dwellers tend to be singles and couples without children. A large portion of their income is discretionary and their life-style includes frequent dining out. According to the National Restaurant Association, singles spend more than half of their food budget dining out. Married couples spend only 37% of their food budget eating out.[8] Suburbanites spend their money on housing, automobiles, and children. Dining out is reserved for weekends and special occasions. Thus, income alone can be misleading as a segmentation variable.

Income segmentation is commonly believed to be one of the primary variables affecting pricing strategies. Price is not solely determined by income, but there is often a close correlation. The St. Moritz On-The-Park hotel in New York City has combined income and geographical segmentation variables. This hotel charges rates at least half those charged by competitors and appeals heavily to middle-income international travelers.[9]

A study of Singapore hotels showed that income was not as strong a segmentation variable as purpose of the visit.[10] This demonstrates the importance of studying and clearly understanding the relative importance of segmentation variables on a market-by-market approach. It is very dangerous to assume that income or any other segmentation variable will be of equal importance in all markets.

Psychographic Segmentation

Psychographic segmentation divides buyers into different groups based on social class, life-style, and personality characteristics. People in the same demographic group can have very different psychographic profiles.

The Claire Tappan Lodge near Sugar Bowl ski area on the northern shore of Donner Lake was built by the Sierra Club in the 1930s. This lodge appeals to individuals within a common psychographic segment. Guests represent varying ages and income brackets, but all have a common interest in seminars hosted by this cozy lodge, such as outdoor photography, orienteering, and nature.

Social Class.   In Chapter 7 we described the six American social classes and explained that social class has a strong effect on preferences for cars, clothes, home furnishings, leisure activities, reading habits, and retailers. Afternoon tea at the Ritz-Carlton is aimed at the upper-middle and upper classes. A neighborhood pub near a factory targets the working class. The customers of each of these establishments would probably feel uncomfortable in the other establishment.

Life-style.   Chapter 7 also showed the influence of people's life-styles on the goods and services that they buy. Marketers are increasingly segmenting their markets by consumer life-styles. For example, night clubs are designed with certain clientele in mind: young singles wanting to meet the opposite sex, singles wanting to meet the same sex, and couples wanting to avoid the singles bars and enjoy each other's company.

The Kempinski Group of German Hotels selected market segments based on social class and life-style for hotels in New York, Boston, and Washington, D.C. Kempinski decided on a market niche of upscale business travelers who appreciate and can afford smaller European-style hotels with Old World-style service.[11]

Personality.   Marketers also use personality variables to segment markets, endowing their products with personalities that correspond with those of consumers. For example, Southwest Airlines developed a promotion showing seniors having fun scooting around on snowmobiles. The setting of the ad would have been just as appropriate for 20-year-olds. Southwest was appealing to active seniors, who still viewed themselves as young. The airline was appealing to the kid inside all adults.

Behavior Segmentation

In **behavior segmentation**, buyers are divided into groups based on their knowledge, attitude, use, or response to a product. Many marketers believe that behavior variables are the best starting point for building market segments.

Occasions.   Buyers can be grouped according to occasions when they get the idea, make the purchase, or use a product. Occasion segmentation helps firms to build product usage. For example, air travel is triggered by occasions related to business, vacation, or family. Airline advertisements aimed at the business traveler often incorporate service, convenience, and on-time-departure benefits in the offer. Airline marketing aimed at the vacation traveler utilizes price, interesting destinations, and prepackaged vacations. Airline marketing aimed at the family market often shows children traveling alone to visit a relative, under the watchful eye of an airline employee. A message of this nature is particularly relevant to the single-parent segment.

Occasion segmentation can help firms to build product usage. For example, Mother's Day has been promoted as a time to take your mother or wife out to eat. St. Patrick's Day has been promoted as a night of cele-

Caesars Pocono Resorts target the honeymoon market. This room features a two-story champagne glass shaped spa and a heart-shaped tub. Courtesy of Caesars Pocono Resorts.

bration. Monday holidays, such as Labor Day and Memorial Day, have been promoted as times to enjoy a mini vacation. These are examples of occasion marketing.

The honeymoon market represents an occasion with excellent potential for the hospitality industry. In many cultures the honeymoon trip is paid for by parents or other family members. As a gift, the honeymoon package may contain upscale products and services such as a hotel suite and first-class airfare.

Some hotels, such as those in the Pocono Mountains of Pennsylvania, specialize in the honeymoon market. In some cases, rooms are equipped with heart-shaped beds and champagne-glass-shaped spas. The Japanese honeymoon market is particularly important to the hospitality industry of Guam, Hawaii, New Zealand, and Australia. Group honeymoon tours have proved to be successful, in which several Japanese newlyweds participate in a tour of one or more destinations.

One of the most unusual examples of occasion segmentation is the "Room at the Inn" program offered by Doubletree Hotels of Canadian Pacific Hotels and Resorts. Doubletree offers free short-term lodging for travelers needing emergency lodging between Thanksgiving and Christmas. These are persons who travel to visit loved ones undergoing emergency medical treatment. Local hospitals, the Red Cross and United Way provide referrals of eligible guests.

Benefits Sought.   Buyers can also be grouped according to the product benefits they seek. After studying patrons and nonpatrons of three types of restaurants—family-popular, atmosphere, and gourmet—one researcher concluded that there are five major appeal categories for restaurant customers.[12] The relative importance of food quality, menu variety, price, atmosphere, and convenience factors across each group was studied. It was found that patrons of family-service restaurants sought convenience and menu. Variety patrons of atmosphere restaurants ranked food quality and atmosphere as the top attributes. Patrons of gourmet restaurants valued quality.

Knowing the attributes or benefits sought by customers is useful in two ways. First, restaurant marketers understand what to provide and promote in order to attract a specific segment. Second, identification of customer types is possible. Profiles of a firm's current market can be used to identify potential customers, clones of their present market. One study was able to classify consumers who would use a certain type of restaurant with over 80% accuracy.[13] This type of information reduces waste in advertising and increases effectiveness.

User Status.   Many markets can be segmented into nonusers, former users, potential users, first-time users, and regular users of a product. High-market-share companies such as major airlines are particularly interested in keeping regular users and attracting potential users. Potential users and regular users often require different marketing appeals.

Usage Rate.   Markets can also be segmented into light-, medium-, and heavy-user groups. Heavy users are often a small percentage of the market but account for a high percentage of total buying. Using beer as an example, 16% of the U.S. population accounts for 88% of total beer consumption. Heavy users drink more than seven times as much beer as light users. This illustrates the well-known 80–20 rule, which states that in many businesses or industries a high percent of the business is generated by a low percent of the clientele. Researchers have discovered that 4.1% of airline travelers account for 70.4% of total airline trips, while 7.9% of pleasure trip users of hotels and motels account for 59.4% of room nights.[14]

One of the most controversial programs ever employed by the hospitality and travel industries to ensure heavy patronage by key customers is the frequent flyer or frequent guest program. Many professors, consultants, and industry executives seriously question the long-run value of these programs. However, the results of one study of frequent guest programs concluded that, "While it is expensive to maintain frequent guest programs, they seem to be effective in keeping a large lucrative portion of the business travel market coming back to those hotels that offer such programs. Therefore, unless the industry as a whole drops these programs, it appears that individual chains will be forced to maintain them as a means of encouraging and maintaining customer loyalty."[15]

Clearly, marketers are eager to identify heavy users and build a marketing mix to attract them. Too many firms spread their marketing resources evenly across all potential customers. Seasoned marketers identify heavy users and focus marketing strategies toward them.

Loyalty Status.   A market can also be segmented on the basis of consumer loyalty. Consumers of hospitality products can be loyal to brands, such as Courtyard by Marriott or to companies such as American Airlines. Others are only somewhat loyal. They may be loyal to two or three brands or favor one brand but buy others. Still other buyers show no brand loyalty at all. They want variety or simply buy whichever brand is cheapest or most convenient. These individuals will stop at a Ramada Inn or Holiday Inn depending on which one they see first when looking for a motel.

In the hospitality and travel industries, marketers attempt to build brand loyalty through *relationship marketing*. Whereas manufacturing companies often lack direct contact with their customers, most hospitality and travel marketers have direct contact with their customers. They can develop a guest history database and use this information to customize offers and customer communications.

One restaurant keeps a file on its frequent customers, detailing their preferred captain, wines, table choice, last visit, and even their appearance (making it easier for restaurant employees to recognize them). VIP customers are given a special reservation phone number by this restaurant. Individuals who call that number are immediately identified as key customers and treated accordingly.

A review of marketing strategies for resorts in the 1990s suggested that the first and most basic strategy was "to keep and expand the current market base. To encourage vital repeat business, resorts should stay in contact with their former guests through direct mail that lets them know of special events, discount offers, and new programs and facilities."[16]

Buyer Readiness Stage.   At any given time, people are in different stages of readiness to buy a product. Some are unaware of the product; some are aware; some are informed; some want the product; and some intend to buy. The relative number in each stage makes a big difference in designing a marketing program.

A group travel operator wanted to sell long-haul destinations to incentive travel planners who normally purchased close-by destinations. Travel planners were aware of the long-haul product but were uninterested. The group travel operator implemented a direct marketing campaign in an attempt to change short-haul into long-haul buyers. The objective of the campaign was to convince incentive travel planners to visit the travel operator's booth at an upcoming travel show. As a result of the mail campaign, personal contact at the booth, and follow-up sales calls, a significant number of travel planners became convinced that long-haul incentive trips to exotic destinations were appropriate for some of their customers. The group travel operator attributed nearly $400,000 in sales increases to the campaign.[17]

Requirements for Effective Segmentation

Although there are many ways to segment a market, all are not equally effective. For example, buyers of restaurant meals could be divided into blond and brunette customers. But hair color does not affect the purchase of restaurant meals. Furthermore, if all restaurant customers buy the same number of meals each month, believe all restaurant meals are of equal quality, and are willing to pay the same price, the company would not benefit from segmenting this market.

To be useful, market segments must have the following characteristics:

- **Measurability.** The degree to which the segment's size and purchasing power can be measured. Certain segmentation variables are difficult to measure, such as the size of the segment of teenagers who drink primarily to rebel against their parents.

- **Accessibility.** The degree to which segments can be accessed and served. One of the authors found that 20% of a college restaurant's customers were frequent patrons. However, frequent patrons lacked any common characteristics. They included faculty, staff, and students. There was no usage difference among part-time, full-time, or class-year of the students. Although the market segment had been identified, there was no way to access the heavy-user segment.

- **Substantiality.** The degree to which segments are large or profitable enough to serve as markets. A segment should be the largest possible homogeneous group economically viable to support a tailored marketing program. For example, large metropolitan areas can support many different ethnic restaurants, but in a smaller town, Thai, Vietnamese, and Moroccan food restaurants would not survive.

- **Actionability.** The degree to which effective programs can be designed for attracting and serving segments. A small airline, for example, identified seven market segments, but its staff and budget were too small to develop separate marketing programs for each segment.

Segmentation reveals market opportunities available to a firm. The company then selects the most attractive segment or segments to serve as targets for marketing strategies to achieve desired objectives.

Market-coverage Alternatives

A firm can adopt one of three market-coverage strategies: undifferentiated marketing, differentiated marketing, and concentrated marketing. The arrows in Figure 9-3 indicate that a company has developed a marketing mix aimed at a particular segment or market. The mix has been developed from research gained from the market or members of a particular segment.

Undifferentiated Marketing

Using an **undifferentiated marketing** strategy, a firm ignores market segmentation differences and goes after the whole market with one market offer. It focuses on what is common in the needs of consumers, rather than on differences. It designs a marketing plan that will reach the greatest number of buyers. Mass distribution and mass advertising serve as the basic tools to create a superior image in consumers' minds.

Undifferentiated marketing provides cost economies. The narrow product line keeps down production, inventory, and transportation costs. The undifferentiated advertising program holds down advertising costs. The neglect of segmentation holds down marketing research costs and product development costs.

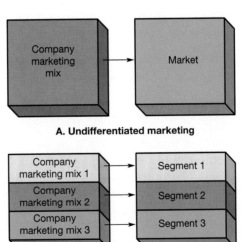

A. Undifferentiated marketing

B. Differentiated marketing

Figure 9-3
Three alternative market-coverage strategies.

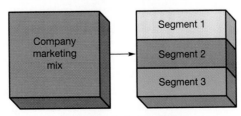

C. Concentrated marketing

Most modern marketers have strong doubts about this strategy in today's competitive environment. It is difficult to develop a product or brand that will satisfy all or even most consumers. When several firms aim at the largest segments, the inevitable result is heavy competition. Small firms generally find it impossible to compete directly against giants and are forced to adopt market-niche strategies. Larger segments may become less profitable due to heavy marketing costs, including the possibility of price cutting and price wars. In recognition of this problem, many firms target smaller segments or niches where product differentiation is appreciated.

The U.S. beer industry is an example. Smaller breweries cannot directly compete with Budweiser, Miller, and Coors. Smaller firms cannot achieve the distribution of the Big 3, nor can they match advertising and sales promotion budgets. Instead, a proliferation of micro breweries has occurred. Each micro brewery serves a limited market area and many depend on a company-owned pub or restaurant as the primary distribution center.

A similar situation exists within the world's commercial aviation industry. This is an oligopolistic industry with a few giant carriers. Many smaller "flag" carriers exist only because some nations feel they must have a national airline and are willing to subsidize it.

Within the North American market, several new niche market airlines have emerged, such as Casino Express that flies between Denver, Colorado, and Elko, Nevada, or Spirit Airlines based in Atlantic City. These airlines are unlikely to pose a direct threat to American, Delta, United, or U.S. Air. One of the last start-up airlines to pose such a threat was People's Express, which was unable to withstand the intense competition from major carriers when it expanded from a regional to a national carrier.

Differentiated Marketing

Using a **differentiated marketing** strategy, the firm targets several market segments and designs separate offers for each. Accor Hotels, a French company, operates under 12 trade names and manages several brands and types of hotels. Included in its brands are international luxury hotels (Sofitel), three-star hotels (Novotel), two-star hotels (Ibis), limited-service hotels (Formula One), and extended-stay hotels aimed at the elderly (Hotelia). This segmentation has allowed Accor to open 474 hotels in France. Accor states in its annual report that it hopes to become the world's foremost hotel group by the year 2000.[18] In 1990, it took another step toward achieving this goal by purchasing another brand, Motel Six.

Differentiated marketing typically produces more total sales than undifferentiated marketing. Accor gets a higher hotel room market share with three different brands in one city than if it only had one brand in that city. Sofitel attracts the upscale business traveler, Novotel attracts the midscale traveler, while Formula One attracts the families and the budget traveler. Accor offers a different marketing mix to each target market. At the same time, its costs are higher. It has to have marketing plans, marketing research, forecasting, sales analysis, promotion planning, and advertising for each brand. Thus companies must weigh increased sales against increased costs in considering a differentiated marketing strategy.

Concentrated Marketing

A third market-coverage strategy, **concentrated marketing**, is especially appealing to companies with limited resources. Instead of going for a small share of a large market, the firm pursues a large share of one or more small markets.

There are many examples of concentrated marketing. Rosewood Hotels concentrates on the high-priced hotel room market. Motel 6 concentrates on the low end. Through concentrated marketing, firms achieve a strong market position in the segments that they serve, thanks to their greater knowledge of those segments' needs and the special reputation the firm acquires. The firm also enjoys many operative economies because of specialization in production, distribution, and promotion. If the segment is well chosen, the firm can earn a high rate of return on investment.

At the same time, concentrated marketing involves higher than normal risks. The particular market segment can turn sour. For example, Victoria Station's menus were heavily concentrated on red meat items. When consumers started eating less red meat, Victoria Station's customer count plummeted. Additionally, meat prices jumped. Victoria Station's most profitable product, alcoholic beverages, also began a sales decline as a result of drunk driving campaigns. Thus it experienced declining and less profitable sales. For these reasons, many companies prefer to operate in two or more markets.

Choosing a Market-coverage Strategy

Companies need to consider several factors in choosing a market-coverage strategy. One factor is the **company's resources**. When the company's resources are limited, concentrated marketing makes the most sense. Another factor is the **degree of product homogeneity**. Undifferentiated marketing is more suited for homogeneous products. Products that can vary in design, such as restaurants and hotels, are more suited to differentiation or concentration. The product's life-cycle stage must also be considered. When a firm introduces a new product, it is practical to launch only one version, and undifferentiated marketing or concentrated marketing makes the most sense. For example, the early McDonald's restaurants had a very limited selection, compared to their present menu selection. In the mature stage of the product life cycle, differentiated marketing becomes more feasible. Another factor is **market homogeneity**. If buyers have the same tastes, buy a product in the same amounts, and react the same way to marketing efforts, undifferentiated marketing is appropriate. Finally, **competitors' strategies** are important. When competitors use segmentation, undifferentiated marketing can be suicidal. Conversely, when competitors use undifferentiated marketing, a firm can gain an advantage by using differentiated or concentrated marketing.

Identifying Attractive Market Segments

Suppose that a company decides on concentrated marketing. It must now identify the most attractive segment to select as a target. The company must collect data on various market segments, such as current dollar sales, pro-

Marketing Highlight 9-1

The Business Traveler

The business traveler is the hotel industry's largest segment, accounting for over half of all hotel room revenues. This market is better educated, more affluent, and employed in sales, managerial, or professional positions. The business traveler reads more and watches less television than the average American. The number one reason for making a business trip is for sales.

In selecting a hotel, business travelers give attention to a convenient location, cleanliness and service, the room rate, and reputation. Desirable room amenities include good-quality mattresses, heavy bath towels, a desk, and a telephone with no charge for local calls and no surcharges for long-distance calls. The no charge for local calls is an important factor for the salesperson.

Business travelers say that they would be very likely to use the hotel restaurant, a free continental breakfast (if offered), and no smoking rooms. Over half the business travelers pay more than $50 a night and about 11% pay more than $100 a night. A surprising finding is that over 60% of business travelers make their own reservations. Toll-free numbers are very important to business travelers. Those not booking reservations themselves use travel agents or secretaries. Information on the business traveler helps hotels to develop a marketing offer to attract this segment.

One way of subsegmenting this large segment is through prices that travelers are willing to pay. Those seeking economy lodging are usually traveling salesmen, self-employed, or government workers. This group's daily expenditures are limited by their organization or, in the case of the self-employed, it comes directly out of their income. This group will trade off other features, such as a hotel restaurant, to get a clean comfortable room for under $50. La Quinta, Red Roof Inns, Hampton Inns, and Fairfield Inns have targeted this segment.

The next segment is the mid-priced business traveler. A broad range of full-service hotels pursue this segment. They include Courtyard by Marriott, Hilton, Holiday Inns, Marriott, and Ramada. Notice that Marriott has two products going after this market. Courtyard is at the lower end of the range, while Marriott hotels are at the upper end of the range. Marriott felt it could not cover this segment adequately with just one product.

The upscale business traveler would be attracted to Four Seasons, Ritz-Carlton, Stouffers, and Westin. These hotels offer extra services and amenities that the upscale business wants. They are able to cover the costs generated by these extra features by charging more for their rooms.

As the hotel market becomes more competitive, chains will develop further brands and variations aimed at well-defined market segments.

Source: George Taininecz, "1990 Business Traveler Survey," *Hotel and Motel Management* (June 25, 1990 [205(1)]), p. 29; Kenneth Ray and James L. Haskett, "Fairfield Inn," Harvard Case Study 9-689-092 (October 1989); James R. Abbey, *Hospitality Sales and Advertising* (Educational Institute of the AH&MA: East Lansing, Mich., 1989), pp. 389–402; and Arch Woodside, Victor J. Cook, Jr., and William Mindale, "Profiling the Heavy Traveler Segment," *Journal of Travel Research*, 25, no. 4, (April 1987), pp. 9–14.

jected sales growth rates, expected profit margins, strength of competition, and marketing channel needs. No segment is likely to be best in all these dimensions, so trade-offs would have to be made.

After the company identifies the more objectively attractive segments, it must decide which segments fit best with its business strengths. For example, the military market may be highly attractive, but the company may have had no experience selling to the military. That same company may have expertise in selling to the consumer market. Thus the company

Radisson created the Radisson Business Class, a bundle of products to attract the corporate customer. Their business class includes a full breakfast, daily newspaper, free movies, complimentary coffee, data port for computers, free telephone access, and immediate priority fax. Courtesy of Radisson Hospitality Worldwide.

seeks a segment that is attractive in itself and for which it has the necessary business strengths to succeed. It seeks segments in which it possesses the greatest strategic advantage.

Once a company has chosen its target market segments, it must decide what positions to occupy in those segments.

POSITIONING FOR A COMPETITIVE ADVANTAGE

Market Positioning

A product's position is the way the product is defined by consumers on important attributes—the place the product occupies in consumers' minds relative to competing products. Consumers are overloaded with information about products and services. They cannot reevaluate products every time they make a buying decision. To simplify buying decision making, consumers organize products into categories—they "position" products and companies in their minds.

Marketers do not want to leave their products' positions to chance. They plan positions that will give their products the greatest advantage in selected target markets and then design marketing mixes to create the planned positions. In the fast-food hamburger business, Wendy's promotes never frozen meat, hot off the grill; Burger King is known for its flame-broiled food, and Rally's double drive through uses low price to position itself in the marketplace.[19]

Positioning Strategies

Marketers can follow several positioning strategies. They can position their products based on **specific product attributes**. Motel Six advertises its low price; Hilton advertises its locations. Products can also be positioned on the

needs they fill or the **benefits they offer**. Bennigans advertises itself as a fun place, while many bars promote their image as a meeting place for members of the opposite sex (or same sex). Marketers can also position for **certain classes of users**, such as a hotel advertising itself as a women's hotel.

A product can be positioned **against an existing competitor**. In the "Burger Wars," Wendy's ran its "Where's the beef" campaign against McDonald's and Burger King, while Burger King used its flame-broiled campaign against McDonald's. Taco Bell positioned itself as an alternative to typical fast-food meals. Seven Up successfully positioned itself as the "Uncola" at a time cola beverages were engaged in a fierce battle for market share dominance. The strategy of Taco Bell and Seven Up has many applications in the hospitality industry.

Finally, products can be positioned against another **product class**. For example, McDonald's "You deserve a break campaign" tells the customer to come to McDonald's rather than cook at home. Cruise ships have positioned themselves against other vacation alternatives, such as destination resorts, and customers have positioned B&B's as an alternative to all other forms of lodging. Conference centers have consistently positioned their product against hotels with conference facilities.

The hotel industry should take warning from the plight of mighty IBM. Few competitors found it possible to directly attack IBM for market share. IBM was dominant in mainframe computer, in its sales/distribution force, and in the position it held in the minds of the business community. Competitors attacked IBM with flanking or guerrilla attacks rather than a frontal assault. Little by little, niche competitors began to chew at the computer market through specialized software, PCs, specialty computers, and specialty service. IBM suddenly found it was surrounded by competitors who had captured niche markets at the same time that the demand for its traditional products was softening.

Traditional hotels with a ballroom, conference seminar rooms, full-service restaurant, a bar, an exercise room, and other product offerings are experiencing the IBM phenomenon. Market-niche players in the hospitality industry continue to attack full-service hotels with specialized products such as conference centers, specialized F&B outlets, fitness centers, B&Bs, all-suite lodging, condo hotels, and meeting/seminar rooms within convention centers, and even athletic arenas.

The Asian market such as Hong Kong or Singapore has consisted largely of deluxe five-star full-service hotels with world-class competitors such as The Peninsula, Mandarin, Shangrila, Regent, Hilton International, and Hyatt Hotels. Less expensive hotel properties existed, but these predominantly appealed to nearby markets and to GIT (group inclusive tour) segments. As rack rates increased in these markets and as customer familiarization with these destinations grew, niche products have begun to emerge.

The YMCA is a surprising niche competitor in Hong Kong. The YMCA enjoys a good location near the harbor and has been remodeled to meet the needs of American, European, and Australian guests. Occupancy and guest satisfaction in the YMCA remain high and serve as a warning to traditional five-star luxury properties that guests are willing to accept alternative lodging products.

When two or more firms pursue the same position, each must seek further differentiation, such as "a business hotel for a lower cost" or "a business hotel with a great location." Each firm must build a unique bundle of competitive advantages that appeals to a substantial group within the segment. This subpositioning is often called *niche marketing*.

Most cruise lines offer a multi-day cruise experience with stops at several ports. A few niche cruise lines have found it profitable to offer a one-day cruise with no ports of call. The QE-2 (Queen Elizabeth 2) has successfully developed a market niche as the Rolls Royce of cruise ships with costs of several thousand dollars and lengthy cruise times.

Choosing and Implementing a Positioning Strategy

The positioning task consists of three steps: identifying a set of possible competitive advantages upon which to build a position, selecting the right competitive advantages, and effectively communicating and delivering the chosen position to a carefully selected target market.

A company can differentiate itself from competitors by bundling competitive advantages. It gains **competitive advantage** by offering consumers lower prices than competitors for similar products or by providing more benefits that justify higher prices.[20] Thus a company must compare its prices and products to those of competitors and continuously look for possible improvements. To the extent that it can do better than its competitors, the company has achieved a competitive advantage.

Club Med used a successful bundling strategy of offering all services other than retail purchases to a young market segment that was unfamiliar with tipping, ordering from a menu, selecting wines, and asking a concierge for help in acquiring a tennis lesson. Club Med bundled all these products/services and eliminated the use of money at their resorts. Instead of dollars, pesos, or francs, Club Med's international guests could buy a round of drinks with beads given to them at check in.

In some cases, unbundling of products has also worked as a positioning tactic. Until the early 1970s, many destination resorts sold only a bundled product known as The American Plan (AP) in which all or most of the resort's services such as F&B were included. Consumer preferences changed as many guests no longer wanted three daily meals and a Friday evening formal dance included in a package. Resort managers who observed this behavior change began to differentiate their properties by offering a Modified American Plan (MAP) in which lunch was not included or a European plan that did not include any meals.

Not every company faces an abundance of opportunities for gaining a competitive advantage. Some companies can identify only minor advantages, which are often easily copied and therefore highly perishable. These companies must continue to identify new potential advantages and introduce them one by one to keep competitors off balance. Few or perhaps no companies can achieve a major permanent advantage, but instead gain smaller advantages that help them build their market share over time. Hotels, resorts, and restaurants sometimes believe that their locations on a beach, near an airport, next to a ski hill, or in the central business district provide them with a permanent advantage. History clearly depicts a different scenario. Beaches erode or become polluted, ski hills lose their popularity, airports move, and central business districts lose their appeal. In many cases the management of hospitality companies with perceived permanent advantages lose interest in customers and employees, thus further contributing to their inevitable demise.

Product Differentiation

A company can differentiate its product or offer products similar to competitors. Today most products try to differentiate themselves from their competitors. In what ways can a company differentiate its offer from those of competitors? A company can differentiate along the lines of physical attributes, services, personnel, location, or image.

Physical Attribute Differentiation. Classic hotels that have been renovated, such as the Sheraton Place in San Francisco, the Palmer House in Chicago, the Waldorf Astoria in New York, and The Raffles in Singapore differentiate themselves on the grandeur of the past. Their physical environment offers something a newly constructed hotel cannot match. Planet Hollywood with its memorabilia from the motion picture industry and Hard Rock Cafe with its music memorabilia offer environments that competitors will have a hard time duplicating. MGM airlines offered a plane that was designed to serve first-class passengers only. The plane had a stand-up bar, couches, and other physical features that were not found in the first-class sections of major domestic carriers.

Service Differentiation. Some companies differentiate themselves on service. For example, Sheraton provides an in-room check-in service. Red Lobster allows its customers to call from home and put their name on the waiting list, reducing the amount of time that they have to wait at the restaurant. Some restaurants offer home delivery as a point of differentiation. By providing services that will benefit its target market, a company can achieve differentiation.

Personnel Differentiation. Companies can gain a strong competitive advantage through hiring and training better people than their competitors do. Thus Singapore Airlines enjoys an excellent reputation largely because of the grace of its flight attendants. Herb Kelleher, of Southwest Airlines, claims that a competitor possibly could replicate their low-cost system, but a competitor will never be able to create a spirit similar to the spirit of Southwest's employees.[21]

Personnel differentiation requires that a company select its customer-contact people carefully and train them well. These personnel must be competent—they must possess the required skills and knowledge. They need to be courteous, friendly, and respectful. They must serve customers with consistency and accuracy. And they must make an effort to understand customers, to communicate clearly with them, and to respond quickly to customer requests and problems.

Location Differentiation. In the hospitality and travel industries location can provide a strong competitive advantage. For example, hotels facing Central Park in New York City have a competitive advantage over those hotels a block away with no view of the park. Motels that are located right off of a freeway exit can have double digit advantages in percentage of occupancy over hotels a block away. Restaurants on the top of a mountain advertise their views as a competitive advantage and restaurants with an ocean view do the same. International airlines often use their location as a point of differentiation in their home markets. For example, Qantas promotes itself as Australia's airline and has a strong following in its home market. Hospitality and travel firms should look for benefits created by their location and use these benefits to differentiate themselves from their market.

Image Differentiation.   Even when competing offers look the same, buyers may perceive a difference based on company or brand images. Thus companies need to work to establish images that differentiate them from competitors. A company or brand image should convey a singular or distinctive message that communicates the product's major benefits and positioning. Developing a strong and distinctive image calls for creativity and hard work. A company cannot implant an image in the public's mind overnight using a few advertisements. Chili's has developed an image as a casual and fun neighborhood restaurant. This message is conveyed by their advertising, menu, the physical atmosphere, and the employees. The image must be supported by everything that the company says and does.

Studebaker's positioned itself as a singles night club for adults over 25 (product class and user) naming itself after a car. The name Studebaker and the use of a Studebaker auto in the facility had no meaning to a younger market segment who had very possibly never seen this automobile on the streets and highways. Thus the word Studebaker meant something to their target market, but held little meaning for younger markets.

Selecting the Right Competitive Advantages

Suppose that a company is fortunate enough to discover several potential competitive advantages. It now must choose the ones upon which it will build its positioning strategy. It must decide how many differences to promote and which ones.

How Many Differences to Promote?   Many marketers think that companies should aggressively promote only one benefit to the target market. Ad man Rosser Reeves, for example, said a company should develop a unique selling proposition (USP) for each brand and stick to it. Each brand should pick an attribute and tout itself as *number one* on that attribute. Buyers tend to remember *number one* better, especially in an overcommunicated society. Thus Motel 6 consistently promotes itself as the lowest-priced national chain and Ritz-Carlton promotes itself as a value leader. What are some number one positions to promote? The major ones are best quality, best service, lowest price, best value, and best location. A company that hammers away at a position that is important to its target market and consistently delivers on it probably will become the best known and remembered.

Other marketers think that companies should position themselves on more than one differentiating factor. A restaurant may claim it has the best steaks and service. A hotel may claim it offers the best value and location. Today, in a time when the mass market is fragmenting into many small market segments, companies are trying to broaden their positioning strategies to appeal to more segments. For example, The Boulders, in Arizona, promotes itself as a top golf resort and as a luxury resort giving guests a chance to experience the flora and fauna of the Sonora Desert. By doing this, the Boulders can attract both golfers and nongolfers.

However, as companies increase the number of claims for their brands, they risk disbelief and a loss of clear positioning. In general, a company needs to avoid three major positioning errors. The first is **underpositioning**, or failing to ever really position the company at all. Some companies discover that buyers have only a vague idea of the company or that they do not really know anything special about it. Many independent hotels trying to capture an international market are underpositioned. The Seoul Plaza Hotel, a luxury hotel in Seoul, is not well known in Europe or North America. To establish positions in distant markets, hotels like the Seoul Plaza are affiliating with marketing groups such as "Leading Hotels of the World" and "Preferred Hotels." The second positioning error is **overpositioning**, or giving buyers a too narrow picture of the company. Finally, companies must avoid **confused positioning**, leaving buyers with a confused image of a company. For example, Burger King has struggled for years to establish a profitable and consistent position. Since 1986, it has fielded five separate advertising campaigns, with themes ranging from "Herb the nerd doesn't eat here" and "This is a Burger King town," to "The right food for the right times" and "Sometimes you've got to break the rules." This barrage of positioning statements has left consumers confused and Burger King with poor sales and profits.[22]

Which Differences to Promote?   Not all brand differences are meaningful or worthwhile. Not every difference makes a good differentiator. Each difference has the potential to create company costs as well as customer benefits. Therefore, the company must carefully select the ways in which it will distinguish itself from competitors. A difference is worth establishing to the extent that it satisfies the following criteria:

- *Important.* The difference delivers a highly valued benefit to target buyers.
- *Distinctive.* Competitors do not offer the difference, or the company can offer it in a more distinctive way.
- *Superior.* The difference is superior to other ways that customers might obtain the same benefit.
- *Communicable.* The difference is communicable and visible to buyers.
- *Preemptive.* Competitors cannot easily copy the difference.
- *Affordable.* Buyers can afford to pay for the difference.
- *Profitable.* The company can introduce the difference profitably.

Many companies have introduced differentiations that failed one or more of these tests. The Westin Stamford Hotel in Singapore advertises that it is the world's tallest hotel, a distinction that is not important to many tourists—in fact, it turns many off.

Some competitive advantages may be quickly ruled out because they are too slight, too costly to develop, or too inconsistent with the company's profile. Suppose that a company is designing its positioning strategy and has narrowed its list of possible competitive advantages to four. The company needs a framework for selecting the one advantage that makes the most sense to develop.

Communicating and Delivering the Chosen Position

Once having chosen positioning characteristics and a positioning statement, a company must communicate their position to targeted customers. All of a company's marketing mix efforts must support its positioning strategy. Thus, if a company decides to build service superiority, it must hire service-oriented employees, provide training programs, reward employees for providing good service, and develop sales and advertising messages to broadcast its service superiority.

Building and maintaining a consistent positioning strategy is not easy. Many counterforces are continuously at work. Advertising agencies hired by the company may not like a selected position and may overtly or covertly work against it. New management may not understand the positioning strategy. Budgets may be cut for critical support programs such as employee training or sales promotion. The development of an effective position requires a long-run, consistent program with continuous support by management, employees, and vendors.

Companies normally develop a memorable statement to communicate their desired position. Burger King's "Have it your way" lets customers know that they can get their choice of condiments. La Quinta's "Just Right over Night" catches the attention of travelers coming in by car and needing overnight accommodation, but not needing a full-service hotel. Avis Auto Rental originally positioned itself with a statement and strong supportive program to convince the customer, "We're only No. 2 so we try harder." This also positioned Avis with the number one company, Hertz, and away from Budget, Dollar, National, and Thrifty. These statements aim to create a positive image in the target customer's mind.

A company's positioning decisions determine who its competitors will be. When setting its positioning strategy, the company should review its competitive strengths and weaknesses and select a position that places it in a superior position vis-à-vis its chosen competitors.

Chapter Review

I.   Market. A market is the set of all actual and potential buyers of a product.

II.   The target marketing process involves three steps, market segmentation, market targeting, and positioning.

    1) Market segmentation is the process of dividing a market into distinct groups of buyers who might require separate products and/or marketing mixes.

2) Market targeting is the process of evaluating each segment's attractiveness and selecting one or more of the market segments.

3) Positioning is the process of developing a competitive positioning for the product and an appropriate marketing mix.

III.   **Market Segmentation**

1)   **Bases for Segmenting a Market.** There is no single way to segment a market. A marketer has to try different segmentation variables, alone and in combination, hoping to find the best way to view the market structure.

a) **Geographic segmentation** calls for dividing the market into different geographic units, such as nations, states, regions, counties, cities, or neighborhoods.

b) **Demographic segmentation** consists of dividing the market into groups based on demographic variables such as age, gender, family life cycle, income, occupation, education, religion, race, and nationality.

c) **Psychographic segmentation** divides buyers into different groups based on social class, life-style, and personality characteristics.

d) **Behavior segmentation** divides buyers into groups based on their knowledge, attitude, use, or response to a product.

2)   **Requirements for Effective Segmentation**

a) **Measurability:** The degree to which the segment's size and purchasing power can be measured.

b) **Accessibility:** The degree to which segments can be accessed and served.

c) **Substantiality:** The degree to which segments are large or profitable enough to serve as markets.

d) **Actionability:** The degree to which effective programs can be designed for attracting and serving segments.

IV.   **Market Targeting.** Segmentation reveals market opportunities available to a firm. The company then selects the most attractive segment or segments to serve as targets for marketing strategies to achieve desired objectives.

1)   **Market-coverage Alternatives**

a) **Undifferentiated marketing strategy:** An undifferentiated marketing strategy ignores market segmentation differences and goes after the whole market with one market offer.

b) **Differentiated marketing strategy:** The firm targets several market segments and designs separate offers for each.

c) **Concentrated marketing strategy:** Concentrated marketing strategy is especially appealing to companies with limited resources. Instead of going for a small share of a large market, the firm pursues a large share of one or more small markets.

2)   **Choosing a Market-coverage Strategy.** Companies need to consider several factors in choosing a market-coverage strategy.

a) **Company resources:** When the company's resources are limited, concentrated marketing makes the most sense.

b) **Degree of product homogeneity:** Undifferentiated marketing is more suited for homogeneous products. Products that can vary in design, such as restaurants and hotels, are more suited to differentiation or concentration.

c) **Market homogeneity:** If buyers have the same tastes, buy a product in the same amounts, and react the same way to marketing efforts, undifferentiated marketing is appropriate.

d) **Competitors' strategies:** When competitors use segmentation, undifferentiated marketing can be suicidal. Conversely, when competitors use undifferentiated marketing, a firm can gain an advantage by using differentiated or concentrated marketing.

V.   Market Positioning. A product's position is the way the product is defined by consumers on important attributes—the place the product occupies in consumers' minds relative to competing products.

1) **Positioning Strategies**

a) **Specific product attributes:** Price and product features can be used to position a product.

b) **Needs products fill or the benefits they offer:** Marketers can position products by the needs that they fill or the benefits that they offer. For example, a restaurant can be positioned as a fun place.

c) **Certain classes of users:** Marketers can also position for certain classes of users, such as a hotel advertising itself as a women's hotel.

d) **Against an existing competitor:** A product can be positioned against an existing competitor. In the "Burger Wars," Burger King used its flame-broiled campaign against McDonald's, claiming that people prefer flame-broiled burgers over fried burgers.

2) **Positioning Task Consists of Three Steps.** Identifying a set of possible competitive advantages upon which to build a position, selecting the right competitive advantages, and effectively communicating and delivering the chosen position to a carefully selected target market.

3) **Communicating and Delivering the Chosen Position.** Once having chosen positioning characteristics and a positioning statement, a company must communicate their position to targeted customers. All of a company's marketing mix efforts must support its positioning strategy.

DISCUSSION QUESTIONS

1. Explain the process of market segmentation, market targeting, and market positioning.

2. What variables are used for market segmentation in restaurants? Are the same variables used for market segmentation in airlines?

3. Chose a major hotel brand and explain how their marketing offer meets the wants of their target market.

4. Why is usage rate an important segmentation variable?

5. Some restauranteurs want to develop a restaurant with something for everyone. Why is this a dangerous policy?

6. Are some characteristics of market segments more important than others, or are measurability, accessibility, substantiality, and actionability equally important? Why?

7. Explain the advantages and disadvantages of undifferentiated, differentiated, and concentrated marketing. Can you think of an example when each might be appropriate for a restaurant firm?

8. What roles do product attributes and perceptions of attributes play in the positioning of a product? Can an attribute common to several competing brands contribute to a successful positioning strategy?

KEY TERMS

Accessibility   The degree to which a market segment can be reached and served.

Actionability   The degree to which effective programs can be designed for attracting and serving a given market segment.

Age and life-cycle segmentation   Dividing a market into different age and life-cycle groups.

Behavior segmentation   Dividing a market into groups based on consumers' knowledge, attitude, use, or response to a product.

Benefit segmentation   Dividing the market into groups according to the different benefits that consumers seek from the product.

Competitive advantage   An advantage over competitors gained by offering consumers greater value either through lower prices or by providing more benefits that justify higher prices.

Concentrated marketing   A market-coverage strategy in which a firm goes after a large share of one or a few submarkets.

Demographic segmentation   Dividing the market into groups based on demographic variables such as age, gender, family size, family life cycle, income, occupation, education, religion, race, and nationality.

Differentiated marketing   A market-coverage strategy in which a firm decides to target several market segments and designs separate offers for each.

Geographic segmentation   Dividing a market into different geographical units such as nations, states, regions, counties, cities, or neighborhoods.

Income segmentation   Dividing a market into different income groups.

Market   The set of all actual and potential buyers of a product.

Market positioning   Formulating competitive positioning for a product and a detailed marketing mix.

Market segmentation   Dividing a market into direct groups of buyers who might require separate products or marketing mixes.

Market targeting   Evaluating each market segment's attractiveness and selecting one or more segments to enter.

Measurability   The degree to which the size and purchasing power of a market segment can be measured.

Micromarketing   A form of target marketing in which companies tailor their marketing programs to the needs and wants of narrowly defined geographic, demographic, psychographic, or benefit segments.

Occasion segmentation   Dividing the market into groups according to occasion when buyers get the idea, make a purchase, or use a product.

Product position   The way the product is defined by consumers on important attributes; the place the product occupies in consumers' minds relative to competing products.

Psychographic segmentation   Dividing a market into different groups based on social class, lifestyle, or personality characteristics.

Sex segmentation   Dividing a market into different groups based on sex.

Substantiality   The degree to which a market segment is large or profitable enough.

Target market   A set of buyers sharing common needs or characteristics that the company decides to serve.

Undifferentiated marketing   A market-coverage strategy in which a firm decides to ignore market segment differences and go after the whole market with one market offer.

REFERENCES

1. FAYE RICE, "How Carnival Stacks the Decks," *Fortune*, 11, no. 21. (January 16, 1989), pp. 108–116; AND PAULA SCHNORBUS, "Liner Notes," *Marketing and Media Decisions*, 22, no. 1 (January 1987), pp. 63–72.

2. WILLIAM R. SWINYARD AND KENNETH D. STRUMAN, "Market Segmentation: Finding the Heart of Your Restaurant's Market," *Cornell Hotel and Restaurant Administration Quarterly*, 27, no. 1 (May 1986), p. 96.

3. JOHN JESITUS, "The Regional Page: Diners Search for that Down-home Flavor," *Hotel and Motel Management*, 207, no. 1 (January 13, 1992), pp. 25–26.

4. DAVID KALISH, "McTargeting," *Marketing and Media Decisions*, 24, no. 4 (April 1989), pp. 28–29.

5. REGINA MCGEE, "What Do Women Business Travelers Really Want?," *Successful Meetings*, 37, no. 9 (August 1988), pp. 55–57.

6. LISA WELLS, "Hotels Warily Woo Women Travelers," *Advertising Age,* 56, no. 59 (August 1, 1985), p. 4.

7. "Who's Dining Out?," *Cornell Hotel and Restaurant Administration Quarterly,* 26, no. 3 (November 1985), p. 4.

8. GARY M. STERN, "Solo Diners," *Restaurants USA,* 10, no. 3 (March 1990), pp. 15–16.

9. ROBERT SELWITZ, "St. Moritz Drops Rates to Hit Niche," *Hotel and Motel Management,* 207, no. 3 (February 24, 1992), pp. 2 and 25.

10. SUBHASH C. MEHTA AND VERA ARIEL, "Segmentation in Singapore," *Cornell Hotel and Restaurant Administration Quarterly,* 31, no. 1 (May 1990), p. 83.

11. ROBERT SELWITZ, "Lufthansa's Hotel Connections Take Flight," *Hotel and Motel Management,* 206, no. 12 (July 8, 1991), pp. 3 and 36.

12. ROBERT C. LEWIS, "Restaurant Advertising: Appeals and Consumers' Intentions," *Journal of Advertising Research,* 21, no. 5 (October 1981), pp. 69–75.

13. Ibid.

14. VICTOR J. COOK, JR., William Mindak, and Arch Woodside, "Profiling the Heavy Traveler Segment," *Journal of Travel Research,* 25, no. 4 (April 1987), pp. 9–14.

15. KEN W. MCCLEARY AND PAMELA A. WEAVER, "Are Frequent-guest Programs Effective?," *Cornell Hotel and Restaurant Administration Quarterly,* 32, no. 2 (August 1991), p. 45.

16. WILLIAM P. WHELIHAN III AND KYE-SUNG CHON, "Resort Marketing Trends in the 90's," *Cornell Hotel and Restaurant Administration Quarterly,* 32, no. 2 (August 1991), p. 58.

17. DAVID TONNISON, "Marketing to Marketers," *Industrial Marketing Digest,* 12, no. 2 (1987), pp. 67–72.

18. *Accor* Annual Report (1988).

19. For more reading on positioning, see YORAM WIND, "New Twists for Some Old Tricks," *Wharton Magazine* (Spring 1980), pp. 34–39; DAVID A. AAKER AND J. GARY STANSBY, "Positioning Your Product," *Business Horizons* (May–June 1982), pp. 56–62; AND REGIS MCKENNA, "Playing for Position," *Inc.* (April 1985), pp. 92–97.

20. See MICHAEL PORTER, *Competitive Advantage* (New York: Free Press, 1980), Chap. 2. For a good discussion of the concept of competitive advantage and methods for assessing it, see GEORGE S. DAY AND ROBIN WENSLEY, "Assessing Advantage: A Framework for Diagnosing Competitive Superiority," *Journal of Marketing* (April 1988), pp. 1–20.

21. Mobilizing People for Breakthrough Service (video), Boston: Harvard Business School Management Productions, 1993.

22. GAIL DEGEORGE AND MARK LANDLER, "Tempers Are Sizzling over Burger King's New Ads," *Business Week* (February 2, 1990), p. 33; AND PHILIP STELLY, JR., "Burger King Rule Breaker," *Adweek,* (November 9, 1990), pp. 24, 26.

Designing and Managing Products

*I*n the early 1980s, Wendy's spent more than 3 years testing a concept for breakfast. Wendy's vice-president of research and development at the time, Jim Stubblefield, stated that Wendy's previous failure at breakfast made them "extra cautious." He felt the reason for the previous failure was that Wendy's was offering a "me too" breakfast. The objectives for the new breakfast menu were quality and uniqueness.

Wendy's chose three items: an omelette made to order with a choice of fillings, French toast, and a breakfast sandwich. The products were taste-tested at Wendy's headquarters. The R&D equipment testing lab chose the equipment to produce the new products. Next, Wendy's tested the products in a few stores and gave free samples to customers to get their reactions. At the same time, Wendy's tested the production capability of an actual Wendy's unit by producing the items in a store during the night. As a result of these tests, Wendy's made some refinements and test marketed the breakfasts in a few stores. Revisions were made based on these tests, for example, premade omelette shells filled to order. Wendy's decided to cook the omelettes to order so that customers could see their omelette cooking on the grill. They revised the menu to include a scrambled egg platter and changed the format of the breakfast sandwich. The revised menu was tested in Columbus, Ohio, getting customer input on the new variations. Finally,

271

Wendy's introduced the breakfast on a store-by-store basis. By January 1983, it had been introduced in 70 units. The company planned the first television advertisement for the spring of 1983.

Wendy's continued to move cautiously with its breakfast menu for the next 2 years. Finally, in the summer of 1985 it rolled out a multimillion dollar advertising campaign for its breakfast. Despite research and cautious entry, the breakfast failed. Wendy's developed a system to produce made-to-order omelettes in 90 seconds. Yet they failed to consider what would happen when a group of customers came in at the same time. When omelettes were cooked to order, the wait could exceed several minutes. As one analyst put it, this was no longer a fast-food business. David Thomas, the founder of Wendy's, said "We made every omelette to order. Our competitors make things up and put them under a heat lamp. We just could not compete with that." He added, "I think we made a mistake. I don't think our testing was as accurate as it should have been".

During the development of its breakfast, Wendy's put its new breakfast program through seemingly exhaustive testing. It had developed a unique and quality product. The delivery time was fast compared to a family restaurant such as Denny's, but not fast enough for a fast-food restaurant. Also, cooking the items to order made it difficult, if not impossible, to purchase the items through the drive-through window. Thus sales were also lost from this growing segment of the business. Even with significant research efforts and test marketing, products fail.

Introducing a new product is a complex process. It is difficult to consider all the variables. In research and test marketing you want to answer as many questions as possible, to increase a product's chances of success or remove a product failure before it moves to the commercialization stage.[1]

Chapter 10 addresses some of the most visible aspects of marketing: how products are developed and managed.

The product itself is defined in the first section of this chapter. This complex concept includes the **core product**, the **facilitating product**, the **supporting product**, and the **augmented product**. Next we discuss the issues associated with hospitality and travel products: **accessibility, atmosphere**, and **customer interaction with the service delivery system**.

Then we discuss the concept of **branding**. This is followed by a section on product development. We discuss the stages of the **new-product development process: idea generation, idea screening, concept development and testing, marketing strategy, business analysis, product development, test marketing**, and **commercialization**.

Next we follow this section with a discussion of the stages of the **product life cycle, product development, introduction, growth, maturity**, and **decline**, and the need to match marketing strategies to help to manage a product's life cycle. The chapter concludes with a discussion of the **product deletion process**.

A room at the Four Seasons in Toronto, a Hawaiian vacation, McDonald's French fries, a vacation package in Bali, a catered luncheon, a bus tour of historic sites, and a convention in a modern convention center with group rates in a nearby hotel are all products.

WHAT IS A PRODUCT?

Consider the variety of products in a typical casino hotel.

Casino products
    Slot machines: 5¢, 10¢, 25¢, $1.00, $5.00
    Video poker: many varieties
    Gaming Tables: baccarat, blackjack, poker, chemin de fer, roulette, craps
    Others: various numbers games, bingo, off-track betting

Hotel products
    Rooms: single, double, suites, poolsides, cabana
    Food and Beverage: mini bars, poolside lounges, in-room service, vending machines, restaurants, cocktail lounges
    Special services: executive center, tour desk, fitness center

Food and beverage products
    Menu: Individual a la carte items
    Individual dinners
    Buffets
    Group dinners
    Dessert items
    Nonalcoholic beverages
    Alcoholic beverages

Now consider the endless possibilities for bundling various casino/hotel products to create new products.

> Package A   Three-night package: room, breakfasts, $25 in chips for use in casino, five free drinks, and ground transportation

> Package B   Honeymooners package: suite, bottle of champagne, all meals (in-room service), $25 in chips, ground transportation, flowers in room, and a photograph of newlyweds at poolside.

Possibilities for bundling hospitality products are limited only by creativity. If a hospitality firm such as a moderately priced hotel feels it has exhausted possibilities for bundling its own products, a cooperative program can be developed with a noncompeting firm, such as a restaurant, a theater, or a bus line. Hospitality Franchise Systems, Inc. (parent company of Ramada, Park Inn International, Super 8 Motel, Days Inn, and Howard Johnson) signed an agreement with Pizza Hut to provide in-room pizza delivery to all HFS grand hotels in exchange for a payment for each pizza delivered to the properties. With nearly 400,000 rooms in the HFS system, this product represented substantial revenue potential for Pizza Hut and HFS.[2]

We define the term product as follows:

> A product is anything that can be offered to a market for attention, acquisition, use, or consumption that might satisfy a want or need. It includes physical objects, services, places, organizations, and ideas.

This definition refers to the planned component of the product that the firm offers. Besides the planned component, the product also includes an unplanned component. For example, a consumer entered a restaurant in Dallas and was greeted by the hostess, who presented him with a menu. When he opened his menu, he saw a dead roach stuck to the inside. After receiving this unexpected bonus, the consumer decided to leave the restaurant. The restaurant certainly did not plan on having a dead roach in the menu. The product the customer receives is not always as management plans.

PRODUCT LEVELS

Hospitality managers need to think about the product on four levels: the **core product**, the **facilitating product**, the **supporting product**, and the **augmented product**.

Core Product

The most basic level is the **core product**, which answers the following question: What is the buyer really buying? Every product is a package of problem-solving services. Theodore Levitt pointed out that buyers "do not buy quarter-inch drills; they buy quarter-inch holes." And as all good steak houses have learned, "Don't sell the steak—sell the sizzle." Marketers must uncover the core benefit to the consumer of every product and sell these benefits, rather than merely selling features.

Facilitating Products

Facilitating products are those services or goods that must be present for the guest to use the core product. A first-class corporate hotel must have check-in and check-out services, telephones, a restaurant, and valet service, for instance. In a limited-service economy hotel, facilitating services might be no more than check-in and check-out service and public phones on the property. Product design requires an understanding of the target market and the facilitating services that they require.

Supporting Products

Core products require facilitating products, but they do not require supporting products. **Supporting products** are extra products offered to add value to the core product and to help to differentiate it from the competition. In a corporate hotel, a business center or a full-service health spa are supporting products that may help to draw customers to the hotel. The distinction between facilitating and supporting products is not always clear. Facilitating products for one market segment may be supporting products for another. For example, while families may not require restaurants and valet service when staying at a hotel, business travelers depend on them. Hyatt was among the first chains to offer a broad line of bathroom amenities, including shampoo, conditioners, and several choices of soap. When it introduced these amenities, they were supporting the core product—rooms. Today, in Hyatt and similar hotels, amenities have become facilitating products. Other hotels began to match Hyatt's amenity packages and soon travelers began to expect them in this class of hotel. Hilton spent 2 years analyzing consumer trends before developing its amenity package, which costs the company $225,000 on an average night.[3]

Bob Burns, the founder of Regent International Hotels, personally selected products that would enhance the chain's luxury image and provide differentiation. Thus, guests in the Regent of Hong Kong find full-size bottles of quality shampoo in the bathroom. Orange juice is a common menu item in hotels and restaurants throughout the world, but Bob Burns insisted that Regent Hotels serve fresh-squeezed orange juice in keeping with his concept of luxury service. Burns had studied and worked in the hotel industry for years, including a position as general manager of the upscale Kahala Hilton Resort in Hawaii. He had talked with thousands of guests over the years and felt he knew what they wanted.

Ideally, firms should choose supporting products that are not easily matched by competition. They should also be able to deliver supporting services in a professional manner. For example, some mid-scale hotels offer room service because they see it as a competitive advantage in attracting the business traveler. But the unprofessional delivery of supporting products can do more harm than good. Many mid-priced hotels offering room service lack a designated area in the kitchen for room-service carts, a room-service coordinator to answer the phone and write up the tickets, and designated room-service waiters. Necessary equipment and personnel are assembled at the time of the order and, as one might imagine, the results are sometimes disastrous. The person answering the phone lacks the proper training needed to ask the right questions, for example, how the steak is to be cooked, the type of salad dressing the customer would like, and the type of potatoes desired. After taking the order, the next step is to find someone to set up the cart and take the order up to the room. Likely candidates are the bellperson, bus person, or a service person from the dining room. The first two choices are not properly trained, but may quickly jump at the opportunity to gain a tip. Because they are not trained, the bellperson and bus person may forget essential items such as salt and pepper, sugar, forks, and napkins when setting up the cart. To further damage the hotel's image, the guest puts the tray in the hallway after finishing the meal. The tray will sit in the hallway until housekeeping picks it up the next morning.

In summary, supporting products do not offer a competitive advantage if they are not properly planned and implemented. They must meet or exceed customer expectations to have a positive effect.

Augmented Product

The **augmented product** includes accessibility, atmosphere, customer interaction with the service organization, customer participation, and customers' interaction with each other. These elements combine with the core, facilitating, and supporting products to provide the augmented product (see Figure 10-1).

From a managerial standpoint the core product provides a focus for the business; it is the reason for being. Facilitating products are those that are essential for providing the core product to the target market. Supporting products can help position a product. According to Christian Gronroos, a services marketing expert, the core, facilitating, and supporting products determine what the customer receives, but not how they receive it.[4] The delivery of the service affects the customer's perception of the service, illustrated by the room service example above. The augmented service offering combines what is offered with how it is delivered.

PRODUCT ISSUES

In the hospitality industry the customer usually comes to the service system, the hotel or restaurant. Here employees and customers interact with the service delivery system, which creates unique issues for the augmented hospitality product. We will now take a look at some of these issues.

Accessibility

Motel 6 locates its properties along a major highway because its customers arrive by automobile. Sheraton locates many of its hotels in the central business district because its guests are often business persons who use airlines. In a large city, many people will not travel over 10 minutes to go to a casual restaurant. There are usually ample choices within 10 minutes. Therefore, in urban areas restaurants must be within a 10-minute drive time of their market. On a divided highway, median strips can make a fast-food restaurant on the other side of the road appear inaccessible. Drivers may prefer to continue to another fast-food restaurant on their side of the road, rather than go to the next light and make a U-turn. Accessibility also includes hours of operation. A business that is not open is inaccessible to the customer. A hotel health club that opens at 7:00 A.M. does not help the

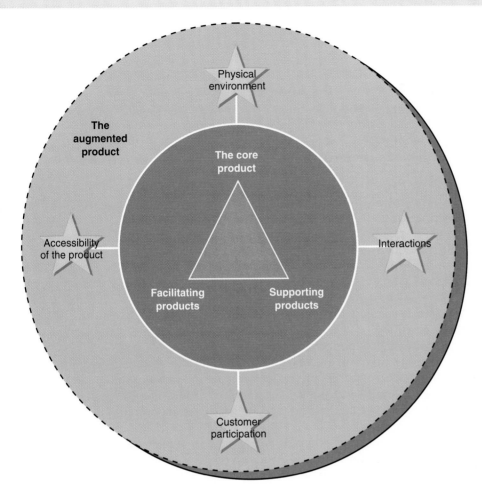

Figure 10-1
Product levels. *Source:*
Adapted from Gronroos, C.
(1987): *Developing the
Service Offering—A Source of
Competitive Advantage.* In
Surprenant, C., ed., *Add Value
to Your Service.* Chicago:
American Marketing
Association, p. 83.

business person who wants to work out at 6:00 A.M., eat breakfast, and go
to an 8:00 A.M. business appointment. One of the main augmentations of a
hospitality product is accessibility.

Atmosphere: The Physical Environment

Atmosphere is a critical element in services. It can be the customer's reason
for choosing to do business with an establishment. Burgundy's, a restaurant in
Houston, lacked street appeal and went out of business. The restaurant was
located in a strip shopping center with a glass panel exterior wall common in
many strip centers. The owners carpeted the concrete floor, put in booths,
installed a sign over the door, and opened the restaurant. Perhaps they felt
their food quality and service would attract customers. But few customers ever
reached the restaurant. The restaurant's exterior lacked identity or character
and was not inviting to potential customers. Conversely, T.G.I. Friday's has
used atmosphere effectively. Their brightly painted buildings with red and
white awnings suggest a casual restaurant with a friendly atmosphere.

Atmosphere is appreciated through the senses. Sensory terms provide
descriptions for the atmosphere of a particular set of surroundings. The

main sensory channels for atmosphere are sight, sound, scent, and touch. Specifically,

> The main **visual** dimensions of atmosphere are *color, brightness, size,* and *shape.*
> The main **aural** dimensions of atmosphere are *volume* and *pitch.*
> The main **olfactory** dimensions of atmosphere are *scent* and *freshness.*
> The main **tactile** dimensions of atmosphere are *softness, smoothness,* and *temperature.*

The following examples illustrate how sensory terms are used to describe particular surroundings. The typical atmosphere of an upscale French restaurant is subdued, quiet, and orderly. The typical atmosphere of a discotheque is bright, noisy, loud, and dynamic.

Atmosphere can affect purchase behavior in at least four ways. First, atmosphere may serve as an attention-creating medium. For example, El Torito uses a Mexican-style building to attract attention. The Casa Bonita Mexican Restaurant in Denver, Colorado, expanded the Mexican theme to include artificial volcanoes and a replica of the diving cliffs of Acapulco from which divers perform for dinner patrons.

Second, atmosphere may serve as a message-creating medium to the potential customer. The tile roof and stucco Spanish exterior architecture lets the prospective customer know that El Torito is a Mexican restaurant. The cheerful, informal appearance suggests a restaurant that is casual without being fast-food.

Third, atmosphere may serve as an effect-creating medium. Colors, sounds, and textures directly arouse visceral reactions that stimulate the purchase of a product. At El Torito and Casa Bonita bright colors and music create a festive atmosphere conducive to selling margaritas.

Finally, environment can be a mood-creating medium. An environmental psychologist has described environments as high load and low load.[5] High and low refer to the information that one receives from the environment. Bright colors, bright lights, loud noises, crowds, and movement are typical elements of a high-load environment, while their opposites are characteristic of a low-load environment.[6] A high-load environment creates a playful, adventurous mood, while low-load environments create a relaxing mood. Vacationers going to Las Vegas are likely to react positively to a high-load environment that offers the excitement that they were expecting to find. The front desk of the Flamingo Hilton is adjacent to the hotel's casino. While waiting to check in, guests hear the sounds of the casino, watch the players, and feel the excitement. On the other hand, business travelers, who often wish to relax in a homelike setting after a busy day, tend to prefer low-load environments. From the lobby of the Luxeford in Houston, guests can view the club area, with its comfortable stuffed chairs, end tables, and reading materials, a relaxing refuge for the tired executive.

The environments of many cities such as New York, Hong Kong, Tokyo, and Mexico City are by nature high load. Many of the successful hotels and restaurants in these cities purposely create a low-load atmosphere as a refuge. Conversely, many cities and towns exude low-load atmospheres, otherwise

Corporate hotels such as the Hilton at Short Hills use a low-load environment. Courtesy of Hilton Hotels Corporation.

referred to as dull and boring. Visitors to these towns are often surprised to find a successful restaurant or night club in which the level of excitement, color, and movement seem completely out of character. Managers of a company in Florence, South Carolina, were worried when they learned that an important buyer from London had unexpectedly arrived on a Saturday and would spend the weekend alone in their town. They need not have been concerned; the Englishman discovered several country western dance halls and pronounced that he had never before enjoyed such a great weekend.

Atmosphere must be considered when creating hospitality products. As marketers we should understand what the customer wants from the buying experience and what atmospheric variables will fortify the beliefs and emotional reaction that the buyers are seeking or in some cases, escaping. Will the proposed atmosphere effectively compete in a crowded market?[7]

Customer Interaction with the Service Delivery System

The customer participates in the delivery of most hospitality and travel products. There are three phases to this involvement: **joining, consumption,** and **detachment.**[8] In the joining stage the customer makes the initial inquiry contact. When designing products we must make it easy for people to learn about the new product. This information must be delivered in a professional way. Wyatts Cafeterias provide an example of a well-planned joining phase. When Wyatts decided to expand their product line by offering take-out meals, a special take-out counter that allowed customers to bypass the cafeteria queue was developed.

The **joining** stage is often enhanced through sampling. Visitors to foreign countries are often reluctant to order a full meal of native foods. The Inter-Continental Hotel of Jakarta, Indonesia, took steps to introduce visitors to the local cuisine by selling sample plates of selected native foods from a typical native pushcart in the afternoon cocktail area of the hotel adjacent to the lobby. This innovation created excitement, enhanced the atmosphere, introduced guests to native foods served in the hotel's restaurant, and served as a profit-making product line.

The **consumption phase** takes place when the service is consumed. In a restaurant it occurs when the customer is dining; in a hotel, when an individual is a guest. Designers of hospitality products must understand how guests will interact with the product. The employees, customers, and physical facilities are all part of the product. A business hotel that opens a concierge floor aimed at the luxury market must train its employees to meet the expectations of this new class of traveler. In addition to employee customer interaction, hospitality firms also have to consider how customers will interact with each other during the consumption stage. A business hotel in Houston located near Astroworld, a large amusement park, developed a package for the summer family market. The package proved to be so popular that some of the hotel's main market, business travelers, were driven away. The noise of the children in the hallways and the lobby changed the atmosphere. Gone was the comfortable atmosphere desired by the business traveler.

Physical features, layout, and signage can also be used to help customers interact with the product. In many hotels, finding your way to a meeting can be frustrating. This problem can be overcome by proper attention to directional signage. Signage can also be used to make customers aware of the existence of supporting products. Guests may leave a hotel not realizing that it had a health club or a business center. It does no good to invest in supporting products if guests aren't aware of their existence.

Occasionally, even the best designed signage is not observed or understood. Guests who appear lost in the Orlando Peabody Hotel are very apt to discover that an employee, including the general manager, will personally escort them to their destination. This does not occur by accident. Training and positive reinforcement in hotels such as the Peabody ensure that this type of service is an integral part of the hotel's product.

The **detachment phase** is when the customer is through using the product and departs. For example, in a hotel guests may need a bellperson to help with the bags. They will need to settle their account and require transportation to the airport. International travelers may need an airport departure tax stamp.

Thinking through these three stages helps management to understand how the customer will interact with the service delivery system, resulting in a product designed to fit the needs of the customer. For example, some hotels, where it is legal, purchase and resell airport departure tax stamps. The guest does not have to wait in line at the airport, and the hotel has eliminated one concern for the guest. Although the hotel does not receive income from reselling departure stamps, the guest leaves with a good impression. Similarly, well-managed international hotels will ask the guests if they have their passports and airline tickets and if they have cleared their safety deposit box when they are checking out. Managers should think through and then experience the joining, consumption, and detachment phases of their guests.

Customer Interaction with Other Customers

An area that is drawing the interest of hospitality researchers is the interaction of customers with each other. An airline flight on Friday afternoon from Dallas to Houston was sold out with a number of people on standby. Some on standby were construction workers returning home. They worked on jobs in Dallas during the week and had come straight from their job sites. The airline's ground crew, in an effort to maximize revenue, put a construction worker in an empty first-class seat. The passenger paying a premium to sit in first class did not appreciate a worker in dirty construction clothes in the next seat. Hospitality organizations must manage the interaction of customers to ensure that some customers do not negatively affect the experience of others.

The issue of customer interaction is a serious problem for hotels and resorts. The FIT guest (independent, non-tour) consistently objects to the presence of large GIT (group-inclusive tours). This problem is magnified if the GIT guests represent a different culture, speak a foreign language, or are from an age group years different from FIT guests.

The Shangrila Hotel of Singapore dealt successfully with this problem by constructing three different hotel properties on the same ground. The tower hotel serves GIT and lesser-revenue FITs. The Bougainvillea section serves a more upscale guest, and a third executive property is exclusively for use by very upscale guests. Interaction between the three groups is limited to the common outdoor swimming pool.

Ski resorts are facing a serious problem of guest interaction. Traditionally, skiers have been a fairly homogeneous group with common cultural norms, even though they arrive from widely separated geographic areas. German, French, Japanese, American and Mexican skiers tended to have societal commonalities despite differences in language.

The arrival of the snowboard changed this congenial mix of guests. Skiers began to complain that they must share the slopes with individuals dressed in baggy counterculture clothing who often show blatant disregard for slope-side courtesy. The management of ski resorts were suddenly faced with a serious problem. Resorts such as Aspen responded by refusing entry to snowboarders; others, such as Heavenly Valley in California/Nevada, refused entrance to part of the terrain.

The problem for management is compounded by the fact that a ski family often has a preteen or teenage member who wants to snowboard while other members wish to ski. The resort feels that if snowboarders are denied admittance the family will go elsewhere. This problem is certain to grow as the percentage of snowboarders increases. Some observers feel that the ultimate answer will be to develop separate snowboard resorts, but others feel this is unrealistic since snowboarders tend not to have the disposable income or spending habits of skiers.

Participation

Involving the guest in service delivery can increase capacity, improve customer satisfaction, and reduce costs. Hampton Inns serves a cold breakfast buffet. The combination of cold food and self-service means breakfast can be served with little labor cost. The Green Valley Athletic Club in Las Vegas installed a device that releases the locker key when the membership card is placed in a slot. Attendants at the towel counter no longer have to ask each member which locker they would like, negotiate alternatives when the member's favorite locker is not available, collect the member's card, issue the key, and return their card when the member is finished with the locker. Now they simply give out towels. The members are happy because they can pick out a locker in an uncrowded area, and the club's management is pleased because they were able to reduce the number of attendants at the towel counter.

Hardee's chain of hamburger restaurants features a self-service condiment bar at which guests can pile on tomatoes, lettuce, onions, cheese, and other condiments. The additional costs of the self-service condiment bar are offset by reduced labor costs and increased capacity of the systems. Furthermore, guests perceive that they are getting a good value. The employee taking the order has only to ask what size hamburger is desired. The counter person does not have to recite the list of condiments and wait while customers make up their minds. Cooks do not have to make sure that they get the correct condiments on each hamburger. They simply cook the burgers and put them on buns.

Hospitality products can be designed to involve customers in the service in other ways to reduce costs. Wendy's easily accessible trash cans encourage self-busing. When the Luxeford Hotel in Houston was designed, it was decided not to employ bellpersons, a service normally available in business class hotels. Through research, it was discovered that most individual business travelers arrived with light baggage, often no more than a hanging bag and a briefcase. Guests were quite willing to carry this luggage to their rooms. Housepersons equipped with pagers could assist the few guests that requested bell service.

One issue related to customer participation is how much input the customer will have in the design of the product. This is the issue of **standardization versus customization**. **Standardization** has several cost-reducing benefits. Employees need fewer skills and are easier to train when products are standardized. For example, a banquet cook working from a standardized selection of five dinner choices needs fewer skills than a chef who works at a hotel that offers customized client meals. Standardization also cuts down on the equipment and inventory needed, reduces costs, and adds to product consistency. McDonald's is a master at the efficient use of standardization.

In general, when people pay more for a product, they expect to have choices. A marketer targeting upscale markets must offer consumers more choice. Guests at luxury hotels expect menus of the day created by the chef and banquets themed to fit the occasion. When developing products, the degree of standardization and customization depends on the positioning and goals for the new product.

Standardized products offering a good value to their target markets include fast-food restaurants and limited-service hotels. They are easy to replicate and lend themselves well to multisite expansion. Conversely, highly customized products such as Caesar Ritz Hotels and Maxim's Restaurants cannot be easily reproduced. As unique products, they are able to draw customers throughout the region. An effective strategy for highly customized products is to expand the geographic base of their market.

The product a company offers is very complex. It is more than an airplane flight, a cruise, a hotel room, or a meal. It starts with the first contact with the company and ends after the guest has paid the bill and departs. A reservation line that puts the customer on hold for 2 minutes, a front-desk clerk who assigns the wrong type of room, a guest who cannot find the hotel's Spanish restaurant due to poor directions given by the housekeeper, or a person who has to wait for a cab for 30 minutes after leaving the restaurant can all influence the guest's perception of the product. When developing a product, one must think of the core product, the facilitating product, the supporting product, and the augmented product.

BRAND DECISIONS

Branding has long been popular in consumer goods. Some brands have become so powerful that they are used as generic terms for the product itself. Aspirin, shredded wheat, and cellophane were all brand names at one time. The real growth of branding came after the Civil War with the growth of national firms and national advertising media. Some of the early brands still survive, notably Borden's, Quaker Oats, Vaseline, and Ivory Soap. Most national brands in the hospitality industry are less than 30 years old. Today, branding has become a powerful force in the hospitality industry. Paul Slattery, a director of Kleinworth Benson Securities Ltd. of London, predicts that the hotel industry will see the growth of megachains.[9]

A brand is a name, term, sign, symbol, design, or a combination of these elements that is intended to identify the goods or services of a seller and differentiate them from those of competitors. A *brand name* is the part of a brand that can be vocalized. Examples are Disneyland, Hilton, Club Med, and Sizzler. A *brand mark* is the part of a brand that can be recognized but is not utterable, such as a symbol, design, or distinctive coloring or lettering. Examples are McDonald's golden arches and Hilton's H. A *trademark* is a brand or part of a brand that is given legal protection; it protects the seller's exclusive rights to use the brand name or brand mark.

Conditions That Support Branding

The following five conditions contribute to the branding decision:

1. The product is easy to identify by brand or trademark.
2. The product is perceived as the best value for the price.
3. Quality and standards are easy to maintain.
4. The demand for the general product class is large enough to support a regional, national, or international chain. Developing a critical mass to support advertising and administrative overhead is important.
5. There are economies of scale.[10]

We shall review these here.

The Product Is Easy to Identify by Brand or Trademark

Hotel and restaurant chains provide many examples of easily identifiable features. The red and white awnings and distinctive painting of T.G.I. Friday's and Holiday Inn's green sign are recognizable to customers. Most freeway billboards are directional signs relying on brand identification. They simply display the brand name and/or the brand mark and directions to the outlet.

The development of a brand name is a key element in developing the identity of the brand. Among the desirable characteristics of a brand name are these:

1. It should suggest something about the product's benefits and qualities. Examples: Dairy Queen, Comfort Inns, Pizza Hut, Burger King, American Airlines.

2. It should be easy to pronounce, recognize, and remember. Short names help. Examples: Wendy's, Hilton, The Shuttle (United's limited-service airline).

3. It should be distinctive. Examples: El Torito, Avis, Bennigan's.

4. For larger firms looking at future expansion into foreign markets, the name should translate easily into foreign languages. Some firms have found that their names have a negative meaning when translated into the language of the countries into which they want to expand.

5. It should be capable of registration and legal protection.

In 1990, Quality International changed its name to Choice Hotels International. The name Choice is short, easy to remember, and conveys a benefit. It also supports the segmentation strategy of the company. Choice offers four major brands: Sleep, Comfort, Quality, and Clarion (Figure 10-2). Additionally, Friendship, Econo Lodges, and Rodeway Inns were purchased by Choice. The full name, Choice Hotels International, conveys the current international position of the company with hotels in 19 countries on five continents.

Figure 10-2
Brand positioning strategy. Courtesy of Choice Hotels International. SLEEP®, COMFORT®, QUALITY®, CLARION®, FRIENDSHIP®, ECONO LODGE®, and RODEWAY® are registered service marks and trademarks of Choice Hotels International, Inc.

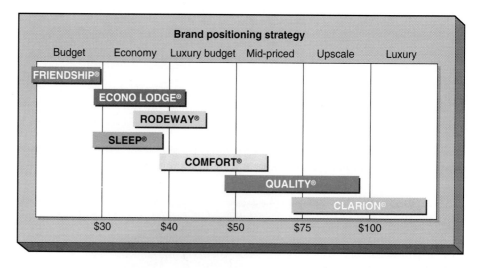

Sometimes a company will outgrow its original name.[11] Name changes by major chains include Western International to Westin and Hilton Hotels to Hilton Hotels and Resorts. Societal changes often prompt the need for a name change. During the railroad era lasting until the 1960s in the United States, many restaurants and hotels associated themselves with this primary mode of transportation. "Choo Choo" bars, Terminal, Station, Track One, Locomotives, Caboose, and other railroad terms were commonly associated with the hospitality industry. The same phenomenon is slowly but surely occurring with the airline industry as names such as the Cockpit Lounge or the Jet restaurant, have been dropped.

Companies may wish to change their image through their logos, without changing their name. Hyatt recently changed its logo. The new logo matches the company's leading-edge image and capitalizes on its strongest symbol, the Hyatt name. Darryl Hartley-Leonard, president of Hyatt International at the time of the change, explained that there was a gap between consumer perception of their logo and the hotel chain. Research showed that consumers perceived Hyatt to be stylish, contemporary, innovative, and high quality. Conversely, they perceived their logo to be dull and old-fashioned. The new logo was created to fit the chain's consumer image. In major chains such as Hyatt, a logo change that will affect all signage on all hotels, supplies, and merchandise will cost millions of dollars.[12] Hyatt invested over $8 million in this change.

Once a name has been chosen, it must be protected. Quality International (now Choice Hotels International) once chose the name McSleep for its line of budget hotels. Quality changed the name to Sleep Inns as a result of legal action by McDonald's.[13] Companies realize they must protect their trade names or risk losing exclusive use.

Choice has developed a logo so that each of its brands can be easily identified. Courtesy of Choice Hotels International. SLEEP®, COMFORT®, QUALITY®, CLARION®, FRIENDSHIP®, ECONO LODGE®, and RODEWAY® are registered service marks and trademarks of Choice Hotels International, Inc.

The Product Is Perceived as the Best Value for the Price

A brand name derives its value from consumer perceptions. Brands attract consumers by developing a perception of good quality and value. La Quinta developed a good image with the overnight business traveler, while Embassy Suites developed an image of good value for those wanting an all-suites hotel. Earlier in Chapter 6 we provided an example of how Marriott carried out extensive research to ensure that Fairfield Inns would be perceived as giving good value. Customers must perceive the brand as a better value than other existing choices.

The concept of a brand name extends to tourist destinations. Vail, Aspen, Acapulco, Palm Springs, and the French Riviera have developed strong reputations, consumer perceptions, and expectations. Individuals who promote and develop tourist destinations must assume responsibility for enhancing and ensuring favorable brand images.

Strict building codes, promotional coordination, presentation of historic sites, and protection against environmental degradation are essential to the success of tourist destinations. Chambers of commerce, visitor promotion associations, town councils, county commissioners, environmental groups, and historical societies play a vital role in protecting and enhancing the brand image of a destination.

Quality and Standards Are Easy to Maintain

To be successful, a large multiunit brand such as Pizza Hut, Holiday Inn, Chili's, or Nathan's Hot Dogs must develop system-wide standards to meet the expectations of the customer. If the brand is successful in developing an image of quality, customers will expect quality in all outlets carrying the same brand name. Inconsistent standards and policies will detract from the value of the brand. Consistency and standardization are critical factors.

Consumers often become brand loyal. The major benefit of branding comes from the development of loyal customers. They purchase the brand whenever it is available; thus the greater the availability, the greater the power of the brand name. Most major hotel chains try to have locations at major destinations in their market areas. Some chains in the United States have opened hotels that they knew would not be profitable for years in order to provide a hotel for their customers in a major city.

McDonald's in Paris attracts Parisians, Germans, Americans, and other nationalities from around the world who are familiar with the McDonald's name. The golden arches have become one of the most powerful brand

Best Western has developed a name and logo that are recognized internationally. This is a photo of the Best Western in Winsford, England. Courtesy of Best Western International, Inc.

marks in the world. McDonald's created a demand for its product and then developed more than 14,000 stores to meet this demand.

Not all brands are as successful as McDonald's. Peter Yesawich, president of Robinson, Yesawich, & Pepperdine, claims that the success of a brand depends on creating a clear differentiation in the customer's mind. Yesawich states that advertising must communicate the perception of a new product. The new brand must communicate benefits to the customer.[14] Robert Hazzard, CEO of Choice Hotels International, says that "people will go for a good deal. The problem is you've got to tell them what a good deal is." Hazzard claims that other hotel brands fail to differentiate themselves—tell why they offer a better deal than their competition—in their advertising. He states that "Holiday Inns had Bugs Bunny jumping across a swimming pool, likewise other major chains had television spots that failed to say here is the benefit, to you the consumer. In our ads we had Vanna White, hostess of Wheel of Fortune, coming out of a suitcase saying, 'Stay with us, not only do you get a comfortable room, but you get a thousand dollars in free discount coupons'".[15]

The Demand for the General Product Class Is Large Enough to Support a Regional, National, or International Chain

New products are generally developed to serve a particular market niche. Later the product may be expanded to encompass multi-niches, or the original niche may grow in market size until it is a huge market share product such as McDonald's.

The product class of limited-service hotels developed as a small niche within the hotel market but grew until it encompassed many brand names, including limited-service brands of hotel chain companies, such as Hampton Inn (Promus), Ramada Express, and Fairfield Inn (Marriott).

Some hospitality products are strictly regional in nature. Biscuitville, the Waffle House, and Bo Jangles are restaurant chains that have enjoyed considerable success in southern states but have not expanded nationally. In a nation as large as the United States a strong regional brand is worth multimillions of dollars in sales. As regional tastes cross boundaries, firms that were once considered to be geographically limited have expanded nationwide and even internationally.

La Quinta Inns of San Antonio, Texas, has entered Mexico with a strategy of bypassing large cities such as Monterrey and instead concentrating on smaller cities, such as Leon and Aguascalientes. Because La Quinta is based near the Mexican border and has many Spanish-speaking employees, the company believed that starting a Mexican operation made good sense. "We're pretty well geared up for this kind of thing" stated Gary L. Mead, president and COO.[16]

Demand estimation for a general product class such as all-suite hotels, roasted chicken, or Mexican foods is not a precise science, but examples abound of entrepreneurs who successfully envisioned a growing demand for a product class, such as those who built Boston Chicken.

The management of Pepsico envisioned a strong national chain of fast-food Mexican food restaurants known as Taco Bell. Many observers of the fast-food industry believe that the product class Chinese food is large enough to support a national chain. General Mills is currently working on the development of a chain of Chinese restaurants, and Panda Express has had some success in this area.

Youth hostels are important lodging establishments in many parts of the world, but have been slow to be accepted in the United States. They were originally developed to provide traveling students with low-cost lodging. Typically, they offer Spartan accommodations, with guests often sharing sleeping and bathing areas. In Australia they are called backpacker's hotels and cater to a broad age group of travelers, all seeking economy lodging. As the demand for this type of accommodation increases, there may be sufficient economic opportunity for a regional or national chain of youth hostels.

There Are Economies of Scale

Branding costs money. The company promoting a brand name has to develop standards, systems, and quality assurance programs. The brand name must be promoted. To justify expenditures for administration and advertising, the brand should provide economies of scale. Typical economies of scale include reduced promotional costs, since all brand units in the area of influence of the advertising benefit from the promotion. Management information systems, reservation systems, national purchasing contracts, and common architectural designs are ways in which brands can provide economies of scale.

Quincy's Steak House and Red Roof Inns appear to follow a strategy of developing multiple units within an area within a short period of time. The number of units within an area serves as a promotional tactic since the public suddenly sees several. Word-of-mouth promotion is a direct result. The cost of advertising in local or regional media such as newspaper, television, and radio broadcast can be allocated among several units. A single stand-alone restaurant or hotel lacks the mass impact of multi-units and does not have the advertising budget to make an impact in a regional or national market.

A chain of beef restaurants known as Victoria Station was instantly popular due to quality food, moderately priced menus, and an unusual ambience in railroad box cars. Unfortunately, the chain ultimately failed. One reason was a franchising program that allowed franchisees to develop Victoria Station units virtually anywhere in the Unites States and its possessions without ensuring that multiple units existed in the area. A single unit in the Hawaiian Islands lacked essential economies of scale, as did other single units scattered throughout the nation.

NEW-PRODUCT DEVELOPMENT

A company has to be good at developing new products. It also has to be good at managing them in the face of changing tastes, technologies, and competition. Every product seems to go through a life cycle: it is born, passes through several phases, and eventually dies as younger products come along that better serve consumer needs.

The product life cycle presents two major challenges. First, because all products eventually decline, a firm must find new products to replace aging ones (the problem of new-product development). Second, the firm must understand how its products age and change marketing strategies as products pass through life-cycle stages. We will first look at the problem of finding and developing new products and then at the problem of managing them successfully during their life cycles.

Given the rapid changes in tastes, technology, and competition, a company cannot afford to rely only on its existing products. Customers want and expect new and improved products. Competition will do its best to provide them. For example, Kentucky Fried Chicken developed its Lite'n Crispy skinless fried chicken in response to consumer demand for more nutritious fast-food meals. The product contained 20% less fat than its regular fried chicken. KFC tested the product in five cities during 1990 and rolled it out on a national basis in 1991. Kyle Craig, president of Kentucky Fried Chicken USA, stated that, "This is a very important positioning move for us in positioning KFC as a contemporary concept." He said that it gave Kentucky Fried Chicken a product that the other fried chicken chains did not have.[17] Unfortunately, this product did not gain sufficient customer interest to warrant retaining it as a permanent part of the KFC product line. Market success is by no means assured for any product despite professional research and development.

All hospitality companies must continuously be alert to trends and ready to try new products. Every company needs a new-product development program. One expert estimates that half of the profits of all U.S. companies come from products that didn't exist 10 years ago.

A company can obtain new products in two ways. One is through acquisition—buying a whole company, a patent, or a license to produce someone else's product. As the cost of developing and introducing major new products climbs, many companies decide to acquire existing brands rather than create new ones. Thus Accor acquired Motel 6, Ladbroke acquired Hilton International, Choice acquired Rodeway, Econo Lodge, and Friendship Inns, and Pepsico acquired KFC, Pizza Hut, and Taco Bell.

A company can also obtain new products through new-product development—by setting up its own research and development department. By new products we mean original products, product improvements, product modifications, and new brands that the firm develops through its own R&D efforts. In this chapter, we will concentrate on new-product development.

In a 2-year period, 1990–1991, 1000 hotels and motels in the United States failed[18] according to one estimate. Max Schnallinger has been involved in the development of 200 restaurants; one of his latest restaurants is China Max in Hong Kong. He claims nine out of ten restaurants in the United States fail. Why do so many new products fail? There are several reasons. A high-level executive might push a favorite idea in spite of poor marketing research findings. Or if the idea is good, the market size may have been overestimated. Or the actual product was not designed as well as it should have been. Or it has been incorrectly positioned in the market, priced too high, or advertised poorly. Sometimes the costs of product development are higher than expected, or competitors fight back harder than expected.

Thus companies face a problem: they must develop new products, but the risk of failure is high. The solution lies in strong new-product planning and in setting up a systematic new-product development process for finding and nurturing new products. The major steps in this process are shown in Figure 10-3.

IDEA GENERATION

New-product development starts with idea generation, the systematic search for new ideas. A company typically has to generate many ideas to find a few good ones. The search for new product ideas should be systematic rather than haphazard. Otherwise, the company risks finding new ideas that will not be compatible with its type of business.

The company should carefully define the new-product development strategy. The strategy should state what products and markets to emphasize. It should also state what the company wants from its new products, whether it be high cash flow, market share, or some other objective. For example, McDonald's added salads to defend against the threat of market share loss from Wendy's salad bar, while Pizza Hut added individual pizzas to attract lunch customers. Finally, the strategy should state the amount of effort that is to be devoted to developing original products, changing existing products, and imitating competitors' products.

To obtain a flow of new product ideas, the company must tap several idea sources. Major sources of new product ideas are discussed next.

Internal Sources. One study found that more than 55% of all new-product ideas come from within the company. Companies can find new ideas through formal research and development, or company executives can brainstorm new-product ideas. The company's salespeople are another good source, because they are in daily contact with customers. Guest-contact employees, who are in a position to get feedback from customers, are another excellent source of product ideas. Just as managers look for new ideas when they visit other restaurants or hotels, employees who care about their jobs do the same thing. Often management never takes advantage of this resource by asking the employees to share their observations.

Within the hotel industry, new-product decisions are made at both the corporate and the property levels. New-product decision makers at the corporate level include mid-level to top management. In some cases, individuals not directly employed by the company but closely affiliated with it, such as bankers, lawyers, and consultants, become involved in this process.

Decision makers at the property level often include the owner if the hotel is not owned by the chain. In some cases the owner is represented by

Figure 10-3
Major stages in new product development.

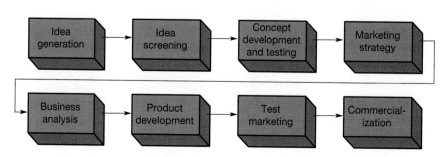

someone such as a president. Others involved in the process are general manager, department managers, and directors of various areas. Often, a corporate vice-president from the chain may participate in the process.

Customers. Almost 28% of all new product ideas come from watching and listening to customers. Consumer needs and wants can be examined through consumer surveys. The company can analyze customer questions and complaints to find new products that better solve consumer problems. Company management or salespeople can meet with customers to obtain suggestions. Managers gain insight into guest needs by walking around the hotel or restaurant and talking with customers. Finally, consumers often create new products on their own. Companies can benefit by finding these products and putting them on the market. Pillsbury gets promising new recipes through its annual Bake-Off. One of Pillsbury's four cake-mix lines and several variations of another came directly from Bake-Off winners' recipes. The owner of a country inn held a dinner party for her friends. She asked guests to bring their favorite dishes and enough copies of the recipes so that all the guests could have a copy. This provided an interesting evening as well as several menu ideas for the country inn.

Many upscale hotels hold a weekly cocktail reception for special guests. The general manager and managers of various departments serve as hosts. This provides management with an opportunity to informally ask these guests for suggestions as to how the hotel can continue to provide outstanding service. Since these guests visit hotels throughout the world and are often innovators in their respective fields, their opinions and ideas are valuable and respected.

Competitors. About 27% of new-product ideas come from analyzing competitors' products. Many companies buy competing new products, see how they are made, analyze their sales, and decide whether they should bring out new products of their own. A company can also watch competitor's ads and other communications to obtain clues about new products. When taking a competitor's idea, one should be able to do it as least as good as the originator. Customers will compare the copy to the original; if that comparison is negative, the product will suffer.

One can appear to be innovative by picking up ideas from other markets. Michael Turback, formerly of Turback's Inn in Ithaca, New York, made it a point to go to the restaurant show in Chicago and to visit restaurants in New York City to gather ideas for his restaurant. His customers viewed him as an innovator.

Many successful hospitality products have been copied by international entrepreneurs. Often the copy product is of inferior quality and may create a poor reputation for the product class, so when the original company enters the market it must overcome a negative image. In other cases, the foreign company may develop a product that is so successful that it sets the standard for its product class. The restaurant chain Pollo Campero of Central America has become the standard against which competitors such as KFC are compared.

When companies transplant ideas from other areas of the country, they must be careful to take regional cultural and social differences into consideration. A former chef of a restaurant on the California coast, specializing in excellent cuisine served in a casual atmosphere, transported the restaurant's concept to Bryan, Texas. The California restaurant offered fine cuisine at a moderate price. Unfortunately, tastes and spending habits were not the same in the small Texas town. Rather than elegantly prepared seafood, the people of Bryan preferred fried seafood or a steak and potato. What was moderately priced in California was high priced in Bryan. The chef's elegant seafood restaurant has closed and the location now houses a steak house.

Hotel executives can pick up competitive information by staying at a competitor's hotel. Excellent competitive information is available from the annual reports of publicly traded hotel companies. The hotel industry is relatively small. Executives and owners tend to know and associate with their peers from competitive hotels. This is true for most communities. Internationally, general managers of different chains tend to know each other and to swap information. The hotel industry is one of the least secretive industries. Managers can easily obtain competitive information.

Distributors and Suppliers. Distributors are close to the market and can pass along information about consumer problems and new-product possibilities. Suppliers can tell the company about new concepts, techniques, and materials that can be used to develop new products. They can also tell which food products are moving in competitive restaurants and new products ordered by hotels.

Hospitality suites are often sponsored by distributors and suppliers at industry trade shows, seminars, and conferences. It is usually a good idea to visit these suites for purposes of picking up information about trends and competitive strategies, as well as to meet important contacts.

Other Sources. Other idea sources include trade magazines, shows, and seminars; government agencies; new-product consultants; advertising agencies; marketing research firms; university and commercial laboratories; and inventors.

IDEA SCREENING

The purpose of idea generation is to create a large number of ideas. The purpose of the succeeding stages is to reduce the number of ideas. The first such stage is idea screening.

The purpose of screening is to spot good ideas and drop poor ones as soon as possible. Product development costs rise greatly in later stages, so the company wants to proceed only with ideas that will turn into profitable products. Most companies require their executives to write up new-product ideas on a standard form that can be reviewed by a new-product committee. The executives describe the product, the target market, and the competition. They make some rough estimates of market size, product price, development time and costs, manufacturing costs, and rate of return. They also answer the following questions: Is this idea good for our particular company? Does it mesh well with the company's objectives and strategies? Do we have the people, skills, equipment, and resources to make it succeed? Many companies have well-designed systems for rating and screening new-product ideas. Figure 10-4 is a qualitative and quantitative screening work sheet developed by Tom Feltenstein of the American Restaurant Marketing Group.

The idea or concept screening stage is the appropriate time to carefully review the question of *product line compatibility*. A common error in

Qualitative screening worksheet

1. Proposed new product _____
2. General description _____
3. Company objectives it will meet _____
4. Role it will play: _____ new entree _____ side dish _____ new product category
5. Key strengths or opportunities _____
6. Key weaknesses or threats _____
7. Expected impact on sales: _____ increase traffic _____ increase frequency
   trade up _____ draw new customer group(s) _____ increase average check
8. Yearly sales goal _____ Profit-impact goal _____
9. Items it will cannibalize _____ To what degree _____
10. Target customers _____
11. Day part(s) affected _____
12. Target price _____ Target portion size _____
13. Key ingredients _____
14. Estimated food costs _____
15. Expected production required _____
16. Current equipment required _____
17. New equipment required _____
18. Space required _____
19. Labor required _____
20. Additional employees required _____
21. Special training required _____
22. Negative effects on current production _____
23. Negative effects on staff _____
24. Similar competitive items _____
25. Likely competitive response _____
26. Key benefits _____
27. Key disadvantages _____
28. Required for development:
    a. facilities _____
    b. budget _____
    c. personnel _____
    d. special expertise _____
    e. time _____

Quantitative screening worksheet

CRITERIA	RATING (A)	WEIGHT (B)	TOTAL (A x B)
Image			
Menu approach			
Overall company goals			
Company strengths			
Company opportunities			
Desired role			
Level of quality			
Pricing			
Current customers			
Targeted customers			
Services			
Specialties			
Menu voids			
Day-part voids			
Production procedures			
Labor content			
Equipment			
Space availability			
Suppliers			
Developmental capabilities			
TOTAL			

Each new product idea is rated on a scale of 1 (low) to 5 (high) on each of the criteria. Then a weight of 1 to 5 is assigned to each criterion. The product of the rating and the weight gives a total score for the product on each criterion. The sum of these scores gives a final grand total for comparison with other proposed products.

Figure 10-4

Qualitative and quantitative screening worksheets. Reprinted by permission of Elsevier Science, Inc. from "New Product Development in Food Service: A Structural Approach," by Tom Feltenstein, *Cornell Hotel and Restaurant Administration Quarterly*, vol. 27, no. 3, pp. 66–67. ©1986 by Cornell University.

new-product development is to introduce products that are incompatible with the company. The following describes major compatibility issues. How will the product assist us to

- Fulfill our mission?
- Meet corporate objectives?
- Meet property objectives?
- Protect and promote our core business?
- Protect and please our key customers?
- Better utilize existing resources?
- Support and enhance existing product lines?

Concept Development and Testing

Surviving ideas must now be developed into product concepts. It is important to distinguish among a product idea, a product concept, and a product image. A *product idea* envisions a possible product that company managers might offer to the market. A *product concept* is a detailed version of the idea stated in meaningful consumer terms. A *product image* is the way consumers picture an actual or potential product.

Major restaurant chains cannot afford to place an untested menu in all their restaurants. Burger King, like others, uses test market restaurants in selected cities. The Piedmont area of North Carolina was used as a test market for American Fries. Apparently, the product performed poorly, because it disappeared from the menus. Hotels commonly introduce new-product ideas to selected floors and to selected properties.

Concept Development. In the late 1970s, Marriott recognized that the urban market for its current hotel products was becoming saturated. They needed a hotel concept that would work in secondary sites and suburban locations. Marriott decided to focus its assets on the company's core business, lodging, through the development of a new product.

This was a product idea. Customers, however, do not buy a product idea; they buy a product. The marketer's task is to develop this idea into alternative product concepts, determine how attractive each is to customers, and choose the best one.

The concept for the new product was called Courtyard by Marriott. Marriott selected persons from different areas of the company to manage the development of this new product. The company conducted extensive competitor and market analysis and, as a result of this research, developed the following conceptual framework for the project:

1. It would be tightly focused for the transient market.
2. It would house fewer than 150 rooms.
3. It would project a residential image. (Through their research Marriott identified a major segment of hotel users who did not like hotels! These consumers preferred homelike settings.)
4. It would not have significant cannibalization of Marriott's other hotels.

5. It would have a limited-menu restaurant.

6. Public and meeting spaces would be limited.

7. It would be a standardized product with five to eight in a region.

8. The Marriott name would be attached for recognition and a halo effect.[19] A halo or umbrella effect refers to the carryover of a corporate or brand name to other products. The name Nabisco has a halo effect for many products, from Oreo cookies to shredded wheat.

Concept Testing. Concept testing occurs within a group of target consumers. New-product concepts may be presented through word or picture descriptions. Marriott tested their concept for the Courtyard Motel using a statistical technique called conjoint analysis. This involved showing potential target guests different motel configurations and having them rank them from the most to the least desirable. The rankings were statistically analyzed to determine the optimal motel configuration.[20]

In most cases, however, simpler consumer attitude surveys are used. Suppose that 10% of the consumers said they "definitely" would buy and another 5% said "probably." The company would project these figures to the population size of this target group to estimate sales volume. But the estimate would be uncertain, because people do not always carry out their stated intentions.

Unfortunately, the Marriott example is far too rare within the hospitality industry. The corporate headquarters of major hotel, resort, and restaurant chains do engage in professional concept testing, but smaller chains and individual properties often pass over this critical stage. They often move directly from product idea to full implementation.

In some cases, intuition or luck proves to be correct and the new product is a winner, thus placing the company well ahead of competition. However, the history of the hospitality industry has proved that in many cases the idea needed the evidence of concept testing, because the product proved to be a disastrous mistake. In the case of a tactical product decision, such as a hotel room amenity or a new room-service beverage, there may be relatively little damage from an incorrect new-product decision. This is not true of new-product decisions involving heavy capital expenditures, such as a new ship for a cruise line or a new destination resort. These decisions involve multimillions of dollars and have sometimes proved so disastrous that hospitality companies have been forced into bankruptcy. The expenditure of a few thousand dollars and a few extra months for concept testing might prove invaluable in the long run.

Marketing Strategy

The next step is marketing strategy development—designing an initial marketing strategy for introducing the product into the market. The marketing strategy statement consists of three parts. The first part describes the target market, the planned product positioning, and the sales, market share, and profit goals for the first few years. The target markets for Courtyard by Marriott were business travelers who wanted moderately priced, high-quality rooms and pleasure travelers who wanted a safe, comfortable room.

The second part of the marketing strategy statement outlines the product's planned price, distribution, and marketing budget for the first year. Statistical software enabled Marriott to build sophisticated models. These models provided information on pricing and expected market share based on these prices. The segmentation information gave Marriott the information it needed for marketing the hotels.

The third part of the marketing strategy statement describes the planned long-run sale, profit goals, and marketing-mix strategy over time.

Business Analysis

Once management decides on the product concept and marketing strategy, it can evaluate the business attractiveness of the proposal. Business analysis involves a review of the sales, costs, and profit projections to determine whether they satisfy the company's objectives. If they do, the product can move to the product-development stage.

To estimate sales, the company should look at the sales history of similar products and should survey market opinion. It should estimate minimum and maximum sales to learn the range of risk.

After preparing the sales forecast, management can estimate the expected costs and profits for the product. The costs are estimated by the R&D, operations, accounting, and finance departments. The analysis includes the estimated marketing costs. The company then uses the sales and costs figures to analyze the new product's financial attractiveness.

The tools in Figure 10-5 can assist managers in their business analysis.

Product Development

If the product concept passes the business test, it moves into product development. Here the product concept develops into a prototype of the product. Up to now it existed only as a word description, a drawing, or a mock-up. This step, which calls for a large increase in investment, will show whether the product idea can be turned into a workable product. The company will develop one or more physical versions of the product concept. It hopes to find a prototype that meets the following criteria:

1. Consumers perceive it as having the key features described in the product concept statement.
2. It performs safely under normal use.
3. It can be produced for the budgeted costs.

Developing a successful prototype can take days, weeks, months, or even years. Marriott built a Courtyard room prototype with portable walls. They developed three room types: a standard, a short, and a narrow configuration. The consumers liked the overall concept. They rejected the narrow version, but did not object to the short version, which Marriott estimated would save close to $100,000 per hotel.

One problem with developing a prototype is that the prototype is often limited to the core product. Many of the intangible aspects of the

CORPORATE   Effect on Corporate Image
             Long Run Compatibility/Cannibalism
             Finance—Millions
             Corporate Form—Ownership, Franchise, Contracts
             Marketing—Compatibility w/other Company Products
             Human Resources
             Others

PROPERTY   Effect on Property's Image
             Effect on Corporate Image
             Compatibility w/Existing Product Line
             Financing—"0" to over $1,000,000
             Cash Flow/Profits
             Compatibility—Operations—w/Various Departments
                (particularly Human Resources)
             Timing—Product Life Cycle
             Customer/Guest—Reaction

PROPERTY—NEW PRODUCT EVALUATION

Objectives		*Expected Resources Required*	
$	_____	$ Capital Investment	_____
Volume	_____	Personnel	
Expected Effect on:	_____	Existing—Full Time	Days _____
			$
Margins	_____	New—Full Time	Days _____
			$
Occupancy	_____	Existing—Part Time	Day + $
Yield	_____	New—Part Time	Day + $
Average Daily Rates	_____	Materials—Not Covered in Capital Investment	
Other Cash Flow	_____	$	
Etc.	_____	Units	
Other—Qualitative Objectives		Support	
_____		Promotional	$ _____
_____		Administrative	$ _____
_____		Other	$ _____

Figure 10-5
New product decision factors.

product, such as the performance of the employees, cannot be included. Marketers have to remember that they must try to give the prospective customer an idea of the intangible aspects of the product, including the supporting and facilitating goods and services.

Test Marketing

If the product passes functional and consumer tests, the next step is market testing. Market testing is the stage in which the product and marketing program are introduced into more realistic market settings.

Market testing allows the marketer to gain experience in marketing the product, to find potential problems, and to learn where more information is needed before the company goes to the great expense of full introduction. Market testing evaluates the product and the entire marketing program in real market situations. The product, its positioning strategy, advertising, distribution, pricing, branding, packaging, and budget levels are evaluated during market testing. The company uses market testing to learn how consumers and dealers will react to handling, using, and repurchasing the product. Market testing results can be used to make better sales and profit forecasts.

The amount of market testing needed varies with each new product. Market testing costs can be enormous, and market testing takes time during which competitors may gain an advantage. When the costs of developing and introducing the product are low or when management is already confident that the new product will succeed, the company may do little or no product testing. Minor modifications of current products or copies of successful competitor products might not need testing. The company may do considerable market testing if one of these conditions is present: The introduction of a new product requires a large investment, or management is not sure of the product or the marketing program. Some products and marketing programs are tested, then withdrawn, changed, and retested many times over a period of several years before they are finally introduced. The costs of market tests are high, but they are often small compared with the costs of making a major mistake.

Marriott chose Atlanta as a test market for its first Courtyard by Marriott, which opened in 1983. The test market model contained different-sized rooms to gain consumer perceptions. Marriott discovered that the rooms could be smaller than they had originally planned. The guests said that they wanted doors on the closets. The test model had doorless closets, which was common in that category.

Commercialization

Market testing gives management the information it needs to make a final decision about whether to launch the new product. If the company goes ahead with commercialization, it will face high costs. It may have to spend between $10 million and $100 million for advertising and sales promotion alone in the first year. For example, McDonald's spent more than $5 million dollars per week on advertising during the introduction of its McDLT sandwich.

In launching a new product, the company must make four decisions: when, where, to whom, and how.

When?

The first decision is whether it is the right time to introduce the new product. In Marriott's case the test market hotel experienced an occupancy of 90%.

Marketing Highlight 10-1

Radisson Hotels Develops Its Own Pizza Company as a Competitive Move

Hotel customers were opting to call Domino's or other local pizza companies as an alternative to room service. For under $15, guests could receive a meal for two including beverages and tip. On most room-service menus, two hamburgers, two soft drinks, room service charge, and a tip would come to well over $20. Many guests viewed pizza as both a preferable meal and a much better value.

Hotel managers throughout the country watched as Domino's delivery vehicles pulled up to hotels and delivery persons in Domino's uniforms carried pizza boxes to their hotel's guest rooms. This was an embarrassment for the hotel as well as a loss of revenue. Hotels across the country—the Hilton Southwest in Houston, the Midland Hotel in Chicago, and the Grand Hyatt in Washington to name a few—began offering their own room-service pizza.

Radisson went one step further. Radisson developed its own pizza company, Napolizza Pizza. Promotion for the pizza in the guest room is a local number, rather than the hotel's room service number. Hotel managers wanted to give the impression that the pizza was produced by a pizza restaurant, not the hotel. The prices are competitive with the local market. The delivery persons have a distinct uniform, jacket, and cap with the Napolizza logo.

Customers dissatisfied with the high price of room service saw pizza delivery as an alternative. Radisson finally fought back by offering an alternative to high-priced room service menus. They developed their own pizza to keep outside suppliers from gettting their guests' food dollars.

Some hotels, rather than produce their own pizza, have developed an alliance with a pizza retaurant. Some Marriott locations use Pizza Hut; Hospitality Franchise Systems (HFS) has worked out a deal with Pizza Hut to deliver to 900 of its hotels. Typically, these agreements involve a commission paid to the hotel for each pizza sold. Now when a pizza delivery truck pulls up to the hotel, the hotel is getting something out of it.[21]

Where?

The company must decide whether to launch the new product in a single location, a region, several regions, the national market, or the international market. Few companies have the confidence, capital, and capacity to launch new products into full national distribution. Instead they develop a planned market rollout over time. Small companies in particular tend to select an attractive city and put on a blitz campaign to enter the market. They may enter other cities one at a time. Large companies may decide to introduce their product into one region and then move to the next. Companies with national distribution networks, such as auto companies, often launch their new models in the national market. Marriott decided to introduce the Courtyard in regional markets of five to eight. By January 1986, they had 300 sites open, under contract, or under construction.

To Whom?

Within the rollout markets, the company must target its distribution and promotion to the best prospect groups. Management should have determined profiles of prime prospects during earlier market testing. It must now

Courtyard by Marriott.
Courtesy of Marriott
International, Jim Burtnett,
photographer.

fine-tune its market identification, looking for early adopters, heavy users, and opinion leaders.

How?

The company must develop an action plan for introducing the new product into the selected markets and spend the marketing budget on the marketing mix.

Product Development through Acquisition

Large companies will sometimes buy a small restaurant chain rather then develop their own new concepts. They are able to watch the fledgling chain grow. They sit back and observe its customer base, volume of sales per unit, and how easy or difficult it is to open new stores. When they are convinced that the new chain looks like a winner and makes a good strategic fit with their organization, the large company simply buys the chain. This is what Brinker International did when they purchased Romano's Macaroni Grill, and Pepsico purchased Chevy's and California Pizza Kitchen. This method of product development reduces the risk considerably for large companies, who have the assets to purchase and then develop the chain. This acquisition strategy has a new class of restaurant entrepreneurs, those who try to develop a chain with the specific purpose of getting it going and selling it to a large chain.

Another technique is to purchase distressed chains. The mismanagement of a chain and resulting poor performance can drive the market value of the chain down. These chains become attractive targets for companies who feel they can turn them around. This is what Pepsico did when they purchased KFC and Taco Bell.[22] Thus, rather than develop your own products, another option is to purchase new products.

After launching a new product, management wants the product to enjoy a long and lucrative life. Although the product is not expected to sell forever, managers want to earn enough profit to compensate for the effort and risk. To maximize profits, a product's marketing strategy is normally reformulated several times. Strategy changes are often the result of changing market and environmental conditions as the product moves through the **product life cycle** (PLC).

The product life cycle is marked by five distinct stages (Figure 10-6):

1. **Product development** begins when the company finds and develops a new product idea. During product development, sales are zero and the company's investment costs add up.

2. **Introduction** is a period of slow sales growth as the product is being introduced into the market. Profits are nonexistent in this stage because of the heavy expenses of product introduction.

3. **Growth** is a period of rapid market acceptance and increasing profits.

4. **Maturity** is a period of slowdown in sales growth because the product has achieved acceptance by most of its potential buyers. Profits level off or decline because of increased marketing outlays to defend the product against competition.

5. **Decline** is the period when sales fall off quickly and profits drop.

Not all products follow this S-shaped product life cycle. Some products are introduced and die quickly. For example, trendy nightclubs will often have a short life cycle, with a steeper curve, fried vegetables are an example of a menu product that had a short life and a steep curve. They were very popular in the early 1980s, but by the end of the decade they had lost their popularity. Hotels often start into decline and then through a major renovation regain their popularity, and a new growth stage. Diners popular in the fifties and then replaced by fast-food chains, became a popular style of restaurant again in the 1980s. Other products may stay in the mature stage for a very long time.

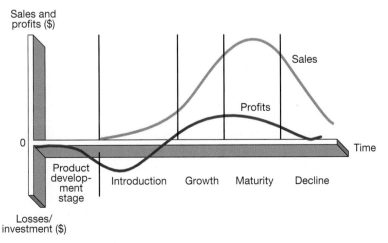

Figure 10-6
Sales and profits over the product's life from inception to demise.

PRODUCT
LIFE-CYCLE
STRATEGIES

The PLC concept can describe a product class (fast-food restaurants), a product form (fast-food hamburgers), or a brand (Wendy's). The PLC applies differently in each case. Product classes have the longest life cycles. The sales of many product classes stay in the mature stage for a long time. Product forms, on the other hand, tend to have the standard PLC shape. Product forms such as the drive-in restaurant and roadside tourist court pass through a regular history of introduction, rapid growth, maturity, and decline. A specific brand's life cycle can change quickly because of changing competitive attacks and responses.

The PLC concept is a useful framework for describing how products and markets work. But using the PLC concept for forecasting product performance or for developing marketing strategies presents some practical problems. For example, managers may have trouble identifying a product's current life-cycle stage, determining when it has moved into the next stage, and enumerating the factors that affect how it will move through the stages. In practice, it is very hard to forecast the sales level at each PLC stage, the length of each stage, and the shape of the PLC curve.

Most marketing texts feature the PLC, yet very few managers claim that they use it in the development of marketing strategy.[23] There are two explanations for this. First, managers make strategic decisions based on the characteristics of each stage of the product life cycle, without using the product life cycle itself as a tool of the product life cycle. The second reason is that accurate prediction of the shape of the product life cycle is impossible. Many products do not follow the typical curve.

The product life cycle is not a predictive tool to determine the length of a product's useful life. It is instead a means of conceptualizing the effect of the market, the environment, and competition and understanding how that product may react to various stimuli.[24] Recognizing that products have life cycles with identifiable stages can provide insights into how to manage the cycle to extend its life. Unmanaged products travel along the life cycle with little resistance. Environmental and competitive changes move a product through its life cycle, and companies must react to keep their products viable. Victoria Station moved quickly through its product life cycle, but McDonald's has been able to extend by modifying the product concept. The McDonald's of today is a different concept than the McDonald's of the 1960s. The menu and the store design are different. McDonald's has evolved from stands with no seating into fast-food restaurants with attractive indoor seating areas and playgrounds for children. The company also changed its distribution strategy. In addition to its traditional suburban locations, McDonald's has developed international, urban, and institutional locations such as hospitals and colleges.

Many observers thought McDonald's would peak in the mid-1970s.[25] Often, when a product begins to peak in sales, management assumes that it has started its decline stage. The downturn could be attributable to many factors: ineffective marketing support, competition, economic conditions, or lack of market development. If managers, wearing "product life-cycle blinders," do not investigate these reasons, they risk seeing the product life cycle as the cause of the slowdown.[26] Fortunately, the management of McDonald's was not wearing life-cycle blinders; they kept growth going.

Using the PLC concept to develop marketing strategy can be difficult. Strategy is both a cause and a result of the product's life cycle: the product's current PLC position suggests the best marketing strategies, and the resulting marketing strategies affect product performance in later life-cycle stages. Yet when used carefully, the PLC concept can help in developing good marketing strategies for different stages of the product life cycle.

We looked at the product development stage of the product life cycle earlier. We will now examine strategies for each of the other life-cycle stages.

Introduction Stage

The introduction stage starts when the new product is first made available for purchase. Introduction takes time, and sales growth is apt to be slow. Some products may linger in the introduction stage for many years before they enter a stage of rapid growth; suite hotels followed this pattern. Many companies take what Theodore Levitt calls the "used apple policy." They watch others go into the market first as pioneers. When suite hotels were introduced, many players sat on the sidelines until the product proved itself in the marketplace. Being a pioneer involves risk, but those who sit on the sidelines may watch others build market share quickly if the product is hot. The pioneers are then in an excellent position to defend their market share against attacks by late arrivals.

In the introductory stage, profits are negative or low because of the low sales and high distribution and promotion expenses. A company needs capital to attract distributors and "fill the pipelines." Promotion spending is high to inform consumers of the new product and encourage them to try it.

In the introductory stage, there are only a few competitors who produce basic versions of the product, since the market is not ready for product refinements. The firms focus on selling to buyers who are ready to buy, usually the higher-income groups. Prices tend to be on the high side because of low output, production problems, and high promotion and other expenses.

Growth Stage

If the new product satisfies the market, it will enter the growth stage, and sales will start climbing quickly. The early adopters will continue to buy, and later buyers will start following their lead, especially if they hear favorable word of mouth. Competitors will enter the market, attracted by the opportunity for profit. They will introduce new product features, which will expand the market. The increase in competitors leads to an increase in the number of outlets, and sales jump.

Prices remain where they are or fall only slightly. Companies keep their promotion spending at the same or at a slightly higher level to meet competition and continue educating the market. Profits increase during this growth stage as promotion costs are spread over a large volume, more efficient systems are developed, and corporate management costs are spread over a larger number of units.

The firm uses several strategies to sustain rapid market growth as long as possible:

1. The firm improves product quality and adds new product features and models.
2. It enters new market segments.
3. It enters new distribution channels.
4. It shifts some advertising from building product awareness to building product conviction and purchase.
5. It lowers prices at the right time to attract more buyers.

In the growth stage, the firm faces a trade-off between high market share and high current profit. By investing heavily in product improvement, promotion, and distribution, it can capture a dominant position. But it sacrifices maximum current profit in the hope of making this up in the next stage.

Maturity Stage

At some point a product's sales growth slows down, and the product enters the maturity stage. This stage normally lasts longer than the previous two stages, and it poses strong challenges to marketing management. Most products are in the maturity stage of the life cycle, and, therefore, most of marketing management deals with the mature product.

The slowdown in sales growth causes supply to exceed demand. This overcapacity leads to greater competition. Competitors begin lowering prices, and they increase their advertising and sales promotions. "Burger wars" and "pizza wars" are the result of these products being in the mature stage. In the mature stage, real sales growth for a product form is about the same as population growth. The only way to increase sales significantly is to steal customers from the competition. Thus price battles and heavy advertising are often the means used to do this, both of which result in a drop in profit. Weaker competitors start dropping out. The industry eventually contains only well-established competitors in the main market segments, with smaller competitors pursuing the niche markets.

A good offense is the best defense. The product manager should not simply defend the product, but should consider modifying target markets, the product, and the marketing mix.

Market Modification. At this point the aggressive product manager tries to increase consumption of the product. The manager looks for new users and market segments and ways to increase usage among present customers. McDonald's added breakfast, salads, desserts, and chicken sandwiches in its effort to attract new users and increase use. Product managers may also reposition the brand to appeal to a larger or faster-growing segment. When drunk-driving campaigns reduced alcoholic beverage consumption, Bennigan's emphasized its food, changing the image from a fun place to drink to a fun place to dine.

Product Modification. The product manager can also change product characteristics—product quality, features, or style—to attract new users and stimulate more usage. A strategy of quality improvement aims at increasing

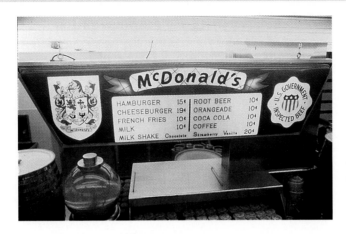

This is McDonald's original menu. One of the ways McDonald's has avoided going into decline is through the development of new products. Courtesy of McDonald's Corporation.

the performance of the product—its durability, reliability, speed, or taste. This strategy is effective when quality can be improved, when buyers believe the claim of improved quality, and when enough buyers want higher quality.

Marketing-mix Modification. The product manager can also try to improve sales by changing one or more marketing-mix elements. Prices can be cut to attract new users and competitors' customers. A better advertising campaign can be developed. Aggressive sales promotion—trade deals, cents-off, gifts, and contests—can be used. The company can move into larger market channels, using mass merchandisers, if these channels are growing. The company can also offer new or improved services to the buyers.

Decline Stage

Sales of most product forms and brands eventually decline. The decline may be slow, as in the case of Steak and Ale, or rapid, as in the case of Victoria Station. Sales may plunge to zero, or they may drop to a low level and continue there for many years.

Sales decline for many reasons, including technological advances, shifts in consumer tastes, and increased competition. As sales and profits decline, some firms withdraw from the market. Those remaining may reduce the number of their product offerings. They may drop smaller market segments and marginal trade channels. They may cut the promotion budget and reduce their prices further.

Carrying a weak product can be very costly to the firm, and not just in terms of reduced profit. There are also hidden costs. A weak product may take up too much of management's time. It often requires frequent price and inventory adjustments. The advertising and sales-force attention consumed by the weak product could be used to make the healthy products more profitable. Its failing reputation can shake customer confidence in the company and its other products. But the biggest cost may well lie in the future. Keeping weak products delays the search for replacements, creates a lopsided product mix, hurts current profits, and weakens the company's foothold on the future.

For these reasons, companies must pay more attention to their aging products. Regularly reviewing sales, market shares, costs, and profit trends for each of its products will help to identify products in the decline stage.

For each declining product, management has to decide whether to maintain, harvest, or drop it. Management may decide to harvest the product, which means reducing various costs. For example, as restaurants featuring red meat products fell out of favor with customers, Steak and Ale closed some of its marginal restaurants, but maintained its more profitable locations. The company even developed new restaurants in areas where customers still sought a good steak when they went out to eat. If successful, harvesting will increase the company's profits in the short run. Or management may decide to drop the product from the line. It can sell it to another firm or simply liquidate it at salvage value. If the company plans to find a buyer, it will not want to run down the product through harvesting.

PRODUCT DELETION

As we have seen, the product life cycle illustrates that most products will become obsolete, lose their attractiveness in the marketplace, and have to be replaced. One danger of the product life cycle is that a product may be replaced prematurely. Products take time, effort, and money to introduce. Only about half of all new products become profitable. When a company has a winner, it wants to receive the maximum benefit from this product. Management will not want to delete it while profit potential exists. If a product is no longer viable, it is important to terminate that product, rather than continue to pour time and resources into reviving it.

Thus, understanding the product deletion process is just as important as understanding product development. The Strawberry Patch, a successful restaurant in Houston, served a chicken breast topped with sautéed mushrooms. This dish enjoyed success for more than 10 years. When sales started to drop and the decline continued, it appeared that the product was no longer in favor with the restaurant's customers. Management asked customers about the dish and they responded that it was too greasy. When the sautéed mushrooms were poured over the chicken breast, the butter collected at the bottom of the plate. In the 1970s, this was viewed as a nice sauce, but by the 1980s the butter was viewed as excess fat. As the restaurant's customers became more health conscious, the dish became less popular. The restaurant revitalized the dish by removing the sautéed mushrooms and garnishing the chicken with fresh sliced mushrooms. If management of the Strawberry Patch had been wearing life-cycle blinders, they would have deleted the product.

The deletion analysis is a systematic review of a product's projected sales and estimated costs associated with those sales (see Figure 10-7). If a product appears to no longer be profitable, the analysis looks at possible ways to make modifications and return it to profitability. If the analysis indicates the product should be deleted, there are three choices: phase-out, run-out, or drop it immediately.[26]

Phase-out is the ideal method; it enables the product to be removed in an orderly fashion. For example, a menu item would be replaced on the next revision of the menu. A **run-out** would be used when sales for an item are low and costs exceed revenues, such as the case of a restaurant serving a crabmeat cocktail with sales of only one or two items per week. If the restaurant decides to delete the product, it may chose to deplete its

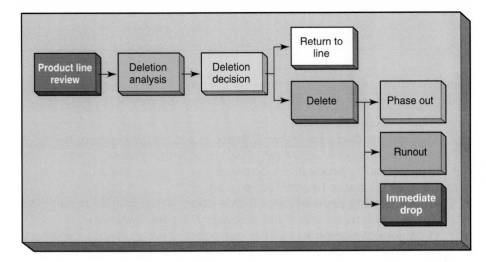

Figure 10-7
Product deletion process.
Source: Martin L. Bell,
*Marketing: Concepts and
Strategy,* 3rd ed., p. 267;
©1979, Houghton Mifflin
Company; used by permis-
sion, Mrs. Marcellette (Bell)
Chapman.

existing stock of crabmeat rather than reorder. The last option is an immediate **drop**. This option is usually chosen when the product may cause
harm or customer dissatisfaction. When a menu item draws a large number
of complaints, it is best to drop the item, rather than continue to create
unhappy customers.

The political aspects of dropping a product often lead to a product
being left on the menu longer than it should be. For example, if the bouill-
abaisse is the general manager's own recipe, the food and beverage manager may be reluctant to remove the dish from the menu. Deletion of a menu
item can also be viewed as a failure. If the resident manager of a hotel
fought to include an item on the menu, strong arguments may be made
against its deletion. Politics must be addressed when conducting a deletion
analysis.

The issue of dropping a product is particularly complex in the case of
the properties of a hotel chain. Management is usually quite aware of individual properties that should be dropped from the chain affiliation due to
deterioration of the property or the neighborhood in which the property is
located. In many cases it is impossible or impractical to quickly close the
hotel or drop it from chain affiliation.

- Contracts may prohibit a quick close.
- The hotel may be a historic property or have sentimental attach-
  ments to the community and to management.
- Closure might negatively affect the community.
- The hotel may be owned by the chain, and a buyer may not be
  readily available.
- Special relationships may exist between the franchisee and the
  franchisor.

Despite difficulties in closing hotels or disassociating properties from a
chain, eventually the inevitable must occur. As in the previous example of
menu items, it is best to make this hard decision as quickly as possible.

Chapter Review

I.   Product. A product is anything that can be offered to a market for attention, acquisition, use, or consumption that might satisfy a want or need. It includes physical objects, service, places, organizations, and ideas.

II.   Product Levels

1) Core product answers the question of what is the buyer really buying. Every product is a package of problem-solving services.

2) Facilitating products are those services or goods that must be present for the guest to use the core product.

3) Supporting products are extra products offered to add value to the core product and to help to differentiate it from the competition.

4) Augmented products include accessibility (geographical location and hours of operation), atmosphere (visual, aural, olfactory, and tactile dimensions), customer interaction with the service organization (joining, consumption, and detachment), customer participation, and customers' interactions with each other.

III.   Product Considerations

1) Accessibility. How accessible the product is in terms of location and hours of operation.

2) Atmosphere. Atmosphere is a critical element in services. It is appreciated through the senses. Sensory terms provide descriptions for the atmosphere as a particular set of surroundings. The main sensory channels for atmosphere are sight, sound, scent, and touch.

3) Customer Interactions with the Service System. Managers must think about how the customers use the product in the three phases of involvement: joining, consumption, and detachment.

4) Customer Interaction with Other Customers. Customers become part of the product you are offering.

5) Participation. Involving the guest in service delivery can increase capacity, improve customer satisfaction, and reduce costs.

IV.   Reasons Companies Use Brands and Identify the Major Branding Decisions. Brand is a name, term, sign, symbol, design, or a combination of these elements that is intended to identify the goods or services of a seller and differentiate them from those of competitors.

1) Conditions That Support Branding

a) The product is easy to identify by brand or trademark.

i) It should suggest something about the product's benefits and qualities.

ii) It should be easy to pronounce, recognize, and remember.

iii) It should be distinctive.

iv) For larger firms looking at future expansion into foreign markets, the name should translate easily into foreign languages.

v) It should be capable of registration and legal protection.

b) The product is perceived as the best value for the price. A brand name derives its value from consumer perceptions. Brands attract consumers by developing a perception of good quality and value.

c) Quality and standards are easy to maintain. If the brand is successful in developing an image of quality, customers will expect quality in all outlets carrying the same brand name. Consistency and standardization are critical factors for multi-unit brand.

d) The demand for the general product class is large enough to support a regional or national chain. New products are generally developed to serve a particular market niche. Later the product may be expanded to encompass multiniches, or the original niche may grow in market size until it is a huge market share product.

e) There are economies of scale. The brand should provide economies of scale to justify expenditures for administration and advertising.

V.   New-product Development

1)   Product Life Cycle Presents two Challenges:

a) All products eventually decline.

b) The firm must understand how its products age and change marketing strategies as products pass through life-cycle stages.

2)   New-product Development Strategy:

a) A company has to develop new products in order to survive. New products can be obtained through acquisition or through new-product development.

3)   New-product Development Process:

a) **Idea generation** gains ideas from internal sources, customers, competitors, distributors and suppliers.

b) **Idea screening:** The purpose of screening is to spot good ideas and drop poor ones as soon as possible.

c) **Concept development and testing**: Surviving ideas must now be developed into product concepts. These concepts are tested with target customers.

d) **Marketing strategy development:** There are three parts to the marketing strategy statement. The first part describes the target market, the planned product positioning, and the sales, market share, and profit goals for the first 2 years. The second part outlines the product's planned price, distribution, and marketing budget for the first year. The third part describes the planned long-run sales, profit, and the market-mix strategy over time.

e) **Business analysis:** Business analysis involves a review of the sales, costs, and profit projections to determine whether they satisfy the company's objectives.

f) **Product development:** Product development turns the concept into a prototype of the product.

g) **Marketing testing:** Market testing is the stage in which the product and marketing program are introduced into more realistic market settings.

h) **Commercialization:** The product is brought into the marketplace.

VI.   Product Life-cycle Stages

1)   Product development begins when the company finds and develops a new product idea.

2) Introduction is a period of slow sales growth as the product is being introduced into the market. Profits are nonexistent in this stage.

3) Growth stage is a period of rapid market acceptance and increasing profits.

4) Maturity stage is a period of slowdown in sales growth because the product has achieved acceptance by most of its potential buyers.

5) Decline stage is the period when sales fall off quickly and profits drop.

DISCUSSION QUESTIONS

1. Define the product that a customer receives in exchanges with the following businesses:
   a. A fast-food restaurant
   b. A sit-down service restaurant
   c. A stay in a four-star hotel

2. Use a product from the hospitality or travel industries to explain the following terms:
   a. Facilitating product
   b. Supporting product
   c. Augmented product

3. ARAMARK, a large contract food-service company, is introducing branded food as part of its campus feeding. Why would ARAMARK pay a royalty to Burger King when it is capable of making its own hamburgers very efficiently.

4. As a hotel or restaurant manager, how would you gain new-product ideas?

5. Less than one-third of new-product ideas come from the customer. Does this percentage conflict with the marketing concept's philosophy of "find a need and fill it"? Why or why not?

6. If you were the director of new-product development for a national fast-food chain, what factors would you consider in choosing cities for test marketing a new sandwich. Would the place where you live be a good test market? Why or why not?

7. Answer the following questions:
   a. How can knowledge of the product life cycle help a restaurant manager manage menu offerings?
   b. Apply the concept of the product life cycle to a hotel. How does a company keep its products from going into the decline stage?

KEY TERMS

Actual product A product's parts, styling, features, brand name, packaging, and other attributes that combine to deliver core product benefits.

Augmented product Additional consumer services and benefits built around the core and actual products.

Brand A name, term, sign, symbol, or design, or a combination of these, intended to identify the goods or services of one seller or group of sellers and to differentiate them from those of competitors.

Business analysis A review of the sales, costs, and profit projections for a new product to find out whether they satisfy the company's objectives.

Commercialization Introducing a new product into the market.

Concept testing New-product concepts are tested with a group of target consumers to find out if the concept has strong consumer appeal.

Decline stage The product life-cycle stage when a product's sales decline.

Growth stage The product life-cycle stage when the new product's sales start climbing quickly.

Idea generation The systematic search for new-product ideas.

Idea screening New-product ideas are screened in order to spot good ideas and drop poor ones as soon as possible.

Introduction stage The product life-cycle stage when the new product is first distributed and made available for purchase.

Marketing strategy development Designing an initial marketing strategy for a new product based on the product concept.

Marketing testing The stage of new-product development when the product and marketing program are tested in more realistic market settings.

Maturity stage The stage in the product life cycle when sales growth slows or levels off.

New-product development The development of original products, product improvements, product modifications, and new brands through the firm's own R&D efforts.

Product Anything that can be offered to a market for attention, acquisition, use, or consumption that might satisfy a want or need. It includes physical objects, services, persons, places, organizations, and ideas.

Product concept A detailed version of the new-product idea stated in meaningful consumer terms.

Product design The process of designing a product's style and function: creating a product that is attractive; easy, safe, and inexpensive to use and service; and simple and economical to produce and distribute.

Product development Developing the product concept into a physical product in order to assure that the product idea can be turned into a workable product.

Product idea An idea for a possible product that the company can see itself offering to the market.

Product image The way consumers picture an actual or potential product.

Product life cycle (PLC) The course of a product's sales and profits over its lifetime. It involves five distinct stages: product development, introduction, growth, maturity, and decline.

Product line A group of products that are closely related either because they function in a similar manner, are sold to the same customer groups, are marketed through the same types of outlets, or fall within given price ranges.

Product mix (or product assortment) The set of all product lines and items that a particular seller offers for sale to buyers.

Test marketing The stage of new-product development in which the product and marketing program are tested in more realistic market settings.

Trademark A brand or part of a brand that is given legal protection; the trademark protects the seller's exclusive rights to use the brand name or brand mark.

Unsought goods Consumer goods that the consumer either does not know about or knows about but does not normally think of buying.

REFERENCES

1. JULIE LIESCO, "The Taste of Time," *Restaurants and Institutions* (February 1, 1983), pp. 79–84.

2. 1993 Annual Report, Hospitality Franchise Systems, Inc., 339 Jefferson Road, P.O. Box 278, Parsippany, N.J. 07054-0278, pp. 3–4.

3. KARL ALBRECHT AND LAWRENCE J. BRADFORD, *The Service Advantage* (Dow Jones-Irwin, Homewood, Ill., 1990), p. 69.

4. CHRISTIAN GRONROOS, *Service Management and Marketing* (Lexington, Mass.: Lexington Books, 1990).

5. ALBERT MEHRABIAN, *Public Places and Private Spaces* (New York: Basic Books, 1976).

6. BERNARD BOOMS AND MARY J. BITNER, "Marketing Services by Managing the Environment," *Cornell Restaurant and Hotel Administration Quarterly* (May 1992), pp. 35–39.

7. See PHILIP KOTLER, "Atmospherics as a Marketing Tool," *Journal of Retailing*, 49, no. 4, (Winter 1973–1974), pp. 48–64.

8. GRONROSS, *Service Management and Marketing*.

9. PAUL SLATTERY, "Hotel Branding in the 1990's", *EIU Travel and Tourism Analyst*, no. 1 (1991), pp. 23–35.

10. E. JEROME MCCARTHY AND WILLIAM D. PERREAULT, JR., *Basic Marketing* (Homewood, Ill.: Irwin, 1990), p. 236.

11. ROBERT SELWITZ, "Quality Takes on 'Choice' Name", *Hotel and Motel Management*, 205, no. 14 (August 20, 1990).

12. SUSAN M. BARD, "New Logo Rises at Hyatt," *Hotel and Motel Management*, 205, no. 15 (September 10, 1990), pp. 1, 117.

13. TOM ICHNIOWSKI, "Hey, Little Spender, Have These Motels Got a Deal for You," *Business Week*, Issue 3024 (November 2, 1987), p. 63.

14. GLENN WITHIAM, "Hotel Companies Aim for Multiple Markets," *Cornell Hotel and Restaurant Administration Quarterly*, 26, no. 3 (November 1985), pp. 39–51.

15. EDWARD C. ACHORN, "The Game of Choice", *Lodging*, 15, no. 2 (October 1990), pp. 26–30.

16. LAURA E. KEETON, "La Quinta Plans Mexican Venture with 22 Hotels," *Wall Street Journal*, (September 23, 1994), p. B3.

17. SCOTT HUME, "KFC 'skins' the Fat off New Chicken Entry," *Advertising Age*, 62, no. 4 (January 28, 1991), p. 9.

18. MORRIS E. LASKY, "Hotel/Motel Workouts: Ask Fundamental Questions to Uncover Problems," *Commercial Lending Review*, 5, no. 2 (Spring 1990), pp. 44–48.

19. The Marriott example and this list were drawn from CHRISTOPHER W. L. HART, "Product Development: How Marriott Created Courtyard," *Cornell Hotel and Restaurant Administration Quarterly*, 27, no. 3 (November 1986), pp. 68–69; and JERRY WIND, PAUL E. GREEN, DOUGLAS SHIFFLET, AND MARSHA SCARBROUGH, "Courtyard by Marriott: Designing a Hotel Facility with Consumer-based Marketing," *Interfaces*, 19, no. 1 (January–February), pp. 25–47.

20. J. L. HESKETT AND R. HALLOWELL, *Courtyard by Marriott*, Harvard Case 9-693-036, Harvard Business School Publishing: Boston, 1993.

21. MEGAN ROWE AND CARLO WOLF, "Top tips for rough times; hospitality industry tips," *Lodging Hospitality*, 49, no. 1, (January 1993), p. 36, Edwin McDowell, "Fast food fills menu for many hotel *chains*," *New York Times*, January 9, 1992, Section D, Page 1, and Chad Rubel, "Hotels help lodgers who help themselves," *Marketing News,* May 8, 1995, p. 5.

22. BRADFORD T. HUDSON, "Innovation through Acquisition," *Cornell Hotel and Restaurant Administration Quarterly*, 35, no. 2 (June 1994), pp. 82–87.

23. THEODORE LEVITT, *The Marketing Imagination* (New York: Free Press, 1986), p. 173.

24. See JOHN E. SMALLWOOD, "The Product Life Cycle: A Key to Strategic Marketing Planning," in *Strategic Marketing*, Barton A. Weitz and Robin Wensley, eds. (Boston: Kent Publishing, 1984), pp. 184–192; NARIMAN K. DHALLA AND SONIA YUSPEH, "Forget the Product Life Cycle Concept," *Harvard Business Review* (January–February 1976), pp. 102–112; and CHRISTOPHER W. HART, GREG CASSERLY, AND MARK J. LAWLESS, "The Product Life Cycle: How Useful?" *Cornell Hotel and Restaurant Quarterly*, 25, no. 3 (November 1984), pp. 54–63.

25. ROBERT C. LEWIS AND RICHARD E. CHAMBERS, *Marketing Leadership in Hospitality* (New York: Van Nostrand Reinhold), p. 314.

26. DHALLA AND YUSPEH, "Forget the Product Life Cycle Concept," pp. 102–112.

27. WILLIAM PRIDE AND O. C. FERRELL, *Marketing*, Houghton Mifflin Company: Boston, 1995, pp. 312–313.

Internal Marketing

11

The Sheraton Perth is one of Perth, Australia's finest hotels. Barry Urquhart, a services management consultant, was looking forward to celebrating his niece's wedding at the hotel. Urquhart does not drink beverages containing caffeine, except on special occasions when he enjoys a cappuccino. Relaxing after the wedding dinner, Urquhart decided to forget his diet. When the banquet staff was serving the after-dinner tea and coffee, he asked the server for a cappuccino. He realized it was not part of the set menu and said he would be happy to pay for it. The server replied that the rest of the guests would first have to be served. Urquhart felt that this was reasonable, since it would take time to prepare his special order. Later he noticed that all the guests were served, and he was without a cappuccino. When the server was reminded of the order, a reply was given that the supervisor had refused the order. Urquhart became irritated and asked to speak to this person. The supervisor then appeared and explained that the reception dinner was a set menu, and cappuccino was not on the menu. Urquhart again explained that he was willing to pay for the cappuccino and wait for it to be prepared. The supervisor replied that cappuccino was available only from the restaurant downstairs and company policy did not allow it to be brought upstairs. When Urquhart asked the banquet supervisor if he knew the slogan placed next to every Sheraton bed, the supervisor said that he didn't. "At the Sheraton, little things mean a lot," was the slogan.

Urquhart now says his image of the whole Sheraton network has been altered. He had been a guest in Sheraton Hotels throughout the world. When he had asked for similar service in the past, he had received it. The sign by the bed meant something to him as a guest. It reinforced his belief that Sheraton delivered good service. On his niece's wedding day he understood that sometimes little things really do not mean a lot to some of the hotel's staff. In the future, he wondered, how he would identify those Sheratons where little things do mean a lot? Sheraton has an excellent reputation as a five-star hotel chain in the Asia–Pacific region, but all it took was one banquet supervisor to put uncertainty about Sheraton in Urquhart's mind. The supervisor thought he was carrying out company policy by preventing an employee from fulfilling a guest's request.[1] This example shows how employees can influence guest satisfaction. When a company's external guest communications conflict with its employee communications, problems are inevitable.

The chapter starts with a discussion of why internal marketing, marketing directed internally to the firm's employees, is important.

Internal marketing is implemented through a four-step process, establishment of a **service culture**, development of a **marketing approach to human resource management**, **dissemination of marketing information to employees**, and implementation of a **reward and recognition system**. Each of these steps is discussed in detail in the chapter.

The chapter concludes with a discussion of **nonroutine transactions**.

Everyone has a story to tell about the time he or she received poor service at a hotel or restaurant. Customer service expert John Tscholl tells about the one and only time he stayed in one of Marriott's Courtyard Inns.[2] He was never given an emergency message that his father-in-law had suffered a heart attack nor did he receive his wake-up call the next morning. He said that he will never return to a Courtyard Inn and has told this story to thousands of Marriott's customers and potential customers. Marriott spent much time and effort developing the Courtyard concept, but a well-designed concept and good physical facilities are not enough. If the hotel's employees do not perform to expectations, guests will not return.

Stories are not always negative. Most travelers have stories to tell about employees who gave them excellent service. These two examples show how hotels can retain customers by solving their needs and recognizing employees who do something extra for the hotel. Barry Urquhart also tells of the time he went back to his room and walked out on the balcony to get a breath of fresh air, only to hear cries for help coming from several stories up. The balcony door had shut, locking the guest out of the room. Urquhart called the front desk, and in a few minutes the guest was let back in the room. The next day the hotel delivered a bottle of champagne to Urquhart's room to thank him for making them aware of the problem.[3] This unexpected gift increased positive feelings about the hotel.

Karl Albrecht, co-author of *Service America*, was staying in a hotel in Sydney. He requested a late check-out so he could hold a business meeting in his room. Unfortunately, the hotel was fully booked and the room was needed for guests arriving that afternoon. The manager made provisions for him to use a conference room free of charge. Albrecht offered to pay but the hotel refused. The future business the hotel received from Karl Albrecht—and the positive word of mouth—more than equaled the lost revenue.[4]

Marketing in the hospitality and travel industries must be embraced by all employees; it cannot be left up to the marketing or sales department. Marketing should be part of the philosophy of the organization, and the marketing function should be carried out by all line employees. In manufacturing firms the marketing function is often carried out by a marketing department, since many employees do not interact with the customer. In service industries the line employees carry out a majority of the marketing function (see Figure 11-1).

Managers must understand that bad service encounters receive more attention than good ones. When guests have been treated badly, they respond by talking about the incident. A study done by the Technical Assistance Research Program found that when people have a good experience they tell five people. If they have a bad experience, they tell ten.[5] Spreading positive word of mouth is difficult. A few negative stories can offset many good stories. The goal is to have every guest's expectations met or exceeded.

The front-desk clerk, dining room service person, door attendant, and concierge all influence whether the guest departs satisfied. Their attitude, appearance, and willingness to handle the guest's requests help form an impression of the hotel. Employees deliver the products of hospitality organizations, and through their delivery they become part of the product. It is often hard to differentiate the tangible part of the product of competing companies. Steak dinners and hotel rooms in the same price range tend to be similar. Product differentiation often derives from the people who deliver the service. In the hospitality industry, most marketing activity is carried out by employees outside the marketing department, not the marketing staff. The hotel's marketing program brings guests to the hotel. The hotel's staff must turn the first-time guest into a repeat customer. There is a positive relationship between the number of repeat guests and profit. Research has shown that a 5% increase in retention can lead to 25% to 125% increases in the bottom line.[6]

Richard Normann of The Service Management Group says that a key ingredient in almost all service companies is some innovative arrangement or formula for mobilizing and focusing human energy.[7] Normann developed the term, **moments of truth,** which Jan Carlzon of SAS later popularized. A

Figure 11-1
The relationship between the marketing function and the marketing department. *Source:* Christian Gronroos, "Designing a Long Range Marketing Strategy for Services," *Long Range Planning,* April 1980, p. 40.

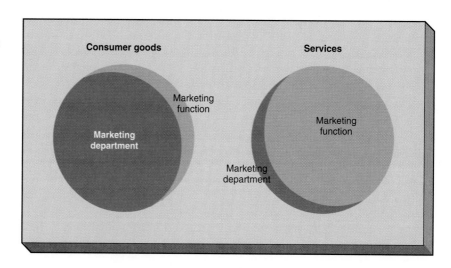

moment of truth occurs when employee and customer have contact. Normann states that when this occurs what happens is no longer directly influenced by the company. It is the skill, motivation, and tools employed by the firm's representative and the expectations and behavior of the client that together create the service delivery process.[8] Norman borrowed the idea from bullfighters who used the term to describe the moment when the bullfighter faces the bull in the ring. In spite of all his training and preparation, a wrong move by the bullfighter, or an unanticipated move by the bull can result in disaster. Similarly, when employees and customers interact, a careless mistake by the employee or an unanticipated request by the guest can result in a dissatisfied guest.

The hospitality industry is unique in that **employees are part of the product.** The hotel must have a staff that will perform well during moments of truth. When people think of marketing, they usually think of efforts directed externally toward the marketplace, but a hotel or restaurant's first marketing efforts should be directed internally to employees. Managers must make sure that employees know their products and believe that they are good value. The employees must be excited about the company that they work for and the products they sell. Otherwise, it will be impossible for the guests to become excited. External marketing brings customers into the hotel but does little good if the employees do not perform to the guest's expectations.

Marketers must develop techniques and procedures to ensure that employees are able and willing to deliver quality service. The internal marketing concept evolved as marketers formalized procedures for marketing to employees. Internal marketing ensures that employees at all levels of the organization experience the business and understand its various activities and campaigns in an environment that supports customer consciousness.[9] The objective of internal marketing is to enable employees to deliver satisfying products to the guest. As Christian Gronroos notes, "The internal marketing concept states that the internal market of employees is best motivated for service-mindedness and customer-oriented performance by an active, marketing-like approach, where a variety of activities are used internally in an active, marketing-like and coordinated way."[10] Internal marketing uses a marketing perspective to manage the firm's employees.[11] **Internal marketing** is marketing aimed internally at the firm's employees.

Internal marketing is a process that involves the following steps:

THE INTERNAL MARKETING PROCESS

1. Establishment of a service culture
2. Development of a marketing approach to human resource management
3. Dissemination of marketing information to employees
4. Implementation of a reward and recognition system

Service Culture

An internal marketing program flows out of a service culture. A service marketing program is doomed to failure if its organizational culture does not support serving the customer. An article in a recent issue of *The*

Australian, a national newspaper, reported that four firms had pumped $2 million into customer service programs with little result.[12] One reason these customer service efforts failed was that the companies' culture was not service oriented. The companies carried out the customer service programs because they thought that they would produce satisfied customers and make the firm more money. These firms soon discovered that a good customer-service program involves much more than working with line employees. *An internal marketing program requires a strong commitment from management.*

A major barrier to most internal marketing programs is middle management. Managers have been trained to watch costs and increase profits. Their reward systems are usually based on achieving certain cost levels. Imagine a hotel's front-desk clerks returning from a training session, eager to help the guests. They may take a little extra time with the customers or perhaps give away a health club visit to help a dissatisfied guest recover from an unsatisfactory experience at the hotel. The front-office manager, who has not been through similar training, may see the extra time spent as unproductive and the services given away as wasteful.

If management expects employees' attitudes to be positive toward the customer, management must have a positive attitude toward the customer and the employees. Too often organizations hire trainers to come in for a day to get their customer-contact employees excited about providing quality customer service. The effect of these sessions is usually short-lived because the organizations do little to support the customer-contact employees. Managers tell receptionists to be helpful and friendly, yet often the receptionists are understaffed. The greeting developed to make receptionists sound sincere and helpful—"Good morning Plaza Hotel, Elizabeth speaking, how may I help you?"—becomes hollow when it is compressed into 3 seconds with a "Can you please hold?" added to the end. The net result from the guest's perspective is to wait fourteen rings for the phone to be answered and then receive a cold, rushed greeting. Management must develop a **service culture**. A culture that supports customer service through policies, procedures, reward systems, and actions.

An **organizational culture** is the pattern of shared values and beliefs that gives members of an organization meaning, providing them with the rules for behavior in the organization.[13] Every organization has a culture. In some companies it may be weak. In well-managed companies, everyone in the organization embraces the culture. A strong culture helps organizations in two ways. First, it directs behavior. Employees know how to act and what is expected of them. Second, a strong culture gives employees a sense of purpose and makes them feel good about their company.[14] They know what their company is trying to achieve and how they are helping the company achieve that goal.

Culture serves as the glue that holds an organization together. When an organization has strong culture, the organization and its employees act as one. But a company that has a strong culture may not necessarily have a service culture. A strong service culture influences employees to act in customer-oriented ways and is the first step toward developing a customer-oriented organization.

Herb Kelleher, the CEO of Southwest Airlines, spends time on Southwest's planes with employees and customers. Courtesy of Southwest Airlines.

Developing a customer-oriented organization requires a commitment from management of both time and financial resources. The change to a customer-oriented system may require changes in hiring, training, reward systems, and customer complaint resolution, as well as empowerment of employees. It requires that managers spend time talking to both customers and customer-contact employees. Management must be committed to these changes. A service culture does not result from a memorandum sent by the CEO. It is developed over time through the actions of management. For example, a hotel manager who spends time greeting guests and inquiring about their welfare during morning check-out and afternoon check-in demonstrates caring about guests.[15]

In some companies, including Hyatt, McDonald's, and Hertz, management spends time working alongside customer-contact employees serving customers. This action makes it clear to employees that management does not want to lose touch with operations and that managers care about both employees and customers. An internal marketing program that is developed without the support of management will be unproductive. Organizations cannot expect their employees to develop a customer-oriented attitude if it is not visibly supported by company management.

Weak Culture.   In firms that have weak corporate cultures, there are few or no common values and norms. Employees are often bound by policies and regulations, though these policies may make no sense from a customer-service perspective. As a result, employees become insecure about making decisions outside the rules and regulations.[16] Because there are no established values, employees do not know how the company wants them to act, and they spend time trying to figure out how to behave. When they do come up with a solution, they must get their supervisor's permission before applying it to the problem. Supervisors, in turn, may feel the need to pass the responsibility upward. During the decision process the guest is kept waiting minutes, hours, days, or even months to receive a reply. In a company with a strong service culture, employees know what to do and they do it. Customers receive a quick response to their questions and quick solutions to their problems.

La Quinta Motor Inns brings employees from each of its 18 regions to corporate headquarters for brainstorming sessions. The purpose of these sessions is to (1) demonstrate appreciation for employees and (2) emphasize that all employees are empowered to do what is necessary to meet guest expectations.[17] When a firm **empowers** employees, it moves the authority and responsibility to make decisions from the supervisor to the line employees.

A fast-food restaurant had a policy of not letting the public use its business phone, though there were no public phones on the premises. One evening a man who had been assaulted several blocks from the restaurant asked if he could use the phone. The employees refused and turned the man away. The policy manual said that guests were not to use the phone. Their corporate culture had trained them to act by the book. They were incapable of making a decision that went against the company's written policies. The press featured this as a great story about the insensitivity of a business toward a member of the community. The restaurant received negative publicity because of its employee's action. It was fortunate to avoid a suit.

When you come into contact with an organization that has a strong service culture, you recognize it right away. In the Marriott culture, there is an instinctive and automatic impulse to turn toward the customer in making decisions about how to run the organization. Chairman J. Willard "Bill" Marriott Jr., is consistent in his preaching, teaching, and reminding people about the customer and about service.[18] Four Seasons Hotels had two hotels in Houston, the Four Seasons and the Inn on the Park. When a guest entered either of these hotels, they received a genuinely warm reception from the employees, who sincerely wanted to make their guests comfortable. There is a difference in the feeling a guest receives between an employee who is required to memorize a greeting and recite it back to the guests and an employee who has a genuine interest in guests and personally communicates this. The employees at the Four Seasons' hotels were genuine; they reaffirmed the guest's decision to stay at the hotels.

Turning the Organizational Structure Upside Down.   The conventional organizational structure is a triangular structure. For example, in a hotel the CEO (chief executive officer) and COO (chief operating officer) are at the peak of the triangle. The general manager is on the next level, followed by department heads, supervisors, line employees, and the customers (see Figure 11-2). Ken Blanchard, author of *One Minute Manager*, states that the problem with a conventional organizational structure is that everyone is working for their boss. Employees want do well in the organization. Thus line employees are concerned with what their supervisors think of their performance, department heads are concerned with how the general manager views them, and the general managers want the corporate office to think highly of them. The problem with this type of organization is that everyone is concerned with satisfying people above them in the organization, and very little attention is paid to the customer.[19]

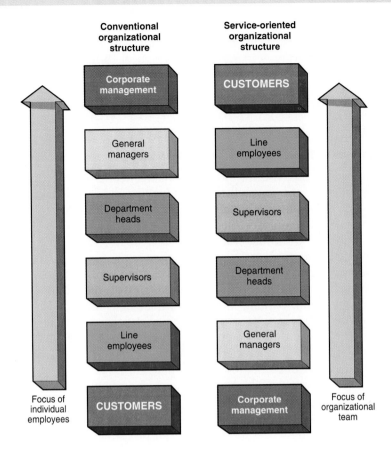

Figure 11-2
Turning the organizational structure upside down.

When a company has a service culture, the organizational chart is turned upside down. The customers are now at the top of the organization and corporate management is at the bottom of the structure. In this type of organization, everyone is working to serve the customer. Corporate management is helping their general managers to serve the customer, general managers are supporting their departments in serving the customer, department heads are developing systems that will allow their supervisors to better serve the customer, and supervisors are helping line employees serve the customer.

A bellperson at a Ritz-Carlton hotel delivered baggage to a guest about an hour after they had checked in due to an error. After he had delivered the luggage, he told his supervisor. The supervisor apologized to the guests and noted in the hotel's computer that this guest had experienced a problem and should receive exceptional service during the rest of his stay.[20] This seems like a rational way to handle the problem, but it is really an extraordinary event. In a hotel with a conventional organizational structure, if any employee makes a mistake, they hope their supervisor never finds out about it; they may even try to cover it up. They know if their supervisor does find out about a mistake they may be reprimanded. The Ritz-Carlton has a service culture; they have turned the organizational structure upside down. The bellperson was concerned about the guest and knew his supervisor would take action that would enable the hotel to recover from his mistake. The supervisor was not afraid to communicate the department's mistake to other departments. When you turn the organization upside down, everyone works to serve the guest. When you have a conventional organizational structure, everyone works to please the boss.

A Marketing Approach to Human Resource Management

Creating Jobs That Attract Good People

Managers must use the principles of marketing to attract and retain employees. They must research and develop an understanding of their employees' needs, just as they examine the needs of customers. Not all employees are the same. Some employees seek money to supplement their incomes; others are looking for work that will be their sole source of income. Marketers can use marketing research techniques to segment the employee market, choosing the best segments for the firm and developing a marketing mix to attract those segments. For employees, the marketing mix is the job, pay, benefits, location, transportation, parking, hours, and intangible rewards, such as prestige and perceived advancement opportunities. Just as customers look for different attributes when they purchase a product, employees look for different benefits. Some may be attracted by flexible working hours, others are attracted by good health insurance benefits, while still others may be attracted by child-care facilities. Flexible working hours for office or housekeeping positions, cafeteria-style benefit programs in which employees design their own benefit package, and child care can all be used to attract a certain type of employee. Advertising should be developed with prospective employees in mind, building a positive image of the firm for present and future employees and customers. Employees chose employers and leave them the same way that guests select certain hotels and then decide to switch. It is expensive to lose both guests and employees.[21] Using a marketing approach to develop positions and company benefits helps to attract and maintain good employees.

The cost of employee turnover was estimated in the late 1980s to average $2100 for an hourly position. This means turnover would cost over $400,000 for a hotel with a 100% turnover and 200 employees. This cost is undoubtedly higher today.[22] A reduction in turnover can result in hundreds of thousands of dollars in savings.

La Quinta Motor Inns examined the problem of burn-out at management levels and reduced this problem from 36% to 21% annually. The company identified four principal factors as critical in helping to reduce the problem.[23]

Selection. La Quinta maintains strict standards and has a policy of hiring couples. Prospective couples go through an extensive interview process.

Orientation. Each selected couple must complete an intensive 13-week training program plus on-the-job training as fill-in managers.

Stability. The management team (couples) cannot request a transfer before completion of 2 years at a property. La Quinta discovered that frequent transfer contributes to high turnover.

Training. La Quinta's executive vice-president for development, Anne Binns Bliss, stated, "You have to select and keep people that you want to be part of your team." La Quinta believes strongly in ongoing training for employees.

The problem of burnout was studied in the restaurant industry with the following conclusions:

1. More chain restaurant managers than hotel food and beverage managers suffered from burnout.
2. Assistant managers were more prone than general managers.
3. General managers were more likely to suffer from depersonalization than assistant managers.
4. Burnout was higher among singles than married people.
5. Men were less likely to experience burnout than women.
6. Good communication on the part of general managers seems to reduce burnout among assistant managers.[24]

These conclusions seem to indicate that burnout is not consistent among groups and different types of restaurants. Training programs and employee motivational programs obviously must be customized to meet the needs of different employee groups. Just as a single marketing strategy is unlikely to attract all market segments, a single approach to dealing with employees is equally likely to fail.

Students enrolled in college/university hospitality programs clearly demonstrate that many factors in addition to salary and benefits are important to them when selecting an employer. Nonmonetary variables of interest to hospitality students when selecting an employer are (by rank order) as follows:

1. Chance for promotion and growth
2. Work that keeps me interested
3. A chance for increasing responsibility
4. Good working condition
5. Feeling in on things, being a part
6. Full appreciation of work done
7. Job security
8. Good training program
9. Personal loyalty to worker by company
10. Good salary
11. Nice people to work with
12. Good fringe benefits
13. Access to superior
14. Geographical location
15. Reasonable hours
16. Sympathetic help with personal problems[25]

The Hiring Process.   Employee turnover rates of 100% or more are common in the hospitality industry. Organizations with high turnover rates cannot develop a service culture. In companies with high turnover, managers tend to put very little effort into hiring, basing their decisions on whether the job candidate will work for a small wage and can fill schedule vacancies.

If you want friendly, courteous service, you must hire friendly, courteous people. Hospitality firms that deliver good service seem to follow this advice. These firms understand that it is difficult to train people to be friendly. It is possible to provide employees with the technical skills needed for the job, but difficult to train them to be friendly and caring.

Swissair carefully screens its applicants, selects candidates for personal interviews and puts them through a 5- to 6-hour selection process. The airline then puts successful applicants on probation for a 3-month period. They invest a great deal in each candidate because they realize that it is better to spend money choosing the right employee than trying to repair mistakes caused by poor employees. Swissair understands the importance of hiring the right employees.[26]

From dishwasher to auditor, people seeking jobs at Guest Quarters hotels must complete four interviews, including one with the hotel's general manager. "We're not hiring," says Robert T. Foley, Guest Quarter's senior vice-president for human resources. "We're entering into a fifty–fifty relationship with them. We will pay fairly and give them a good benefit plan. Their commitment to us is that they be customer-oriented."[27]

Disney World allows its best employees—its star "cast members"—to pick future employees. Disney gives cast members who will be used in the selection process 3 weeks of training. They are then turned loose in a 45 minute interview session to select potential new employees. James Poisant, a former manager at Disney World, explains that employees chose employees who mirror their own values. "In 45 minutes the cast members pick up on who's fooling and who's genuine."[28]

Days Inns initiated a program to hire greater numbers of older workers for its reservation center in Atlanta. Older workers designed and distributed flyers and worked at a job fair where they registered participants, conducted tours, answered questions about their jobs, and acted as enthusiastic recruiters for Days Inns.[29]

An effective internal marketing program demands close cooperation between marketing and human resource management. Hiring and training, traditionally the responsibility of human resource management, are key areas in any internal marketing program. A marketinglike approach to human resource management starts with hiring the right employees. Selection methods that identify customer-oriented candidates are used as part of the hiring process.

Teamwork.   Employees who are not customer-oriented often try to pass the responsibility for serving employees to others. They are not team players. In companies that practice internal marketing, if one employee makes an error, other employees try to cover it before the guest notices. In these organizations, guests do not have to understand the hotel's organization and business to ensure that their needs are met. The front desk will handle most requests, relaying the guest's desire to the appropriate department. In restaurants that have used internal marketing to create a service culture, staff cover for each other. Employees who see that a guest needs something will serve the guest, even though it may not be their table.

Organizations that lack teamwork create an uncomfortable environment for the guest. For example, a guest called the front desk of Las Hadas, a five-star resort in Mexico, and asked for extra towels. The front desk clerk answering the telephone acted puzzled. Surely a guest would know to call housekeeping for towels. The operator stated that this was the front desk, not housekeeping, told the guest to call housekeeping, and hung up. Many restaurant guests have asked for a drink while they are sitting at their tables looking over the dinner menu. The response to some of these guests is that they have mistaken the food-service person for a cocktail service person. Food service then tells the customer to redirect their request to cocktail service and departs, leaving the guest's needs unfilled. In both of the above incidents, the first employee contacted should have taken care of the customer's request and passed it along to the appropriate person. This is referred to as *ownership of the problem*. In Ritz-Carlton, the first employee to receive a guest request or complaint "owns" it. The employee is responsible for making sure that guests receive what they need by following up with other departments involved and then contacting the guest to make sure everything was satisfactory. Customers should not have to learn the hotel or restaurant's organizational chart. They should not have to redirect their request for service to another employee. Hiring procedures need to identify these employees who are team players.

Older employees were one group that surprised some managers by their willingness to support other employees. Some managers believed that the elderly might not be willing to cooperate with much younger workers or to accept direction from a youthful supervisor. Kentucky Fried Chicken and McDonald's were among the first hospitality firms to prove the invalidity of these assumptions. A survey of National Restaurant Association members demonstrated that older workers were regarded to have better relations with guests and fellow employees than the "average employees".[30]

The Importance of Initial Training

While staying at a franchised Holiday Inn, a guest asked the desk clerk about the management company: How many hotels did they manage? Where were they located? The employee was unable to answer either question. On another occasion a conversation was overheard between a guest and the dining-room hostess of a Ramada Inn. The guest asked for a recommendation concerning a good place to eat in the area. Managers would hope that the host would first suggest the hotel's restaurant and then mention other restaurants in the area. Instead, the hostess said she had just moved to the area and had not yet found a good place to eat. Too often employees know nothing about the hotel they work for or its products and other items of interest to guests. If employees are not enthusiastic about the company they work for and the products they sell, it will be difficult to create enthusiastic customers.

To be effective, employees must receive information regularly about their company. The company's history, current businesses, its mission statement and vision are important for employees to know. They must be encouraged to feel proud of their new employer. Desire to contribute to the company's success must be instilled in them. At Disney all new employees take a course called "Traditions," in which they learn about the company, its founder, and its values and beliefs. Employees then receive specific training for their particular assignments. Disney trains its ticket takers for 4 days, because the company wants them to be more than ticket takers; they want them to be cast members. The term *cast members* implies they are members of a team. Like other Disney cast members, they are putting on a performance. While they work in the ticket booths, guests will ask many questions. They must know the answers to these questions or be able to find them quickly. Disney understands the importance of these moments of truth. They provide their staff with extensive training before the first moment of truth is faced.[31] Disney has become so well known for its training and human resource management that it now conducts courses for other companies.

Opryland Hotel has developed a training program for new employees that begins with an orientation designed to instill pride in the history, culture and stature of the hotel. The purpose of the orientation process is to create an inspiring atmosphere and build a solid work commitment that helps reduce turnover. According to Marc Clark, the director of training at Opryland, "the new employee orientation program and all employee policies are built on a foundation of a sincere service attitude. If employees, particularly managers, are not serving guests directly, then they should be serving those who are."[32]

The Homestead in Virginia's Allegheny Mountain region is a resort heavy with tradition. Guests feel the nearly 100 years of tradition through the architecture and the customs such as "gentlemanly sports" and afternoon tea, but principally through the employees. The vision of Mr. H. H. Ingalls Jr., president, is "to preserve what is wonderful about this place and to communicate and serve it effectively to guests." Ingalls credits the Homestead employees for earning a five-star designation for the hotel. In praise he stated, "The support of our employees is like the support of a large family. They deliver the kind of service people expect."

This feeling of being a member of a family is precisely the effect successful companies like Disney World, Opryland Hotel, and The Homestead have created and that all members of the hospitality industry must strive to attain.

Continuous Training.   Two principal characteristics have been identified in companies that lead their industries in customer service: They emphasize cross-training and they insist that everybody share certain training experiences. Delta Airlines flight attendants must learn several back-office jobs before they start their careers as attendants.[33] Most hotel training programs for college graduates rotate new employees through all departments in the hotel. This gives the trainees an insight into the importance of each department and how they work together to provide customer service. James Coney Island, a fast-food restaurant chain, cross-trains its employees so that they understand all the positions in the restaurant. Embassy Suites

Hotels goes a step further, providing employees an opportunity to increase their wages based on the number of positions they have mastered.

Companies must make sure that their employees are familiar with all the products the organization sells. For example, all restaurant employees should be prepared to tell guests about the restaurant's Sunday brunch, even those who do not work on Sundays. A restaurant service person in a hotel should be able to give directions to the hotel's health club. Often employees do not have knowledge of products in their own areas because they have never been given the opportunity to sample them. When a service person does not know how an item tastes, it promotes the perception that the employee or management does not care about the customer.

A front-desk clerk said that she felt uneasy when guests asked her about the show in the hotel's night club. The hotel had stressed the importance of promoting it favorably, but did not give the front-desk employees an opportunity to see the show. As a result, the front-desk clerk would tell the guest that it was a great show. Sometimes, the guest would start asking specific questions about the show. When this happened, her answers usually reflected her lack of firsthand knowledge about the show and made her feel foolish. It would have been wise for the hotel to provide an opportunity for front-desk employees to see the show. They could have enthusiastically promoted the show with firsthand knowledge, instead of cringing when someone asked about the show. They may have even promoted the show on their own, rather than waiting for a guest to ask about it.

In well-managed restaurants, employees know the menu. They are trained to direct guests to the menu selections that will best suit their taste and instructed in how to sell the choices on the menu. Every restaurant should have tastings where employees sample the products that they are selling. Product training is a continuous learning process; it should be part of every company's employee training.

Product training sometimes must extend into the visual arts. The Grand Hyatt of Hong Kong is a magnificent hotel with caring and well-trained personnel. Yet even here there is room for additional training. The Grand Hyatt is truly an art museum within a hotel, as the decor features sculpture, paintings, and other fine works of visual art. Unfortunately, none of the employees seems to have sufficient knowledge of these expensive and carefully selected art pieces to discuss them with inquiring guests. If exquisite art is part of the product, it should be part of the training. Guests will be impressed and employees will gain pride in the hotel.

This results in the circular effect of creating satisfied and proud employees who in turn create satisfied guests. The results of a study of this circular effect clearly demonstrated that "as employee's job satisfaction, job involvement and job security improve, their customer focus also improves."[34]

Insurance executives checking out of the Sheraton Boca Raton locked their keys in the car. The car was blocking traffic and the executives had a plane to catch. The bellman telephoned the car's make and serial number to a nearby locksmith, and the hotel staff rolled the car out of traffic. Fifteen minutes after the bellman's call, the locksmith arrived with replacement keys.[35] The employees were successful in handling the problem

The Hyatt Sanctuary Cove develops its employees through training programs that are open to all employees, allowing employees from one department to learn about other departments. Courtesy of Sanctuary Cove, Queensland, Australia.

because they were prepared for such an incident. They knew that a car blocking the entrance could cause problems, so they stored a car jack attached to a dolly nearby. The bell staff knew the phone numbers of nearby locksmiths. They also understood the importance of keeping guests informed to relieve anxiety. Throughout this event, they kept the insurance executives informed of what was going on. Leaving the Sheraton Boca Raton could have been a disaster; instead, it provided an exciting incident that enabled the staff to show their professionalism and further convince the guests that they had indeed chosen the right hotel.

The Hyatt Sanctuary Cove in Australia has adjusted its training programs. Training is now conducted by each department instead of by a trainer from the human resources department. Departments decide what their training needs are and develop programs to fill those needs. The hotel also allows any employee to attend any training session and posts all training sessions on the employee bulletin board so that every employee can review the hotel's training program for the coming month. During a visit to the Hyatt, an accounting department employee was observed training a food-service waiter on the hotel's computerized food and beverage accounting system. It became obvious from their conversation that each was learning about the other's department and how the departments could better support each other.

The development of a good training program can start organizations on an upward spiral. A research study found that service quality is inversely related to staff turnover. Properly trained employees can deliver quality service, which helps the image of the firm, attracting more guests and employees to the organization. Some firms ask why they should spend money training employees if they are just going to leave. This can turn into a self-fulfilling prophecy for firms that have this attitude. The employees are not properly trained and thus not capable of delivering quality service. Not being able to deliver good service, they will feel uncomfortable in their jobs and quit. Unfortunately, this reinforces employers' beliefs that they should not spend money training their employees. But not investing in employee training programs leads to a cycle of high employee turnover and guest dissatisfaction.

Hospitality companies with a strong commitment to employee training are well advised to make this philosophy well known to all employees in action and in word. The Centennial Hotel Management Company of Canada has a written statement of human resources philosophy that includes orientation and training. This statement is an excellent internal marketing tool.[36]

Orientation
- The purpose of Centennial Hotel orientation is to assure the new employee that he or she has made the right decisions, and to build a strong sense of belonging to the company, the team, and the industry.
- Orientation assures the employees that the company provides the support that they require to be successful. It is also a time to share the values of Centennial Hotel and to introduce the facilities of the hotel.

Training
- Centennial Hotel is committed to providing consistent basic training throughout the company, as well as continuous upgrading. Training is for everyone, and must be planned, systematic and comprehensive. The success of training must be measurable.

Dissemination of Marketing Information to Employees

Often the most effective way of communicating with customers is through customer-contact employees. They can suggest additional products, such as the hotel's health club or business center, and they can upsell when it is to the guest's benefit. Employees often have opportunities to solve guest problems before these problems become irritants. To do this, they need information. Unfortunately, many companies leave customer-contact employees out of the communication cycle. The director of marketing may tell managers and supervisors about upcoming events, ad campaigns, and new promotions, but some managers may feel employees do not need to know this information.

Beth Lorenzini of Restaurants and Institutions states, "Promotions designed to generate excitement and sales can do just the opposite if employees aren't involved in planning and execution."

Monica Kass, sales and marketing coordinator for Lawry's The Prime Rib, Chicago, says that employees and marketing people who develop promotion must communicate. Lawry's increased its Thanksgiving day sales by 48% through employee involvement. Lawry's invited all the "wait staff" to a Thanksgiving dinner a week before Thanksgiving. This was the same meal it was serving to guests on Thanksgiving day. The dinner not only served as a festive affair to get everybody into the Thanksgiving holiday mood, but it also served as a training tool. Employees knew exactly what was going to be served on Thanksgiving day, including wines that went well with the meal. The management of Lawry's also asked the staff for their input as to how to make the promotion run smoothly. On Thanksgiving day, each wait person was given a corsage or a boutonniere. Like the employees at Lawry's, all staff should be informed about promotions. They should hear about promotions and new products from management, not from advertisements meant for external customers. [37]

The actions of management are one way an organization communicates with its employees. Management at all levels must understand that employees are watching them for cues about expected behavior. If the general manager picks up a piece of paper on the floor, other employees will start doing the same. A manager who talks about the importance of employees working together as a team can reinforce the desire for teamwork through personal actions. Taking an interest in employees' work, lending a hand, knowing employees by name, and eating in the employee cafeteria are actions that will give credibility to the manager's words.

Hospitality organizations should use printed publications as part of their internal communication. Most multiunit companies have an employee newsletter, and larger hotels usually have their own in-house newsletters. Besides mass communication, personal communication is important to the effective communication of new products and promotional campaigns. Leonard Berry suggests having two annual reports—one for stockholders and one for employees. His suggestion is now being implemented by many firms.[38]

McDonald's initiated a "talking" annual report on videotape complete with commercials. This unusual and creative approach to presenting the required annual report proved to be an excellent means for reaching stockholders and employees. When introduced, it also produced a wealth of free publicity in major news media.

Ongoing communication between management and employees is essential, not just group meetings but regular individual meetings between the employee and management. Every customer-contact employee communicates with hundreds of customers. Managers should meet with these employees to gain customer need insights and determine how the company can make it easier for the employee to serve the customer.

Ansett Airlines in Australia provides an example of what can happen when employees are not informed of changes in the company's marketing plans. A traveler called Ansett to ask the airline about a promotion that they had just read about in a newspaper advertisement. The airline representative did not know anything about the promotion and asked the caller how he found out about the promotion. When the caller stated that he had read it in today's newspaper, the airline representative explained that that was why she had not heard about it. She stated it would be several days before she would get a copy of the details of the promotion. Hospitality organizations often spend time and effort developing campaigns for specific markets, which are effective in enticing customers. But if customers must deal with employees who are uninformed and cannot provide them with information, they may walk away dissatisfied.

Front-desk clerks are the communication center of the hotel, yet they frequently do not know the names of entertainers or the type of entertainment featured in the hotel's lounges. They may also be unaware of special marketing promotions. The roof-top lounge of the Westin Oaks Hotel in Houston was known for having good entertainment. When the hotel was called to find out who was playing in the lounge, the front-desk clerk gave the name of an unfamiliar group. When asked what type of music they played, the clerk had no idea.

Hotels can use technology and training to provide employees with product knowledge. Technology can be used to develop a database. Information can be readily accessible to employees, who should then be trained in the hotel's products and services. Finally, employees can be encouraged to try the company's products. They can eat in the restaurants, stay overnight in the hotel, and receive special previews of lounge entertainment. It is much more convincing if the front-desk employee can give a potential guest firsthand information rather than reading a description.

Employees should receive information on new products and product changes, marketing campaigns, and changes in the service delivery process. All action steps in the marketing plan should include internal marketing. For example, when a company introduces a new mass media campaign, the implementation plan should include actions to inform employees about the campaign. The first time most employees see company advertisements is in the media where the advertisement is placed. Before the advertisements appear in the media, the company should share the ad with its employees. Managers should also explain the objective of the campaign and the implications.

One of the authors once worked in a restaurant whose owner decided to install a computer system without any discussion with the staff. The system was first used during a busy lunch period, and the restaurant had given the staff almost no prior training. The system did not perform well, and the staff grew determined to get rid of it. They found the system was sensitive to grease spots on the check. If a service person got butter on a check, the guest would be charged for all sorts of extra items. Some staff would deliberately put grease spots on their checks to develop false charges for the customer. When the customer complained about the bill, the server would explain to the guest the problems that they were having with the new system. Customers quickly sided with the service personnel, and within 3 months the owner was forced to eliminate the new system. If management has consulted employees before installation, the employees might have supported the computer. Management could have shown the employees how the system would help them better serve the guest by automatically adding their tickets and keeping them current. This would have created employee support. Instead, without the proper information and training, employees were determined from the beginning to get rid of the computer.

Reward and Recognition

Employees must know how they are doing to perform effectively. Communication must be designed to give them feedback on their perfor-

Marketing Highlight 11-1

Walt Disney Enterprises— A Highly Responsive Organization

Service companies—hotels, hospitals, colleges, banks, and others—are increasingly recognizing that their marketing mix consists of five Ps, that is, product, price, place, promotion, and people. And people may be the most important P! The organization's employees are in constant contact with consumers and can create good or bad impressions.

Organizations are eager to learn how to "turn on" their inside people (employees) to serve their outside people (customers). Here is what the Disney organization does to market positive customer attitudes to its employees.

1. The personnel staff at Disney extends a special welcome to new applicants. Those who are hired are given written instructions on what to expect—where to report, what to wear, and how long each training phase will be.

2. On the first day, new employees report to Disney University for an all-day orientation session. They sit four to a table, receive name tags, and enjoy coffee, juice, and pastry while they introduce themselves and get acquainted. The result is that each new employee immediately knows three other people and feels part of a group.

3. The employees are introduced to the Disney philosophy and operations through the latest audiovisual presentations. They learn that they are in the entertainment business. They are "cast members" whose job it is to be enthusiastic, knowledgeable, and professional in serving Disney's "guests." Each division is described, and the new employees learn how they will each play a role in producing the "show." Then they are treated to lunch, tour the park, and are shown the recreational area set aside for the employees' exclusive use. That area consists of a lake, recreation hall, picnic area, boating and fishing facilities, and a large library.

4. The next day, the new employees report to their assigned jobs, such as security hosts

mance. An internal marketing program includes service standards and methods of measuring how well the organization is meeting these standards. The results of any service measurement should be communicated to employees. Sheraton, Marriott, and other major hotel companies survey their guests to determine their satisfaction level with individual attributes of the hotel. One researcher found that simply communicating information collected from customers changed employee attitudes and performance.[39] Customer-service measurements have a positive effect on employee attitudes if results are communicated and recognition is given to those who serve the customer well. If you want customer-oriented employees, seek out ways to catch them serving the customer, and reward and recognize them for making the effort.[40]

Most reward systems in the hospitality and travel industry are based on meeting cost objectives such as achieving a certain labor cost or food cost. They are also based on achieving sales objectives. A few companies are now starting to give rewards based on customer satisfaction, but these

(police), transportation hosts (drivers), custodial hosts (street cleaners), or food-and-beverage hosts (restaurant workers). They will receive a few days of additional training before they go "on stage." When they have learned their function, they receive their "theme costumes" and are ready to perform.

5. The new employees receive additional training on how to answer questions guests frequently ask about the park. When they don't have the answer, they can dial switchboard operators who are armed with thick fact books and stand ready to answer any question.

6. The employees receive a Disney newspaper called *Eyes and Ears*, which features news of activities, employment opportunities, special benefits, educational offerings, and so on. Each issue contains a generous number of pictures of smiling employees.

7. Each Disney manager spends a week each year in "cross-utilization," that is, giving up the desk and heading for the front line, such as taking tickets, selling popcorn, or loading or unloading rides. In this way, management stays in touch with running the park and maintaining quality service to satisfy the millions of visitors. All managers and employees wear name badges and address each other on a first-name basis, regardless of rank.

8. All exiting employees answer a questionnaire on how they felt about working for Disney and any dissatisfactions they might have. In this way, Disney's management can measure its success in producing employee satisfaction and, ultimately, customer satisfaction.

No wonder the Disney people are so successful in satisfying their "guests." Management's attention to its employees helps the latter feel important and personally responsible for the "show." The employees' sense of "owning this organization" spills over to the millions of visitors with whom they come in contact.

Source: See N. W. Pope, "Mickey Mouse Marketing," *American Banker*, (July 25, 1979); and "More Mickey Mouse Marketing," *American Banker*, (September 12, 1979).

---

companies are the exception, not the rule. If companies want to have customer-oriented employees they must reward them for servicing the customer. Reward systems and bonuses based on customer satisfaction scores are one method of rewarding employees based on serving the customer.

NONROUTINE TRANSACTIONS

A good internal marketing program should result in employees who can handle nonroutine transactions, such as Barry Urquhart's request for a cappuccino. Training programs and manuals can prepare employees to handle normal or routine transactions with customers. Internal marketing programs will help them deal with guests in a positive and friendly manner. But not all transactions are routine. In this chapter, we discussed Barry Urquhart's request for a cappuccino, Karl Albrecht's request for a late check-out when the hotel was full, and the hotel guest who locked his keys in his car. One benefit of an internal marketing program is that it provides employees with the right attitude, knowledge, communication skills, and authority to deal with nonroutine transactions. The ability to handle nonroutine transactions separates excellent hospitality companies from mediocre ones. A nonroutine transaction is a guest transaction that is unique and usually experienced for the first time by the employees. The number of possible nonroutine transactions is so great that they cannot be covered in a training manual.

Management must be willing to give employees the authority to make decisions that will solve guests problems. Management should exhibit confidence in their ability to hire and train employees by trusting the employees' ability to make decisions. Simon Cooper, president of Delta Hotels and resorts, a 25-location chain headquartered in Toronto, believes that having staff do nothing but control other staff reflects poorly on the organization. He states that the job of an assistant housekeeper is to go around and check that the maids are doing their job. Having that position is an admission that we can't hire the right people. Cooper says that Delta has successfully eliminated that position. They have a few assistant housekeepers, who are now in training positions. When their housekeepers finish a room, they know the next person in it will be a guest. Cooper states that the degree of trust makes them far better workers.[41] When we trust employees, they solve guest problems more effectively and create less causes for the guest to complain.

Hospitality companies that rely on rigid policies and procedures rather than motivated, well-trained, and empowered employees have little hope of achieving maximum guest satisfaction. This sentiment was expressed very well by Robert C. Lewis.[42]

> The success of the internal-marketing concept ultimately lies with management. Lower-level employees cannot be expected to be customer-conscious if the management above them does not display the same focus. Operations-oriented managers who concern themselves primarily with policies and procedures, often instituted without regard to the customer, undermine the firm's internal-marketing effort, reducing employee's jobs to mechanical functions that offer little in the way of challenge, self-esteem or personal gratification. Moreover, by requiring employees to adhere rigidly to specific procedures, the operations-oriented manager ties their hands and restricts their ability to satisfy the customer.

The issue of nonroutine transactions will become increasingly important in the future. Hospitality firms are now using technology to serve routine customer transactions. This use of technology will become even more pervasive. Computerized check-in, video check-out, and robotics will be adapted to the hospitality industry, so employees will find themselves dealing more frequently with nonroutine tasks. Self-confident guests will take advantage of technology designed to enhance and hasten guest service. The uncertain guest or guests with problems will wish to deal with an employee. As the workplace becomes more automated, employees will take a greater role in answering questions and solving guests' problems. They must also be prepared to handle nonroutine transactions.

As Parasuraman says, "Customer service earned through several satisfactorily performed routine transactions can be badly damaged by just one botched attempt at processing a nonroutine transaction. No amount of written procedures, guidelines, or specifications can prevent the occurrence of such botched attempts; only true organizational dedication to customer satisfaction can."[43] A strong service culture enables employees to make decisions required to handle non-routine transactions.

Chapter Review

I. **Internal Marketing**
   1) The hospitality industry is unique in that **employees are part of the product.**
   2) Marketers must develop techniques and procedures to ensure that employees are able and willing to deliver quality service.
   3) Internal Marketing is marketing aimed internally at the firm's employees.

II. **The Internal Marketing Process**
   1) Establishment of a Service Culture
      a) A **service culture** is an organizational cultural that supports customer service through policies, procedures, reward systems, and actions.
      b) An **organizational culture** is a pattern of shared values and beliefs that gives members of an organization meaning, providing them with the rules for behavior in the organization.
      c) **Turning the organizational chart upside down.** Service organizations should create an organization that supports those employees who serve the customers.
   2) Development of a Marketing Approach to Human Resource Management.
      a) **Creating positions that attract good employees.**
      b) A **hiring process** that identifies and results in hiring service-oriented employees.
      c) **Initial employee training** designed to share the company's vision with the employee and supply the employee with product knowledge.
      d) **Continuous employee training** programs.

III. **Dissemination of Marketing Information to Employees**
   1) Often the most effective way of communicating with customers is through customer-contact employees.
   2) Employees should hear about promotions and new products from management, not from advertisements meant for external customers.
   3) Management at all levels must understand that employees are watching them for cues about expected behavior.
   4) Hospitality organizations should use printed publications as part of their internal communication.

5) Hotels can use technology and training to provide employees with product knowledge.

6) Employees should receive information on new products and product changes, marketing campaigns, and changes in the service delivery process.

IV. **Implementation of a Reward and Recognition System**

1) Employees must know how they are doing to perform effectively. Communication must be designed to give them feedback on their performance.

2) An internal marketing program includes service standards and methods of measuring how well the organization is meeting these standards.

3) If you want customer-oriented employees, seek out ways to catch them serving the customer, and reward and recognize them for making the effort.

V. **Nonroutine Transactions**

1) A good internal marketing program should result in employees who can handle nonroutine transactions.

2) One benefit of an internal marketing program is that it provides employees with the right attitude, knowledge, communication skills, and authority to deal with nonroutine transactions.

3) A nonroutine transaction is a guest transaction that is unique and usually experienced for the first time by the employees.

4) Management must be willing to give employees the authority to make decisions that will solve guests' problems.

DISCUSSION QUESTIONS

1. Why are employees called internal customers?
2. What is a service culture? Why is it a requirement for an internal marketing program?
3. Discuss the possible ways marketing techniques can be used by human resource managers.
4. What are the benefits of explaining advertising campaigns to employees before they appear in the media?
5. The handling of nonroutine transactions will separate excellent hospitality companies from mediocre ones. Discuss this statement.

KEY TERMS

Cast members A term used for employees. It means that employees are part of a team that is performing for the guests.

Cross-training Training employees to do two or more jobs within the organization.

Customer-contact employees Employees that come in direct contact with the customer.

Empowerment When a firm *empowers* employees, it moves the authority and responsibility to make decisions to the line employees from the supervisor.

Internal marketing Marketing aimed internally at the firm's employees.

Moments of truth A moment of truth occurs when the employee and the customer have contact.

Nonrountine transaction A guest transaction that is unique and usually experienced for the first time by the employees.

Organizational culture The pattern of shared values and beliefs that gives members of an organization meaning and provides them with the rules for behavior in that organization.

Service culture An organizational culture that supports customer service through policies, procedures, reward systems, and actions.

REFERENCES

1. BARRY URQUHART, *Serves You Right* (Kalamunda, Wash.: Marketing Focus, 1991), pp. 83–85.

2. JOHN TSCHOLL, *Achieving Excellence through Customer Service, (Englewood Cliffs, N.J.: Prentice Hall, 1991).*

3. *Urquhart,* Serves Your Right, *p. 86.*

4. *KARL ALBRECHT AND RON ZEMKE,* Service America! *(Homewood, Ill.: Dow-Jones Irwin, 1985), p. 127–128.*

5. *Tschohl,* Achieving Excellence, p. 3.

6. Harvard studies

7. RICHARD NORMANN, *Service Management: Strategy and Leadership in Service Businesses* (New York: John Wiley & Sons, 1984), p. 33.

8. Ibid., p. 9.

9. WILLIAM R. GEORGE AND CHRISTIAN GRONROOS, "Developing Customer-conscious Employees at Every Level; Internal Marketing," in *The Handbook of Marketing for the Service Industries* Carole A. Congram, ed. (New York: American Management Association), pp. 85–100.

10. CHRISTIAN GRONROOS, *Strategic Management and Marketing in the Service Sector*, Cambridge, Mass: Marketing Science Institute, 1983, as cited in C. Gronroos, *Service Management and Marketing*, Lexington, Mass: Lexington Books, 1990, p. 223.

11. Ibid., p. 85.

12. *The Australian*, October 10, 1990.

13. S. M. DAVIS, *Managing Corporate Culture* (Cambridge, Mass.: Ballinger, 1985).

14. TERRENCE E. DEAL AND ALLAN A. KENNEDY, *Corporate Cultures.* (Reading, Mass.: Addison-Wesley, 1982), pp. 15–16.

15. A. PARASURAMAN, *Corporate Culture,* p. 44.

16. CHRISTIAN GRONROOS, *Services Management and Marketing* (Lexington, Mass.: Lexington Books, 1990), p. 242.

17. JOHN J. HOGAN, "Turnover and What to Do about It," *Cornell Hotel and Restaurant Administration Quarterly*, 33, no. 1 (February 1992), p. 41.

18. KARL ALBRECHT, *At America's Service* (Homewood, Ill.: Dow-Jones Irwin, 1988), p. 130.

19. Ibid., p. 107; and NATHAN TYLER, *Service Excellence*, Tape 2 (Boston, Mass.: 1987).

20. JAMES L. HESKETT, W. EARL SASSER, AND LEONARD A. SCHLESINGER, *Saving Customers with Service Recovery* (video tape) (Boston, Mass.: Harvard Business School Management Productions, 1994).

21. LEONARD L. BERRY, "The Employee as Customer," *Journal of Retail Banking*, 3, no. 1 (1981), pp. 33–40.

22. HOGAN, "Turnover," p. 40.

23. Ibid., p. 41.

24. DENNIS REYNOLDS AND MARY TABACCHI, "Burnout in Full Service Chain Restaurant," *Cornell Hotel and Restaurant Administration Quarterly*, 34, no. 2 (April 1993), p. 68.

25. KEN W. MCCLEARLY AND PAMELA A. WEAVER, "The *Job* Offer: What Today's Graduates Want," *Cornell Hotel and Restaurant Administration Quarterly*, 28, no. 4 (February 1988), p. 31.

26. LELE, MILIAND, *The Customer Is Key* (New York: John Wiley & Sons, 1987), p. 252.

27. WILLIAM H. DAVIDOW AND BRO UTTAL, *Total Customer Service* (New York: Harper & Row Publishers, 1989), p. 123.

28. TSCHOHL, *Achieving Excellence*, p. 113.

29. FREDERICK J. DE MICCO AND ROBERT D. REID, "Older Worker, A Hiring Resource for the Hospitality Industry," *Cornell Hotel and Restaurant Administration Quarterly*, 29, no. 1 (May 1988), p. 56.

30. Ibid., p. 58.

31. N. W. POPE, "Mickey Mouse Marketing," *American Banker* (July 25, 1979), as included in: W. EARL SASSER JR., CHRISTOPHER W. L. HART, AND JAMES L. HESKETT, *The Service Management Course, Cases and Reading* (New York, N.Y.: The Free Press, 1991), pp. 649–654.

32. MARC CLARK, "Training for Tradition," *Cornell Hotel and Restaurant Administration Quarterly,* 31, no. 4 (February 1991), p. 51.

33. DAVIDOW AND UTALL, *Total Customer Service*, p. 128.

34. JOHN R. DIENHART AND MARY B. GREGOIRE, "Job Satisfaction, Job involvement, Job Security and Customer Focus of Quick Service Restaurant Employees," *Hospitality Research Journal*, 16, no. 2 (1993), p. 41.

35. CHRISTOPHER W. L. HART, JAMES L. HESKETT, AND W. EARL SASSER, JR., *Service Breakthroughs* (New York: The Free Press, 1990), p. 109.

36. MICHAEL K. HAYWOOD, "Effective Training: Toward a Strategic Approach," *Cornell Hotel and Restaurant Administration Quarterly,* 33, no. 6 (December 1992), p. 46.

37. BETH LORENZINI, "Promotion Success Depends on Employee's Enthusiasm," *Restaurants and Institutions* (February 12, 1992), pp. 59+.

38. BERRY, "Employee as Customer," pp. 33–40.

39. ALBRECHT AND ZEMKE, *Service America!,* p. 142.

40. CHIP R. BELL AND RON ZEMKE, *Managing Knock Your Socks off Service* (New York: American Management Association, 1992), p. 169.

41. CARLA B. FURLONG, *Marketing for Keeps* (New York: John Wiley & Sons, 1993), pp. 79–80.

42. ROBERT C. LEWIS, "Hospitality Marketing: The Internal Approach," *Cornell Hotel and Restaurant Quarterly*, 30, no. 3 (November 1989), p. 43.

43. A. PARASURAMAN, "Customer-Oriented Corporate Cultures are Crucial to Services Marketing Success," *Journal of Services Marketing*, 1, no. 1 (Summer 1987), pp. 33–40.

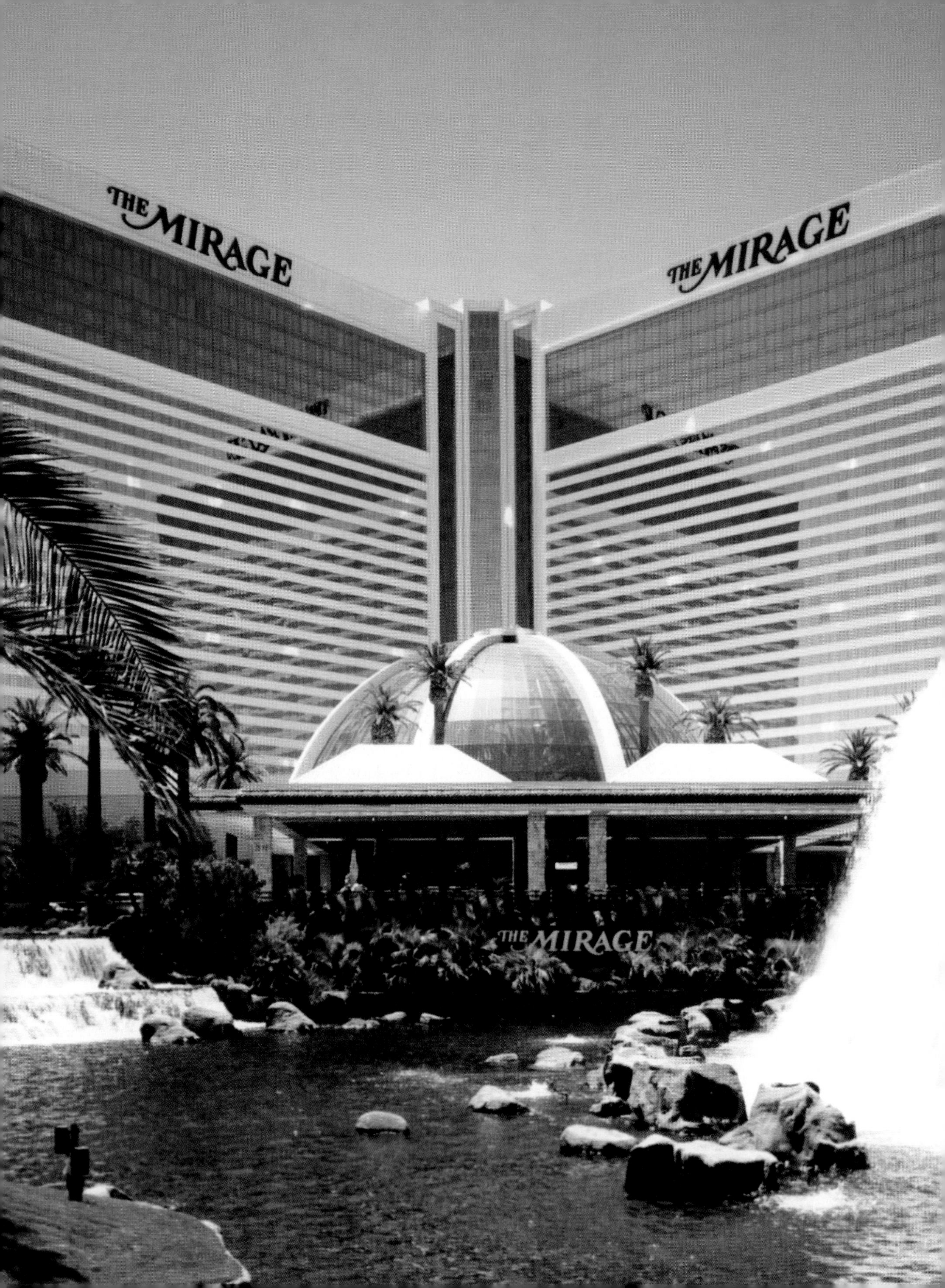
THE MIRAGE
THE MIRAGE
THE MIRAGE

Building Customer Satisfaction through Quality

*I*n January 1990, Hampton Inns began advertising a **service guarantee**. *The guarantee offered a free night's stay if the guest was dissatisfied. Most hotel managers are strongly opposed to offering such guarantees; they feel the hotel will end up giving away rooms to dishonest customers who claim that they were not satisfied just to get their money back. Because of this attitude among hotel managers, the move by Hampton Inns was a bold one. The company had faith in their guests' honesty and in their employees' ability to deliver a quality product. This trust in their guests and employees gave them a competitive advantage over hotel companies without a service guarantee.*

A survey of Hampton Inns' customers found that more than 85% of the guests viewed the guarantee as appealing: the guests ranked it as one of the ten most important attributes of the hotel. Ninety-nine percent of the guests who invoked the guarantee said that they would give the chain another chance, and a tracking study revealed that almost 40% of those guests returned to the Hampton Inns within a relatively short period. When management feels that the guest is taking advantage of the guarantee without a valid reason, a note is made in Hampton Inns' database. When these guests call to make a reservation, the operator tells the guest that they will be happy to take their reservation; however, the guarantee will not be valid. Thus a few guests may take advantage of the system one or two times and then they are eliminated from the system.

Hampton Inns tracked the costs of its guarantee. They found that about 2% of their guests representing 157,000 room nights came to the hotel in 1990 because of the guarantee. These guests generated $7 million in sales, and guests who returned after invoking the guarantee represented another $1 million in sales. During the year, Hampton Inns paid out $350,000 to customers who invoked the guarantee. In 1991 Hampton Inns put its sales generated by the guarantee at $18 million, while compensation paid to customers invoking the guarantee remained constant.[1]

One reason for the success of Hampton Inns' guarantee is that the company regularly performs quality audits. Hampton Inns realized that its guarantee could be a financial disaster if it did not provide a product that would satisfy its guests. Their audit includes a corporate employee posing as a guest invoking the guarantee. The employee tracks how the Inn resolves the problem and if they follow up with the guest to make sure that everything is satisfactory.[2]

The guarantee also had an effect on the hotel's employees. When asked to make comments about their job, almost 50% suggested (unaided) that the guarantee made them work harder. The employees also stated that it gave them the confidence to solve guest problems on their own without waiting for a manager's approval. Management claimed that the guarantee made Hampton Inns a better place to work and improved employee morale. The service guarantee provides an example of how hospitality firms are focusing on improving the quality of the services they offer.[3] It also provides evidence that employees prefer working for a company that helps them deliver a quality product and satisfy their customers.

Some managers are afraid of a guarantee because they expect customers will unfairly take advantage of the guarantee to get a free meal or a free room. This will happen, but researchers estimate there will be 19 legitimate complaints for every cheater.[4] Hampton Inns controls cheating by advising guests who are suspected of cheating and have invoked the guarantee on more than one occasion that they are welcome as guests, but they will no longer be offered the guarantee. The real danger with guarantees is from businesses who offer a guarantee but do not provide a satisfactory product.

Chapter 12 reviews a key trend in marketing for the twenty-first century: the trend toward the use of relationship marketing to improve customer satisfaction.

We frame the chapter by reinterpreting the marketing concept, stressing the need to offer real **customer value** and **customer satisfaction** in order to compete effectively.

We discuss the fact that marketers usually focus on attracting new users, but most also retain current customers by developing relationship marketing.

Next we discuss different definitions of quality. **Product features** that enhance customer satisfaction and **freedom from deficiencies** are discussed as types of quality.

Next, a service quality model that includes **technical quality, functional quality**, and **societal quality** is presented. We discuss how functional quality or the process of delivering the service can become a point of differentiation for the firm. Societal or ethical quality is an important component of quality that managers often overlook.

The five-gap model of service quality is presented as a way of relating quality to management actions. Through this discussion we show managers how they can identify and eliminate quality gaps. Next, retaining customers, avoidance of price competition, retention of employees, and reduction of costs are discussed as benefits of service quality.

Finally, we present a program to develop service quality in a hospitality organization.

INTRODUCTION

Today's companies face their toughest competition in decades, and things will only get worse in years to come. In previous chapters, we have argued that to succeed in today's fiercely competitive marketplace, companies will have to move from a *product and selling philosophy* to a *customer and marketing philosophy*. This chapter spells out in more detail how companies can go about winning customers and outperforming competitors. The answer lies in the marketing concept—in doing a better job of *meeting and satisfying customer needs*.

To succeed, or simply to survive, companies need a new philosophy. To win in today's marketplace, companies must be **customer centered**; they must deliver superior value to their target customers. They must become adept in *building customers*, not just *building products*. They must be skillful in *market engineering*, not just *product engineering*.

Too many companies think that obtaining customers is the job of the marketing or sales department. But winning companies have come to realize that marketing cannot do this job alone. In fact, although it plays a leading role, marketing can be only a partner in attracting and keeping customers. The world's best marketing department cannot successfully sell poorly made products that fail to meet consumer needs. The marketing department can be effective only in companies in which all departments and employees have teamed up to form a competitively superior *customer value delivery system*.

Consider McDonald's. People do not swarm to the world's 14,000 McDonald's restaurants only because they love the chain's hamburgers. Consumers flock to the McDonald's system, not just to its food products. Throughout the world, McDonald's finely tuned system delivers a high standard of what the company calls QSCV—quality, service, cleanliness, and value. The system consists of many components, both internal and external.

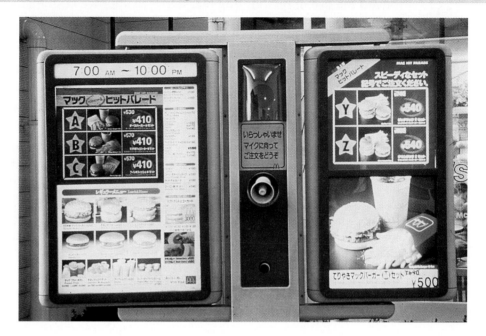

McDonald's consistency is one of the main reasons for its global acceptance. There is little variation in its products within a region, its restaurants are clean, and its service is quick. Courtesy of McDonald's.

McDonald's is only effective to the extent that it successfully partners with its employees, franchisees, suppliers, and others to jointly deliver exceptionally high customer value.

This chapter discusses the philosophy of customer-value-creating marketing and the customer-focused firm. It addresses several important questions: What are customer value and customer satisfaction? How do leading companies organize to create and deliver high value and satisfaction? How can companies keep current customers as well as get new ones? How can companies practice total quality marketing?

DEFINING CUSTOMER VALUE AND SATISFACTION

Consumers buy from the firm that they believe offers the highest **customer delivered value**—the difference between *total customer value* and *total customer cost*. The customer derives value from the core products, the service delivery system, and the company's image. These components make up *total customer value*. The costs to the customer include *money, time, energy, and physic costs* (see Figure 12-1). For example, a business traveler will value a nonstop flight over a direct flight that makes a stop because of the reduced travel time. They may avoid certain airports as connecting points because they are large and require a lot of walking. Thus, going from the East Coast of the United States to the West Coast, they may prefer to change planes in Memphis rather than Dallas. Finally, they will prefer an airline that has a good on-time record and a good customer service record. This can reduce the physic cost of worrying if the plane and baggage will arrive on time.

Thus consumers form judgments about the value of marketing offers and make their buying decisions based on these judgments. *Customer satisfaction* with a purchase depends on the product's performance relative to a buyer's expectations. A customer might experience various degrees of satisfaction. If the product's performance falls short of expectations, the cus-

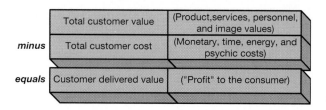

	Total customer value	(Product, services, personnel, and image values)
minus	Total customer cost	(Monetary, time, energy, and psychic costs)
equals	Customer delivered value	("Profit" to the consumer)

Figure 12-1
Customer delivered value.

tomer is dissatisfied. If performance matches expectations, the customer is satisfied. If performance exceeds expectations, the customer is highly satisfied or delighted.

But how do buyers form their expectations? Expectations are based on the customer's past buying experiences, the opinions of friends and associates, and marketer and competitor information and promises. Marketers must be careful to set the right level of expectations. If they set expectations too low, they may satisfy those who buy but fail to attract enough buyers. In contrast, if they raise expectations too high, buyers are likely to be disappointed. For example, Holiday Inn ran a campaign a few years ago called "No Surprises," which promised consistently trouble free accommodations and service. However, Holiday Inn guests still encountered a host of problems, and the expectations created by the campaign only made customers more dissatisfied. Holiday Inn had to withdraw the campaign.

Still, some of today's most successful companies are raising expectations and delivering performance to match. These companies embrace *total customer satisfaction*. For example, Ritz-Carlton views the Baldrige Award as a milestone in its quality journey, not the finish line. Hampton Inns offers a guarantee, and Southwest Airlines consistently has one of the highest on-time arrival rates in the industry. These companies aim high because they know that customers who are *only* satisfied will still find it easy to switch suppliers when a better offer comes along.

Although the customer-centered firm seeks to deliver high customer satisfaction relative to competitors, it does not attempt to *maximize* customer satisfaction. A company can always increase customer satisfaction by lowering profits. In addition to customers, the company has many stakeholders, including employees, dealers, suppliers, and stockholders. Spending more to increase customer satisfaction might divert funds from increasing the satisfaction of these other "partners." Thus the purpose of marketing is to generate customer value profitably. Ultimately, the company must deliver a high level of customer satisfaction while at the same time delivering at least acceptable levels of satisfaction to the firm's other stakeholders. This requires a very delicate balance: the marketer must continue to generate more customer value and satisfaction but not "give away the house."[5]

RETAINING CUSTOMERS

Beyond building a stronger relation with their partners in the supply chain, companies today must work to develop stronger bonds and loyalty with their ultimate customers. In the past, many companies took their customers for granted. Customers often did not have many alternative suppliers, or the other suppliers were just as poor in quality and service, or the market was growing so fast that the company did not worry about fully satisfying its customers. A company could lose 100 customers a week but gain another 100 customers and consider its sales to be satisfactory. Such a company, operating on a "leaky bucket" theory of business, believes that there will always be enough customers to replace the defecting ones. However, this high *customer churn* involves higher costs than if a company retained all 100 customers and acquired no new ones. Another problem is that the dissatisfied customers are spreading negative word of mouth. This makes it increasingly difficult to gain the 100 new customers per week. In businesses that depend on local business, such as a neighborhood restaurant, it soon becomes impossible to gain an equal amount of replacement customers.

Cost of Lost Customers

Companies must pay close attention to their customer defection rate and undertake steps to reduce it. First, the company must define and measure its retention rate. Next, the company must identify the causes of customer defection and determine which of these can be reduced or eliminated. Not much can be done about customers who leave the region or about business customers who go out of business. But much can be done about customers who leave because of poor service, poor quality food, or prices that are too high. The company needs to prepare a frequency distribution showing the percentage of customers who defect for different reasons.

Companies can estimate how much profit they lose when customers defect unnecessarily. For an individual customer, this is the same as the *customer's lifetime value*. Ritz-Carlton knows its repeat customers are worth over $100,000 over their lifetime. A restaurant customer can be worth several thousand dollars worth of business, and a travel agency customer can generate over $50,000 during their lifetime with the agency. The lifetime value is calculated by measuring how much a member of a market segment produces per year, on average, and multiplying this amount by the average life of a member of that segment. The average life is determined through surveys or guest history. People move, get transferred, change companies, and become dissatisfied; thus the average life for an individual business traveler might be 4 years. The average life of a restaurant customer might be only 3 years in a transient community. Hotel chains with a guest history system can track the lifetime value of guests to the chain, not just an individual hotel. The lifetime varies by location and market segment; it is unique to an individual business.

The company needs to figure out how much it would cost to reduce the defection rate. If the cost is less than the lost profits, the company should spend that amount to reduce customer defections. Today, outstanding companies go all out to retain their customers. Many markets have settled into maturity, and there are not too many new customers entering most categories. Competition is increasing and the costs of attracting new customers are rising. In these markets, it might cost five times as much to attract a new customer as to keep a current customer happy. Offensive marketing typically costs more than defensive marketing, because it takes a great deal of effort and spending to coax satisfied customers away from competitors.

Unfortunately, classic marketing theory and practice centers on the art of attracting new customers, rather than retaining existing ones. The emphasis has been on creating *transactions*, rather than *relationships*.

Discussion has focused on *presale activity* and *sale activity*, rather than on *postsale activity*. Today, however, more companies recognize the importance of retaining current customers. According to one report, by reducing customer defections by only 5%, companies can improve profits anywhere from 25% to 85%.[6] Unfortunately, however, most company accounting systems fail to show the value of loyal customers.

Thus, although much current marketing focuses on formulating marketing mixes that will create sales and new customers, the firm's first line of defense lies in customer retention. And the best approach to customer retention is to deliver high customer satisfaction that results in strong customer loyalty.

Resolving Customer Complaints

Resolving customer complaints is a critical component of customer retention. One study by TARP found that if a customer has a major complaint, 91% will not buy from you again, but if it was resolved quickly, 82% of those customers will return. The complaint resolution drops the customer defection from 91 out of a hundred to 18 out of a hundred. With resolution of minor complaints the defection rate can be reduced to less than 5 out of 100.[7] In complaint resolution there are two important factors. First, if you resolve a complaint, do it quickly; the longer to takes to resolve the higher the defection rate. Second, seek out customer complaints.

For example, a businesswoman had just returned from an overseas trip. After a good night's sleep in a New York hotel she was ready for an American breakfast. She dialed room service and her breakfast was delivered promptly. A cheerful waiter wheeled the table into the room and positioned it so that the woman could look out the window. He opened the heating compartment and pulled out the breakfast that the woman had been waiting for, a full, hot American breakfast. The waiter handed the woman the bill, and she promptly signed the bill and added a handsome tip. Now she was ready to start her breakfast.

The waiter said, "I'm sorry you will have to pay cash." She explained that she did not have any money with her and pulled out her credit cards, getting the American Express gold card she had used to check into the hotel. The waiter called on the phone and after 5 minutes it was resolved that the woman could use her credit card. The woman, now upset, sat down to a cold breakfast.[8]

A meeting planner ordered a bus to take a group of club managers on a tour of a country club. The bus was ordered for a 9:30 A.M. departure on Saturday morning. The bus company usually scheduled the buses to arrive at least 15 minutes before the departure time. The meeting planner became concerned when the bus had not arrived by 9:20. He called the dispatcher at the bus company. The dispatcher told him in a matter of fact way that the bus drivers were still sleeping and they would not be there until 11:00 A.M. It seems they were working with a tour that did not get through until 2:30 A.M. the previous night and federal regulations called for at least 8 hours off between trips. The dispatcher hung up after explaining the reason for the delay. The meeting planner called a fleet of taxi cabs to transport his group so that they would make the 10 A.M. appointment. He then called back to cancel the bus. On Monday he called the bus company to get his money back. The bus company required payment in full when the bus was reserved. He was told he would not be entitled to a refund, since the bus was canceled with less than 24 hours notice. After several weeks of phone calls and a letter, the bus company agreed to refund the money. Six months later the meeting planner received another check for $125 and an apology from the national sales manager.

The bus company had refunded the money and paid $125 and still lost the customer. After 6 months, the meeting planner had found another bus company and was satisfied with their service. He was not about to change. If the bus company had promptly refunded the money and offered $125 toward the meeting planner's next trip, they might have been able to salvage the customer. The waiter, at the New York Hotel, could have told the businesswoman he was sure her signature would be fine and left, telling her to enjoy her meal. He then could have resolved the problem outside her room. This would have resulted in the woman enjoying the meal she was looking forward to. In both these cases the customer received a resolution to the problem, but it came too late.

Another critical area in complaint resolution is that most customers do not complain. They do not give managers a chance to resolve their problem. They just leave and never come back. Managers must develop ways to encourage customers to complain. Methods to seek complaints include customer hot lines that encourage customers to call about problems that they are having. Customer comment cards encourage customers to discuss problems that they had with the product. Managers can train employees to look out for guests that look dissatisfied and try to find out their problems. A service guarantee is another way of getting customers to complain; in order to invoke the guarantee, they have to complain.

When a customer does complain, management should be grateful. They should remember that most customers do not complain. The complaining customer gives management a chance to resolve the complaint. Complaints that come in by letter should be responded to quickly by a letter or phone call. If you respond by letter, customize part of the letter acknowledging the customer's specific complaint and what will be done to prevent it from happening again. A resolution to the complaint should be offered to the guest. A more effective way of resolving the complaint can be through the use of the telephone. Today, it often costs less to make a telephone call than it does to send out a letter. The telephone call allows personal contact with the guest and allows the manager to probe, finding out exactly what happened to the guest. The worst thing a company can do is send out a form letter that shows no empathy to the guest's problem.

Bob Martin, a professor at UNLV, was spending a summer as an administrative assistant at a resort. One day while he was in the general manager's office, the manager began complaining about a stack of customer complaint letters he had to answer. The manager further stated he hated to answer complaint letters. The manager also indicated it was a waste of time, since he would be lucky if 5% returned to the hotel. Bob picked up the stack of letters and said "I will take care of this." As he left, he said, "I will get all of them back."

ROYAL CARIBBEAN

March 2, 1995

Mr. & Mrs. C. Wirt
200 Apple Lane
Schaumburg,
Illinois 60193
U.S.A.

Dear Mr. & Mrs. Wirt:

Thank you for taking the time to complete our Guest Questionnaire upon check-out recently. We trust that you had a wonderful time and that we will have the opportunity of welcoming you back to Sandals Royal Caribbean - **the # 1 Fully Ultra All Inclusive in the Caribbean** in the not too distant future.

We have noted the areas with which you expressed concern, i.e. "some food colder than it should, main hot tub should be 104 degrees, include more vegetarian options" and assure you that we are investigating these with a view to taking prompt remedial action. It is through comments like yours that we are able to improve our facilities and keep our "extended family" (you, our guests), happy and satisfied.

We ask that you advise us when you will be returning to Sandals Royal Caribbean to experience firsthand, our improved product.

Yours sincerely,

EARL R. FOSTER
GENERAL MANAGER

P.O. Box 167, Mahoe Bay, Montego Bay, Jamaica, W.I.
Telephone: (809) 953-2231, 953-2232 Fax: (809) 953-2788

THE CARIBBEAN'S #1 ULTRA ALL-INCLUSIVE® LUXURY RESORTS FOR COUPLES ONLY
SANDALS MONTEGO BAY • SANDALS ROYAL CARIBBEAN • SANDALS NEGRIL • SANDALS OCHO RIOS • SANDALS DUNN'S RIVER • SANDALS INN / JAMAICA • SANDALS ANTIGUA • SANDALS ST. LUCIA • SANDALS INN / ST. LUCIA • SANDALS BARBADOS
Unique Vacations is the Worldwide Representative for Sandals Resorts. 1-800-SANDALS

When customers fill out a comment card, managers should respond. There should be a personalized section to the response, to let the customer know you understand their concerns. This is an example of a customized response to a guest, awaiting the general manager's review and signature.

Bob Martin developed a letter that acknowledged receipt of their complaint and thanked the guests for taking the time to write. He apologized for the problem and mentioned what the resort was doing to correct the problem. He offered the guest a complimentary room and asked them to call the executive secretary to make their reservation. This made the guest feel important and allowed the resort to track returning guests. He closed by saying that he hoped other guests would not be the only ones to benefit from the corrections made as a result of the complaint letter, but that they would return again as a valued guest. By the end of the summer, 90% of the writers had returned or made reservations to return. The lifetime value of these guests was over $100,000 in revenues. The complaint resolution also turned a lot of negative word of mouth advertising into positive word of mouth advertising. In fact, some of the returning guests had talked another couple into coming with them. Resolving complaints is one of the easiest ways to plug up a hole in a "leaky bucket." It is an effective way of preventing customer defection. Managers should seek complaints and quickly resolve them.

Relationship Marketing

Relationship marketing involves creating, maintaining and enhancing strong relationships with customers and other stakeholders. Increasingly, marketing is moving away from a focus on individual transactions and toward a focus on building value-laden relationships and marketing networks. Relationship marketing is oriented more toward the long term. The goal is to deliver long-term value to customers, and the measure of success is long-term customer satisfaction. Relationship marketing requires that all the company's departments work together with marketing as a team to serve the customer. It involves building relationships at many levels—economic, social, technical, and legal—resulting in high customer loyalty.

We can distinguish five different levels of relationships that can be formed with customers who have purchased a company's product, such as a meeting or a banquet:

- *Basic.* The company salesperson sells the product but does not follow up in any way.
- *Reactive.* The salesperson sells the product and encourages the customer to call whenever he or she has any questions.
- *Accountable.* The salesperson phones the customer a short time after the booking to check with the customer and answer questions. During and after the event, the salesperson solicits from the customer any product improvement suggestions and any specific disappointments. This information helps the company to continuously improve its offering.
- *Proactive.* The salesperson or others in the company phone the customer from time to time with suggestions about improvements that have been made or creative suggestions for future events.
- *Partnership.* The company works continuously with the customer and with other customers to discover ways to deliver better value.

What specific marketing tools can a company use to develop stronger customer bonding and satisfaction? It can adopt any of three customer value-building approaches.[9] The first relies primarily on adding *financial benefits* to the customer relationship. For example, airlines offer frequent-flyer programs, hotels give room upgrades to their frequent guests, and supermarkets give patronage refunds.

Although these reward programs and other financial incentives build customer preference, they can be easily imitated by competition and thus may fail to differentiate the company's offer permanently. The second approach is to add *social benefits* as well as financial benefits. Here company personnel work to increase their social bonds with customers by learning individual customers' needs and wants and then individualizing and personalizing their products and services. They turn their *customers* into *clients*: Customers may be nameless to the institution; clients cannot be nameless. Customers are served as part of the mass or as part of larger segments; clients are served on an individual basis. Customers are served by anyone who happens to be available; clients are served by the professional assigned to them.[10]

The third approach to building strong customer relationships is to add structural ties as well as financial and social benefits. For example, airlines developed reservation systems for travel agents. Frequent guests have special phone lines that they can call. Airlines have developed lounges for their first-class customers, and some will send a limousine to deliver them to the airport. Here are the main steps in establishing a relationship marketing program in a company:

- *Identify the key customers meriting relationship management:* Choose the largest or best customers and designate them for relationship management. Other customers can be added who show exceptional growth or who pioneer new industry developments.

- *Assign a skilled relationship manager to each key customer:* The salesperson currently servicing the customer should receive training in relationship management or be replaced by someone more skilled in relationship management. The relationship manager should have characteristics that match or appeal to the customer.

- *Develop a clear job description for relationship managers:* Describe their reporting relationships, objectives, responsibilities, and evaluation criteria. Make the relationship manager the focal point for all dealings with and about the client. Give each relationship manager only one or a few relationships to manage.

- *Have each relationship manager develop annual and long-range customer relationship plans:* These plans should state objectives, strategies, specific actions, and required resources.

- *Appoint an overall manager to supervise the relationship managers:* This person will develop job descriptions, evaluation criteria, and resource support to increase relationship manager effectiveness.

When it has properly implemented relationship management, the organization begins to focus on managing its customers as well as its products. At the same time, although many companies are moving strongly toward relationship marketing, it is not effective in all situations:

> When it comes to relationship marketing…you don't want a relationship with every customer….In fact, there are some bad customers. A company should selectively develop customer relationships: figure out which customers are worth cultivating because you can meet their needs more effectively than anyone else.[11]

THE ULTIMATE TEST: CUSTOMER PROFITABILITY

Ultimately, companies must judge which segments and which specific customers will be profitable. Marketing is the art of attracting and keeping *profitable customers*. Yet companies often discover that between 20% and 40% of their customers are unprofitable. Furthermore, many companies report that their most profitable customers are not their largest customers but their mid-sized customers. The largest customers demand greater service and receive the deepest discounts, thereby reducing the company's profit level. The smallest customers pay full price and receive less service, but the costs of transacting with small customers reduce their profitability. In many cases, mid-sized customers who pay close to full price and receive good service are the most profitable. This helps to explain why many large firms that once targeted only large customers are now invading the middle market.

A company should not try to pursue and satisfy every customer. For example, if business customers of Courtyard (Marriott's less expensive motel) start asking for Marriott-level business services, Courtyard should say no. Providing such service would only confuse the respective positionings of the Marriott and Courtyard systems.

Some organizations try to do anything and everything customers suggest. Yet, while customers often make many good suggestions, they also suggest many courses of action that are unactionable or unprofitable. Randomly following these suggestions is fundamentally different from market focus—making a disciplined choice of which customers to serve and which specific combination of benefits and price to deliver to them (and which to deny them).[12]

What makes a customer profitable? We define a *profitable customer* as person, household, or company whose revenues over time exceed, by an acceptable amount, the company costs of attracting, selling, and servicing that customer. Note that the definition emphasizes lifetime revenues and costs, not profit from a single transaction.

Customer satisfaction and company profitability are linked closely to product and service quality. Higher levels of quality result in greater customer satisfaction, while at the same time supporting higher prices and often lower costs. Therefore, *quality improvement* programs normally increase profitability. The well-known profit impact of marketing strategies (PIMS) studies show a high correlation between relative product quality and profitability.[13]

The Link between Marketing and Quality

On June 24, 1980, NBC aired the television program "If Japan Can, Why Can't We?" This program introduced W. Edwards Deming to the American public. Deming is credited as the man responsible for leading the Japanese on their successful quest for quality. Japanese auto makers invaded the American markets in the 1970s and gained a significant market share, in part because of the superior quality of Japanese cars. During that time, Sony became known for its superior quality in televisions, and Japanese cameras took over the 35mm market, again based on their quality. This invasion by the Japanese started a quality revolution in the United States and elsewhere.

A study of 50 of America's largest firms by Price Waterhouse found that quality and customer service were top priorities for these firms.[14]

Quality service has emerged as an important area in hospitality management. The number of articles on quality in the hospitality industry dramatically increased in the late 1980s. In 1992, Ritz-Carlton became the first hospitality company to win the Malcolm Baldrige National Quality Award. This award was established by the U.S. Congress in 1987 and is awarded annually to recognize companies that have achieved excellence through adherence to quality improvement programs.[15] Ritz-Carlton's success in the Baldrige Award competition helped to accelerate the growing interest of hospitality firms in service quality.

Philip Crosby states in *Quality is Free* that quality is conformance to specifications, an act controlled by the firm.[16] Other researchers claim that customers determine quality. These researchers define quality as meeting or exceeding the guest's expectations. Still others view moving from the standards of a two-star hotel to a four-star hotel as improving quality. But is this really quality improvement? And is quality free as Philip Crosby claims, or does it cost money? Initial discussions of quality often raise more questions than they answer. We will now define quality, look at quality models, provide a link between quality and marketing, explain why quality is important, and discuss how hospitality firms can improve the quality of their products.

Quality in the hospitality industry requires a different focus from quality in manufacturing firms. Hospitality products are produced and consumed simultaneously, while production and consumption in manufacturing firms are separated by time and distance. This gives manufacturing firms time to inspect and discard defective products before customers receive them. Defective products cost a firm money, but not as much as the customer who defects. In the hospitality industry during periods of peak demand, quality controls become difficult to carry out. Thus, achieving quality in the hospitality industry is a challenging task.

The following example illustrates how mistakes can occur during busy periods. A guest made a reservation for a room at the Marriott Hotel in Surfers Paradise, Australia. The new hotel offered a special promotional rate to people who lived in the area to familiarize them with its services, creating positive word of mouth. The guest was informed by the hotel that check-in could occur after 2 P.M. When the guest arrived at 2:30, the front-desk clerk stated that there were no rooms available and asked the guest to check back in a little while. After waiting an hour, the desk clerk said that the room was ready. The guest proceeded to the room, opened the door, saw a group of people in the room, and returned to the front desk, where the clerk was informed of the situation. Puzzled, the clerk checked the computer again, and then made a few phone calls. The clerk found that a salesperson had been showing the room to potential guests and had not bothered taking it out of order. Normally, this would not have created a problem, but on the day of the incident, there was a backlog of guests waiting for rooms. As the rooms were released by the housekeeping department, they were assigned to guests. The front-desk clerk explained what had happened and asked the guest to return to the room. Later, champagne and strawberries arrived with an apologetic note from the manager.

The hospitality industry involves a high degree of contact and coordination between employees and guests. Total quality can never be achieved. Employees will make mistakes and systems will fail. The pursuit of quality is a never-ending journey, but today it is a journey that every hospitality organization must take. Through total quality programs, managers strive to eliminate failures and increase the guests' perception of product quality. Companies that fail to provide quality products can incur significant costs.

After finishing college, a new food and beverage manager arrived at the University Center at Ohio University. Shortly thereafter, the university's food-service workers went on strike. This meant management had to train unskilled students to fill all the positions in the operation. The center had been trying for some time to sell the Rotary Club on using its facilities for their evening dinner meeting, and when they finally decided to try out the center, the event fell in the middle of the strike.

Recognizing the importance of the event, the new food and beverage manager developed a special menu of beef stroganoff made with beef tenderloin. In college the young manager had learned a good beef stroganoff uses beef tenderloin. A famous chef had given a guest demonstration in the foods class, after which students commented to the professor in charge of the course that the beef stroganoff was wonderful. The instructor, unimpressed with the chef's talents, replied that anyone could make good beef stroganoff if they used tenderloin.

The sauce was excellent. The salads were well presented and the manager looked forward to converting the Rotary Club to a regular customer. As the event unfolded, the manager observed that most guests were leaving a large portion of the beef stroganoff on their plates. Suddenly the manager realized that in haste a bag of stew meat cubes had been grabbed instead of the beef tenderloin cubes. The university center lost the group due to poor quality and lack of quality control. That group would have been worth $7,000 a year or $35,000 over a 5-year period, an expensive mistake that illustrates the importance of quality.

WHAT IS QUALITY?

A distinction can be made between two types of quality: **product features** that enhance customer satisfaction and **freedom from deficiencies** that increase customer satisfaction.[17] The first type of quality, product features, adds to the cost of the product. Customers must either be willing to pay for the added costs of additional product features or these features must make them more loyal. For example, lettuce and tomato is found only on McDonald's more expensive hamburgers. Hotel rooms on concierge floors have more features than standard rooms and command a higher price. La Quinta Inns offers free local telephone calls to encourage loyalty among salespeople.

The expectations of guests are formed by company image, word of mouth, the company's promotional efforts, and price. A guest paying $35 for a room at a Motel 6 will have different expectations than a guest paying $250 for a room at the Four Seasons Hotel in Washington, D.C. The person staying at the Motel 6 could be perfectly satisfied. The room features meet their expectations. The first type of quality, product features, relates to guest expectations. People staying in a Motel 6 may perceive it as the best quality motel for under $40. They are not comparing it to a Four Seasons Hotel. Both the guests of a Motel 6 and a Four Seasons Hotel will expect the room to be free from deficiencies. For example, guests at the Four Seasons and those at a Motel 6 are both likely to get upset if they return in the evening to rooms that have not been made up.

There is another way to view quality. A distinction can be made between **technical** and **functional quality**. Technical quality refers to what the customer is left with after the customer employee interactions have been completed. For example, technical quality relates to the guest room in the hotel, the meal in the restaurant, and the car from the rental agency. Functional quality is the process of delivering the service or product. While the service is being delivered, customers go through many interactions with the firm's employees. A guest makes a reservation, is greeted by the door attendant, is escorted to the front desk by a bellperson, checks in with the desk clerk, and is escorted to the room. The experience of checking into a hotel is an example of functional quality. Excellent functional quality may make up for a room that is not quite up to expectations. If functional quality is unpleasant, a high-quality room might not overcome the guests' previous dissatisfaction.

A consultant asked Sheraton hotel managers to identify pictures of their competitors' rooms. They were given photographs of four hotel rooms and names of eight competitors. The managers were then asked to put a name by the hotel room. The rooms were chosen as typical examples of competitors' hotel rooms, yet most managers failed to match more than one room correctly. This exercise was not used to evaluate the managers, but to show that in hotels of the same class, the differentiating factor is not technical quality, it is functional quality. A model of service quality using technical and functional quality as determinants of total quality is shown in Figure 12-2.[18]

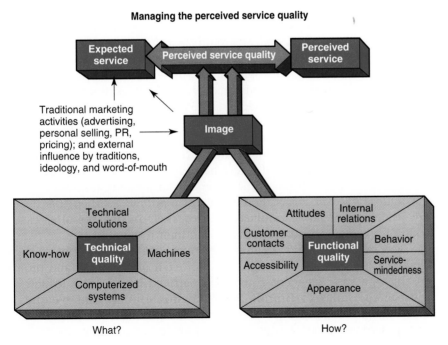

Managing the perceived service quality

Figure 12-2
Managing the perceived service quality. *Source:* Grönroos, Christian (1982): *Strategic Management and Marketing in the Service Sector,* Helsingfors, Finland: Swedish School of Economics and Business Administration, p. 79.

In the mid-1970s, Barker Enterprises owned and managed the Ramada Inn in Shreveport, Louisiana. There were hotels in Shreveport that offered as good, if not better, core products: rooms, food, and beverage at a similar price. Yet the Ramada Inn gained more than its fair share of the market. This was not due to superior rooms than other hotels in the same class, but because of the way that particular Ramada Inn delivered its products to the guest. The front-desk staff greeted repeat customers by name and made all guests feel welcome. The Shreveport Ramada Inn excelled at service delivery and was rewarded for its efforts.

We have now discussed four components of service quality: product features, freedom from deficiencies, functional quality, and technical quality. There is one other type of quality—**societal (ethical) quality**. Societal quality is a credence quality; it cannot be evaluated by the consumer before purchase and is often impossible to evaluate after purchase.

Some products can provide satisfaction in the short term, but may have long-term adverse effects for their users. For example, McDonald's french fries were proclaimed as the best in the world. One reason they were so popular was that they were fried in beef fat, which added flavor. When the public became aware that animal fats were not desirable, McDonald's changed the ingredients of their frying oil. In the 1970s chemical antioxidants were commonly used by restaurants to keep salads crisp and potatoes white. Antioxidants allowed restaurants to produce products that were more acceptable to the consumer, but the product could have long-term adverse health effects. In these examples, the product component that increased satisfaction in the short term could create long-run problems for the customer.

Some hotel managers do not know the location of their fire plans. Other managers know where the plans are but do not train employees to carry out the fire plan. This lack of life safety management will have no impact on the guests unless a fire occurs. The guest can leave the hotel feeling perfectly satisfied, ready to return, and may recommend the hotel to others. An airline may skimp on maintenance to save costs, a fact that will never be noticed by the customer unless there is a crash and the resulting investigation uncovers poor maintenance standards. Airlines and hotels that do a good job in preventive maintenance and safety training usually do not advertise the fact, since it relates to a negative aspect of their products.

Firms must consider ethical responsibilities when developing products and services, avoiding product features that can cause harm and adding those that eliminate potential safety hazards. Often these features may not immediately affect customer satisfaction, but in the long term they can prevent undesirable situations. Restaurant owners have learned this the hard way, watching negative publicity destroy their businesses after cases of food poisoning or hepatitis were traced to their restaurants.

The original Braniff Airlines experienced a similar problem. Braniff installed a clock in the passenger cabin of each of its aircraft and promised passengers a cash payment if the plane arrived late. During a flight from Houston to Dallas, a Braniff plane encountered severe weather and crashed. A great hue and cry then erupted from the public that Braniff was more concerned about on-time arrivals than passenger safety. Service guarantees, such as Hampton Inns' guarantee, can be very positive features of a hotel or restaurant. However, when creating the guarantee, managers must think about the possible consequences to the company's image. This is particularly true where the guarantee involves time, and employees may be perceived to be rushing to beat the clock. Earlier in the book we mentioned that Domino Pizza's 30-minute guarantee resulted in a lawsuit and unfavorable publicity. A driver unfortunately was involved in a serious accident during a delivery. In court it was contended that this occurred due to the 30-minute service guarantee.

Third-world hospitality enterprises that maintain strict safety and health regulations usually find that the market responds in a very positive manner, particularly if they serve guests from industrialized nations. During a false alarm, guests in a major hotel in Tegucigalpa, Honduras, discovered that the fire stairs were blocked with used furniture and the ground floor door was locked. Surveys among residents of third-world nations often show that safety is a primary reason for selecting an airline. Safety is seldom listed as a primary decision factor by passengers of industrialized nations.

A company's corporate image affects how customers perceive quality. Customers of a firm that has a good image may overlook minor mistakes as being atypical. The perceived quality of the service will be enhanced for firms that have a good corporate image and diminished for firms with a poor one. Societal quality relates design and delivery of safe products for the guest and society. A firm has a responsibility to its publics to provide societal quality. This makes good ethical sense and in the long run is good for the business.

Quality is made up of the following components: technical, functional, and societal. The manager must remember that in the end the customer perceptions of the delivered quality are what is important. Customers evaluate delivered service against their expectations. If perceived service meets expectations, they view the service as good quality. If perceived service falls short of expectations, they view the service as poor. Expectations are formed by prior experience with the product, word of mouth, the firm's external communication, and publicity.

THE FIVE-GAP MODEL OF SERVICE QUALITY

A widely used model of service quality is known as the five gap model (Figure 12-3). This model defines service quality as meeting customer expectations. In the words of those who developed the model, "knowing what customers expect is the first and possibly the most critical step in delivering service quality. Stated simply, providing service that customers perceive as excellent requires that a firm know what customers expect."[19] This model is closely linked to marketing since it is customer based. The model has five gaps, explained in the section that follows.

Gap 1: Consumer Expectations versus Management Perception

Hospitality executives may fail to understand what consumers expect in a service and which features are needed to deliver high-quality service. When

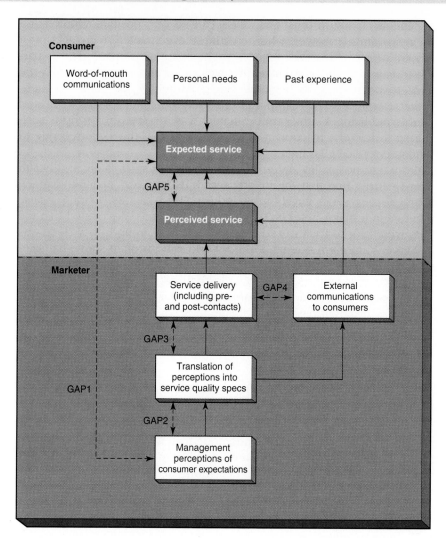

Figure 12-3
Conceptual model of service quality—the gap analysis model.

management does not understand what their customers want, a gap 1 exists. For example, a manager may develop a system to ensure that all guests wait no longer than 15 minutes to check in. However, if guests start getting upset after 10 minutes, this system will cause dissatisfaction. Talking to guests before developing the check-in system would enable the manager to learn that the critical time was 10 minutes, not 15 minutes. Marriott Hotels observed that guests were not using the complimentary bath crystals provided as a bathroom amenity. They discontinued the bath crystals in favor of cable television, a more important benefit to most guests than bath crystals.[20] Originally, management felt that bath crystals would be considered a benefit. However, after observing their guests, it was found that guest satisfaction could be increased by offering a different service.

Many firms conduct initial studies to find out what their market wants, but later they become internally focused and oblivious to the fact that customers' needs have changed. If customer needs change but the product does not, the marketing mix becomes less attractive to the target market,

Gap 1 is reduced when managers talk to customers. Courtesy of United Airlines.

and gap 1 has increased. Managers should walk around their operations, talk with customers, and encourage feedback. Management can also gain information on customers from marketing information systems.

Gap 2: Management Perception versus Service Quality Specifications

Gap 2 occurs when managers know what their customers want but are unable or unwilling to develop systems that will deliver it. Several reasons have been given for gap 2: (1) inadequate commitment to service quality, (2) lack of perception of feasibility, (3) inadequate task standardization, and (4) absence of goal setting.[21]

Some companies look for short-term profits and are unwilling to invest in people or equipment. This almost inevitably causes service quality problems. Hotel owners who are reluctant to provide enough operating capital can be a cause of gap 2 errors. For example, the hotel owner who budgets for just enough linen to get by may discover that the linen inventory quickly drops below critical levels as linen is stolen and destroyed. A visitor experienced this in Ft. Lauderdale, Florida. The guest returned from a walk on the beach to a freshly cleaned room, started to get ready to take a shower, and noticed that there were no towels in the room. The guest called housekeeping and explained that he had to take a shower to get ready for a business appointment and there were no towels in the room. Housekeeping apologized, saying they were short on towels. In about 15 minutes a housekeeper arrived with towels, causing the guest to arrive late for the appointment. Incidents such as this detract from positive guest experience, create unnecessary tasks, and decrease employee morale. In this case, hotel management knew that the linen inventory was low, but the owner either did not want to invest the money or did not have the money to properly supply the hotel.

Sometimes managers feel that improving an existing problem is not feasible. For example, most business guests want to check out after breakfast. They are usually in a hurry to get started with the day's business. Many hotel managers understand this, but accept a 10- to 20-minute wait as the best that they can do, as they are unwilling to hire extra employees to help during the rush period. Bill Marriott Jr. felt the problem was important enough to develop a system to solve it and invented Express Check-outs.[22] Guests receive their bills the evening before. If they are accurate, the guests simply dropped them off with their keys at the front desk. Today, most hotel chains use some type of express check-out system. Some hotels make use of technology and allow the guest to check the accuracy of bills on their television screens and check out using in-room television equipment. The express check-out system was developed by a person who viewed reducing check-out queues as a challenge, rather than a problem that was an inherent part of the system. Bill Marriott eliminated this gap 2 error. Bill Marriott demonstrated that capital is not the only cure for a gap 2 problem. Innovative thinking can also eliminate gap 2 problems. Sometimes we need to look for unconventional solutions to the problem. Translating customer needs into service specifications is critical to service quality.

Finally, goals must be accepted by employees. Management must show its support through measurement of results, communication, and rewarding employees for superior service.

Gap 3: Service Quality Specifications versus Service Delivery

Gap 3 is referred to as the service-performance gap.[23] Gap 3 occurs when management understands what needs to be delivered and appropriate specifications have been developed, but employees are unable or unwilling to deliver the service.

Gap 3 errors occur during moments of truth, when the employee and the customer interact. Service operations that use machines to deliver service are less likely to have gap 3 errors. Machines do not make human errors, and guests expect less from machines. For example, a person using a computerized check-in station in a hotel does not expect the machine to give her a cheerful greeting and be able to give directions to the coffee shop. Employees, however, are expected to act cheerfully and solve the guest's problems. When they do not, guests may perceive a problem with functional quality.

Gap 3 errors can be minimized through internal marketing programs. Management of the human resource functions (hiring, training, monitoring working conditions, and developing reward systems) is important in reducing gap 3 errors.

Bernard Booms likes to tell the story of the flight attendant who received a complaint from a passenger. When the flight attendant responded to a passenger's call button, the passenger complained that his baked potato was bad. The flight attendant reached over, picked up the passenger's potato, and spanked it while saying, "Bad potato, bad potato." She returned the potato to the passenger's tray and walked away. This anecdote provides a humorous story, but at the time the passenger probably had trouble seeing humor in the flight attendant's actions. This type of gap 3 error occurs when employees are under stress, resulting from too much contact with too many customers.

Gap 4: Service Delivery versus External Communications

Gap 4 is created when the firm promises more in its external communications than it can deliver. Earlier in the book we mentioned the advertising campaign put on by the government of Bermuda, inviting travelers to enjoy the attractions of the island during its uncrowded low season. Visitors were disappointed when they discovered that many attractions were closed during the off season. Marketers must make sure that operations can deliver what they promise.

During the last week of ski season, skiers were surprised to find that only half the runs on one side of the mountain had been groomed. This was particularly annoying and even dangerous, since the half-grooming occurred on intermediate runs where less than expert skiers might suddenly encounter bad conditions. The runs had been perfectly groomed all season until that final week. Late-season arrivals undoubtedly felt they had been slighted.

The Regent of Fiji encountered a severe problem when a military takeover occurred and discouraged tourism. A consultant, Chuck Gee, dean of the School of Travel Industry Management at the University of Hawaii, was hired to advise during this crisis. Chuck's advice was, "Do nothing different. Do not reduce your staff, your lighting, your food quality or your service." When asked why, Chuck's answer was that the Regent had positioned itself as a luxury resort and must continue to offer that level of service even if only one guest appeared. He further explained that the Regent knew that there were risks when it entered this market and must now be prepared to accept them and pay the price to continue as an upscale resort.

Lack of consistency can also cause gap 4 problems. Hotel policies were discussed during a marketing seminar. After the seminar a manager from La Quinta told of a problem with a guest when the cashier refused to cash a personal check. The check was over the limit La Quinta had set for personal checks. However, the guest had cashed a check for the same amount during a previous stay at a La Quinta Inn. The first desk clerk had given the implicit message that it was okay to cash personal checks for that amount. The clerk may have known the guest, had enough cash, and felt the guest should receive a favor. This clerk did not realize that problems were being developed for the next La Quinta. Customers expect chains to have similar products and policies. Inconsistency results in gap 4 errors.

Gap 5: Expected Service versus Perceived Service

Gap 5 is a function of the others. As any of the other gaps increase in size, gap 5 also increases. It represents the difference between expected quality and perceived quality.

The expected quality is what the guest expects to receive from the company. The perceived service is what the guest perceives he received from the company. If the guest receives less than he expected, the guest is dissatisfied.

The five-gap service model provides insights into the delivery of quality service. By studying this model, we can develop an understanding of the potential problem areas related to service quality. This insight will help to close any gaps that may exist in our operations.

BENEFITS OF SERVICE QUALITY

Firms that have a higher market share and better perceived quality than competitors can earn returns dramatically higher than those of firms with smaller market share and inferior quality. In the book, *The PIMS Principles*, the authors identify a link between quality and profitability. They illustrate this through Figure 12-4. As we can see from the figure, firms with high market share and high quality have the greatest return on investment.

Retaining Customers

High quality builds loyal customers and creates positive word of mouth. It is an important factor in the purchase decision. It determines customer satisfaction, which affects repeat business and word of mouth. Studies have shown that it costs four to six times as much to create a customer as it does to maintain an existing one. If a potential client is happy with an existing hotel, it is difficult to convince him to use another. Often a substantial reduction in price by a competitor will not be enough to encourage a client to switch. Hotel salespeople may have to wait until a competitive hotel makes a mistake before they can convince a client to try their hotel. This may take months or even years. During this time the salesperson is making calls, leaving specialty advertising materials, and inviting the potential client to breakfast or lunch at the hotel. The hotel is spending money on advertising and public relations and sending potential clients direct-mail pieces. The hotel may spend several thousands of dollars trying to obtain a client to use their products. If a major client decides to use the hotel, the money spent on marketing is well invested. However, if a potential client tries the hotel and perceives the quality of service to be inferior, he or she will leave. When this happens, all marketing efforts that went into getting this customer have been wasted.

A satisfied customer will also spread a recommendation by word of mouth. On average, one satisfied guest will tell five others, while a dissatisfied guest will tell ten or more people. Just to balance positive word of

Figure 12-4
Relative quality boosts rates of return.

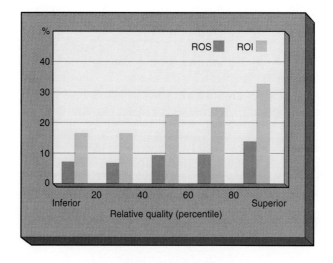

mouth with negative word of mouth, two or more customers must leave feeling good about the service for every person who feels the quality of service is poor. The market perceives a hotel or restaurant that receives mixed reviews as mediocre. The hotel striving to build an excellent reputation must do much better.

Hospitality firms that seek excellent quality set a goal of zero errors. A 200-room hotel can have more than 50,000 guests during the year. Most hoteliers feel that 90% conformance to standards is satisfactory.[24] If housekeepers clean the rooms according to the hotel's specifications 90% of the time in a 200-room hotel, 5000 guests a year may receive rooms that were not cleaned to specifications. Perhaps half the guests will never notice the nonconformance. If 2500 noticed the errors and half of those guests do not return, the hotel lost 1250 customers. If each of these customers has a potential lifetime revenue stream to the hotel of $1000, the hotel lost $125,000 in future revenue because of housekeeping errors. Repeating the exercise with food and beverage, front desk, and reservations, it is easy to see that dollars lost from poor quality can be significant.

Avoidance of Price Competition

Frank Perdue, a well-known chicken producer, once said, "Customers go out of their way to buy superior products, and you can charge them a toll for the trip."[25] The PIMS data showed that firms in the top third in quality could charge 5% to 6% higher than those in the bottom third. High quality can help to avoid price competition and help to maximize potential revenue.

A restaurant with a reputation for good-quality food and service is in a much stronger competitive position than one with a reputation for inconsistent or poor quality. The restaurant with the good image can count on positive word of mouth and repeat customers to bring in new business. The restaurant with a poor reputation will not get its fair share of repeat customers and will receive more negative word of mouth than positive. Restaurants in this situation often revert to price discounting through two-for-one coupons and other means.

Hospitality companies sometimes fail to concentrate on what the customer really wants. Having newspapers delivered to one's hotel door appeals to more guests than a health club costing thousands of dollars to build and maintain.

The executive housekeeper of a 1400-room hotel was asked why the hotel did not install retractable clotheslines since so many guests desired them. The reply was, "They are too much trouble."[26]

Differentiating products in the hospitality industry is sometimes as easy as simply asking guests what they really want.

Retention of Good Employees

Employees appreciate working in operations that are well run and produce quality products. Front-desk clerks do not enjoy receiving guest complaints. Absenteeism, turnover, and loss of employee morale are listed as costs of poor quality.[27] Two researchers developed a list of reasons recent graduates of hotel and restaurant management schools gave for quitting their jobs.

One reason cited by the graduates was the lack of quality in the organization.[28] When an operation has good quality, it can retain good employees. Recruiting is easier and training costs are reduced.

Reduction of Costs

Costs associated with quality include internal and external costs and quality system costs. Internal costs are those associated with correcting problems discovered by the firm before the product reaches the customer. The following are examples of internal costs: An air conditioner breaks down because of improper maintenance and the guest room is placed out of order until it is repaired. A cook prepares fried grouper instead of the grilled grouper ordered by the guest. The server discovers the mistake when he picks up the food in the kitchen and has the cook grill a new piece of fish.

External costs are associated with errors that the customer experiences. They can be very expensive when the customer decides not to return because of a service problem. Here are some examples of external costs: A restaurant manager gives guests a free bottle of wine because they complained about slow service. A guest receives a complimentary breakfast because it took room service an hour to deliver the meal. A guest receives a complimentary fruit basket because the front-desk clerk assigned a dirty room. A group has problems with the hotel's audiovisual service and cancels future bookings. Unfortunately, it is more difficult to detect errors before they reach the customer because of simultaneous production and consumption in the hospitality industry.

A quality service system does not come without costs. However, these are usually less than those associated with the internal and external costs resulting from poor-quality service. Some examples of the costs of a quality system: customer service audits, training, management meetings with employees and customers, and the introduction of new technology. These costs can be viewed as investments in the future of the company. They help to ensure that customers return. Internal costs, on the other hand, neither add to nor detract from customer satisfaction. They are simply money down the drain. External costs associated with errors are often high. A firm may go to great expense to maintain the goodwill of a customer who has received a poor-quality product. Sometimes these efforts are not successful, and the firm loses the customer's business forever.

DEVELOPING A SERVICE QUALITY PROGRAM

A service quality program involves a cooperative effort between marketing and operations. To develop quality service, a firm must follow certain principles. It is not in the scope of this text to provide a detailed procedure for developing total quality management. However, these 10 principles of quality service offer a framework for a quality service program.[29]

1. Leadership

The CEO of the organization must have a clear vision for the company, but it is not enough to have a vision. The CEO must also communicate that vision and convince employees to believe in and follow it. Domino's was almost destroyed because Monaghan and his partner had disparate visions for the company. Monaghan envisioned a company based on the delivery concept, while his partner insisted on a sit-down service concept. Finally, Monaghan took over the company and united it under his vision.[30]

Good leaders communicate their dedication to service quality through actions visible to both employees and customers. When one thinks of good quality, several names come to mind—Bill Marriott, Isadore Sharp of Four Seasons, Horst Schulze of Ritz-Carlton, Doug Roth of Bistro 110 in Chicago, Robert Del Grande of Cafe Annie in Houston, Joseph Baum of the Rainbow Room in New York, and Norm Brinker of Brinker International. These leaders pay attention to detail, spend time in their hotels and restaurants, talk to employees and customers, and do not accept compromises on service quality. They are committed to service quality, and they show it through their actions.

2. Integrate Marketing throughout the Organization

The marketing concept states that marketing should be integrated throughout the organization. Tom Fitzgerald, vice-president of corporate marketing for ARAMARK Services, believes that marketing functions in a hospitality organization are the responsibility of people outside the marketing department. He challenges marketing executives to recognize this and avoid creating a large, separate marketing department. Marketing must be integrated into operations.[31]

3. Understand the Customer

Customers perceive quality. Companies with quality products know what the market wants. The product must be designed for and aimed at a target market. Firms must understand the needs of target markets.

Mr. Steak restaurant conducted marketing research to determine the needs of their "empty nester" customer segment. The results showed that this important customer group resented standing in line to pay. For years, the standard operating procedure at Mr. Steak had been to present guests with the check and expect them to take it to the cash register. In response to the research information, Mr. Steak changed its procedures by giving guests their choice of taking the check to the register or having the server take it for them.[32]

4. Understand the Business

Delivering quality service takes teamwork. Employees must realize how their job affects the rest of the team. Many firms that deliver quality service use cross-training. Cross-training exposes employees to different perspectives and encourages them to view the operation from other perspectives. They see how their jobs affect those of other employees and how they affect the customer. They begin to understand the business.

5. Apply Operational Fundamentals

The organization has to be well planned and managed. This starts with the design of the concept. Earlier in the book we discussed Marriott's planning process for Courtyard Inns. Courtyard Inns were designed so that their features provided benefits for a selected market segment. Systems are required to provide management information and to enable the hotel to operate. Examples of these systems include hiring and training procedures, purchasing procedures, management information systems, property information systems, reservation and front-office systems, equipment maintenance systems, quality control systems, and production procedures for the kitchen. Companies that deliver quality service have good operational procedures.

6. Leverage the Freedom Factor

In first-class restaurants and four- and five-star hotels, guests expect more customized service. The service delivery system has to be flexible. Employees must have the freedom to shape the delivery of the service to fit the needs of their guests. They should not be bound to strict procedures and inflexible rules. Managers should support and guide the staff, rather than provide barriers with rules and regulations that prevent the employees from serving the customer.

7. Use Appropriate Technology

Technology should be used to monitor the environment, help operational systems, develop customer databases, and provide methods for communication with customers. The Ritz-Carlton Hotel Company, winner of the Malcom Baldrige award for service excellence, has developed a computerized guest history profile that provides information on 240,000 repeat guests. The Ritz-Carlton collects daily production reports from 720 work areas in the hotel. These reports serve as an early warning system to identify problems that might impede customer service. Other information used by Ritz-Carlton includes annual guest room preventive maintenance cycles and percentage of check-ins with no queuing. This hotel company effectively utilizes advanced technology, from an automated building and safety system to computerized reservation system, for the purpose of ensuring a continuously high level of guest satisfaction.[33]

8. Good Human Resource Management

In the section on internal marketing, we discussed the need to hire the right people. Employees must be capable of delivering the services promised to the customer.

9. Set Standards, Measure Performance, and Establish Incentives

The most important way to improve service quality is to set service standards and goals and then teach them to employees and management. These standards must be continuously improved. Employees who deliver good service should be rewarded.

10. Feedback the Results to the Employees

The results of your measurements should be communicated to all employees. This should be done through communications from top management and as a part of departmental meetings. Employees should know what guests like and what they do not like. They should also know the areas that are improving and those that are not improving.

A study of quality assurance programs in hotels showed that "the rewards of quality assurance were worth the initial investment." Nevertheless, some hotels reported that such programs did not work. Three basic reasons existed for these failures: (1) a lack of top-middle management commitment, (2) departure of the person responsible for quality assurance, and (3) a change in the hotel's ownership.[34]

QUALITY
ASSURANCE
PROGRAM
FAILURES

Chapter Review

I.   To win in today's marketplace, companies must be **customer centered**: they must deliver superior value to their target customers.

II.   Consumers buy from the firm that they believe offers the highest **customer delivered value**, the difference between *total customer value* and *total customer cost.*

    1) The customer derives **value** from the core products, the service delivery system, and the company's image.

    2) The **costs** to the customer include *money, time, energy, and physic costs.*

III. **Retaining Customers**

    1) The Cost of Lost Customers. Companies should know how much it costs when a customer defects, this is the same as the customer's lifetime value.

    2) Resolving Customer Complaints. Resolving customer complaints is a critical component of customer retention.

    3) Relationship Marketing. Relationship marketing involves creating, maintaining, and enhancing strong relationships with customers and other stakeholders.

IV.   Customer Profitability. Ultimately, companies must judge which segments and which specific customers will be profitable. Marketing is the art of attracting and keeping *profitable customers.*

V.   What is quality? There are several views of product quality. One is based on product features, another is based on freedom from deficiencies, and a third is based on categories.

    1) Product Features. Some view product features that enhance customer satisfaction as a way of measuring quality. According to this, a luxury hotel has a higher level of quality than a limited-service hotel.

    2) Freedom from Deficiencies. Freedom from deficiencies is another way of viewing quality. According to this view, a limited-service hotel and a luxury hotel could both be quality products if the product they offered was free of deficiencies.

3) Three Categories of Service Quality. A third view divides quality into three categories.

 a) **Technical Quality** refers to what the customer is left with after the customer-employee interactions have been completed.

 b) **Functional Quality** is the process of delivering the service or product.

 c) **Societal Quality** is a credence quality; it cannot be evaluated by the consumer before purchase and is often impossible to evaluate after purchase.

VI. Five-gap Model of Service Quality

1) Gap 1: Consumer Expectations versus Management Perception. Gap 1 occurs when hospitality executives fail to understand what consumers expect in a service and which features are needed to deliver high-quality service.

2) Gap 2: Management Perception versus Service Quality Specifications. Gap 2 occurs when managers know what their customers want but are unable or unwilling to develop systems that will deliver it.

3) Gap 3: Service Quality Specifications versus Service Delivery. Gap 3 is referred to as the service-performance gap. Gap 3 occurs when management understands what needs to be delivered and appropriate specifications have been developed, but employees are unable or unwilling to deliver the service.

4) Gap 4: Service Delivery vs. External Communications. Gap 4 is created when the firm promises more in its external communications than it can deliver.

5) Gap 5: Expected Service vs. Perceived Service. Gap 5 is a function of the other gaps. It increases as any of the other gaps increase in size. It represents the difference between expected quality and perceived quality.

VII. Benefits of Service Quality

1) Retaining Customers. High quality builds loyal customers and creates positive word of mouth.

2) Avoidance of Price Competition. The PIMS data show that firms in the top third in quality could charge 5% to 6% higher than those in the bottom third. High quality can help to avoid price competition and help to maximize potential revenue.

3) Retention of Good Employees. Employees appreciate working in operations that are well run and produce quality products. When an operation has good quality, it can retain good employees. Recruiting is easier and training costs are reduced.

4) Reduction of Costs.

 a) **Internal costs** are those associated with correcting problems discovered by the firm before the product reaches the customers.

 b) **External costs** are associated with errors that the customers experience.

 c) **Quality system costs** are costs viewed as investment in the future of the company to ensure that customers return.

VIII. Developing a Service Quality Program

1) Leadership. The CEO of the organization must have a clear vision for the company, but it is not enough just to have a vision. The CEO must also communicate that vision and convince employees to believe in it and follow it.

2) Integrate Marketing throughout the Organization. The marketing concept states that marketing should be integrated throughout the organization.

3) Understand the Customer. Companies with quality products know what the market wants.

4) Understand the Business. Delivering quality service takes teamwork. Employees must realize how their jobs affect the rest of the team.

5) Apply Operational Fundamentals. The organization has to be well planned and managed.

6) Leverage the Freedom Factor. Employees must have the freedom to shape the delivery of the service to fit the needs of their guests.

7) Use Appropriate Technology. Technology should be used to monitor the environment, help operational systems, develop customer databases, and provide methods for communication with customers.

8) Good Human Resource Management. Employees must be capable of delivering the services promised to the customer.

9) Set Standards, Measure Performance, and Establish Incentives. The most important way to improve service quality is to set service standards and goals and then teach them to employees and management. Employees who deliver good service should be rewarded.

IX. Quality Assurance Program Failures. Three reasons exist for failure:

1) A lack of top-middle management commitment.

2) Departure of the person responsible for quality assurance.

3) A change in the hotel's ownership.

DISCUSSION QUESTIONS

1. Think of a time when you purchased a hospitality or travel product such as an airline flight, hotel room, or meal and had a problem. How did the company resolve the problem (if they did)? Was the complaint resolution satisfactory, why or why not?

2. "When it comes to relationship marketing you do not want a relationship with every customer." Explain what this statement means.

3. Does McDonald's have a quality product? Explain your answer and include the criteria you used to evaluate quality.

4. Choose a hospitality or travel product you are familiar with and explain which components of the product would comprise technical quality, functional quality, and societal quality.

5. In the 5-Gap Model of service quality explain what causes Gap 1 and how this gap can be reduced.

6. Describe a time when you have had a problem with a Gap 4 problem. For example, what the business promised you was different from what you received. Use a hospitality or travel product for your example.

7. How does good quality increase *employee* satisfaction?

KEY TERMS

Customer delivered value The difference between total customer value and total customer cost.

Customer satisfaction Customer satisfaction with a purchase depends on the product's performance relative to a buyer's expectations. If performance matches expectations, the customer is satisfied.

Expected service The service that the customer feels he will receive from a service provider.

Five-gap model of service quality The five-gap model of service quality proposes that the smaller the gap between expected service and perceived service the higher the quality of service. In the model, the gap between perceived service and expected service is shown to be a function of four other gaps.

Freedom from deficiencies A type of service quality that focuses on conformance to specifications.

Freedom factor The freedom factor refers to the amount of authority employees have to make decisions.

Functional quality The quality of the process of delivering the service.

Perceived service The service the guest feels that she received from a service provider.

Product features Product features that enhance customer satisfaction is one type of service quality.

Relationship marketing Relationship marketing involves creating, maintaining, and enhancing strong relationships with customers and other stakeholders.

Societal (ethical) quality Societal (ethical) quality refers to delivering products that will not cause harm to the customer or society as a whole. It is a type of quality that often goes unobserved by the guest.

Technical quality The quality of the core product that the guest receives in the transaction. In a hotel it is the hotel room. In a restaurant it is the meal.

Total customer cost The costs to the customer include *money, time, energy, and physic costs.*

Total customer value The customer derives value from the core products, the service delivery system, and the company's image. These components make up *total customer value.*

REFERENCES

1. CHRISTOPHER W. L. HART, *Extraordinary Guarantees* (New York: American Management Association, 1993), pp. 164–165.

2. HART, *Extraordinary Guarantees*, pp. 97–98.

3. This section draws heavily from CHRISTOPHER W. L. HART, "Hampton Inns Guests Satisfied with Satisfaction Guarantee," *Marketing News*, 25, no. 3 (February 4, 1991), p. 7.

4. HART, *Extraordinary Guarantees*, p. 175.

5. THOMAS E. CARUSO, "Got a Marketing Topic? Kotler Has an Opinion," *Marketing News* (June 8, 1992), p. 21.

6. FREDERICK F. REICHHELD AND W. EARL SASSER, JR., "Zero Defections: Quality Comes to Services," *Harvard Business Review*, no. 5 (September–October 1990), pp. 105–111.

7. *Feelings Consultant Marketing Manual* (Bloomington, MN: Better Than Money Corporation, undated). The Technical Research Programs Institute (TARP) does studies on customer complaints and the success of compliant resolution.

8. LINDA M. LASH, *The Complete Guide to Customer Service* (New York: John Wiley and Sons, 1989), pp. 68–69.

9. LEONARD L. BERRY AND A. PARASURAMAN, *Marketing Services: Competing Through Quality* (New York: The Free Press, 1991), pp. 136–42.

10. JAMES H. DONNELLY, JR., LEONARD L. BERRY, AND THOMAS W. THOMPSON, *Marketing Financial Services—A Strategic Vision* (Homewood, Il: Dow Jones-Irwin, 1985), p. 113.

11. THOMAS E. CARUSO, "Kotler: Future Marketers Will Focus on Customer Data Base to Compete Globally," *Marketing News* (June 8, 1992), p. 21.

12. MICHAEL J. LANNING AND LYNN W. PHILLIPS, "Strategy Shifts Up a Gear," *Marketing* (October 1991), p. 9.

13. ROBERT D. BUZZELL AND BRADLEY T. GALE, *The PIMS Principles: Linking Strategy to Performance* (New York: The Free Press, 1987), Chap. 6.

14. HOWARD SCHLOSSBER, "U.S. Firms: Quality is the Way to Satisfy," *Marketing News*, 25, no. 3 (February 4, 1991), p. 1.

15. CHARLES PARTLOW, "How Ritz-Carlton Applies TQM," *Cornell Hotel and Restaurant Quarterly*, 34, no. 3 (August 1993), pp. 16–24.

16. PHILIP CROSBY, *Quality is Free*, (New York: Mentor, 1980).

17. J. M. JURAN, *Juran on Quality by Design* (New York: Free Press, 1992), p 9.

18. CHRISTIAN GRONROOS, *Strategic Management and Marketing in the Service Sector* (Bromely, Kent, England: Chartwell-Bratt, 1983), p. 48.

19. LEONARD L. BERRY, A. PARASURAMAN, AND VALARIE A. ZEITHAML, *Quality Service*, (New York: Free Press, 1990), p. 51.

20. JURAN, *Quality by Design,* p. 91.

21. DAVID R. BENNETT, LEONARD L. BERRY, and CARTER W. BROWN, *Service Quality* (Homewood, Il.: Dow Jones-Irwin, 1989), pp. 71–72.

22. KEITH D. DENTON, *Quality Service* (Houston: Gulf Publishing Company, 1989), p. 77.

23. Ibid, p. 89.

24. STEPHEN S. HALL, *Quality Assurance in the Hospitality Industry* (Milwaukee, WI: ASC Quality Press, 1990), p. 23.

25. BUZZEL AND BRADLEY, *The Pims Principles*, p. 120.

26. ROBERT C. LEWIS AND MICHAEL NIGHTINGALE, "Targeting Service to your Customer," *Cornell Hotel and Restaurant Administration Quarterly*, 31, no. 2, p. 21.

27. CHRISTOPHER W. L. HART, JAMES L. HESKETT, AND W. EARL SASSER, JR., *Service Breakthroughs* (New York: Free Press, 1990); AND H. JAMES HARRINGTON, *Poor Quality Cost* (New York: ASQC Quality Press, 1987).

28. ROBERT A. BRYMER AND DAVID V. PAVESIC, "Job Satisfaction: What's Happening to the Young Managers," *Cornell Hotel and Restaurant Administration Quarterly*, 30, no. 4 (February 1990), pp. 90–96.

29. DENTON, *Quality Service*, pp. 139–155.

30. Ibid, p. 140.

31. BERRY AND PARASURAMAN, *Marketing Services*, pp. 78–79.

32. BONNIE J. KNUTSON, "Ten Laws of Customer Satisfaction," *Cornell Hotel and Restaurant Administration Quarterly*, 29, no. 3 (November 1988), p. 16.

33. CHARLES G. PARTLOW, "How Ritz-Carlton applies TQM," *Cornell Hotel and Restaurant Administration Quarterly*, 34, no. 4 (August 1993), p. 19.

34. TAMER T. SALANEH AND JOHN R. WALKER, "The QA Payoff," *Cornell Hotel and Restaurant Administration Quarterly*, 30, no. 4 (February 1990), p. 59.

Pricing Products: Pricing Considerations, Approaches, and Strategy

*A*s I pulled into the gravel parking lot I knew immediately that the Mexicatessan was a warm, friendly Mexican restaurant. There was nothing new here—and I don't mean that in a negative way. Nothing looked new but it all looked comfortable, well worn with the passage of time.

The front entrance is laden with business cards stapled over the last 30 years. A World War II photo of the owner adorns one wall and Mexican motifs line the walls and ceiling—right next to the window air conditioners. Somehow this all looked familiar although I knew I had never been to the Mexicatessan before.

This is how Sally Bernstein, the restaurant reviewer for the Houston Post, *described the Mexicatessan in an article celebrating the restaurant's thirtieth birthday. Mr. and Mrs. Herrera established the Mexicatessan in 1957. The restaurant, located in a lower-middle-class neighborhood, attracts both locals and Houston's rich and famous. In the early 1980s the restaurant's profitability started to drop. Herrera worked long hard hours, producing a quality product that his customers enjoyed; but he received very little reward for his time and investment. He had a good product, a good location, and a strong following. The problem was pricing. The prices at the Mexicatessan were far below competition. Herrera wanted to offer good value and he felt he had to keep his prices below the chains. He used*

price to gain a competitive advantage against the chain's expensive buildings and their large regional advertising budgets.

Instead of attracting and maintaining loyal customers, the Mexicatessan's low prices almost destroyed the business. The prices were not high enough to produce sufficient cash flow to keep the restaurant in good repair. Herrera was unable to receive financial reward for his efforts. After several years of struggling, the owner commissioned a research project to see how he could increase his cash flow. The research suggested his prices were 50% less than the competition, while his customers thought the food quality was better. Herrera decided to increase his prices so that they were only 10% less than the competition. He felt this price difference and his food quality would offset the competitive advantages of the chains. He set out achieving his strategy through a series of planned price increases. Because achieving his target would mean price increases of 70% or more on some items, the first price increase was about 25%, with subsequent price increases gradually moving him to his desired pricing levels. Over a 3-year period from 1982 to 1985, the menu prices increased by 40% to 70%. This was a bold move at a time when Houston was in the middle of a decade-long recession.

After the price increases, the Mexicatessan's revenues increased at a higher percentage than the price increases, indicating that there was little resistance to the price increases. His customers still thought they were getting good value. The price increases allowed Herrera to put a new roof on the building, hire additional staff, decorate the restaurant's interior, and receive a good return on his investment. This case study demonstrates the importance of price. Operations that charge too little often do not have money to maintain the business, although they have many customers and appear prosperous.

Herrera was lucky. It is easier to move up the price of a product that is underpriced than it is to lower the price of an overpriced product. Companies that overcharge create a negative attitude among those who have tried their products. Even when prices are lowered, customer attitudes may remain unchanged. Pricing must be a carefully planned management process.

Chapter 13 provides an overview of factors that affect pricing and compares general pricing approaches.

To start, we will consider pricing as one element of the marketing mix and show how it can be used to support broader marketing objectives.

We will follow with a discussion of **costs**, **including variable costs**, **fixed costs**, and **total costs** and demonstrate that costs set the floor for a company's price.

The chapter continues with a discussion of the **external factors affecting pricing**, including consumer perceptions of price and the price–demand relationship. We will then discuss cost-plus pricing, breakeven analysis, product-bundle pricing, buyer-based pricing, and competition-based pricing.

We will then build on this discussion by detailing **specific pricing strategies**.

These strategies include pricing new products, including prestige pricing, market-skimming, market-penetration approaches, and product-bundle pricing.

Price adjustment strategies, including yield management, psychological pricing, and promotional pricing, will be discussed next.

Finally, we conclude with the topics of **initiating price changes** and **responding to price changes**.

Price is the only marketing mix element that produces revenue. All others represent cost. Some experts rate pricing and price competition as the number one problem facing marketing executives. Pricing is the least understood of the marketing variables. Yet pricing is controllable in an unregulated market. Pricing changes are often a quick fix made without proper analysis. The most common mistakes include pricing that is too cost oriented, prices that are not revised to reflect market changes, pricing that does not take the rest of the marketing mix into account, and prices that are not varied enough for different product items and market segments. A pricing mistake can lead to a business failure, even when all other elements of the business are sound. Every manager should understand the basics of pricing.

Simply defined, **price** is the amount of money charged for a good or service. More broadly, price is the sum of the values consumers exchange for the benefits of having or using the product or service.

All for-profit organizations and many nonprofit ones must set prices on their products or services. Price goes by many names:

> Price is all around us. You pay rent for your apartment, a rate when you stay overnight in a hotel, tuition for your education, and a fee to your physician or dentist. Airlines, railways, taxis, and bus companies charge you a fare. The bank charges interest for using their money. The price for driving your car on Florida's Sunshine State Parkway is a toll. The price of a front desk clerk is a wage, while a bartender receives a wage and tips. A real estate agent who sells a restaurant charges a commission. Finally, income taxes are the price for the privilege of making money.[1]

It is important for marketers and managers to have an understanding of price. Charging too much chases away potential customers. Charging too little can leave a company without enough revenue to properly maintain the operation. Equipment wears out, carpets get stained, and painted surfaces need to be repainted. A firm that does not produce enough revenue to maintain the operation will eventually go out of business. This chapter will examine factors that hospitality marketers must consider when setting prices, general pricing approaches, pricing strategies for new products, product mix pricing, initiating and responding to price changes, and adjusting prices to meet buyer and situational factors.

FACTORS TO CONSIDER WHEN SETTING PRICES

Internal and external company factors affect a company's pricing decisions. Figure 13-1 illustrates these. Internal factors include the company's marketing objectives, marketing mix strategy, costs, and organization. External factors include the nature of the market, demand, competition, and other environmental constraints.

Internal Factors Influencing Pricing Decisions

Marketing Objectives

Before establishing price, a company must select a product strategy. If the company has selected a target market and positioned itself carefully, its marketing mix strategy, including price, will be more precise. For example, Four Seasons positions its hotels as luxury hotels and charges a room rate that is higher than most. Motel 6 and Red Roof Inns have positioned themselves as limited-service motels, providing rooms for budget-minded travelers. This market position requires charging a low price. Thus past decisions on market positioning have a major influence on price.

The clearer a firm is about its objectives, the easier it is to set price. Examples of common objectives are survival, short-run profit maximization, market-share maximization, and product-quality leadership.

Survival   Companies troubled by too much capacity, heavy competition, or changing consumer wants set survival as their objective. In the short run, survival is more important than profit. Hotels often use this strategy when the economy slumps. A manufacturing firm can reduce production to match demand. During a recession a 300-room hotel still has 300 rooms to sell each night, although the demand has dropped to 140 a night. The hotel tries to ride out the slump in the best way possible by cutting rates and trying to create the best cash flow possible under the conditions. This strategy inevitably directly affects immediate competitors and sometimes the entire industry. Competitors in the hospitality industry are highly cognizant of price changes and will usually respond if they feel threatened.

Figure 13-1
Factors affecting price decisions.

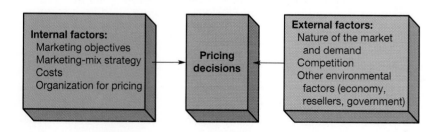

Internal factors:
Marketing objectives
Marketing-mix strategy
Costs
Organization for pricing

→ Pricing decisions ←

External factors:
Nature of the market and demand
Competition
Other environmental factors (economy, resellers, government)

Continental Airlines and other troubled air carriers lowered prices while in bankruptcy or after emerging in an effort to gain market share. Continental offered a special "Peanut Fare" in several of its markets, particularly the East Coast. Competitors such as U.S. Air directly and immediately responded with matching price cuts. The result of most price wars is a reduction in profit for all members engaged in the war.

Observers of the hospitality industry have sometimes suggested that competition using a survival pricing strategy should be carefully monitored but not necessarily emulated. In the previous case of a troubled 300-room hotel, the relative importance of that property to the total market must be understood. If the hotel is one of two in a market such as a small town, the effect of price discounting could be considerable. On the other hand, if the hotel is in Orlando, Florida, it is one of many and represents a fraction of the total room supply.

It sometimes makes sense to allow a competitor to lower prices and skim off the budget-conscious customers, leaving more profitable business for competitors who do not lower prices, particularly if the member using a survival strategy is a small player. The effect of 300 rooms on a market of 30,000 would indeed be small.

Current Profit Maximization   Many companies want to set a price that will maximize current profits. They estimate what demand and costs will be at different prices and choose the price that will produce the maximum current profit, cash flow, or return on investment, seeking current financial outcomes rather than long-run performance. For example, a company may purchase a distressed hotel at a low price. The objective becomes to turn the hotel around, show an operating profit, and then sell. If the hotel owners can achieve a successful turnaround, they may receive a good capital gain.

Some entrepreneurs develop a restaurant concept with the objective of selling the concept to a major chain. They realize that the concept's viability must be proved through a small chain that produces a high net profit. If they can do this, they may attract the attention of a major corporation. The pricing objective in this case is current profit maximization.

Market-share Leadership   Other companies want to obtain a dominant market-share position. They believe that a company with the largest market share will eventually enjoy low costs and high long-run profit. Thus prices are set as low as possible. Marriott strives to be the market-share leader in its class. When it opens a new hotel, Marriott builds market share as quickly as possible. For example, Marriott opened its resort on Australia's Gold Coast with $99 rates; 6 months later the hotel charged almost twice this rate. Low opening rates created demand. As the demand increased, low-revenue business was replaced with higher. Such a strategy uses price and other elements of the marketing mix to create the awareness of better value than the competition.

Product-quality Leadership   The Ritz-Carlton chain has a construction or acquisition cost per room that often exceeds $250,000. Besides a high capital investment per room, luxury chains have a high cost of labor per room. Their hotels require well-qualified staff and a high employee/guest ratio to provide luxury service. They must charge a high price for their product.

Groen, a manufacturer of food-service equipment, is known for its high-quality steam-jacketed kettles. Kitchen designers specify Groen equipment because of its known quality. The company can demand a high price

Four Seasons Hotels use non-price factors in their advertisements. They feature product attributes that will create value for their target market. Courtesy of Four Seasons–Regent Hotels and Resorts.

for its equipment because of its perceived quality. To maintain its quality, Groen must have a well-engineered product comprised of high-quality materials. It also must have the budget to ensure that it maintains its position as a quality leader.

Quality leaders such as Ritz-Carlton and Groen charge more for their products, but they also have to continuously reinvest in their operations to maintain positions as quality leaders.

A bowl of chili and a beverage might not exceed $5 or $6 in many restaurants, but the Red Sage Restaurant in Washington, D.C., charges $13 to $18 for its Southwestern cuisine. Patrons pay for more than just a bowl of chili. This two-story restaurant cost $5 million to re-create the wide open spaces of the west. More than 100 craftsmen and artists were employed to create stunning original designs, such as murals of horses and a cloud sculpture that flashes blue lightning.[2]

Other Objectives   A company also might use price to attain other more specific objectives. A restaurant may set low prices to prevent competition from entering the market or set prices at the same level as its competition to stabilize the market. Fast-food restaurants may temporarily reduce prices to create excitement for a new product or draw more customers into a restaurant. Thus pricing may play an important role in helping to accomplish the company's objective at many levels.

The case of two upscale restaurants in New York, both owned by former major league baseball players, offers an example of contrasting pricing strategies.[3] Mickey Mantle's restaurant purposely established a high price for alcoholic beverages. "A beer here isn't cheap" said John Lowy, co-owner. "We charge $3.75 or $4.00. It keeps out the kids. This is a high-exposure place. If something bad happened, it would get out real quick."

An opposite pricing strategy is employed at Rusty Staub's Restaurant. Rusty's pricing philosophy for wine is unique for the industry. He believes that "the better the wine the less the markup." "We work on a thin margin," said Staub. "A lot of people in the industry say you should charge at least three times the cost of the wine. But we're way under that. I want people to know we're one of the great-value restaurants."

Which pricing philosophy is correct, Mantle's or Staub's? It all depends on the objectives each of the owners was attempting to meet. An analysis of the two strategies 1 or 2 years later might show that both were wrong, both were winners, or only one succeeded. There is never one pricing strategy that is right for all competitors in the hospitality industry.

Marketing Mix Strategy

Price is only one of many marketing mix tools a company uses to achieve its marketing objectives. Price must be coordinated with product design, distribution, and promotion decisions to form a consistent and effective marketing program. Decisions made for other marketing mix variables may affect pricing decisions. For example, resorts that plan to distribute most of their rooms through wholesalers must build enough margin into their room price to allow them to offer a deep discount to the wholesaler. Owners usually refurbish their hotels every 5 to 7 years to keep them in good condition. Prices must cover the costs of future renovations.

A firm's promotional mix also influences price. A restaurant catering to conventioneers receives less repeat business than a neighborhood restaurant and must advertise in city guides targeted to conventioneers. Managers of restaurants who do not consider promotional costs when setting prices will experience revenue/cost problems.

Companies often make pricing decisions first. Other marketing mix decisions are based on the price a company chooses to charge. For example, Marriott saw an opportunity in the economy market and developed Fairfield Inns using price to position the motel chain in the market. Fairfield Inns' target price defined the product's market, competition, design, and product features. Companies should consider all marketing mix decisions together when developing a marketing program.

Costs

Costs set the floor for the price a company can charge for its product. A company wants to charge a price that covers its costs for producing, distributing, and promoting the product. Beyond covering these costs, the price has to be high enough to deliver a fair rate of return to investors. Therefore, a company's costs can be an important element in its pricing strategy. Many companies work to become the low-cost producers in their industries. McDonald's has developed systems for producing fast food efficiently. A new hamburger franchise would have a hard time competing with McDonald's on cost. Effective low-cost producers achieve cost savings through efficiency rather than cutting quality. Companies with lower costs can set lower prices that result in greater market share. Lower costs do not always mean lower prices. Some companies with low costs keep their prices the same as competitors, providing a higher return on investment.

Costs take two forms, fixed and variable. Fixed costs (also known as overhead) are costs that do not vary with production or sales level. Thus, whatever its output, a company must pay bills each month for rent, interest, and executive salaries. Fixed costs are not directly related to production level. Variable costs vary directly with the level of production. For example, a banquet produced by the Hyatt in San Francisco has many variable costs; each meal may include a salad, rolls and butter, the main course, a beverage, and a dessert. In addition to the food items, the hotel provides linen for each guest. These are called variable costs because their total varies with the number of units produced. Total costs are the sum of the fixed and variable costs for any given level of production. In the long run, management must charge a price that will at least cover total costs at a given level of sales.

Managers sometimes forget that customers are not concerned with a business's operating costs; they seek value. The company must watch its costs carefully. If it costs the company more than competitors to produce and sell its product, the company must either charge a higher price or make less profit.

Many hospitality companies are developing sophisticated models and software to better understand costs and their relations to price. Embassy Suites recognizes this relationship and believes that the most valuable guest is not necessarily the one who pays the highest price for a suite. A contribution model developed by Embassy Suites now examines costs to acquire and service guests, such as room labor costs, advertising, special promotions, and other associated costs.

Organizational Considerations

Management must decide who within the organization should set prices. Companies handle pricing in a variety of ways. In small companies, top management, rather than the marketing or sales department, often sets the prices. In large companies, pricing is typically handled by a corporate department or by regional or unit managers, under guidelines established by corporate management. A hotel develops a marketing plan that contains monthly average rates and occupancies for the coming year. Regional or corporate management approves the plan. The hotel's general manager and sales manager are then responsible for achieving these "averages." In times of high demand, they can achieve rates significantly above their projected average, while in periods of low demand, they will be below their objective. Management may have some freedom in the prices it charges for different groups, but at the end of the financial period they are responsible for achieving their overall pricing and occupancy objectives.

Many corporations within the hospitality industry now have a revenue management department with responsibility for pricing and coordinating with other departments that influence price. Airlines, cruise lines, auto rental companies, and many hotel chains have developed revenue management departments. According to Brian Rice, the director of revenue planning and analysis for Royal Caribbean Cruise Line, the development of a revenue management department was an evolutionary process.

> To practice effective revenue management we needed to make sure that our pricing structures were supportive of what we were doing in inventory management and that sales was targeting the same market segments we needed to push. Now we have got to the point where we meet weekly with the sales group to set priorities, we also work with advertising, inventory management and reservations.[4]

The potential rewards are enormous from professional revenue management in a large hospitality company. According to Brian Rice, "If the average yield at Royal Caribbean goes up by $1 a day, it is worth $5.5 million and 100% of it goes to the bottom line." Brian conservatively estimated the monetary benefits of "baby-sitting" the revenue on a day-to-day basis at Royal Caribbean at over $20 million per day.[5]

External Factors Affecting Pricing Decisions

Market and Demand

While costs set the lower limits of prices, the market and demand set the upper limit. Both consumer and channel buyers such as tour wholesalers balance the product's price against the benefits it provides. Thus, before setting prices, a marketer must understand the relationship between price and demand for a product.

Royal Caribbean Cruises has developed a revenue management department with the responsibility for price and coordinating with other departments that influence price. Courtesy of Royal Caribbean Cruises, Ltd.

Rudy's was one of the finest restaurants in Houston. It prospered during Houston's boom in the 1970s and early 1980s. In 1982, oil prices plummeted, sinking Houston's oil-dependent economy into a recession. It remained in a depressed state for the rest of the decade. The demand for fine dining fell and Rudy's suffered. Its lunches were just breaking even. Management considered a price increase as a way to push revenue above the break-even point. On the surface this may have seemed like a good idea: just charge each customer $5 more and the revenue would move above break-even. This tactic assumed the market was price inelastic.

Business had dropped at Rudy's because people could no longer afford their prices. An increase in price would have further reduced the size of the market that could afford the restaurant's prices. Another restaurant in Houston adapted its pricing tactics to fit the recession. La Colombe d'Or offered a three-course meal for the spot price of a barrel of oil. When the morning price of oil was $12.62 a barrel, they charged $12.62 for a meal that cost $20 to $25 in comparable restaurants. The promotion gained the restaurant national and local publicity. The meal was a loss leader since most guests ordered wine with their meal. The restaurant frequently booked business luncheons, and the host of a business luncheon generally does not force guests to order the cheapest item on the menu. As a result, La Colombe d'Or sold many meals at regular prices and had healthy wine sales. Yet even with the loss leader the owner realized that other prices must offer value.

Market price determinants can often be highly misleading when viewed as a snapshot in time. It is essential to regularly review market conditions and respond in accord. The 1994 World Cup Soccer tournament offered a surprise to hoteliers in tournament cities. Hotels had reserved large blocks of rooms for expected tournament spectators, but were forced to release them with heavy discounts. In Orlando, single rooms were cut to $39 from $60 and in Chicago to $69 from $100. What happened?

1. Hotels lost many potential bookings after Japan, France, and England, homes to large numbers of affluent soccer fans, failed to make the championships. Third-world championship countries simply could not provide a large number of visitors.

2. An estimated 30% of soccer fans were VFR (visiting friends and relatives) travelers. These individuals stayed in private homes.

3. The perceived high price of rooms in these cities caused soccer fans to book rooms outside the city.[6]

Cross Selling and Upselling

The owner of La Colombe d'Or utilized **cross selling**, one of the basics of effective revenue management. Cross-selling opportunities abound in the hospitality industry. A hotel can cross sell F&B, exercise room services, and executive support services such as FAX and can even sell retail products ranging from hand-dipped chocolates to terry-cloth bath robes. A ski resort can cross sell ski lessons and dinner sleigh rides.

Upselling is also part of effective yield management. This occurs through training of sales and reservations employees to continuously offer a higher-priced product, rather than settling for the lowest price. One proponent of upselling believes that any hotel can increase its catering revenue by 15% through upselling.[7]

Hundreds of upselling opportunities exist. They simply must be recognized and programs implemented to ensure their success. The common practice of offering after-dinner coffee can be turned into an upselling opportunity by offering high-image upgraded presentations of coffee and tea rather than the standard pot of coffee. Gourmet coffee sales are expected to reach or exceed 30% of U.S. coffee sales.[8]

Price changes are easy to make and are often seen as a quick fix to a complex problem. Although it is easy to increase or decrease prices, it is hard to change a perception that your price is incorrect. Pricing decisions require a good understanding of the customer, market factors including the economic environment, and competition.

In this section, we will look at how the price–demand relationship varies for different types of markets and how buyer perceptions of price affect pricing decisions. We will also discuss methods for measuring the price–demand relationship.

Pricing in Different Markets

The seller's pricing freedom varies with different types of markets. Economists recognize four types of markets: pure competition, monopolistic competition, oligopolistic competition, and pure monopoly. Under pure competition, the market consists of many buyers and sellers trading in a uniform commodity such as wheat, copper, or financial securities. A pure monopoly consists of one seller. The seller may be a government monopoly, such as the postal service, a private regulated monopoly, such as a power company, or a private nonregulated monopoly, such as Du Pont when it introduced nylon.

Most hospitality firms operate in monopolistic competition or oligopolistic competition. Under monopolistic competition, the market consists of many buyers and sellers who trade over a range of prices rather than a single market price. A range of prices occurs because sellers can differentiate their offers to the buyers. Either the physical product can be varied in quality, features, or style or the accompanying service can be varied. Buyers see differences in the sellers' products and will pay different prices. Sellers develop differentiated offers for different customer segments and, besides price, freely use branding, advertising, and personal selling to set their offers apart. Because there are many competitors, each firm is less affected by competitors' marketing strategies than in oligopolistic markets. For example, in a large city there are many sit-down service restaurants. Each restaurant is differentiated by price and nonprice factors.

Under oligopolistic competition the market consists of a few sellers who are highly sensitive to each other's pricing and marketing strategies. The sellers are few because it may be difficult to enter the market. Each seller is alert to competitors' strategies and moves. If a major airline cuts its fares by 10%, it will quickly attract additional customers. Other airlines will cut their fares in reaction to the competition. On the other hand, if an oligopolist raises its price, its competitors might not follow the lead. The oligopolist would then have to retract its price increase or risk losing its customers to competition.

Consumer Perceptions of Price and Value

In the end, it is the consumer who decides whether a product's price is right. When setting prices, management must consider how consumers perceive price and the ways these perceptions affect consumers' buying decisions. Pricing decisions, like other marketing decisions, must be buyer oriented.

"We can't see the value of our product" explains Carlos Talosa, senior vice-president of Operations at Embassy Suites. "We can only set price. The market value is set by our customers and our ability to sell to it." According to Talosa, "Even in recessionary times, consumers aren't necessarily buying the cheapest options, but they are demanding value for their dollars and rightly so. If you aren't value-selling, then you are giving away precious assets."[9]

Pricing requires more than technical expertise. It requires creative judgments and awareness of buyers' motivations. Effective pricing opens doors. It requires a creative awareness of the target market, why they buy, and how they make their buying decisions. Recognition that buyers differ in these dimensions is as important for pricing as it is for effective promotion, distribution, or product policy.

When consumers buy a product, they exchange something of value (money) for something else of value (the benefits of having or using the product). Effective, buyer-oriented pricing involves understanding the value consumers place on the benefits that they receive from the product. Such benefits include both actual and perceived benefits. When a consumer buys a meal at an upscale restaurant, it is easy to figure out the value of the meal's ingredients. But it is very difficult to measure the value that customers will give to this product. Some guests come for the service, and others put great value on the chef's ability. Still others may value the restaurant's prestige and atmosphere. If customers perceive that the price is greater than the product's value, they will not buy.

Marketers must try to look at the consumer's reasons for choosing a product and set price according to consumer perceptions of its value. Because consumers vary in the values that they assign to products, marketers often vary their pricing strategies for different segments. They offer different sets of product features at different prices. For example, a quarter-pound hamburger might cost $3 at McDonald's, $6 at a sit-down service restaurant such as Bennigan's, and $9 in an exclusive city club.

Buyer-oriented pricing means that the marketer cannot design a marketing program and then set the price. Good pricing begins with analyzing consumer needs and price perceptions. Managers must consider other marketing mix variables before setting price. Most hotel and restaurant concepts are designed by identifying a need in the marketplace. The product concept usually contains a price range that the market is willing to pay. La Quinta Inns identified a market that did not value many amenities found in a full-service motel—the commercial traveler staying for one night. These guests did not use cocktail lounges, hotel restaurants, and banquet and meeting facilities. By eliminating these features, La Quinta saved money in both construction and operating costs. They passed these savings along to the customer as lower prices, offering the same sleeping room at a lower price than mid-scale hotels.

Consumers tend to look at the final price and then decide whether they received a good value. For example, two people dining in a restaurant receive their bill and see that it is $80. The diners then decide whether they were satisfied during the postpurchase evaluation. Rather than going over each item on the menu individually and judging its value, they judge the entire dining experience against the cost of that experience. If a restaurant offers a good value on food but a poor value on wine—charging $5 a glass for house wine, for instance—a couple who consumed six glasses of wine may feel that the check total is too high when $30 for wine is added to the bill.

The general manager of a five-star hotel in Kuala Lumpur, Malaysia, experienced a serious situation that nearly resulted in the closing of this hotel. A sultan's son and five guests appeared in the hotel's cocktail lounge late one evening and ordered three rounds of the "finest cognac" in the house without asking or being informed of the price. When the bill was presented, a price of $150 per glass or $2250 for three rounds seemed exorbitant even to a future sultan. The next day the hotel's general manager received calls from well-placed government officials suggesting that the practices of the hotel must be reviewed as well as its license to operate.

The situation was calmed by eliminating the bar charges and hand delivering a bottle of the cognac along with apologies to the sultan's son. The hotel policy was also changed to discretely give all guests ordering expensive drinks a written menu with prices before pouring rounds.

Melvyn Greene, a hotel marketing consultant, once interviewed guests immediately after they had paid their bills and were leaving the hotel. Only about one-fifth could remember the room rate they had just paid. They could, however, state whether they had received good value. Most of the guests had stayed for more than one day, made phone calls, and used the hotel's food and beverage outlets. The room rate was only one part of the charges of their total bill. They tended to accept the charges and sign their charge card.[10] The guests based their perception of value on the total dollar amount of the bill, the products they had received, and their satisfaction with those products.

Different market segments evaluate products differently. Managers must provide their target markets with product attributes that the target market will value and eliminate those features that do not create value. Then they have to price the product so that it will be perceived to be a good value by the desired target market. For some markets, this means modest accommodations at a low price; for other markets, this means excellent service at a high price. Perceived value is a function of brand image, product attributes, and price.

Analyzing the Price–Demand Relationship

Each price a company can charge will lead to a different level of demand. The demand curve illustrates the relationship between price charged and the resulting demand. It shows the number of units the market will buy in a given period at different prices that might be charged. In the normal case, demand and price are inversely related, that is, the higher the price, the lower the demand (see Figure 13-2). Thus the company would sell less if it raised its price from P_1 to P_2. Consumers with limited budgets will usually buy less of something if its price is too high.

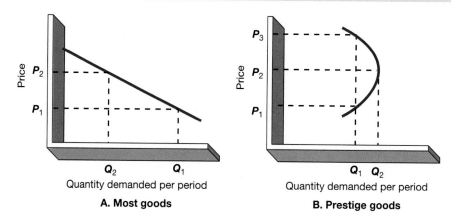

Figure 13-2
Two hypothetical demand
schedules.

Most demand curves slope downward in either a straight or a curved line. But for prestige goods, the demand curve sometimes slopes upward. For example, a luxury hotel may find that by raising its price from P_1 to P_2, it will sell more rooms rather than fewer: consumers do not perceive it as a luxury hotel at the lower price. However, if the hotel charges too high a price (P_3), the level of demand will be lower than at P_2.

Most company managers understand the basics of a demand curve, but few are able to measure their demand curves. The type of market determines the type of demand curve. In a monopoly, the demand curve shows the total market demand resulting from different prices. But if the company faces competition, its demand at different prices will depend on whether competitors' prices remain constant or change with the company's own prices. Here we will assume that competitors' prices remain constant. Later in this chapter, we will discuss what happens when competitors' prices change.

Estimating demand curves requires forecasting demand at different prices. For example, a study by Economic Intelligence Unit (EIU) estimated the demand curve for holiday travel in Europe. Their findings suggested that a 20% reduction in the price of visiting a holiday destination increases demand by 35%. A 10% reduction in price increases demand by 23%, while a 5% decrease results in a 15% increase in demand.[11] The EIU study used vacation destinations in the Mediterranean and assumed that other variables were constant.

Researchers can develop models that assume that other variables remain constant. For managers, things are not that simple. In normal business situations, other factors affect demand along with price. These factors include competition, the economy, advertising, and sales effort. If a resort cut its price and then advertised, it would be hard to tell what portion of the increased demand came from the price decrease and what portion came from the advertising. Price cannot be isolated from other factors.

Economists show the impact of nonprice factors on demand through shifts in the demand curve, rather than movement along it. Suppose that the initial demand curve is D_1 (see Figure 13-3). The seller is charging P and selling Q_1 units. Now suppose that the economy suddenly improves or the seller doubles its advertising budget. Higher demand is reflected through an upward shift of the demand curve from D_1 to D_2. Without changing the price, P, the demand has increased.

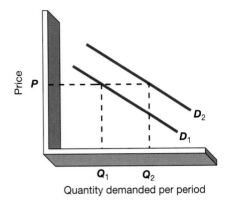

Figure 13-3
Effects of promotion and other non-price variables on demand shown through shifts of the demand curve.

Price Elasticity of Demand

Marketers also need to understand the concept of price elasticity—how responsive demand will be to a change in price. Consider the two demand curves in Figure 13-4. In Figure 13-4a a price increase from P_1 to P_2 leads to a small drop in demand from Q_1 to Q_2. In Figure 13-4b, however, the same price increase leads to a large drop in demand from Q_1 to Q_2. If demand hardly varies with a small change in price, we say the demand is inelastic. If demand changes greatly, we say the demand is elastic.

$$\frac{\% \text{ change in quantity demanded}}{\text{price elasticity of demand}} = \% \text{ change in price}$$

Suppose that demand falls by 10% when a seller raises its price by 2%. Price elasticity of demand is therefore −5 (the minus sign confirms the inverse relation between price and demand) and demand is elastic. If demand falls by 2% with a 2% increase in price, then elasticity is −1. In this case, the seller's total revenue stays the same: The seller sells fewer items, but at a higher price that preserves the same total revenue. If demand falls by 1% when the price is increased by 2%, then elasticity is −1/2 and demand is inelastic. The less elastic the demand, the more it pays for the seller to raise price.

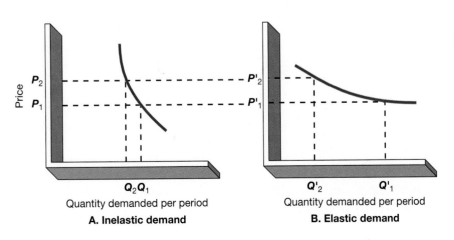

Figure 13-4
Inelastic and elastic demand.

What determines the price elasticity of demand? Buyers are less price sensitive when the product is unique or when it is high in quality, prestige, or exclusiveness. Chains try to differentiate their brand to create a perception of uniqueness. Consumers are also less price sensitive when substitute products are hard to find. After the closure of the Neil House in downtown Columbus, Ohio, Stouffer's Hotel became one of the few places in the central business district to hold a major banquet function. With supply down, they could charge more for their banquets. They maintained this advantage until new hotels were built and the market became competitive.

If demand is elastic rather than inelastic, sellers will generally consider lowering their prices. A lower price will produce more total revenue. This practice makes sense when the extra costs of producing and selling more products do not exceed the extra revenue.

Factors Affecting Price Sensitivity[12]

We will now look at some factors that affect price sensitivity. These include the unique value effect, the substitute awareness effect, the business expenditure effect, the end-benefit effect, the total expenditure effect, the shared cost effect, the sunk investment effect, the price quality effect, the price spread effect, and price points.

Unique Value Effect In Houston the Pappas family has converted failed locations into successful restaurants, taking what had been dead restaurants and turning them into businesses with a 1-hour-long wait on week nights. The Pappas family developed these restaurants during a recession, when other restauranteurs were complaining about lack of business and using two-for-one coupons to lure customers. The Pappas family did not have to use coupons or other price discounts to sell their food. They created a perception of value by giving large portions of food at a moderate price, which appealed to the upper lower class and the middle class. As Ralph Hitz said, give them value and you will create volume.

Creating the perception that your offering is different from those of your competitors avoids price competition. In this way the firm lets the customer know it is providing more benefits and offering a value that is superior to that of competitors, one that will either attract a higher price or more customers at the same price.

The K&W chain of cafeterias in North Carolina offers a consistent and fairly predictable menu of basic items such as chicken breast, prime rib, and family-style vegetables and desserts. Customers sometimes can be heard complaining about the lack of menu creativity, but they consistently return. K&W has discovered a price/value relationship that is recognized and appreciated by a broad spectrum of the people in North Carolina.

Substitute Awareness Effect The existence of alternatives of which buyers are unaware cannot affect their purchase behavior. For example, one of the authors attended a conference in Melbourne, Australia, and made a reservation at a mid-scale hotel. The accommodations were satisfactory but not special. Walking around the town, a new luxury-suite hotel was discovered featuring a special introductory price, equivalent to the author's room rate. The author would have preferred this hotel, but it was not part of his awareness set.[13]

Hotel restaurants often charge more for meals based on the substitute awareness effect. The guest who arrives in the evening, being unfamiliar with the city, will usually have breakfast in the hotel. The guest knows that a better value probably exists elsewhere, but is unfamiliar with other restaurants in the city. Although the breakfast in the hotel may cost twice as much as a meal in a nearby restaurant, the search costs—the time it would take to find the restaurant and the travel time to it—are greater than the dollar savings of the meal.

Restaurants that target the convention market or out-of-town guests use the substitute awareness effect to their advantage. These restaurants have large advertisements in the city's entertainment magazines that are distributed in the hotels. They are often not the choice of the local resident, who perceives them as overpriced, but they do attract hotel guests who are unaware of alternatives. There must be a continuous source of uninformed customers to use the substitution effect as the rationale for charging premium prices.

When consumers discover products offering a better value, they switch to these products. Many hotel restaurants are empty in the evening. They are perceived as overpriced by the local market. Hotel guests have time during the day to find alternatives. These hotels often view food and beverage as a required amenity, rather than an opportunity to compete for local business. A better philosophy is to use food and beverage as a means to attract customers.

Business Expenditure Effect   When someone else pays the bill, the customer is less price sensitive. An executive, fully reimbursed for all travel expenses, is unlikely to be attracted to a discount rate offer for a hotel room and a restaurant offering a $9.99 dinner special. This individual would probably prefer to stay in an upscale hotel, have room-service breakfast, and eat lunch and dinner in a more expensive restaurant. When setting rates, management needs to know what the market is willing to pay. If their hotel can attract executives who have a generous travel allowance and are willing to pay high room rates, they are leaving money on the table by offering discounts.

Airlines will offer a second business class ticket free when one is purchased at full price. Hotels will offer bonus frequent flyer miles. Both of these promotions are taking advantage of the business expenditure effect. The airline knows that the business will pick up the full fare ticket and the business traveler will be able to take a companion along for free. The hotel knows that since the traveler's company will pay for the hotel room, cutting prices by a few dolars might not bring in extra business travelers, but giving the business traveler bonus frequent flyer miles—which they can use for vacation trips—will. The business expenditure effective has numerous applications in the hospitality and travel industry.

Many hotels use information about corporate per diem rates to determine rate structures and identify target markets that are willing to pay the price. For example, when the Mandarin Oriental chain entered the U.S. market with a hotel in San Francisco, a survey of potential corporate clients was conducted to learn their per diem rates. From this information, target markets were identified.

End-Benefit Effect   Customers are more price sensitive when the price of the product accounts for a large share of the total cost of the end benefit. For example, a Japanese couple paying $2000 in air fare to travel to Australia will pay $150 a night for a luxury ocean-front hotel. The $150 is a small cost of the end benefit (their vacation). Many families driving to the Gold Coast from Sydney (a 500-mile trip) are looking for less expensive accommodations. These families are often on a limited budget and will prefer a less expensive motel a few blocks from the ocean.

When the Japanese couple goes to Dreamworld (a theme entertainment park), they will pay the $29 per person entrance fee without hesitation. The $58 admission fee is a small portion of the price of their vacation. However, the local family of four looking for weekend entertainment may view the $29 adult charge and $19 charge for children as high. In this case, the $96 entry fee amounts to a large portion of their entertainment expenses. To attract the local customer, Dreamworld offers yearly passes for just twice the single admission charge and second visit passes for $8, which allow the purchaser to enter anytime during the next 3 months. Dreamworld knows that if it were to raise its prices by 20% it would lose more local customers than international travelers. Thus it is important for Dreamworld to know its customer mix. If 75% of Dreamworld's customers are local residents, Dreamworld must be cautious about its price increases. It is common for tourist attractions such as Dreamworld to provide special rates for local residents. For example, a water slide near Disney World in Orlando, Florida, offered a special rate to families who could produce a local driver's license.

Upscale hotels can use the end-benefit effect as a tool to convince potential customers to pay an additional amount for hotel rooms. A company holding a two-day sales meeting may spend $500 in air fare, pay $250 in salary per day, and spend $50 in materials and $50 in speakers fees per participant. Thus, before room, food, and beverage costs, $1000 is invested in each participant. A smart hotel sales person may convince the meeting planner to upgrade by pointing out that the hotel costs are a small portion of the total costs. The sales presentation might be structured like this:

> And the difference between our luxury accommodations and the hotel accommodations you're considering is only $30 per night or $60 per participant, which is a small portion of your total cost per participant. Don't you think it's worth $60 to instill pride in your employees and show them that you care enough about them to put them in one of the best hotels in the city? Surely, the attitude difference this will create in the participants will play a significant role in the total success of the conference. Let's get the contracts drawn up for your sales meeting right now while we still have the space.

When working with price, the end-benefit price is an important concept to consider. The end-benefit price identifies price-sensitive markets and provides opportunities to overcome pricing objections when the product being sold is a small cost of the end benefit. To take full advantage of this effect, remember that many purchases have nonmonetary costs. For example, a mother planning the wedding of her daughter wants everything to be perfect and to avoid any embarrassing moments. High emotional involvement often makes the buyer less price sensitive.

Total Expenditure Effect   The more someone spends on a product, the more sensitive he or she is to the product's price. For example, limited-service chains such as Hampton Inns, Red Roof Inns, and La Quinta have made a successful effort to appeal to salespersons. The travel expenses of a salesperson can be significant, especially for those who average 2 to 3 days a week away from home. A salesperson who saves just $20 a night can realize annual savings of more than $2000. This savings adds to the profit of salespeople on straight commission. Companies that pay the expenses of their salespeople can save $2000 times the number of salespeople that they employ. Thus a company with 12 salespeople can save $24,000.

The total expenditure effect is useful in selling lower-price products or products that offer cost savings to volume users. The hotel concepts mentioned above provide salespeople with the benefits that they seek in a hotel: clean comfortable rooms, security, free telephone calls, and a coffee shop nearby.

The total expenditure effect is a dominant decision-making force for thousands of travelers who are provided with a set figure per trip. Many truckers are given a predetermined amount of cash such as $500 for a trip. Expenditures over that level are not reimbursed.

Not all motels desire the business of truckers, but those who do are highly cognizant of the fixed expenditure of their guests. They realize that ample parking for a 16-wheeler, a clean room with two beds, and a reasonable price will attract business.

Hotels that cater to upscale travelers frequently feature one king-sized bed in a room since few individuals on unlimited or high-expense accounts wish to share a room. Quite the opposite is true of individuals such as truckers or pipeline construction teams with fixed expenditure travel budgets. A $40 room shared by two extends a fixed budget.

Shared Cost Effect   Purchasers are less price sensitive when they are sharing the cost of the purchase with someone else. In the case of travel products, the government shares costs by allowing deductions from taxes. Many airlines offer a second ticket free with the purchase of a business-class ticket. This package is attractive to business travelers who might prefer to take a companion along on a trip. Although the business-class ticket may cost more than twice the amount of a discounted coach seat, the cost is tax deductible if the trip is for business purposes. The after-tax price of the business-class seats may be less than the cost of two economy seats if the companion's ticket is not tax deductible.

Another example is extending conferences with a weekend vacation component. Delegates to a conference that ends Friday may choose to spend the weekend at the resort or hotel if the hotel offers a special leisure package. This package is especially attractive because the airfare for the person attending the conference is usually tax deductible or paid by the company. The total cost of the vacation is reduced, since the expenses were shared.

Sunk Investment Effect   Purchasers who have an investment in products that they are currently using are less likely to change for price reasons.

For example, if IBM has held its last 10 regional sales meetings at the Omni in Atlanta, the company will have invested much time working with the hotel's conference service staff. The staff will know exactly how IBM wants rooms set up, which menus the conference planners prefer, the arrival patterns of the guests, and so on. IBM will also have worked with the staff to avoid repetition of any mistakes made during the previous conferences. IBM's meeting planners may have invested weeks of time working with Omni's staff. Because of this, they may be hesitant to change even if another hotel offers a lower price.

The sunk investment effect is one reason it can be difficult to get companies to change hotels. Once the company finds a hotel that performs well and meets its needs, price becomes less of an issue. On the other hand, a hotel that frequently turns over its convention service and sales staffs will require the corporate meeting planner to educate new staff members regularly. Here the meeting planner has no sunk investment; the planner will entertain other offers and make a decision based on price.

The concept of sunk investment combined with elasticities of demand for various customer segments provides a powerful argument for maintaining high prices for corporate customers. Eric Orkin, a pioneer in pricing and yield management, argues that some hotel chains have erred in following the lead of car rental companies by offering large corporations special discounts at all hotels within their chain. Orkin contends that this practice provides the lowest rates to those most able to pay and that it inevitably leads to similar moves by competitors, thus removing any advantage. Adding to this negative strategy is the fact that it often spreads to mid-sized customers, thus further decreasing revenue.[14]

Price Quality Effect   Consumers tend to equate price with quality, especially when they lack any prior experience with the product. For example, a friend may recommend that you stay at the Grand Hotel on your trip to Houston. If you call to make the reservation and they offer you a $49 weekend rate, you may perceive this rate as too low for the class of hotel that you want and select another. The Grand Hotel may have met all your needs, but, because of the low price, you assumed it would not.

A high price can also bring prestige to a product, because it limits availability. Restaurants where the average check is more than $100 per person for dinner would lose many of their present customers if they lowered their prices. In cases where price is perceived to relate to quality or where price creates prestige, a positive association between price and demand may exist with some market segments. For example, the Gosforth Park Hotel, an upscale hotel in Newcastle, England, found that occupancy increased as their rates increased.[15]

Competitors' Prices and Offers

Competitors' prices and their possible reactions to a company's own pricing moves are other external factors affecting pricing decisions. A meeting planner scheduling a meeting in Chicago will check the price and value of competitive hotels. Because of this, a hotel salesperson must learn the price, quality, and features of each competitor's offer. A hotel might do this in several ways: It can send out comparison shoppers to price and compare other competitors' products. It can review competitors' price lists and sample their products. The hotel can also ask buyers how they view the price and quality of each competitor's hotel or restaurant.

Once a company is aware of its competitors' prices and offers, it can use this information as a starting point for deciding its own pricing. For example, if a customer perceives that the Sheraton in Singapore is similar to the Hilton, the Sheraton must set its prices close to those of the Hilton or lose that customer. Additionally, the Sheraton would have to charge less than more luxurious hotels and more than those that are not as good. Sheraton uses price to position its offer relative to its competitors' offers.

Other External Factors

When setting prices, the company must also consider other factors in the external environment. Economic factors such as inflation, boom or recession, and interest rates affect pricing decisions. They affect both the costs of producing a product and consumer perceptions of the product's price and value. For example, in the 1970s, menu prices were commonly increased several times a year due to inflation. An alternative to raising price is reducing cost by changing menu items. For example, the recession of 1990–1991 forced many restaurants to reduce their prices. Most could not offer the same product at a lower price and survive. The restaurants created new menus with lower-cost items, items that could be sold at a lower price.

The Persian Gulf War of 1991 caused international travel to come to a standstill as people responded to terrorist threats. Even the American Society of Travel Agents (ASTA) canceled its annual conference. After the war was over, airlines and hotels used price as a tool to increase demand. Truste House Forte Hotels offered travelers 30% off its published rates at properties in Europe, North America, and the Caribbean.[16]

When reacting to environmental pressures created by the macroenvironment, a company must consider the impact its pricing policies will have on its microenvironment. For example, members of the distribution channel are often affected by price changes. In the fall of 1990, American Airlines offered its frequent flyers a $50 round-trip companion fare. United Airlines reacted by offering a $25 companion fare, followed by Northwest, which offered a buy-one-get-one-free fare. Travel agents found themselves reissuing hundreds of tickets, for no additional commissions, so that their clients could take advantage of these promotions. Some airline promotions resulted in travel agents rewriting tickets at a reduced fare, requiring that they do additional work, only to lose commissions. The travel agents grew irritated with the airlines over these promotions.[17]

All areas of the environment can affect pricing. Meeting new government regulations can cause costs to increase, or governments can streamline processes, reducing costs. If pro-environmental groups succeed in getting pesticides banned, food prices may increase. Marketers must know the laws concerning price and make sure that their pricing polices are legal (see Marketing Highlight 13-1). Marketers must use environmental knowledge gained through marketing information systems in making pricing decisions.

Marketing Highlight 13-1

Price Fixing

Federal legislation on price fixing states that sellers must set prices without talking to competitors. Otherwise, price collusion is suspected. Price fixing is illegal per se—that is, the government does not accept any excuses for price fixing. Even a simple conversation between competitors can have serious consequences.

During the 1980s, American Airlines and Braniff were immersed in a price war in the Texas market. Each carrier undercut the other until both were offering absurdly low fares and each was losing money on many flights. In the heat of the battle, American's CEO, Robert Crandall, called the President of Braniff and said: "Raise your ... fares 20 percent. I'll raise mine the next morning." Fortunately for Crandall, the Braniff president warned him off, saying, "We can't talk about pricing!" As it turns out, the phone conversation had been recorded, and the U.S. Justice Department

began action against Crandall and American for price fixing. The charges were eventually dropped— the courts ruled that because Braniff had rejected Crandall's proposal, no actual collusion had occurred, and that a proposal to fix prices was not an actual violation of the law. This case and others like it have made most executives very reluctant to discuss prices in any way with competitors. In obtaining information on competitors' pricing, they rely only on openly published materials, such as trade association surveys and competitors' brochures.

Sources: For more on public policy and pricing, see Louis W. Stern and Thomas L. Eovaldi, *Legal Aspects of Marketing Strategy* (Englewood Cliffs, NJ: Prentice Hall, 1984), Chap. 5; Thomas T. Nagle, *The Strategy and Tactics of Pricing* (Englewood Cliffs, NJ: Prentice Hall, 1987), pp. 321–37; and Robert J. Posch, *The Complete Guide to Marketing and the Law* (Englewood Cliffs, NJ: Prentice Hall, 1988), Chap. 28.

GENERAL PRICING APPROACHES

The price the company charges will be somewhere between one that is too low to produce a profit and one that is too high to produce any demand. Product costs set a floor for the price; consumer perceptions of the product's value set the ceiling. The company must consider competitors' prices and other external and internal factors to find the best price between these two extremes.

Companies set prices by selecting a general pricing approach that includes one or more of these sets of factors. We will look at the following approaches: the cost-based approach (cost-plus pricing, break-even analysis, and target profit pricing), the buyer-based approach (perceived-value pricing), and the competition-based approach (going rate).

Cost-based Pricing

The simplest pricing method is cost-plus pricing—adding a standard markup to the cost of the product. Food and beverage managers often use the cost-plus method to decide wine prices. For example, a bottle of wine that costs $14 may sell for $28, a 100% markup on cost. The gross profit is $14.

Cost as a percentage of selling price is another commonly used pricing technique in the restaurant industry. Some restaurant managers target a certain food cost and then price their menu items accordingly. For example, a manager wanting a 40% food cost will price the items two and a half times greater than their cost. The multiplicand is found by dividing the desired food cost percentage into 100. A manager desiring a 30% food cost would multiply the cost by 3.33. Managers using this type of pricing should realize that a restaurant is not 100% efficient. To make up for spoilage, shrinkage, and mistakes, managers will usually have to price 3 to 4 percentage points below their desired food cost. Thus a manager wanting a 40% food cost would need to price the menu at 36 to 37%. The adjustment figure varies depending on the volume and efficiency of the operation. In high-volume, limited-menu operations, it is lower.

For managers using this technique, it is advisable to use prime cost, the cost of labor and food, when determining menu prices. There is often a trade-off between labor and food costs; thus prime cost is a truer reflection of the cost of producing a menu item. For example, if a restaurant makes its own desserts, the cost of the ingredients is usually cheaper than buying a similar product from a bakery; however, there are no labor costs for the preparation of the purchased product. It is better to look at both labor and food costs to determine prices.

Does using standard markups to set prices make logical sense? Generally, no. Any pricing method that ignores current demand and competition is not likely to lead to the best price. Some restauranteurs use the same markup percentage despite the cost of the item. For example, using a 100% markup, a bottle of wine that costs $6 would sell for $12, while a bottle that costs $15 would sell for $30. In the first case the gross profit is $6; in the second case it is $15. The costs of serving each bottle of wine are identical, except for the carrying costs. It would be smart to reduce the markup on the higher-priced bottles if doing so would sell more wine. Here it would make more sense to price the wine based on demand and optimum profitability, instead of using a straight markup. If there is a demand for five bottles per night at $24, selling the wine at $24 that costs $15 will create more profit than two bottles at $30.

Most managers who use the cost as a percentage of selling price to price their menus use this technique to develop a target price. They adjust the individual prices for menu items based on factors such as what the market will bear, psychological pricing, and other techniques discussed in this chapter.

Markup pricing remains popular for many reasons. First, sellers are more certain about costs than about demand. Tying the price to cost simplifies pricing and managers do not have to adjust as demand changes. Second, because many food and beverage operations tend to use this method, prices are similar and price competition is minimized.

Break-even Analysis and Target Profit Pricing

Another cost-oriented pricing approach is break-even pricing, in which the firm tries to determine the price at which it will break even. Some firms use a variation of break-even pricing called target pricing, which targets a certain return on investment.

Target pricing uses the concept of a break-even chart (see Figure 13-5). For example, a buffet restaurant may want to make a profit of $200,000. Their break-even chart shows the total cost and total revenue at different levels of sales. Suppose that fixed costs are $300,000, and variable costs are $10 per meal. Variable costs are added to fixed costs to find total costs, which rise with volume. Total revenue starts at zero and rises with each unit sold. The slope of the total revenue reflects the price. If the restaurant sells 50,000 meals at a price of $20, for example, the company's revenue is $1 million.

At the $20 price the company must sell at least 30,000 units to break even; that is, at this sales level, total revenues will equal total costs of $600,000. If the company wants a target profit of $200,000, it must sell at least 50,000 meals, or 137 meals a day. This level of sales will provide $1 million of revenue to cover costs of $800,000, plus $200,000 in target profits. On the other hand, if the company charges a higher price, say $25 per meal, it will need to sell only 33,334 meals, or 92 a day, to meet its target profit. The higher the price, the lower the company's break-even point.

The selling price less the variable cost represents the gross profit or contribution that the sale makes toward offsetting fixed costs. The formula for the break-even (BE) point is

$$BE = \frac{\text{fixed costs}}{\text{contribution (selling price − variable cost)}}$$

In the previous example,

$$BE = \frac{\$300,000}{\$10\ (\$20\ \text{selling price} - \$10\ \text{variable cost})}$$

$$= 30,000\ \text{meals}$$

Figure 13-5
Breakeven chart for determining target price.

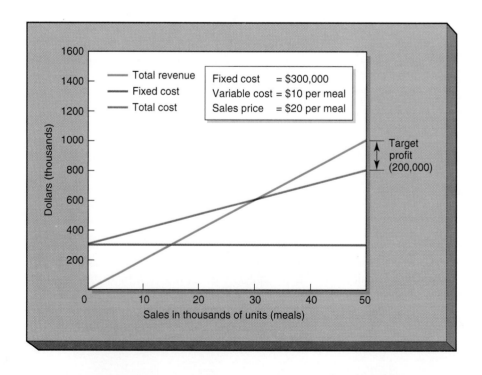

Hotels use the concept of contribution margin to set rates when demand drops. Hotels will set low rates, rationalizing that at least they are covering their variable costs. This can be effective if it creates additional demand.

However, some hotels try to steal business during good times by cutting rates. Figure 13-6 is a spread sheet that shows the increase in occupancy needed to make up for a reduction in rate. This chart illustrates the difficulty of recuperating from any substantial cut in prices in an inelastic market. At 70% occupancy, a hotel that lowers its rate from $75 to $60 (20%) will need to increase its occupancy to 95.5% to offset the decrease in price.[18]

Much depends on the relationship between price and demand. For example, suppose the company calculates that, given its current fixed and variable costs, it must charge a price of $30 for the product to earn its desired target profit. But marketing research shows that few consumers will pay more than $25 for the product. In this case, the company must trim its costs to lower the break-even point so that it can charge the lower price that consumers expect.

Buyer-based Pricing

An increasing number of companies are basing their prices on the product's perceived value. Perceived-value pricing uses the buyers' perceptions of value, not the seller's cost, as the key to pricing. The company uses the nonprice variables in the marketing mix to build perceived value in the buyers' minds, setting price to match the perceived value.

The price of rate-cutting

Present occupancy	Reduction in present rate				
	5%	10%	15%	20%	25%
	Occupancy required to make up for reduction				
76%	81.4%	87.7%	95.0%	103.6%	114.0%
74	79.3	85.4	92.5	100.9	111.0
72	77.1	83.1	90.0	98.2	108.0
70	75.0	80.8	87.5	95.5	105.0
68	72.9	78.5	85.0	92.7	102.0
66	70.7	76.2	82.5	90.0	99.0
64	68.6	73.8	80.0	87.3	96.0
62	66.4	71.5	77.5	84.5	93.0
60	64.3	69.2	75.0	81.8	90.0
58	62.1	66.9	72.5	79.1	87.0
56	60.0	64.6	70.0	76.4	84.0
54	57.9	62.3	67.5	73.6	81.0
52	55.7	60.0	65.0	70.9	78.0
50	53.6	57.7	62.5	68.2	75.0

(Based on cost of operating additional occupied rooms equal to 25% of present rate)

Figure 13-6
The price of rate-cutting.
Source: The Horwath Accountant, vol. 47, no. 7, 1967, p. 8.

Wendy's offers a number of products for under $1.00 to create a perception of value with their customers. Courtesy of Wendy's.

Consider the various prices different restaurants charge for the same items. A consumer who wants a cup of coffee and a slice of apple pie may pay $1.50 at a drugstore counter, $2.50 at a family restaurant, $4 at a hotel coffee shop, $6 for hotel room service, and $7 at an elegant restaurant. Each succeeding restaurant can charge more because of the value added by each type of service.

Any company using perceived-value pricing must learn the value in the buyers' minds for different competitive offers. Sometimes researchers ask consumers how much they would pay for each benefit added to the offer. One method of identifying how much customers are willing to pay involves using a technique called trade-off analysis. Researchers ask buyers how much they would pay for a hotel room with and without certain amenities. This information provides an idea of which features add more value than they cost. If the seller charges more than the buyers' perceived value, its sales will suffer. Many companies overprice their products, resulting in poor sales. Other companies underprice. Underpriced products sell very well, but they produce less revenue than they would if the company raised its price to the perceived-value level.

A study of meeting planners provided evidence that meeting planners perceived a greater value in paying $200 for a room than $175. Apparently planners, like many guests, associate quality with higher prices.[19]

The price of a hotel room may vary according to the type of customer. The hotel may have a rate for individual business guests, a group rate for groups of 10 or more, and a convention rate for associations that want to hold large functions at the hotel. If a hotel has the objective of maintaining 60% occupancy at an average rate of $90, it will need to determine its mix of customers and the average rate per segment. For example, it might develop the following mix to achieve a $90 rate:

	Percent of Business	*Average Rate*
Business	30%	$100
Corporate Group	40%	$90
Association	30%	$80

To achieve its target rate of $90, the hotel would have to sell above the average rate in peak times to compensate for discounted prices during off-peak times. It is important to develop target rates and keep on track toward meeting these goals. If the hotel offers a group 100 rooms for three nights at a rate of $75, they will need to make up $4500 (100 rooms × 3 nights × $90 target rate − 300 × $75 actual rate) in revenue. They must either sell to other groups above the $90 target rate, sell more business rooms at the $100 rate, or increase the targeted occupancy rate and sell additional rooms.[20, 21]

A successful guest price mix depends on carefully studying the behavior profiles of major guest segments. For most hospitality companies, this begins with a separation of guests into leisure and business segments. Such segmentation of each category may then occur, providing greater information about these major guest categories. Undoubtedly, the most important distinguishing profile characteristics of these two major segments is their relative degree of price elasticity. In general, business travelers exhibit inelastic price behavior and leisure travelers an elastic price response.

Competition-based Pricing

Going-rate Pricing

A strategy of going-rate pricing is the establishment of price based largely on those of competitors, with less attention paid to costs or demand. The firm might charge the same, more, or less than its major competitors. Some firms may charge a bit more or less, but they hold the amount of difference constant. For example, a limited service hotel chain may charge $10 more than Motel Six in markets where they compete. This form of pricing is quite popular. When elasticity is hard to measure, firms feel that the going price represents the collective wisdom of the industry concerning the price that will yield a fair return. They also feel that holding to the going price will avoid harmful price wars.

New-product Pricing Strategies

Pricing strategies usually change as the product passes through its life cycle. The introductory stage is especially challenging. Several options exist for pricing new products: prestige pricing, market-skimming pricing, and market-penetration pricing.

PRICING
STRATEGIES

Prestige Pricing

Hotels or restaurants seeking to position themselves as luxurious and elegant will enter the market with a high price that will support this position. Nightclubs may charge a cover charge to attract a certain type of clientele and create an image of exclusiveness. In each of these cases, lowering the price would reposition the business, resulting in a failure to attract the target market.

Market-skimming pricing

Price skimming is setting a high price when the market is price insensitive. Price skimming can make sense when lowering the price will create less revenue. For example, the owner of the only motel in a small town in Louisiana can set high prices if there is more demand than rooms. Price skimming can be an effective short-term policy. However, one danger is that competition will notice the high prices consumers are willing to pay and enter the market, creating more supply and eventually reducing prices. Price skimming is common in industries with high research and development costs, such as pharmaceutical companies and computer firms. It is seldom possible for an extended period of time in the hospitality industry due to the relative ease of entry by competitors.

Market-penetration Pricing

Rather than setting a high initial price to skim off small but profitable market segments, other companies set a low initial price to penetrate the market quickly and deeply, attracting many buyers and winning a large market share. Theodore Zinck's, a cocktail lounge in downtown Dallas, opened with prices about 20% lower than the competition. Management had negotiated a low lease, giving Zinck's a competitive advantage. Competitors could not match Zinck's lower prices because of their higher overhead. The policy allowed Zinck's to attract many customers quickly.

Several conditions favor setting a low price: The market must be highly price sensitive so that a low price produces more market growth, there should be economies that reduce costs as sales volume increases, and the low price must help keep out competition.

Product-bundle Pricing

Sellers who use product-bundle pricing combine several of their products and offer the bundle at a reduced price. For example, hotels sell specially priced weekend packages that include room, meals, and entertainment or offer commercial rates that include breakfast and a newspaper. Price bundling can promote the sales of products consumers might not otherwise buy, but the combined price must be low enough to convince them to buy the bundle. Ideally, the items added to the core service create more value to the customer than they cost to provide. For example, in 1993 British Airways featured a television ad that showed a representative negotiating low rates with a hotel manager. The airline ended up purchasing the hotel room at about half the original asking price. The ad's message was that if

McDonald's bundles its sandwiches with a drink and french fries. This makes it easier and faster for guests to order and promotes the sales of french fries.

you book a vacation through British Airways you will receive excellent hotel accommodations at bargain prices.

Product-bundle pricing is a strategy that has been well developed by cruise lines, tour wholesalers and casinos. Cruise lines typically offer fly–cruise or fly–drive–cruise packages in which the services of an auto rental company, airline, cruise line, and hotel are combined at a price well under the cost of purchasing each separately.

Hotel casino operations often use product-bundle pricing for the purpose of attracting gamblers who spend heavily in the gaming area. The hotel room may be priced below cost and used as a loss leader. Food, beverages and entertainment are often included in the bundle and may also be priced below cost or given free.

Price-adjustment Strategies

Companies usually adjust their basic prices to account for various customer differences and changing situations. We will look at the following adjustment strategies: discount pricing and allowances, discriminatory pricing, yield management, psychological pricing, promotional pricing, and geographical pricing.

Volume Discounts

Most hotels have special rates to attract customers who are likely to purchase a large quantity of hotel rooms, either for a single period or throughout the year. Hotels usually offer special prices or provide free goods for association and corporate meeting planners. As an example, suppose that a convention held by an industry association is attended by people who pay their own room charges. The association may prefer to receive a free room night for every 20-room nights booked, rather than a room rate that is $5 lower. They can use the free nights for their staff and invited speakers, reducing the association's total costs. Besides group rates, hotels offer corporate rates to companies that will guarantee their use of the hotel for an agreed-upon number of room nights each year.

Discounts Based on Time of Purchase

A seasonal discount is a price reduction to buyers who purchase services out of season, when the demand is lower. Seasonal discounts allow the hotel to keep demand steady during the year. Hotels, motels, and airlines offer seasonal discounts during selling periods that are traditionally slower. Airlines often offer off-peak prices, based on the time of day or the day of the week that the passenger flies. International flights adjust the price according to seasonal demand. A flight from Auckland to Sydney may cost $599 round trip during the Christmas season, while in July the same flight may cost $329. Restaurants offer early-bird specials to attract customers before their normal rush. Unfortunately, the various discount rates offered by a company sometimes clash to negate the desired positive effects. Restaurants commonly offer senior-citizen discounts, but would also like to induce this market segment to visit the restaurant early in the evening before the rush begins. Senior citizens often feel no reason to accept the early-bird special since they will qualify for a discount at peak hours.

Discriminatory Pricing

The term discriminatory pricing often invokes mental images of discrimination against individuals on the basis of race, religion, gender, or age. Sex-based price discrimination has historically served as a promotional tactic in night clubs and bars that offer a ladies night or ladies-only coupon by which prices of admission or for drinks are heavily discounted. In California, a suit was filed against an establishment that offered ladies-only discounts. The court ruled against the owner of the establishment under the Civil Rights Act.[22] Other illegal forms of discrimination sometimes come to mind, such as violation of antitrust. These perceptions are incorrect! Discriminatory pricing refers to segmentation of the market and pricing differences based on price elasticity characteristics of these segments. Price discrimination as used in this chapter is legal and is viewed by many as highly beneficial to the consumer.

Companies often adjust basic prices to allow for differences in customers, products, and locations. In discriminatory pricing, the company sells a product or service at two or more prices, although the difference in price is not based on differences in cost.

Suppose, for example, that a steak dinner has a menu price of $20 and the demand is 100 dinners at this price. If the restaurant lowers the price to $14, demand increases to 200 dinners. If the variable costs for preparing and serving the dinner are $8, the gross profit in each case will be $1200. However, if we assume that of the 200 persons willing to pay $14 for the steak 100 were part of the group willing to pay $20, $600 of potential income is lost from these 100 customers.

Price discrimination works to maximize the amount that each customer pays. In the case above, we would charge $20 to customers willing to pay $20. Those who are willing to pay $14 would be charged $14. How do we do this? We can't ask the customer, "Would you like to pay $20 or would you like to pay $14?" Obviously, everyone would say $14. Instead, we give different prices to different segments, offering the highest price to those segments that are less price sensitive. For example, our standard price is $20 for the dinner. We offer an early-bird special of $14 to diners arriving before 6 P.M. An individual who works until five probably is unwilling to rush home and rush to the restaurant to take advantage of the discount. This customer prefers to relax at home after work and arrive at the restaurant at 8 P.M. However, retired persons who may be more price sensitive, but less time sensitive, would be attracted by this special. The restaurant could also choose to send a coupon in a direct-mail coupon package to prospective customers. The price-sensitive customers would keep the coupon and use it the next time that they went out to eat. Many people who receive the coupon would throw it away. These customers do not want to be bothered with filing the coupon and then looking for it when they want to go out to eat. To these customers the $6 savings is not worth the hassle of using the coupon. Price discrimination discriminates in favor of the price-sensitive customer.

The supersaver fares on airlines usually require an advance purchase and a stay over a weekend. The weekend stay eliminates most business travelers, while the advance purchase eliminates family emergencies and business trips made on short notice. Airlines know that business travelers and those traveling for emergencies are less price sensitive, that is, they exhibit inelastic price behavior. Airlines offer low fares with the leisure traveler in mind. The leisure traveler uses discretionary income to pay for travel and as a result is more price-sensitive than the business traveler. A reduction in price often results in additional demand from the leisure segment.

Table 13-1 shows the prices available on a typical flight. Notice coach seats range from $629 to $129 for a senior citizen who has purchased tickets in advance through a multiple coupon book. The lower fares are aimed at the price sensitive leisure traveler. Like the airlines, many hotels discriminate between the leisure and business segments. Hotels in central business districts that cater to business travelers suffer low occupancy on weekends. Many of these hotels have developed lower-priced weekend packages to entice the leisure traveler.

Low variable costs combined with fluctuations in demand make price discrimination a useful tool for smoothing demand and bringing additional revenue and profits to most businesses. This form of pricing uses lower prices to attract additional customers, without lowering the price for everyone.

Major sectors of the hospitality industry, such as airlines, hotels, cruise lines, and railroads, are faced with enormous fixed costs. Companies in these sectors are faced with the need to fill seats or beds. Richard Hanks, vice-president of revenue management for the Marriott Corporation believes that "our greatest opportunity cost is an empty room." Marriott has designed a pricing system based on discriminatory pricing to fill rooms and maximize revenue opportunities. Marriott refers to the concept as "fencing."[23] The purpose behind fencing is to keep price-inelastic customers from using rates designed for price-elastic segments.

Table 13-1

Examples of Airfare Categories
for a Flight from Detroit to Los Angeles

FIRST-CLASS: 32 SEATS, 36 FARES

Examples of first-class fares

$944, normal first-class fare

$849, normal fare with 10% senior-citizen discount

$629, free upgrade from full coach fare for Worldperks Gold member

$305 or $239, free upgrade on 14-day advance purchase excursion fare for Worldperks Gold member; limited number of seats at each fare

Free, Worldperks frequent-flier award ticket

COACH CLASS: 256 SEATS, 22 FARES

Examples of coach fares

$629, normal fare

$566, normal fare with 10% senior-citizen discount

$466 or $238, one-way military fare; limited number of seats at each fare

$309, bereavement fare

$239, excursion fare with 14-day advance purchase

$189, visit USA fare, good for foreign travelers

$179, excursion fare (sale currently in effect) with seven-day advance purchase

$129, senior-citizen travel based on coupon booklet

SPECIAL FARES

Convention fares, usually 5% off lowest excursion fare or 40% off normal coach fares

Group fares, specially negotiated for group travel; generally close to lowest excursion fare

Bulk fares, special deals for tour operators

Tour fares, for travelers on a tour package, such as a cruise

Corporate fares, negotiated with certain corporations; can be from 10% to 35% off the full coach or first-class fare

Reprinted with permission of *The Detroit News.*

Fencing at Marriott is accomplished by establishing restrictions that allow customers to self-select price discriminatory rates that are best for them. Such fences include advance reservations and nonrefundable advance purchases. These policies permit price-sensitive customers to enjoy lower rates and inelastic segments to pay full fare without restrictions.

Richard Hanks strongly defends this strategy.

The fact of the matter is, if it weren't for incremental leisure guests, business guests would have to pay a higher price for their rooms in order for the hotel to meet financial obligations. I'd have to offer all our guests a $79 room, but in order to cover the costs of the hotel and ensure returns to our investors we must differentiate. The bottom line is this: either we accommodate both guests, one paying $79 and one paying $125, or we ask the business guests to pay $145. These are the choices.[24]

To successfully price discriminate, the following criteria must be met:

1. Different groups of consumers must have different responses to price; that is, they must value the service differently.

2. The different segments must be identifiable and a mechanism must exist to price them differently.

3. There should be no opportunity for individuals in one segment who have paid a lower price to sell their purchases to other segments.

4. The segment should be large enough to make the exercise worthwhile.

5. The cost of running the price discrimination strategy should not exceed the incremental revenues obtained. This is partly a function of criterion 4.

6. The customers should not become confused by the use of different prices.[25]

Yield Management   One application of discriminatory pricing is yield management. A yield management system is used to maximize a hotel's yield or contribution margin. This is done by the rates that a hotel will charge and the number of rooms available for each rate based on projected occupancies for a given period. These systems help hotels achieve the maximum contribution margin based on the demand for hotel rooms. The concept behind yield management is to effectively manage revenue and inventory by pricing differences based on the elasticity of demand for selected customer segments.

An effective yield management system establishes fences to prohibit customers from one segment receiving prices intended for another. For example, business travelers on an expense account exhibit somewhat inelastic price behavior. Leisure travelers are commonly more price sensitive (price elastic). A typical fencing strategy for leisure travelers would be to require a Friday and Saturday night stay with a 30-day advance reservation. This effectively fences out business travelers, who then pay higher rates to stay during a business week with little or no advance reservations.

Yield management involves the development and use of different rate classes based on the projected demand for the service. These rates are used to maximize yield. The formula for yield* is

$$\frac{\text{room nights sold}}{\text{room nights available}} \quad \text{x} \quad \frac{\text{actual average room rate}}{\text{room rate potential}} \quad = \quad \text{yield}$$

---

*Reprinted with permission from *Yield Management: Strategies and Tactics*, ©1990, by the Educational Institute of the American Hotel and Motel Association, P.O. Box 1240, East Lansing, MI 48826.

A hotel with sufficient history can project occupancy based on current booking patterns. If low occupancy is projected, the hotel will keep lower rate classes open to increase occupancy. The lower rates will typically use price discrimination techniques that favor the leisure traveler. Sheraton, for example, has 21-day advance supersaver rates. The idea is to create extra demand with low rates attracting guests that the hotel would not have received otherwise. If the projected occupancy is high, the lower rates will be closed and only the higher rate classes will be accepted. Today, several computerized systems are available that automatically project occupancy levels for a given date and suggest pricing levels for each day. It is common for a yield management system to increase revenues by at least 5%. Reservations for Hyatt's Regency Club concierge floors climbed 20% after Hyatt implemented yield management. One Hilton hotel increased its average transient rate by $7.50 with no reduction in occupancy the first month after installing a yield management system.[26]

Yield management systems must be based on sound marketing. They should be developed with the long-term value of the customer in mind. One early yield management system cut off reservations from travel agents when projected occupancy for a given date was high. This was done to eliminate travel agency commissions when the hotel could sell the rooms. This system saves money in the short term by saving travel agency commissions. However, in the long term the hotel could lose a significant portion of its travel agency business. Think of the person who wants to stay at the Regal Hotel in Orlando and fly to Orlando on Delta. The travel agent informs the client that the airline is confirmed, but no rooms are available at the Regal, so a reservation was made at the Gator Hotel. The client calls the Regal only to find that rooms are available. The client now thinks the travel agent is pushing the Gator Hotel and gets upset with the travel agent. The travel agent becomes upset with the Regal and refuses to book future business with them. The Regal gains short-run extra revenue but loses the travel agent's business in the long term. Yield management programs should focus on long-term profitability, not just the maximization of one day's revenue.

With some yield management systems, customers staying a longer period can be charged more than those staying only a few nights. Normally, one might expect a concession for longer stays. Sometimes the longer stay may take the guest into a period of high occupancy. These yield management systems average the occupancy over the guest's stay. For example, based on the occupancy levels in the following table, a guest checking in May 8 and checking out May 10 would be quoted a $65 rate as the lowest available rate. A guest checking in May 8 and checking out May 12 would be quoted $85 as the lowest available rate, since the hotel can sell rooms for the 10th and the 11th at a minimum of $105 a night. Under this system the staff must be well trained to explain rate differences to the guest.

Projected Occupancy

May 8	60%	May 10	85%
May 9	60%	May 11	90%

Yield management systems can be useful in managing the number of rooms available for transient demand. Most hotels have a base of transient demand composed of individual guests who pay a high rate. Some of these transient guests are business persons who may stay in the hotel several times during the year. Groups make their reservations well in advance of the transients; thus a sales person sometimes wants to take the sure business. When group business displaces transient business, the average rate drops and some displaced transient guests may never return, deciding to stay at an alternative hotel. Yield management systems help eliminate the problem of displaced transient guests by projecting the number of transient rooms that will be used on any given date.

Yield management systems, if used properly, can provide extra revenue. A good yield management system benefits both the hospitality company and the guest. It opens low-rated rooms for the leisure traveler during times of low occupancy and saves rooms during periods of peak demand for the business traveler willing to pay full rates. The company gains, since yield management focuses on maximizing revenue, not cutting costs.

A yield management system requires the availability of good data. This has forced many hospitality companies to go back to the basics and develop sound information-retrieval systems for internal data, such as booking patterns, and to develop and use better forecasting methods. The end result is that, without even using yield management, the company is in a far better position to make intelligent management decisions.

An effective yield management system depends on several variables.[27, 28] These are the ability to segment markets, perishable inventory, ability to sell product in advance, fluctuating demand, low marginal sales costs, high marginal production costs (can easily add another room), booking pattern data, information on demand pattern by market segment, an overbooking policy, knowledge of effect of price changes, a good information system for internal and external data, and ability to fence customer segments.

Regarding the ethics of yield management, many industry observers and consumer advocates have voiced concern. Steve Hall, executive director of the International Institute for Quality and Service in Tourism, has responded to these concerns.[29] "Revenue management is important, it is honorable, it is ethical and it is fair."

Psychological Pricing

Psychological pricing considers the psychology of prices and not simply the economics. Earlier in the chapter we discussed the relationship between price and quality. Prestige can be created by selling products and services at a high price.

Another aspect of psychological pricing is reference prices; these are prices that buyers carry in their minds and refer to when they look at a given product. A buyer's reference price might be formed by noting current prices, remembering past prices, or assessing the buying situation. Popular products often have reference prices. For a given type of restaurant, most consumers have a preconceived idea about the price or price range of certain items, such as a cup of coffee, a strip steak, or a hamburger. For example, a pizza chain may advertise its medium pizza for a price that they know is $2 less than the competition to establish a reference price for pizza eaters. But their price for beverages and extra items will be the same as competition. The reference item creates the perception of value; consequently, little would be gained by cutting the price of the other items.

Customers tend to simplify price information by ignoring end figures. For instance, there is greater perceived distance between $0.69 and $0.71 than there is between $0.67 and $0.69. Consumers also tend to round figures. One restaurant study found that consumers round prices ranging from $0.86 to 1.39 to a dollar, from $1.40 to 1.79 to a dollar and a half, and from $1.80 to 2.49 to two dollars. If this is the case, there may be little change in demand caused by a price increase of $0.30 from $1.45 to $1.75, but there may be a significant decrease in demand between $1.75 and $2.05.

The length of the field is another consideration. The jump from $0.99 to $1 or the jump from $9.99 to $10 can be perceived as a significant increase although it is only $0.01. Taco Bell's value prices were all under $1, and therefore only two digits. Some psychologists argue that each digit has symbolic and visual qualities that should be considered in pricing. For example, because the number 8 is round, it creates a soothing effect; while 7 is angular, thus creating a jarring effect.[30, 31]

Promotional Pricing

When companies use promotional pricing, they temporarily price their products below list price—and sometimes even below cost. Promotional pricing takes several forms. Fast-food restaurants will price a few products as loss leaders to attract customers to the store in the hope that they will buy other items at normal markups. Donut shops may offer coffee for 25 cents, knowing that a customer will usually buy at least one donut. A Jack-in-the-Box offers three hamburgers for a dollar, knowing that they will sell french fries and a soft drink with each order. During slow periods, hotels may offer a special promotional rate to increase business. Rather than just discount prices, well-managed hotels will create special events. A Valentine's weekend special including a room, champagne upon arrival, a dinner for two, and breakfast in the room; or a theater package including a room, tickets to a play, dinner for two, and breakfast for two. These promotions give the guest a reason to come; the bundle of products adds value for the customer. The promotion creates a positive image, whereas straight price discounting can create a negative image.

The gaming industry is particularly aware of the importance of product bundling and promotional pricing. Bruce Rowe, director of gaming information technology development at Promus Companies, the parent of Harrah's, stated that, "We are in the adult entertainment business, our main product offering is gambling and there are many components that support it such as hotels, entertainment facilities, and restaurants." Harrah's views hotel rooms as a means to entice and enable customers to gamble. "All patrons are welcome to stay in the hotel," said Rowe, "but to maximize revenue, casinos must ensure that rooms are readily available for the most profitable gaming customers."[32]

Hotel pricing at Harrah's reflects the fact that the company's main product offering is gaming, and a hotel room is only a supporting product for gaming.

Price Spread Effect

The restaurant industry has historically employed a rule of thumb that the highest-price entree should be no more than 2.5 times as expensive as the lowest-price entree. The rationale is that if the price span is too great customers will predominantly purchase the low-price items, which probably carry the lowest margins. A study at Cornell University in the Terrace Restaurant tended to confirm that this rule of thumb is indeed correct.[33]

Price Points

The concept of price points is well known and used throughout the retail industry. Some restaurant operators, particularly chain operations with sit-down menus, also employ the concept. Price points are important to the hospitality industry.[34]

Retailers and restauranteurs cannot offer the customer all possible product offerings. A retailer cannot maintain sufficient inventory to offer shoes at prices varying by only $1.00 between $29.95 and $32.95. Instead of offering selections at $29.95, $30.95, $31.95, and $32.95, a retailer will select one price point, such as $32.95, and no others in that range. The idea behind this is to simplify inventory and to force consumers who wanted a pair of shoes at $29.95 to pay $32.95. It is felt that the consumer is actually willing to pay $32.95 if that is the only available price point within a certain price range.

A restaurant operator must also make similar price point decisions. A steak house cannot offer $1 price points between $11.95 and $21.95 for a steak. Instead, the manager must select cuts and price points that will satisfy customers and maximize revenue. There is no reason to offer an $11.95 price point cut if customers are willing to pay $12.95.

Price points vary by retailer and by restaurant. J.C. Penny and Ponderosa Steak Houses both have price points that they feel are psychologically best suited for their customers. Saks of Fifth Avenue and Ruth's Chris steak restaurants have different price points for their customers.

Initiating Price Changes

After developing their price structures and strategies, companies may face occasions when they want to cut or raise prices.

Initiating Price Cuts

Several situations may lead a company to cut prices. One is excess capacity. Unable to increase business through promotional efforts, product improvement, or other measures, a hotel may resort to price cutting. In the late 1970s, many companies dropped "follow-the-leader pricing"—that is, charging about the same price as their leading competitor—and aggressively cut prices to boost sales. As the airline, hotel, rental car, and restaurant industries have learned in recent years, cutting prices in an industry loaded with excess capacity generally leads to price wars as competitors try to regain market share.

Companies may also cut prices in a drive to dominate the market or increase market share through lower costs. Either the company starts with lower costs than its competitors, or it cuts prices in the hope of gaining market share through larger volume. In January 1991, Burger King launched a promotion to cut the price of its Burger Buddies, two 1-ounce hamburgers, from 89 cents to 29 cents. The fast-food restaurant hoped that the price promotion would increase store traffic. They also made sure that they would not lose money on the promotion by requiring customers to buy french fries and a soft drink to get the Burger Buddies at the 29-cent price. Taco Bell started the pricing trend several years earlier when it slashed prices on its basic products to 59 cents. McDonald's entered the price war with 59-cent hamburgers, french fries, and soft drinks.

In mid-1991, Taco Bell sought to become the value leader in the fast-food industry by introducing a line of snack items for 39 cents. The new menu items were rolled out after test marketing in Los Angeles, Dallas/Fort Worth, Oklahoma City, and Youngstown, Ohio. The new items lowered check averages, but required the same amount of labor to make as the larger items. Taco Bell claimed that the products overcame these disadvantages by expanding their customer base.[35]

Initiating Price Increases

On the other hand, many companies have had to raise prices in recent years. They do this knowing that price increases may be resented by customers, dealers, and their own sales force. However, a successful price increase can greatly increase profits. For example, if the company's profit margin is 3% of sales, a 1% price increase will increase profits by 33% if sales volume is unaffected.

A major factor in price increases is cost inflation. Increased costs squeeze profit margins and lead companies to regular rounds of price increases. Companies often raise their prices by more than the cost increase in anticipation of further inflation. Companies do not want to make long-run price agreements with customers. They fear that cost inflation will reduce profit margins. For example, hotels prefer not to quote a firm price for conventions booked 3 years in advance. Another factor leading to price increases is excess demand. When a company cannot supply all its customers' needs, it can raise its prices, ration products to customers, or both. When a city hosts a major convention, hotels may charge rates that are twice the average room rate. They know that the demand for hotel rooms will be great and they can take advantage of this demand.

In passing price increases on to customers, the company should avoid the image of "price gouger." It is best to increase prices when customers perceive the price increase to be justified. Restaurants had an easier time implementing increased menu prices after the price of beef jumped, because their customers noticed this price increase in the supermarket. If food prices are going down, while the other costs of operating a restaurant are going up, it is difficult to gain customer acceptance of the need for a price increase. Restaurant managers should try to time price increases so that they will be perceived as justified by customers, such as when increases in the price of food receive media attention, after an increase in the minimum wage, or when inflation is in the news. Price increases should be supported with a company communication program informing customers and employees why prices are being increased.

Buyer Reactions to Price Changes

Whether the price is raised or lowered, the action will affect buyers, competitors, distributors, and suppliers. Price changes may also interest the government. Customers do not always put a straightforward interpretation on price changes. They may perceive a price cut in several ways. For example, what would you think when you see a restaurant advertising a buy-one-meal-get-one-free special? If you know the restaurant and have a positive feeling, you might be attracted. Someone who doesn't know the restaurant may feel it is having trouble attracting customers or that there is something wrong with the food or service. Or you might wonder if portion size has been reduced or inferior-quality food was being served. Remember, buyers often associate price with quality when evaluating hospitality products that they have not directly experienced.

Similarly, a price increase that would normally lower sales may have a positive meaning for buyers. A nightclub that increases its cover charge from $5 to $10 might be perceived as the "in place" to go.

Competitor Reactions to Price Changes

A firm considering a price change has to worry about competitors' reactions. Competitors are most likely to react when the number of firms involved is small, when the product is uniform, and when buyers are well informed.

One problem with trying to use price as a competitive advantage is that competitors can neutralize the price advantage by lowering their prices. In a competitive market where supply exceeds demand, this often sets off price wars in which the industry as a whole loses. In the United States, Burger King and McDonald's are locked in a fierce battle for market share. When one of these fast-food giants cuts its price, the other usually follows. Ninety-nine-cent Big Macs are matched by 99-cent Whoppers.

In early 1991, British Airways cut its 30-day advance purchase fares by 33%. Delta and Pan Am matched British Airways. TWA more than matched the British Airways offer by slashing its fares to London by 50%. British Airways lost the competitive advantage of lower fares when competitors quickly matched its price.[36]

Competitors may choose to retaliate in different markets. For example, when Southwest Airlines cut prices on its Houston to San Antonio flights, its competitors reacted by cutting prices on their Houston to Dallas flights. The Houston to Dallas flights were Southwest's bread and butter. By hitting here, the competition hurt Southwest more than they could have by matching prices on the Houston to San Antonio route. Competitors may also react to a price cut with nonprice tactics. When Continental Airlines offered a "chicken-feed" discount fare, the competition responded by not booking their connecting passengers on Continental's flights. Continental was forced to rescind its price cuts. Before cutting prices, it is essential to consider competitive reactions. As we mentioned at the beginning of the chapter, price is a very flexible element of the marketing mix. It can easily be matched by the competition. A firm that lowers its price and has it matched by competition loses both its competitive advantage and profit.[37]

Trade Ally Reactions to Price Changes

Earlier mention has been made of the reaction of travel agents to heavy discounting by airlines. This is an example of trade ally reactions.

The hospitality and travel industry represent such an interconnected and interdependent group of firms that pricing actions by major participants such as airlines, cruise lines, and ski resorts have a domino effect on others.

Shoeshine attendants sometimes complain that a dramatic cut in airfares is bad for business. Airports are jammed with people wearing sneakers, sandals, and other footwear that requires no polish. Business travelers are lost in the crowd and may not see the shoeshine stands due to the traffic.

Suppliers to firms that offer deep discounts may also be asked to offer special discounts or risk losing business. Independent firms such as limousine services and food vendors may be tempted to raise prices due to increased traffic.

Communities such as resorts and convention cities are greatly concerned by the pricing activities of airlines, ski resorts, and other principal players and may be expected to exert considerable pressure on managers concerning their pricing strategies. They want to keep prices low to encourage tourism. Besides pressure for low prices from some local governments, governments also view the hospitality industry as a source of income by local, state, and federal governments. Visitors to a region are seldom voters in that area and are therefore viewed as excellent tax revenue sources by elected officials. Room taxes, airport departure taxes, sales taxes, and other imaginative taxes directly add to the price of a hospitality product. In some heavily taxed areas, taxation and visitor tariffs may add 20% to the price.

This situation often requires strong political action by the hospitality industry and supportive groups such as local retailers. Hotels in New York State won a 3-year battle to repeal a 5% tax on rooms. Hotels in New York City were particularly hard hit. Guests will still be forced to pay 14.25% plus a $2 surcharge on hotel rooms. Hoteliers argued that the tax was a major factor in driving convention and meeting business from the city.

Following the repeal of the 5% tax, Stephen Morello, president of the New York Convention and Visitors Bureau, stated, "Tomorrow we'll be calling the 44 conventions worth $52 million that said they couldn't come to New York City last year because of the tax."[38]

In addition to governmental taxation, private associations may levy a surcharge. Organizers of the 1994 World Cup soccer tournament levied a surcharge for travelers who booked reservations through this organization. Many soccer fans discovered that they could save money by reserving their own rooms and avoided the organization surcharge.[39]

Responding to Price Changes

Here we reverse the question and ask how a firm should respond to a price change by a competitor. The firm needs to consider several issues. Why did the competitor change the price? Was it to gain more market share, to use excess capacity, to meet changing cost conditions, or to lead an industry-wide program change? Does the competitor plan to make the price change temporary or permanent? What will happen to the company's market share and profits if it does not respond? Are other companies going to respond? What are the competitors' and other firms' responses likely to be to each possible reaction?

Besides these issues, the company must make a broader analysis. It must consider its own product's stage in the life cycle, its importance in the company's product mix, the intentions and resources of the competitor, and possible consumer reactions to price changes.

In 1989 when Marriott's Fairfield Inns were just getting started, they offered a special $19.95 coupon, $16 less than their average daily rate. Their competitors decided not to match the rate because Fairfield had only 30 hotels at the time. Joan Ganje-Fischer, vice-president of Super 8, said that if a major chain such as Super 8, Econo Inns, or Days Inns offered the $19.95 special it would catch the attention of the other organizations. A price war would be the likely result of such a cut by a major chain. But since Fairfield Inns consisted of only 30 units, major competitors were unwilling to reduce rates across their hundred-plus motel chains. Fairfield Inns used size to their advantage, recognizing that the larger chains would be unwilling to give up revenue from hundreds of hotels and thousands of rooms to match the price of a 30-unit chain.

At the end of a pilot strike against United Airlines, the company announced a refund of half the cost of any flight taken during a 1-week period. United wanted to attract customers who were forced to use other airlines when it cut service during the strike. By limiting price reductions to 1 week, United avoided getting into a price battle. Competitors who were doing well because of United Airlines' plight chose not to discount fares and conceded United the lower fares for a week.[41]

These examples show how companies can avoid competitive reactions to price changes by carefully planning those changes.

Chapter Review

I.   **Factors to Consider When Setting Price**
    1) **Internal Factors**
        a) **Marketing objectives:**
        Survival: It is used when the economy slumps or a recession is going on. A manufacturing firm can reduce production to match demand and a hotel can cut rates to create the best cash flow.
        Current profit maximization: Companies may choose the price that will produce the maximum current profit, cash flow, or return on investment, seeking financial outcomes rather than long-run performance.
        Market-share leadership: When companies believe that a company with the largest market share will eventually enjoy low costs and high long-run profit, they will set low opening rates and strive to be the market-share leader.
        Product-quality leadership: Hotels like the Ritz-Carlton chain charge a high price for their high-cost products to capture the luxury market.

Other objectives: Stabilize market, create excitement for new product, draw more attention.

b) Marketing-mix strategy: Price must be coordinated with product design, distribution, and promotion decision to form a consistent and effective marketing program.

c) Costs

Fixed costs: costs that do not vary with production or sales level.

Variable costs: costs that vary directly with the level of production.

d) Organizational considerations: Management must decided who within the organization should set price. In small companies; this will be top management; in large companies, pricing is typically handled by a corporate department or by a regional or unit manager under guidelines established by corporate management.

2) **External Factors**

a) Nature of the market and demand

Cross selling: selling the company's other products to the guest.

Upselling: occurs through training of sales and reservation employees to continuously offer a higher-priced product that will better meet the customer's needs, rather than settling for the lowest price.

b) Pricing in different markets: There are four types of markets:

Pure competition: The market consists of many buyers and sellers trading in a uniform commodity

Monopolistic competition: The market consists of many buyers and sellers who trade over a range of prices, rather than a single market price.

Oligopolistic competition: The market consists of a few sellers who are highly sensitive to each other's pricing and marketing strategies.

Pure monopoly: The market consists of one seller; it could be government monopoly, a private regulated monopoly, or a private non-regulated monopoly.

c) Consumer perception of price and value: It is the consumer who decides whether a product's price is right. The price must be buyer oriented. The price decision requires a creative awareness of the target market and recognition of the buyers' differences.

d) Analyzing the price–demand relationship: Demand and price are inversely related; the higher the price, the lower the demand. Most demand curves slope downward in either a straight or a curved line. The prestige goods demand curve sometimes slopes upward.

e) Price elasticity of demand: If demand hardly varies with a small change in price, we say that the demand is inelastic; if demand changes greatly, we say that the demand is elastic. Buyer are less price sensitive when the product is unique or when it is high in quality, prestige, or exclusiveness. Consumers are also less price sensitive when substitute products are hard to find. If demand is elastic, sellers will generally consider lowering their prices to produce more total revenue. The following factors affect price sensitivity.

Unique value effect: Creating the perception that your offering is different from those of your competitors avoids price competition.

Substitute awareness effect: Lack of the awareness of the existence of alternatives reduces price sensitivity.

Business expenditure effect: When someone else pays the bill, the customer is less price sensitive.

End-benefit effect: Consumers are more price sensitive when the price of the product accounts for a large share of the total cost of the end benefit.

Total expenditure effect: The more someone spends on a product, the more sensitive he or she is to the product's price.

Shared cost effect: Purchasers are less price sensitive when they are sharing the cost of the purchase with someone else.

Sunk investment effect: Purchasers who have an investment in products that they are currently using are less likely to change for price reasons.

Price quality effect: Consumers tend to equate price with quality, especially when they lack any prior experience with the product.

f) **Competitor's price and offers:** When a company is aware of its competitors' price and offers, it can use this information as a starting point for deciding its own pricing.

g) **Other environmental factors:** Inflation, boom, or recession, interest rates, government purchasing, birth of new technology.

II. General Pricing Approaches

1) Cost-based Pricing. Cost-plus pricing: adding a standard markup to the cost of the product.

2) Break-even Analysis and Target Profit Pricing.

3) Buyer-based Pricing. Companies base their prices on the product's perceived value. Perceived-value pricing uses the buyers' perceptions of value, not the seller's cost, as the key to pricing.

4) Competition-based Pricing. Competition-based price is based on the establishment of price largely against those of competitors, with less attention paid to costs or demand.

III. Pricing Strategies

1) Prestige Pricing. Hotels or restaurants seeking to position themselves as luxurious and elegant will enter the market with a high price that will support this position.

2) Market-skimming Pricing. Price skimming is setting a high price when the market is price insensitive. It is common in industries with high research and development costs, such as pharmaceutical companies and computer firms.

3) Marketing-penetration Pricing. Companies set a low initial price to penetrate the market quickly and deeply, attracting many buyers and winning a large market share.

4) Product-bundle Pricing. Sellers using product-bundle pricing combine several of their products and offer the bundle at a reduced price. Most used by cruise lines.

5) Volume Discounts. Hotels have special rates to attract customers who are likely to purchase a large quantity of hotel rooms, either for a single period or throughout the year.

6) Discounts Based on Time Of Purchase. A seasonal discount is a price reduction to buyers who purchase services out of season when the demand is lower. Seasonal discounts allow the hotel to keep demand steady during the year.

7) Discriminatory Pricing. Refers to segmentation of the market and pricing differences based on price elasticity characteristics of the segments. In discriminatory pricing, the company sells a product or service at two or more prices, although the difference in price is not based on differences in cost. It maximizes the amount that each customer pays.

8) Psychological Pricing. Psychological aspects like prestige, reference prices, round figures, and ignoring end figures are used in pricing.

9) Promotional Pricing. Hotels temporarily price their products below list price, and sometimes even below cost, for special occasions, such as introduction or festivities. Promotional pricing gives guests a reason to come and promotes a positive image for the hotel.

IV. **Price Changes**

1) Initiating Price Cuts. Reasons for a company to cut price: excess capacity, unable to increase business through promotional efforts, product improvement, follow-the-leader pricing, and to dominate the market.

2) Initiating Price Increases. Reasons for a company to increase price: cost inflation or excess demand.

3) Buyer Reactions to Price Changes. Competitors, distributors, suppliers, and other buyers will associate price with quality when evaluating hospitality products they have not experienced directly.

4) Competitor Reactions to Price Changes. Competitors are most likely to react when the number of firms involved is small, when the product is uniform, and when buyers are well informed.

5) Responding to Price Changes. Issues to consider: reason, market share, excess capacity, meet changing cost conditions, lead an industry-wide program change, temporary versus permanent.

DISCUSSION QUESTIONS

1. One way of increasing revenue is through upselling. Give examples from the hospitality or travel industries of when upselling can result in a more satisfied guest.

2. You have just been hired as the dining room manager at a local hotel. The manager asks you to evaluate the menu prices to see if they need to be adjusted. How would you go about this task?

3. A number of factors affecting price sensitivity are discussed in this chapter. Provide some examples of the application of these factors in hospitality or travel businesses.

4. Many restaurants have unbundled their products to lower prices. For example, some restaurants which normally included a salad bar with all meals now offer a dinner price which includes the salad bar and a lower a la carte which does not. Why do you think these restaurants are unbundling their products? When is price bundling effective?

5. Give an example of an effective use of price discrimination. Be sure and support why you think it is a good example.

6. Does yield management create and maintain customers, or is it a short term approach to increasing revenue?

7. Airlines and hotels give bonus frequent flyer miles, gifts, and free companion tickets to attract the business traveler. These promotions are often provided in lieu of a price cut. The traveler benefits personally, while their company does not get the benefit of lower rates. Is this ethical?

KEY TERMS

Break-even pricing (target profit pricing)
Setting price to break even on the costs of making and marketing a product, or to make the desired profit.

Cost-plus pricing Adding a standard markup to the cost of the product.

Demand curve A curve that shows the number of units the market will buy in a given time period at different prices that might be charged.

Experience curve (learning curve) The drop in the average per-unit production cost that comes with accumulated production experience.

Fixed costs Costs that do not vary with production or sales level.

Going-rate pricing Setting price based largely on following competitors' prices rather than on company costs or demand.

Monopolistic competition A market in which many buyers and sellers trade over a range of prices rather than a single market price.

Oligopolistic competition A market in which there are a few sellers who are highly sensitive to each other's pricing and marketing strategies.

Perceived-value pricing Setting price based on buyers' perceptions of value, rather than on the seller's cost.

Price The amount of money charged for a product or service, or the sum of the values consumers exchange for the benefits of having or using the product or service.

Price elasticity A measure of the sensitivity of demand to changes in price.

Pure competition A market in which many buyers and sellers trade in a uniform commodity; no single buyer or seller has much effect on the going market price.

Pure monopoly A market in which there is a single seller; it may be a government monopoly, a private regulated monopoly, or a private nonregulated monopoly.

Total costs The sum of the fixed and variable costs for any given level of production.

Variable costs Costs that vary directly with the level of production.

Yield management Yield management is a pricing method using price as a means of matching capacity with demand. The goal of yield management is to optimize the yield or contribution margin.

REFERENCES

1. DAVID J. SCHWARTZ, *Marketing Today: A Basic Approach*, 3rd ed. (New York: Harcourt Brace Jovanovich, 1981), pp. 270–273.

2. DENEFE JANET, "Yearning for Learning," *F&B Magazine*, 2, no. 1 (March/April 1994), p. 13.

3. JACK SMITH, "Of Fame and Fundamentals," *F&B Magazine*, 2, no. 1 (March/April 1994), pp. 34–35.

4. "Royal Caribbean Breaks Through," *Scorecard: The Revenue Management Quarterly* (Third Quarter, 1992), Aeronomics Inc., Atlanta, Ga., p. 3.

5. Ibid., p. 6.

6. RHONDA RICHARDS, "Hotels See Slow Soccer Tournament Bookings," *U.S.A. Today* (May 24, 1994), p. 4B.

7. HOWARD FEIRTAG, "Up Your Property's Profits by Upselling Catering," *Hotel and Motel Management*, 206, no. 14 (August 19, 1991), p. 20.

8. GAIL BELLAMY, "Hot Stuff: Upselling Coffee and Tea," *Restaurant Hospitality*, 75, no. 2 (February 1991), pp. 120–124.

9. "Embassy's Suite Deal," *Scorecard; The Revenue Management Quarterly* (Second Quarter, 1993), Aeronomics Inc., Atlanta, Ga., p. 3.

10. MELVYN GREENE, *Marketing Hotels and Restaurants into the 90's* (New York: Van Nostrand Reinhold Company, 1987).

11. ANTHONY EDWARDS, "Changes in Real Air Fares and Their Impact on Travel," *EIU Travel and Tourism Analyst*, (1990, 2), pp. 76–85.

12. This sections draws on THOMAS T. NAGLE, *The Strategy and Tactics of Pricing* (Englewood Cliffs, N.J.: Prentice Hall, 1987).

13. Cite NAGLE.

14. Eric B. Orkin, "Strategies for Managing Transient Rates," *Cornell Hotel and Restaurant Administration Quarterly*, 30, no. 4 (February 1990), p. 39.

15. MELVYN GREENE, *Marketing Hotels and Restaurants into the 90's*, p. 47.

16. "Trusthouse Sets 30% Discount off Rack Rates," *Travel Weekly*, 50, no. 18 (March 4, 1991), p. 13.

17. ISAE WADA, "Agents Irate over Airlines 2-for-1 Fares," *Travel Weekly*, 29, no. 96 (November 29, 1990), p. 1.

18. JEROME VALLEN AND GARY K. VALLEN, *Check-in Checkout* (Dubuque, Iowa: William C. Brown, 1991).

19. Leo M. Renaghan and Michael Z. Kay, "What Meeting Planners Want: The Conjoint-analysis Approach," *Cornell Hotel and Restaurant Administration Quarterly*, 28, no. 1 (May 1987), p. 73.

20. GREENE, *Marketing Hotels and Restaurants into the 90's*, p. 42.

21. JOHN E. H. SHERRY, "Sex-based Price Discrimination: Does It Violate Civil Rights Laws?," *Cornell Hotel and Restaurant Administration Quarterly*, 35, no. 2 (April 1994), pp. 16–17.

22. RICHARD O. HANKS, ROBERT G. CROSS, AND PAUL R. NOLAND, "Discounting in the Hotel Industry: A New Approach," *Cornell Hotel and Restaurant Administration Quarterly*, 33, no. 1 (February 1992), p. 23.

23. "Rational Pricing at Marriott," *Scorecard: The Revenue Management Quarterly* (Third Quarter, 1993), p. 4.

24. JOHN E. G. BATESON, *Managing Services Marketing* (Dryden Press: Fort Worth, Ind., 1992), p. 339.

25. ERIC B. ORKIN, "Boosting Your Bottom Line with Yield Management," *Cornell Hotel and Restaurant Quarterly*, vol. 28 no. 4, (1988), pp. 52–56.

26. SHERYL E. KISNER, "The Basics of Yield Management," *Cornell Hotel and Restaurant Administration Quarterly*, 30, no. 3 (November 1989), pp. 15–18.

27. "The Ethics of Revenue Management," *Scorecard: The Revenue Management Quarterly* (Third Quarter, 1993), Aeronomics Inc., Atlanta, Ga, p. 9.

28. This section drew heavily on "Pricing Considerations in Menu Expansion and New Product Development," presented at the *National Restaurant Association's Marketing Research Group Meeting* (New Orleans, September 21, 1981).

29. "High Stakes at Harrah's," *Scorecard: The Revenue Management Quarterly* (First Quarter, 1993), Aeronomics Inc., Atlanta, Ga., p. 3.

30. JOANN CARMIN AND GREGORY X. NORKUS, "Pricing Strategies for Menus: Magic or Myth," *Cornell Hotel and Restaurant Administration Quarterly*, 31, no. 3 (November, 1990), p. 50.

31. Ibid.

32. RICHARD MARTIN, "Taco Bell Rolls out a New 39-Cent Snack Menu," *Nation's Restaurant News* 25, no. 25 (June 24, 1991), p. 3; RICHARD MARTIN, "McDonald's Kicks off Value Menu Blitz," *Nation's Restaurant News*, 25, no. 1 (January 7, 1991), p. 3; SCOTT HUME, "Burger King Backs Low-price Buddies," *Advertising Age*, 61, no. 53 (December 24, 1990), p. 2.

33. ISAE WADA, "TWA Slashes Transatlantic Fares by Half," *Travel Weekly*, 50, no. 14 (February 18, 1991), p. 1+.

34. NAGLE, *The Strategy and Tactics of Pricing*, pp. 95–96.

35. "NYC: Tax Cut, CHRAQ News and Reviews," *Cornell Hotel and Restaurant Administration Quarterly*, 35, no. 4 (August 1994), p. 6.

36. RHONDA RICHARDS, "Hotels See Slow Soccer Tournament Bookings," p. 4B.

37. "Fairfield Cuts Rates to Gain Stronger Presence," *Hotel and Motel Management* (June 19, 1989), p. 1+.

38. JOHN A. QUELCH AND MELANIE D. SPENCER, "United Airlines: Price Promotion Policy" (Harvard Business Case 586-089, 1986).

Managing Capacity and Demand

14

Qantas, Australia's international airline, is experiencing a demand bonanza. Its market area in the Pacific Basin contains some of the fastest-growing economies in the world, including Japan, Australia, and the four newly industrialized countries of Hong Kong, Singapore, South Korea, and Taiwan. The area's growth rate for air travel far exceeds world averages. Industry forecasts suggest that Pacific Basin air travel will grow at 10% to 14% per year and that the area will capture a 40% share of all international air passenger traffic by the year 2000.

Such explosive growth presents a huge opportunity for Qantas and the other airlines serving the Pacific Basin. But it also presents some serious headaches. To take advantage of the growing demand, Qantas must first forecast it accurately and prepare to meet it. Air travel demand has many dimensions. Qantas must forecast how many and what kinds of people will be traveling, where they will want to go, and when. The airline must project total demand, as well as demand in each specific market that it plans to serve. And Qantas must estimate what share of this total demand it can capture under alternative marketing strategies and in various competitive circumstances. Moreover, it must forecast demand not just for next year, but also for the next 2 years, 5 years, and even further.

Forecasting air travel demand is no easy task. Many factors affect how often people travel and where they go. To make accurate demand forecasts,

Qantas must first anticipate changes in the factors that influence demand: worldwide and country-by-country economic conditions, demographic characteristics, population growth, political developments, technological advances, competitive activity, and many other factors. Qantas has little or no control over many of these factors.

Demand can shift quickly and dramatically. For example, relative economic growth and political stability in Japan, Australia, and the other Pacific Basin countries have caused a virtual explosion in demand for air travel there. Ever increasing numbers of tourists from around the world are visiting these areas. In Australia, foreign tourism more than doubled between 1984 and 1988, and it is expected to triple between 1988 and the year 2000. People from the Pacific Basin countries are also traveling more. Almost 12 million Japanese took holidays abroad in the mid 1990s, a 10% increase over previous years. Forecasting demand in the face of such drastic shifts can be difficult.

To make things even more complicated, Qantas goes beyond forecasting demand to anticipate the factors that can affect its ability to meet that demand. For example, what airport facilities will be available in the future? How will this availability affect Qantas? Will there be enough skilled labor to staff and maintain its aircraft? While the demand in the Pacific Basin has skyrocketed, the support system has not. A shortage of runways and terminal space already limits the number of flights Qantas can schedule. As a result, Qantas may decide to purchase fewer but larger planes. Fewer planes would require fewer crews, and larger planes can hold more passengers at one time, making flights more profitable.

Qantas bases many important decisions on its forecasts. Perhaps the most important decision involves aircraft purchases. To meet burgeoning demand, Qantas knows that it will need more planes. But how many? At a cost of $150 million for each new Boeing 747-400, ordering even a few too many planes can reduce profits. But, if Qantas buys too few planes, it has few short-run solutions. It usually takes about 2 years to get delivery of a new plane.

If Qantas overestimates demand by even a few percentage points, it will be burdened with costly overcapacity. If it underestimates demand, it could miss out on profit opportunities and disappoint customers.

Ultimately, for Qantas the forecasting problem is more than a matter of temporary gains or losses of customer satisfaction and sales. It's a matter of survival. Thus Qantas has a lot flying on the accuracy of its forecasts.[1]

When a company finds an attractive market, it must estimate the market's current size and future potential carefully. The company can lose a lot of profit by overestimating or underestimating the market. Once a firm has a forecast of demand, it must then try to match its capacity with the projected demand. This chapter discusses measuring demand and then presents techniques to manage capacity and demand.

Measuring market demand starts with a clear understanding of the market involved.

The chapter starts with a section on **market definition** followed by a discussion of different techniques for **forecasting demand**. The chapter ends with a discussion of techniques used to **manage capacity and demand**.

The Qantas example shows the importance of forecasting demand. Like airlines, hotel companies have to commit large amounts of capital to build capacity. Long-term planning ensures that future demand will fit the company's expansion programs. Short-term forecasting is important to ensure that each hotel or restaurant maximizes its capacity. The inability to inventory products means that, if today's capacity does not match today's demand, problems can arise for the company. Businesses must turn guests away when demand exceeds capacity. If demand is less than capacity, hotel rooms go unsold and restaurant seats are empty. Many restaurants have gone out of business because they were built to handle a capacity that ended up being two to three times their demand. In many cases a smaller restaurant with less overhead would have survived. Fast-food chains are developing smaller units with a capacity that will match the demand of secondary markets. In the long run, firms must match capacity with demand.

Staffing is another important reason for forecasting. Understaffing results in poor customer service and delays that may send customers somewhere else. Overstaffing is expensive, and in tipped positions, it can result in employee dissatisfaction. Thus forecasting and adjusting the business to fit the forecasted demand are essential to a well-run business.

Market demand measurement calls for a clear understanding of the market involved. The term *market* has acquired many meanings over the years. In its original meaning, a market was a physical place where buyers and sellers gathered to exchange goods and services. Medieval towns had market squares to which sellers brought their goods and buyers shopped for them. In today's cities, buying and selling occurs in what are called shopping areas rather than markets.

DEFINING THE MARKET

To an economist, the term *market* describes all the buyers and sellers who transact over some good or service. Thus the limited-service hotel market consists of all the consumers who use limited-service hotels and the companies who supply limited-service hotel rooms. The economist is interested in the structure, conduct, and performance of each market.

To a marketer, a market is the set of all actual and potential buyers of a product or service. A **market** is the set of buyers, and the **industry** is the set of sellers. The size of the market hinges on the number of buyers who might exist for a particular market offer. Potential buyers for something have three characteristics: **interest, income**, and **access**.

Consider the market for Carnival Cruises. To assess its market, Carnival first must estimate the number of customers who have a potential interest in going on a cruise. To do this, the company could conduct a random sampling of consumers and ask the following question: "Do you have an interest in taking a cruise?" If one person out of ten says yes, Carnival can assume that 10% of the total number of consumers are the potential market for cruises. The **potential market** is the set of consumers that professes some level of interest in a particular product or service.

Consumer interest alone is not enough to define the cruise market. Potential consumers must have enough income to afford the product. They must be able to answer yes to the following question: "Can you afford to purchase a cruise?" The higher the price, the fewer the number of people who can answer yes to this question. Thus market size depends on both interest and income.

Access barriers further reduce the cruise market size. If Carnival markets its cruises in remote areas not served by travel agents, the number of potential customers in these areas is limited. The **available market** is the set of consumers that has interest, income, and access to the product.

For some market offers, Carnival might have to restrict sales to certain groups. A particular state might not allow the signing of a contractual agreement by anyone under the age of 21. The remaining adults make up the **qualified available market**—the set of consumers that has interest, income, access, and qualifications for the product.

Carnival now has the choice of going after the whole qualified available market or concentrating on select segments. Carnival's **served market** is the part of the qualified available market that it decides to pursue. For example, Carnival may decide to concentrate its marketing efforts on the East Coast, the Chicago area, and the Southwest. These areas become its served market.

Carnival and its competitors will end up selling a certain number of cruises in their served market. The **penetrated market** is the set of consumers that has bought cruises.

Figure 14-1 brings these market concepts together with some hypothetical numbers. The bar on the left of the figure shows the ratio of the potential market—all those who are interested—to the total market. Here the potential market is 10%. The bar on the right shows several possible breakdowns of the potential market. The available market—those who have interest, income, and access—is 40% of the potential market. The qualified available market—those who can meet the legal requirements—is

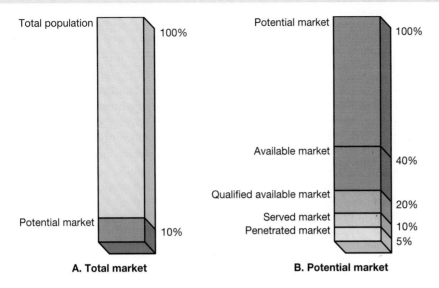

Figure 14-1
Levels of market definition.

50% of the total available market (or 20% of the potential market). Carnival concentrates its efforts on 50% of the qualified available market—the served market, which is 10% of the potential market. Finally, Carnival and its competitors already have penetrated 50% of the served market (or 5% of the potential market).

These market definitions are a useful tool for marketing planning. Carnival's management can take a number of actions if they are not satisfied with current sales. It can lobby to get the age for signing a legal contract lowered. It can expand its markets in North America or in other areas of the world. Carnival can lower its prices to expand the size of the potential market. It can try to attract more buyers from its served market through stronger promotion or distribution efforts to target current customers. Or it can try to expand the potential market by increasing advertising to convert noninterested consumers into interested consumers. This is what Carnival did when it created the "Fun Ships."

Market Areas for Restaurants

In the restaurant industry, it is common to describe market areas geographically and call them **trade areas**. Trade areas vary by type of restaurant and area description. For example, in rural areas it is common for people to make a 100-mile round trip to dine at a favorite restaurant. In contrast, 90% of the customers of a fast-food restaurant in a residential area of a major city live within 3 miles of the restaurant. People are not willing to spend a great deal of time getting a fast-food meal. But, if they eat at a specialty restaurant, such as a Hard Rock Cafe, they are willing to drive across town. Thus Hard Rock Cafe's trade area may encompass a 15-mile radius. A McDonald's in the same town may define its trade area as a 3-mile radius.

John Melaniphy, a restaurant site location expert, describes the trade area of a restaurant as an area that provides 85% of the restaurant's business. Restaurants that serve out-of-town guests can examine customers' zip codes and find out where their guests are staying while they are visiting the city.[2] He gives other factors that influence the trade area of a restaurant.[3] Topography defines trade areas. Rivers, lakes, or mountains may set boundaries. Psychological barriers can also exist. For example, expressways, airports, and industrial parks may create barriers. Demographic differences in neighborhoods can also create psychological barriers. For example, residents of a lower-class neighborhood may feel more comfortable eating in their own neighborhood than eating in a restaurant in an upper-middle-class neighborhood, even though both restaurants are the same distance from their houses and have the same average check.

Competition has a big impact on the trade area. Sometimes competition from the same chain may define a trade area. For example, in a city that has eight McDonald's, an adjacent McDonald's may set the boundaries of the trade area for another.

Traffic flows and road patterns also help define trade areas. Accessibility is an important consideration: the better the access the more extensive the trade area. People also become accustomed to traveling in certain directions and are more likely to travel 4 miles to a restaurant that they pass every day going to work than 4 miles in a direction that they infrequently travel. Thus a knowledge of normal traveling routes to major employment and shopping areas is useful in determining a trade area.

MEASURING CURRENT MARKET DEMAND

We now turn to some practical methods for estimating current market demand. Marketers will want to estimate three different aspects of current market demand: *total market demand, area market demand*, and *actual sales and market shares*.

Estimating Total Market Demand

The **total market demand** for a product or service is the total volume that would be bought by a defined consumer group in a defined geographic area in a defined time period in a defined marketing environment under a defined level and mix of industry marketing effort.

Total market demand is not a fixed number, but a function of the stated conditions. One of these conditions, for example, is the level and mix of industry marketing effort. Another is the state of the environment. Part A of Figure 14-2 shows the relationship between total market demand and these conditions. The horizontal axis shows different possible levels of industry marketing expenditure in a given time period. The vertical axis shows the resulting demand level. The curve represents the estimated level of market demand for varying levels of industry marketing expenditure. Some base sales (called the *market minimum*) would take place without any marketing expenditures. Greater marketing expenditures would yield higher levels of demand, first at an increasing rate and then at a decreasing rate. Marketing expenditures above a certain level would not cause much more demand, suggesting an upper limit to market demand called the *market potential*. The industry market forecast shows the level of market demand corresponding to the planned level of industry marketing expenditure in the given environment.[4]

The distance between the market minimum and the market potential shows the overall sensitivity of demand to marketing efforts. We can think of two extreme types of markets, the *expandable* and the *nonexpandable*. An expandable market, such as the market for air travel, is one whose size is affected by the level of industry marketing expenditures. In terms of Figure 14-2, in an expandable market, the distance between Q_1 and Q_2 would be fairly large. A nonexpandable market, such as the market for opera, is one whose size is not much affected by the level of marketing expenditures; the distance between Q_1 and Q_2 would be fairly small. Organizations selling in a nonexpandable market can take **primary demand**—total demand for all brands of a given product or service—as a given. They concentrate their marketing resources on building **selective demand**—demand for *their* brand of the product or service.

Given a different marketing environment, we must estimate a new demand curve. Figure 14-2 shows the relationship of market demand to the environment. A given level of marketing expenditure will always result in more demand during prosperity than it would during a recession. The main point is that marketers should carefully define the situation for which they are estimating market demand.

Estimating Area Market Demand

Companies face the problem of selecting the best sales territories and allocating their marketing budget optimally among these territories. Therefore, they need to estimate the market potential of different cities, states, and even national markets (see Marketing Highlight 14-1). Two major methods are available: the *market-buildup method* and the *market-factor index method*. The market-buildup method calls for identifying all the potential buyers in each market and estimating their potential purchases. The market-factor index method is used in the fast-food industry.

Figure 14-2
Market demand.

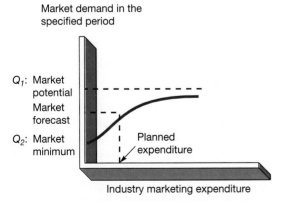

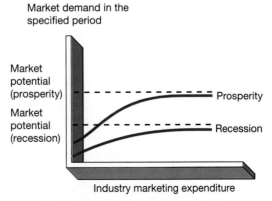

A. Market demand as a function of industry marketing expenditure (assumes a marketing environment of prosperity)

B. Market demand as a function of industry marketing expenditures (under prosperity vs. recession)

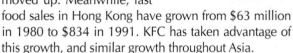

Marketing Highlight 14-1

KFC Finds More Potential in Asia Than in the United States

Kentucky Fried Chicken's success in Asia dramatizes the case for becoming a global firm. Had PepsiCo's KFC Corporation remained only a domestic U.S. business, its overall fortunes would have fallen. In 1991, for example, its U.S. sales fell 5 percent as health-minded American consumers reduced their intake of fried foods and as other fast-food competitors moved up. Meanwhile, fast food sales in Hong Kong have grown from $63 million in 1980 to $834 in 1991. KFC has taken advantage of this growth, and similar growth throughout Asia.

Not so in Asia. KFC, not McDonald's, is the fast-food leader in China, South Korea, Malaysia, the Middle East, Thailand, and Indonesia, and it is second to only McDonald's in Japan and Singapore. KFC's 1,800 outlets average $1.2 million per store, about 60 percent more than its average U.S. stores. No wonder KFC plans to double its number of Asian outlets during the next five years.

Why is KFC so successful in Asia? First, many of the large Asian cities have a growing concentration of young middle-class urban workers with rising incomes. Fast-food outlets represent a step up from buying food at hawkers' stalls, and Asians are willing to pay more for the quality and comfort of sitting in a well-decorated, American-style restaurant. Second, Asian women have been entering the labor force in large numbers, leaving them with less time for cooking meals at home. Third, chicken is more familiar to the Asian palate than burgers, and more available than beef. Further, chicken faces none of the religious strictures that beef faces in India or that pork faces in Muslim countries.

KFC serves its standard chicken, mashed potatoes, and cole slaw throughout Asia but has offered a few adaptations, such as Hot Wings, a spicier chicken, in Thailand, and fried fish and chicken curry in Japan.

Clearly, companies must increasingly view the world as their market. They must identify those areas that promise the greatest potential sales and profit growth, whether in their neighborhood, state, nation, or the world beyond.

Sources: See Andrew Tanzer, "Hot Wings Take Off," *Forbes* (January 18, 1993), p. 74, and Li Lan and Mahmood A. Khan, "Hong Kong's Fast-Food Industry," *Cornell Hotel and Restaurant Quarterly,* June 1995, pp. 34–41.

A common method for calculating area market potential is to identify market factors that correlate with market potential and combine them into a weighted index.

Many companies compute additional area demand measures. Marketers now can refine state-by-state and city-by-city measures down to census tracts or ZIP code centers. Census tracts are small areas about the size of a neighborhood, and ZIP code centers (designed by the U.S. Post Office) are larger areas, often the size of small towns. Information on population size, family income, and other characteristics is available for each type of unit. Marketers can use these data for estimating demand in neighborhoods or other smaller geographic units within large cities.

Estimating Actual Sales and Market Shares

Besides estimating total and area demand, a company will want to know the actual industry sales in its market. Thus it must identify its competitors and estimate their sales. The industry's trade association often will collect and publish total industry sales, although not listing individual company sales separately. In this way, each company can evaluate its performance against the industry as a whole. Suppose that the company's sales are increasing at a rate of 5% a year and industry sales are increasing at 10%. This company is actually losing its relative standing in the industry.

Forecasting is the art of estimating future demand by anticipating what buyers are likely to do under a given set of conditions. For example, an association wants to book 100 rooms for three nights in a 250-room hotel next year. They will pay $95 per room per night. The current rate structure of the hotel is as follows: rack rate $150, corporate rate $125, and average rate $105. Should the manager take the 300 room nights at a low rate or does the manager turn down this request for $28,500 of business. Without forecasting, it is difficult to answer this question. Forecasts help managers maximize their profits.

Most markets do not have a stable industry or company demand, so good forecasting becomes a key factor in company success. Poor forecasting can lead to overstaffing and excess inventories or understaffing and running out of products. The more unstable the demand, the more the company needs accurate forecasts and elaborate forecasting procedures.

Forecasting Methods

Many firms base their forecasts on past sales. They assume that the causes of past sales can be uncovered through statistical analysis and that analysts can use the causal relations to predict future sales. One popular method, **time-series analysis**, consists of breaking down the original sales into four components—trend, cycle, season, and erratic components—and then recombining these components to produce the sales forecast. **Trend** is the long-term, underlying pattern of growth or decline in sales resulting from basic changes in population, capital formation, and technology. It is found by fitting a straight line through past sales.

Cycle captures the medium-term wave movement of sales resulting from changes in general, economic, and competitive activity. The cyclical component can be useful for medium-range forecasting. Cyclical swings, however, are difficult to predict because they do not occur at regular intervals.

Season refers to a consistent pattern of weekly, monthly, or quarterly sales movements within the year. In the hospitality industry, we usually think of seasonal changes on a yearly basis, but weekly and hourly sales changes are important. The seasonal component can be related to weather factors, holidays, and trade customs. The seasonal pattern provides a norm for forecasting short-range sales. Yield management depends on forecasting demand by day, by flight or cruise, and by hour of the day. Historical sales patterns are carefully analyzed, such as examining sales for Tuesdays of the second week of September or total passengers and the mix of passengers on flight 482 each Wednesday afternoon at 3:30. Forecasting in the airline industry is further complicated by the presence of interconnecting stops. Large hospitality companies such as airlines, hotel chains, and car rental firms, such as Hertz, depend on sophisticated software to analyze huge volumes of data.

Finally, **erratic events** include fads, strikes, snowstorms, earthquakes, riots, fires, and other disturbances. These components, by definition, are unpredictable and should be removed from past data to reveal the more normal behavior of sales. Most of these events cannot be accurately forecasted, but a few, such as snowstorms and strikes, lend themselves to short-run forecasting. Hotel managers in Washington, D.C., know that, if a major snowstorm is predicted for the city, room demand will increase. Visitors will be unable to leave the city and will want to retain their rooms. Office workers may be unable to return home and will also want a room. Managers who have a knowledge of the past behavior of demand when erratic events occurred can factor this into their thinking in times of crisis management.

The first step in managing demand is understanding the factors that affect the demand of the firm's market segments. The payday of a major employer may drive area customer demand. For example, in north Dallas the Friday and Saturday nights after a payday at Texas Instruments are much busier than nonpayday weekends. There also may be seasonal variations. The Boulders, a resort in Arizona, charges more than $500 a room in season, yet closes in July and August because of a lack of demand for rooms at less than half this price. Holiday periods have a positive influence on demand at most resorts. Business travel drops off between mid-December and mid-January, during the summer period, and over weekends. Although there is fluctuation in demand, much of the fluctuation can be explained. Managers must understand the factors that drive demand and build it into their forecasts.

Suppose that a 250-room hotel had an occupancy of 76%, selling 69,350 room nights during the year at an average rate of $80. During the last 7 years the number of room nights sold and average rate have both increased by 5%. The hotel has undergone two expansions to keep up with the growth. This information suggests that next year the hotel will sell 72,818 room nights (69,350 $\times$ 1.05) at an average rate of $84 (1.05 $\times$ $80). The manager first has to determine whether the hotel has the capacity to handle the increase. If the hotel sold out to business travelers from Tuesday to Thursday during February through May and September through October, it is unrealistic to expect that the growth will continue at a 5% rate since it will be constrained by capacity. The only opportunity to increase occupancy is during the low-demand periods.

Let us assume that a recession is expected next year. As a result, the number of room nights is expected to drop by 10%, and the average rate is expected to decrease by 15% as competitors cut their rates to attract customers. If the manager did not factor in the recession and projected based solely on past information, the occupancy and average room rate would be greatly overstated. Taking the recession into consideration, the forecast will call for a lower occupancy at a greatly reduced room rate.

When a forecast calls for a decrease in sales, it is important to document the reasons for the decrease. This is especially true of regional recessions. A regional economy with a heavy dependence on one industry can suffer a regional recession when that industry declines, while the rest of the country enjoys prosperity. When the hotel management sends its forecast showing a decline in sales to the home office, it will be rejected unless it is well supported. In many cases when a director of sales has presented a marketing plan calling for a decrease in sales without supporting documents to defend the projected decrease, corporate management required the director of sales to increase the forecast. In this scenario, the hotel fails to meet the revised forecast, and the director of sales is fired for not meeting the sales goal. Managers must forecast accurately and provide information to support their forecasts.

Statistical Demand Analysis

Time-series analysis views past and future sales as a function of time, rather than as a function of any real demand factors. But many factors affect the sales of any product. **Statistical demand analysis** is a set of statistical procedures used to discover the most important real factors affecting sales and their relative influence. The factors most commonly analyzed are prices, income, population, and promotion.

Statistical demand analysis consists of expressing sales (Q) as a dependent variable and trying to explain sales as a function of several independent demand variables $X_1, X_2, ..., X_n$. That is,

$$Q = f(x_1, x_2, ..., X_n)$$

Using a technique called multiple-regression analysis, various equation forms can be statistically fitted to the data in the search for the best predicting factors and equation.[5]

For example, a restaurant near Marquette University in Milwaukee, Wisconsin, found that its sales were explained by whether Marquette University was in session and the previous week's sales.[6]

$$Q = 2614.3 + 1610.7X_1 + 0.2605X_2$$

where X_1 is a dummy variable* indicating whether Marquette was in session, with 1 given when it was in session and 0 used when it was not in session and X_2 is last week's sales. For example, if Marquette had just finished a term and management wanted to predict sales for next week when last week's sales were $6000, forecast sales for next week would be

$$
\begin{aligned}
Q &= 2614.3 + 1610.7X_1 + 0.2605X_2 \\
&= 2614.3 + 1610.7(0) + 0.2605(6000) \\
&= 2614.3 + 0 + 1563 = \$4177.30
\end{aligned}
$$

The manager could also expect a gradual decline in sales (since the previous week's sales will be falling) as activity around the campus slows

---

*The researcher used a dummy variable to give a value to nominal data; it is called a dummy variable because the value is given by the researcher.

down. For example, if the restaurant achieved the forecasted sales of $4177.30, the next week's projected sales would be $3702.49. The decline is due to the drop in the previous week's sales from $6000 to $4176.30. Sales for the restaurant when the university is not in session will level off at $3535 in the sixth week of the break.

Two cautions apply to the use of regression in forecasting. First, the above equation will not be sensitive to extraordinary events. For example, on parents' weekend the restaurant may generate very high sales. The equation does not include parents' weekend as a variable; therefore, it is unable to project sales accurately for this event. The sales for the week after parents' weekend will be overstated since the figure for the previous week (parents' weekend) will be extraordinarily high. Second, it is dangerous to forecast outside the range of the different variables used to build the forecast. For example, if a manager examines the relationship between advertising and room sales, the manager may find that room sales increase $5 for every dollar spent on advertising. If the hotel advertising expenditures had ranged from $75,000 to $150,000, we could not necessarily expect this relationship to hold up for advertising expenditures of $250,000, since this level of advertising has not been tested.

The above cautions illustrate two types of errors caused by the misuse of regression analysis. Statistical demand analysis can be very complex, and the marketer must take care in designing, conducting, and interrupting such analysis. Yet constantly improving computer technology has made statistical demand analysis an increasingly popular approach to forecasting.

Two other forecasting techniques used in the hospitality industry are moving average and exponential smoothing. A **moving average** is the average of a set number of previous periods (n); this average is used to predict sales for the next period. For example, if a restaurant had sales of $12,000, $12,500, $13,000, and $12,500 over the last 4 weeks, using a 4-week moving average, the sales forecast for the next week would be $12,500.

$$\frac{\$12,000 + \$12,500 + \$13,000 + \$12,500}{4} = \$12,500$$

A limitation of moving averages is that the latest period used in the average has the same weight as the current period. **Exponential smoothing** is a simple, but useful mathematical technique, which allows recent periods to be weighted.[7]

The forecasting techniques presented in this chapter represent a few of the techniques used by managers. It is not within the scope of this book to provide a detailed explanation of all forecasting techniques. We simply want to illustrate that tools are available to assist managers with their forecasts.

MANAGING CAPACITY

Managers have two major options for matching capacity with demand: change capacity or change demand. For example, an airline can change capacity on a heavily traveled route by assigning a larger plane to the route. If a larger plane is not available, they can reduce demand by eliminating discounted fares. This section will discuss capacity management, and the next section will focus on demand management.

Corporate management is responsible for matching capacity with demand on a long-term basis, while unit managers are responsible for matching capacity with fluctuations in short-term demand. The techniques presented in this section assist in managing short-term demand. The actions managers can take to adjust to short-term capacity include the following:

1. Involve the customer in the service delivery system.
2. Cross-train employees.
3. Use part-time employees.
4. Rent or share extra facilities and equipment.
5. Schedule downtime during periods of low capacity.
6. Extend service hours.
7. Use technology.[8]
8. Use price.

Involve the Customer in the Service Delivery System

Getting the customer involved in service operations expands the number of people that one employee can serve, thus expanding the capacity of the operation. The concept has wide acceptance in food and beverage operations, but modern technology is responsible for its increasing use in the accommodation sector.

Food and beverage operations can develop systems that permanently involve customers in service delivery or use customer involvement as a way to increase capacity during extremely busy periods. Many convention hotels have self-service food and beverage operations. Examples of kiosks or self-service coffee shops can be found in the Loew's Anatole in Dallas, the Wyndham Greenspoint in Dallas, and Stouffer's Hotel in Orlando. These operations can serve many people in a short time. They feature premade sandwiches and salads, enabling the operator to build a buffer inventory. When a meeting breaks and a number of the participants want a meal or snack, these operations have the capacity to serve many people quickly.

On the rooms side, hotels have taken advantage of technology that enables the customer to check in through a computer. Guests who choose to use the computer avoid standing in line at the front desk, which takes pressure off the lines. The above examples illustrate how managers can use customers to increase the capacity of service delivery systems.

Some fast-food operations have customers get their own drinks, making it possible for employees to handle more customers. It is particularly effective for a restaurant when the food is customized for the guest and the guest has to wait for the food. Examples of this type of restaurant are Burger King, Subway, and Taco Bell. The task occupies customers during their wait, reducing the perceived wait.

Besides permanent service delivery systems, hotels and restaurants can develop temporary systems for periods of unusually high demand. In

Chapter 2 we gave the example of hotels increasing their capacity by offering special buffets on Mother's Day. Some hotels also serve breakfast buffets when they know that the house will be full and that there are large meetings booked without a breakfast function. The breakfast buffet allows them to move people in and out of the restaurant. Using customers as self-servers is one way hospitality firms can increase their capacity.

Cross-train Employees

In a hotel the demand for all services does not rise and fall in unison. One outlet may experience sudden strong demand while other areas enjoy normal levels. When managers cross-train their employees, they can shift employees to increase the capacity. A hotel restaurant that does only 30 to 40 covers a night cannot justify more than two service people, even though it may have 80 seats. However, such low staffing levels mean that the restaurant may have a difficult time serving more than 60 guests, especially if they arrive at about the same time. Having front-desk staff and banquet staff that are trained in a la carte service means that the restaurant manager has a group of employees that can be called on if demand for the restaurant on any particular night exceeds the capacity of two service people. It also provides the manager with a group of substitute service people who can fill in should a regularly scheduled employee call in sick. Cross-training employees gives the operation flexibility by allowing the business to increase capacity by shifting employees and can help to prevent the organization from reducing capacity when an employee calls in sick.

Use Part-time Employees

Managers can use part-time employees to expand capacity during an unusually busy day or meal period or during the busy months of the year for seasonal businesses. Summer resorts hire part-time staff to work during the summer period. They reduce their staff during the slower seasons and either reduce staff further or close during the low season. Part-time employees allow a hotel or restaurant to efficiently increase or decrease its capacity. Part-time employees can also be used on an on-call basis. Hotels usually have a list of banquet waiters to call for large events. Part-time employees give an organization the flexibility to adjust the number of employees to the level required to meet demand.

Rent or Share Extra Facilities and Equipment

Businesses do not have to be constrained by space limitations or equipment limitations. A hotel with an opportunity to book a 3-day meeting from Tuesday to Thursday may have to turn down the business because all the function space is booked Wednesday evening and there is no space for the group's Wednesday evening dinner. Rather than lose the group, a creative solution would be to suggest the group go outside the hotel for a unique dinner experience. In Paris, the alternative might be a dinner cruise on the Seine. In Arizona it might be an outdoor steak fry, while in Hong Kong it could be a dinner at Jumbo, the famous floating restaurant.

This Clock Tower in Bermuda doubles as a meeting room. Hotels can expand their meeting space by use of off-premise locations for functions. Courtesy of the Bermuda Department of Tourism.

Hotels and restaurants can also work with sister properties. In Fiji, the Regent and Sheraton are within walking distance of each other on Denru Island, and EIE owns both hotels. Although different companies manage the hotels, they work together if it means getting a piece of business for the island. Omni has three hotels on Canton Road in Hong Kong. These hotels refer business to each other. When a property is capacity constrained, alliances with other businesses can be beneficial to both.

Catering firms often purchase only the amount of equipment that they will regularly use. When they have a busy period, they rent equipment. Renting, sharing, or moving groups to outside facilities can increase capacity to accommodate short-term demand.

Schedule Downtime during Periods of Low Capacity

Businesses in seasonal resorts have periods of high and low demand. The actions we have discussed so far enable a business to increase capacity to meet peak demand. There are also cases when a business needs to handle low-demand periods as efficiently as possible by decreasing capacity. One way to decrease capacity is to schedule repairs and maintenance during the low season. Employees can take vacations during periods of low demand or be utilized for other activities. Wet n' Wild, a water park in Las Vegas, uses employees to print and collate its marketing material during the off season. As a result, several key employees can be kept on the payroll year round. The employees develop and build marketing kits to be used in the coming season. Shifting activities is one way of reducing the negative effects of slow periods and ensuring maximum capacity during busy periods. Training can also be scheduled for slow periods.

Extend Service Hours

Restaurants and entertainment facilities can increase capacity by extending their hours. A hotel coffee shop that is full by 7:30 A.M. may find it useful to open at 6:30 A.M. instead of 7:00. If five tables arrive in the first half-hour, these should be free in about a half-hour, allowing the restaurant to have more tables available during the peak period. Leaps and Bounds, a child's entertainment center that is normally closed at night, offers all-night parties for groups of 20 or more. When the demand exists, they supply the capacity by opening at night. Fast-food operations have expanded their capacity by opening for breakfast. Many businesses can increase their capacity by expanding their hours of operation.

Use Technology

Phone systems with automatic wake-up capability allow many guests to receive wake-up calls simultaneously. Although a wake-up call from a computer is impersonal, it ensures that guests in large hotels receive their wake-up calls in a timely and accurate manner. Technology will become increasingly important as advances are made in robotics. Technology also makes it easier to involve the customer in the service delivery system.

Use Price

As previously discussed, there is a relationship between pricing strategy and capacity management. Car rental firms attempt to manage capacity through the use of one-way drop fees. A spokesperson for Avis said, "You lose too much business if your cars are in another part of the country and everyone wants to rent from you."

Alamo Rent-A-Car offered daily rates in Houston as low as $18, but if the car was driven into Louisiana and dropped at New Orleans, the cost would be an additional $600.[9] Conversely, rent-a-car companies may offer low or no drop-off rates to areas where they need cars.

MANAGING DEMAND

In an ideal situation, managers simply expand capacity to meet demand. However, during a city-wide convention, a hotel may receive requests for rooms that exceed its capacity. The Saturday before Christmas, a restaurant could book more banquets if it had space, and during a summer holiday a resort could sell more rooms, if it had them. All successful hospitality businesses become capacity constrained. Capacity management allows a business to increase its capacity, but it will not prevent situations where demand exceeds capacity. Besides managing capacity, managers must manage demand. The following strategies for managing demand will be discussed.

1. Use price to create or reduce demand.
2. Use reservations.
3. Overbook.
4. Use queuing.
5. Shift demand.

6. Change the salesperson's assignment.
7. Create promotional events.

Use Price to Create or Reduce Demand

Pricing is one method used to manage demand. In Chapter 12 we saw that price is inversely related to demand for most products. Managers can create more demand for a product by lowering its price. To create demand, restaurants offer specials on slow days. For example, some Subway restau-

Airlines have many different fare classes. Lower fare classes are closed when demand is high and opened when demand is low. Courtesy of Southwest Airlines.

THE LOW
LOWER
LOWEST
FARES IN THE AIR.

Unrestricted Fare, One-Way
$69
Sacramento to LAX

14-Day Advance Purchase Fare, One-Way
$59
Sacramento to LAX

Friends Fly Free
FREE
Sacramento to LAX

As the airline that invented low fares, it's only natural that we offer you a *choice* of low fares. So here goes: First, there's our low everyday, unrestricted fare—good on every seat, every flight, every day. Next, our lower 14-day advance purchase, no stayover fare—the fare that doesn't penalize you if your plans change because it's fully refundable. And finally, our Friends Fly Free fare. The only fare that lets you bring along a friend, absolutely free, with the purchase of a roundtrip unrestricted-fare ticket. (Tickets are fully refundable and reservations are required.) So fly Southwest Airlines. And pick your favorite low.

SERVICE STARTS SEPTEMBER 7

SOUTHWEST
THE *Low Fare Airline*™
Call your travel agent or 1-800-I-FLY-SWA.

Seats are limited and some restrictions apply on 14-day fare and Friends Fly Free. Does not include Passenger Facility Charge of $6 roundtrip. ©1994 Southwest Airlines

rants, a submarine sandwich shop, offer two-for-one specials on Tuesdays. Port of Subs (a competitor) offers special discounts after 5 P.M., because most people do not eat sandwiches for the evening meal. Resorts lower prices during the off season, and city hotels offer weekend specials. As mentioned in Chapter 12, managers must make sure that the market segments attracted by the lower price are their desired targets.

When demand exceeds capacity, managers raise prices to lower demand. On New Year's Eve, many restaurants and nightclubs offer set menus and packages that exceed the normal average check. They realize that, even with higher prices, demand remains sufficient to fill to capacity. Chapter 13 described two pricing techniques used to manage demand: price discrimination and yield management.

Use Reservations

Hotels and restaurants often use reservations to monitor demand. When it appears that they will have more demand than capacity, managers can save capacity for the more profitable segments. Reservations can also limit demand by allowing managers to refuse any further reservations when capacity meets demand.

Although reservations in restaurants can help manage demand, they can also decrease capacity. This is the reason high-volume mid-priced restaurants do not usually take reservations. A group may arrive 10 minutes late or one couple of a two-couple party may arrive on time and wait 20 minutes at the table until the other shows up. The estimated times of customer arrival and departure may not fit precisely, resulting in tables remaining empty for 20 minutes or more. In high-priced restaurants, guests expect to reserve a table and have it ready when they arrive. Customers of mid-priced restaurants have different expectations, allowing popular restaurants to increase their capacity by having customers queue and wait for the next available table. Queues allow managers to inventory demand for short periods of time and fill every table immediately when it becomes available, eliminating dead time.

A few restaurants serve patrons on long picnic style tables similar to those in German beer halls. Customers are mixed together even though they may not know one another. This system helps with the issue of capacity, but has definite restrictions for use in the marketplace.

To maximize capacity, some restaurants accept reservations for seating at designated times. For example, they may have six o'clock, eight o'clock, and ten o'clock seatings. When customers call to make a reservation, the receptionist makes them aware of the seating times and lets them know that the table is theirs for up to 2 hours. After 2 hours, another party will be waiting to use the table. The use of seatings increases capacity by ensuring that the restaurant will have three turns and by shifting demand. As the eight o'clock seating fills, managers can shift demand to either six or ten o'clock depending on the customer's preference.

In cases where demand is greater than capacity, guests can be asked to prepay or make a deposit. For example, some New Year's Eve parties at hotels and restaurants require that guests purchase their tickets in advance. Resorts often require a nonrefundable deposit with a reservation. By requiring an advance payment, managers help to ensure that revenue matches capacity. If a customer fails to arrive, the resort does not lose revenue.

Reservation systems can be very complex. It is not within the scope of this text to explore the variations of reservations for hotels, restaurants, and other hospitality organizations.

Overbook

Not everyone who reserves a table or books a room shows up. Plans change and people with reservations become no shows. Overbooking is another method that hotels, restaurants, trains, and airlines use to match demand with capacity. Hotel managers who limit reservations to the number of available rooms frequently find themselves with empty rooms. For example, at one hotel 20% of guests holding nonguaranteed reservations and 5% of those holding guaranteed reservations typically do not honor those reservations. If this hotel had 80 guaranteed reservations and 40 nonguaranteed reservations, it will, on average, be left with 12 empty rooms. For a hotel with an average room rate of $75, this can mean a potential annual loss of more than $500,000 in room and food and beverage revenue.

Overbooking must be carefully managed. When a hotel fails to honor its reservations, it risks losing the future business of guests whose reservations are not honored and possibly the business of their companies and travel agents. Usually, it is better to leave a room unoccupied than to fail to honor a reservation.

Developing a good overbooking policy minimizes the chance of walking a guest. This requires knowing the no-show rate of different types of reservations. Groups who reserve rooms should be investigated to see what percent of their room block they have filled in the past. One study found that reservations made one day before arrival and on the day of arrival had a higher no-show rate than reservations made much earlier.[10] Through an analysis of the types of reservations, the time when the reservation is made, and the segment making the reservation, a model can be built to develop an overbooking policy.

Some hotels do nothing for the traveler whose reservation is not honored. However, many hotels find alternative accommodations, pay for one night's stay at the new hotel, and provide transportation to the hotel. They may also give the guest a free phone to inform those back home of the new arrangements and keep the guest's name on their information rack so that they can refer any phone calls the guest may receive to the hotel where the guest is staying. Smart managers try to get turned-away guests back by offering a free night's stay at their hotel the next day. Hotels that are careless in handling their reservations can be held liable. In one case a travel agent, Rainbow Travel Service, reserved 45 rooms with the Fontainebleau Hilton for clients going to the Miami-Oklahoma football game. The Fontainebleau walked a number of Rainbow's clients and Rainbow sued for damage to its reputation. A jury awarded the travel agency $250,000. The jury believed the Fontainebleau should have altered their policy of overbooking by 15% because of the demand created by the football weekend.[11]

Overbooking is one method of managing demand. It can increase demand by compensating for no shows, but managers should use it judiciously. Turning away guests who have reservations destroys long-term relationships with customers, their companies, and their travel agents.

Amtrak faces a particularly difficult management problem regarding no shows. Amtrak overbooks only 5% to 10% of seats because its trains leave once a day and too much overbooking would strand passengers. Airlines can place an overbooked passenger on the next flight, so the reservations systems of airlines don't declare a flight oversold until it has been overbooked by 20%.[12]

Booking Curve Analysis

Yield management professionals include booking curve analysis in the decision making process. An awareness of booking curves is important to sales and marketing managers throughout the hospitality industry.

Convention and conference planners witness a pattern in which reservations occur. Assume that a conference is announced and promoted 90 days prior to the conference date. A certain percentage of reservations will occur in stages during the 90 days. In recent years, planners complain that the booking curve has shortened, with most reservations occurring near the conference date. Organizers of a conference on yield management noticed that 80% of the reservations were made 10 days or less prior to the conference. This is a nightmare situation for a conference organizer and the hotel, because attendance predictions must be delayed.

Information regarding when reservations or orders occur should be routinely documented and stored by hospitality marketers. An analysis of booking curves provides valuable information for use in forecasting and better managing capacity. Figure 14-3 shows how booking curve analysis is used in the hotel industry.

Use Queuing

Earlier in this chapter, the taking of reservations was mentioned as a method of inventorying demand. When capacity exceeds demand and guests are willing to wait, queues will form. Sometimes guests make the decision to wait; in other cases they have no choice. For example, when the host tells a restaurant guest that there will be a 40-minute wait, the guest can either go somewhere else or accept the wait. At check-in, hotel guests may not have a choice. A taxi has dropped them at the hotel where they have made a reservation. They have told their business associates where they will be staying. As a result, they will endure the 20-minute wait at check-in.

Voluntary queues, such as waits at restaurants, are a common and effective way of managing demand. Good management of the queue can make the wait more tolerable for the guest. Always overestimate the wait. It is better to tell guests it will be a 35-minute wait, when the estimated wait is 30 minutes, than to tell them they will have a 20-minute wait. Some managers fear that if the wait is too long they will lose guests, so they "shorten" the wait time. Once customers have accepted the wait time, they may sit down and have a drink, but they tend to keep their eyes on their watches. When their names have not been called after the allotted time, they run up

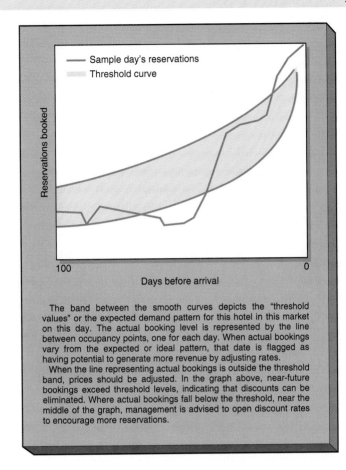

The band between the smooth curves depicts the "threshold values" or the expected demand pattern for this hotel in this market on this day. The actual booking level is represented by the line between occupancy points, one for each day. When actual bookings vary from the expected or ideal pattern, that date is flagged as having potential to generate more revenue by adjusting rates.

When the line representing actual bookings is outside the threshold band, prices should be adjusted. In the graph above, near-future bookings exceed threshold levels, indicating that discounts can be eliminated. Where actual bookings fall below the threshold, near the middle of the graph, management is advised to open discount rates to encourage more reservations.

Figure 14-3
Booking curve analysis. Reprinted by permission of Elsevier Science Inc. from "The Yield Management Approach to Hotel Room Pricing," by Walter J. Relihan, III, *Cornell Hotel and Restaurant Administration Quarterly,* vol. 30, no. 1, p. 43, ©1989 by Cornell University.

to the host and ask where they are on the list. When guests wait longer than they were told they would, they go to their dining table upset and in a mood that makes them tend to look for other service failures. It can be difficult for the restaurant to recover from this initial failure, and many guests leave with memories of an unsatisfactory experience.

If the host tells guests it will be a 35-minute wait and then seats them in 30 minutes, the guests will be delighted. If a guest decides not to accept the wait, the host can suggest a time when the wait will be shorter.

In general, the higher the level of service, the longer the guest is willing to wait. Twenty minutes for sit-down service might be acceptable, while a five-minute wait at a fast-food restaurant will be unacceptable. Fast-food restaurants must raise their capacity to meet demand or lose customers.[13]

David Maister, a service expert, provides the following tips for the management of a waiting line.[14]

Unoccupied Time Feels Longer Than Occupied Time

The Showboat Hotel has a magician who entertains guests waiting to check in at the front desk. The entertainment makes a 10-minute wait pass very quickly. Entertainment parks have characters who talk to kids in waiting lines, occupying time and making the wait pass faster. Restaurants send customers waiting for a dinner table into their cocktail lounge, where a cocktail and a conversation make the time pass more quickly. The Rio Hotel places television monitors over the line for their buffet. The monitors promote different products that the resort has to offer, such as their entertainment and other food and beverage outlets. These are a few examples of how managers can occupy guests' time and make their wait more enjoyable.

Unfair Waits Are Longer Than Equitable Waits

Guests can become upset and preoccupied with a wait if they feel that they are being treated unfairly. Restaurants with a limited number of large tables try to maximize the capacity of these tables. For example, rather than put a party of four at a table for six, the restaurant will seat a party of six at the table, even if there are several parties of four in front of them. This sometimes leads to anger on the part of the guests in the passed-over party of four. Because they were next, they feel the host should seat them next. In such cases, the host should explain what is going on to the next party in line. Another example of an unfair wait is when a guest who has been waiting for 20 minutes to check in finally reaches the front of the line. Just as he is starting to give the details of his reservation to the front desk clerk, the phone rings. The phone is promptly answered by the clerk, who gets involved in a 10-minute conversation with the caller. Marriott has started a policy of removing phones from the front desk to avoid this distraction and eliminate unfair waits.

Maister states that the customer's sense of equity is not always obvious and needs to be managed. Whatever priority rules apply, the service provider must make vigorous efforts to ensure that these rules match with the customer's sense of equity, either by adjusting the rules or by convincing the client that the rules are appropriate.

Shift Demand

It is often possible to shift the demand for banquets and meetings. A sales manager may want to set up a sales meeting for the end of October or the beginning of November and knows that, when the hotel is called to check availability, a date must be given. Suppose that October 31 is picked, although it could have been October 24 or November 7 just as easily. Twenty rooms will be needed the night before and a meeting room the day of the event. The hotel is forecast to sell out on October 31, but presently has rooms available. The smart manager asks whether October 31 is a firm date. If the date is flexible, the manager will shift the date to a period when the hotel is not projected to sell out.

Change the Salesperson's Assignment

In hotels, the director of sales assigns salespeople to specific segments. If a soft spot is forecast 2 months in the future, the director of sales can focus more effort on short-term business in an attempt to fill the soft period. This can be accomplished by shifting a salesperson from the association market, which books a year or more out, to the corporate market, which can produce bookings in a month or less.

Create Promotional Events

An object of promotion is to shift the demand curve to the left. Casinos have slot tournaments and table game tournaments during their slow periods as a way of building up business. The Sheraton Inn in Steamboat Springs, Colorado, developed "The Way It Wuz Days" to promote summer business. This campaign brought local businesses together to develop summer business for this seasonal ski resort. During slow periods, creative promotions can be an effective way of building business.

Chapter Review

I.   Definition of Market. A market is the set of all actual and potential buyers of a product or service. A market is the set of buyers, and the industry is the set of sellers.

    1) Potential buyers have three characteristics: interest, income, and access.

    2) The potential market is the set of consumers that professes some level of interest in a particular product or service.

    3) The available market is the set of consumers that has interest, income, and access to the product.

    4) The qualified available market is the set of consumers that has interest, access, and qualifications for the product.

    5) The served market is the part of the qualified available market the seller decides to pursue.

    6) The penetrated market is the set of consumers that has bought the company's product.

II.   Measuring Current Market Demand. Marketers will want to estimate three different aspects of current market demand: *total market demand, area market demand*, and *actual sales and market shares.*

    1) The total market demand for a product or service is the total volume that would be bought by a defined consumer group in a defined geographic area in a defined time period in a defined marketing environment under a defined level and mix of industry marketing effort.

    2) Estimating area demand helps companies to select the best sales territories and allocate their marketing budget optimally among these territories.

    3) A company will want to know the actual industry sales in its market. Thus it must identify its competitors and estimate their sales to estimate the **actual industry sales and their market share**.

III.   Forecasting Future Demand. Forecasting is the art of estimating future demand by anticipating what buyers are likely to do under a given set of conditions. Two methods commonly used for forecasting are time-series analysis and statistical demand analysis.

    1) Time-series analysis consists of breaking down the original sales into four components: trend, cycle, season, and erratic components.

2) **Statistical demand analysis** is a set of statistical procedures used to discover the most important real factors affecting sales and their relative influence.

IV. **Managing Capacity.** Corporate management is responsible for matching capacity with demand on a long-term basis, while unit managers are responsible for matching capacity with fluctuations in short-term demand.

1) **Involve the Customer in the Service Delivery System.** Getting the customer involved in service operations expands the number of people that one employee can serve, thus expanding the capacity of the operation.

2) **Cross-train Employees.** Cross-training employees gives the operation flexibility, allowing the business to increase capacity by shifting employees, and can help to prevent the organization from reducing capacity when an employee calls in sick.

3) **Use Part-time Employees.** Managers can use part-time employees to expand capacity during an unusually busy day or meal period or during the busy months of the year for seasonal businesses.

4) **Rent or Share Extra Facilities and Equipment.** Businesses do not have to be constrained by space limitations or equipment limitations.

5) **Schedule Downtime during Periods of Low Capacity.** One way to decrease capacity is to schedule repairs and maintenance during the low season.

6) **Extend Service Hours.** Businesses can increase capacity by extending their hours.

7) **Use Technology.** Technology can be used to increase the capacity of systems. One example is the automatic wake-up call system in hotels that can make hundreds of wake-up calls in an hour.

8) **Use Price.** Price can be used to adjust capacity in companies using mobile products such as rental car companies.

V. **Managing Demand**

1) **Use Price to Create or Reduce Demand.** In most cases price and demand are inversely related.

2) **Use Reservations.** Hotels and restaurants often use reservations to monitor demand. When it appears that they will have more demand than capacity, managers can save capacity for the more profitable segments. Reservations can also limit demand by allowing managers to refuse any further reservations when capacity meets demand.

3) **Overbook.** Not everyone who reserves a table or books a room shows up. Plans change and people with reservations become no shows. Overbooking is another method that hotels, restaurants, trains, and airlines use to match demand with capacity.

4) **Booking Curve Analysis.** An analysis of booking curves provides valuable information for use in forecasting and better managing capacity.

5) **Queuing.** Voluntary queues, such as waits at restaurants, are a common and effective way of managing demand. Good management of the queue can make the wait more tolerable for the guest.

6) **Shift Demand.** It is often possible to shift the demand for banquets and meetings.

7) **Change the Salesperson's Assignment.** If a soft spot is forecast 2

months in the future, the director of sales can focus more effort on short-term business in an attempt to fill the soft period.

8) Create Promotional Events. An object of promotion is to shift the demand curve to the left.

DISCUSSION QUESTIONS

1. In market measurement and forecasting, which is the more serious problem, to overestimate demand or to underestimate it?
2. If you were opening a restaurant, how would you determine the trade area?
3. You are the director of sales of a 300-room hotel catering to the business traveler. What process would you use to forecast sales for the coming year?
4. Give some examples of how hospitality organizations involve customers in the service delivery process.
5. Should restaurants charge customers who have reservations and do not show?
6. Is it ethical for hotels to overbook?

KEY TERMS

Available market The set of consumers that has interest, income, and access to a particular product.

Cycle Cycle captures the medium-term wave movement of sales resulting from changes in the general economic and competitive activity.

Forecasting The art of estimating future demand by anticipating what buyers are likely to do under a given set of conditions.

Industry The set of the sellers of a product.

Market The set of all actual and potential buyers of a product.

Moving average The average of a set number of previous periods (n); this average is used to predict sales for the next period.

Penetrated market The set of consumers that has already purchased a particular product.

Potential market The set of consumers that has professed some level of interest in a particular product.

Qualified available market The set of consumers that has interest, income, access, and qualifications for a product.

Statistical demand analysis A set of statistical procedures used to discover the most important real factors affecting sales and their relative influence.

Season A consistent pattern of sales movements within the year.

Served market Those consumers who have interest, income, access, and qualifications for the product or service.

Time-series analysis Consists of breaking down the original sales into four components—trend, cycle, season, and erratic components—and then recombining these components to produce the sales forecast.

Trade area The area from which a restaurant draws 85% of its customers.

Trend The long-term, underlying pattern of growth or decline in sales resulting from basic changes in population, capital formation, and technology.

REFERENCES

1. See HAMISH MCDONALD, "Caught on the Hop," *Far Eastern Economic Review* (February 18, 1988), pp. 72–73; "Qantas Embarks on Major Fleet Expansion Plan," *Aviation Week and Space Technology* (June 20, 1988), pp. 39, 42–43; MICHAEL WESTLAKE, "Stand-by Room Only," *Far Eastern Economic Review* (June 2, 1988), pp. 72–75; AND PAUL PROCTOR, "Pacific Rim Carriers Struggle to Cope with Impending Traffic

Boom," *Aviation Week and Space Technology* (November 20, 1989), pp. 110–111. Additional information provided by Qantas Airways Ltd., April 1993.

2. JOHN C. MELANIPHY, *Restaurant and Fast-Food Site Selection* (New York: Wiley, 1992).

3. Ibid., pp. 55–71.

4. For further discussion see GARY L. LILIEN, PHILIP KOTLER, AND K. SRIDHAR MOORTHY, *Marketing Models* (Englewood Cliffs, New Jersey, 1992).

5. See DONALD S. TULL AND DEL I. HAWKINS, *Marketing Research: Measurement and Method* (New York: Macmillan, 1990).

6. FRANK FORST, "Forecasting Restaurant Sales Using Multiple Regression and Box–Jenkins Analysis," *Journal of Applied Business Research*, 8, no. 2, (Spring 1992), pp. 15–19.

7. For a more detailed discussion of forecasting techniques, see RAYMOND S. SCHMIDGALL, *Hospitality Industry Managerial Accounting* (East Lansing, Mich.: Educational Institute of the American Hotel and Motel Association, 1990), pp. 317–365; AND DAVID MERCER, *Marketing* (Oxford, England: Alden Press, 1992), pp. 194–241.

8. See CHRISTOPHER H. LOVELOCK, *Managing Services* (Englewood Cliffs, New Jersey: Prentice Hall, 1992); AND ROBERT G. MURDICK, BARRY RENDER, AND ROBERTA S. RUSSELL, *Service Operations Management* (Boston, Mass.: Allyn and Bacon, 1990).

9. JONATHAN DAHL, "Tracking Travel," *Wall Street Journal*, (September 27, 1994), sec. B, p. 1.

10. CAROLYN U. LAMBERT, JOSEPH M. LAMBERT, AND THOMAS P. CULLEN, "The Overbooking Question: A Simulation," *Cornell Hotel and Restaurant Administration Quarterly*, 30, no. 2 (August 1989), pp. 15–20.

11. MARK PESTRONK, "Finding hotels liable for walking guests," *Travel Weekly*, 49, no. 37 (May 7, 1990), pp. 37+.

12. JONATHAN DAHL, "Tracking Travel," sec. B, p. 1.

13. CAROLYN U. LAMBERT AND THOMAS P. CULLEN, "Balancing Service and Costs through Queuing Analysis," *Cornell Hotel and Restaurant Administration Quarterly*, 28, no. 2 (August 1987), pp. 69–72.

14. DAVID H. MAISTER, "The Psychology of Waiting Lines," *Service Encounter*, edited by John A. Czepiel, Michael R. Solomon, and Carol F. Surprenant (Lexington, Mass: D. C. Heath, 1985).

CHILE

PANAMA

PERU

ECUADOR

GUATEMALA

CHILE

BRAZIL

ECUADOR

EL SALVADOR

GUATEMALA

CHILE

ECUADOR

PERU

ECUADOR

VENEZUELA

COSTA RICA

COLOMBIA

COLOMBIA

BRAZIL

JELA

BRAZIL

VENEZUELA

CHILE

BRAZIL

NICARAGUA

MEXICO

Distribution Channels

*I*n 1991 Little Caesar's negotiated a strategic alliance with Kmart, one of the largest discount chains in the United States. According to the agreement, Kmart would replace other in-store food service with 1200 Little Caesar's over a 5-year period. Kmart would gain a brand-name restaurant for shoppers instead of the generic cafeteria/food bar previously featured. Little Caesar's would gain additional distribution and hoped that, once exposed to Little Caesar's in Kmart, the customer would also buy from traditional Little Caesar's stores. Kmart also agreed to contribute to Little Caesar's national advertising fund thus providing improved media opportunities to Little Caesar's. The management of Little Caesar's was elated.

Some franchisees were not impressed. Initially, they were upset because the agreement included carry-out sales when they had thought it would be in-store consumption only. They felt that carry-out sales would be direct competition with their stores. In response, a group of disgruntled franchisees formed the Association of Little Caesar's Franchisees (ALCF), which claimed to represent 70 franchisees who operated more than 550 stores of the 4000-unit chain. The ALCF claimed that some members had seen sales dip as much as 20% after a Kmart store opened. The ALCF also complained that Kmarts, located in the same mall as a Little Caesar's, were allowed to install a competitive Little Caesar's. A town of 5000 in North

Carolina had two Little Caesar's franchises, a new one in the Kmart and the original franchisee. The ALCF also complained that the agreement stipulated that Kmart had to contribute to national advertising, but not to the local fund. Some ALCF members felt that Kmart took away their customers while benefiting from the dollars they spent on local advertising. The ALCF was so bitter that they collected a monthly membership fee for a legal fund to bring legal action against Little Caesar's.

Not all franchisees were upset. Many thought the association with Kmart was a good move and would expose Little Caesar's name to millions of Kmart shoppers.

The Little Caesar's case shows that distribution systems are delicately balanced: What is good for one member of the channel may not be good for another, resulting in conflict and power struggles. Managers must give careful thought to the choice of distribution channels, as this can have long-term effects.[1]

Chapter 15 presents a general outline of the key concepts of distribution channels and provides an overview of the major distribution channels in the hospitality and travel industries.

First, we look at the nature of **distribution channels** and the **functions** that channels perform. Then we discuss **marketing intermediaries** used by the hospitality and travel industries.

Next we discuss how channel members **interact** and how they **organize** to do the work of the channel. We identify major distribution channel **alternatives** open to a company.

We conclude by explaining how companies **select**, **motivate**, and **evaluate** channel members.

NATURE AND IMPORTANCE OF DISTRIBUTION SYSTEMS

If we view properties as the heart of a hotel company, then distribution systems can be viewed as the company's circulatory system.[2] Distribution systems provide a steady flow of customers. A well-managed distribution system can make the difference between a market share leader and a company struggling for survival. Many hospitality companies are making greater use of the marketing channels available to them. For example, Ritz-Carlton receives a significant share of business from travel agents because of aggressively developing this channel. Marriott entered a marketing alliance with New Otani Hotels, giving Marriott exposure to Japanese travelers in North America. In return, New Otani gained Marriott's marketing expertise to help reach Americans traveling to Japan.[3] In today's competitive environment it is not enough to count on a central reservation system and your own sales force. Companies must develop increasingly complex distribution networks.

Competition, a global marketplace, electronic distribution techniques, and a perishable product have increased the importance of distribution. Innovative ways of approaching new and existing markets are needed. Globalization has meant that many hotel companies must choose foreign partners to help them market or distribute their products. Sheraton built an alliance with the Welcome Group in India, which manages Sheraton Hotels on the Indian subcontinent. New electronic distribution methods have resulted in the growth of international reservation systems such as Utell. Finally, the importance of distribution has increased because hospitality products are perishable. RCI, a time-share exchange company, uses its large membership base to negotiate special hotel rates for its members. The agreement works well for both parties: Hotels have a chance to sell rooms during a soft period, and RCI can offer its members a benefit.

NATURE OF DISTRIBUTION CHANNELS

A *distribution channel* is a set of independent organizations involved in the process of making a product or service available to the consumer or business user.[4] Development of a distribution system starts with the selection of channel members. Once members have been selected, the focus shifts to managing the channel. Distribution networks in the hospitality industry consist of contractual agreements and loosely organized alliances between independent organizations.[5]

Why Are Marketing Intermediaries Used?

Why does Shenago China sell its chinaware to restaurants through an intermediary? Doing so means giving up control over pricing the products. But Shenago also gains advantages from selling through an intermediary. The company does not have to maintain several display rooms and a large sales force in every major city. Instead, a restaurant supply company displays, promotes, and makes personal sales calls. The restaurant supply house sells hundreds of other items. Their large assortment makes them a convenient supplier to the restaurant industry. The sales potential from their product assortment allows them to make personal sales calls, send catalogs, and provide other support for the products that they represent. Selling through wholesalers and retailers usually is much more efficient than direct sales.

The use of intermediaries depends on their greater efficiency in making goods available to target markets. Through their contacts, experience, specialization, and scale of operation, intermediaries normally offer more than a firm can on its own. Figure 15-1 shows one way that intermediaries can provide economies. Part A shows three producers, each using direct marketing to reach three customers. This system requires nine different contacts. Part B shows three producers working through one distributor.

Figure 15-1
How a distributor reduces the number of channel transactions.

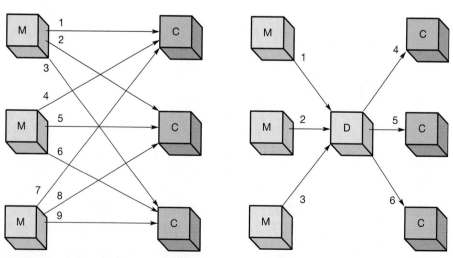

A. Number of contacts without a distributor
M x C = 3 x 3 = 9

M = Manufacturer   C = Customer

B. Number of contacts with a distributor
M x C = 3 + 3 = 6

D = Distributor

This system requires only six contacts. A restaurant manager can make one call to a restaurant supply house and order a French knife, a dozen plates, a case of candles, a dozen oyster forks, a case of wine glasses, and a case of cocktail napkins. Each of these items is produced by a different manufacturer, but they are all available through one phone call. To the purchaser, this means access to small quantities of products, since these become part of a large order. This reduces inventory requirements, number of deliveries, and number of processed invoices.

Distribution Channel Functions

A distribution channel moves goods from producers to consumers. It overcomes the major time, place, and possession gaps that separate goods and services from those who would use them. Members of the marketing channel perform many key functions:

- *Information.* Gathering and distributing marketing research and intelligence information about the marketing environment.
- *Promotion.* Developing and spreading persuasive communications about an offer.
- *Contact.* Finding and communicating with prospective buyers.
- *Matching.* Shaping and fitting the offer to the buyer's needs, including such activities as manufacturing, grading, assembling, and packaging.
- *Negotiation.* Agreeing on price and other terms of the offer so that ownership or possession can be transferred.
- *Physical distribution.* Transporting and storing goods.
- *Financing.* Acquiring and using funds to cover the costs of channel work.
- *Risk taking.* Assuming financial risks such as the inability to sell inventory at full margin.

The first five functions help to complete transactions. The last three help to fulfill the completed transactions.

All these functions have three things in common: They use scarce resources, they can often be performed better through specialization, and they can be shifted among channel members. Shifting functions to the intermediary may keep producer costs and prices low, but intermediaries must add a charge to cover the cost of their work. To keep costs low, functions should be assigned to channel members who can perform them most efficiently. For example, many airlines encourage passengers to use travel agents. The travel agents answer the passenger's questions, issue the ticket, collect the payment, and when the passenger's plans change they reissue the ticket. Travel agents are also conveniently located, and many will deliver a ticket to their clients the same day it is booked. It would not be economically feasible for an airline to set up a similar distribution system.

Number of Channel Levels

Distribution channels can be described by the number of channel levels. Each layer that performs some work in bringing the product and its ownership closer to the final buyer is a *channel level*. Because the producer and the final consumer both perform some work, they are part of every channel. We use the number of intermediary levels to show the length of a channel. Figure 15-2 shows several consumer distribution channels.

Channel 1, called a **direct marketing channel**, has no intermediary level. It consists of a manufacturer selling directly to consumers. For example, a restauranteur may buy produce directly from the grower at a farmer's market. Channel 2 contains one level. In consumer markets, this level is typically a retailer. The Fisherman's Pier restaurant in Geelong, near Melbourne, Australia, purchases its fish from a fisherman's co-op. The co-op markets the fish, allowing the fishers to specialize in fishing, not marketing.

Many of the agricultural products purchased by the hospitality industry come from cooperatives. In the United States, Sunkist, Diamond Walnuts, and Land o' Lakes butter are all producer cooperatives. New

Figure 15-2
Business to consumer and business to business marketing channels.

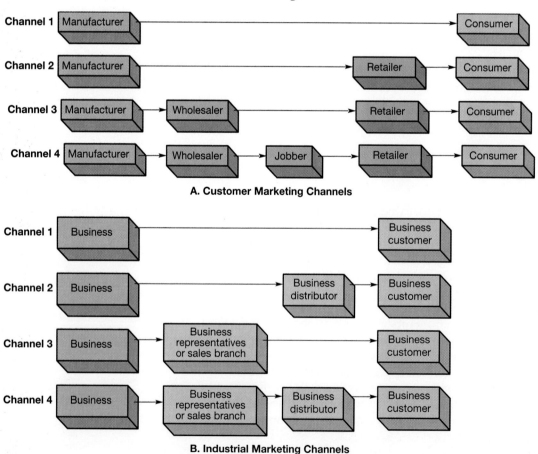

A. Customer Marketing Channels

B. Industrial Marketing Channels

Zealand Milk Products Company is also a cooperative and sells dried milk and cheese throughout Southeast Asia and Latin America.

Channel 3 contains two levels. In consumer markets, these are typically a wholesaler and a retailer. This type of channel is used by smaller manufacturers. Channel 4 contains three levels. The jobber buys from wholesalers and sells to smaller firms that are not served by larger wholesalers. From the producer's point of view, a greater number of intermediaries in the channel means less control and more complexity.

All the institutions in the channel are connected by several types of flows. These include the physical flow of products, the flow of ownership, payment flow, information flow, and promotion flow. These flows can make channels with only one or a few channels very complex.

MARKETING INTERMEDIARIES

Many specialized channels are available to hospitality and travel organizations. We will discuss the following components of a hospitality or travel distribution system: travel agents, tour operators, tour wholesalers, specialists, hotel sales representatives, incentive travel agents, government tourist associations, consortia and reservation systems, and electronic distribution systems. A manager must choose the intermediaries that will make up the distribution system and the number of levels that the distribution system will have.

Travel Agents

One way of reaching a geographically diverse marketplace is through travel agents. There are more than 32,000 travel agents in the United States who, in 1993, booked more than $93 billion of travel services, $56 billion of air travel, $14 billion in cruises, $10.4 billion of hotel services, $6.6 billion of car rentals, and $0.5 billion of other services. Half of travel agents' business clients and two-thirds of their leisure customers seek advice in choosing hotel accommodations.[6] Today, some chains generate more than one-third of their room sales from travel agents. Travel agents book more than 95% of cruises, 90% of airline tickets, 50% of car rentals, and 25% of hotel rooms.[7]

Hotels interested in travel agency business are listed in airline reservation systems and hotel guides. Hotels also send information packages to travel agents that include collateral material and hotel news, including updates about hotel packages, promotions, and special events. Hotels also invite travel agents to visit the property on familiarization tours (fam trips). Airlines assist with fam trips by providing free airfare. Fam trips must be well organized.[8] Finally, promotional campaigns can be directed at travel agents through travel agent publications such as *Travel Weekly, Travel Trade,* and *Travel Agent.* The use of promotional campaigns targeted at travel agents will be discussed in Chapter 16.

Hotels seeking travel agent business must make it easy for agents to make reservations. Providing toll-free reservation numbers is essential to servicing travel agents. Hotels that generate many bookings from travel agents have a separate number dedicated to business travel. Travel agents like to be paid quickly. Hotels that want travel agent business will process commissions rapidly. Hyatt guarantees payment within 1 week of the guest's departure.[9] Foreign chains are now paying commissions in the travel agent's local currency, eliminating the need for the agent to go through the costly process of converting a commission check. On a $50 commission foreign currency check, the travel agent stands to lose nearly the full amount because most banks charge a minimum of $30 to $40 per transaction for processing and converting checks drawn on a foreign bank.

Hospitality providers who serve travel agents must remember that agents entrust the hotel with their customers. In *Travel Weekly*'s 1994 travel agency market survey, travel agents rated reputation for honoring reservations as the most important factor in choosing a hotel. Other important factors are listed in Table 15-1.[10] Hotels must do everything possible to make a favorable impression on guests booked through travel agents to ensure future business from that agent. When business is obtained through an intermediary, the hospitality provider, such as a hotel or cruise line, has two customers, the guest and the intermediary.

The majority of cruise lines will not sell directly to the ultimate consumer, but insist that bookings be made through travel agents or tour operators.

"Travel agents are changing the way they make hotel reservations. They are turning away from toll-free telephone numbers to booking hotel rooms directly through computer systems. Travel agents' computer systems, which were referred to as computer reservation systems (CRSs) for years, are now called global distribution systems (GDSs) because of their global reach."[11] These systems allow hotels to display information concerning their properties for use by travel agents when making reservations. In 1992, 377,000 travel agents throughout the world were using GDS.[12]

Companies are a major source of travel bookings. The volume of U.S. corporate travel in 1994 reached $130 billion. Each penny of that represents a cost that corporations would like to reduce. Consequently, companies make arrangements with travel agents and in some cases set up their own travel agency.

Table 15-1

Factors Very Important to Agencies Selecting a Hotel

Reputation for honoring reservations	90%*
Reputation for good guest service	83%
Ease of collecting commission	77%
Room rates	76%
Prior success with booking clients at a particular hotel	76%
Efficiency of hotel's reservations system	70%
Commission rate	64%
Special rates with a particular hotel	61%
Bookable through computerized reservations system	48%
Relationship with hotel sales representative	31%
Client requests for hotel offering frequent stay programs	26%

Source: Travel Weekly, 53, no. 65, p. 118.
* Percentage of agencies

Many organizations sign an exclusive agreement with one travel agency, and employees are required to book through this firm. The travel agency assumes responsibility for locating the least expensive travel alternatives for the company. Software programs such as Prelude, Dacoda, Maestio, PDQ, and Maximizer enable companies to bypass the frequent-flyer or airline preference of an employee if a cheaper fare is available on another carrier. It is estimated that when the lowest available fare is not used corporations incur an average of $141 in unnecessary costs per trip. The software also enables companies to determine which employees frequently violate corporate travel policies by booking higher-priced fares and rooms.[13]

Tour Wholesalers

Tour wholesalers assemble travel packages usually targeted at the leisure market. These generally include transportation and accommodations, but may include meals, ground transportation, and entertainment. In developing a package, a tour wholesaler contracts with airlines and hotels for a specified number of seats and rooms, receiving a quantity discount. The wholesaler also arranges transportation between the hotel and the airport. Retail travel agents sell these packages. The tour wholesaler has to provide

---

Marketing Highlight 15-1

Top Ten Ideas for Working with Travel Agents

- Pay commissions promptly. Be sympathetic to agents' need for prompt payment and take action on their behalf.
- Make a company-wide commitment to the agent market, starting from the top.
- Educate your staff to the importance and the special needs of the agent market.
- Initiate a trading-places program for your hotel staff and travel agents to foster better understanding of each other's needs and responsibilities.
- Recognize and reward agents who book your hotel frequently.
- Through sales brochures, electronic listings, and hotel directory advertising, provide agents with detailed information on the facilities and services that your hotel offers. Include information on booking and commission procedures.

- Work with your local tourism organizations to initiate familiarization trips for travel agents.
- Be sure to qualify agents asking for a free or reduced-rate visit.
- Create educational opportunities for agents by sponsoring seminars on how to plan meetings or incentive packages.
- Provide information on special events, packages, and promotions as far in advance as possible so that agents will be able to sell them. If you offer last-minute "specials" to consumers, inform agents as well.

Reprinted by permission of Elsevier Science, Inc. from "Hotels and Travel Agents, the New Partnership," by Christopher Schulz, *Cornell Hotel and Restaurant Administration Quarterly*, 35, no. 3, (April 1994), p. 45, ©1994 Cornell University.

a commission for the travel agent and give consumers a package that is perceived to be a better value than what they could arrange on their own. Additionally, tour operators have to make a profit for themselves. The profit margin on each package is small. Generally, wholesalers must sell 85% of the packages available to break even.[14] This high break-even point leaves little room for error. As a result, it is not uncommon for a tour wholesaler to go broke. Thus it is important that hospitality providers check the history of the tour operator, receive a deposit, and get paid promptly. Additional security is provided by dealing with tour operators who are members of the U.S. Tour Operators Association (USTOA). USTOA requires its members to post a $100,000 indemnity bond for its consumer payments protection program. This ensures refund of tour deposits and payments in the event of financial failure of any of its members.[15]

With the increased number of international resorts, tour wholesalers are becoming a powerful member of the distribution channel. It is impossible for travel agents to know every resort. Instead, they rely on catalogs provided by tour wholesalers. If a couple wants to holiday on Saipan, they will be given the catalog of a tour operator covering Micronesia. The catalog will contain a selection of several luxury hotels, four-star hotels, three-star hotels, and tourist hotels. The wholesaler writes a description of each. The hotel may provide information, but the tour operator decides on the description of the hotel that goes in the brochure.

If a couple wants to stay at a luxury hotel, the brochure may only include three luxury hotels. Others are eliminated from consideration and will not be part of the couple's awareness set. The couple will choose a resort that seems to offer the best value based on the information provided by the tour wholesaler. Thus the tour wholesaler exerts a powerful force over resorts, especially remote international markets.

Specialists: Tour Brokers, Motivational Houses, and Junket Reps

Tour brokers sell motorcoach tours, which are attractive to a variety of markets. Tours through New England to view the fall foliage, trips to college and sporting events, tours built around Mardi Gras, and regularly scheduled tours of the Washington, D.C., area are examples of popular motorcoach trips. Some motorcoach tours are seasonal, some are based on one event, and others are year round. For hotels on their routes, motorcoach tours can provide an important source of income.[16]

Motorcoach tours are very important to museums and historic restorations such as Historic Colonial Williamsburg in Virginia. Hospitality providers such as historic restorations, hotels, and destination cities usually participate in a travel conference sponsored by the American Bus Association. Booth space is rented, and salespeople representing these providers scramble to make appointments with bus tour companies that serve their area.

Motivational houses provide incentive travel offered to employees or distributors as a reward for their efforts. Companies often use incentive travel as a prize for employees who achieve sales goals or for the sales team achieving the highest sales. The incentive trip is usually to a resort area and includes first-class or luxury properties. For resorts or up-market properties in destination cities, such as New York, San Francisco, Chicago, or Boston, motivational houses represent an effective distribution channel. Ways of reaching tour brokers and incentive houses include trade magazines and trade associations, such as the National Tour Association and the Society of Incentive Travel Executives.[17]

Junket reps serve the casino industry as intermediaries for premium players. Junket reps maintain lists of gamblers who like to visit certain gaming areas, such as Reno, Las Vegas, or Atlantic City. Junket reps work with one or a few casinos rather than the entire industry. They are paid a commission on the amount the casino earns from the players or in some cases on a per player basis. Members of a junket receive complimentary or low-cost hospitality services, including air transportation, ground transportation, hotel lodging, food and beverage, and entertainment. The amount of complimentary services received depends on the amount players gamble in the casino.

Hotel Representatives

Hotel representatives sell hotel rooms and hotel services in a given market area. It is often more effective for hotels to hire a hotel representative than use their own salesperson. This is true when the market is a distant one and when cultural differences may make it hard for an outsider to penetrate the market. For example, a corporate hotel in Houston may find that it is more effective to hire a hotel representative in Mexico City than to send a sales manager there. Hotel sales representatives should represent noncompeting hotels. They receive a straight commission, a commission plus a salary, or a combination of both. It takes time for a hotel representative to learn a company's products and inform the market about them. The choice of a hotel representative should not be taken lightly. Frequent changes in hotel representatives are not cost efficient or effective.

National, State, and Local Tourist Agencies

These agencies are an excellent way to get information to the market and gain room bookings. National associations promote tourism within their own countries. Their impact can be important to hotel chains that have locations throughout the country. State agencies promote the state resources and attractions overseas, nationally, and in the state itself. State tourist agencies usually have tourist information centers strategically located throughout the state, often at entrance points. Regional associations can also help the independent and chain operators.

Consortia and Reservation Systems

Reservation systems such as Loews Representation International, Steigenberger Reservation Service, and International Reservations and Information Consortium are expanding their services. Reservation systems provide a central reservation system for hotels. They usually provide the system for small chains or provide an overseas reservation service, allowing international guests to call a local number to contact the hotel.

In ski areas, the ski resort may operate the hotel's reservation system. The resort will book hotel reservations at independent hotels or motels for a commission such as 15%. Since the resort commonly has its own lodging, independent hotel and motel managers sometimes fear the power of this organization and may refuse to cooperate in joint promotional efforts, since they do not wish to share their database.

A *consortium* is a group of hospitality organizations that is allied for the mutual benefit of the members. Marketing is often the reason why consortia are formed. The consortium allows a property to be independent in ownership and management, while gaining the advantages of group marketing. An example of a consortium is Leading Hotels of the World. The distinction between consortia and reservation services is becoming blurred as reservation services such as SRS, Utell, and Supranational are now expanding into marketing activities. It is a natural evolution for reservation systems to add additional services once they have a critical number of hotels as subscribers.

In 1990, the top five consortia, as measured by rooms represented, were Utell, Supranational, Logis de France, Leading Hotels of the World, and Golden Tulip. Utell, primarily a reservation service, represented more than 1.3 million rooms from 6500 member hotels. One feature of Utell is its UtellVision, a system that allows reservation agents throughout the world to see pictures of a property on their computer terminals. Utell also operates the Hotel and Travel Roadshows. This organization markets hotels to the incentive market, conference planners, tour operators, corporate meeting planners, travel agents, and wholesalers. Logis de France is an association of more than 4000 small one-, two-, and three-star hotels in France. Logis de France is a consortium, with hotels identifying themselves as members of the organization through signage on the hotel and road signs.

Consortia and reservation systems are providing increased marketing coverage for hotel organizations. Frances Martin, managing editor of *Hotels*, reports that the top 25 consortia more than tripled the number of rooms represented between 1989 and 1990, to 1,955,486 rooms. Membership in an organization such as Logis de France may be the main promotion and distribution effort of a small country inn, while Utell is part of a sophisticated marketing program used by major chains. It allows chains to increase their accessibility to travel agents and international markets. As the globalization of business continues, consortia will become an even more powerful marketing tool.[18]

Regions are also developing consortia to promote their area as a tourism attraction. For example, tourist attractions in the Bath area of the United Kingdom have formed the Association of Bath and District Leisure Enterprises (ABLE). This type of cooperative allows smaller hospitality organizations to develop and distribute promotional material. Travel agents have formed consortia to negotiate lower rates for hotel rooms, airlines, and other tourist products. One of the larger travel agent consortia is Woodside Management Systems. Consortia can also develop vertical marketing systems by negotiating special prices on supplies that members may use.[19]

Airline-based Reservation Systems

Another type of computerized reservation system serves as a product catalog for travel agents and other distributors of hospitality products. These reserva-

Airline reservation systems such as Worldspan make travel products available to travel agents and corporate travel planners around the world.

tions were developed by the airlines to promote sales. Originally, the information provided was biased toward the flights of the system's developer. Regulation has eliminated that bias, and now systems must list flights according to their departure times. Ninety-six percent of the travel agents in the United States are connected to at least one computer reservation system. The most popular systems in the United States are Apollo, developed by United Airlines; Sabre, developed by American Airlines; and System One, developed by Continental Airlines, and Worldspan, owned by affiliates of Delta Airlines,

Northwest Airlines, and TWA. British Airways developed an international system, merging it with Apollo. This system, called Galileo, is now one of the major international systems. Another major international system, Amadeus, was developed by Lufthansa and Air France. Hotel companies, rental car companies, and other tourist products can gain listings on these reservation systems, making it easy for travel agents to sell their products.[20]

Airlines may also serve as tour operators. An airline such as Air New Zealand offers farm/ranch or bed and breakfast packages for the FIT (foreign independent traveler) market. Visitors to New Zealand can book auto rentals or camper rentals and reservations with these specialized lodging providers through the tour desk of Air New Zealand.

The Internet

Many hospitality firms are now using the internet to distribute their products. "All of us are interested in getting on the information superhighway because we know the channels of travel distribution are changing," said Nancy Vaughn, Best Western's director of corporate communications.[21] Hotel companies and tourist destinations can make color brochures available to millions of travelers.

Internet users can view various brochures; if they see something that interests them, they can save the information on their computer, including the color photos. If they decide to make a reservation, they can do it over the internet. Mary Sweenson, managing director of worldwide communications for Best Western, said the internet allows Best Western to reach the 72% of their customers who do not use a travel agent.[22]

Restaurant companies are also using the internet as a distribution channel. Pizza Hut developed PizzaNet, an on-line ordering system in California. TerraNet was developed in Boston for customers wanting home delivery of restaurant meals. The database allows the user to search by restaurant name or type of food. The internet user then gets information on the menu, including color photos of the dishes. The customer can select either take-out or delivery. After they have made their selection, they will get the amount owed, including any delivery charges.[23] The capability of transmitting color photographs to millions of people across the globe makes the internet an exciting new distribution channel.

Customer to Supplier Electronic Systems

Customers are now able to book their rooms and function space through specially designed software packages. For example, Meeting Services Network (MSN) contains details on room count, meeting space, and amenities at 7500 hotels, convention centers, conference centers, and resorts. Meeting planners will be able to bypass the hotel sales force by using such systems.

The International Association of Conference Planners has an on-line database that allows meeting planners to select the type of conference center desired. The addition of reservation service capability in such systems directly affects the sales and reservations departments.

Global distribution systems may allow large corporations and meeting planners to avoid all travel intermediaries and make reservations electronically throughout the world.

Guest to hotel, a technology that may allow guests to directly interface with hotels, airlines, car rental firms, and other hospitality/travel suppliers, appears to be near at hand. One possible application is the use of seat space on an airline as a workstation, entertainment center, and reservations medium. In the future, airline passengers flying from San Francisco to Hong Kong may be able to pull up on a screen pictures and descriptions of Hong Kong hotels in their price bracket, make reservations while in flight, and receive confirmations.

The application of direct consumer-to-supplier technology could dramatically affect the use of travel intermediaries such as travel agents (see Marketing Highlight 15-2).

CHANNEL BEHAVIOR AND THE ORGANIZATION

Distribution channels are more than simple collections of firms tied together by various flows. They are complex behavioral systems in which people and companies interact to accomplish goals. Some channel systems consist of formal interactions among loosely organized firms. Others consist of formal interactions guided by strong organizational structures. Channel systems do not stand still. New types surface and new channel systems evolve. We will now look at channel behavior and how members organize to do the work of the channel.

Channel Behavior

A distribution system consists of dissimilar firms that have banded together for their common good. Each channel member is dependent on the others, playing a role in the channel and specializing in performing one or more functions.

Ideally, because the success of individual channel members depends on general channel success, all channel firms should work together. They should understand and accept their roles, coordinate their goals and activities, and cooperate to attain overall channel goals. By cooperating, they can more effectively understand and serve the target market.

But individual channel members rarely take such a broad view. They are usually more concerned with their own short-run goals and their dealings with the firms operating closest to them in the channel. Cooperating to achieve overall channel goals sometimes means giving up individual company goals. Although channel members are dependent on each another, they often act alone in their own short-run best interests. They frequently disagree on the roles each should play—on who should do what for which rewards. Such disagreements over goals and roles generate channel conflict.

Horizontal conflict is conflict between firms at the same level of the channel. For example, some Pizza Inn franchisees may complain about other Pizza Inn franchisees cheating on ingredients and giving poor service, thereby hurting the overall Pizza Inn image.

Vertical conflict, which is more common, refers to conflicts between different levels of the same channel. At the beginning of this chapter we mentioned the agreement between Little Caesar's and Kmart. For Little Caesar's, this agreement provided a great opportunity to increase sales and add 1200 new outlets to its distribution system. However, to some Little Caesar's franchisees it meant an erosion of their sales.

Marketing Highlight 15-2

The Hilton Model

Hilton Hotels has initiated a number of comprehensive programs designed to serve agents while bolstering agent recognition and appreciation. Their initiatives include the following:

- **Centralized reservation systems.** Hilton's toll-free Private Travel Agent Reservation Line assists agents with inquiries and reservations for Hilton Hotels nationwide. Staffed by 40 reservationists trained exclusively for work with travel agents, the line offers around-the-clock information every day. Hilton's other central reservation services include automated services, such as Sabre, Apollo, System One, Datas II, and Covia's Inside Availability; expanded rate categories; automatic rate updates; rate returns; contests; and other marketing messages.

- **Centralized commission payment.** Hilton gives agents consolidated payments for bookings at Hilton Hotels nationwide. Commission checks are issued biweekly for hotels enrolled in Hilton's central commission program, and all other commissions are paid within 48 hours of guest check-out. Check statements include commission amount, folio number, hotel name, number of nights, and guest name. Hilton identifies which rates are commissionable at the time of reservation.

- **Hilton fam club.** Recognizing the importance of agent familiarization trips, Hilton introduced its chain-wide "fam" policy, which extends to agents a 50% savings off the minimum rack rate at each Hilton Hotel.

- **Hilton Direct.** The Hilton Direct toll-free customer service and meeting arrangement system offers agents information on availability and rates of hotel conference facilities within 24 hours of any inquiry.

- **Travel agent help desk.** The toll-free help line provides agents with research on commission payments, assistance with CRS bookings and format questions, and comprehensive assistance with Hilton's travel agent marketing and sales programs.

- **Travel agent advisory board.** Comprising nine travel industry professionals and five Hilton executives, the agent advisory board provides feedback for the company's travel agent programs and ensures that relations between travel agents and hotels continue to improve.

Reprinted by permission of Elsevier Science Inc. from "Hotels and Travel Agents, the New Partnership," by Christopher Schulz, *Cornell Hotel and Restaurant Administration Quarterly*, 35, no. 2, ©1994 by Cornell University.

Some conflict in the channel takes the form of healthy competition. Without it, the channel could become passive and noninnovative. But sometimes conflict can damage the channel. For the channel as a whole to perform well, each channel member's role must be specified, and channel conflict must be managed. Cooperation, assignment of roles, and conflict management are attained through strong channel leadership. The channel will perform better if it contains a firm, agency, or mechanism that has the power to assign roles and manage conflict.

Today, the complexity of channels has made it more difficult to manage channel members and act in the best interest of all channel members. Some forms of conflict are the result of management not thinking about how marketing decisions will affect all of a firm's channel members. For example, Embassy Suites had to modify a promotion it developed with Hertz offering cash payments to Hertz customers, who were renting cars and staying overnight. The promotion offered Hertz's customers with a confirmed hotel reservation a cash voucher if they would switch to an Embassy Suites Hotel. Embassy Suites saw an opportunity to reach hotel customers who were making an immediate purchase, and Hertz saw an opportunity to build business by offering its customers a cash bonus. It seemed like a good idea for both companies, but the American Society of Travel Agents protested the agreement. They felt that the hotel chain was unfairly taking commissions away from travel agents who had made the original reservations.[24] Both Embassy Suites and Hertz failed to recognize the negative impact that the promotion would have on one of their channel members, the travel agent.

In a large company the formal organizational structure assigns roles and provides needed leadership. But in a distribution channel made up of independent firms, leadership and power are not formally set. Traditionally, distribution channels have lacked the leadership needed to assign roles and manage conflict. In recent years, new types of channel organizations have appeared to provide stronger leadership and improved performance.[25]

Channel Organization

Historically, distribution channels have been loose collections of independent companies, each showing little concern for overall channel performance. These conventional distribution systems have lacked strong leadership and have been troubled by damaging conflict and poor performance.

Growth of Vertical Marketing Systems

One of the biggest recent channel developments has been the vertical marketing systems that have emerged to challenge conventional marketing systems. Figure 15-3 contrasts the two types of channel arrangements.

A **conventional distribution channel** consists of one or more independent producers, wholesalers, and retailers. Each is a separate business seeking to maximize its own profits, even at the expense of profits for the system as a whole. No channel member has much control over the other members, and no formal means exists for assigning roles and resolving channel conflict. For example, most hotels pay a commission to travel agents. No formal contract is signed between the hotel and every agent. The hotel simply communicates its policy and can, if it wishes, make rooms unavailable to travel agents on a temporary basis.

By contrast, a **vertical marketing system** (VMS) consists of producers, wholesalers, and retailers acting as a unified system. One channel member either owns the others, has contracts with them, or wields so much power that they all cooperate.[26] The vertical marketing system can be dominated by the producer, wholesaler, or retailer. VMSs were originally developed to control channel behavior and manage channel conflict. Another

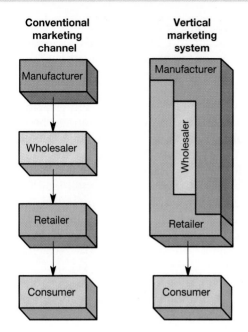

Figure 15-3
Major types of vertical
marketing systems.

major benefit is economies through size, bargaining power, and elimination of duplicated services. VMSs have become dominant in consumer marketing, serving as much as 64% of the total market.

We will now look at the three major types of VMSs shown in Figure 15-3. Each type uses a different means for setting up leadership and power in the channel. In a corporate VMS, coordination and conflict management are attained through common ownership at different levels in the channel. In an administered VMS, leadership is assumed by one or a few dominant channel members. In a contractual VMS, they are attained through contractual agreements among channel members.

A **corporate VMS** combines successive stages of production and distribution under a single ownership. For example, Red Lobster has its own food-processing plants and distributes food products to its restaurants. Breweries in Great Britain own pubs, which serve only the beers of the owner brewery. Gallo, the world's largest wine maker, does much more than simply turn grapes into wine:

> The Gallo brothers own Fairbanks Trucking Company, one of the largest intrastate truckers in California. Its 200 semis and 500 trailers are constantly hauling wine out of Modesto and raw materials back, including … lime from Gallo's quarry east of Sacramento. Alone among wine producers, Gallo makes bottles—two million a day—and its Midcal Aluminum company spews out screw tops as fast as the bottles are filled. Most of the country's 1,300 or so wineries concentrate on production to the neglect of marketing. Gallo, by contrast, participates in every aspect of selling short of whispering in the ear of each imbiber. The company owns its distributors in about a dozen markets and probably would buy many … more … if the laws in most states did not prohibit doing so.[27]

BEST TWO LETTERS ON YOUR KEYBOARD.

Best
Western

YOUR BEST BET IS A BEST WESTERN.
For information or reservations, call our Travel Agent Help Desk at 1-800-334-7234.

Your computer is more powerful than you think. Just type in BW and it can reach every Best Western in the world. This reservation access code allows you to make and confirm reservations, compare rates, check availability and obtain information about all our new programs and amenities.

You'll find we've introduced some new frequent traveler clubs. And that's just one of our many changes. We're also spending more than a billion dollars upgrading hotels worldwide. We've enacted tough new inspection standards at 3,400 locations in more than 50 countries.

And you can bring them all up on the screen with just the touch of a button. Well, two buttons.

Best Western is a type of contractual VMS. It provides its members with marketing services, such as this reservation access code allowing travel agents who make reservations from their computers. Courtesy of Best Western International, Inc., and Lord, Dentsu and Partners.

An **administered VMS** coordinates successive stages of production and distribution—not through common ownership or contractual ties but through the size and power of the parties. For example, in the 1970s a popular beer brand gained an exclusive right to supply draft beer in a restaurant or bar through the power of its brand. The producer would not allow a bar serving its beer on tap to serve any others, claiming that other beers on the same line could reduce the quality of their product. They argued that other beer companies might use dirty tools to clean the lines and set the pressure improperly. They used their brand power to eliminate competition.

The world's airline industry has been affected by administered VMSs since the birth of the industry. Many nations continue to cling to a subsidized national carrier known as a flag carrier. These airlines often exert an inordinate amount of power over reservations systems, tour operators, and travel agencies within their respective nations.

The third type of VMS is contractual. A **contractual VMS** consists of independent firms at different levels of production and distribution who join through contracts to obtain economies or sales impact. A contract with a hotel representative would be an example of a contractual VMS. An important form of contractual VMS is franchising.

Franchising

"Franchising is a method of doing business by which a franchisee is granted the right to engage in offering, selling, or distributing goods or services under a marketing format which is designed by the franchisor. The franchisor permits the franchisee to use its trademark, name, and advertising."[28] Franchising has been the fastest-growing retailing form in recent years. The 500,000 plus franchise operations in the United States now account for about one-third of all retail sales and may account for one-half by the year 2000.[29]

Franchises have been popular forms of distribution for both hotels and restaurants. Some popular hotel franchises include Choice Hotels, Holiday Inns, Days Inns, Sheraton Inns, and Hilton Inns. Restaurant franchises include McDonald's, Burger King, Kentucky Fried Chicken, Pizza Hut, and T.G.I. Friday's. Franchises have been responsible for shifting the restaurant business from individual operators to multiunits. Franchised restaurant companies had sales of $79 billion in 1991 and accounted for more than half of all restaurant sales. They achieved this through a network of 106,000 locations.[30]

For the right to use the name, methods of operation, and other benefits that come with the franchise, the franchisee pays an initial fee, a royalty, and a marketing fee. In the case of hotels, a fee for use of the central reservation system is also charged. Embassy Suites charges an initial fee of $500 per room with a minimum fee of $100,000. The royalty is 4% of gross room revenue, the marketing fee is 2% of gross room revenue, and the reservation fee is 1% of gross room revenue.[31] Note that these percentages are gross percentages. Using gross revenue allows the franchisor to collect fees from unprofitable businesses. The franchisor can verify gross receipts through tax reports.

The following information from the 1993 Annual Report of Hospitality Franchise Systems tells just how profitable franchising can be.

Wow ... what a year!

1993 was the year Hospitality Franchise Systems, Inc. became the world's largest and most successful hotel franchisor. It was a year in which we acquired two hotel franchise systems, set industry records for internal growth, entered into strategic alliances with other travel providers as well as preferred vendors, and extended our business into the rapidly expanding gaming industry.

As the parent company of Days Inn, Howard Johnson, Park Inn, Ramada and Super 8, HFS' unique combination of financial stability and rapid growth are primarily attributable to the fact that the royalty portion of franchise fees, which is calculated as a percentage of hotel room revenue, represents the majority of the Company's earnings. Marketing and reservation fees paid by our franchisees cover all of the variable expenses of marketing and reservation system support. These characteristics create high operating leverage so that virtually every dollar of increased royalties primarily created a $32 million or 111% increase in income before income taxes and extraordinary loss in 1993 compared with 1992. Earnings per share before extraordinary loss increased from $.45* in 1992 to $.68* during 1993, even though our outstanding shares increased 15% from 43.8 million to 50.1 million.

The equity market recognized this accomplishment during 1993, causing the Company's stock price to rise from $9.63* to $26.56.* Perhaps our most important achievement was creating $900 million in increased shareholder value. The credit markets also took note of HFS' progress; during the year the Company's debt was rated "investment grade" by both Moody's Investors Service, Inc. and Standard & Poor's Corporation, enabling HFS to significantly reduce its cost of funds.

*Restated to give effect for a two-for-one stock split effected in the form of a dividend approved by the Board of Directors on February 18, 1994 to stockholders of record on March 14, 1994. *Source:* 1993 Annual Report, Hospitality Franchise Systems, Inc., 339 Jefferson Road, P.O. Box 278, Parsippany, N.J. 07054-0278.

The initial fee and the royalty depend on the brand equity of the franchise. For example, McDonald's is recognized as a fast-food restaurant around the world. People in London, Paris, Hong Kong, and New York recognize McDonald's. The stronger the market position is, the more valuable the brand name. Thus a McDonald's franchise offers more value than a Mr. Quick franchise. Other advantages of a franchise include management assistance, quality control, accounting systems, marketing, access to capital, architectural plans, and group buying.

Marriott moved from a company-owned Courtyard by Marriott to an aggressive franchising program in 1990. Mike Ruffer, executive vice-president with Marriott, stated, "We're looking forward to growing our own brand and gaining additional distribution in the 1990s, but we can't do it ourselves." The additional distribution Marriott was seeking included central business district locations and resorts. In 1992, the Courtyard by Marriott in Chicago became the first Courtyard to be developed in a central business district.[32]

Franchising is used in smaller restaurant chains to help them retain managers. It is difficult for a small chain to compete with opportunities that a large chain offers its managers. Some small chains combat career opportunities the large chains offer by helping their best managers get their own store through franchising. This allows the chain to keep managers who might otherwise grow bored and unchallenged. A well-conceived franchise provides benefits for both the franchisor and the franchisee. Table 15-2 provides the costs of different mid-scale lodging and restaurant franchises.

Alliances

Alliances are another form of contractual agreement. Alliances are developed to allow two organizations to benefit from each other's strengths. In the beginning of the chapter we mentioned the alliance between the Welcome Group and Sheraton Hotels. It would be difficult if not impossible for Sheraton to go into India by itself because of that nation's regulation of foreign-owned business. The Welcome Group offered Sheraton an Indian partner. Additionally, the Welcome Group had a good reputation in India and understood how to do business there. Sheraton offered the Welcome Group a name that was known to the international business traveler. Sheraton offered training and management support systems. Thus both partners benefited from the alliance.

Alliances by two or more noncompeting firms are a popular and effective way of expanding markets. For example, restaurants are developing alliances with convenience stores and hotel properties to distribute their products. 7-Eleven Stores sell Dunkin' Donuts in 2000 of its stores. Embassy

Table 15-2

Hotel and Restaurant Franchise Costs

HOTEL FRANCHISES

CHAIN	HEADQUARTERS	TOTAL FRANCHISED PROPERTIES/ROOMS	ADDITIONAL PROPERTIES/ROOMS (BY YEAR END)	FEE STRUCTURE (US $)
Ramada		649/103,359	88/10,795	Initial: $350/room, $35,000 minimum Royalty: 4% gross rooms revenue Ad/marketing: combined with reservation fee, see reservation fee Reservation: combined with ad fee, 4.5% gross rooms revenue
Days Inn of America		1,397/142,671	181/8,500	Initial: $350/room, $35,000 minimum Royalty: 6.5% gross rooms revenue Ad/marketing: included in royalty fee Reservation: 2.3% gross rooms revenue and initial entry charge to gain access (lesser of $100 per room or $10,000)
Holiday Inn Worldwide	Atlanta	1,751/336,212	43/5,046	Initial: $30,000/room; $75,000 Crowne Plaza Royalty: 5% Ad/marketing: 1.5%, Crowne Plaza, Express, 2% Reservations: 1%
Best Western International	Phoenix	3,349/273,851	92/10,000	Initial: $25,000 minimum/100 rooms Royalty: annual dues/$21,626 for 100 rooms Reservation: 25 cents/room/day, first year, then fee based on prior year's room nights booked Ad/marketing: annual dues/$2949 for 100 rooms
Choice Hotels International Comfort	Silver Springs, MD	2,661/239,696 1,081/189,403	219/28,088 49/5,220	Initial: $300/room, $40,000 minimum $50,000 for suites Royalty: 5% of gross rooms revenue Ad/marketing: 1.3% of gross rooms revenue, plus 28 cents per room per day (for all brands) Reservation: 1% gross rooms revenue, plus $1 per night confirmed through system (all brands)

CHAIN	HEADQUARTERS	TOTAL FRANCHISED PROPERTIES/ROOMS	ADDITIONAL PROPERTIES/ROOMS (BY YEAR END)	FEE STRUCTURE (US $)
Embassy Suites		47/11,267	3/383	Initial: $500 per suite, $100,000 minimum; Royalty: 4% gross suite revenue; Ad/marketing: 2.125% gross suites revenue; Reservation: 1.5% gross suites revenue
Fairfield Inns by Marriott		44/4,000	17/1,500	Initial: $375/room new builds; $200/room conversion; Royalty: 4% room sales; Ad/marketing: 2.5% of room sales; Reservation: 1% of room sales and $2/reservation

Source: Hotel Motel Management, vol. 208, no. 16, August 16, 1993, pp. 16+. Copyright Advanstar Communications. All rights reserved.

RESTAURANT FRANCHISES

FRANCHISE SYSTEM	FRANCHISE FEE	ROYALTY %	ADVERTISING ROYALTY (%)	TOTAL INVESTMENT[a] ($000s)	ESTIMATED 1991 AVERAGE UNIT VOLUME ($000s)	INVESTMENT/SALES RATIO (U.S. ONLY)
Applebee's Neighborhood Grill & Bar	30,000	4.0	3.0	400	1749	0.23
Arby's	25–37,000	3.5–4	0.1	525–850	651	1.10
Burger King	25,000	4.0	4.0	1000	1,061	0.94
Domino's Pizza	1–3,000	5.5	3.3	75–150	510	0.22
KFC	20,000	4.0	4.5	600–800	676	1.04
McDonalds	$22,500	3.5	4.0	575	1,715	0.37
Pizza Hut	up to 15,000	3–4	1[b]	N/A	631	N/A
Subway Sandwiches & Salads	7,500	8.0	2.5	40	270	0.15
TGI Friday's	50,000	4.0	2–4	2000–2500	3,588	0.63

Source: Restaurant Business, March 20, 1992, pp. 62–3.

[a] Includes cash and debt
[b] 2% of first 15K

471

Suites has Red Lobster restaurants located in its hotels. Chain fast-food operations located in convenience stores allow the store to offer brand-name products, and the chain gains additional high-traffic distribution points. Many consumers perceive hotel restaurants to be overpriced and of poor quality. The introduction of well-known chain restaurants into hotels overcomes this problem.

Airlines are developing alliances to access customers in other parts of the world and to provide their customers with new destination opportunities. For example, SAS developed an alliance with Continental Airlines to give it access to the U.S. market. Before the alliance, SAS served only a handful of U.S. cities. Since the alliance, Continental's U.S. flights can be used to feed into SAS's flights to Europe. Continental gained the SAS passengers flying into Newark and other U.S. gateways, who will now use Continental to reach their final destination in the United States.

The National Motorcoach Network, a marketing consortium of motor-coach operators, has developed a Partner Program to bring charter business to preferred hotels. Now tour operators sometimes extend their trips to include an overnight stay. In the past, operators preferred a day trip to staying overnight in an unfamiliar hotel. A network representative visits all participating hotels before they are accepted. The alliance brings business to the hotels and provides motorcoach operators with negotiated rates at hotels that meet their standards.[31]

Growth of Horizontal Marketing Systems

Another channel development is **horizontal marketing systems**, in which two or more companies at one level join to follow a new marketing opportunity.[34] By working together, companies can combine their capital, production capabilities, or marketing resources to accomplish more than can one company working alone. For example, Seaworld offers tickets at a discount to an automobile club, which promotes these discount tickets as one benefit for its members. In return, Seaworld gains access to several hundred thousand automobile club members. In another example, Sears and McDonald's joined forces to market the McKids line of "fun clothes for small fries." McDonald's franchisees and Sears stores worked together to develop local promotion programs. Such symbiotic marketing arrangements have increased in number in recent years, and the end is nowhere in sight.

American Express, the Coeur D Alene resort, and K2 Skis worked together to offer a free pair of skis at check-in if the guest booked an American Express "Ski Week Holiday."

Growth of Multichannel Marketing Systems

In the past, many companies used a single channel to sell to a single market or market segment. Today, with the proliferation of customer segments and channel possibilities, more companies have adopted multichannel distribution. Such multichannel marketing occurs when a single firm sets up two or more marketing channels to reach one or more customer segments.[35]

For example, McDonald's sells through a network of independent franchisees, but owns more than one-fourth of its outlets. Thus the wholly owned restaurants compete to some extent with those owned by McDonald's franchisees.

The multichannel marketer gains sales with each new channel, but also risks offending existing channels. Existing channels can cry "unfair competition" and threaten to drop the marketer unless it limits competition or repays them in some way. For example, franchisees have brought lawsuits against franchisors who have developed competing operations in their market area.

**CHANNEL
DESIGN
DECISIONS**

We will now look at several channel decision problems facing marketers. In designing distribution channels, marketers struggle between what is ideal and what is practical. Designing a channel system calls for analyzing consumer needs, setting the channel objectives and constraints, identifying major channel alternatives, and evaluating them.

Analyzing Consumer Service Needs

Designing the distribution channel starts with determining the services that consumers in various target segments want. The Victoria House in Belize caters to customers from the United States. Its customers do not want to call Central America to reserve a room, but need an easy way to communicate with the hotel. In response, the Victoria House aligned with a Houston travel agent with a toll-free number. The travel agent receives reservations directly from guests and from other travel agents throughout the United States, relaying the information to the Victoria House.

A large resort such as the Fiesta Americana in Puerto Villarta, Mexico, might consider aligning with a wholesaler. The wholesaler would put together a package that includes airfare, rooms, and ground transportation and distribute it through travel agents. In doing so, the wholesaler provides a package that gives guests everything they need to travel with no worry about finding their way around a foreign country.

To design an effective channel, the company must understand the services its customers require and then balance the needs of those customers against the feasibility and costs of meeting them. The hotel must be able to cover costs associated with the channel and maintain an attractive price.

Setting Channel Objectives and Constraints

Channels for goods-producing firms move the product from the firm to the customer. Distribution channels for the hospitality industry move the customer to the hotel, cruise ship, or restaurant. They provide the right information to the right people at the right time and allow the purchase decision to be made in advance of product consumption. Someone who wants to take a Caribbean cruise in February can walk into a travel agent's office in Atlanta, receive information about the variety of different Caribbean cruises, and reserve a space.

In most hotels, several segments will be identified, each with different needs. The company should decide which segments to serve and the best channels to use. The company wants to minimize total channel cost. The company's channel objectives are also influenced by its products, company characteristics and policies, middlemen characteristics, and environmental factors.

Product Characteristics A large convention hotel requires channels equipped to give technical information on holding a convention at the hotel. The hotel may hire a representative to distribute its product in cities not covered by its sales force. A budget hotel chain with limited food and beverage selection has a simple product aimed at a mass market. It may decide to distribute its product by developing horizontal systems with an automobile association or an association such as AARP (American Association of Retired People).

Company Characteristics and Policies The size of a company will shape its channel design. An independent chain or small hotel chain many join a consortium to increase marketing clout. A larger company may benefit from developing a company—a controlled vertical marketing system. Some airlines have developed their own meeting-planning departments or companies to plan meetings for clients in cities that they serve, giving the airline an inside track on business travel.

Middleman Characteristics The company must find middlemen who are willing and able to perform the needed tasks. In general, middlemen differ in their abilities to handle promotion, customer contact, and credit. For example, hotels can hire hotel representatives at a low cost per customer because several clients share the total cost. However, the selling effort behind the product is less intense than if the company's own sales force did the selling.

Environmental Factors Finally, environmental factors affect channel decisions. For example, the increase in the use of home computers and the development of on-line databases for the consumer have opened new channels for hospitality and travel firms. Consumers can make and pay for travel reservations over their computers. They can also gain information about travel options, including color pictures of a destination's attractions and hotels, over the Internet.

Responsibilities of Channel Members

The company and its intermediaries must agree on the terms and responsibilities of each channel member. For instance, hotels make it clear to travel agents which rates are commissionable and the amount of commission to be paid, and they often guarantee to pay the commission within a certain number of days. McDonald's provides franchisees with promotional support, a record-keeping system, training, and general management assistance. In turn, franchises must meet company standards for physical facilities, cooperate with new promotional programs, provide requested information, and buy specified food products. To avoid disputes, it is important that companies have an explicit arrangement in writing with their channel members.

Suppose that a company has identified several channel alternatives and wants to select the one that will best satisfy its long-run objectives. The firm must evaluate each alternative against economic, control, and adaptive criteria.

Economic Criteria

Each channel will produce different levels of sales and costs. For example, a hotel might consider hiring an independent sales representative to cover a specific market. The first step is to determine sales levels that would be produced by a company sales force and then compare them with those expected from a sales representative. If the hotel sales force understands the market, it can do a better job for the following reasons: (1) The sales force tends to be more motivated because it sells only the company's products and has excellent product knowledge. (2) It is usually more aggressive, since the future of the company depends on its success. (3) It is likely to take pride in the products it is selling and be enthusiastic.

The independent sales representative is more useful in markets that are unfamiliar to the company's sales force. For example, a sales representative in Mexico City will better understand the culture of the market and how to approach it. Customers in Mexico City may prefer dealing with a Mexican, rather than an outsider. Some customers prefer dealing with a company that represents several different hotels.

The level of sales that a channel member is likely to achieve must be evaluated against cost. Contracting with a sales representative in Mexico may be much more cost effective than sending a salesperson to Mexico City. Through the sales representative, the hotel has a phone contact and an office in Mexico City. The maintenance of a sales office in Mexico would not be cost effective for most hotel chains. On the other hand, most large hotel chains based in the United States can afford to have their own sales office in New York because of the size of the market.

Control Criteria

An important consideration in the choice of channels is control. Using sales representatives offers less control than building your own sales force. Sales representatives may prefer to sell rooms in other hotels because it requires less effort. They may eschew smaller customers, preferring instead to call on larger companies who can use most of the hotels that they represent.

Control is also an important consideration in franchising and choosing multiple-channel members. One problem with franchising is that a company sacrifices some control to gain wider distribution. The company may have trouble getting franchisees to add new products or to participate in promotions. Some companies have problems getting their franchisees to meet quality control standards.

When a firm adds multiple channels, it must consider the rights of existing channel members. Often, existing channel members limit their activities with new channel members. For example, earlier in the chapter we talked about the promotion between Embassy Suites Hotel and Hertz. The promotion was modified because it went against the interests of another channel member, the travel agent.

Adaptive Criteria

Each channel involves a long-term commitment and loss of flexibility. A hotel firm using a sales representative in Mexico City may have to sign a 5-year contract. During this 5-year period, the hotel company may develop an alliance with an airline or hotel company based in Mexico. The sales representative in Mexico City may become unnecessary, but the company will be unable to end the relationship until the contract has ended. There is often a trade-off between the benefits created by developing a long term alliance and the loss of flexibility that often comes with such alliances. Understanding the trade-offs and how the market place might change in the future can help a manager make decisions regarding the length of contractual agreements with channel members.

CHANNEL MANAGEMENT DECISIONS

Once the company has reviewed its channel alternatives and selected the best, it must implement and manage the chosen channel. Channel management calls for selecting and motivating individual intermediaries and evaluating their performance.

Teamwork, entrepreneurial managerial behaviors, and proactive marketing policies and activities are highly influential in providing customer satisfaction.[36] It is important to work with channel members as a team to create high customer satisfaction.

Selecting Channel Members

Companies vary in their ability to attract qualified intermediaries. Well-known hotel companies that have a reputation for paying commissions promptly and honoring the reservations of travel agents will have no trouble gaining the support of travel agencies. A new hotel chain with only a few hotels will have difficulty getting most of the country's 32,000 travel agents to sell its chain. It would be wiser for the new chain to choose one travel agency chain or work in key cities that are likely to generate business.

Just as a company carefully chooses its employees, it should also carefully choose channel members. These firms will represent the company and will be partially responsible for the company's image. When selecting channel members, the company's management will want to evaluate each firm's growth and profit record, profitability, cooperativeness, and reputation. When contracting with a hotel sales representative, the hotel company will want to investigate the number and type of other hotels that the firm represents. It will also want to investigate the size and quality of its work force.

Motivating Channel Members

A company must continuously motivate its channel members. Just as a firm must market to its employees, it must also market to its intermediaries. Most firms use positive incentives during times of slow demand. For example, during slow periods, hotel or rental car companies often increase the percentage of commission that they pay. Keeping channel members informed about the company's products is another way to motivate channel members. Hotels with sales representatives must keep them informed about changes in facilities and new products.

Evaluating Channel Members

A company must regularly evaluate the performance of its intermediaries. McDonald's, for example, has 300 field consultants who daily visit franchisees, complimenting them on what they are doing right and making suggestions for improving others (for example, biscuits that slope "a few degrees to one side"). Checking on intermediaries is a delicate business. Sometimes problems may be due to improper support from the supplier. Companies need to evaluate the support that they are giving their channel members and make necessary adjustments.

Underperforming intermediaries need to be counseled. They may need more training or motivation. If they do not shape up, it might be better to terminate them.

A producer must do more than design a good channel system and set it into motion. The system will require periodic modifications to meet the marketplace. Modification becomes necessary when consumer buying patterns change, markets expand, products mature, new competition arises, and new, innovative distribution channels emerge.

Three levels of channel modification can be distinguished. Change may involve *adding or dropping individual channel members, adding or dropping particular market channels,* or *developing a totally new way to sell goods in all markets.*

Modifying channel arrangements requires an incremental analysis. What would the firm's profits look like with the present distribution system and under the modified system?

A hotel may decide to drop representatives that are not producing. Representatives may be replaced by new ones or by the hotel's salespeople. An independent hotel may decide to become part of Leading Hotels of the World to gain access to new markets. Another may drop its affiliation with a reservation system because it is not producing.

Dropping channel members is not always easy. In some foreign markets, particularly third-world markets such as El Salvador, there is a problem of potential monetary payment to independent representatives who are dismissed. In the United States and Canada it is assumed that an independent rep paid only through commission is not an employee of the company. This is not the case in some nations, where courts may rule that the independent rep was in reality dependent on a foreign firm for its livelihood although paid in commissions. Therefore, eliminating this rep may create severe economic hardship, and the foreign company will need to pay a severance fee that may amount to tens of thousands of dollars.

MODIFYING CHANNEL ARRANGEMENTS

BUSINESS LOCATION

One of the most important aspects of distribution for hospitality organizations is location. For businesses whose customers come to them, the business must be conveniently located. Many retailers will say that the three secrets of successful retailing are "location, location, and location." There is no single formula for location. A good location for a Ritz-Carlton Hotel will be different from that of a Motel 6 or a Burger King. Restaurant sites tend to be evaluated

The Waldorf Astoria promotes its prime location.

"At the heart of the meeting place of the world stands The Waldorf Astoria, the flagship of Hilton Hotels, a marvelous and soothing environment where the quality and service of yesterday still exist today. Approach on Park Avenue and stand for a moment outside. You're at the center of the center of it all, bounded by the theaters of Broadway, the country's most fashionable shopping district along Fifth Avenue, the United Nations, the collected commerce of the world."

Source: A promotional brochure from The Waldorf Astoria, a Hilton Hotel. Courtesy of Hilton Hotels Corporation.

on the ability of the local area to provide business. Hotel sites are evaluated on the attractiveness of their location to persons coming to that destination. In both cases, location depends on the firm's marketing strategy. Each firm will have its own set of location evaluation characteristics.

In general, there are four steps in choosing a location. The first is understanding the marketing strategy and target market of the company. La Quinta motels cater to the traveling salesperson and other mid-class hotel guests arriving primarily by automobile. Locations are typically along freeways outside major metropolitan areas. They are close enough to the central business district to offer convenient access, yet far enough away to allow economic purchase of the site. Hyatt, on the other hand, caters to groups and the business person who often arrives by plane. Hyatt hotels are often located in the heart of the central business district. The location decision, like other marketing decisions, cannot be separated from the marketing strategy.

The second step of the selection is regional analysis, which involves the selection of geographic market areas.[37] A restaurant chain may plan to expand into a new metropolitan market. They may need to find a region that will support at least five new stores. A business hotel chain expanding into Southeast Asia may target key cities such as Singapore, Bangkok, Kuala Lumpur, and Jakarta. The chain wants to have a presence in major cities of the region so that business travelers can stay in the chain as they travel throughout the region.

A firm would want to make sure that a region has sufficient and stable demand to support the hotel(s) or restaurant(s). A growing area with a diverse economic base is attractive. Houston's hotels and restaurants suffered in the 1980s when oil prices plummeted because of the area's heavy dependence on one industry. During a 10-year period, many hotels were taken over by lenders. Areas based on one industry are often attractive when that industry is in favor, but are highly vulnerable when that industry suffers.

This is equally true when tourism and hospitality are the primary industries. Miami Beach experienced industry problems when some European tourists were assaulted or killed. The ski industry and ski resort towns depend on the whims of nature. Too little or too much snow can create major economic problems.

Once the firm has chosen a geographic region, the next step is to select an area within that region. If a restaurant chain wants to open five restaurants in a metropolitan area, it must choose sites at which to place its restaurants. The chain will look at the demographic and psychographic characteristics of the area. Competition and growth potential of the different areas will be evaluated. The result will be a choice of five areas within the region that seem most promising.

Finally, the firm will choose individual sites. A key consideration in site analysis is compatible businesses. A restaurant or hotel will look for potential demand generators. For a hotel these can be major office complexes, airports, or integrated retail, residential, and business complexes. A restaurant may look for residential communities, shopping centers, or motels without food and beverage facilities. Demand generators vary depending on the target markets of the business. It is important for firms to have a good profile of their customers when they look for customer sources within a given area.

In addition to demand generators, a firm will also look at competitors. If there is an adequate supply of similar restaurants or hotels, the site will usually be rejected. Hotels have entered saturated markets, just to gain a presence in that city. Competition is not always a negative factor. Restaurants often tend to be clustered, creating a restaurant row. This can be beneficial. Customers going to one restaurant are exposed to a selection of others.

Site evaluation includes accessibility. Is the site easily accessible by traffic going in different directions or do uncrossable medians create a barrier?

Is the site visible to allow drivers to turn? Speed of traffic is also a factor. The slower the traffic is, the longer the visibility. Restaurant sites at intersections with a stoplight have the benefit of exposure to waiting drivers. The desirability of the surroundings is another consideration. Is the area attractive? If the site is in a shopping center, is the center well maintained? Other considerations for the site include drainage, sewage, utilities, and size.

Often, companies will develop a profile of preferred sites. For example, Carl's Jr. restaurant, a fast-food hamburger restaurant, developed this profile:

Free-standing location in a shopping center.

Free-standing corner location (with a signal light at the intersection).

Inside lot with 125-foot minimum frontage.

Enclosed shopping mall.

Population of 12,000 or more in a 1-mile radius (growth areas preferred).

Easy access of traffic to location.

Heavy vehicular/pedestrian traffic.

An area where home values and family income levels are average or above.

Close to offices and other demand generators.

A parcel size of 30,000 to 50,000 square feet.

No less than 2 or 3 miles from other existing company locations.[38]

The choice of a site is often determined by a checklist, statistical analysis, or a combination of both. A checklist usually contains items such as those listed in the profile above and specific building requirements. Items such as building codes, signage restrictions, availability of utilities, parking, and drainage are also included in a checklist. A common type of statistical analysis used in site selection is regression analysis. The dependent variable in the equation is sales, and the independent variables are factors that contribute to sales. Typical independent variables might include population within the market area, household income of the market, competitors and attributes of the location.

Location is a key attribute for a hotel or restaurant. The location must not only be viable at the present time, but must continue to be good throughout the life of the business.

Chapter Review

I.   Nature of Distribution Channels. A distribution channel is a set of independent organizations involved in the process of making a product or service available to the consumer or business user.

II.   Reasons That Marketing Intermediaries Are Used. The use of intermediaries depends on their greater efficiency in marketing the goods available to target markets. Through their contacts, experience, specialization, and scale of operation, intermediaries normally offer more than a firm can on its own.

III. **Distribution Channel Functions.**

    1) Information. Gathering and distributing marketing research and intelligence information about the marketing environment.

    2) Promotion. Developing and spreading persuasive communications about an offer.

    3) Contact. Finding and communicating with prospective buyers.

    4) Matching. Shaping and fitting the offer to the buyers' needs.

    5) Negotiation. Agreeing on price and other terms of the offer so that ownership or possession can be transferred.

    6) Physical Distribution. Transporting and storing goods.

    7) Financing. Acquiring and using funds to cover the cost of channel work.

    8) Risk Taking. Assuming financial risks, such as the inability to sell inventory at full margin.

IV. **Number of Channel Levels.** The number of channel levels can vary from direct marketing, through which the manufacturer sells directly to the consumer, to complex distribution systems involving four or more channel members.

V. **Marketing Intermediaries.** Marketing intermediaries available to the hospitality industry and travel industry include travel agents, tour operators, tour wholesalers, specialists, hotel sales representatives, incentive travel agents, government tourist associations, consortia and reservation systems, and electronic distribution systems.

VI. **Channel Behavior**

    1) Channel Conflict. Although channel members depend on each other, they often act alone in their own short-run best interests. They frequently disagree on the roles each should play—on who should do what for which rewards.

        ***a)*Horizontal conflict:** Conflict between firms at the same level.

        ***b)*Vertical conflict:** Conflict between different levels of the same channel.

VII. **Channel Organization.** Distribution channels are shifting from loose collections of independent companies to unified systems.

    1) Conventional Marketing System. A conventional marketing system consists of one or more independent producers, wholesalers, and retailers. Each is a separate business seeking to maximize its own profits, even at the expense of profits for the system as a whole.

    2) Vertical Marketing System. A vertical marketing system consists of producers, wholesalers, and retailers acting as a unified system. VMSs were developed to control channel behavior and manage channel conflict and its economies through size, bargaining power, and elimination of duplicated services. There are three major types of VMSs: corporate VMS, administered VMS, and contractual VMS.

        ***a)*Corporate:** A corporate VMS combines successive stages of production and distribution under a single ownership.

        ***b)*Administered:** An administered VMS coordinates successive stages of production and distribution, not through common ownership or contractual ties, but through the size and power of the parties.

c) **Contractual:** A contractual VMS consists of independent firms at different levels of production and distribution who join through contracts to obtain economies or sales impact.

   i) **Franchising:** Franchising is a method of doing business by which a franchisee is granted the right to engage in offering, selling, or distributing goods or services under a marketing format that is designed by the franchisor. The franchisor permits the franchisee to use its trademark, name, and advertising.

   ii) **Alliances:** Alliances are developed to allow two organizations to benefit from each other's strengths.

3) Horizontal Marketing System. Two or more companies at one level join to follow new marketing opportunities. Companies can combine their capital, production capabilities, or marketing resources to accomplish more than one company working alone.

4) Multichannel Marketing Systems. A single firm sets up two or more marketing channels to reach one or more customer segments.

VIII. Channel Design Decisions

1) Analyzing Consumer Needs. Designing the distribution channel starts with determining what services consumers in various target segments want.

2) Setting the Channel Objectives and Constraints. Factors to consider in setting channel objectives include product characteristics, company characteristics, and marketing intermediaries.

3) Responsibilities of Channel Members. The company and its intermediaries must agree on the terms and responsibilities of each channel member.

4) Identifying Major Channel Alternatives. The firm must evaluate each alternative against economic, control, and captive criteria.

IX. Channel Management Decisions

1) Selecting Channel Members. When selecting channel members, the company's management will want to evaluate each potential channel member's growth and profit record, profitability, cooperativeness, and reputation.

2) Motivating Channel Members. A company must continuously motivate its channel members.

3) Evaluating Channel Members. A company must regularly evaluate the performance of its intermediaries and counsel underperforming intermediaries.

4) Modifying Channel Arrangements. Modification becomes necessary when consumer buying patterns change, markets expand, products mature, new competition arises, and new, innovative distribution channels emerge.

X. Business Location. There are four steps in choosing a location:

1) Understanding the Marketing Strategy. The target market of the company.

2) Regional Analysis. The selection of geographic market areas.

3) Choosing the Area within the Region. Demographic, psychographic characteristics, and competition are factors to consider.

4) Choosing the Individual Site. Compatible business, competitors, accessibility, drainage, sewage, utilities, and size are factors to consider.

DISCUSSION QUESTIONS

1. Discuss how you think technology will change distribution channels in the hospitality and travel industries.

2. Explain how international travel changed distribution channels in the hospitality and travel industries.

3. What are the major differences between a distribution channel for a business making tangible products and a firm producing hospitality and travel products?

4. Can a business have too many channel members? Explain your answer.

5. Explain the difference between a tour wholesaler and a travel agent.

6. Why is franchising such a fast-growing form of retail organization?

KEY TERMS

Administered VMS A vertical marketing system that coordinates successive stages of production and distribution, not through common ownership or contractual ties, but through the size and power of one of the parties.

Agent A wholesaler who represents buyers or sellers on a more permanent basis, performs only a few functions, and does not take title to goods.

Broker A wholesaler who does not take title to goods and whose function is to bring buyers and sellers together and assist in negotiation.

Channel conflict Disagreement among marketing channel members on goals and roles—on who should do what and for what rewards.

Channel level A layer of middlemen that performs some work in bringing the product and its ownership closer to the final buyer.

Contractual VMS A vertical marketing system in which independent firms at different levels of production and distribution join together through contracts to obtain more economies or sales impact than they could achieve alone.

Corporate VMS A vertical marketing system that combines successive stages of production and distribution under single ownership; channel leadership is established through common ownership.

Direct marketing Marketing through various advertising media that interact directly with consumers, generally calling for the consumer to make a direct response.

Direct-marketing channel A marketing channel that has no intermediary levels.

Direct-mail marketing Direct marketing through single mailings that include letters, ads, samples, foldouts, and other "salespeople on wings" sent to prospects on mailing lists.

Distribution channel (marketing channel) A set of interdependent organizations involved in the process of making a product or service available for use or consumption by the consumer or business user.

Electronic shopping Direct marketing through a two-way system that links consumers with the seller's computerized catalog by cable or telephone lines.

Exclusive distribution Giving a limited number of dealers the exclusive right to distribute the company's products in their territories.

Franchise A contractual association between a manufacturer, wholesaler, or service organization (a franchiser) and independent business people (franchisees) who buy the right to own and operate one or more units in the franchise system.

Franchise organization A contractual vertical marketing system in which a channel member called a franchiser links several stages in the production–distribution process.

Horizontal marketing systems A channel

arrangement in which two or more companies at one level join together to follow a new marketing opportunity.

Integrated direct marketing Direct-marketing campaigns that use multiple vehicles and multiple stages to improve response rates and profits.

Intensive distribution Stocking the product in as many outlets as possible.

Marketing database An organized set of data about individual customers or prospects that can be used to generate and qualify customer leads, sell products and services, and maintain customer relationships.

Multichannel marketing Multichannel distribution, as when a single firm sets up two or more marketing channels to reach one or more customer segments.

Retailers Businesses whose sales come *primarily* from retailing.

Retailing All activities involved in selling goods or services directly to final consumers for their personal, nonbusiness use.

Telemarketing Using the telephone to sell directly to consumers.

Vertical marketing system (VMS) A distribution channel structure in which producers, wholesalers, and retailers act as a unified system; either one channel member owns the others, or has contracts with them, or has so much power that they all cooperate.

Wholesalers Firms engaged *primarily* in wholesaling activity.

Wholesaling All activities involved in selling goods and services to those buying for resale or business use.

REFERENCES

1. MILFORD PREWITT, "Little Caesar's Licensees Debate Kmart Deal," *Nations Restaurant News*, 25, no. 23 (June 10, 1991), pp. 1, 3; MILFORD PREWITT, "Little Caesars, Kmart Deal Riles Franchisee Group", *Nations Restaurant News*, 26, no. 21 (May 25, 1992), pp. 1, 40.
2. E. RAYMOND COREY, FRANK V. CESPEDES, AND V. KASTURI RANGAN, *Going to Market* (Harvard Business School Press: Boston, 1989), p. xxvii.
3. AMY RICCIARDI, "Marriott, Otani Enter Marketing Pact," *Travel Weekly*, 51, no. 12 (February 10, 1992), p. 3.
4. LOUIS W. STERN AND ADEL I. EL-ANSARY, *Marketing Channels*, 3rd. ed. (Englewood Cliffs, N.J.: Prentice Hall, 1988), p. 3.
5. COREY ET AL., *Going to Market*.
6. MARLEE CROCKER, *Agency Marketplace*, pp. 28–41; ANDREW ADLER, "The Leisure Market," pp. 46–49; SHULY KUSTANOWITZ, "The Business Market," pp. 70–72, in U.S. Travel Agency Survey 1994, *Travel Weekly*, 53, no. 65 (August 18, 1994).
7. CHRISTOPHER SCHULZ, "Hotels and Travel Agents, the New Partnership," *Cornell Hotel and Restaurant Administration Quarterly*, 35, no. 2 (April 1994), p. 45.
8. For more information on familiarization trips, see "How to Plan and Program Travel Agent Familiarization Tours," undated, published by the Hotel Sales and Marketing Association, Washington, D.C.
9. JAMES R. ABBEY, *Hospitality Sales and Advertising* (East Lansing, Mich: Educational Institute of the American Hotel and Motel Association, 1989).
10. FRAN GOLDEN, "Room for Growth," *Travel Weekly*, 53, no. 65 (August 18, 1994), p. 118.
11. RITA MARIE EMMER, CHUCK TAUCK, SCOTT WILKINSON, AND RICHARD G. MOORE, "Marketing Hotels Using Global Distribution Systems," *Cornell Hotel and Restaurant Administration Quarterly*, 34, no. 6 (December 1993), p. 80.
12. Ibid., p. 85.
13. JONATHAN DAHL, "Many Bypass the New Rules of the Road," *Wall Street Journal*, (September 29, 1994), sec. B, pp. 1 and 3.
14. MICHAEL M. COLTMAN, *Tourism Marketing* (Van Nostrand Reinhold: New York, 1989).
15. CHUCK Y. GEE, JAMES C. MAKENS, AND DEXTER J. L. CHOY, *The Travel Industry* (Van Nostrand Reinhold: New York, 1989).
16. For more information on tour brokers, see "HSMA/Group Tour Information Manual" (Washington, D.C.: Hotel Sales and Marketing Association, undated).
17. COLTMAN, *Tourism Marketing*.
18. FRANCE MARTIN, "Consortia Extend Hotels' Regional, Global Reach," *Hotels*, 25, no. 9 (July 1991), pp. x; CHRIS BAUM, "How Utell Reacts to the Market," *Hotels*, 25, no. 9 (September 1991), pp. 73–74; JAMES CARPER, "The New Brand of SRS," *Steigenberger Hotels*, 25, no. 10 (October 1991), pp. 72–74.
19. See J. C. HOLLOWAY AND R. V. PLANT *"Marketing for Tourism"* (Pittman, London, 1992), pp. 124–126.
20. Ibid., p. 135; and ALAN FREDERICKS, "Agency Automation," Travel Agency Survey 1992, *Travel Weekly*, 51, no. 65 (August 13, 1992) pp. 87–90.
21. KEN WESTERN, "Internet Inn: Best Western Marketing

on Network," *Arizona Republic* (January 31, 1995), p. E1.

22. DAVID VIS, "Best Western Is Latest Hotel Chain to Market Properties on Internet," *Travel Weekly*, 54, no. 8 (January 30, 1995), pp. 1, 53.

23. MICHELLE JOHNSON, "Technically Speaking, Plugged In," *Boston Globe* (September 9, 1994), p. 87.

24. DINAH A. SPROTZER, "Hotel Chain Shifts Policy on Coupons," *Travel Weekly*, 51, no. 8 (January, 27, 1992), p. 1+.

25. See IRVING REIN, PHILIP KOTLER, AND MARTIN STROLLER, *High Visibility* (New York: Dodd, Mead, 1987).

26. LOUIS STERN AND ADEL I. EL-ANSARY, *Marketing Channels*, 3rd. ed. (Englewood Cliffs, N.J.: Prentice Hall, 1988), p. 3.

27. JACYLN FIERMAN, "How Gallo Crushes the Competition," *Fortune* (September 1, 1986), p. 27.

28. ANDY KOSTECKA, Franchising in the Economy (Washington, D.C.: U.S. Printing Office, January 1987), p. 2.

29. See LAURA ZINN, "Want to Buy a Franchise? Look before You Leap," *Business Week* (May 23, 1988), pp. 186–187; and "Why Franchising Is Taking off," *Fortune* (February 12, 1990), p. 124.

30. FRANCHISE REPORT, *Restaurant Business*, 90, no. 5 (March 20, 1991), pp. 106–117; "The Top One Hundred," *Restaurant Business*, 90, no. 17 (November 20, 1991), pp. 116–132.

31. FRANCHISE FACT FILE, *Lodging Hospitality* (July 1991), pp.49–53.

32. RUSSELL SHAW, "Marriott Moves Courtyard into Franchise Mode," *Hotel and Motel Management*, 206, no. 1 (January 14, 1991), pp. 1, 60.

33. BILL POLING, "Motorcoach Network Launches Partner Program for Hotels," *Travel Weekly*, 51, no. 83 (October 15, 1992), p. 7.

34. See LEE ADLER, "Symbiotic Marketing," *Harvard Business Review* (November–December 1966), pp. 59–71; and P. VARADARAJAN AND DANIEL RAJARATNAM, "Symbiotic Marketing Revisited," *Journal of Marketing* (January 1986), pp. 7–17.

35. See ROBERT WEIGAND, "Fit Products and Channels to Your Markets," *Harvard Business Review* (January–February 1977), pp. 95–105.

36. FRANCESE PAULA, "Breaking the Rules: Delivering Responsive Service," *Hospitality Research Journal*, 16, no. 2 (1993), p. 69.

37. See AVIJIT GOSH, *Retail Management* (Chicago: Dryden Press, 1990), pp. 216–249.

38. DONALD E. LUNDBERG, *The Restaurant: From Concept to Operation* (Wiley, 1985), p. 35.

Promoting Products: Communication and Promotion Policy

*O*n October 23, 1993, two-hundred thousand people watched a multimillion dollar pyrotechnic show. Later that evening and the next morning, hundreds of millions of people would see glimpses of the same show on their television. The event was the implosion of the Dunes hotel, a publicity event to celebrate the opening of the Treasure Island Resort in Las Vegas. Mirage Resorts, the parent company of the Treasure Island, purchased the Dunes property for future expansion. Steve Wynn, CEO of Mirage Resorts, developed a plan to prematurely raze the 10-story sign and 23-story north tower of the Dunes. The empty buildings were going to have to be razed at some point, so why not raze them as part of an opening celebration for the Treasure Island.

 Today, building implosions are a common and cost-effective way of clearing land. Thus, if the Dunes implosion was to attract the media's attention, it would have to be extraordinary. Steve Wynn hired a pyrotechnics expert and developed a spectacular show. The show included 6 minutes of fireworks set from the building's roof. This was followed by explosions of fireballs, representing cannon shots from a replica of the HMS Britannia at the Treasure Island. These cannon shots first hit the 10-story Dunes' sign, bringing it to the ground. Then they hit the building, igniting 550 gallons of aviation fuel and sending flames shooting up the building. Finally, 365 pounds of dynamite was detonated, sending the building to the ground.

Besides this event, the resort placed an ad that appeared on all three major television networks simultaneously. As viewers changed channels, they saw the same message, hinting of the opening of a wonderfully mysterious place. This unique placement of the ads created its own publicity. The resort also placed one-page ads featuring a skull and cross bones in key cities throughout the country. Steve Wynn purchased an hour of network time from NBC at a cost of $1.7 million to show "The Adventure Begins." This was an infomercial in the form of a movie, which featured the implosion of the Dunes. The movie was shot at the Treasure Island and subtly takes viewers on a tour of the property. The purchase of the time ensured that his production would be aired on the desired date. Some cost was offset through the sale of commercials. Wynn timed the show for the end of January. The opening and the Christmas and New Year holidays would ensure good business until January. Wynn thus timed it to generate interest in the hotel during what could be a slack period. After NBC broadcast the movie, Mirage Resorts then featured "The Adventure Begins" as a choice on in-room television in the Mirage and Treasure Island.[1]

Most hotels and restaurants do not have $4 million to spend on opening promotions. However, the techniques applied by the Treasure Island apply to all operations. The opening promotion of the Mirage was well planned and creative. Maximum benefit was gained from every promotional dollar spent because of preplanning. The resort used several different media and integrated its publicity and advertising efforts. To be effective, promotional efforts must be well planned and well executed.

Chapter 16 explains communication and promotion strategy, the basic underpinnings of all efforts to promote products.

We start with **determining the response** that we are seeking from the target audience, which may be **awareness, knowledge, liking, preference, conviction,** or **purchase.** We continue with guidelines on **choosing a message,** including **content, structure, format,** and **choosing media,** including **personal** and **nonpersonal communications channels.**

We continue by reviewing the basic methods for **setting a total promotional budget: affordable, percentage of sales, competitive parity,** and **objective and task** methods. We consider the nature of each promotional tool: **advertising, personal selling, sales promotion,** and **public relations.** Finally, we conclude by considering factors in setting the **promotion mix: type of product and market, push** versus **pull strategies, buyer readiness states,** and **product life-cycle stage.**

Chapter Preview

Modern marketing calls for more than developing a good product, pricing it attractively, and making it available to target customers. Companies must also continuously communicate with their present and potential customers. Every company is inevitably cast into the role of communicator and promoter.

What is communicated should not be left to chance. To communicate effectively, companies often hire advertising agencies to develop effective ads, sales-promotion specialists to design sales-incentive programs, and public relations firms to develop corporate images. Salespeople are trained to be friendly, helpful, and persuasive. For any company the question is not whether to communicate, but how much to spend and in what ways.

A modern company manages a complex marketing communications system. The company communicates with its marketing intermediaries, consumers, and various publics. Intermediaries communicate with their consumers and publics. Consumers communicate with each other by word of mouth and with members of other publics. Meanwhile, each group provides feedback to every other group.

A company's total marketing communications program, called its **promotion mix,** consists of a specific blend of advertising, sales promotion, public relations, and personal selling to achieve advertising and marketing objectives. The four major promotion tools are defined next:

Advertising: Any paid form of nonpersonal presentation and promotion of ideas, goods, or services by an identified sponsor.

Sales promotion: Short-term incentives to encourage the purchase or sales of a product or service.

Public relations: Building good relations with the company's various publics by obtaining favorable publicity, developing a good corporate image, and handling or heading off unfavorable rumors, stories, and events.

Personal selling: Oral presentation in a conversation with one or more prospective purchasers for the purpose of making sales.[2]

Within these categories are specific tools, such as sales presentations, point-of-purchase displays, specialty advertising, trade shows, fairs, demonstrations, brochures, literature, press kits, posters, contests, premiums, and coupons. At the same time, communication goes beyond these specific promotional tools. The product's design, its price, the shape and color of its package, and the stores that sell it all communicate something to buyers. Although the promotion mix is the company's primary communication activity, the entire marketing mix—promotion, product, price, and place—must be coordinated for greatest communication impact.

This chapter looks at two questions: *What are the major steps in developing effective marketing communication? How should the promotion budget and mix be determined?* Chapter 17 focuses on mass communication tools—advertising and sales promotion. Chapter 18 looks at public relations. Chapter 19 examines the sales force as a communication and promotion tool.

STEPS IN DEVELOPING EFFECTIVE COMMUNICATION

Marketers must understand how communication works. Communication involves the nine elements shown in Figure 16-1. Two elements are the major parties in a communication: the sender and the receiver. Another two are the major communication tools: the message and the media. Four are major communication functions: encoding, decoding, response, and feedback. The last element is noise in the system. These elements are defined next and applied to a Taco Bell television ad:

Sender: The party sending the message to another party, in this case, Taco Bell.

Figure 16-1
Elements in the communication process.

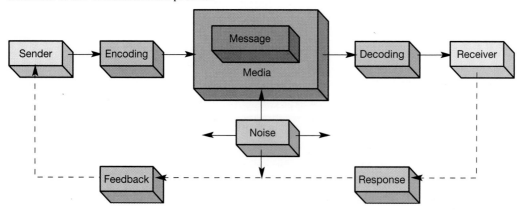

Encoding: The process of putting thought into symbolic form. Taco Bell's advertising agency assembles words and illustrations into an advertisement that will convey the intended message.

Message: The set of symbols that the sender transmits—the actual Taco Bell advertisement.

Media: The communication channels through which the message moves from sender to receiver, in this case, television and the specific television programs that Taco Bell selects.

Decoding: The process by which the receiver assigns meaning to the symbols encoded by the sender. A consumer watches the ad and interprets the words and illustrations that it contains.

Receiver: The party receiving the message sent by another party—the consumer who watches the Taco Bell ad.

Response: The reactions of the receiver after being exposed to the message—any of hundreds of possible responses, such as the consumer likes Taco Bell better, is more likely to eat at Taco Bell next time, or … nothing.

Feedback: That part of the receiver's response communicated back to the sender. Taco Bell's research shows that consumers like and remember the ad, or consumers write or call Taco Bell praising or criticizing the ad or Taco Bell's products.

Noise: The unplanned static or distortion during the communication process that results in the receiver getting a different message than the sender sent; for example, the consumer has poor TV reception or is distracted by family members while watching the ad.

This model points out the key factors in good communication. Senders must identify the audiences that they want to reach and the responses that they seek. They must be good at encoding messages that take into account how the target audience decodes them. They must send the message through media that reach target audiences. And they must develop feedback channels so that they can assess the audience's response to the message.

Thus the marketing communicator must make the following decisions: (1) identify the target audience, (2) determine the response sought, (3) choose a message, (4) choose the media through which to send the message, (5) select the message source, and (6) collect feedback.

Identifying the Target Audience

A marketing communicator starts with a clear target audience in mind. The audience may be potential buyers or current users, those who make the buying decision, or those who influence it. The audience may be individuals, groups, special publics, or the general public. The target audience will heavily affect the communicator's decision on what will be said, how it will be said, when it will be said, where it will be said, and who will say it. For example, The Hotel Nikko Chicago targets the business traveler. To do this they place a full page color advertisement in *Fortune*, a magazine read by many business people. The headline of the ad reads;

> "The Chicago Business Hotel.
> Redefined."

The ad discusses and provides photographs of the hotel's features that will be perceived to be benefits by the business traveler. These features include: an excellent location for the business traveler, an executive business center, a fully staffed fitness center, and guest rooms with spacious work areas.

The target audience for many hospitality firms may remain fairly steady for several years and then suddenly change. In far too many cases, advertising directors and agencies respond slowly to these changes, thus negating communication effectiveness.

In the early 1990s the U.S. airline industry began to witness a dramatic change in the profile of air travelers. The proportion of business travelers, which includes people who pay full economy or first-class fares, fell from 52% in 1982 to 40% in 1994, with no end in sight for the decline.[3] This was due to four trends:

1. Middle management ranks were cut through industry restructuring.
2. Areas that normally supplied business travelers, such as consulting, defense, and sales, were down.
3. Video conferencing and other new telecommunications technology had reduced the need for business travel.
4. Companies with private jets learned to use them more efficiently, reducing their need for commercial aviation.

The full-service airlines, U.S. Air, Delta, United, and American, were left with two basic strategic decisions concerning a target audience.

Alternative A: Advertise/promote to the profitable business segment and hope to take market share from other full-service carriers.

Alternative B: Advertise/promote to a mix of business and leisure customers, recognizing that the leisure passenger was less profitable.

Determining the Response Sought

Once a target audience has been defined, the marketing communicator must decide what response is sought. Of course, in most cases the final response is purchase. But purchase is the result of a long process of consumer decision making. The marketing communicator needs to know where the target audience stands in relation to the product and to what state it needs to be moved.

The Indian tribes of South Dakota wished to significantly increase tourist visitation to their reservations. Their objectives were

- To provide guests for B&B operations.
- To increase the market for Indian products.
- To participate in other tourism-related incomes.
- To correct misconceptions about the American Indian. It was deemed important to show that the Lakota, Dakota, and Nakota people are living cultures.

This combination of economic and cultural education objectives led to the development of the Alliance of Tribal Tourism Advocates (ATTA) as a communication vehicle. Instead of depending on the State of South Dakota Department of Tourism or other organizations, Indians would promote themselves. "If you want to visit an Indian, the best person to talk with is a native American," said Ronald L. Neiss, acting director of ATTA and a member of the Rosebud Sioux Tribal Council.[4]

The target audience may be in any of six buyer readiness states: awareness, knowledge, liking, preference, conviction, or purchase, which are shown in Figure 16-2.

Awareness

First, the communicator must be able to gauge the target audience's awareness of the product or organization. The audience may be totally unaware of it, know only its name, or know one or a few things about it. If most of the target audience is unaware, the communicator tries to build awareness, perhaps by building simple name recognition. This process can begin with simple messages repeating the name. Even then, building awareness takes time. Suppose that an independent restaurant named The Hungry Hunter opens in a northern suburb of Houston. There are 50,000 people within a 3-mile radius of the restaurant. Initially, the restaurant will have little name recognition. The Hungry Hunter may set an objective of making 40% of the people living within 3 miles of the restaurant aware of its name.

Red Roof Motels utilize the color of their roofs and locations with good visibility near freeways to create awareness. Another Red Roof strategy is to simultaneously develop several properties in an area. This has a "mushroom" effect, as motorists suddenly see Red Roof Inns everywhere. Restaurant chains such as Quincy's use a similar strategy.

Awareness communication is a never ending responsibility. People forget names of other people, places, and products. A product must have *top-of-mind* awareness. It is of little value to a company if it is eventually remembered following 20 competitors.

Dress is a rich form of communication whose value is repeatedly demonstrated within the hospitality industry. For that reason it is difficult to understand why many hotels and restaurants permit the attitude that any clothing is acceptable as long as it is clean. It is equally strange that many companies adopt a bland uniform that is virtually nondistinguishable from those of competitors.

Singapore Airlines instantly communicates with the public that it offers a unique, professional, and somewhat exotic service. Female flight atten-

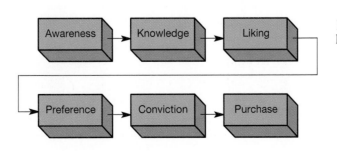

Figure 16-2
Buyer readiness states.

dants (Singapore girl) and their Batik uniforms have become an image and standard that is instantly recognized and appreciated by passengers. Airlines within western nations would undoubtedly face serious union and public relations problems by using a Singapore girl approach in advertising and public relations. It is important to recognize that Canadian, U.S., and European carriers are in competition with airlines such as Singapore Air, Cathay Pacific, and Thai Air. Western carriers do not need to copy Singapore girl, but they must find effective ways to instantly communicate with the same customer base.

It is impossible not to be aware of the Luxor Hotel/Casino in Las Vegas. This hotel is a 30-story pyramid topped by a spotlight with an intensity of 40 billion candles. If somehow people miss that they will not miss the 100-foot-tall sphinx at the entrance, whose eyes shoot laser images on the spray of a spectacular fountain. Inside the hotel there is a 29 million-

Bermuda uses the slogan "Bermuda. A Short Trip to the Perfect Holiday." Most of the consumer advertisements for Bermuda mention that Bermuda is less than 2 hours away. The Bermuda Department of Tourism knows that most people are aware of Bermuda, but many people do not know that it is only about 2 hours off the east coast of the United States. Courtesy of the Bermuda Department of Tourism and DDB Needham Worldwide, Inc.

cubic-foot atrium, a model of King Tut's tomb, a laser show, seven restaurants, and a River Nile. You would literally have to be blind to miss the Luxor Hotel/Casino.

Product awareness is a major objective of highway billboard advertising. The time span that a motorist can devote to reading a billboard is so limited that brand or product awareness reinforcement is virtually the only purpose for this medium.

The Atlantic City expressway leads to the hotels and casinos of that city. Two billboards by competing hotel/casinos were placed at the last available location before entering the city. A billboard by Showboat said "Free Parking—The only casino/hotel in Atlantic City with Free Parking." A competing billboard by Resorts International featured a smiling portrait of Merv Griffin, who said, "The Best Buffet Just Got Better."

The two competitors used very different product differentiation tactics, but both wanted the visitors to be knowledgeable of a unique product feature. Which was most effective? It is probably impossible to ever know. Both could fail had they selected product features unimportant to the visitors. Chances are good that both hotel/casinos understood their markets and decided to make them aware of a single critical product feature.

Knowledge

The target audience might be aware of the company or product but know little else. The Hungry Hunter specializes in wild game, but the market may not be aware of this. The restaurant may decide to select product knowledge as its first communication objective.

The chain of Ruth's Chris Steak House restaurants uses a simple slogan and advertises on a quarter-page in airline in-flight magazines. The message is directed at frequent flyers who deserve a "sizzling reward." The advertisement features a color photo of a very thick steak, a list of restaurant addresses, and the slogan of Ruth's Chris Steak House—*"Home of Serious Steaks."* This simple message quickly gives the reader knowledge of restaurant location, size of the steak, and seriousness of the restaurant as a steak house.

Liking

If target audience members know the product, how do they feel about it? We can develop a range of preference such as a "likert scale" covering degrees of liking, for example, "dislike very much," "dislike somewhat," "indifferent," "like somewhat," and "like very much." If the market is unfavorable toward the Hungry Hunter, the communicator must learn why and then develop a communication campaign to create favorable feelings. If unfavorable feelings are based on real problems, such as slow service, then communication alone cannot do the job. The Hungry Hunter will have to fix its problems and then communicate its renewed quality.

In some geographical markets a restaurant with the name Hungry Hunter might face extreme hostility. Markets with a high concentration of animal rights, antihunting consumers could pose such severe problems that entry would be unwise. Communication within such markets could be negative, resulting in highly undesirable local and even national or worldwide publicity.

Benihana, the Japanese restaurant, is aware that Americans like the restaurant and that, despite occasional trade disputes, Americans like Japanese people. One of Benihana's more colorful communication tactics is the use of a hot-air balloon designed to look like a Japanese male with a black, turn-down mustache and a red hat prominently displaying the name Benihana.

Preference

A target audience might like the product but not prefer it to others. In this case, the communicator must try to build consumer preference. The communicator will promote the product's quality, value, performance, and other features. The communicator can check on the campaign's success by measuring audience preferences after the campaign. If the Hungry Hunter finds that many of the area residents like the name and concept but choose other restaurants, it will have to identify those areas where its offerings are better than for competing restaurants. It must then promote its advantages to build preference among possible customers.

Conviction

A target audience might prefer the product but not develop a conviction that they should purchase the product now. Marketers have a responsibility to turn favorable attitudes into conviction, because conviction is closely linked with purchase.

A public relations tactic that has proved effective for many restaurants is to work with local nonprofit groups such as a Rotary Club and the Red Cross. For example, a restaurant offers a special dinner such as spaghetti and salad on an off-night, such as Monday. Members of the local Rotary Club sell tickets and proceeds go to the Red Cross. Those buying the tickets now have a conviction that they should go to the restaurant. Some may still not go if the restaurant appears to be dirty or if they hear that the food is bad. But, normally, conviction leads to purchase consumption.

Purchase

Finally, some members of the target audience might have conviction but not quite get around to making the purchase. They may wait for more information or plan to act later. The communicator must lead these consumers to take the final step. Actions might include offering the product at a low price, offering a premium, or letting consumers try it on a limited basis. The Hungry Hunter may provide a "Tuesday Night Special," offering prime rib or its seafood of the day for $9.95 instead of the usual price of $14.95.

Choosing a Message

Having defined the desired audience response, the communicator turns to developing an effective message. Ideally, the message should get **attention**, hold **interest**, arouse **desire**, and obtain **action** (a framework known as the **AIDA** model). In practice, few messages take the consumer all the way from awareness to purchase, but the AIDA framework does suggest the desirable qualities of a good message.

In putting the message together, the marketing communicator must solve three problems: what to say (message content), how to say it logically (message structure), and how to say it symbolically (message format).

Message Content

The communicator has to figure out an appeal or theme that will produce a desired response. There are three types of appeals.

Rational appeals relate to audience self-interest. They show that the product will produce desired benefits. Occasionally, rational appeals are overlooked. This is the traditional problem of missing the forest because of the trees. The city of Denver received considerable negative feedback from large potential conventions because it did not have a 1000-room convention hotel; yet development costs were too high to justify building such a structure.

The problem was solved when the existing 511-room Hyatt Regency and the 613-room Marriott Hotel, one block apart, joined forces to jointly market their properties as a 1000-room hotel suitable for conventions. By marketing the two hotels as one, several customer benefits became apparent, such as elimination of duplicate planning meetings, a single bill combining charges at both hotels, free telephone calls between the two hotels, combined service staffs, and posting of events at both hotels.[5]

Emotional appeals attempt to provoke emotions that motivate purchase. These include fear, guilt, and shame appeals that entice people to do things that they should (brush their teeth, buy new tires) or stop doing things they shouldn't (smoke, drink too much, overeat).

Emotional appeals are widely used by resorts and hotels to stimulate cross purchases.

- Commercials on in-room television, posters and desk-top tents promote the health center and the need to reduce stress and work off "pounds gained from eating in the hotel."
- "Think of the Spouse and Kids at Home." This theme is widely used to promote a myriad of products available in the hotel, from hand-dipped chocolates to a stuffed animal.

This appeal is also used to convince the business guests to purchase a vacation for the family at one of the chain's resort properties.

Moral appeals are directed to the audience's sense of what is right and proper. They are often used to urge people to support such social causes as a cleaner environment, better race relations, equal rights, and aid to the needy.

Moral appeals clearly are used by a subsector of the lodging industry; the religious camp and retreat sector. Members of this sector range from a monastery with half a dozen guest rooms to summer camps for children and luxurious resort-style hotels, such as that developed by a minister near Charlotte, North Carolina.

Moral appeals usually dwell on the need for spiritual renewal in the right environment with fellow believers. These organizations communicate through religious leaders, previous guests, and advertisements in religious publications.

Message Structure

The communicator must also decide how to handle three message structure issues. The first is whether to draw a conclusion or leave it to the audience. Early research showed that drawing a conclusion was usually the most effective. More recent research, however, suggests that in many cases the advertiser is better off asking questions and letting buyers come to their own conclusions.

The second message structure issue is whether to present a one- or two-sided argument. Usually, a one-sided argument is more effective in sales presentations except when audiences are highly educated and negatively disposed.

The third message structure issue is whether to present the strongest arguments first or last. Presenting them first creates strong attention but may lead to an anticlimactic ending.[6]

Message Format

The communicator also needs a strong format for the message. In a print ad, the communicator has to decide on the headline, copy, illustration, and color. To attract attention, advertisers can use novelty and contrast, eye-catching pictures and headlines, distinctive formats, message size and position, and color, shape, and movement. If the message is to be carried over the radio, the communicator has to choose words, sounds, and voices. The "sound" of Tom Bodett promoting Motel 6 is different from an announcer promoting Hyatt.

If the message is to be carried on television or in person, all these elements, plus body language, must be planned. Presenters plan their facial expressions, gestures, dress, posture, and hair style. If the message is carried on the product or its package, the communicator has to watch texture, scent, color, size, and shape. For example, color plays a major communication role in food preferences. When consumers sampled four cups of coffee that had been placed next to brown, blue, red, and yellow containers (all the coffee was identical, but the consumers did not know this), 75% felt that the coffee next to the brown container tasted too strong, nearly 85% judged the coffee next to the red container to be the richest, nearly everyone felt that the coffee next to the blue container was mild, and the coffee next to the yellow container was seen as weak.

The restaurant chain Angel's Diner employs the use of its menus as a format to transmit more than product and price information. The back of each menu contains 15 Golden Rules and a color picture of gift merchandise for sale in the diner. Guests are encouraged to take miniature menus home.

Message Source   Messages delivered by attractive sources achieve higher attention and recall. Advertisers often use celebrities as spokespeople, such as Michael Jordan for McDonald's. Celebrities are likely to be effective when they personify a key product attribute. But what is equally important is that the spokesperson have credibility.

The use of living personalities to serve as spokespeople for a company or product carries inherent problems.

- Celebrities are often difficult to work with and may refuse to participate in important media events or to pose under certain conditions.
- Living personalities are sometimes publicly embarrassed.

The Peabody Hotel Group has successfully used ducks in its advertising campaigns. This ad associates the ducks with different organizations that have held their meetings at the Peabody Orlando. The Peabody uses the names of the organizations as a form of testimonial. Courtesy of Peabody Hotels and Turkel Schwartz & Partners.

Qantas Airlines has been successful using a kangaroo and a koala bear as symbols. McDonald's has effectively used the imaginary Ronald McDonald, and Embassy Suites used Garfield. Animals and cartoon characters are dependable and unlikely to create negative publicity.

Choosing Media

The communicator must now select channels of communication. There are two broad types of communication channels: personal and nonpersonal.

Personal Communication Channels

In personal communication channels, two or more people communicate directly with each other. They might communicate face to face, person to audience, over the telephone, or even through the mail. Personal communication channels are effective because they allow for personal addressing and feedback.

Some personal communication channels are directly controlled by the communicator. For example, company salespeople contact buyers in the target market. But other personal communications about the product may reach buyers through channels not directly controlled by the company. These might include independent experts making statements to target buyers, such as consumer advocates and consumer buying guides. Or they might be neighbors, friends, family members, and associates talking to target buyers. This last channel, known as word-of-mouth influence, has considerable effect in many product areas.

Personal influence carries great weight for products that are expensive, risky, or highly visible. Hospitality products are often viewed as being risky, since they cannot be tried out beforehand. Therefore, personal sources of information are often sought before someone purchases a travel package, selects a restaurant, or stays at a hotel.

Companies can take several steps to put personal communication channels to work. They can devote extra effort to selling their products to well-known people or companies, who may in turn influence others to buy. They can create opinion leaders—people whose opinions are sought by others—by supplying certain people with the product on attractive terms. Finally, the firm can work to manage word-of-mouth communication by finding out what consumers are saying to others, taking appropriate actions to satisfy consumers, correcting problems, and helping consumers to seek information about the firm and its products.[7]

A common form of personal communication used by hotels and cruise lines is to invite key guests, prospective customers, and members of the community to dine with the captain or general manager. A creative and always successful version is to dine in the kitchen, where guests are greeted by the chef, given samples of dishes being prepared, and made to feel "right at home."

The Condado Plaza Hotel and Casino in San Juan, Puerto Rico, uses one of the oldest and most effective means of communications, a personal letter. A personal letter is sent by the president on quality paper in an executive-sized envelope to prior hotel guests. As an added incentive for the guest to return, a coupon good for $100.00 in hotel services is enclosed. This time-proved method of communication remains effective in an age of fax, mail, and information superhighways.

An adaptation of this technique was used by the new general manager of the Palace Hotel in Beijing, China, Peter L. J. Finamore. The manager was transferred from a sister property in Hong Kong and sent his new business card along with a bright yellow and red greeting card that said, "Keep this card—and see you—at the Palace Hotel Beijing." Members of hotel management meet thousands of guests, drop-by visitors, and others during the year. In many cases, particularly in Asia, cards are exchanged. The card collection should serve as a personal database for the manager, who can later use it to keep in touch with guests and prospective guests. Visitors to

Beijing, particularly first-time visitors, would welcome the opportunity to become a guest in a hotel run by an "old friend."

Nonpersonal Communication Channels

Nonpersonal communication channels are media that carry messages without personal contact or feedback. They include media, atmospheres, and events. Major **media** consist of print media (newspapers, magazines, direct mail), broadcast media (radio and television), and display media (billboards, signs, posters). **Atmospheres** are designed environments that create or reinforce the buyer's leanings toward purchasing a product. The lobby of a five-star hotel contains a floral display, original works of art, and luxurious furnishings to reinforce the buyer's perception that the hotel is a five-star hotel. **Events** are occurrences staged to communicate messages to target audiences. Public relations departments arrange press conferences, grand openings, public tours, and other events to communicate with specific audiences.

The Scanticon Princeton (a conference center) used its lobby as a gallery for original artworks by members of the Princeton Artists Alliance. This resulted in excellent publicity, including a full-page story with pictures and the address of Scanticon Princeton in the Sunday edition of a major Philadelphia newspaper.

Nonpersonal communication directly affects buyers. In addition, using mass media often indirectly affects buyers by causing more personal communication. Mass communications affect attitudes and behavior through a two-step flow of communication. In this process, communications first flow from television, magazines, and other mass media to opinion leaders and then to the less active sections of the population. This two-step flow process means that the effect of mass media is not as direct, powerful, and automatic as once supposed. Rather, opinion leaders step between mass media and their audiences. Opinion leaders are more exposed to mass media and carry messages to people who are less exposed.

The two-step flow concept challenges the notion that people's buying is affected by a trickle down of opinions and information from higher social classes. Because people mostly interact with others in their own social class, they pick up fashions and other ideas from people like themselves who are opinion leaders. The two-step flow concept also suggests that mass communicators should aim their messages directly at opinion leaders, letting them carry the message to others.

The restaurant in the Lakewood, Colorado, Sheraton Convention Hotel offered a strange and negative message to a potentially important market segment. A large sign at the restaurant's entrance said, "Breakfast Special $3.00 for guest; $5.00 for nonguest." When the receptionist was asked why the price difference existed, the answer was, "It's a marketing tactic to encourage guests to eat here."

The hotel is located on Union Avenue, a busy four-lane street in the center of office complexes. Denny's, the nearest sit-down breakfast restaurant, is located on the other side of the street. Guests are unlikely to drive or walk there, crossing four busy lanes of traffic, if the breakfast price in the hotel is reasonable; yet they might invite local business associates to meet them for breakfast in the hotel, only to face a potentially embarrassing situation.

The $3.00 price might entice local office workers to eat at the restaurant, but it may upset hotel guests. It would take a lot of $3.00 breakfasts to make up for an upset business traveler that decided not to come back to the hotel. Serious thought must be given to any message that will be seen or heard by potential customers. It is very easy to seriously offend customers and increasingly difficult to create messages that are positive and effective.

Selecting the Message Source

The message's impact on the audience is also affected by how the audience views the sender. Messages delivered by highly credible sources are persuasive. For example, pharmaceutical companies want doctors to tell about their products. Memphis used prominent people to promote that city as a convention and meeting site. A video was produced in which convention planners, tour wholesalers, and association officials endorsed the city as an ideal convention location.

The use of a golf course by recognized golf pros and celebrities is a means of achieving positive communication with average golfers. Interestingly, in the case of downhill skiing it appears that use of a resort by celebrities such as Hollywood stars is more effective than use by members of the national ski team.

What factors make a source credible? The three factors most often found are expertise, trustworthiness, and likability. Expertise is the degree to which the communicator appears to have the authority needed to back the claim. Doctors, scientists, and professors rank high on expertise in their fields. Trustworthiness is related to how objective and honest the source appears to be. Friends, for example, are trusted more than salespeople. Likability is how attractive the source is to the audience. People like sources who are open, humorous, and natural. Not surprisingly, the most highly credible source is a person who scores high on all three factors—expertise, trustworthiness, and likability.

Dave Thomas serves as an excellent message source for Wendys. After all, he built the company and looks like a jolly uncle and someone who probably never told a lie in his life. Donald J. Trump does not communicate in the same folksy manner as Dave Thomas. Trump is known as a wealthy person of high social prestige with many real estate holdings. An advertisement in the *Wall Street Journal* for the Plaza Hotel appeared more as an announcement that a proud parent would make of a son or daughter graduating from the Air Force Academy.

Donald J. Trump
Presents
The Plaza Hotel
Rated the Best Business Hotel
in North America
For the Fourth Consecutive Year
by Business Traveler International,
and Voted Best U.S. Hotel
by the Robb Report
For the third Consecutive Year

The media, the message, and the spokesperson were in harmony for the Plaza.

Collecting Feedback

After sending the message, the communicator must evaluate its effect on the target audience. This involves asking the target audience whether they remember the message, how many times they saw it, what points they recall, how they felt about the message, and their past and present attitudes toward the product and company. The communicator would also like to measure behavior resulting from the message—how many people bought a product, talked to others about it, or visited the store.

Figure 16-3 shows an example of feedback measurement. Looking at hotel brand *A*, we find that 80% of the total market was aware of it, that 20% of those who were aware had tried it, but that only 20% of those who tried it were satisfied. These results suggest that, although the communication program created awareness, the product failed to give consumers the satisfaction expected. The company should therefore try to improve the product while continuing the successful communication program. With hotel brand *B*, the situation was different: only 40% of the total market was aware of it. Only 10% of those had tried it, and 80% of those who tried it were satisfied. In this case, the communication program needed to be stronger to take advantage of the brand's power to create satisfaction.

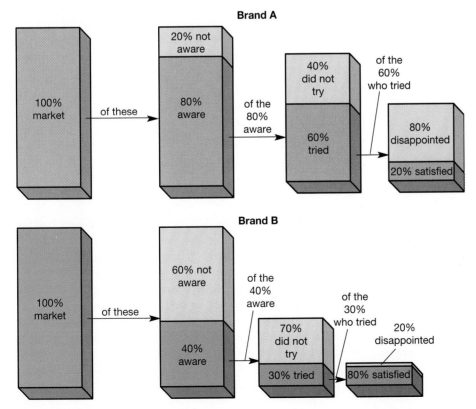

Figure 16-3
Feedback measurements for two brands.

SETTING THE TOTAL PROMOTION BUDGET AND MIX

We have looked at the steps in planning and sending communications to a target audience. But how does the company decide on the total promotion budget and its division among the major promotional tools to create a promotion mix?

Setting the Total Promotion Budget

One of the hardest marketing decisions facing companies is how much to spend on promotion. John Wanamaker, the department store magnate, once said, "I know that half of my advertising is wasted, but I don't know which half. I spent $2 million for advertising, and I don't know if that is half enough or twice too much."

How do companies determine their promotion budget? Four common methods are used to set the total budget for advertising: (1) the affordable method, (2) the percentage of sales method, (3) the competitive parity method, and (4) the objective and task method.[8]

Affordable Method

Many companies use the affordable method: They set a promotion budget at what they think the company can afford. One executive explained this method as follows: "Why it's simple. First, I go upstairs to the controller and ask how much they can afford to give this year. He says a million and a half. Later, the boss comes to me and asks how much should we spend and I say 'Oh, about a million and a half.'"[9]

Unfortunately, this method of setting budgets completely ignores the effect of promotion on sales volume. It leads to an uncertain annual promotion budget, which makes long-range marketing planning difficult. Although the affordable method can result in overspending on advertising, it more often results in underspending.

Percentage of Sales Method

Many companies use the percentage of sales method, setting their promotion budget at a certain percentage of current or forecasted sales, or they budget a percentage of the sales price. Some firms use this method because it is easy. For example, some restauranteurs know that the mean expenditures for promotion for restaurants is 4%. Therefore, they set their promotion budget at 4%.

A number of advantages are claimed for the percentage of sales method. First, using this method means that promotion spending is likely to vary with what the company can "afford." It also helps management to think about the relationship between promotion spending, selling price, and profit per unit. Finally, it supposedly creates competitive stability because competing firms tend to spend about the same percentage of their sales on promotion.

However, in spite of these claimed advantages, the percentage of sales method has little justification. It wrongly views sales as the cause of promotion, rather than as the result. The budget is based on availability of funds, rather than on opportunities. It may prevent increased spending sometimes needed to turn around falling sales. Because the budget varies with year-to-year sales, long-range planning is difficult. Finally, the method does not provide a basis for choosing a specific percentage, except past actions or what competitors are doing.

Competitive Parity Method

Other companies use the competitive parity method, setting their promotion budgets to match competitors' outlays. They watch competitors' advertising or get industry promotion spending estimates from publications or trade associations and then set their budgets based on the industry average.

Two arguments are used to support this method. First, competitors' budgets represent the collective wisdom of the industry. Second, spending what competitors spend helps to prevent promotion wars. Unfortunately, neither argument is valid. There are no grounds for believing that competition has a better idea of what a company should be spending on promotion. Companies differ greatly and each has its own special promotion needs. Furthermore, there is no evidence to indicate that budgets based on competitive parity prevent promotion wars.

Objective and Task Method

The most logical budget setting method is the objective and task method. Using this, marketers develop their promotion budgets by (1) defining specific objectives, (2) determining tasks that must be performed to achieve these objectives, and (3) estimating the costs of performing them. The sum of these costs is the proposed promotional budget.

The objective and task method forces management to spell out its assumptions about the relationship between dollars spent and promotional results. It is also the most difficult method to use, since it can be hard to determine which tasks will achieve specific objectives. So management must consider such questions even though they are hard to answer. With the objective and task method, the company sets its promotion budget based on what it wants to accomplish.

Setting the Promotion Mix

The company must now divide the total promotion budget among the major promotional tools—advertising, personal selling, sales promotion, and public relations. It must carefully blend the promotion tools into a coordinated promotion mix that will achieve its advertising and marketing objectives. Companies within the same industry differ greatly in how they design their promotion mixes. Thus a company can achieve a given sales level with varied mixes of advertising, personal selling, sales promotion, and public relations.

Companies are always looking for ways to improve promotion by replacing one promotion tool with another that will do the same job at less expense. Many companies have replaced a portion of their field sales activities with telephone sales and direct mail. Others have increased their sales promotion spending in relation to advertising to gain quicker sales.

Designing the promotion mix is even more complex when one tool must be used to promote another. Thus, when McDonald's decides to run Million Dollar Sweepstakes in its fast-food outlets (a sales promotion), it has to run ads to inform the public.

Many factors influence the marketer's choice of promotion tools.

Nature of Each Promotion Tool

Each promotion—advertising, personal selling, sales promotion, and public relations—has unique characteristics and costs. Marketers must understand these characteristics to correctly select their tools.

Advertising. Because of the many forms and uses of advertising, generalizing about its unique qualities as a part of the promotion mix is difficult. Yet several qualities can be noted. Advertising's public nature suggests that the advertised product is standard and legitimate. Because many people see ads for the product, buyers know that purchasing the product will be publicly understood and accepted. Advertising also allows the seller to repeat a message many times. Large-scale advertising by a seller says something positive about the seller's size, popularity, and success.

Advertising can be used to build a long-term image for a product (such as Four Seasons or McDonald's ads) and also stimulate quick sales (as when Embassy Suites in Phoenix advertises a promotion for the July 4 week). Advertising can reach masses of geographically dispersed buyers at a low cost per exposure.

Advertising also has shortcomings. Although it reaches many people quickly, advertising is impersonal and cannot be as persuasive as a company salesperson. Advertising is able to carry on only a one-way communication with the audience, and the audience does not feel that it has to pay attention or respond. In addition, advertising can be very costly. Although some forms, such as newspaper and radio advertising, can be done on small budgets, other forms, such as network TV advertising, require very large budgets.

A critical challenge faced by hotel marketers is creating an immediate awareness of brand name to ensure that their properties are included in the traveler's evoked set of lodging choices. The evoked set of brand preferences and the relative impact of advertising and prior stay were investigated in a study of frequent travelers. It was found that chains whose names were well established in a traveler's evoked set most often won the traveler's business. There was little influence on chain name recall of prior stay without ad exposure nor influence on ad exposure without prior stay. The combined effect of ad exposure and prior stay was an important influence on brand selection.[10]

Personal Selling. Personal selling is the most effective tool at certain stages of the buying process, particularly in building buyer preference, conviction, and purchase. Compared with advertising, personal selling has several unique qualities. It involves personal interaction between two or more people, allowing each to observe the other's needs and characteristics and make quick adjustments. Personal selling also lets all kinds of relationships spring up, ranging from a matter of fact selling relationship to a deep personal friendship. The effective salesperson keeps the customer's interests at heart to build a long-term relationship. Finally, with personal selling the buyer usually feels a greater need to listen and respond, even if the response is a polite "no thank you."

These unique qualities come at a cost. A sales force requires a longer-term company commitment than advertising; advertising can be turned on and off, but sales force size is harder to vary. Personal selling is the company's most expensive promotion tool, costing industrial companies an average of $225 per sales call.[11] American firms spend up to three times as much on personal selling as they do on advertising.

Sales Promotion.   Sales promotion includes an assortment of tools, coupons, contests, cents-off deals, premiums, and others, and these tools have many unique qualities. They attract consumer attention and provide information that may lead the consumer to buy the product. They offer strong incentives to purchase by providing inducements or contributions that give additional value to consumers. And sales promotions invite and reward quick response. Advertising says "buy our product." Sales promotion says "buy it now."

Companies use sales promotion tools to create a stronger and quicker response. Sales promotion can be used to dramatize product offers and to boost sagging sales. Sales promotion effects are usually short-lived, however, and are not effective in building long-run brand preference.

Public Relations.   Public relations offers several advantages. One is believability. News stories, features, and events seem more real and believable to readers than do ads. Public relations can reach many prospects who avoid salespeople and advertisements. The message gets to the buyers as news, rather than as a sales-directed communication. And, like advertising, public relations can dramatize a company or product.

A relatively new addition to the promotion mix is the infomercial. This is a hybrid between advertising and public relations. Companies provide interesting stories on videotape for use on television during periods of light viewing, such as early morning. Infomercials provide enough information to keep the attention of viewers combined with a "soft" approach to product or brand advertising.

Hospitality marketers tend to underuse public relations or use it only as an afterthought. Yet a well-thought-out public relations campaign used with other promotion mix elements can be very effective and economical.

Factors in Setting the Promotion Mix

Companies consider many factors when developing their promotion mix, including the following: type of product and market, push versus pull strategy, buyer readiness state, and product life-cycle stage.

Type of Product and Market.   The importance of different promotion tools varies among consumers and commercial markets. When hospitality firms market to consumer markets, they spend more on advertising and sales promotion and often very little on personal selling. Hospitality firms targeting commercial organizations spend more on personal selling. In general, personal selling is more heavily used with expensive and risky goods and in markets with fewer and larger sellers. A meeting or convention is customized for the organization putting on the event. It takes a skilled salesperson to put together a package that will give clients what they want at an appropriate price that will provide good revenue for the company.

Push versus Pull Strategy.   The promotional mix is heavily affected by whether a company chooses a push or pull strategy. The two strategies are contrasted in Figure 16-4. A push strategy involves "pushing" the product through distribution channels to final consumers. The manufacturer directs its marketing activities (primarily personal selling and trade promotion) at channel members to induce them to order and carry the product and to promote it to final consumers. For example, Dollar Rent-A-Car offered travel agents a 15% commission instead of 10% to persuade them to order its brand for clients. Continental Plaza Hotels and Resorts developed a promotion that gave travel agents an extra $10 in addition to their normal commission for bookings. A push strategy provides an incentive for channel members to promote the product to their customers or push the product through the distribution channels.

Using a pull strategy, a company directs its marketing activities (primarily advertising and consumer promotion) toward final consumers to induce them to buy the product. For example, Sheraton placed an ad for its Hawaiian properties in the Phoenix, Arizona, paper. Interested readers were instructed to call their travel planner or ITT Sheraton. If the strategy is effective, consumers will purchase the product from channel members, who will, in turn, order it from producers. Thus, under a pull strategy, consumer demand "pulls" the product through the channels.

Buyer Readiness State.   Promotional tools vary in their effects at different stages of buyer readiness. Advertising, along with public relations, plays a major role in the awareness and knowledge stages, more important than

Figure 16-4
Push versus pull promotion strategy.

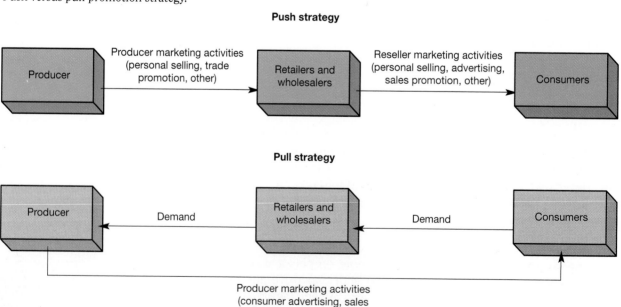

that played by "cold calls" from salespeople. Customer liking, preferences, and conviction are more affected by personal selling, which is closely followed by advertising. Finally, closing the sale is primarily accomplished with sales calls and sales promotion. Only personal selling, given its high costs, should focus on the later stages of the customer buying process.

Product Life-cycle Stage.   The effects of different promotion tools also vary with stages of the product life cycle. In the introduction stage, advertising and public relations are good for producing high awareness, and sales promotion is useful in product early trial. Personal selling must be used to get the trade to carry the product in the growth stage; advertising and public relations continue to be powerful, while promotion can be reduced because fewer incentives are needed. In the mature stage, sales promotion again becomes important relative to advertising. Buyers know the brands, and advertising is needed only to remind them of the product. In the decline stage, advertising is kept at a reminder level, public relations is dropped, and salespeople give the product only a little attention. Sales promotion, however, may continue to be strong.[12]

Chapter Review

I.   Promotion Mix. A company's total marketing program consisting of advertising, sales promotion, public relations, and personal selling.

II.   Four Major Promotion Tools
    1)   Advertising. Any paid form of nonpersonal presentation and promotion of ideas, goods, or services by an identified sponsor.
    2)   Sales Promotion. Short-term incentives to encourage purchase or sales of a product or service.
    3)   Public Relation. Building good relations with the company's various publics by obtaining favorable publicity, developing a good corporate image, and handling or heading off unfavorable rumors, stories, and events.
    4)   Personal Selling. Oral presentation in a convention with one or more prospective purchasers for the purpose of making sales.

III.   Major Steps in Developing Effective Marketing Communication
    1)   Sender. The party sending the message to another party.
    2)   Encoding. The process of putting thought into symbolic form.
    3)   Message. The set of symbols that the sender transmits.
    4)   Media. The communication channels through which the message moves from sender to receiver.
    5)   Decoding. The process by which the receiver assigns meaning to the symbols encoded by the sender.
    6)   Receiver. The party receiving the message sent by another party.
    7)   Response. The reactions of the receiver after being exposed to the message.
    8)   Feedback. That part of the receivers's response communicated back to the sender.

        9) Noise. The unplanned static or distortion during the communication process that results in the receiver getting a different message than the sender sent.

IV. Decisions That the Marketing Communicator Must Make

    1) Identify the target audience.

    2) Determine the response sought. Six buyer readiness states: awareness, knowledge, liking, preference, conviction, and purchase.

    3) Choose a message.

        a) AIDA model. The message should get attention, hold interest, arouse desire, and obtain action.

        b) Three problems that the marketing communicator must solve:

            i) Message content (what to say). There are three types of appeals.

                a) Rational appeals: They relate to audience self-interest. They show that the product will produce desired benefits.

                b) Emotional appeals: They attempt to provoke emotions that motivate purchase.

                c) Moral appeal: They are directed to the audience's sense of what is right and proper.

            ii) Message structure (how to say it).

                a) Whether to draw a conclusion or leave it to the audience.

                b) Whether to present a one- or two-sided argument.

                c) Whether to present the strongest arguments first or last.

            iii) Message format (how to say it symbolically).

                a) Visual ad: Using novelty and contrast, eye-catching pictures and headlines, distinctive formats, message size and position, color, shape, and movement.

                b) Audio ad: Using words, sounds, and voices.

                c) Message source: Using attractive sources to achieve higher attention and recall, such as using celebrities.

    4) Choose the media through which to send the message.

        a) Personal communication channels: Personal communication is used for products that are expensive and complex. It can create opinion leaders to influence others to buy.

        b) Nonpersonal communication channels: They include media (print, broadcast, and display media), atmospheres, and events.

    5) Select the message source. Messages delivered by highly credible sources are persuasive. Expertise, trustworthiness, and likability are three factors that make a source credible.

    6) Collect feedback. Evaluating the effects on the targeted audience.

V. Determining the Promotional Budget

    1) Four Common Methods for Setting the Total Promotion Budget

        a) Affordable method: A budget is set based on what management thinks they can afford.

        b) Percentage of sales method: Companies set promotion budget at a certain percentage of current or forecasted sales or a percentage of the sales price.

        c) Competitive parity method: Companies set their promotion budgets to match competitors.

        d) Objective and task method: Companies develop their promotion budget by defining specific objectives, determining the tasks that must be performed to achieve these objectives, and estimating the costs of performing them.

2) Understanding the Nature of Each Promotion Tool and Setting the Promotion Mix

   a) *Advertising:* It suggests that the advertised product is standard and legitimate; it is used to build a long-term image for a product and to stimulate quick sales. However, it is also considered impersonal, one-way communication.

   b) *Personal selling:* It builds personal relationships, keeps the customers' interests at heart to build long-term relationships, and allows personal interactions with customers. It is also considered the most expensive promotion tool per contact.

   c) *Sales promotion:* It includes an assortment of tools: coupons, contests, cents-off deals, premiums, and others. It attracts consumer attention and provides information. It creates a stronger and quicker response. It dramatizes product offers and boosts sagging sales. It is also considered short-lived.

   d) *Public relations:* It has believability. It reaches prospective buyers and dramatizes a company or product.

3) Factors in Setting the Promotion Mix

   a) *Type of product and market:* The importance of different promotional tools varies among consumers and commercial markets.

   b) *Push versus pull strategy*

   i) *Push strategy:* The company directs its marketing activities at channel members to induce them to order, carry, and promote the product.

   ii) *Pull strategy:* A company directs its marketing activities toward final consumers to induce them to buy the product.

   c) *Buyer readiness state:* Promotional tools vary in their effects at different stages of buyer readiness.

   d) *Product life-cycle stage:* The effects of different promotion tools also vary with stages of the product life-cycle.

DISCUSSION QUESTIONS

1. Discuss the factors that may prevent someone from receiving the message intended by the communication. What strategies can be employed to minimize this possibility?

2. Explain the difference between promotion and advertising.

3. Why is it important to identify your target audience when developing marketing communications? Provide an example of a communication from a hospitality or travel company that does a good job of communicating with a specific market segment. The example can be any form of communication, for example, an advertisement, a sales promotion, or publicity.

4. Why do large hotels spend a major part of their promotional budget on personal selling?

5. Recently, a number of restaurants have shifted some of their promotional budget from advertising to public relations. What benefits does public relations offer that would make restau-

rants spend more on public relations?

6. The percentage of sales method is one of the most common ways of setting a promotional budget. What are some advantages and disadvantages of this method?

7. Find an example of a promotion for a hospitality company that uses the push promotion strat-

egy. Explain how the company is using the strategy.

8. Apply the four major tools in the marketing communication mix to a hospitality or travel company by showing how a company can use all these tools.

KEY TERMS

Advertising   Any paid form of nonpersonal presentation and promotion of ideas, goods, or services by an identified sponsor.

Affordable method   Setting the promotion budget at what management thinks the company can afford.

Atmospheres   Designed environments that create or reinforce the buyer's leanings toward consumption of a product.

Buyer readiness states   The stages consumers normally pass through on their way to purchase, including awareness, knowledge, liking, preference, conviction, and purchase.

Competitive parity method   Setting the promotion budget to match competitors' outlays.

Emotional appeals   Message appeals that attempt to stir negative or positive emotions that will motivate purchase; examples include fear, guilt, shame, love, humor, pride, and joy appeals.

Events   Occurrences staged to communicate messages to target audiences, such as news conferences or grand openings.

Media   Nonpersonal communications channels, including print media (newspaper, magazines, direct mail), broadcast media (radio, television) and display media (billboards, signs, posters).

Moral appeals   Message appeals that are directed to the audience's sense of what is right and proper.

Nonpersonal communication channels   Media that carry messages without personal contact or feedback, including media atmosphere and events.

Objective and task method   Developing the promotion budget by (1) defining specific objectives, (2) determining the tasks that must be performed to achieve these objectives, and (3) estimating the

costs of performing these tasks; the sum of these costs is the proposed promotion budget.

Percentage of sales method   Setting the promotion budget at a certain percentage of current or forecasted sales or as a percentage of the sales price.

Personal communication channels   Channels through which two or more people communicate directly with each other, including face to face, person to audience, over the telephone, or through the mail.

Personal selling   Oral presentation in a conversation with one or more prospective purchasers for the purpose of making sales.

Promotion mix   The specific mix of advertising, personal selling, sales promotion, and public relations a company uses to pursue its advertising and marketing objectives.

Public relations   Building good relations with the company's various publics by obtaining favorable publicity, building up a good corporate image, and handling or heading off unfavorable rumors, stories, and events.

Pull strategy   A promotion strategy that calls for spending a lot on advertising and consumer promotion to build up consumer demand; if successful, consumers will ask their retailers for the product, the retailers will ask the wholesalers, and the wholesalers will ask the producers.

Push strategy   A promotion strategy that calls for using the sales force and trade promotion to push the product through channels; the producer promotes the product to wholesalers, the wholesalers promote to retailers, and the retailers promote to consumers.

Rational appeals   Message appeals that relate to the audience's self-interest and show that the product will produce the claimed benefits; examples include appeals to product quality, economy, value, or performance.

Sales promotion Short-term incentives to encourage purchase or sales of a product or service.

Word-of-mouth influence Personal communication about a product between target buyers and neighbors, friends, family members, and associates.

REFERENCES

1. DAVID BAINES, "A Mogul and His Mirage Are a Reality Placing Their Bets," *Vancouver Sun* (March 3, 1994), p. A1.; SCOTT CRAVEN, "Dunes Hotel Brought Down in the Face of New Mega Resorts," *Phoenix Gazette* (October 28, 1993), Metro Age, B6; JEFFERSON GRAHAM, "Vegas Casino Opens with a Blast," *USA Today* (October 27, 1993), Life p. 1D; JAMIE MCKEE, "New Resorts Spend Millions to Reach National audience," *Las Vegas Business Press*, 10, no. 37 (November 1, 1993), p. 1.

2. These definitions, except for sales promotion, are from *Marketing Definitions: A Glossary of Marketing Terms* (Chicago: American Marketing Association, 1960). Also, PETER D. BENNETT, *Dictionary of Marketing Terms* (Chicago: American Marketing Association, 1988).

3. HOWARD BANKS, "A Sixties Industry in a Nineties Economy," *Forbes*, 153, no. 10 (May 9, 1994), p. 108.

4. KONNIE LE MAY, "South Dakota Tribes Beating Tomtoms to Drum up Increased Tourist Trade," *Star-Ledger*, Section Eight (May 8, 1994), p. 6.

5. STEVE RAABE, "2 Hotels Link up for Sales," *Denver Post*, Business Section C (May 4, 1994), p. 1C.

6. For more on message content and structure, see LEON G. SCHIFFMAN AND LESLIE LAZAR KANUK, *Consumer Behavior*, 4th ed. (Englewood Cliffs, N.J.: Prentice Hall, 1991), Ch. 10; AND FRANK R. KARDES, "Spontaneous Inference Processes in Advertising: The Effects of Conclusion Omission and Involvement on Persuasion," *Journal of Consumer Research* (September 1988), pp. 225–233.

7. K. MICHAEL HAYWOOD, "Managing Word of Mouth Communications," *Journal of Services Marketing* (Spring 1989), pp. 55–67.

8. For a more comprehensive discussion on setting promotion budgets, see MICHAEL L. ROTHSCHILD, *Advertising* (Lexington, Mass.: D. C. Heath, 1987), Ch. 20.

9. Quoted in DANIEL SELIGMAN, "How Much for Advertising?" *Fortune* (December 1956), p. 123.

10. MICHAEL S. MORGAN, "Traveler's Choice: The Effects of Advertising and Prior Stay," *Cornell Hotel and Restaurant Administration Quarterly*, 32, no. 4 (December 1991), pp. 40–49.

11. "The Rise (and Fall) of Cost per Call," *Sales and Marketing Management* (April 1990), p. 26.

12. For more on advertising and the product life cycle, see JOHN E. SWAN AND DAVID R. RINK, "Fitting Market Strategy to Product Life Cycles," *Business Horizons* (January–February 1982), pp. 60–67.

Promoting Products: Advertising, Direct Marketing, and Sales Promotion

17

"*Hi, Tom Bodett for Motel 6 here. I'm sitting in room 201 in Yuba City, California, and it's wild. We're watching color TV, I'm talkin' on the phone and my family's thumbing through the Yellow Pages. I'm tellin' you, we're having a Ball.*" This is an excerpt from one of the most successful radio campaigns for a hospitality company, Motel 6's campaign featuring Tom Bodett. The following is one of the spots from the series.

> *Hi, Tom Bodett for Motel 6 with a plan for anyone whose kids are on their own now. Take a drive, see some of the country and visit a few relatives. Like your sister Helen and her husband Bob. They're wonderful folks always happy to pull the hide-a-bed out for you, but somehow the smell of moth-balls just isn't conducive to gettin' a good night's sleep. And since Bob gets up at 5:30, well that means you do, too. So here's the plan. Check into Motel 6. 'Cause for around 22 bucks, the lowest prices of any national chain, you'll get a clean, comfortable room, and Helen and Bob'll think you're mighty considerate. Well you are, but maybe more important, you can sleep late and not have to wonder if the towels in their bathroom are just for decora-tion. My rule of thumb is, if they match the tank and seat cover, you better leave 'em alone. Just call 505-891-6161 for reservations. I'm Tom Bodett for Motel 6. Give my best to Helen and Bob and we'll leave the light on for you.*

For 24 years, Motel 6 never had an advertising campaign. Price and word of mouth brought in guests. This strategy worked well against inde-pendents and small regional chains. Eventually, other low-priced chains

emerged and price was no longer a point of differentiation for Motel 6. Occupancy of the hotel dropped from 81% in 1981 to 69.5% in 1985. In 1985, Kohlberg, Kravis, Roberts and Company purchased Motel 6. KKR hired Joe McCarthy to run Motel 6, and McCarthy hired Hugh Thrasher to head up marketing. In February 1986, McCarthy awarded their advertising contract to The Richards Group in Dallas.

The advertising agency spent almost one year conducting research. They held scores of focus groups to find out who stays at a Motel 6, what they like, and what they dislike about Motel 6. The 6 in Motel 6 stands for $6 a day, the original price of a Motel 6 room in 1962. To provide a room for $6, the original hotels where built inexpensively, with few conveniences. In 1985, when KKR took over, Motel 6 did not offer rooms with telephones, and it cost $1.49 to have the television turned on. In the early hotels, television sets were coin operated, and guests paid by the hour. In 1986, the price of a room was $17.95 systemwide, regardless of location. Guests paid cash in advance, because Motel 6 didn't take credit cards. There was a charge for children sharing the same room with their parents. Families paid a rate determined by a complicated formula. Guests had to write to the hotel for a reservation, because there was no central reservation system. The advertising agency found that all these factors were guest irritants.

Information obtained from the research was used to redesign the company's marketing mix. Phones were added, and free local phone service was offered. There was no service charge for hook-up to long-distance calls. The order for 50,000 phones by Motel 6 was AT&T's largest phone order by a public company. The addition of phones made Motel 6 more attractive to salespeople and added a sense of security for the leisure traveler, both for themselves and in knowing that families could reach them. The charge for television was dropped, and the room charge for children staying in the same room was also dropped. The price of a room was changed from a standard price across all geographic markets to one that reflected local market conditions. When management felt they had developed a product that was right for the market, Motel 6 started its radio advertising campaign in November 1986. In October 1986, Motel 6 had consumer awareness of less than 10%. By the end of the year, radio spots had lifted awareness to more than 50%. Revenues went from $256 million in 1986 to more than $425 million in 1989. Occupancy jumped from 66.7% to 72.7% in 1987, ending a 6-year decline marked by an occupancy drop of almost 15 points.

The success of the advertising campaign was attributed to consumer research and marketing mix changes. It was not until Motel 6 adjusted the product to market demand that advertising was initiated. The campaign allowed Motel 6 to reposition their properties from a cheap place to stay to a motel chain offering value for the dollar. They went from almost no awareness in the marketplace to a product with more than 50% awareness. Profits increased from an $18.7 million loss in 1986 to a $5.3 million profit in 1988.[1]

Chapter 17 discusses the ways products are promoted through advertising, direct marketing, and sales promotion.

First, we survey the major decisions in advertising, including **setting objectives and budget; creating and evaluating the advertising message; selecting advertising media** based on research, frequency, and impact; and **choosing media types, vehicles, and timing**.

Next we discuss **direct marketing**, and why it has grown in popularity, including direct marketing's role in relationship marketing. This section concludes with an overview of **integrated direct marketing** and the development of a **marketing database system**.

The chapter concludes with a review of **sales promotion**, beginning with objectives, and looking at **consumer-promotion, trade-promotion, and business-promotion tools**.

ADVERTISING

We define advertising as any paid form of nonpersonal presentation and promotion of ideas, goods, or services by an identified sponsor. The hospitality and travel industries spend billions of dollars on advertising. In 1993, the top hospitality and travel advertisers were McDonald's ($736.6 million), Wendy's ($168.3), Marriott ($132.6 million), and Delta Airlines ($113.4 million).[2]

Advertising is a good way to inform and persuade, whether the purpose is to sell Hilton International Hotels around the world or to get residents of Kuala Lumpur, the capital of Malaysia, to stay at a nearby resort on the island of Langkawi. Organizations have different ways of managing their advertising. The owner or the general manager of an independent restaurant usually handles the restaurant's advertising. Most hotel chains give responsibility for local advertising to the individual hotels, while corporate management is responsible for national and international advertising. In some corporate offices, the director of marketing handles advertising. Other firms might have advertising departments to set the advertising budget, work with an outside advertising agency, and handle direct-mail advertising and other advertising not done by the agency. Large companies commonly use an outside advertising agency, because it offers several advantages (see Marketing Highlight 17-1).

MAJOR DECISIONS IN ADVERTISING

Marketing management must make five important decisions in developing an advertising program. These decisions are listed in Figure 17-1 (on page 520) and discussed next.

Objectives Setting

The first step in developing an advertising program is to set advertising objectives. Objectives should be based on information about the target market,

Marketing Highlight 17-1

How Does an Advertising Agency Work?

Madison Avenue is a familiar name to most Americans. It's a street in New York City where some major advertising agency headquarters are located. But most of the nation's 10,000 agencies are found outside New York, and almost every city has at least one agency, even if it's a one-person shop. Some ad agencies are huge—the largest U.S. agency, Young & Rubicam, has annual worldwide billings (the dollar amount of advertising placed for clients) of more than $6 billion. Dentsu, a Japanese agency, is the world's largest agency with billings of more than $10 billion.

Advertising agencies were started in the mid-to-late 1800s by salespeople and brokers who worked for the media and received a commission for selling advertising space to various companies. As time passed, salespeople began to help customers prepare their ads. Eventually, they formed agencies and grew closer to the advertisers than the media. Agencies offered more advertising and marketing services to their clients.

Even companies with strong advertising departments use advertising agencies. Agencies employ specialists who can often perform advertising tasks better than the company's own staff. Agencies also bring an outside point of view to solving the company's problems, along with the experience of working with different clients and situations. Agencies are partly paid from media discounts and often cost the firm very little. Since a client can drop its agency at any time, most agencies work hard to do a good job. Smaller clients are generally charged a fee because they often do not use much commissionable media.

Full-service Ad Agencies. Advertising agencies usually have four departments: *creative*, which develops and produces ads; *media*, which selects media and places ads; *research*, which studies audience characteristics and wants; and *business*, which handles the agency's business activities. Each account is supervised by an account executive; staff members in each department are usually assigned to work on one or more accounts.

Agencies often attract new business through their reputation or size. Generally, however, a client invites a few agencies to make a presentation for its business and then selects one of them.

Ad agencies have traditionally been paid through commissions and some fees. Under this system, the agency receives 15% of the media cost as a rebate. Suppose that the agency buys $60,000 of magazine space for a client. The magazine bills the advertising agency for $51,000 ($60,000 less 15%), and the agency bills the client for $60,000, keeping the $9000 commission. If the client bought space directly from the magazine, it would pay $60,000, because commissions are only paid to recognized advertising agencies.

Both advertisers and agencies have become increasingly unhappy with the commission system. Larger advertisers complain that they pay more for the same services received by smaller ones simply because they place more advertising. Advertisers also believe that the commission system drives agencies away from low-cost media or noncommissionable media and short advertising campaigns. Agencies are unhappy because they perform extra services for an account without receiving additional revenue. As a

positioning, and marketing mix. Marketing positioning and mix strategies define the role that advertising must perform in the total marketing program.

An advertising objective is a specific communication task to be accomplished with a specific target audience during a specific period of time. Advertising objectives can be classified by their aim: to **inform, persuade, or remind**. **Informative advertising** is used heavily when introducing a

result, the trend is now toward paying either a straight fee or a combination commission and fee. Some large advertisers are tying agency compensation to the performance of the agency's advertising campaigns. Today, only about 35% of companies still pay their agencies on a commission-only basis.

Another trend is also hitting the advertising agency business. In recent years, as growth in advertising spending has slowed, many agencies have tried to keep growing by acquiring other agencies, thus creating huge agency-holding companies. One of the largest of these megagroups, Saatchi & Saatchi PLC, includes several large agencies—Saatchi & Saatchi Compton, Ted Bates Worldwide, DFS Dorland Worldwide, and others—with combined billings exceeding $15 billion. Many agencies have also sought growth by diversifying into related marketing services. These new megagroup agencies offer a complete list of integrated marketing and promotion services under one roof, including advertising, sales promotion, public relations, direct marketing, and marketing research.

Specialized Ad Agencies. The hospitality and travel industries often uses the services of specialized ad agencies. The *specialty advertising agency* offers a variety of merchandise, such as coffee mugs, dishes, luggage, and thousands of other items used in sales promotions and employee incentive programs. Some observers feel that this form of agency is primarily a broker of products.

The *incentive agency* is important to the hospitality and travel industries as a provider of guests. Again, many observers feel it should not properly be classified as an ad agency.

The *brochure ad agency* once again is an enterprise that many feel is incorrectly called an ad agency. This company specializes in the production and delivery of travel-industry-related brochures. Brochure ad agencies acquire and maintain rack space in restaurants, truck stops, motel lobbies, museums, and other places frequented by highway travelers. Restaurants, motels, and tourist attractions who depend on transient highway customers often view the work of these agencies as highly valuable.

Special Location Agencies. In New Zealand and Australia a highly unusual specialized ad agency has developed. Some individuals find the work of this agency to be intrusive. This company acquires the rights to the back of the door in public restrooms and places ads in this location.

Other specialized ad agencies have acquired advertising space that should be considered by members of the hospitality and travel industries. These include airport advertising, ball field advertising, transit advertising on public conveyance, and shelter advertising (ad space on bus stop shelters and benches). Given the wide diversity of members of the hospitality and travel industries, virtually every specialized media probably has a useful role for some firm.

Sources: See Walecia Konrad, "A Word from the Sponsor: Get Results—Or Else", *Business Week* (July 4, 1988), p. 66; "Saatchi Leads Top 11 Megagroups", *Advertising Age* (March 29, 1989); and R. Craig Endicott, "Ad Age 500 Grows 9.7%," *Advertising Age* (March 26, 1990), pp. S1–S2.

---

new product category and when the objective is to build primary demand. When an airline opens a new route, its management often runs full-page advertisements informing the market about the new service. Stouffer Hotels ran a two-page spread in *Business Travel News* introducing the new Stouffer Concourse Hotel in Atlanta. The ad targeted corporate meeting planners, giving them information on function space, conference rooms, and other

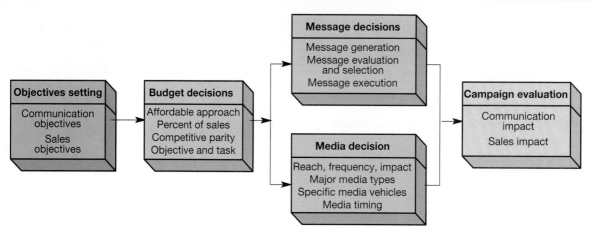

Figure 17-1
Major advertising decisions.

features of the hotel. Junior's Deli, in the Westwood section of Los Angeles, uses direct-mail campaigns to create new customers. New residents in the neighborhood receive a gift certificate for a Deli Survival Kit, which contains a chunk of beef salami, two types of cheese, a loaf of fresh rye bread, and a homebaked dessert. The kit is absolutely free, with no purchase required, but the certificate must be redeemed at the restaurant. More than 1000 new neighbors come in to claim their kits each year. Thus the kit not only informs potential customers about the restaurant, but results in visits to the restaurant by customers who sample its products.[3]

Persuasive advertising becomes more important as competition increases and a company's objective becomes building selective demand. Some persuasive advertising has become comparison advertising, which compares one brand directly or indirectly with one or more other brands. For example, Ramada Inn ran a $6 million campaign directed at Holiday Inns in 1992. The ad's theme, "Ramada's in, Holiday's out," was a hard-hitting message suggesting that Ramada offers more value than Holiday Inns. The initial spot offered Holiday Inn customers a $5 rebate if they switched to Ramada Inns. The vice-president of Hospitality Franchise Systems, the parent company of Ramada Inns said, "You've got to steal share out there. The economy is in a sewer. You have got to be pretty aggressive."[4]

Burger King has used direct-comparison advertising against McDonald's. Table tents in Burger King show a picture of a hamburger. Inside the hamburger is a white circle depicting the size of a McDonald's hamburger compared to Burger King's. The copy read, "The only one who won't like our new burger is McDonald's. The new Burger King 2.8oz flame broiled hamburger has 75% more beef than McDonald's hamburger."

The use of direct-comparison advertising is a controversial subject. Many marketers believe that comparison ads are not appropriate as they obviously draw attention to the competitor, rather than strictly to the company's product. An unwritten rule of using comparison ads is that the prestige brands and market share leaders should never use this tactic because it draws attention to competitors and causes the customer to question the value of the market share leader or prestige brand.

Reminder advertising is important for mature products, because it keeps consumers thinking about the product. Expensive McDonald's ads on television are designed to remind people about McDonald's, not to inform or persuade them. The Old Spaghetti Warehouse, a restaurant chain based in Dallas, sends customers a postcard thanking them for their patronage. The postcard features a message, such as "Till We Meet Again" or "Can't Stop Thinking About You." A handwritten thank you from the manager appears on each card.[5] The personalized thank you card creates goodwill and reminds the customer about the restaurant.

For an advertising campaign to create long-term sales, the product advertised must create satisfied customers. One mistake frequently made by the owners of new restaurants is advertising before the operation has gone through a shakedown period. The owners, eager to get a return on their investment, advertise before the restaurant's staff is properly trained and the restaurant's systems are tested under high-demand situations.

Because most people look forward to trying a new restaurant, advertising campaigns are usually effective, resulting in waits during peak periods. However, success can be short lived when restauranteurs deliver poor-quality food, poor service, or poor value. Dissatisfied customers quickly spread negative word of mouth to potential customers, who are eager to find out about the new restaurant. Frequently, advertising a noncompetitive product will quicken the product's death through negative word. The owner of a restaurant in Houston who went through this experience and ultimately went out of business blamed his loss on fickle customers. In his words, "The restaurant used to have waits every night of the week. Now, the restaurant is empty. I can't believe how fickle customers are." The customers weren't fickle; in fact, they knew exactly what they wanted: good food and good service. These were things the restaurant did not offer when they first opened.

The president of a hospitality marketing, advertising, and public relations firm believes that

> The implementation of an effective advertising campaign is one of the fastest ways to jeopardize the performance of a mediocre property. You must first be sure that the property can live up to the promises your advertising makes. If your property or service is inconsistent with the claims made, the money you spend to generate additional business will probably do little more than increase the number of dissatisfied guests.[6]

Even highly satisfied customers need frequent reminders. Ski and scuba diving resorts share a common problem. Satisfied guests often fail to return because they wish to experience new slopes and new dive areas. Years may pass before the guest is ready to return. Reminder advertising can shorten that period of time.

Setting the Advertising Budget

After determining advertising objectives, a company can establish an advertising budget for each product. The role of advertising is to affect demand for a product. The company wants to spend the amount needed to achieve the sales goal. Four commonly used methods for setting the advertising budget were discussed in Chapter 15. Here we will describe some specific factors that should be considered when setting a budget:

Stage in the Product Life Cycle. New products typically need large advertising budgets to build awareness and gain consumer trial. Mature brands usually require lower budgets as a ratio to sales.

Market Share. High-market-share brands usually require greater advertising expenditures as a percentage of sales than low-share brands. Building a market or taking share from competitors requires larger advertising budgets than maintaining current share.

Competition and Clutter. In a market with many competitors and heavy advertising support, a brand must be advertised more frequently to be heard above the noise of the market.

Advertising Frequency. Larger advertising budgets are essential when many repetitions are needed to present the brand's message.

Product differentiation. A brand that closely resembles others in its product class (pizza, limited-service hotels, air travel) requires heavy advertising to set it apart. When a product differs greatly from those of competitors, advertising can be used to communicate differences to consumers.

How much impact does advertising really have on consumer purchases and brand loyalty? One study found that advertising increased purchases by loyal users but was less effective in winning new buyers. The study found that advertising appears unlikely to have a cumulative effect that leads to loyalty. Features, displays, and especially price have a stronger impact on response than advertising.[7]

These findings were not well received by the advertising community, and several advertising professionals attacked the study's data and methodology. They claimed that the study primarily measured short-run sales effects and thus favored pricing and sales promotion activities that tend to have a more immediate impact. Most advertising, on the other hand, takes many months or even years to build strong brand positions and consumer loyalty. Long-run effects are difficult to measure. This debate underscores the fact that the measurement of sales results from advertising remains in its infancy.

Message Decisions

The message decision is a third decision in the advertising management process. A large advertising budget does not guarantee a successful advertising campaign. Two advertisers can spend the same amount on advertising with dramatically different results. Studies have shown that creative advertising messages can be more important than the number of dollars spent. No matter how big the budget, advertising can succeed only if its message gains attention and communicates well.

Good advertising messages are especially important in today's costly and cluttered advertising environment. The average consumer has 22 television stations from which to choose, plus about 11,500 magazines in the United States. Add the countless radio stations and a continuous barrage of direct-mail ads and out-of-home media and the result is consumers bombarded with ads at home, work, and all points in between.[8]

All this advertising clutter bothers some consumers and causes big problems for advertisers. Take, for instance, the situation facing network television advertisers. They typically pay $100,000 to $200,000 for 30 seconds of advertising time during a popular prime-time TV program and even more if it is an especially popular program or event like the Super Bowl ($1,000,000). In such cases, their ads are sandwiched in with a clutter of 60 other commercials, announcements, and network promotions per hour.

Until recently, television viewers were an almost captive audience for advertisers. Viewers had only a few channels from which to choose. Those who found the energy to get up and change channels during unwelcome commercial breaks usually found only more of the same on other channels. With the growth in cable TV, VCRs, and remote-control units, today's viewers have many more options. They can avoid ads altogether by watching commercial-free cable channels. They can "zap" commercials by pushing the fast-forward button during taped programs, instantly turn off the sound during a commercial, or "zip" around the channels. Advertisers take such "zipping" and "zapping" seriously. One expert predicts that, by the year 2000, 60% of all TV viewers may be regularly tuning out commercials.[9]

Thus, just to gain and hold attention, today's advertising messages must be better planned and more imaginative, entertaining, and rewarding to consumers. Creative strategy will play an increasingly important role in advertising success. Developing a creative strategy requires three message steps: generation, evaluation and selection, and execution.

Message Generation

Hotels, resorts, B&Bs, and cruise lines face an inherent barrier to effective communication with the customer. This is the intangibility of the product. A hotel's product is experienced only at or after the time of purchase. This characteristic of services in general poses genuine challenges for message creation. As the editor of the *Cornell Quarterly* pointed out, "An advertisement can depict a product—a food item, a desk, an exercise machine—but how does one illustrate a hotel stay?"[10]

Creative people have different ways of developing advertising messages. Many start by talking to consumers, dealers, experts, and competitors. Others imagine consumers using the product and determine the benefits that consumers seek. Although advertisers create many possible messages, only a few will be used.

Marketing managers bear a responsibility to critically review the message, the media, and the illustration and creative concepts recommended by the advertising agency. A fine line sometimes exists between responsible review and unwarranted intrusion into the professional work of advertising agencies. Marketing managers for client companies such as a hotel or excursion train are expected to know their products, customers, and employees better than any ad agency. In the final analysis, they must assume responsibility for messages that fail to effectively motivate customers or offend employees. On the brighter side, they can also shine in the glory of creative, well-received advertising.

(MUSIC UP)

ANNCR: (VO) Was it aeons of isolation from the rest of the world?

Or was it the way the wind blew?

Or the way the rain fell?

Was it the angle of the sun?

Or was it a bird blown off course

that found its way here

with a single seed that grew...

...and changed the course of history?

Somehow we just evolved differently.

AUSTRALIA
FEEL THE WONDER

Australia. Feel the wonder.

1-800-395-7000

For your free 130-page travel planner, call 1-800-395-7000.

Story boards like this one are used to convey television advertising messages before the ad is produced on film. Courtesy of Australia Tourist Commission.

Message Evaluation and Selection

The advertiser must evaluate possible appeals on the basis of three characteristics. First, messages should be meaningful, pointing out benefits that make the product more desirable or interesting to consumers. Second, appeals should be distinctive. They should tell how the product is better than competing brands. Finally, they must be believable. Making message appeals believable is difficult, because many consumers doubt the truth of advertising. One study found that, on average, consumers rate advertising messages as "somewhat unbelievable."

Message Execution

The impact of the message depends on what is said and how it is said—message execution. The advertiser has to put the message across in a way that wins the target market's attention and interest. Advertisers usually begin with a statement of the objective and approach of the desired ad.

The advertising agency's creative staff must find a style, tone, words, and format for executing the message. Any message can be presented in different execution styles, such as the following:

1. Slice-of-life shows one or more people using the product in a normal setting. Bennigan's developed a television ad showing friends enjoying an evening at Bennigan's.

2. Life-style shows how a product fits with a life-style. For example, an airline advertising its business class featured a businessperson sitting in an upholstered chair in the living room, having a drink, and enjoying the paper. The other side of the ad featured the same person in the same relaxed position with a drink and a paper in one of the airline's business class seats.

3. Fantasy creates a wonder world around the product or its use. For instance, Cunard's Sea Goddess features a woman lying in a raft in the sea, with the luxury liner anchored in the background. A cocktail server in tuxedo is walking through the ocean carrying a drink for the woman.

The use of fantasy has also occurred in the development of resort hotels. Disney may have started the trend with hotels on the property of Disney World, but Hyatt Corporation, Westin Hotels and Resorts, and many others have adopted the concept. Such hotels are designed to surround the guests with a fantasy ambience, including costumed employees, entertainment, and dramatic physical structures, such as waterfalls, a pyramid, or a miniature Amazon river. Fantasy hotels are expensive to build and maintain, with costs per room running $300,000 or more and 2000 or more employees.

The human psyche is receptive to fantasy. Archaeologists often have difficulty discerning whether cave paintings represent fantasy or sights really observed. Children's books, cartoons, and top-selling novels are fantasy. It is not surprising that fantasy advertising is effective within an industry that appeals to one's desire to escape.

4. Mood or image builds a mood or image around the product, such as beauty, love, or serenity. No claim is made about the product except through suggestion. Bally's resort in Las Vegas developed an advertisement designed to change its image after its $37 million renovation. The headlines in the ad were "To them a watch does more than tell time, A car is not merely transportation, And their resort is Bally's in Las Vegas."

5. Musical shows one or more people or cartoon characters singing a song about the product. Many cola ads have used this format. Delta Airlines used music effectively in its "We Love to Fly and It Shows" campaign. Certain cultures seem particularly receptive to the use of theme songs and sing-along melodies in advertisements. Australians often use simple but catchy melodies in their advertisements. Brazilians often use adaptations of samba music, particularly music that was popular during carnival.

6. Personality symbol creates a character that represents the product. The character might be created by the company, such as McDonald's Ronald McDonald, or real, such as Tom Bodett of Motel 6.

Advertising agencies will present mock-ups of ad concepts for the client to review. Marketing managers must critically review the message, the media, illustrations, and creative concepts recommended by the advertising agency. These are two mock-ups presented to Grand Heritage Hotels—both were rejected by Grand Heritage. Grand Heritage is a collection of elegant luxury hotels with historical significance located in North America and Europe, including The Pontchartrain in New Orleans, The Brazilian Court in Palm Beach, Florida, Thornbury Castle in Avon, England, and The Hotel Royal Monceau in Paris.

The purpose of this ad is to attract inquiries from potential clients interested in Grand Heritage managing their hotel. The ad has attractive graphics, but they detract from the message. Grand Heritage wants to convey to potential clients that their management team will perform and produce results. However, an ad conveying an image of business performance would create a more positive image than a circus performer.

This ad is very creative and draws an analogy between Grand Heritage's success in the hotel business and what would happen if it went into the farming business. The problem is that Grand Heritage's luxury image and a farmer standing in a field are incompatible.

    7. Technical expertise shows the company's expertise with the product. Hotels often use this style in advertisements directed toward meeting and convention planners, emphasizing that they have the technical expertise to support the meeting planner. American Airlines make heavy and frequent use of expertise, particularly that of its pilots and mechanics.

    8. Scientific evidence presents survey or scientific evidence that the brand is better or better liked than one or more other brands. During the month of May 1992, Northwest Airlines had the highest percentage of on-time arrivals, the lowest level of mishandled baggage, and the lowest level of customer complaints of the seven largest airlines, according to the Department of Transportation air travel consumer report. Northwest took advantage of this achievement by developing an advertisement using the DOT survey results.

Northwest, however only included the top seven airlines. Southwest, the eighth largest airline had actually beaten Northwest in of these categories. Southwest developed a humorous ad to counteract Northwest's claim, stating that their official corporate response was "Liar, liar. Pants on fire." And they used DOT results to back their claim.

The restaurant industry is facing either a dilemma or an opportunity, depending on one's viewpoint. The U.S. Food & Drug Administration is considering requiring restaurants to back up claims for dishes labeled healthy or light by including nutritional information. Hyatt Hotels Corporation assembled a team of six chefs and a nutritionist to create a new line, Cuisine Naturelle, listing information such as calories, carbohydrates, cholesterol, sodium, protein, and fat. Cuisine Naturelle now represents 30% of lunch orders and 10% of breakfasts and dinners where it is offered.[11]

Does this imply that the restaurant industry will need to switch advertising to describe the nutritional value of its products, rather than the excitement, taste, and enjoyment? If a restaurant advertises one line as healthy, does this imply that the rest of its products are unhealthy? Will warning labels have to be attached to a milk shake, prime rib, or french fries, just as they now appear on cigarette packages? These are questions of genuine concern to the restaurant industry.

9. Testimonial evidence features a highly believable or likable source endorsing the product. After Tip O'Neill retired as majority leader of the U.S. Senate, Choice Hotels developed an ad using the well-known politician in a testimonial about the value offered by the company's senior citizen discount.

The advertiser must also choose a tone for the ad. Hyatt always uses a positive tone, with ads that say something very positive about its own products. They avoid humor that might take attention away from the message. By contrast, Motel 6 and Red Roof ads are humorous.

Memorable and attention-getting words must also be found. For example, the themes listed on the left of the table on the page 529 would have had much less impact without the creative phrasing on the right.

Finally, format elements will make a difference in an ad's impact and cost. A small change in design can make a big difference in an ad's effect. The illustration is the first thing the reader notices. That illustration must be strong enough to draw attention. Then the headline must effectively entice the right people to read the copy. The copy, the main block of text in the ad, must be simple but strong and convincing. These three elements must effectively work together. Even then, a truly outstanding ad will be noted by less than 50% of the exposed audience. About 30% of the exposed audience will recall the main point of the headline.

After lengthy deliberation at the highest executive levels, and extensive consultation with our legal department, we have arrived at an official corporate response to Northwest Airlines' claim to be number one in Customer Satisfaction.

"Liar, liar. Pants on fire."

Okay. We lost our temper for a moment. Northwest Airlines didn't really lie. And, its pants aren't actually on fire. Northwest simply excluded Southwest Airlines from its comparison.

Fact. According to the U.S. Department of Transportation's Consumer Report for May, the real leader in Customer Satisfaction is Southwest Airlines. That means we received the fewest complaints per 100,000 passengers among all Major airlines, including Northwest Airlines.

More facts. The Department of Transportation's

Consumer Report also shows Southwest Airlines best in On-time Performance (highest percentage of systemwide domestic flights arriving within 15 minutes of schedule, excluding mechanical delays), best in Baggage Handling (fewest mishandled bags per 1,000 passengers), as well as best in Customer Satisfaction, from January through August 1992.

It's all there in black and white.

Fly the real No. 1. You'll know there's no substitute for satisfaction. Call Southwest Airlines or your travel agent for reservations.

SOUTHWEST AIRLINES℠
Just Plane Smart™
1-800-I-FLY-SWA (1-800-435-9792)

© Southwest Airlines 1992

Southwest countered Northwest's claim that they had won the "triple crown" with this advertisement. Courtesy of Southwest Airlines.

THEME	CREATIVE COPY
Take a break from cooking.	"You Deserve a Break Today." (McDonald's)
Add some fun to your day by eating lunch away from the office.	"Throw Away the Old Bag." (The Chancery, Milwaukee)
Have a fast-food hamburger prepared with the condiments you select.	"Have it your way." (Burger King)
If you just need a room to sleep in overnight, why pay for extra features you will never use?	"Just Right, Overnight." (La Quinta)
We don't rent as many cars, so we have to do more for our customers.	"We're number two, so we try harder." (Avis)
Our employees love what they are doing, and it shows in the high quality of their work.	"We love to fly and it shows." (Delta Airlines)

Approximately 25% will remember the advertiser's name, and fewer than 10% will have read most of the body copy. Less than outstanding ads will not achieve even these results.

Media Decision

The fourth step is to choose the media to carry the message. The major steps in media selection are (1) deciding on reach, frequency, and impact; (2) choosing among major media types; (3) selecting specific media vehicles; and (4) deciding on media timing.

Deciding on Reach, Frequency, and Impact

To select media, the advertiser must decide what reach and frequency are needed to achieve advertising objectives. *Reach* is a measure of the percentage of people in the target market who are exposed to the ad campaign during a given period of time. For example, the advertiser might try to reach 70% of the target market during the first year. *Frequency* is a measure of how many times the average person in the target market is exposed to the message. For example, the advertiser might want an average exposure frequency of three. The advertiser must also decide on desired media *impact*, the qualitative value of message exposure through a given medium. For products that must be demonstrated, television messages using sight and sound are more effective. The same message in one magazine (*Newsweek*) may be more believable than in another (the *National Enquirer*).

Suppose that the advertiser's product has the potential to appeal to a market of 1 million consumers. The goal is to reach 700,000 consumers (70% of 1 million). Because the average consumer will receive three exposures, 2.1 million exposures (700,000 $\times$ 3) must be bought. If the advertiser wants exposures of 1.5 impact (assuming 1.0 impact is the average), a rated number of exposures of 3.15 million (2.1 million $\times$ 1.5) must be bought. If 1000 exposures with this impact cost $10, the advertising budget must be $31,500 (3150 $\times$ $10). In general, the more reach, frequency, and impact that the advertiser seeks, the larger the advertising budget will have to be.

Gross rating points (GRP) show the gross coverage or duplicated coverage of an advertising campaign. GRPs are determined by multiplying reach times frequency. In the example above, an ad with a reach of 700,000 and frequency of three exposures would produce 210 gross rating points if the market was 1 million. Each gross rating point is equal to 1% of the market.

Choosing among Major Media Types

The media planner has to know the reach, frequency, and impact of each major media type. The major advertising media are summarized in Table 17-1. The major media types, in order of advertising volume, are newspapers, television, direct mail, radio, magazine, and outdoor. Each medium has advantages and limitations.

McDonald's Purchases 20,000 Outdoor Boards

In 1992, McDonald's purchased 20,000 outdoor boards to display the message, "Great food, great value at McDonald's." This is believed to be the largest single buy of outdoor boards. Traditionally, local McDonald's stores and franchisees purchased outdoor advertising as part of their local store marketing, with little outdoor advertising having been purchased by the chain's corporate office. In 1991, outdoor advertising accounted for only 1 percent of McDonald's national media expenditures. Many locally purchased outdoor boards were directional signs, designed to let drivers know where McDonald's restaurants were located and when to exit the highway.

The use of outdoor boards appealed to McDonald's because it allowed them to convey a single national message along with a localized message on promotions, products, and prices. James Keller, vice-president of marketing for Gannett, said the ability to customize boards to local marketing needs is one of the strengths of outdoor advertising.[12]

Media planners consider many factors when making their media choices, including the media habits of target consumers. Radio and television, for example, are the best media for reaching teenagers. The nature of the product also affects media choices. Resorts are best shown in color magazines. Fast-food ads targeted at young children are best on television. Different types of messages may require different media. A message announcing a Mother's Day buffet would be conveyed effectively on radio or in newspapers. A message that contains technical data, such as an ad explaining the details of a travel package, might be disseminated most effectively in magazines or through direct mail. Cost is also a major factor in media choice. While television is very expensive, newspaper advertising costs much less. The media planner looks at both the total cost of using a particular medium and at the cost per thousand exposures, that is, the cost of reaching 1000 people.

Ideas about media impact and cost must be reexamined regularly. For many years, television and magazines dominated the media mixes of national advertisers, while other media were neglected. Recently, costs and clutter (competition from competing messages) have increased while audi-

Table 17-1
Profiles of Major Media Types

MEDIUM	VOLUME IN BILLIONS	PERCENTAGE	EXAMPLES OF COST	ADVANTAGES	LIMITATIONS
Newspapers	30.7	23.4	$29,800 for one page, weekday Chicago Tribune	Flexibility; timeliness; good local market coverage; broad acceptance; high believability	Short lift; poor reproduction quality; small pass-along audience
Television	29.4	22.4	$1500 for 30 seconds of prime time in Chicago	Combines sight, sound, and motion; appealing to the senses; high attention; high reach	High absolute cost; high clutter; fleeting exposure; less audience selectivity
Direct mail	25.4	19.3	$1520 for the names and addresses of 40,000 veterinarians	Audience selectivity; flexibility; no ad competition within the same medium; personalization	Relatively high cost; junk mail image
Radio	8.7	6.6	$700 for 1 minute of drive time (during commuting hours, A.M. and P.M.) in Chicago	Mass use; high geographic and demographic selectivity; low cost	Audio presentation only; lower attention than television; nonstandardized rate structures; fleeting exposure
Magazines	7.0	5.3	$84,390 for one page, four colors, in Newsweek	High geographic and demographic selectivity; credibility and prestige; high-quality reproduction; long life; good pass-along readership	Long ad purchase lead time; some waste circulation; no guarantee of position
Outdoor	1.0	0.8	$25,500 per month for 71 billboards in metropolitan Chicago	Flexibility; high repeat exposure; low cost; low competition	No audience selectivity; creative limitations
Other	29.1	22.2			
Total	131.3	100.0			

Sources: Columns 1 and 2 reprinted with permission from Robert J. Cohen, "Ad Gains Could Exceed 6% This Year," *Advertising Age,* (May 3, 1993), p. 4.

ences have dropped. As a result, many marketers have adopted strategies targeted at narrower segments, and TV and magazine advertising revenues have leveled off or declined. Advertisers have increasingly turned to alternative media, ranging from cable TV to outdoor advertising.

Given these and other media characteristics, the media planner must decide how much of each type of media to buy. Table 17-2 is a comparison of Marriott and Wendy's media expenditures.

Selecting Specific Media Vehicles

The media planner must now choose the best specific media vehicles within each general media type. For example, television vehicles include "Friends," "Sixty Minutes," and the "CBS Evening News." Magazine vehicles include *Newsweek*, *Travel and Leisure*, *The New Yorker*, and *Town and Country*. If advertising is placed in magazines, the media planner must look up circulation figures and the costs of different ad sizes, color options, ad positions, and frequencies for various specific magazines. The planner then evaluates each magazine on such factors as credibility, status, reproduction quality, editorial focus, and advertising submission deadlines. The media

Table 17-2
Comparison of Marriott's and Wendy's Use of Media[13]

MEDIA	MARRIOTT	WENDY'S
Magazine	4,261,000	5,000
Sunday magazine	471,000	0
Newspaper	20,279,000	0
Outdoor	295,000	1,915,000
Network TV	0	41,954,000
Spot TV	10,094,000	39,518,000
Syndicated TV	0	8,424,000
Cable TV	2,955,000	2,386,000
Network radio	3,594,000	0
Spot radio	6,175,000	215,000
Total measured media	48,911,000	94,416,000
Total unmeasured media	90,800,000	29,700,000
Total media	139,711,000	124,116,000

Terms used in the table:
Unmeasured media is an estimate of direct mail, sales promotion, couponing, special events, and other promotional activities.
Network TV is advertising on the major networks: ABC, CBS, NBC.
Spot TV is TV purchased on a market-by-market basis.
Syndicated TV includes satellite-distributed syndicated TV and Fox Broadcasting Company.
Cable TV includes CNN, ESPN, Family Channel, MTV: Music Television, WTBS, USA Network, and other such channels.

planner decides which vehicles give the best reach, frequency, and impact for the money.

Media planners also compute the cost per thousand persons reached by a vehicle. If a full-page, four-color advertisement in *Newsweek* costs $100,000 and *Newsweek*'s readership is 3.3 million people, the cost of reaching each 1000 persons is $28. The same advertisement in *Business Week* may cost only $57,000, but reach only 775,000 persons, at a cost per thousand of about $74. The media planner would favor magazines with the lower cost per thousand for reaching target consumers.

The media planner must also consider the costs of producing ads for different media. Whereas newspaper ads can cost very little to produce, flashy television ads may cost millions. The average cost of producing a single 30-second television commercial is $180,000. Some ads with special effects can cost over $1 million for a 30-second spot.[14]

The media planner must thus balance media cost measures against several media impact factors. First, costs should be balanced against the media vehicle's audience quality. For a corporate hotel advertisement, *Business Week* would have a high-exposure value; *People* would have a low-exposure value. Second, the media planner should consider audience attention. Readers of *Vogue*, for example, typically pay more attention to ads than do readers of *Newsweek*. Third, the planner assesses the vehicle's editorial quality; *Time* and the *Wall Street Journal* are more believable and prestigious than the *National Enquirer*.

Media planners are increasingly developing more sophisticated measures of effectiveness and using them in mathematical models to arrive at the best media mix. Many advertising agencies use computer programs to select the initial media and then make further media schedule improvements based on subjective factors not considered by the media section model.[15]

Deciding on Media Timing

The advertiser must also decide how to schedule advertising over the course of a year. For a hotel or resort, effective advertising requires knowledge of the origin of its guests and how far in advance they make their reservations. If guests living in Connecticut make their reservations in November to go to a Caribbean resort in January, it will not be effective for a resort to advertise in December after consumers have already made their vacation plans. Restaurants with a strong local demand may decide to vary their advertising to follow the seasonal pattern, to oppose the seasonal pattern, or to be the same all year. Most firms do some seasonal advertising.

Finally, the advertiser must choose the pattern of the ads. Continuity means scheduling ads evenly within a given period. Pulsing means scheduling ads unevenly over a given time period. Thus 52 ads could either be scheduled at one per week during the year or pulsed in several bursts. Those who favor pulsing feel that the audience will learn the message more completely and that money can be saved. Once they have done a burst of ads, they remove themselves from the advertising market. A company could use a 6-month burst of advertising, for example, to regain its past sales growth rate. This finding led Budweiser to adopt a pulsing strategy.[16]

Marketing Highlight 17-2

Association Advertising

Hospitality firms often belong to an association such as a local chamber of commerce, hotel/motel association, or restaurant association. They may also belong to independent promotional associations such as the Australian Dine Out, Preferred Hotels, or Leading Hotels.

Sooner or later the manager of every hotel, restaurant, B&B, and other hospitality enterprise must decide whether to join an association and, if so, what degree of cooperation to provide. There is a wide diversity of opinion covering the possible benefits from advertising and promotion through an association such as the local visitors bureau. Some associations distribute free magazines or newspapers to visitors that are read and used. Others seem to provide ineffective support.

Remember that any funds given to associations come directly from the company's advertising budget. A decision to join and support an association must be based on an evaluation of possible gains for the company, not simply on an emotional plea to support the group.

The marketing power of hospitality chains offers a genuine threat to independents. An independent hotel, for instance, cannot hope to match the spending levels or brand-building thrust of chains.

Organizations such as Preferred Hotels exist to provide a group identity for independent hotel members. Organizations such as Preferred may also offer a frequent-flyer program, worldwide directory, promotional programs for intermediaries such as travel agents, and central reservations. For some member hotels, such as the Captain Cook Hotel in Alaska, the Preferred Hotels' central bookings accounts for 80% of transient bookings. Preferred Hotels annually spends over $1 million in advertising to promote member luxury hotels and another $3 million in cooperative advertising. Associations also exist for budget hotels, such as Friendship Inns. Friendship charges members a royalty per room, such as 49 cents per room, of which 30% goes toward advertising.[17]

Road Blocking. Advertisers can sometimes use a tactic known as road blocking to help ensure that an intended audience receives the advertising message. The tropical island resort, Great Keppel in Queensland, Australia, knew that its audience in Brisbane, Sydney, and Melbourne listened to certain FM rock stations. Great Keppel purchased drive time radio spots for the same exact time on all rock stations in the three markets. This prevented listeners from switching stations to avoid the advertisement.

Campaign Evaluation

Managers of advertising programs should regularly evaluate the communication and sales effects of advertising.

Measuring the Communication Effect

Measuring the communication effect reveals whether an ad is communicating well. Called copy testing, this process can be performed before or after an ad is printed or broadcast. There are three major methods of advertising pretesting. The first is direct rating, in which the advertiser exposes a consumer panel to alternative ads and asks them to rate the ads. Direct ratings show how well the ads attract attention and how they affect consumers. Although it is an imperfect measure of an ad's actual impact, a high rating indicates a potentially effective ad. In portfolio tests, consumers view or listen to a portfolio of advertisements, taking as much time as they need. The interviewer then asks the respondent to recall all the ads and their contents. The recall can either be aided or unaided by the interviewer. Recall level indicates the extent to which an ad stands out and how well its message is understood and remembered. Laboratory tests use equipment to measure consumers' physiological reactions to an ad: heartbeat, blood pressure, pupil dilation, and perspiration. The tests measure an ad's attention-getting power, but reveal little about its impact on beliefs, attitudes, or intentions.

There are two popular methods of posttesting ads. Using recall tests, the advertiser asks people who have been exposed to magazines or television programs to recall everything they can about the advertisers and products that they saw. Recall scores indicate the ad's power to be noticed and retained. In recognition tests, the researcher asks readers of, for instance, a given issue of a magazine to point out what they have seen. Recognition scores can be used to assess the ad's impact in different market segments and to compare the company's ads with competitors'.

Measuring the Sales Effect

What quantity of sales are caused by an ad that increases brand awareness by 20% and brand preference by 10%? The sales effect of advertising is often harder to measure than the communication effect. Sales are affected by many factors besides advertising, such as product features, price, and availability. One way to measure sales effect is to compare past sales with past advertising expenditures. Another is through experiments.

To spend a large advertising budget wisely, advertisers must define their advertising objectives, develop a sound budget, create a good message, make media decisions, and evaluate the results.

Advertising draws much public attention because of its power to affect life-styles and opinions. Advertising faces increased regulation to ensure that it performs responsibly (see Marketing Highlight 17-1).[18]

Direct Marketing

I've always been a strong believer in direct-mail advertising. Direct-mail advertising plays a very important part in the success of a hotel's marketing program. It's an excellent balance to outside sales calls and telephone solicitation. It presents your product to a client without the expense of a personal sales call. In addition, you're able to solicit many more clients than you could individually through direct mail.
Jim Mastrangelo, Director of Sales, Ramada, Inc.[19]

The term direct marketing has taken on new meanings over the years. Originally, it was simply a form of marketing in which products or services moved from the producer to consumer without an intermediate channel of distribution. In this sense, companies that use salespeople are using direct marketing. As the telephone and other media came into heavy use to promote offers directly to customers, direct marketing was redefined by the Direct Marketing Association (DMA): *Direct marketing is an interactive system of marketing which uses one or more advertising media to affect a measurable response and/or transaction at any location.* In this definition, the emphasis is on marketing undertaken to obtain a measurable response, typically an order from a customer. Because of the nature of the transaction, it can also be called direct-order marketing.

Today, many users of direct marketing visualize it as playing a broader role, which can be called direct-relationship marketing.[20] These direct marketers use direct-response advertising media to make a sale and learn about a customer whose name and profile are entered in a customer database, which is used to build a continuing and enriching relationship. The emphasis is on building preferred customer relationships. Airlines, hotels, and others are building strong customer relationships through award programs and are using their customer database to match their offers more carefully to individual customers. They are approaching a stage where offers are sent only to those customers and prospects most able, willing, and ready to buy the product. To the extent that they succeed, higher response rates to promotions will be gained. Marriott Hotels, Resorts & Suites now claims to have the largest hotel database in the world due to the Honored Guests Incentive program.[21]

The following examples illustrate ways in which the hospitality and travel industries are using direct marketing. Continental Airlines sent its OnePass members a coupon for a $198 child's round-trip ticket between any two cities Continental serves in the contiguous United States. American Express offered its members in Houston a discount coupon to Birraporetti's restaurant. The San Diego Convention and Visitors Bureau placed an advertisement in *Travel Weekly*, offering a free "Travel Planner's Guide" to interested travel agents and meeting planners.

Ski Limited, which operates the Killington and Mt. Snow resorts in Vermont and Bear Mountain resort in California, has a database that tracks 2.5 million skiers and adds 250,000 skiers a year. The information includes home addresses, level of skiing ability, and past skiing expenditures. Ski Limited uses this information to determine where skiers come from, when they ski, and what level of services they desire at a resort. This allows the company to promote events aimed at certain segments, such as an amateur race for New York City skiers. In one promotion, 90,000 mid-week lift ticket discount cards were mailed to skiers who lived at least 3 car hours away and normally came to the resort only on weekends. This promotion had a great deal to do with changing ski days so that 50% of the company's revenues now come from midweek customers.[22]

Reasons for Growth of Direct Marketing

There are several reasons for the growth of direct marketing. Direct marketing allows **precision targeting**. A manager promoting a dinner featuring a variety of wines can send a mailing to customers who have purchased a bottle of wine in the restaurant costing more than $50 during the last 6 months. In a properly targeted and executed direct-marketing program, response rates of 10% to 20% are achievable. Thus it is possible to get 50 to 100 sales from a list of 500 qualified names. Normally, one might expect this kind of response after contacting 2000 potential customers.

Personalization is another advantage of direct marketing. Personalization can be expressed in several ways, for example, by personalizing the offer to fit the needs of the target market. This could be as simple as recognizing an interest that a restaurant's customers have in fine wines. Hotels can also develop unique offers directed at individuals, such as offering a special weekend package in celebration of a client's wedding anniversary. McDonald's, Burger King, and other fast-food restaurants develop birthday clubs and send reminder notices to the child's parents before the birthday, offering their restaurant as a location for the child's birthday party. In the last two examples, timing, another advantage of direct mail, helped to personalize the message. The manager can send the message before an individual's birthday or anniversary or when a particular company will be planning its next sales meeting. The message will reach the client at the right moment.

Direct marketing permits **privacy** because the direct marketer's offer and strategy are not visible to competitors. Continental Airline's $198 children's offer is not as likely to be matched by the competition, because it was not announced publicly. By using direct marketing in this way, Continental can sell inventory at a discount without starting a price war. Offers made by airlines to their frequent flyers often call for immediate action. In another instance, Continental offered up to $75 off tickets purchased within 2 weeks. Direct marketing is an excellent way to create immediate results. In periods of low demand, companies can target known customers to produce quick results.

The timeshare resort Eagles Nest located in southwest Florida was a newly opened property coming into the summer or trough season. The management of Eagles Nest wanted to introduce the property to residents within 300 miles and fill rooms in the slack period. A New York list broker provided 15 lists of upscale residents within the 300-mile limit. It was decided to conduct a test market on no more than 20% of the total list. Following the test market, a "rollout" of the remaining 80% would be undertaken. A direct mailing was designed that included a letter describing Eagles Nest and offering a great introductory price and a second envelope. This envelope was closed with a seal that said, "Don't open this till you read the letter."

This creative use of reverse psychology apparently worked in much the same way as telling a small child to stay out of the cookie jar. Inside the sealed envelope were six certificates. Five were redeemable for discounts or gift offerings, such as a free drink. The sixth was a return postage paid reservation card. The results of this campaign amazed everyone. Eagles Nest received sufficient reservations from the test market that a rollout was unnecessary. Despite the fact that many fine Florida resorts offer summer specials, Eagles Nest filled up.[23]

Members of the casino industry such as Bally's of Atlantic City use direct marketing for premium player promotion and for the intermediaries known as junket reps who bring premium players to a casino. Casinos can and do direct special promotions to related junket reps who consistently provide profitable customers for the casino.

Another benefit of direct marketing is **measurability**. In the last chapter we quoted John Wanamaker: "I know half of my advertising is wasted, but I don't know which half." Direct marketing can be measured. If John Wanamaker had used direct marketing, he would have known if he was wasting his money or making a good investment. A manager can track the response to a particular direct-marketing campaign and usually determine the revenue that it produced.

Direct-marketing efforts may be measured in three ways: (1) the number of inquiries generated, (2) the ratio of conversions realized from inquiries generated, and (3) communication impact.[24]

Direct-marketing tools are expanding today with the emergence of fax machines and E mail. Computer-driven communication offers considerable promise as an advertising and sales vehicle. Many companies now communicate directly to key customers through E Mail.

Telemarketing

One form of direct marketing that combines aspects of advertising, marketing research, and personal sales is telemarketing. Telemarketing employs the use of the telephone to reach customers or prospective customers. Skilled telemarketers employ careful time scheduling and tracking systems for calls that require call backs. They also use role playing to practice how they will react to various questions and objections that they are likely to encounter.

Experienced telemarketers carefully study times that are best to call. They study response rates, such as uncompleted calls and cooperative call responses. It is suggested that optimum times for conducting business-to-business telemarketing are after 10:00 A.M. and between 2:00 to 5:00 P.M. except for Monday mornings and Friday afternoons, which are undesirable calling times.[25]

Relationship Marketing

Relationship marketing is an important benefit of direct marketing. Today, airlines, hotels, travel agents, restaurants, and rental car companies operate in very competitive markets. The major way to grow market share is to steal it from the competition. Direct marketing allows companies to develop a strong relationship with their customers, which helps prevent them from switching to competitors. Sheraton Club International offers its members special rates, upgrades based on availability, special amenities, their own floors, and often their own lounge with complimentary beverages. Airlines develop special offers for their frequent flyers. The general manager of a hotel often invites regular guests to an evening cocktail party. Managers recognize that spending money developing loyalty among current customers can be more effective than spending money trying to develop new guests. Studies have shown that it costs four to seven times as much to bring in a new customer as it does to maintain an existing one.

While *any* c*i*t*y*
w*o*uld w*e*lc*o*m*e*
w*i*nter gu*e*sts w*i*th
o*p*en arm*s*, we
*pr*efer to sl*a*m 'e*m*.

The New American City

Pulse-pounding CAVS basketball action, on-court in our brand new Gund Arena—just one reason why Cleveland's jammin' this winter. The RainForest at Cleveland Metroparks Zoo, unforgettable music, comedy and drama in our beautiful theaters, exciting nightlife in The Flats, museums of art, space, history—you name it, it's happening here. Call for your free Greater Cleveland Card and save big on participating area eats, attractions, even hotel stays. So enjoy the weekend—go Cleveland.

Call for your free Cleveland Card and save big!
1-800-BUCKEYE

During the first quarter of 1995 Cleveland received 70,000 visitor information requests, more than the total for all of 1994. Courtesy of Sprecher, Barrett, Bertalot and Company.

Latour Management of Wichita operates four restaurants in Wichita, Kansas. They sent 16,000 postcards to area residences, using a mailing list that profiled current customers in terms of postal code and income. The card offered a free dinner at one of Latour's restaurants, if the recipient dined at the other three. The card featured names of each restaurant and a space for a signature by each restaurant certifying that the diner had purchased a meal. When the diner had three signatures, a free meal was available at the fourth restaurant. Diners had to turn in their cards to receive the free meal. Thus, Latour could update its database using the address label on the card.

Another benefit of the promotion was that it exposed customers of one restaurant to others in the chain. During the first ten days of the campaign, the restaurants signed 500 cards accounting for 1,000 meals.[26]

Mauna Kea resort villas of Hawaii had a very real need to develop relationship marketing with prospective customers. After all, they were selling vacation villas for over $1 million each. Obviously, advertisements in most media would be inappropriate or too expensive. Mauna Kea developed a three-stage direct-mail program aimed at frequent visitors. During stage 1, a quality Japanese lounge jacket and a letter were sent free of charge to each prospect. In stage 2 a beautiful conch shell and again a letter were sent. Stage 3 occurred when the guests arrived at Mauna Kea and reached their rooms. A third letter was conspicuously placed next to a free bottle of champagne. The result was a 40% lead generation response.[27]

Development of Integrated Direct Marketing

Most direct marketers rely on a single advertising vehicle and a one-shot effort to reach and sell a prospect. A one-time mailing offering a weekend package at a hotel is an example of a single-vehicle, single-stage campaign. A single-vehicle, multiple-stage campaign would involve sending successive mailings to a prospect to trigger purchases. For example, restaurants may send four notices to a household to entice the household to try the restaurant. As previously described, Mauna Kea resort villas used a three-stage campaign.

A more powerful approach is to execute a multiple-vehicle, multiple-stage campaign. This technique is known as integrated direct marketing (IDM).[28] Consider the following sequence:

Paid ad with a response channel $\longrightarrow$ Direct mail mechanism $\longrightarrow$ Outbound telemarketing $\longrightarrow$ Face-to-face sales call

The paid ad creates product awareness and stimulates inquiries. The company then sends direct mail to those who inquire. Within 48 to 72 hours following mail receipt, the company phones, seeking an order. Some prospects will place an order; others might request a face-to-face sales call. Even if the prospect is not ready to buy, there is ongoing communication. This use of response compression, whereby multiple media are deployed within a tightly defined time frame, increases impact and awareness of the message. The underlying idea is to deploy select media with precise timing to generate greater incremental sales, while offsetting incremental costs. A direct-mail piece alone may generate only a 2% response, but it is possible to generate responses of 12% or more using integrated direct marketing.[29]

The Delta Chelsea Inn of Toronto initiated an $80 million renovation program, the largest Canadian hotel building project in 18 years. Management wished to reposition the Chelsea as offering "value on a grand scale." An integrated marketing program was selected to meet this objective using direct sales, media advertising to the general public and the trade, public relations programs, trade shows, and internal promotion. As a result the Chelsea was able to maintain its market share position in occupancy and narrow the gap between itself and major competitors.[30]

Spector/Barrett/Bertalot and Company developed an integrated direct marketing campaign for Cleveland. The response mechanism is an 800 number that potential visitors can call to get a free "Cleveland Card." The card offers discounts at major hotels and tourist attractions in the Cleveland area. The promotion was advertised in Detroit, Pittsburgh, and Cleveland. The advertising media consisted of a combination of television and regional newspapers. During the first quarter of 1995 Cleveland received 70,000 visitor information requests, more than the total for all of 1994.[31]

Developing a Marketing Database System

To implement successful integrated direct marketing, companies must invest in a marketing database system. A **marketing database** is an organized collection of data about individual customers, prospects, or suspects that is accessible and actionable for such marketing purposes as lead generation, lead qualification, sale of a product or service, or maintenance of customer relationships.

Building a database involves investing in central and remote computer hardware, data-processing software, information enhancement programs, communication links, personnel to capture data, user training, design of analytical programs, and so forth. The system should be user friendly and available to various departments. For example, in a hotel, reservations, sales, reception, food and beverage, accounting, and the general manager would all need access to the database. Building a database takes time and involves much cost, but when it runs properly, the selling company will achieve much higher marketing productivity.

SALES PROMOTION

Advertising is joined by two other mass-promotion tools: sales promotion and public relations. **Sales promotion** consists of short-term incentives to encourage the purchase or sales of a product or service. Sales promotion includes a variety of promotional tools designed to stimulate earlier or stronger market response. It includes consumer promotion (samples, coupons, rebates, price-off, premiums, contests, demonstrations); trade promotion-buying allowances (free goods, cooperative advertising, and push money); and sales-force promotion (bonuses and contests).

Sales promotion tools are used by most organizations. Estimates of annual sales-promotion spending run as high as $100 billion. Spending has increased rapidly in recent years. Formerly, the ratio of advertising to sales-promotion spending was about 60 to 40. Today, in many consumer packaged-goods companies, the picture is reversed, with sales promotion often accounting for 60% or 70% of all marketing expenditures. Sales promotions are most effective when they are used with advertising or personal selling. Consumer promotions must normally be advertised and can add excitement and pulling power to ads. Trade and sales-force promotions support the firm's personal selling process. In using sales promotions, a company must **set objectives, select the right tools, develop the best program, pretest and implement it,** and **evaluate the results**. These steps will now be discussed.

Setting Sales-promotion Objectives

Sales-promotion objectives vary widely. Consumer promotions can increase short-term sales or they can be used to help build long-term market share. The objective may be to entice consumers to try a new product, lure consumers away from competitors, or hold and reward loyal customers. For the sales force, objectives include building stronger customer relations and obtaining new accounts.

Sales promotions should be consumer franchise building; that is, they should promote the product's positioning and include a sales message. Ideally, the objective is to build long-run consumer demand, rather than to prompt temporary brand switching. If properly designed, every sales-promotion tool has consumer franchise-building potential.

Selecting Sales-promotion Tools

Many tools can be used to accomplish sales-promotion objectives. The promotion planner should consider the type of market, the sales-promotion objectives, the competition, and the costs and effectiveness of each tool. The main consumer- and trade-promotion tools are described next.

Consumer-promotion Tools

The main consumer-promotion tools include samples, coupons, cash refunds, price packs, premiums, patronage rewards, point-of-purchase displays, demonstrations, contests, sweepstakes, and games.

Samples. Samples are offers of a trial amount of a product. Some samples are free. For others, the company charges a small amount to offset its cost. McDonald's offered a cup of coffee and an apple-bran muffin for $1.00. Normally, the coffee and the muffin were offered for 95 cents each. The promotion was designed to get customers to try the muffin. There are some people who do not eat bran muffins and by "charging" 5 cents for the muffin, McDonald's avoided giving the muffin away to customers who would never buy one in the future.

The Inn on the Park in Houston invited potential customers and influential community members to stay in the luxury hotel at no charge. The promotion accomplished two objectives: (1) salespeople were aided in selling corporate contracts, since many of their potential customers had experienced the hotel. (2) Positive word of mouth about the hotel was created. Sampling is the most effective, but also the most expensive, way to introduce a new product.

Sampling by the staff who are employed by a hospitality firm such as a hotel, restaurant, or ski resort can be a very useful educational and promotional device. A thorough knowledge of the product is particularly beneficial to upselling. It is difficult for anyone to recommend a premium-priced Bordeaux or California Merlot if they have no idea how the wine tastes. The sales and reservation staff of a hotel or resort can more convincingly sell a prospect on the idea of upgrading to a poolside, cabana, or suite if they have a personal knowledge of the product.

How does the staff obtain personal knowledge of the product or services of a company? Several successful approaches have been used to accomplish staff product knowledge.

1. Provide continuous training programs. Invite suppliers such as vintners, cheese producers, and gourmet coffee distributors to provide samples and assist with product training.

2. Offer sales and performance incentives that include prizes on the property, such as a five-course meal, a month's use of the health club, or a weekend in the deluxe suite.

3. Create an employee's day in which the staff has full use of the facility. Country clubs often provide a special day in which employees and sometimes their families are treated to exclusive use of the pool, the golf course, the restaurant, and even the ballroom for an evening dance.

4. Share product information with employees through newsletters or

product brochures. Often, product information brochures remain only in the offices of the purchasing department, the F&B manager, or some other executive office.

5. Continuously talk about the company's products and services in a positive and upbeat manner. As humans, people have a tendency to forget the many positive attributes of the facilities and the services that surround us daily.

Preston L. Smith, the president and CEO of Ski Limited, regularly sends memos to company managers urging them to hit the slopes. Smith personally manages to ski over 60 times each season. "Everyone skis here. It's a way of sharing the customer's experience. It's also a way to achieve personal growth because skiing is exhilarating and exciting."[32]

Coupons. Coupons are certificates that offer buyers savings when they purchase specified products. More than 220 billion coupons are distributed in the United States each year, with a total face value of more than $55 billion. Coupons can be mailed, included with other products, or placed in ads. Coupons are most popular in the restaurant industry; however hotel, rental car companies, tourist attractions, and cruise lines also use coupons. American Express cardholders received coupon packs featuring mid- and upscale restaurants. The prestige of American Express allows these restaurants to use coupons without detracting from their image.

Some restaurants have suffered from overcouponing. In the "pizza wars," the major chains fought for market share by distributing coupons at least once a week. Some pizza restaurants posted signs saying that they would honor competitors' coupons, to neutralize the impact of their competitors' advertising. During the pizza wars, the price of pizza dropped to the discounted coupon price for most customers. These customers felt they were getting poor value if they purchased a pizza without a coupon. Overcouponing should be avoided, because it lowers the price so that the coupon no longer offers a competitive advantage.

Besides stimulating sales of a mature product, coupons are also effective in promoting early trial of a new product. For example, when a fast-food chain develops a new product, it often introduces the product in print advertisements featuring a coupon. The coupon provides an incentive and reduces the risk for customers trying the new product.

Joint promotions using coupons create goodwill for those who distribute the coupons and those who redeem them. For example, Aloha Airlines and Pizza Hut sponsored a joint promotion. Aloha Airlines gave passengers a coupon for a free pizza with the purchase of another of equal or greater value. They distributed the coupons on flights that had on-time arrivals.[33]

Many professional marketing consultants and observers of marketing and sales practices feel that too much promotion creates a commodity out of a differentiated product. It is argued that companies spend millions of dollars and years of effort to develop a distinct image and a high level of product differentiation in the minds of consumers, only to have it destroyed by promotions.

In far too many cases, promotions have created an impression that margins were unreasonably high to begin with or the company could not have made this offer. They have also led to coupon wars and other forms of price discounting, all the while detracting from the intrinsic value of the company's product or service.

Premiums. Premiums are goods offered either free or at low cost as an incentive to buy a product. For example, fast-food restaurants often offer a free promotional glass, instead of their normal paper cup. A self-liquidating premium is a premium sold to consumers who request it. McDonald's in Australia offered Batman figures for 95 cents with the purchase of a burger.

Many restaurants, such as Hard Rock Cafes, have discovered that promotional items such as caps, T-shirts, and sweat shirts can be sold at a good profit, thus creating another profit center for the company. Others offer a premium-priced drink or dessert that is served with a special glass or plate. Guests actually pay for the glass or plate in the price of the product, take the "gift" home with them, and are reminded of a pleasant restaurant experience each time it is later seen. Pat O'Brien's in the French Quarter of New Orleans serves a Hurricane in a commemorative glass. These glasses can be seen in homes throughout the world. The name recognition developed through its Hurricane glasses has helped to make Pat O'Briens a major tourist attraction in the French Quarter.

Although Pat O'Brien's gives the glasses to its Hurricane customers, guests sometimes take items as souvenirs. Hotels, resorts, golf clubs, and cruise lines experience significant dollars loses in *product shrink*. This refers to the disappearance of products such as towels, bath robes, soap dishes, and ash trays from rooms or public areas. It is well known that this disappearance is due to theft by guests who rationalize the act as "good promotion for the company" or a "gift for my patronage" or "it's just a souvenir."

Shrink occurs in all levels of properties, including exclusive resorts. The general manager of an upscale Hawaiian resort observed this problem and established a section of the guest shop with products commonly stolen from the hotel. When asked if this move substantially cut down on shrink the answer was, "No, but the margin of profit we make on the sale of the items in the gift shop just about compensates for the cost of the products that walked."

Patronage Rewards. Patronage rewards are cash or other awards for the regular use of a company's products or services. For example, most airlines offer frequent-flyer plans that award points for miles traveled. The points are redeemable for free or upgraded air travel, rental cars, and hotel rooms. Marriott has adopted an "honored guest" plan that awards points for users of their hotels. Some restaurants offer cards that are punched during each visit. After 10 visits the customer receives a free meal or some other reward.

Point-of-Purchase. Point-of-purchase (POP) promotions include displays and demonstrations that take place at the point of purchase or sale. Fox example, a representative of Richmond Estate Wines might offer a taste of their wines in the Robina Tavern package store.

The value of POP has long been recognized by the retailing industry and is making rapid inroads in restaurants, hotels, auto rental companies, and other hospitality industry firms. Hospitality firms have discovered that POP may be used to (1) disseminate information about the company's products or services, and (2) Sell additional products and services, thus adding to gross revenue.

Rack brochures can be used for cross promotions, such as promoting hotels at tourist attractions and visitor centers. A less expensive form of the brochure is a rack card, which can be printed on one or two sides. Courtesy of Bill Bard Associates, Monticello, N.Y.

Hotels use display racks in the lobby to promote other hotels in the chain and additional services, from valet parking to sleigh rides. Restaurants such as Perkins, the Village Inn, and Denny's use the space near the cash register to create eye-catching displays of bakery items and desserts to be taken home by the guests.

Several years ago, Farrells Restaurants in Hawaii discovered a means to add over 10% to the bottom line without decreasing prices or adding new customers. Farrells appealed heavily to families with pre-teenage children. Keeping the customer profile in mind, a decision was made to design a new passageway out of the restaurant before reaching the cash register. This passageway involved walking through thousands of gift, candy, and gum items selected for child irresistibility. This unique and colorful passageway served as a giant POP that added revenue directly to the bottom line.

Contests, Sweepstakes, and Games. Contests, sweepstakes, and games give consumers a chance to win something, such as cash or a trip. A contest calls for consumers to submit an entry—a jingle, guess, or suggestion—to be judged by a panel. A sweepstake calls for consumers to submit their names for a drawing. A game presents consumers with something every time they buy—bingo numbers or missing letters—that may or may not help them win a prize. A sales contest urges dealers or the sales force to increase their efforts, with prizes going to the top performers.

During the 1992 Olympic Games, ITT Sheraton Pacific ran a promotion offering two trips to the Olympic games in Barcelona as its gold prize, five regional holidays as its silver prize, and 10 two-night stays at the Sheraton closest to the winner for the Bronze. The contest featured the slogan "Sleep at a Sheraton and Wake Up in Barcelona." Sheraton gave key clients a kit entitled "Inspired Excellence," which included a commemorative medallion and a luxurious brochure. Many of these kits were hand-delivered by Sheraton salespeople. A separate contest was designed for travel agents, offering them an incentive to promote the contest to their customers. Additionally, point-of-purchase material was displayed at the front desks of Sheraton Hotels. The campaign was supported by television advertising. While this campaign was primarily a sales promotion, it used other areas of the promotional mix for support.

Developing the Sales-promotion Program

The third step in developing a sales promotion is to define the full sales-promotion program. This step calls for marketers to make other decisions. First, they must decide on the size of the incentive. A certain minimum incentive is necessary if the promotion is to succeed. A larger incentive will produce more sales response. The marketer must also set conditions for participation. Incentives might be offered to everyone or only to select groups. Sweepstakes might not be offered in certain states, to families of company personnel, or to persons under a certain age.

The marketer must then decide how to promote and distribute the promotion program. A restauranteur can distribute coupons at the restaurant, by mail, or in an advertisement. Each distribution method involves a different level of reach and cost. The length of the promotion is also important. If the sales-promotion period is too short, prospects who would not buy during that time will be unable to take advantage of it. If the promotion runs too long, the deal will lose some of its "act now" force.

The question of how to distribute a promotional program has resulted in problems for companies. An example is a restaurant that decided to print 10,000 flyers announcing a promotion and have employees stick them under the windshield wiper of cars in a shopping center. The following results occurred: Employees threw most in the dumpster, several auto owners threatened to sue, claiming their wipers had been broken, the owner of the shopping center demanded someone clean up the mess, and finally an employee and a car owner engaged in a fistfight. The employee won the fistfight, but the company paid an out-of-court settlement to the auto owner with a broken nose.[34]

Restaurant promotions often consist of cards, flyers, coupons, and other devices featuring two-for-one specials, 20% off, free drinks or other "hooks." Normally, these bear a date at which the promotion becomes ineffective. In theory, this should work well, but in actuality customers often present coupons months or even years old and became enraged when they are told that the promotion is no longer in effect. A prospective new owner or buyer of any hospitality company should ask if there are outstanding promotions in the community. Many new owners have been shocked to witness a flood of promotional coupons that negatively affected cash flow.

Other problematic media used by hospitality companies include hot air balloons bearing the company's logo that crashed on freeways or atop buildings, road signs that ended up in strange places such as the mayor's lawn, and sponsored bicycle races in which the restaurant rider crashed through a competitor's storefront. In today's, "I'll sue you" environment, it is wise to discuss proposed promotions with an attorney and with the company's insurance agent prior to initiation.

Marketing managers need to set promotion dates, which will be used by production, sales, and distribution. Some unplanned promotions may also be needed, requiring cooperation on short notice.

Finally, the marketer has to decide on the sales-promotion budget. It can be developed in two ways. The marketer can choose the promotions and estimate total cost. However, the more common way is to use a percentage of the total budget for sales promotion. One study found three major problems in the way that companies budget for sales promotion. First, they do not consider cost effectiveness. Second, instead of spending to achieve objectives, they simply extend the previous year's spending, take a percentage of expected sales, or use the "affordable approach." Finally, advertising and sales-promotion budgets are too often prepared separately.[35]

Partnerships can stretch a budget. The Palm, a national upscale steakhouse, developed a promotion with a Chicago car dealer to promote its Chicago restaurant. The car dealer offered a $20 gift certificate for the Palm to all who test drove its luxury model cars. The cost of the certificate was split equally between the partners. The dealership gained an incentive to attract customers with a certificate that was steeply discounted, and the restaurant gained additional customers for $10 per table.[36] Partnerships can also be used to acquire prizes in sweepstakes. Companies will often discount or provide merchandise in exchange for advertising exposure.

Greyhound Lines, Inc., and Hospitality Franchise Systems, Inc., have entered into an agreement to conduct joint marketing programs. Part of the program calls for Greyhound passengers to stay at HFS properties such as Ramada, Days Inn, or Super 8 for lodging and meals.[37]

Pretesting and Implementing

Whenever possible, sales-promotion tools should be pretested to determine if they are appropriate and of the right incentive size. Consumer sales promotions can be quickly and inexpensively pretested; yet few promotions are ever tested ahead of time. Seventy percent of companies do not test sales promotions before initiating them. To test sales promotions, researchers can ask consumers to rate or rank different promotions. Promotions can also be tried on a limited basis in selected geographic test areas.

Companies should prepare implementation plans for each promotion, covering lead time and sell-off time. Lead time is the time necessary to prepare the program before launching it. Sell-off time begins with the launch and ends when the promotion ends.

Evaluating the Results

Even though result evaluation is important, many companies fail to evaluate their sales-promotion programs. Others do so only superficially. Many evaluation methods are available, the most common of which is sales comparisons before, during, and after a promotion. Suppose that a company has a 6% market share before the promotion, which jumps to 10% during the promotion, falls to 5% immediately after, and rises to 7% later. The promotion appears to have attracted new customers and more purchases from current customers. After the promotion, sales fell as consumers used inventories or moved purchases forward. For example, a person planning on traveling to see relatives in New York in June may move the trip forward to April to take advantage of an airline promotion that expires April 30. The long-run rise to 7% means that the airline gained some new users, but if the brand's share returned to the prepromotion level, then the promotion changed only the timing of demand, rather than total demand.

The results of consumer research will demonstrate the kinds of people who responded to the promotion and their postpromotion buying behavior. Surveys can provide information on how many consumers recall the promotion, what they thought of it, how many accepted it, and how it affected their buying patterns. Sales promotions can also be evaluated through experiments that include variables such as incentive value, length, and distribution method.

Clearly, sales promotion plays an important role in the total promotion mix. To use it well, the marketer must define sales-promotion objectives, select the best tools, design the sales-promotion program, pretest, implement, and evaluate the results.

Chapter Review

I.   **Major Decisions in Advertising**

1) **Setting Objectives. Objectives** should be based on information about the target market, positioning, and market mix. Advertising objectives can be classified by their aim: to inform, persuade, or remind.

*a)***Informative advertising** is used to introduce a new product category or when the objective is to build primary demand.

b) **Persuasive advertising** is used as competition increases and a company's objective becomes building selective demand.

c) **Reminder advertising** is used for mature products, because it keeps the consumers thinking about the product.

2) **Setting the Advertising Budget.** Factors to consider in setting a budget are the stage in the product life cycle, market share, competition and clutter, advertising frequency, and product differentiation.

3) **Creating the Advertising Message.** Advertising can only succeed if its message gains attention and communicates well.

a) **Message generation.** Marketing managers must help the advertising agency create a message that will be effective with their target markets.

b) **Message evaluation and selection.** Messages should be meaningful, distinctive, and believable.

c) **Message execution.** The impact of the message depends on what is said and how it is said.

4) **Selecting Advertising Media**

a) **Deciding on reach, frequency, and impact**

b) **Choosing among major media types.** Newspapers, television, direct mail, radio, magazines, and outdoor.

c) **Selecting specific media vehicles.** Costs should be balanced against the media vehicle's: audience quality, ability to gain attention, and editorial quality.

d) **Deciding on media timing.** The advertiser must decide on how to schedule advertising over the course of a year based on seasonal fluctuation in demand, lead time in making reservations, and if they want to use continuity in their scheduling or if they want to use a pulsing format.

5) **Advertising Evaluation.** There are three major methods of advertising pretesting and two popular methods of posttesting ads.

a) **Pretesting**

i) **Direct rating:** The advertiser exposes a consumer panel to alternative ads and asks them to rate the ads.

ii) **Portfolio tests:** The interviewer asks the respondent to recall all ads and their contests after letting them listen to a portfolio of advertisements.

iii) **Laboratory tests:** Use equipment to measure consumers' physiological reactions to an ad.

b) **Posttesting**

i) **Recall tests:** The advertiser asks people who have been exposed to magazines or television programs to recall everything that they can about the advertisers and products that they saw.

ii) **Recognition tests:** The researcher asks people exposed to media to point out the advertisements that they have seen.

c) **Measuring the sales effect.** The sales effect can be measured by comparing past sales with past advertising expenditures and through experiments.

II. **Direct Marketing**

1) **Reasons for the Growth of Direct Marketing**

a) **Precision marketing**

b) **Personalization** through personalizing offers to fit the target market and timing offers to fit the needs of the consumer, such as offers associated with a birthday.

c) **Privacy.** The offer is not visible to competitors.

d) **Immediate results**

e) **Measurability**

2) **Telemarketing** is a form of direct marketing that combines aspects of advertising, marketing research, and personal sales.

3) **Relationship Marketing.** Direct marketing can be used to develop a relationship with customers. It costs four to seven times as much to create a customer as it does to maintain a customer.

4) **Integrated direct marketing** is a more powerful approach to direct marketing through a multiple-vehicle, multiple-stage campaign.

5) **Developing a marketing database system** to implement successful direct marketing; companies must invest in a marketing database system.

III. **Sales Promotion**

1) **Setting Sales-promotion Objectives.** Sales-promotion objectives vary widely and can include increasing short-term sales, increasing long-term sales, getting consumers to try a new product, luring customers away from competitors, or creating loyal customers.

2) **Selecting Sales-promotion Tools.** Many tools can be used to accomplish sales-promotion objectives. The promotion planner should consider the type of market, the sales-promotion objectives, the competition, and the costs and effectiveness of each tool. Common sales-promotion tools include samples, coupons, premiums, patronage rewards, point-of-purchase (POP), contests, sweepstakes, and games.

3) **Developing the Sales-promotion Program.** The following steps are involved in developing a sales-promotion program:

a) Decide on the size of the incentive.

b) Set the conditions for participation.

c) Decide how to promote and distribute the promotion program.

d) Set promotion dates.

e) Decide on the sales-promotion budget

4) **Evaluating the Results.** The company should evaluate the results against the objectives of the program.

DISCUSSION QUESTIONS

1. Is it feasible for an advertising agency to work for two competing clients simultaneously? How much competition between such accounts is too much competition?

2. According to advertising expert Stuart Henderson Britt, good advertising objectives spell out the intended audience, the advertising message, the desired effects, and the criteria for determining whether the effects were achieved (for example, not just "increase awareness" but "increase awareness 20%"). Why should these components be part of the advertising objective? What are some effects that an advertiser wants a campaign to achieve?

3. What are some benefits and drawbacks of comparison advertising? Which has more to gain from using comparison advertising, the market-leading brand or a lesser brand?

4. Describe several ads that you think are particularly effective and compare them with others

that you think are ineffective. How would you improve the less-effective ads?

5. What factors call for more frequency in an advertising media schedule? What factors call for more reach? How can you increase one without either sacrificing the other or increasing your advertising budget?

6. Which forms of sales promotion are most effective in getting consumers to try a product? Which are most effective in building loyalty to a product?

7. Give an example of a good direct marketing campaign. Why do you feel it was effective?

KEY TERMS

Advertising Any paid form of nonpersonal presentation and promotion of ideas, goods, or services by an identified sponsor.

Advertising objective A specific communication *task* to be accomplished with a specific *target* audience during a specific period of *time*.

Advertising specialties Useful articles imprinted with an advertiser's name given as gifts to consumers.

Comparison advertising Advertising that compares one brand directly or indirectly to one or more other brands.

Consumer franchise building promotions Sales promotions that promote the product's positioning and include a selling message along with the deal.

Consumer promotion Sales promotion designed to stimulate consumer purchasing, including samples, coupons, rebates, prices-off, premiums, patronage rewards, displays, and contests and sweepstakes.

Contests, sweepstakes, and games Promotional events that give consumers the chance to win something—such as cash, trips, or goods—by luck or through extra effort.

Continuity Scheduling ads evenly within a given period.

Copy testing Measuring the communication effect of an advertisement before or after it is printed or broadcast.

Coupons Certificates that give buyers a saving when they purchase a product.

Discount A straight reduction in price on purchases during a stated period of time.

Frequency The number of times the average person in the target market is exposed to an advertising message during a given period.

Informative advertising Advertising used to inform consumers about a new product or feature and to build primary demand.

Media impact The qualitative value of an exposure through a given medium.

Media vehicles Specific media within each general media type, such as specific magazines, television shows, or radio programs.

Patronage rewards Cash or other awards for the regular use of a certain company's products or services.

Persuasive advertising Advertising used to build selective demand for a brand by persuading consumers that it offers the best quality for their money.

Point-of-Purchase promotions (POP) Displays and demonstrations that take place at the point of purchase or sale.

Premiums Goods offered either free or at low cost as an incentive to buy a product.

Public relations Building good relations with the company's various publics by obtaining favorable publicity, building up a good corporate image, and handling or heading off unfavorable rumors, stores, and events. Major PR tools include press relations, product publicity, corporate communications, lobbying, and counseling.

Publicity Activities to promote a company or its products by planting news about it in media not paid for by the sponsor.

Pulsing Scheduling ads unevenly in bursts during a time period.

Reach The percentage of people in the target

market exposed to an ad campaign during a given period.

Reminder advertising Advertising used to keep consumers thinking about a product.

Sales promotion Short-term incentives to encourage purchase or sales of a product or service.

Sales-force promotion Sales promotion designed to motivate the sales force and make sales force selling efforts more effective, including bonus-es, contests, and sales rallies.

Samples Offers of a trial amount of a product to consumers.

Trade promotion Sales promotion designed to gain reseller support and to improve reseller selling efforts, including discounts, allowances, free goods, cooperative advertising, push money, and conventions and trade shows.

REFERENCES

1. See CAROL HALL, "King of the Road," *Marketing and Media Decision*, 24, no. 3 (March 1989), pp. 80–86, and MARKE W. CUNNINGHAM AND CHEKITAN DEV, "Strategic Marketing: A Lodging 'End Run'," *Cornell Hotel and Restaurant Administration Quarterly*, 24, no. 3 (August 1992), pp. 36–43.

2. See "The Advertising Fact Book," *Advertising Age* (January 2, 1995).

3. LESLIE ANN HOGG, *Junior's 50 More Promotion's That Work for Restaurant's* (New York: Walter Mathews Associates, Inc.), p. 11.

4. IRA TEINOWITZ, "Ramada Blasts Holiday Inn in Scathing Ads," *Advertising Age*, (January 27, 1992), pp. 3–41.

5. "Spaghetti Warehouse Says Thanks by Mail," *Nations Restaurant News*, 26, no. 13 (March 30, 1992), p. 14.

6. PETER C. YESAWICH, "Execution and Measurement of Programs," *Cornell Hotel and Restaurant Administration Quarterly*, 29, no. 4 (February 1989), p. 89.

7. GERALD J. TELLIS, "Advertising Exposure, Loyalty, and Brand Purchase: A Two-stage Model of Choice," *Journal of Marketing Research* (May 1988) pp. 57–70.

8. See BICKLEY TOWNSEND, "The Media Jungle," *American Demographics* (December 1988), p. 8.

9. CHRISTINE DUGAS, "And Now, a Wittier Word from Our Sponsors," *Business Week* (March 24, 1986), p. 90. Also see FELIX KESSLER, "In Search of Zap-proof Commercials," *Fortune* (January 21, 1985), pp. 68–70; and DENNIS KNEALE, "Zapping of TV Ads Appears Pervasive," *Wall Street Journal* (April 25, 1988), p. 29.

10. WITHIAM GLENN, "Hotel Advertising in the 80's: Surveying the Field," *Cornell Hotel and Restaurant Administration Quarterly*, 27, no. 1 (May 1986), pp. 33–34.

11. MATT MURRAY, "Today's Special: 855 Calories and 19.6 Grams of Fat," *Wall Street Journal, The Marketplace* (September 26, 1994), sec. B, p. 1.

12. SCOTT HUME AND ALISON FAHEY, "McDonald's Readies Major Blast Via Outdoor Boards," *Advertising Age* (March 30, 1992), p. 58.

13. See note 2.

14. JANE MEYERS AND LAURIE FREEMAN, "Marketers Police TV Commercial Costs," *Advertising Age* (April 3, 1989), p. 51.

15. See ROLAND T. RUST, *Advertising Media Models: A Practical Guide* (Lexington, Mass.: Lexington Books, 1986).

16. PHILIP H. DOUGHERTY, "Bud 'Pulses' the Market," *New York Times* (February 18, 1975), p. 40.

17. WITHIAM GLENN, "Unchained Melody: How Independent Hotels Work in Harmony," *Cornell Hotel and Restaurant Administration Quarterly*, 28, no. 2 (August 1987), pp. 78–79.

18. For more on the legal aspects of advertising and sales promotion, see LOUIS W. STERN AND THOMAS L. EOVALDI, *Legal Aspects of Marketing Strategy* (Englewood Cliffs, N.J.: Prentice Hall, 1984), Chaps. 7 and 8.

19. JAMES R. ABBEY, *Hospitality Sales and Advertising* (East Lansing Mich.: Educational Institute, 1989), p. 322.

20. the terms *direct-order* marketing and *direct-relationship* marketing were suggested as subsets of direct marketing by STAN RAPP AND TOM COLLINS in the *Great Marketing Turnaround* (Englewood Cliffs, N.J.: Prentice Hall, 1990).

21. CLARE SAMBROOK, *Marketing, The World's Biggest Hotel Database*, ISSN:0025-3650 (March 4, 1993), p. 19.

22. DAVID H. FREEDMAN, "An Unusual Way to Run a Ski Business," *Forbes*, Issue Number 0015-6914 (December 7, 1992), p. 28.

23. Eagles Nest, The Pete and Pierre Show, Consumer Campaigns, Hake Communications Inc., 224 Seventh St., Garden City, N.Y. 11530.

24. YESAWICH, "Execution and Measurement," p. 91.

25. ROBERT A. MEYER, "Understanding Telemarketing for

Hotels", *Cornell Hotel and Restaurant Administration Quarterly*, 28, no. 2 (August 1987), p. 25.

26. ROBIN LEE ALLEN, "It's in the Mail—Latour's New Campaign, That Is," *Nation's Restaurant News*, 26, no. 17 (April 27, 1992), p. 12.

27. MAUNA KEA, The Pete and Pierre Show, Consumer Campaigns, Hake Communications, Inc., 224 Seventh St., Garden City, N.Y. 11530.

28. See ERNAN ROMAN, *Integrated Direct Marketing* (New York: McGraw-Hill, 1989), p. 108.

29. Ibid., p. 108.

30. NANCY H. ARAB, "Integrated Marketing Repositions Toronto Hotel: Occupancy Soars," *Public Relations Journal*, 47, no. 3 (March 1991), pp. 22-23.

31. "Cleveland Launches City's First Tourism Marketing Campaign," USAE (January 24, 1995), pp. 20+

32. FREEDMAN, "An Unusual Way," p. 27.

33. "Ad Watch," *Nations Restaurant News*, 26, no. 19 (May 11, 1992), p. 12.

34. MICHAEL M. ZEFENER, "Restaurant Advertising, Coupon Claims and Cadillacs," *Cornell Hotel and Restaurant Administration Quarterly*, 29, no. 4 (February 1989), p. 98.

35. ROGER A. STRANG, "Sales Promotion—Fast Growth, Faulty Management," *Harvard Business Review*, July–August 1976, p. 119.

36. STEVE WEISS, "Promotions Trend: Get Yourself a Partner," *Restaurants and Institutions*, 103, no. 26 (November 1, 1993), pp. 78–93.

37. 1993 Annual Report, HFS—Hospitality Franchise Systems Inc., 339 Jefferson Road, P.O. Box 278, Parsippany, N.Y. 07054–0278.

Promoting Products: Public Relations

*T*he launch of Sputnik I in 1957 started a series of successes for the Soviet Union's space program. These achievements became propaganda vehicles promoting the achievements and advantages of communism. Kennedy used the "space gap" between the United States and the Soviet Union to his advantage, claiming that the Republicans had let the Soviet Union pass the United States. He campaigned under the banner of a New Frontier.

After Kennedy's election in 1960 the American space program had some success. In May and July of 1961, America's self-image was boosted by the suborbital flights of Shepard and Grissom. However, the pride these flights provided was short lived. In July 1961, Gherman Titov flew a 17-orbit mission for the Soviets, making the suborbital flights look like child's play.

NASA was eager to build America's pride. It canceled a third suborbital flight and announced that John Glenn would be America's first person to orbit the world. Glenn was well known to most Americans. He had served as a pilot in World II and the Korean War and made headlines in 1957 for setting a new cross-continent flying speed record. As a result of this achievement, he was invited to participate on two television host shows and was the most publicized of the seven U.S. astronauts.

NASA's publicity machine set the stage for the event. It was America's first attempt at an orbital flight with America's most publicized astronaut.

NASA needed to create as much hype as possible to give Americans a sense they were still in the space race. As a result of this hype, over 100 million people were expected to watch the televised launch of Friendship 7.

Bud Grice, a Marriott sales manager, thought about all those people who were expected to watch the launch. What a great way to expose Americans to a growing Marriott corporation. Grice knew that Marriott could not afford television ads, but the idea of all those people watching the coverage of the launch intrigued him; if only Marriott could communicate with an audience of that size.

On February 20 1962, 135 million Americans watched Glenn take off on his 5-hour, three-orbit flight. Grice was one of them and still thinking about the opportunities created by so many people watching a single event. Once the flight was off, cameras switched to the Glenn residence. There were scores of reporters at the residence and the area was a beehive of activity. The Glenns lived in the Washington, D.C., suburb of Arlington, Virginia, not too far from Marriott's corporate headquarters. Grice saw his opportunity. He would have lunch delivered to Mrs. Glenn by Marriott's Hot Shoppes. He put buckets of fried chicken with large Marriott labels in a station wagon and had it delivered to the Glenn residence. The real test would be getting through the police barricades. This proved to be too easy a challenge as the driver simply said he was delivering Mrs. Glenn's lunch. The Marriott vehicle pulled up in front of the residence and the Marriott containers were soon seen by an estimated 100 million Americans still watching television.

In a conversation with President Kennedy after the flight, Glenn stated that he was looking forward to spending some time with his family and that he would like to stay at a Marriott because they were so good to his wife. Marriott again had another public relations (PR) opportunity. They invited Glenn to stay in a complimentary Marriott suite and received additional publicity when the press followed Glenn into the Marriott.

This story illustrates several uses of public relations. First, we are shown how governments use events to promote their ideologies. Second, we see how PR can be planned to take advantage of opportunities. In this case, Grice created an event, serving lunch to Mrs. Glenn, to gain exposure of the Marriott name to millions of viewers. Finally, through being aware of Glenn's desire to stay in a Marriott hotel, Marriott gained additional publicity from the event.[1]

Hospitality and travel customers place a high value on personal sources of information. **Public relations** and **publicity** can be a powerful marketing tool.

This chapter starts with a discussion of the **five different public relations activities: press relations, product publicity, corporate communication, lobbying,** and **counseling**. Next we will discuss **corporate image**. An overview of the public relations process will be presented, followed by an overview of the major tools used in public relations.

PUBLIC RELATIONS

"Public relations, perhaps the most misunderstood part of marketing communications, can be the most effective tool."[2] Definitions for public relations differ widely, but perhaps that by Hilton International offers greatest application for the hospitality industry: "The process by which we create a positive image and customer preference through third-party endorsement."[3]

Public relations is an important marketing tool, which until recently was treated as a marketing stepchild. PR is moving into an explosive growth stage. Companies are realizing that mass marketing is no longer the answer to some of their communication needs. Advertising costs continue to rise, while audience reach continues to decline. Advertising clutter reduces the impact of each ad. Sales promotion costs have also increased as channel intermediaries demand lower prices and better commissions and deals. Personal selling can cost over $500 a call. In this environment, public relations holds the promise of a cost-effective promotional tool. The creative use of news events, publications, social events, community relations, and other public relations techniques offers companies a way to distinguish themselves and their products from their competitors.[4]

The public relations department of cruise lines, restaurant chains, airlines, and hotels is typically located at corporate headquarters. Often its staff is so busy dealing with various publics—stockholders, employees, legislators, and community leaders—that PR support for product marketing objectives tends to be neglected. Many four- and five-star hotel chains have corrected this deficiency by hiring local public relations managers.

In the past it was common for the marketing function and PR function to be handled by two different departments within the firm. Today these two functions are increasingly integrated. There are several reasons for this integration. First, companies are calling for more *market-oriented PR*. They want their PR departments to manage PR activities that contribute toward marketing the company and improving the bottom line. Second, companies are establishing *marketing PR groups* to directly support corporate/product promotion and image making. Thus marketing PR, like financial PR and community PR, serve a special constituency, the marketing department.

MAJOR ACTIVITIES OF PR DEPARTMENTS

PR departments perform the following five activities, not all of which feed into direct product support.

Press Relations

The aim of press relations is to place newsworthy information into the news media to attract attention to a person, product, or service. One reason for the growth of PR in the hospitality industry is its credibility. Most types of publicity are viewed by the consumer as third-party information. A favorable write-up of a restaurant in the local newspaper by the food editor has more impact than an advertisement written by the restaurant's management.

Product Publicity

Publicity is the task of securing editorial space, as opposed to paid space, in print and broadcast media to promote a product or service. Product publicity involves various efforts to publicize specific products. New products, special events, such as food festivals, redesigned products, such as a newly renovated hotel, and products that are popular because of current trends, such as nonfat desserts, are all potential candidates for publicity. Table 18-1 provides an example of a timetable for a public relations campaign for the opening of a new hotel.

Corporate Communication

This activity covers internal and external communications and promotes understanding of the organization. One important marketing aspect of corporate communication is communication directed toward employees, such as company newsletters.

Lobbying

Lobbying involves dealing with legislators and government officials to promote or defeat legislation and regulation. Large companies employ their own lobbyists, while smaller companies lobby through their local trade associations.

Counseling

Counseling involves advising management about public issues and company positions and image.[5] Counseling is important when there may be sensitive issues associated with the business. For example, water is a scarce commodity in Las Vegas. Major resorts with water displays, such as The Mirage, counsel their managers on the resort's water conservation efforts, such as recycling the hotel's waste water to be used in the hotel's fountains.

Table 18-1

Sample Timetable for Preopening Public Relations for a Hotel

This schedule begins 6 months before the hotel opening, at which time the announcement of construction plans and the groundbreaking ceremony will have been completed.

150 to 180 days before opening
1. Hold meeting to define objectives and to coordinate public relations effort with advertising; establish timetable in accordance with schedule completion date.
2. Prepare media kit.
3. Order photographs and renderings.
4. Begin preparation of mailings and develop media lists.
5. Contact all prospective beneficiaries of opening events.
6. Reserve dates for press conferences at off-site facilities.

120 to 150 days before opening
1. Send announcement with photograph or rendering to all media.
2. Send first progress bulletin to agents and media (as well as corporate clients, if desired).
3. Begin production of permanent brochure.
4. Make final plans for opening events, including commitment to beneficiaries.

90 to 120 days before opening
1. Launch publicity campaign to national media.
2. Send mailings to media.
3. Send second progress bulletin.
4. Arrange exclusive trade interviews and features in conjunction with ongoing trade campaign.
5. Begin trade announcement.

60 to 90 days before opening
1. Launch campaign to local media and other media with a short lead time; emphasize hotel's contribution to the community, announcement of donations and beneficiaries, and the like.
2. Send third and final progress bulletin with finished brochure.
3. Commence behind-the-scenes public tours.
4. Hold hard-hat luncheons for travel writers.
5. Set up model units for tours.

30 to 60 days before opening
1. Send preopening newsletter (to be continued on a quarterly basis).
2. Hold soft opening and ribbon-cutting ceremony.
3. Hold press opening.
4. Establish final plans for opening gala.

The month before opening
1. Begin broadside mailing to agents.
2. Hold opening festivities.
3. Conduct orientation press trips.

Source: Reprinted by permission of Elsevier Science Inc. from "Public Relations for the Hotel Opening," by Jessica D. Zive, *Cornell Hotel and Restaurant Administration Quarterly,* vol. 22, no. 1, p. 21, ©1981 by Cornell University.

PUBLICITY

Publicity is a direct function of public relations. Publicity is the task of securing editorial space, as opposed to paid space, in print and broadcast media to promote a product or a service. Publicity is a popular PR tool used in the five activities mentioned above. Some popular uses of publicity are described next.

Product-Related Publicity

Assist in the Launch of New Products.   The development of a new product is a newsworthy event. When The Hard Rock Cafe announced that it was going into the hotel business with the development of the first Hard Rock Hotel, the media covered the event during the initial announcement and the ground-breaking ceremonies. Later, when the hotel opened, a concert staged at the hotel was broadcast on MTV. This concert, the uniqueness of the hotel, and a concert the following day by The Eagles and Sheryl Crow ensured that the opening of the hotel received world wide publicity.

Assist in Repositioning a Mature Product.   New York City had an extremely bad press in the late 1960s and early 1970s. Robert Tisch, former chairman of the New York Convention and Visitors Bureau, writes that back in 1970 people all over the world believed that everything bad happened in New York. It was, they thought, the dirtiest, rudest, noisiest, most crowded city on earth. Fear City, Sin City, Stink City were just a few of the (printable) appellations. Tisch and Robert Gillett decided that they needed to stress all the positive aspects of the city. New York has more than 100 museums, the world's most active theater, 25,000 restaurants, and incomparable sight-seeing attractions.

They selected The Big Apple as the theme of their 1971 marketing campaign. The Big Apple was a term used by entertainers as a synonym for The Big Time. As Tisch states, there may be many apples on the tree, but when you pick New York you have picked the big one.[6] This campaign, along with the "I love New York" campaign by the New York State Department of Commerce, helped attract millions of visitors to New York City.

Build Up Interest in a Product Category.   Companies and trade associations have used PR to rebuild interest in declining commodities like eggs, milk, and potatoes and to expand consumption of such products as tea and orange juice. Pork and veal producers face a continuing need to promote their products and ensure that they are maintained as menu items in face of adverse publicity from health or animal rights groups. Sometimes an entire restaurant type will face adverse publicity, such as that directed against steak/prime rib restaurants or the issue of MSG in Chinese food. The cruise line industry successfully overcame a negative image as a hospitality product suitable only for the geriatric set. The "Loveboat" TV series had a dramatic and positive impact on changing attitudes and perceptions about cruise ships. The tragic sinking of a passenger ferry in Northern Europe in 1994 could well affect traveler interest in this type of vessel throughout the world. Much work will be needed to overcome an image of a "death ship."

Corporate Communication

Influence Specific Target Groups.   Companies can use publicity to build a positive image with specific groups. For example, McDonald's sponsors special neighborhood events in Hispanic and black communities for

Marketing Highlight 18-1

Singapore Suntec Centre

An article about the Singapore International Convention and Exhibition Centre in *Meetings & Conventions* provides a good example of effective publicity. The Centre, nicknamed Suntec, received a feature article in a magazine that targets Suntec's customers. The article included key information about Suntec, such as that the Centre features a 129,000-square-foot convention hall, an exhibition hall of the same size that can be divided into four rooms, a 23,000-square-foot ballroom, a 600-seat auditorium, 26 meeting rooms, and the latest technology in audiovisual systems. The article then described the tourist attractions of Singapore and hotels within walking distance of the Suntec.

Timing

Evaluating this article from a PR standpoint, several aspects make it effective. First, the timing. The article was written about 9 months before Suntec opened. The lead time for many of Suntec's customers will be over a year. Thus the article is timed to start bringing in inquiries for business shortly after the Centre opens. If the PR releases had waited until the Centre opened, business generated by the release would have been at least a year away. The advance publicity allows the Centre to make an announcement 9 months before opening, and certainly the official opening of the Centre will allow for additional PR. Smaller businesses, such as restaurants, do not need a large lead time. Restaurant customers make purchase decisions with short lead times. Many restaurants will have a "soft opening." They will not seek publicity when they initially open, but will get their delivery system fine-tuned. They start their PR campaign with an "official grand opening" when they know that they are ready to provide excellent service to the customer. The timing of a press release is a key success factor.

Media and Message

Media selection is important. In this case the medium was a magazine that has a readership consisting of professionals who make decisions on the sites for major meetings and conventions. It is important that PR be targeted; marketing publicity that is not aimed at an organization's target market has little value. The article included technical information about the Centre, information this professional audience will want. It is important to make sure that the message will be of interest to the audience. Most media make their money from selling advertising. Their advertising rates are based on their circulation or the size of their audience. To keep their circulation, they must print or broadcast messages that will be of interest to their audience. If they receive a press release that is interesting and relevant to their audience, they are likely to use the piece. A different publicity piece should be written for each audience.

Follow Up

The article included a phone number for the Centre, making it easy for a planner to contact the Centre.[7]

good causes. The sponsorship of the events and the publicity generated from the sponsorship builds up a good company image.

Defend Products That Have Encountered Public Problems. After a series of hotel fires made national news, the Adam's Mark Hotel in Houston invited a television crew to come to the hotel and see the latest safety devices incorporated into the hotel. As a result, they received several minutes of coverage on the evening news, showing that the fire safety problem had been addressed.

Tourist destinations are particularly influenced by negative publicity. When disaster hits a region or city, tourists instantaneously learn of the problem and quickly find alternative destinations. In part, tourism recovery

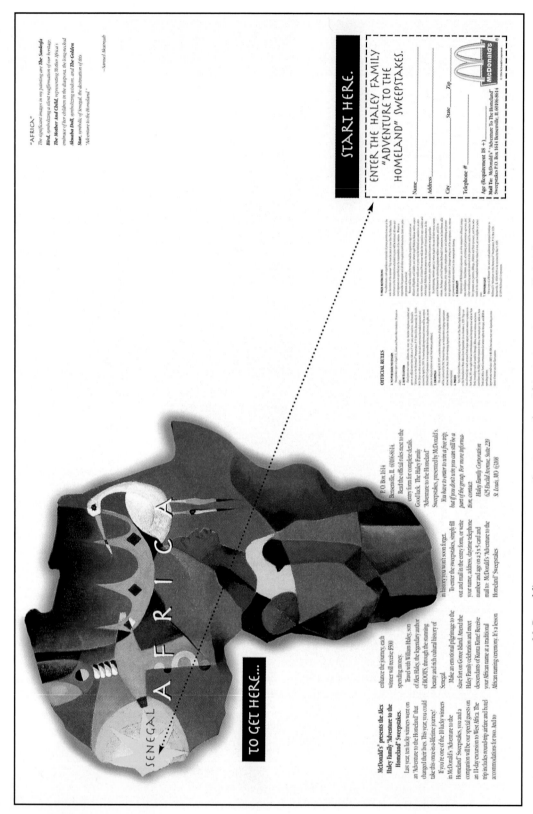

McDonald's sponsors a promotion targeted at African-Americans called "Adventure to the Homeland." Ten winners and their companions will travel to the west coast of Africa with William Haley, the son of Alex Haley, author of Roots. Courtesy of McDonald's Corporation. Original painting titled "Africa," by Samuel Akainyah.

depends on the reintroduction of a tourism destination. The reintroduction must overcome the adverse publicity resulting from the natural disaster, and it may take several years to rebuild business to predisaster levels. The speed of recovery depends on

1. The extent of damage caused by the disaster.
2. The efficiency with which tourism partners bring their facilities back on line.
3. An effective marketing message that clearly states that the destination is once again open (or still is) and ready for business.[8]

In 1992 the Hawaiian Island of Kauai was hit by hurricane Iniki. The world's press presented considerable bad news about the destruction of the resort by the hurricane. Although the problem was severe there was also a problem of misinformation. The head of the Kauai Advertising Group representing the tourist industry said, "Our biggest problem is how we deal with misinformation."[9]

Valuable PR lessons were learned from the disaster on Kauai:

Be available.	Take immediate steps.
Process information quickly.	Install hot-line information.
Be flexible.	Develop and use press releases.
Initiate action.	Be consistent.
Make action communications.	Update reservations.
See the big picture.	Bring travel agents, travel writers, and others to see the recovery.

Build the Corporate Image in a Way That Projects Favorably on Its Products. Choice Hotels International developed the Yellow Ribbon campaign during the war in Iraq. During the promotion, Choice donated $5 for every reservation to the American Red Cross to aid families of U.S. troops in the Persian Gulf.[10]

As the power of mass advertising weakens, marketing managers are turning to PR. In a survey of 286 U.S. marketing managers, three-fourths reported that their companies were using marketing PR. They found it particularly effective in building awareness and brand knowledge, for both new and established products. In several cases, PR proved more cost effective than advertising. Nevertheless, it usually must be planned jointly with advertising. PR needs a sufficient budget. Companies that have a small or no PR budget will have to take money from other areas of the promotional mix to support their PR program.[11]

Clearly, public relations can make a memorable impact on public awareness at a fraction of the cost of advertising. The company does not pay for the space or time obtained in the media. It pays for a staff to develop and circulate stories and manage certain events. If the company develops an interesting story, it could be picked up by all the news media and be worth millions of dollars in equivalent advertising. Furthermore, it would have more credibility than advertising. Some experts say that consumers are five times more likely to be influenced by editorial copy than by advertising.

In the mid 1970s, Braniff Airlines accomplished a PR feat that is still remembered in the airline industry. Braniff decided to retain the services of an artist by the name of Calder. It was decided to paint one of Braniff's airplanes as a flying contemporary art object. This proved to be a brilliant strategy worth millions of dollars in free exposure. The story was used by TV, magazines, newspapers, and radio throughout the world. In Latin America, customers made reservations months in advance to be assured of a seat on this plane.

THE PUBLIC RELATIONS PROCESS

Effective public relations is the result of a process. This process must be integrated with the firm's marketing strategy. One common misconception about public relations and particularly publicity is that quantity is more important than quality. Some public relations firms measure success by the number of articles placed in media. As in other marketing efforts, public relations should be meaningful to the target market.

The public relations process consists of the following steps: research, establishing the market objectives, defining the target audience, choosing the PR messages and vehicles, and evaluating the results.

Research

Before a company can develop a public relations program, it must understand the company's mission, objectives, strategies, and culture. It should know the vehicles that will be effective in delivering messages to the target audience. Much of the information needed by a PR manager will be contained in a well-written marketing plan. Ideally, the PR manager should be involved in the formation of the marketing plan.

The firm's environmental scanning system is another important source of information for the PR manager. Analysis of this information should identify trends and give the firm insights into how they should react to these trends. For example, many hotel and restaurant companies are now showing what they are doing to save and protect the natural environment.

Establishing the Marketing Objectives

Once the PR manager has identified PR opportunities through product experiment and research, priorities can be established and objectives set. Marketing PR can contribute to the following objectives:

Build awareness. PR can place stories in the media to bring attention to a product, service, person, organization, or idea.

Build credibility. PR can add credibility by communicating the message in an editorial context.

Stimulate the sales force and channel intermediaries. PR can help boost sales force and franchisee enthusiasm. Positive stories about a new menu item will make an impression on the customers, employees, and franchisees of a restaurant chain. The publicity Ritz-Carlton receives from winning the Baldrige Award provides their sales force with great ammunition when they make a sales call.

Feature Facility

breakout space for up to 700 people and banquet service for up to 1,120.

Combine this with its professional staff and top-notch standard of service and you have the formula for success.

Grand Geneva's reputation for excellence is well-deserved. After $20 million in renovations and a complete change in ownership, Grand Geneva is planning to get even better.

"All the basics were always here," Hoppe explained. "But they were never taken advantage of."

Grand Geneva, formerly known as "Americana," and remembered as one of Hugh Hefner's last (and most extravagant) Playboy Clubs began in 1968. It was operated by Hefner until 1986 when Americana purchased it.

J&B Realty of Chicago bought Americana and operated it as the "Americana Lake Geneva." In 1989, it made the decision to close the resort except during the summer season. It remained that way until 1993.

Recognizing the resort's potential for excellence, Americana Lake Geneva, was bought by the Marcus Corporation in July 1993.

After Marcus took over, one of its first priorities was the renaming of the resort to reflect its splendor. Lee Berthelsen, president and chief operating officer of Marcus Hotels and Resorts said the name change, based on its uniqueness, was an obvious one.

"The grounds, the two PGA championship golf courses, the architec-

ture, the setting are all grand," Berthelsen said. "Choosing a name to reflect that was simple. And we are making a substantial investment to make sure that every aspect of this resort does indeed live up to its name."

Hoppe said dedication to the philosophy of making each visitor's experience "grand" as well as recent renovations contribute to Grand Geneva's success.

"It was a grand project to undertake and we also want to provide a grand experience," Hoppe said.

In June 1994, the plans became reality. The renovations involved the complete redecoration of 355 guest rooms and suites, the purchase of 4,000 pieces of furniture and the

Photo courtesy of Grand Geneva

Grand Geneva's lobby gives guests an incredible first impression of the resort and hints of the splendor to come.

22   Wisconsin Meetings & Incentives

The Grand Geneva resort received four pages of space in this write-up on Wisconsin meetings and incentives. The magazine targets the resorts markets and thus is an example of well-placed PR. PR pieces such as this have more credibility than advertisements. Courtesy of Sprecher/Barrett and Company.

Hold down promotion costs. PR costs less than direct mail and media advertising. The smaller the company's promotion budget is, the stronger the case for using PR to gain share of mind.

Specific objectives should be set for every PR campaign. The Wine Growers of California hired the public relations firm of Daniel J. Edelman, Inc., to develop a publicity campaign to convince Americans that wine drinking is a pleasurable part of good living and to improve the image and market share of California wines. The following publicity objectives were established: (1) develop magazine stories about wine and place them in top magazines (*Time, House Beautiful*) and in newspapers (food columns, feature sections); (2) develop stories about wine's many health values and direct them to the medical profession; and (3) develop specific publicity for the young adult market, college market, governmental bodies, and various ethnic communities. These objectives were refined into specific goals so that final results could be evaluated.

The Homestead of Hot Springs, Virginia, conducts special weekends that serve as a part of that hotel's promotion mix. These weekends bring members of the media to the resort and give them an event to write about in addition to the resort's amenities. A spring wine and food festival serves as an excellent PR tool for invited guests, including meeting planners and journalists. A seven-course meal with twelve wines served in a formal setting serves as a dramatic event.[12]

The restaurant association in many cities sponsors a Taste of the Town. This event features food from the city's restaurants. The restaurants have a chance for exposure to many potential customers in one evening. The association usually charges an admission fee, which helps to ensure that those attending are interested in finding out about restaurant fare, rather than obtaining a free dinner. The fee is then donated to a charity, providing for additional publicity.

Defining the Target Audience

A relevant message delivered to a target audience by the appropriate vehicle is crucial to the success of any PR campaign. Effective PR practitioners carefully identify the publics that they wish to reach. They then study these publics and find media that can be used as vehicles to deliver their message. They identify issues that will be important to the public and form the message so that it will seem natural and logical to the target audience.

Choosing the PR Message and Vehicles

The PR practitioner is now ready to identify or develop interesting stories about the product or service. If the number of stories is insufficient, the PR practitioner should propose newsworthy events that the company can sponsor. Here the challenge is to *create news*, rather than *find it*. PR ideas include hosting major academic conventions, inviting celebrity speakers, and developing news conferences. Each event is an opportunity to develop a multitude of stories directed at different audiences.

Event creation is a particularly important skill in publicizing fund raising drives for nonprofit organizations. Fund raisers have developed a large repertoire of special events, including *anniversary celebrations, art exhibitions, auctions, benefit evenings, bingo games, book sales, cake sales, contests, dances, dinners, fairs, fashion shows, parties in unusual places, phonathons, rummage sales, tours* and *walkathons*. No sooner is one type of event created, such as a walkathon, than competitors spawn new versions, such a readathons, bikathons, and jogathons. The Fairmont Hotel in New Orleans upgraded its bathroom amenities in 1988, resulting in a disposal problem for the cartons of shampoo it had used before the upgrade. The hotel created an essay contest, with the winner receiving the shampoo. The hotel timed the event to coincide with the Democratic National Convention, when the town would be filled with members of the media. In their press release the Fairmont claimed that the contest gave the Democrats a chance to "wash the Republicans out of their hair." This line and the timing of the event resulted in international coverage of the event.[13]

Trine Palace is a historic restoration of the original governor's mansion when North Carolina was a British colony. Located in New Bern, this attraction annually draws thousands of tourists. The month of December used to be a poor month for attendance with inclement weather and preparation for Christmas occupying the minds of potential visitors. Trine Palace developed a Christmas tour that included actors costumed as the original governor and wife, tables heaped with Christmas food (display only), strolling bagpipe musicians, Christmas candles, holly, and a reception for guests following the tour at which punch and cookies are served. This relatively simple idea has become so successful that December is now among the top attendance months.

New York's Vista Hotel decided to offer a Cajun dinner, but needed a "hook" to make the event authentic and newsworthy. That hook was Paul Prudhomme, the colorful Cajun chef. The Vista arranged to host a publication party for Paul's Cajun cookbook at the hotel during the Cajun dinner. This type of creative thinking creates a great PR event from an otherwise interesting but not particularly newsworthy event.[14]

Implementing the Marketing PR Plan

Implementing publicity requires care. Consider the matter of placing information in media. Exciting information is easy to place. But most press releases are less than great and might not get the attention of busy editors. A chief asset of publicists is their personal relationship with media editors. Public relations practitioners are often ex-journalists who know many media editors and what they want. PR people look at media editors as a market to satisfy so that they will continue to use the company's press releases.

Publicity requires extra care when it involves staging special events, such as testimonial dinners, news conferences, and national contests. PR practitioners need a good head for detail and for coming up with quick solutions when things go wrong. Most hotel corporations have a crisis plan included as part of their PR plan. In this plan they state who can talk to the media and who should not. These plans usually state that staff should not speak to media, but instead direct inquiries to the director of public relations.

Evaluating PR Results

The contribution of PR is difficult to measure, because it is used along with other promotion tools. If it is used before other tools come into action, its contribution is easier to evaluate.

Exposures.   The easiest measure of PR effectiveness is the number of exposures created in the media. Publicists supply the client with a clipping book showing all the media that carried news about the product and a summary statement, such as the following:

Media coverage included 3500 column inches of news and photographs in 350 publications with a combined circulation of 79.4 million; 2500 minutes of air time on 290 radio stations and an estimated audience of 65 million; and 660 minutes of air time on 160 television stations with an estimated audience of 91 million. If this time and space had been purchased at advertising rates, it would have amounted to $1,047,000.[15]

This exposure measure is not very satisfying. There is no indication of how many people actually read, heard, or recalled the message and what they thought afterward. There is no information on the net audience reached, since publications overlap in readership. Because publicity's goal is reach, not frequency, it would be useful to know the number of unduplicated exposures. It is also important that publicity reach target markets. A common weakness of publicity is that persons exposed to the publicity are not part of the company's target market.

Awareness/Comprehension/Attitude Change.   A better measure is the change in product awareness/comprehension/attitude resulting from the campaign (after allowing for the effect of other promotional tools). For example, how many people recall hearing the news item? How many told others about it (a measure of word of mouth)? How many changed their minds after hearing it? The Potato Board learned, for example, that the number of people who agreed with the statement "Potatoes are rich in vitamins and minerals" went from 36% before the campaign to 67% after the campaign, a significant improvement in product comprehension.

Sales-and-Profit Contribution.   Sales-and-profit impact is the most satisfactory measure, if obtainable. A well-planned public relations campaign is usually part of an integrated promotional campaign. This makes it very difficult to isolate the impact of the public relations campaign.

MAJOR TOOLS IN MARKETING PR

Publications

Companies rely extensively on communication materials to reach and influence their target markets. These include annual reports, brochures, cards, articles, audiovisual materials, and company newsletters and magazines. Brochures can play an important role in informing target customers about a product, how it works, and how it is to be assembled. McDonald's developed a series of brochures discussing the quality ingredients that it uses, the actions that it has taken to help protect the environment, and the nutritional content of its products. Thoughtful articles written by company executives can draw attention to the company and its products. Company newsletters and magazines can help build the company's image and convey important news to target markets. Audiovisual materials, such as films, slides-and-sound, and video and audio cassettes are coming into increasing use as promotion tools. The cost of audiovisual materials is usually greater than the cost of printed material, but so is the impact. Many resort destinations use videos to promote their properties. Disney World created a 20-minute video aimed at families considering Disney World as a vacation site. Wet N Wild developed a 4-minute video aimed at travel agents, tour agents, and other members of the distribution channel.

McDonald's developed a creative and potentially trend setting annual report for stockholders on videotape. This contained statements by members of top management as well as commercials. Publicly traded hospitality corporations with thousands of stockholders should consider the annual report and other stockholder communication as opportunities to promote the company's products and services, and not simply information required by law.

Events

Hospitality companies can draw attention to new products or other company activities by arranging special events, such as the Homestead wine and food festival mentioned earlier. Events include news conferences, seminars, outings, exhibits, contests and competitions, anniversaries, and sport and cultural sponsorships that will reach the target publics. Sponsoring a sports event, such as the Coors International Bicycle Class, gives these companies a chance to invite and host suppliers, journalists, distributors, and customers, as well as bring repeated attention to the company's name and products.

News

A major task of PR professionals is to find or create favorable news about the company, its products, and its people. News generation requires skill in developing a story concept, researching it, and writing a press release. But the PR person's skill must go beyond preparing news stories. Getting the media to accept press releases and attend press conferences calls for marketing and interpersonal skills. A good PR media director understands press needs for stories that are interesting and timely and for releases that are well written and attention getting. The media director needs to gain the favor of editors and reporters. As the press is cultivated, it is increasingly likely to provide better coverage to the company.

A proven technique for writing a good press release is to use the Hey-You-See-So approval. Imagine that a teenager saw a friend in front of the high school. The teenager might yell, "Hey (attention getter) Bill and Helen (you), look what I have, three tickets for Saturday's rock concert (see). Let's plan to go (so)." When this simple technique is followed in a press release, effectiveness is increased.

Another journalistic technique is to write a press release in an inverted pyramid form. Think of a pyramid standing on its point and remember that editors can and do shorten a press release to serve space requirements. A press release should be written so that the bulk of the information the company wishes to transmit is contained in the first paragraph. Each additional paragraph simply adds to the original and is less and less damaging to the story if clipped by an editor.

Speeches

Speeches are another tool for creating product and company publicity. Iaccoca's charismatic talks before large audiences helped Chrysler sell its cars. Increasingly, company executives must field questions from the media or give talks at trade associations or sales meetings. These appearances can build or hurt the company's image. Companies are choosing their spokespersons carefully and using speech writers and coaches to help improve the speaking ability of those selected.

The creation of a quality speech is costly for any company. A considerable amount of staff and executive time must be devoted to the project. It therefore makes sense to obtain maximum PR mileage from each speech. This is accomplished by printing copies of the speech or excerpts for distribution to the press, stockholders, employees, and other publics. A speech that is given but not distributed represents a wasted PR opportunity.

Public Service Activities

Companies can improve public goodwill by contributing money and time to good causes. A large company typically will ask executives to support community affairs where their offices and plants are located. In other instances, companies will offer to donate a certain amount of money to a specified cause out of consumer purchases. Called *cause-related marketing*, it is used by a growing number of companies to build public goodwill.[16] Restaurant and hotel chains will donate so much of each sale to a charitable cause for a given amount of time. For example, a fast-food restaurant may donate 5 cents from every sandwich purchased on a certain day to the Muscular Dystrophy Association.

Identity Media

Normally, a company's PR material acquires separate looks, which creates confusion and misses an opportunity to create and reinforce corporate identity. In a society subject to overcommunication, companies must compete for attention. They should strive to create a visual identity that the public immediately recognizes. The visual identity is carried by the company's logos, stationery, brochures, signs, business forms, business cards, buildings, uniforms, dress codes, and rolling stock.

PUBLIC RELATIONS OPPORTUNITIES FOR THE HOSPITALITY INDUSTRY

Public Relations Opportunities for Individual Properties

Public relations is by far the most important promotional tool available to entrepreneurs and individual properties such as a single restaurant, tourist attraction, bed and breakfast, tour operator, or hotel. Seldom can these enterprises afford costly advertising or other promotional programs. Successful PR programs by individual operators have demonstrated winning strategies that can be emulated by others.

Build PR around the Owner/Operator

The owner/operator and the enterprise itself often become one and the same in the minds of customers. Obviously, this strategy holds dangers, such as the death of the owners, but benefits usually exceed risks. Michael Lefever, a professor at the University of Massachusetts, relates the success of a restaurant operator named Joe. The name of this restaurant not surprisingly was Joe's. Joe used to drive a Cadillac with two magnetic signs advertising his restaurant.

Everyone in the community knew Joe and watched for his car as it rolled about town. Joe built his own personal image by wearing white cook's pants, a starched white shirt, and big comfortable black shoes that squeaked. Joe wore this uniform everywhere. If people failed to see Joe coming, they knew by the aroma of his big cigar that he was near. Joe knew the power of visibility and built a gigantic window so that passersby could look directly into the kitchen. Joe had a team of "trained chefs" who knew the value of show biz. They stirred, flipped, and flamed dishes to the delight of all. Joe knew the value of show biz, but most of all he realized the value of "Joe." Joe's most powerful PR asset was that he was always at the restaurant. He called this personal goodwill. Customers came to see Joe. Joe knew them by name and greeted each with a firm handshake. Joe was a pro at "selling Joe."[17]

The owner/operator of a fishing lodge in Costa Rica had been a circus trapeze artist before retiring to the jungles of Costa Rica. Each year, U.S. and Canadian TV and radio talk shows featured this entrepreneur and his fishing lodge. This owner/operator knew that the media is always hungry for a good human interest story.

Individuals successful at promoting themselves often use theatrical costumery such as Joe's squeaky shoes or General MacArthur's corn cob pipe. Ken Hamblin, an African-American columnist and talk show host, is never seen without a hat. Obesity, a wart on the nose, a bony appearance, a limp, a mustache, and dozens of other personal characteristics have been successfully used to build memorable personalities. As increasing numbers of men wear pony tails and earrings, the blue suit and white shirt IBM-type appearance may become a differentiating "costume."

Build PR around Location

Some restaurants and B&Bs are almost impossible to find without a compass and topographical map. Normally, this would be viewed as the kiss of death for a hospitality firm. Hundreds of owners/operators of these enterprises have turned their lemon into a lemonade. The isolation and obscurity of the enterprises is used as a PR tactic.

A restaurant in San Francisco lies directly under a freeway that collapsed during an earthquake. Sure enough, instead of discouraging patrons, interest increased as the restaurant was featured on national TV as the little restaurant that refused to succumb to an earthquake.

The Solitaire Lodge in New Zealand is located on a beautiful but isolated lake. The owner originally felt that U.S. fly fishing fans would find his lodge irresistible. This was not to be, as the owner sadly discovered that fly fishing fans desired rivers not lakes. The owner then changed tactics and successfully promoted the lodge as a great getaway place and a wonderful location to observe Halley's comet free of night light pollution. This unusual twist brought the lodge to the attention of major U.S. newspapers who carried the story free of charge.

Build PR around a Product or Service

Wall Drug Store is a major tourist stop and tourist attraction for the state of South Dakota. Located in a town of less than a thousand residents,

The story has it that an early owner of the historic Peabody Hotel in Memphis went on a hunting trip, had a little too much to drink, and let live ducks loose in the hotel's fountain. When the hotel was being renovated in the 1980s, the new owners played up this historical event into a brilliant PR campaign. The Peabody ducks have received millions of dollars worth of print and broadcast time. Today people from all over still come to see the ducks. Courtesy of Peabody Hotels and Turkel Schwartz & Partners.

Wall Drug daily attracts 15,000 or more visitors during tourist season. Wall Drug was built on free ice water. Before the days of air-conditioned cars, Mr. and Mrs. Ted Hustead, the owners, saw tourists passing by on their way to the Black Hills. These folks looked thirsty and indeed they were. Ted hand painted a few signs saying "Free Ice Water—Wall Drug" and placed them along the highway. Before Ted returned from planting these signs, tourists had already found their way to Wall Drug. They have never stopped coming. Today word of mouth and PR have replaced many of the road signs, but Wall Drug remains the free ice water stop.

The Raffles Hotel in Singapore has a colorful and long history, but most visitors know it as the birthplace of the Singapore Sling. Today the renovated bar serves thousands of Singapore Slings. Even the empty glasses are sold and serve as a PR vehicle throughout the world. Hospitality enterprises throughout the world have built a solid and long-lasting image around a drink, a dessert, a special entree, fireplaces in the guest rooms, and even ducks. The Peabody Hotel of Memphis became well known for a flock of ducks that daily waddled from the rooftop via the elevator to a fountain in the lobby. Today, the duck association continues even for the Orlando property.

The Ramada Inn of Antigua, Guatemala, has a wood-burning fireplace in each guest room. On chilly evenings a staff member appears to light the fireplace in each occupied room.

Unique service also serves as a PR focal point. Usually, this means exceptionally fine service, but sometimes the reverse is true. Occasionally, a bar and grill or a restaurant gains a reputation for having the rudest and sometimes the ugliest wait staff anywhere in the country. A Dallas bar and grill popular with the lunch time business crowd was notorious for its surly staff. Those familiar with the place loved to take unsuspecting newcomers to see how badly their companion could be insulted. Fans of the TV program "Cheers" will recall the disrespectful Carla and how she nevertheless maintained a peculiar charm.

CRISIS MANAGEMENT

Hotels are open 24 hours a day, major airline companies have thousands of flights a day, and fast-food companies serve millions of customers each day. There are times when things go wrong; sometimes it is management's fault and sometimes it is beyond management's control. Managers must realize that things will go wrong; guests will fall asleep while smoking, people will be poisoned by restaurant food, thieves will rob your guests, and planes will crash. A crisis management program will reduce the negative effects of these events.

The first step in crisis management is to take all precautions to prevent negative events from occurring. Good sanitation practices reduce the risk of serving poisoned food. Regular cleaning of kitchen ducts and employee training can eliminate grease fires in the kitchen. Fire prevention and control plans rehearsed by the employees can reduce the risk of a deadly fire. Hotels that train all their employees to look out for suspicious actions and report them to security can reduce the risk of crimes against guests. A well-managed property is the best form of crisis management.

When a crisis does occur, good communication with the press can reduce the impact of negative publicity. For example, a fire in a guest room resulting in no injuries could result in negative or positive publicity. If the hotel provides no information to the press, the headline might read "Regal Hotel Fire Forces Evacuation of 360 Guests." If the hotel contacts the press, the hotel has a chance to tell their story. In this case the hotel could state that there was a hotel fire. "The smoke alarm went off at 12:33 A.M., setting the hotel's fire plan into action. The fire department was called and employees conducted an orderly evacuation of the hotel as a precautionary measure. No one was injured and all guests were able to return to their rooms within 30 minutes. Ms. Roberta Dominquez, the general manager of the Regal, praised the quick action of the employees. She stated that as a result of the hotel's monthly fire drills all employees knew exactly what to do." The headline from this story might read; "Well-trained Employees Quickly Move Guests to Safety."

When a crisis does occur, three things are essential. First, the company should appoint a spokesperson. Other employees should be instructed to refer media to this person. This ensures that the company is giving a consistent story based on facts. Second, if the hotel has a public relations agency, the agency should be contacted. In a major crisis, it is a good idea to seek the help of a public relations firm. Finally, the company should notify the press when a crisis does occur and keep the press updated. The media will learn about the event, so it is best that they find out from the company. Every company should have a crisis management plan and instruct employees in crisis management as part of their initial training.

LOCAL STORE MARKETING

Local store marketing, also called local area marketing or neighborhood marketing, is defined as a low-cost, hands-on effort to take advantage of all opportunities within the immediate trading area to promote and market a business.[17] Although all areas of the promotional mix are used in local area marketing, public relations is the heart of any local area marketing program. Local area marketing is used by both big and very large companies; however, it is an area where small companies can compete just as effectively as large companies. Independently owned businesses, such as restaurants or travel agencies, have an advantage over large companies since the owners become permanent fixtures of the community, whereas the large companies tend to replace their store managers every 2 or 3 years.

Examples of public relations activities included in local store marketing are providing tours of your facility. Primary schools look for places to take their students on field trips. A restaurant or hotel can be an exciting venue. A short tour, followed by a tasting and providing the students with a coupon (so that they can show their parents where they went) can be a good way to create business and goodwill. Many suburban papers have weekly papers; providing a weekly or monthly article on travel, food, or wine is a good way to gain exposure. If the articles are well written, the paper will appreciate the free articles and the writer will gain exposure and credibility in the local market. Being a speaker at meetings of local social and service clubs is another way to gain exposure. During the holiday season a business can become a depository for charities collecting toys for disadvantaged children. But don't accept this task passively. For example, if the local firefighters ask you to collect toys for their campaign, suggest that the campaign be started with a kickoff drive including fire engines, sirens, and firemen in uniform in your parking lot on a Saturday. If they agree, call the local news station and get some television coverage.[19]

A good local area marketing campaign creates goodwill in the community and exposure for the restaurant that will translate into increased business and customer loyalty. Successful local marketers do not give products or money away freely; they evaluate every opportunity and make sure that the effort will be worthwhile. By being creative, managers can ensure that their local marketing efforts will be noticed.

Chapter Review

I.   Definition of Public Relations. The process by which we create a positive image and customer preference through third-party endorsement.

II.   Five Public Relations Activities

1) Press Relations. The aim of press relations is to place newsworthy information into the news media to attract attention to a person, product, or service.

2) Product Publicity. Product publicity involves efforts to publicize specific products.

3) Corporate Communication. This activity covers internal and external communications and promotes understanding of the organization.

4) Lobbying. Lobbying involves dealing with legislators and government officials to promote or defeat legislation and regulation.

5) Counseling. Counseling involves advising management about public issues and company positions and image.

III.   Marketing Public Relations. Publicity is the task of securing editorial space, as opposed to paid space, in print and broadcast media to promote a product or service. Marketing PR goes beyond simple publicity. Marketing PR can contribute to the following tasks:

1) Assist in the Launch of New Products

2) Assist in Repositioning a Mature Product

3) Build up Interest in a Product Category

4) Influence Specific Target Groups

5) Defend Products That Have Encountered Public Problems

IV.   The Public Relations Process

1) Research to Understand the Firm's Mission, Culture, and Target of the Communication

2) Establishing Marketing Objectives

a) Build awareness

b) Build credibility

c) Stimulate the sales force and channel intermediaries

d) Hold down promotion costs

3) Defining the Target Audience

4) Choosing the PR Message and Vehicles, such as Event Creation

5) Implementing the Marketing PR Plan

6) Evaluating PR Results

a) Exposures

b) Awareness/comprehension/attitude change

c) Sales-and-Profit contribution

V.   Overview of the Major Tools in Public Relations

1) Publications. Companies can reach and influence their target market via annual reports, brochures, cards, articles, audiovisual materials, and company newsletters and magazines.

2) Events. Companies can draw attention to new products or other company activities by arranging special events.

3) News. PR professionals cultivate the press to increase better coverage to the company.

4) Speeches. Speeches create product and company publicity, and it is accomplished by printing copies of the speech or excerpts for distribution to the press, stockholders, employees and other publics.

5) Public Service Activities. Companies can improve public goodwill by contributing money and time to good causes, such as supporting community affairs.

6) Identity Media. Companies can create a visual identity that the public immediately recognizes, such as with company's logos, stationery, signs, business forms, business cards, buildings, uniforms, dress code, and rolling stock.

VI.   Public Relations Opportunities for Individual Properties

1) Build PR around the Owner / Operator

2) Build PR around the Location. For instance, the isolation and obscurity of an enterprise can be used as a PR tactic.

3) Build PR around a Product or Service

VII.   Crisis Management

1) Take all precautions to prevent negative events from occurring.

2) When a crisis does occur:

a) Appoint a spokesperson. This ensures that the company is giving a consistent story based on facts.

b) Contact the firm's public relations agency if it has one.

c) The company should notify the press when a crisis does occur and keep the press updated.

DISCUSSION QUESTIONS

1. What is meant by the term public? Can a company have more than one public?

2. Why might it make sense for a hotel chain to shift some of its advertising dollars to public relations?

3. Give some examples of how a hospitality organization might be able to gain publicity.

4. Is publicity free?

5. Compare and contrast publicity with advertising. What are the benefits and drawbacks of each?

KEY TERMS

Corporate communication   This activity covers internal and external communications and promotes understanding of the organization.

Counseling   Counseling involves advising management about public issues and company positions and image.[20]

Lobbying   Lobbying involves dealing with legislators and government officials to promote or defeat legislation and regulation.

Press relations   The aim of press relations is to

place newsworthy information into the news media to attract attention to a person, product, or service.

Product publicity   Product publicity involves various efforts to publicize specific products.

Public relations   The process by which we create a positive image and customer preference through third-party endorsement.[21]

REFERENCES

1. DALE CARTER, *The Final Frontier: The Rise and Fall of the American Rocket State* (London: Verso, 1988); C. Dewitt Coffman, *Marketing for a Full House* (Ithaca, N.Y.: School of Hotel Administration, Cornell University, 1975); JON TRUX, *The Space Race, From Sputnik to Shuttle: The Story of the Battle for the Heavens* (London: New English Library, 1985).

2. JESSICA MILLER, "Marketing Communications," *Cornell Hotel and Restaurant Administration Quarterly*, 34, no. 5 (October 1993), p. 49.

3. IBID.

4. PHILIP KOTLER, "Public Relations versus Marketing: Dividing the Conceptual Domain and Operational Turf," paper presented at the Public Relations Colloquium 1989, San Diego, Calif., January 24, 1989.

5. Adapted from SCOTT M. CUTLIP, ALLEN H. CENTER, AND GLEN M. BROWN, *Effective Public Relations,* 6th ed. (Englewood Cliffs, N.J.: Prentice-Hall, 1985), pp. 7–17.

6. PRESTON ROBERT TISCH, "Why Millions Pick the Big Apple," in *The Complete Travel Marketing Handbook* (Lincolnwood, Ill.: NTC Business Books, 1988), pp. 86–100.

7. JOE DUROCHER, "Recovery Marketing: What to Do after a Natural Disaster," *Cornell Hotel and Restaurant Administration Quarterly, 35*, no. 2 (April 1994), p. 66.

8. IBID., p. 67.

9. BARBARA HOLSOMBACK, "Getting Back on Solid Ground," *ADWEEK* (April 20, 1992), pp. 31–38.

10. Tom Duncan, *A Study of How Manufacturers and Service Companies Perceive and use Marketing Public Relations* (Muncie, Ind.: Ball State University, 1985).

11. WITHIAM GLENN, "Combining Tradition and Innovation," *Cornell Hotel and Restaurant Administration Quarterly*, 32, no. 2 (August 1991), p. 64.

12. KAREN WEINER ESCALERA, "How to Get News out of Nothing," *Lodging* (March 1992), pp. 25–26.

13. MILLER, "Marketing Communications," p. 49.

14. ARTHUR M. MERIMS, "Marketing's Stepchild: Product Publicity," *Harvard Business Review* (November–December 1972), pp. 111–112. Also see KATERINE D. PAINE, "There Is a Method for Measuring PR," *Marketing News* (November 7, 1987), p. 5.

15. For further reading on cause-related marketing, see P. RAJAN VARADARAJAN AND ANIL MENON, "Cause-related Marketing: A Co-alignment of Marketing Strategy and Corporate Philanthropy," *Journal of Marketing* (July 1988), pp. 58–74.

16. MICHAEL M. LEFEVER, "Restaurant Advertising: Coupons, Clauses and Cadillacs," *Cornell Hotel and Restaurant Administration Quarterly, 29*, no. 4 (February 1989), p. 94.

17. National Restaurant Association, *Promoting the Neighborhood Restaurant: A Local Store Marketing Manual* (Chicago: National Restaurant Association, 1988).

18. IBID, p. 69.

19. Adapted from CUTLIP, CENTER, AND BROWN, *Effective Public Relations,* pp. 7–17.

20. MILLER, "Marketing Communications," p. 49.

21. LOREN G. EDELSTEIN, "Suntec Centre: all the More Reason to Meet in Singapore '95," *Meetings and Conventions*, 29, no. 12, 1994, pp. 12+.

Professional Sales

19

*M*any of the world's top salespeople don't carry that title, but daily serve as superior sales role models. Ruth Fertel exemplifies the best. Ruth Fertel founded Ruth's Chris Steak House, billed as "The Nation's Largest Upscale Restaurant Company," with 44 operations selling over 9000 steaks per day and grossing over $110 million annually.[1] Let's briefly examine some of the success characteristics behind Ruth.

Optimism and a Willingness to Overcome Adversity

Ruth earned a degree in chemistry with a minor in physics at Louisiana State University, graduating at age 19. She taught briefly at McNeese Junior College in Lake Charles, Louisiana, but left to marry and raise a family.

Fourteen years later Ruth, by then divorced, reentered the work force as a lab technician at Tulane Medical School. Four years there convinced her that she couldn't earn enough to send her two sons to college, so she decided to go into business for herself. That was in 1965. One day, while scanning the classified section of the local newspaper, Ruth found an ad for a steak house for sale. "I can do that!" she thought to herself, although she had no prior experience and limited funds.

In short order, against the advice of her lawyer, her banker, and her best friend, Ruth mortgaged her home to buy the small restaurant, then called

Chris Steak House. "To show you how naive I was at the time," recalls Ruth, "I was ready to borrow only the $18,000 required to buy the restaurant, but the bank suggested I take an additional $4000 to buy food and supplies!"

Ruth compensated for her lack of experience with plain hard work. It paid off, and the people came. In the first 6 months, she cleared more than double her previous annual salary. Her restaurant soon became popular with the city's media personalities, political leaders, sport figures, and business people. The name "Ruth's Chris" became identified with quality and fine steaks.

Treating Others Correctly

To what does Ruth attribute her success? "It's as simple as following the Golden Rule," says Ruth. "I treat my customers and my associates as I would want to be treated."

Knowing Your Customers

Despite the growth of Ruth's Chris, Ruth Fertel is determined not to lose touch with her clientele. Under her direction, the company distributes 50,000 copies of "Steak House Gang News," a glossy 16-page newsletter to customers. The company has also gathered 10,000 names of customers who want free issues by mail on a quarterly basis. Customer profiles will be among the magazine's features.[2]

Confidence

"I've always had a lot of confidence in my ability to do anything I set my mind to," said Fertel. "I'm not a restauranteur, I'm a business person who owned a restaurant. I just had confidence and never once thought I couldn't do it or would fail."[3]

Honesty

"A verbal contract with Ruth is as good as any contract," said her broker.

Emphasis on Quality

"Get a good product, serve it with a smile at the right price, and take the profits to the bank," said Ruth. Ruth insists that her beef never be frozen to retain its tenderness and flavor. She demands that individual steaks be cut at each restaurant, broiled to diner's tastes, and served sizzling. Portions tend to be huge, 12 to 18 ounces, because Ruth believes that larger cuts of meat hold onto their juices better during cooking. If there's any secret to my business, it's in the quality," says Fertel.[4]

The Word Failure Doesn't Exist

Ruth will not allow any of her restaurants to close, despite economic difficulties. The Houston franchise threatened to shut down following a bad financial year. Fertel herself stepped in and bought the restaurant. She and her team have since turned it around.

Chapter 19 concentrates on the vital area of professional sales.

We start with a discussion of the nature of professional sales within the hospitality industry and the need to establish **salesforce objectives**. Other subjects covered are **salesforce structure** and **size** including **territorial, product, customer**, and **market** structures.

After establishing a **sales structure**, we move to **organizing** the **sales department** including the **inside salesforce**, the **reservations department, electronic** and **telephone sales**, and the **field salesforce**.

This chapter also includes a discussion of **relationship marketing** and **strategic alliances**. We then move to critical aspects of professional sales including **recruiting, training, managing**, and **salesforce**. We conclude with a discussion of **sales negotiating, sales compensation, sales motivation**, quotas, and other **control** techniques.

MANAGEMENT OF PROFESSIONAL SALES

Success or failure within the hospitality industry ultimately rests on the ability to sell. A roadside motel at an intersection of major highways or a popular restaurant with waiting lines is sometimes viewed as being above the need "To Sell." No member of the hospitality industry can accept this as a long-run viewpoint.

Discourteous front-desk clerks and cashiers who would impress Grumpy of the Seven Dwarfs are part of one's sales force. These and all others who face the public can drive away or attract business. In the best cases, they can upsell through suggestive selling, thus increasing the check size by effectively suggesting desserts, special drinks, and even a gift certificate for a friend. Higher-margin suites can be sold instead of the lowest-price room.

Successful owners and managers know that they must continuously sell. County commissioners, tax evaluation officials, planning boards, the press, bankers, and the local visitor center must all be sold on one's hospitality business. Those in the backroom who check credit card reports, care for audiovisual equipment, serve as secretaries, and maintain the physical plant are also part of the sales team.

Libraries could be filled with tales of lost sales or needlessly fractured guest relationships because of a curt response or an unsavory attitude on the part of support staff who mistakenly believe that sales is not their responsibility.

Everyone must sell, but a few individuals have the specific responsibility for ensuring that payrolls can be met, invoices can be paid, and a fair return on investment can be achieved. These are the professional salespeople.

The term *sales representative* covers a broad range of positions in our economy, where the differences are often greater than the similarities. The following classification of sales positions has application in the hospitality industry.

1. **Deliverer.** Positions in which the salesperson's job is predominantly to deliver the product (e.g., restaurant supplies, hotel linens).

2. **Order taker.** Positions in which the salesperson is predominantly an inside order taker (e.g., reservations or fast-food person) or outside order taker (e.g., the restaurant supply person calling on a chef).

3. **Missionary.** Positions in which the salesperson is not expected or permitted to take an order, but is called on only to build goodwill or to educate the actual or potential user. Airline and cruise line salespeople who call on travel agencies, work at trade shows, and conduct other public relations types of work are in effect missionary salespeople.

4. **Technician.** Positions in which the major emphasis is placed on technical knowledge (e.g., the yield management salesperson who is primarily a consultant to client companies such as hotels or airlines).

5. **Demand creator.** Positions that demand the creative sale of tangible products or of intangibles (e.g., most of the hospitality industry).[5]

The positions range from the least to the most creative types of selling. The first jobs call for servicing accounts and taking new orders, while the latter require seeking prospects and influencing them to buy.

This chapter will focus on six major areas.

1. Nature of hospitality sales
2. Sales-force objectives
3. Sales-force structure and size
4. Organizing the sales department
5. Recruiting and training a professional sales force
6. Managing the sales force

NATURE OF HOSPITALITY SALES

Sales personnel serve as the company's personal link to customers. The sales representative is the company to many of its customers and in turn brings back much needed customer intelligence. Personal selling is the most expensive contact and communication tool used by the company.

Cost estimates for making a personal sales call vary depending on the industry and the company, but one conclusion remains constant. However measured, the cost is high! According to *Business Week,* "There are 8 million people in the U.S. workforce who are directly involved in sales and it now costs $250 and up to send any one of them on a call."[6] A nonhospitality company, E. I. du Pont de Nemours and Company, Inc., estimates a cost per field sales call of $500[7] and up, and an even higher estimate of $700 per visit is given by a researcher who included the salesperson's salary, cost of travel, technical support people, and cost of presentations.[8]

Add to this the fact that sales orders are seldom written on the first call and often require five or more calls, particularly for larger orders. The cost of obtaining a new client thus becomes enormously high, as depicted in Table 19-1.

Despite the high cost, personal selling is often the most effective tool available to a hospitality company. Sales representatives perform one or more of the following tasks for their companies:

- **Prospecting.** Sales representatives find and cultivate new customers.
- **Targeting.** Sales representatives decide how to allocate their scarce time among prospects and customers.
- **Communicating.** Sales representatives communicate information about the company's products and services.
- **Selling.** Sales representatives know the art of salesmanship—approaching, presenting, answering objections, and closing sales.
- **Servicing.** Sales representatives provide various services to the customers—consulting on their problems, rendering technical assistance, arranging financing, and expediting delivery.
- **Information gathering.** Sales representatives conduct market research and intelligence work and fill in call reports.
- **Allocating.** Sales representatives decide which customers to allocate scarce products to during product shortages.

The sales representative's mix of tasks varies with the state of the economy. During product shortages, such as a temporary shortage of hotel rooms during a major convention, sales representatives find themselves with nothing to sell. Some companies jump to the conclusion that fewer

Table 19-1
Cost of Obtaining a New Client

NUMBER OF CALLS NEEDED TO CLOSE A SALE	TOTAL COST TO OBTAIN A NEW CLIENT AT VARIOUS ESTIMATES OF COST OF SALES CALL		
	@ $250	@ $500	@ $700
1	$ 250	$ 500	$ 700
2	500	1000	1400
3	750	1500	2100
4	1000	2000	2800
5	1250	2500	3500*
6	1500	3000	4200
7	1750	3500	4900
8	2000	4000	5600
9	2250	4500	6300
10	2500	5000	7000

*Five sales calls seems to be an estimate commonly given to obtain a new client.

sales representatives are then needed. But this thinking overlooks the salesperson's other roles—allocating the product, counseling unhappy customers, and selling the company's other products that are not in short supply. It also ignores the long-run nature of hospitality sales.

Many conventions and conferences are planned years in advance, and hospitality salespeople must often work with meeting and convention planners 2 to 4 years in advance of the actual event. Resorts in the United States have concentrated much of their selling efforts on meetings and conferences, which now represent 35% of their customers.[9] This was not achieved by viewing professional sales as a short-run tactic. A senior analyst with Tourism Canada has demonstrated that Canadian resort salespeople are effective in reaching foreign markets. Guests in Canadian resorts are 60% Canadian and 40% foreign. By comparison, U.S. resorts have a mix of 91% American and 9% foreign.[10] Again, penetrating foreign markets is not accomplished in the short run.

As companies move toward a stronger market orientation, their sales forces need to become more market focused and customer oriented. The traditional view is that salespeople should worry about volume and sell, sell, sell and that the marketing department should worry about marketing strategy and profitability. The newer view is that salespeople should know how to produce customer satisfaction and company profit. They should know how to analyze sales data, measure market potential, gather market intelligence, develop marketing strategies and plans, and become proficient at the use of sales tactics.

Days Inns of America recognizes that the general manager (GM) is responsible for a properties' sales efforts. "It is immensely important that the GM be equipped with the necessary sales and marketing tools" said John Russell, Days Inns president.[11] Chains such as Days Inns, Motel Eight, and Travelodge of Australia must view the GM as the head of sales. Larger hotels and resorts, such as Sheraton, Hilton, Shangila, and Four Seasons, employ professional sales managers. In these cases, the GM is considerably less involved with details of the sales function.

Sales representatives need analytical skills. This becomes especially critical at the higher levels of sales management. Marketers believe that a sales force will be more effective in the long run if members understand marketing as well as selling. The newer concept is basic to the successful use of yield management in the hospitality industry.

This has become very clear as database marketing has gained in importance within the hospitality industry. Group sales have been particularly affected. After viewing the importance of marketing information to sales, a hospitality industry writer with *Hotel and Motel Management* magazine concluded the following:[12]

- Closing sales has more to do with professionalism than anything else.
- Understanding who real prospects are increases sales productivity.
- Sales force members can save hours of time by having information about prospect group clients.
- It is critical to know what groups have a history of booking rooms in your type of hotel.

Hospitality companies typically establish objectives for the sales force. Sales objectives are essential for two reasons.

1. To ensure that corporate goals are met. Goals may include revenue, market share, improving corporate image, and many others.

2. Objectives assist sales force members to plan and execute their personal sales programs. Objectives also help to ensure that a salesperson's time and company support resources such as personal computers are efficiently utilized.

Sales-force objectives must be custom designed annually for each company. Individual sales objectives are established to support corporate goals and marketing and sales objectives. Annual marketing and sales objectives are normally broken into quarterly and monthly objectives. Sales-force members break them down further into personal objectives by day and week.

It is the responsibility of the sales manager to establish and assign objectives to individual salespeople. These are often developed after consultation with the salesperson. An experienced salesperson is in the best position to understand what is happening in the marketplace and to assist the sales manager in formulating realistic objectives.

Occasionally, annual objectives must be changed before year end. This is generally due to a dramatic occurrence, such as the outbreak of war, a natural disaster such as an earthquake, a dramatic change in the economy such as a massive currency devaluation, or new ownership of the hotel.

Although sales objectives are custom designed, there are general objectives commonly employed by members of the hospitality industry.

Sales Volume. Occupancy, passenger miles, and total covers are common measures of sales volume within the hospitality industry. They all mean the same thing: bring is as many customers as possible. An emphasis on volume alone inevitably leads to price discounting, attracting undesirable market segments, cost cutting, and employee unhappiness.

Sales Volume by Selected Segments. Exclusive resorts, charter flight service, and upper-end cruises tend to operate with the philosophy that if one establishes volume objectives but restricts prospecting to highly selective segments, then price and profits will take care of themselves. While appropriate for a few niche players, this thinking cannot be applied to the majority of the hospitality industry. Nevertheless, the concept of establishing sales objectives by specific market segment is viable and basic to effective sales. Sales strategies must continuously be analyzed and reviewed in view of quantitative sales results.

Canadian resort operators targeted the meeting and convention market, with the result that this segment made up 25% of their customer mix, as compared to 35% for U.S. resorts. This led to questions of whether the differences were the result of the sales techniques employed in the two nations.[13]

Sales Volume and Price/Margin Mix. Establish sales volume objectives by product lines to ensure a desired gross profit. This system is the basis for yield management. Salespeople often criticize the system as restrictive and unrealistic. The fact is, it works. British World Airways, Hertz, Sheraton

Hotels, and Royal Caribbean Cruises are representative of the firms who use this system. Whether or not a yield management system is in place, establishing objectives by volume and by price/margin segments leads to improved revenue.

Upselling and Second-chance Selling

Excellent profit opportunities exist for hospitality companies, particularly hotels and resorts, to upgrade price and profit margins by selling higher-priced products such as suites through *upselling*. A related concept is *second-chance selling*, in which the sales department contacts a client who has already booked an event such as a two-day meeting. Opportunities exist to sell additional services such as airport limousine pickup and delivery or to upgrade rooms or food and beverage from chicken to prime rib.

Second-chance selling encourages cooperation and teamwork between departments such as catering, food and beverage, and sales. Hospitality researchers who have studied second-chance selling concluded that "Hoteliers (who do not employ second-chance selling) may be overlooking an opportunity to substantially increase revenues with little additional cost. By establishing specific values for business that has already been booked, hotel managers can encourage salespeople to increase the productivity of existing resources. If salespeople have clearly established goals and objectives for a second chance to increase their rewards, they may work harder to achieve goals."[14]

Opryland Hotel discovered by accident the value of second-chance selling. A new member of the sales force rose to prominence by winning all sales contests. The sales manager discovered that, since this individual lacked a sales client base, common sense dictated another approach. This led the salesperson to recontact clients who had already signed contracts. It also clearly demonstrated the economic value of second-chance selling.

Market Share or Market Penetration

Airlines, cruise lines, major fast-food chains, and rental car companies are highly concerned with market share and market penetration. These concepts have considerably less meaning to many restaurants, hotels, resorts, and other members of the hospitality industry.

The management of most hotels is primarily concerned with measures such as occupancy, average room rate, yield, and customer mix. The corporate marketing department of a chain is, however, likely to be concerned about market share, particularly if it is a dominant chain in a market such as Hawaii. Hilton, Sheraton, Aston Hotels and Resorts, and Outrigger Hotels actively compete for market share in that market.

There is evidence that hotel management companies are increasingly held accountable for clearly defined performance standards. Among these is the level of market penetration. This is a clear departure from the past, when contracts between owners and hotel management companies contained vague references to standards of performance.[15]

As a result, it is very possible that the sales department of hotels and resorts will increasingly be required to measure market potential and will be held accountable for a predetermined level of market penetration. Independent measures of market penetration such as STAR (Smith Travel Research) will undoubtedly assume increased importance in the measurement of hotel sales.

Product-specific Objectives

Occasionally, a sales force will be charged with the specific responsibility to improve sales volume for specific product lines. This objective may be associated with upselling and second-chance selling, but may also be part of the regular sales duties of the sales force. A sales force may be asked to sell more suites, higher-margin coffee breaks, holiday packages, honeymoon packages, or other product lines.

Excellent opportunities for enhanced revenues exist within many hotels and resorts from nonroom sales. Recreation club memberships, including children's programs, are sometimes sold to local residents. A properly designed club membership can generate substantial income from membership fees, dues, and food and beverage revenues. The Boca Raton Resort initiated a Premier Club Membership program that produced membership sales in excess of $40 million the first 3 years.[16]

If management places extreme attention on specific products, there is always a possibility that other product line members will be ignored. A common approach to encourage the sale of specific products is to set objectives for them and to reward performance with bonuses or other incentives.

SALES-FORCE STRUCTURE AND SIZE

The diverse nature of the hospitality industry means that different sales-force structures and sizes have evolved. The structure of a sales force within the airline industry is different from that of a hotel or cruise line. In general, most restaurants do not use a sales force, but depend on other parts of the marketing mix, such as advertising and sales promotion.

The hotel/resort industry traditionally uses a functional, hierarchical structure. Within this structure, hotel departments are organized around particular functions, such as housekeeping or sales. Department managers, including the sales manager, report to a general manager. In smaller hotels such as roadside motels, the GM usually serves as sales manager since the organization is not large enough to support functional departments. Within large hotels and resorts, the sales department may have directors of specialized sales such as a convention and meetings sales director or a corporate accounts sales director. These are organized on a functional basis.

The structure of a hotel sales department depends on the culture of the organization, size of the property, nature of the market, and type of hotel. A casino hotel might contain the same number of rooms as a ski resort hotel yet have a somewhat different organizational structure. Some casino hotels have sales directors who are responsible for working with junket reps and premium players. A resort hotel might have a sales director responsible for working with travel agents and tour wholesalers or with nationwide ski clubs.

The functional organization model for a hotel has been challenged by professors from Purdue, Washington State, and the University of New

Orleans. These individuals feel that the functional organization has several weaknesses.[17]

- **Central decision making.** Authorization by the general manager slows decision making.
- **Difficulty of cross-functional coordination.** Coordination to ensure customer satisfaction requires intradepartment cooperation, which is often different under a functional organizational structure.
- **Unclear responsibility for overall performance.** Sales specialization leads to difficulty in determining overall responsibility and commissions.
- **Need to coordinate cross-functional activities from the top.** Managers in one sales area such as conventions might lack knowledge of food and beverage and thus promise services that cannot be delivered.
- **Limited opportunities for general management training**

The individuals who have challenged the traditional organizational structure believe that a reengineering structure using teams could lead to greater efficiencies. They point to experimentation in structured change by Ritz-Carlton, ITT Sheraton, and Radisson Hotel chains.

The sales-force structures commonly used in the hospitality industry today are described next.

Territorial-structured Sales Force

In the simplest sales organization, each sales representative is assigned an exclusive territory in which to represent the company's full line. This sales structure has a number of advantages. First, it results in a clear definition of the salesperson's responsibilities. As the only salesperson working the territory, he or she bears the credit or blame for area sales to the extent that personal selling effort makes a difference. Second, territorial responsibility increases the sales representative's incentive to cultivate local business and personal ties. These ties contribute to the sales representative's selling effectiveness and personal life. Third, travel expenses are relatively small, since each sales representative travels within a small geographical area.

A territorial sales organization is often supported by many levels of sales management positions. Each higher-level sales manager takes on increasing marketing and administration work in relation to the time available for selling. In fact, sales managers are paid for their management skills rather than their selling skills. The new sales trainee, in looking ahead, can expect to become a sales representative, then a district manager, and then a regional manager, and, depending on his or her ability and motivation, may move to still higher levels of sales or general management.

In designing territories, the company seeks certain territorial characteristics. Territories are easy to administer, their sales potential is easy to estimate, they reduce total travel time, and they provide a sufficient and equitable workload and sales potential for each sales representative. These characteristics are achieved through deciding on territory size and shape.

Territory Size. Territories can be designed to provide either equal sales potential or equal workload. Each principle offers advantages at the cost of some dilemmas. Territories of equal potential provide each sales representative with the same income opportunities and provide the company with a means to evaluate performance. Persistent differences in sales yield by territory are assumed to reflect differences in ability or effort of individual sales representatives. Customer density varies by territory, and territories with equal potential can vary widely in size. The potential for selling cruises in Chicago is larger than in several Rocky Mountain states. A sales representative assigned to Chicago can cover the same sales potential with much less effort than the sales representative who sells in the Rocky Mountain West. The sales representative assigned to the larger and sparser territory is going to end up with either fewer sales and less income for equal effort or equal sales through extraordinary effort. One solution is to pay the Rocky Mountain sales representatives more compensation for the extra effort. But this reduces profits on sales in these territories. Another solution is to acknowledge that territories differ in attractiveness and assign the better or more senior sales representatives to the better territories.

Alternatively, territories might be designed to equalize the sales workload. Each sales representative could then cover his or her territory adequately. This principle results in some variation in territory sales potential. This does not concern a sales force on straight salary. But when sales representatives are compensated partly on commission, territories will vary in their attractiveness even though workloads are equal.

Territory Shape. Territories are formed by combining smaller units, such as counties or states, until they add up to a territory of a given sales potential or workload. Territorial design must take into account the location of natural barriers, the compatibility of adjacent areas, the adequacy of transportation, and so forth. Many companies prefer a certain territory shape because the shape can influence the cost and ease of coverage and the sales representatives' job satisfaction.

The territorial structure sales force is most commonly used by airlines, cruise lines, and rental car companies and at the corporate level by hotel chains. It is not frequently used by individual hotel/resort properties, who instead seem to organize their sales departments by function or type of customer.

Product-structured Sales Force

The importance of sales representatives' knowing their products, together with the development or product divisions and product management, has led many companies to structure their sales force along product lines. Product specialization is particularly warranted when the products are technically complex, highly unrelated, or very numerous.

The mere existence of different company products, however, is not a sufficient argument for specializing the sales force by product. Such specialization might not be the best course if the company's separate product lines are bought by the same customers.

Market-segment-structured Sales Force

Companies often specialize their sales forces along market segment lines. Separate sales forces can be set up by different industries for the convention/meeting segment, the incentive travel market, and other major segments.

The obvious advantage of market specialization is that each sales force can become knowledgeable about specific market segments. The major disadvantage of a market-segment-structured sales force arises when the various members of a segment are scattered throughout the country or the world. This vastly increases the travel costs.

Market-channel-structured Sales Force

The importance of marketing intermediaries, such as wholesalers, tour operators, travel agencies, and junket reps, to the hospitality industry has created sales-force structures to serve marketing channels. Travel agencies account for over 95% of all cruise line sales.[18] A cruise line naturally structures its sales force on a marketing intermediary basis. Commercial airlines receive 90% of their bookings through travel agencies, auto rental firms receive 50%, and hotels about 25%.[19]

Some hotels, such as those near historic sites, receive substantial bookings through motorcoach tour brokers. The location, size, and type of hospitality company greatly affect the relative importance of travel intermediaries. This in turn affects whether a company designs it sales-force structure by travel intermediary.

Aston Hotels and Resorts of Hawaii manages 30 properties with 4500 rooms. These are sold primarily through travel agents and wholesalers who supply 85% to 90% of Aston's business. "I differentiate between my customers who are the travel agents and the consumers who are the people who actually stay in the units," said Andre S. Tatibouet, CEO of Aston Hotels and Resorts.[20]

Customer-structured Sales Force

A customer-structured sales force recognizes that specific customers exist who are critical to the success of the organization. The sales force is usually organized to serve these accounts through a key or national account structure.

When a company sells to many small accounts, it uses a territory-based sales force. However, large accounts (called key accounts, major accounts, or national accounts) are often singled out for special attention and handling. If the account is a large company with many divisions operating in many parts of the country and subject to many buying influences (such as General Motors or Mitsubishi), it is likely to be handled as a national account and assigned to a specific individual or sales team. If the company has several such accounts, it is likely to organize a national account management (NAM) division.

National account management is growing for a number of reasons. As buyer concentration increases through mergers and acquisitions, fewer buyers account for a larger share of a company's sales. Another factor is that many buyers are centralizing their purchases instead of leaving them to the local units. This gives buyers more bargaining power. Still another factor is that, as products become more complex, more groups in the buyer's organization become involved in the purchase process, and the typical salesperson might not have the skill, authority, or coverage to be effective in selling to the large buyer.

Sheraton Hotels noted that business travelers were not shifting from one hotel chain to another as much as in the past. In response, Sheraton developed a reservations system that allowed the establishment of national accounts. When an account number is given, the correct rate for any Sheraton Hotel worldwide is known.

In organizing a national account program, a company faces a number of issues, including how to select national accounts; how to manage them; how to develop, manage, and evaluate a national account manager; how to organize a structure for national accounts; and where to locate national account management in the organization.

Andre Tatibouet of Aston Hotels and Resorts would surely argue that, although his structure does not compensate the guest, it is nevertheless customer directed since it places emphasis on his primary client, the travel agent. Undoubtedly, this is true and reflects the fact that all sales structures must be custom made for the individual hotel. A single sales structure cannot possibly be employed with equal success for all properties within a diverse chain such as Sheraton or Holiday Inn.

Combination-structured Sales Force

Some hotels and resorts have a sales force that is structured by product, market segment, market channel, and customer. This is often a reaction to internal and market forces rather than the result of strategic thinking.

A large hotel might have a catering/banquet sales force (product), a convention/meeting sales force (market segment), a tour wholesales sales force (marketing intermediary), and a national accounts sales force (customer). Proponents of such a sales force feel that it encourages the sales force to reach all or most available customers. They also contend that it is impossible for a single salesperson to understand and effectively sell all the hotel's products to all available customer segments through all marketing channels. Sales specialists can become familiar with major customers, understand trends that affect them, and plan appropriate sales strategies and tactics.

Opponents of this system feel that in many cases this sales force structure indicates that the hotel is trying to be all things to all people in the absence of long-run goals and strategies. They contend that such a structure is difficult to manage and can be confusing to the sales force and the customer, since the same customer may be classified in different areas and thus be handled by more than one salesperson.

Regardless of which structure is used by a hotel or resort, there is a particular market segment that is neglected by many North American hoteliers. Many local markets offer potential, particularly for food and beverage and function room sales. While a resort such as the Greenbriar in a rural area of West Virginia might not have a large local market, this is scarcely the case for most hotels. The Japanese seem to be particularly adept at penetrating this market, because 40% to 50% of Japanese hotel sales are accounted for by parties and other events from local companies.[21] A sales manager must be aware of the local market and develop a sales force structure appropriate for penetrating this market.

Seven months after opening, the Dalmahoy Golf and Country Club Resort near Edinburgh, Scotland, recognized the need for a strong sales effort in the local market and for a combination-structured sales force. Dalmahoy was experiencing low occupancy and less than desirable membership growth. Many factors were involved, such as the Gulf War, a poor economy, and almost no awareness by Edinburgh area golfers. As a member of the UK-based Country Club Hotel Group, Dalmahoy had the assistance of this company's national sales force. The management of Dalmahoy knew that a strong property-level sales effort was also needed and employed two salespersons to serve the local market, plus a travel-trade manager to work with intermediaries to attract overseas business. The result was a 70% occupancy in 1994 compared to 64.5% for hotels in the United Kingdom. This compared to average occupancy of only 32% for the first 7 months before the combination-structured sales force was put in place.[22]

Sales-force Size

Once the company clarifies its sales-force strategy and structure, it is ready to consider sales-force size. Sales representatives are one of the company's most expensive assets.

After determining the type and number of desired customers, a workload approach can be used to establish sales-force size. This method consists of the following steps:

1. Customers are grouped into size classes according to their annual sales volume.
2. The desirable call frequencies (number of sales calls on an account per year) are established for each class.
3. The number of accounts in each size class is multiplied by the corresponding call frequency to arrive at the total workload for the country in sales calls per year.
4. The average number of calls a sales representative can make per year is determined.
5. The number of sales representatives needed is determined by dividing the total annual calls required by the average calls made by a sales representative.

Suppose that the company estimates that there are 1000 A accounts and 2000 B accounts required in the nation, and A accounts require 36 calls a year and B accounts, 12 calls a year. This means that the company needs a sales force that can make 60,000 sales calls a year. Suppose that the average sales representative can make 1000 calls a year. The company would need 60 full-time sales representatives.

The size of a sales force is determined by changes in the market, competition, and corporate strategies and policies. The sales process will also directly affect decisions concerning sales-force size. The following describes several of the factors that influence the size of a hotels' sales force.

Corporate/chain sales support. Several major hotel chains have employed a corporate sales force to reach the meeting/convention/conference market. The concept behind this sales force is that individual hotel properties may not be in a position to search out and track this important market and that a sales force representing the chain can recommend and sell all appropriate hotels within the chain, not simply a single property. In recent years, some chains have begun to question the value of this sales force and may drop this area of sales support. If this occurs, individual properties may find it necessary to employ one or more additional sales-force members to ensure coverage of this important segment.

Use of sales reps. Sales reps have traditionally been used by hotels and resorts to serve distant markets, particularly foreign countries. With the emergence of NAFTA and the growing importance of many foreign markets, several companies are rethinking the use of reps and may substitute salaried sales staff in these markets.

Team selling. Team selling has proved to be an effective and powerful tactic to reach and retain key customers. Its opportunities and limitations are only beginning to be realized in the hospitality industry. It is uncertain how this may affect the size of a sales force.

Electronic sales. Hospitality companies such as Club Med are currently using the Internet. Many observers feel this tool will dramatically change the sales process.

Travel intermediary dependency. Hospitality industry members historically viewed travel intermediaries with mixed emotions. Some hotels may have allowed wholesalers to assume too great a degree of sales power. A study of Caribbean hotels found that "wholesalers play a valuable role in the Caribbean resort hotel industry by helping hotels market and sell their rooms. But in recent years, wholesalers' power has increased, causing operational and financial problems for some Caribbean resort-hotel operators."[23]

In these cases, it may be advisable to increase the size of the sales force and aggressively seek ways to lessen wholesaler dependence. The appropriate size of a hospitality company's sales force cannot be established solely by formula or by comparison to that of competitors. It must be remembered that a sales force is only one tool to accomplish objectives and goals.

The size of a sales force may need to increase to support new marketing strategies. The sales manager then has responsibility to "sell" top management, since a budgetary increase will almost certainly be necessary. Likewise, a professional sales manager must be aware of changing trends and new technology such as database marketing and electronic marketing. Rather than tenaciously supporting a larger-than-necessary sales force, the sales manager must be prepared to downsize and substitute technology when appropriate.

ORGANIZING THE SALES DEPARTMENT

As previously discussed, hospitality companies traditionally design departments along functional lines. It is common to find hotels with several marketing-related departments, such as a sales department, a guest relations department, and an advertising and public relations department, but not a "marketing" department. In recent years, some hotels have given the title sales and marketing to the previously named sales department, but with limited training in marketing for the sales manager.

A sales manager may bear both marketing and sales responsibilities, although it is likely that the department will always emphasize sales. Today's sales managers may have two types of salespeople within their departments: (1) an inside sales force and (2) a field sales force. The term *inside sales* can be misleading because many *field* salespeople spend a great deal of their time inside the hotel calling clients and prospects, meeting with them, making arrangements with other departments, answering mail, and performing many other duties, such as completing sales reports.

Inside Sales Force

Inside salespeople include three types. There are *technical-support persons*, who provide technical information and answers to customers' questions. There are *sales assistants*, who provide clerical backup for the field salespersons. They call ahead and confirm appointments, carry out credit checks, follow up on deliveries, and answer customers' questions when they cannot reach the outside sales rep. And there are *telemarketers*, who use the phone to find new leads, qualify them, and sell to them. Telemarketers can call up to 50 customers per day compared to the 4 or 5 that an outside salesperson can contact. They can be effective in the following ways: cross-selling the company's other products; upgrading orders; introducing new company products; opening new accounts and reactivating former accounts; giving more attention to neglected accounts; and following up and qualifying direct-mail leads.

Telemarketing has found a role in the hospitality industry. Renaissance Cruises has developed and uses a telemarketing sales force to reach individual guest prospects. This is in direct contrast to the majority of the cruise line industry which relies on a field sales force to call on travel agents, rather than on the prospect agent.

Telemarketing has found disfavor among many recipients of these calls. Within the hospitality industry, meeting planners are besieged by hotel sales reps who have done no research concerning the planner. Instead, they commonly begin a conversation with the question, "Do you plan meetings?" Busy meeting planners find this disruptive and frustrating, particularly if frequently called by the same hotel but different sales reps.[24]

Due to the high turnover among hotel salespeople and lack of an updated prospect database, a meeting planner may be called two to three times within 1 year by a hotel's sales reps asking the same questions. Telemarketing, like all sales calls, can be much more productive if the salesperson has basic information concerning the prospect.

Telemarketing failed in one hotel company because members of the sales force were required to perform this function 1 day a week. The hotel's salespeople felt forced into an unpleasant task. The supervisor resigned, management gave up, and the sales force rejoiced.[25]

Another dramatic breakthrough in improving sales force productivity is provided by new technological equipment: desktop and laptop computers, videocassette recorders, videodisks, automatic dialers, electronic mail, fax machines, and teleconferencing. The salesperson has truly gone electronic. This development has been called *sales automation*. Not only is sales and inventory information transferred much faster, but specific computer-based decision support systems have been created for sales managers and sales representatives.

Reservations Department

The reservations department is a very important inside sales area for many hospitality companies because reservationists may speak with 80% of a company's customers. This department is sometimes not viewed as part of the sales team. It is sometimes a separate department and, unfortunately, the reservations and sales departments within a hotel may have little communication. In worst-case scenarios, they may actually find themselves at odds. This is not the case at Hyatt Hotels, where reservations are under sales/marketing.

A study of reservations departments at Hyatt Corporation, American Airlines, and Carnival Cruise Lines revealed that much can be done to improve the effectiveness of this critical inside sales force.[26] The results of this study showed that reservations training was critical. The training program prescribed was remarkably similar to that for any sales position. Hyatt focuses on technical aspects, including how to sell. Hyatt's philosophy is that skills necessary to be an effective salesperson can be taught.

Reservationist candidates at American Airlines are interviewed and hired for their sales ability. Days Inns has a program to hire the elderly and the physically challenged and through training turn them into reservation salespeople. Training your reservationists to be good company representatives and teaching them how to sell will pay back big dividends in the long run.[27]

Electronics and Telephone Sales

A related area of growing importance to hotel sales managers is the management of sales from electronic and telephone distribution systems, such as the 800 number reservation system of a chain or an independent group such as "Preferred Hotels." The importance of sales provided by such distribution systems is likely to grow, particularly as the number of PC owners and users increases and when airlines fully implement in-flight electronic interactive systems for passengers.

The Windsor Hospitality Group of Woodland Hills, California, advocates taking full advantage of electronic distribution channels. Woodland formed strategic alliances with several distributors of global reservation services and regularly screens these services to see how sales for individual properties are doing.[28]

Some hotel chains such as Omni Hotels have signed exclusive agreements with a single reservation service to manage worldwide reservations. Omni appointed Intel International to handle worldwide reservations for its 43 properties in the United States, Mexico, Singapore, and Hong Kong. "With such a spread of destinations, it was important for us to select a reservation facility that could provide international marketing support," said James Schultenower, senior vice-president of sales and marketing for Omni.[29] He went on to say that Omni is integrating the sales and marketing function on a worldwide basis and therefore had to have a system that facilitated rather than complicated the sales/marketing process.

The need for an integrated and *seamless* reservation system has been felt by many hotel chains. Customer reservation systems (CRS) are increasingly required to offer travel agents direct links to a hotel company's entire inventory so that agents can be assured that booking rates won't change when their clients arrive at the hotel. Radisson Hotels in cooperation with Apollo developed *seamless* reservation availability, giving agents the ability to enter Radisson's reservations system, view the entire inventory, and electronically make a reservation.[30]

Many hotel chains and hotel sales managers have realized that they must be equally adept at managing technology as they are at managing people.

Field Sales Force

Today, sales managers face an increasingly complex marketplace, which has created the need to continuously review the organizational design of the field sales force. We will now discuss different types of field sales forces as currently used by hospitality companies.

Commissioned Reps

Hotels and resorts commonly use commissioned sales representatives in distant markets where the market potential does not justify employing a salaried salesperson. A Los Angeles hotel may contract with commissioned sales reps in New York or Miami to reach companies and associations that are known to the local sales reps. Commissioned sales reps normally represent several different properties or chains, but attempt not to represent competing clients. This is sometimes difficult in the case of chains, which have competing properties in the same location.

Foreign markets are commonly served by a commissioned sales rep. Unfortunately the relationship between sales rep and hotel is not always satisfactory. This is often because sales reps are hired without conducting a careful analysis of the reps. Since there is no reason to use a nonperforming or otherwise unsatisfactory sales rep, it is important to follow a few simple rules when working with commissioned sales reps.

1. *Select markets with care.* Distant markets should be selected to match corporate goals and marketing/sales objectives, not simply to have someone represent the company in a location.
2. *Personally visit the market.* Meet with prospective sales reps, examine their offices, check out references, note their personal appearance, ask for a list of current clients, ask for a credit report, and clear the rep through the police and the Better Business Bureau or the equivalent. In general, it is important to be as careful or even

more careful in hiring a sales rep to cover distant markets as in hiring a salaried sales-force member. The United States Travel and Tourism Administration, which is part of the Department of Commerce, maintains offices in several overseas markets. Individuals within these offices are often familiar with local sales reps and may be very helpful. It must be understood that in some third-world nations a commissioned sales rep is considered to be a member of the client company's workforce and dependent on that company for a livelihood. Local courts often decide in favor of the rep and may award the rep large financial settlements in cases such as dismissal for failure to meet performance standards.

3. *Include the sales rep as part of the hotel's sales force.* This requires using adaptation of management tools to be discussed later in this chapter. It is important to occasionally visit the offices of distant sales reps. This requires an adequate budget for travel and may entail considerable effort to convince the GM that such an expenditure of time and money is worthwhile.

Salaried Sales Force

Most hospitality industry sales-force members are paid a salary plus benefits. Additional compensation is sometimes available through commissions, bonus, profit sharing, or other financial remuneration. In some nations, a sales force by law, is paid an additional month's salary at Christmas or New Year and may qualify for benefits unknown to North American companies, such as a month paid vacation each year.

Traditionally, hospitality companies have employed members of the sales force to perform the sales function primarily in an individualized manner. This system continues to be the backbone of a hospitality sales force, but newer forms of organizing a field sales force are gaining acceptance.

Team Sales

Team sales has become a necessity in many industries. The hospitality industry is no exception. The concept of a sales team is two or more individuals working in concert toward a common sales objective. These persons are not necessarily from the same company. The purpose for a team sales approach is to accomplish objectives through the synergism of two or more people that would be impossible or unduly costly through individual sales efforts.

In addition to traditional objectives, such as to increase occupancy in a hotel, other nonquantifiable objectives are sometimes established for teams. These generally deal with enhancing image and goodwill or using the team as a human resource training pool. People from various disciplines and departments are sometimes brought together to improve morale, teach teamwork, and cross educate.

Teams within the hospitality industry have traditionally been used for specific tasks, which include but are not limited to the following:

Today more employees are getting involved in the sales effort through the concept of sales teams. Courtesy of Hilton Hotels Corporation.

Sales blitz

Travel mission

Charity promotions

Community improvement programs

Although teams are used for many purposes, the primary purpose for team sales should be to improve sales and the competitive position of a hotel, airline, cruise line, or other hospitality company. Teams are best used when the needs of the customer or prospect are complex and require the input of specialists. An example might be a large conference that requires the expertise and cooperation of an airline, a golf resort, and a ground transportation company.

Today the concept of team sales is moving beyond once-in-awhile usage, such as during a sales blitz, to the allied concepts of relationship marketing and strategic alliances.

Relationship Marketing and Strategic Alliances

The goal of personal selling has traditionally been viewed as a specific contract with a customer. But in many cases the company is not seeking simply a one-time sale. It has targeted a major customer account that it would like to win and serve for a long period of time. The company would like to demonstrate to the account that it has the capabilities to serve the account's needs in a superior way, particularly if a committed relationship can be formed. The type of selling to establish a long-term collaborative relationship is more complex than a short run, one-time sales approach. Obtaining long-run commitment involves many more agreements than simply closing the sale.[31]

More companies today are moving their emphasis from transaction marketing to relationship marketing. The days of the lone salesperson working his or her territory and being guided only by a sales quota and a compensation plan are numbered. Today's customers are large and often global. They prefer suppliers who can sell and deliver a coordinated set of products and services to many locations, who can quickly solve problems that arise in their different locations, and who can work closely with customer teams to improve products and processes.

Companies recognize that sales teamwork will increasingly be the key to winning and maintaining accounts. Yet they recognize that asking their people for teamwork doesn't produce it. They need to revise their compensation system to give credit for work on shared accounts, they must set up better goals and measures for their sales forces, and they must emphasize the importance of teamwork in their training programs, while at the same time also honoring the importance of individual initiative.

Relationship marketing is based on the premise that important accounts need focused and continuous attention. Salespeople working with customers under relationship marketing must do more than call when they think customers might be ready to place orders. They should monitor key accounts, know their problems, be ready to serve them in a number of ways, and strive to become part of the client's team.

When a relationship management program is properly implemented, the organization will begin to focus as much on managing its customers as on managing its products. At the same time, companies should realize that, while there is a strong and warranted move toward relationship marketing, it is not effective in all situations. Ultimately, hospitality companies must judge which segments and which specific customers will respond profitably to relationship marketing.

The Boca Raton Resort and Club provides an example of the benefits that can accrue from relationship marketing. In 1994, the Cosmetic, Toiletry, and Fragrance Association met at this resort for the twenty-fourth consecutive time. "To keep a national association like CTFA coming back amidst a sea of competitors, our resort cannot merely serve as a site for their conference," explained David Feder, the Boca's senior vice-president of sales and marketing. "We look to ourselves as much more than that: we can actually help associations fulfill their goals and shape their futures."[32]

Strategic alliances are a highly developed form of relationship marketing. Strategic alliances are common between vendor and buyer or between noncompeting vendors and a common buyer. "Alliances are relationships between independent parties that agree to cooperate but still retain separate identities."[33] A strategic alliance may involve sharing a combination of any of the following: confidences, database, market knowledge, planning, resources, risks, security, and technology.

Within the hotel industry, strategic alliances have been defined as "relationships between independent parties that agree to cooperate but still retain separate identities." Three types of strategic alliances have been characterized for the hotel industry.

- **One-night stands.** These are short-term opportunistic relations, such as cross-advertising between a hotel and a restaurant or the selling agreement between Radisson Hotels and Britain's Edwardian Hotels.

- **Affairs.** Medium-term, tactical relationships account for alliances in this grouping. Hotels may participate with airlines in frequent-flyer programs.
- **I Do's.** This is equivalent to marriage. Parties in these arrangements expect long-term commitment. In some cases, equity investment is essential such as the alliance between U.S. Air and British Airways.

Examples of strategic alliances within the hospitality industry include the following:

- An agreement between Carlson Hospitality Group, a division of Carlson Company, Inc., and Hospitality Franchise Systems (HFS) whereby HFS will operate existing food and beverage systems on a franchise or lease basis in Carlson's hotel properties. This agreement includes cooperative buying in which hotel companies can purchase supplies, services, and equipment at reduced prices.[34]
- An agreement between Hostmark International (Denver) and the Management Group (Chicago) to form a partnership to manage hotels. This alliance enables the two companies to approach major financial institutions as a national company, rather than as two regionals.[35]

Strategic alliances have become a necessity due to a variety of factors: globalization, complicated customer needs, large customers with multilocations, the need for technology, highly interdependent vendor/buyer relationships, intensified competition, and low profitability within the hospitality industry.

Strategic alliances directly affect the nature of the professional sales function within hospitality companies. The need for professional sales is dramatically enhanced. Salespeople must be better educated and able to understand sophisticated buyer needs and conduct complex negotiations.

Large customers may require services such as assistance with planning, extended financing, equity participation, and the use of technology, such as EDI (electronic data interchange). In turn, these needs affect the policies and procedures of suppliers. A buyer who demands that all invoices be sent and settled through EDI may create a need for new investment in hardware and software on the part of the suppliers.

Salespeople must be able to understand increasingly sophisticated buyer needs and communicate them to management. In many cases, the real test of a salesperson's skills comes in the ability of that person to convince his or her own management of the need to change policies and procedures.

Top management must often become directly involved in the sales process. As the size of accounts increases and as the negotiation process becomes more complex, top management must become directly involved. In many cases, the negotiation process involves the top management of buyer and seller. Managers who are accustomed to thinking that the sales function is the sole responsibility of the sales department are likely to witness lost sales opportunities and diminished market share.

Salespeople may be responsible for fewer accounts, but must know them in depth. Under strategic alliances, a salesperson may be assigned a few accounts. Previously, salespeople might have had a superficial knowledge of the customer's business. Strategic alliance management requires a detailed knowledge of customers, their competitors, and their industry. Industry- and company-specific expertise becomes very important. Salespeople must know all the major decision makers and influencers. Since the customer will probably make buying decisions with group input, it becomes critical to know and if possible, participate in that group.

Salespeople may be physically located next door or even in the offices of the buyer. The centuries old practice of traveling from a distant office to the client can become extinct with a strategic alliance. Salespeople cannot become part of the customer's team unless they are physically present.

A handful of hospitality companies will always exist who sell on low price and shallow relationships between buyer and seller. These companies scoff at the idea of relationship marketing. Sales success for members of the hospitality industry dedicated to the long-term depends on understanding and fulfilling multiple customer needs, not simply the need for a bargain. Need fulfillment is the basis for all long-run sales success. Relationship marketing simply creates an opportunity for salespeople to exercise customer need fulfillment at a new level of professionalism.

The remainder of this chapter is concerned with the process of sales management. The topics selected for discussion are basic to sales managers of virtually all hospitality companies. Although these concepts have application to the management of an inside sales force, a commission sales force, and team selling, they were developed primarily for the management of a traditional sales force composed of individual salaried salespeople. The majority of the remaining examples in this chapter refer to this traditional form of sales force.

Importance of Careful Selection

At the heart of a successful sales-force operation is the selection of effective sales representatives. The performance difference between an average and a top sales representative can be considerable. One survey revealed that the top 27% of the sales force brought in over 52% of the sales. Beyond the differences in sales productivity are the great wastes in hiring the wrong person. When a salesperson quits, the costs of finding and training a new salesperson plus the cost of lost sales can be substantial. And a sales force with many new people is generally less productive.[36]

What Makes a Good Sales Represenatative?

Selecting sales representatives would be simple if we knew what traits to look for. Most customers say they want sales representatives to be honest, reliable, knowledgeable, and helpful. The company should look for these traits when selecting candidates.

Another approach is to look for traits common to the most successful salespeople in the company. A study of superachievers found that super-sales performers exhibit the following traits: risk taking, powerful sense of

RECRUITING AND TRAINING A PROFESSIONAL SALES FORCE

mission, problem-solving bent, care for the customer, and careful planners.[37] One of the shortest lists of traits concluded that the effective salesperson has two basic qualities: empathy, the ability to feel as the customer does; and ego drive, a strong personal need to make the sale.[38]

Establishing a Profile of Desired Characteristics: Matching the Corporate Culture

The management of each hospitality company has a responsibility to determine a desired sales-force profile. This is not solely the responsibility of a sales manager. The general manager, vice-president marketing/sales, and others should help to determine the preferred characteristics for a sales force. Desired characteristics such as honesty, personal integrity, self-esteem, confidence, inner motivation, and desire to excel must be clearly enunciated by management.

The individual who should first exemplify these is the sales manager. Management selects this individual and then empowers this person with primary responsibility for recruiting, training, motivating, and controlling the sales force.

The rhetoric of most hospitality companies regarding a desired sales force is much the same, but actually putting words into action varies. This is partially attributable to the fact that managers sometimes overlook the importance of their unique corporate culture and simply adopt a generic profile description. All hotels are not alike nor are all cruise lines nor are the members of any hospitality company.

The corporate culture within some organizations is formal and authoritarian. In others, a spirit of spontaneity and fun is encouraged. Substantial differences exist among hospitality firms. Both the employer and the salesperson need to fully recognize that success cannot be realized if the two parties are incompatible. A salesperson might be very successful with InterContinental or Four Seasons Hotels, but unable to adopt to the culture of Ramada or Novotel Hotels.

The Ritz-Carlton Hotel Corporation embraces a corporate philosophy that both the guests it serves and its employees are cultured individuals who should be treated with respect and should be referred to as ladies and gentlemen. This message is transmitted in advertisements for openings, such as an advertisement in the *South China Morning Post* that read as follows: "The Ritz-Carlton Hong Kong, situated in the heart of Central, with 216 guest rooms, offering the finest tradition in hospitality, is now offering committed, energetic, and enthusiastic Ladies and Gentlemen opportunities to fill the following positions:...."[39]

Matching Career Acquisitions with Corporate Objectives

The aspirations of a salesperson must first be clearly understood by that individual and then clearly communicated to the potential employer. The hospitality industry does not generally offer sales positions that allow an individual to become wealthy from commissions or bonus. Salespeople seeking great wealth are well advised to seek careers in commercial real estate or securities. Despite this, the hospitality industry does offer many advantages to a salesperson.

- The industry is fun. Unlike selling funeral plots or cancer insurance, the product is by nature fun and even exciting.
- Clients are generally personable and willing to listen, unlike industries in which the client has little time to talk and exhibits an aggressive knock-you-over attitude.
- Fellow salespeople and other colleagues are generally people oriented, gregarious, and enjoyable.
- Opportunities for travel exist, particularly in sales of airlines, cruise lines, travel agencies, and travel wholesalers.
- Opportunities for movement within the hospitality industry exist. Considerable career movement occurs within the industry. Salespeople move among the various industry members, such as from a hotel or resort to a cruise line or rental car firm.
- Management opportunities exist. Career growth to positions of sales manager are quite feasible. Career growth to vice-presidency of sales or marketing is also possible.

It should be recognized that career promotion to general manager within hotels and resorts from sales historically has not often occurred, but is beginning to occur more frequently. These positions generally call for individuals with broader experience and training, including food and beverage, front desk, and other operational areas.

Neither the salesperson nor the company benefit by disguising true career objectives or the actual corporate culture. Experienced and astute sales managers seem to develop a sixth sense for determining whether a candidate's personality and background truly match the sales position.

Matching Customer and Salesperson

The highly segmented nature of the hospitality industry has led to widely varying concentrations of consumer demographics and psychographics by individual companies. Customers for Princess Hotels are considerably different than those of Motel Six. Major airlines of the world such as British Airways concentrate heavily on business-class customers, while discount carriers historically reach the pleasure traveler.

Some individuals are uncomfortable dealing with travel intermediaries such as tour wholesalers or with the travel departments of major corporations. Others are uncomfortable dealing with a concentration of customers among ethnic, racial, or sexual-preference groups.

Recruiting Process: When to Recruit

The recruitment of professional salespeople is an ongoing process within the hospitality industry. This is the result of two principal factors: high turnover and industry growth.

An effective recruiting process is driven by preestablished standards known as a the *profile* of a desired salesperson. This profile determines the tactics to employ when recruiting, such as the media to use when advertising for salespeople and the type of networking. If low standards are established, then virtually any media is acceptable and one could network by telling passersby on the street that salespeople are needed.

On the other hand, assume that a company establishes the following standards: college degree, 5 years experience, and excellent communication skills. Recruiting individuals with this profile might require the use of specialized media such as the *Wall Street Journal* and selective networking through managers, vendors, and others who know the company. This profile might also predetermine the need for an independent professional sales recruiting firm and the need to pay a significant commission.

The single best source of new salespeople is a company's current sales force. This is true within most industries. Few industries face greater obstacles in recruiting and retaining professional salespeople than life insurance. The Mutual Life Insurance Company of Canada has traditionally experienced good agent retention rates, sometimes double the industry average. One reason has been the heavy involvement of current agents in the recruiting activity.[40]

Sales managers reflect three major philosophies concerning when to recruit.

- *Recruit and train salespeople in a batch process*. Hire more than are needed and wash out the weak ones. This process is expensive and involves considerable management time. It may also necessitate a full-time training director.

- *Recruit only as needed for replacement and growth*. This approach forces management to recruit on a reactive ad hoc basis. Less than desirable candidates are often hired due to the necessity to hire someone.

- *Always recruit*. Set standards very high and never accept anyone who does not meet them. Remain willing to interview an outstanding candidate anytime, even though no openings are listed.

The third philosophy is difficult to maintain due to budgetary constraints. Proponents claim that excellent salespeople will create enough new business for a company to justify hiring them despite budget problems.

Applicant Rating Procedures

Recruiting procedures, if successful, will attract many applicants, and the company will need to select the best ones. The selection procedures can vary from a single informal interview to prolonged testing and interviewing, not only of the applicant but of the applicant's spouse.[41]

Many companies give formal tests to sales applicants. Although test scores are only one information element in a set that includes personal characteristics, references, past employment history, and interviewer reactions, they are weighted heavily by some companies.

Interview Process: How to Interview

Today, throughout many parts of the world, the interview procedure has been complicated by government regulations designed to protect the rights of the interviewee and to assure fairness. Additionally, most large hospitality companies have policies and procedures covering the interview process. It is critical to study and observe all regulations, policies, and procedures before entering the interview process. This extends to the initial stage of announcing or advertising the position. In large organizations, all hiring may be temporarily frozen, except for internal hiring in which salespeople may be recruited from other departments.

Sales-force Training

Sales training is vital to success, yet unfortunately remains a weak link within the hospitality industry. This is particularly problematic for recent graduates with little or no workplace experience. Fortunately, the situation is improving as several hospitality companies now have training programs.

Sales training is not a one-time process, but is instead a career-long endeavor. Continuous training is part of the written philosophy of Singapore Airlines. This company believes that all employees must continuously be trained and retrained, including the basics.

Types of Training Required

Members of a sales force require three types of training:

1. *Product/service training.* Technology creates continuous change within the hospitality industry. Reservation systems, equipment such as airplanes or cruise ships, and entire operational systems change. Service delivery systems, menus, branch locations, and a myriad of other changes require regular and frequent training.

2. *Policies, procedures, and planning training.* As organizations increase in size and complexity, the need for formalized systems and procedures increases. Salespeople are often criticized by other departments for their failure to follow established procedures or conform to policies. Training is essential to ensure that all policies and procedures are understood.

   Effective salespeople continuously wink at some policies and procedures. This is generally done in an effort to quickly satisfy customer needs and close the sale. Unfortunately, a chronic failure to do things the "company way" inevitably leads to problems.

   Hospitality salespeople receive much criticism for their lack of attention to detail in the barrage of paperwork that they must complete. Failure to complete paperwork correctly, on time, and in detail leads to costly errors, customer dissatisfaction, and ill will among other departments.

   Today the sales force of many companies is becoming automated. Sales force members are expected to use computers throughout their career. This trend is likely to continue and will require continuous training of the sales force.

3. *Sales techniques training.* An age-old debate centers on the wisdom of attempting to teach techniques of selling. One camp firmly believes that salespeople are determined by genetics, personality, and motivation, not by training. The other side generally agrees that only a small percentage of individuals make effective salespeople but also contends that their effectiveness can be enhanced by learning sales basics such as the following:

- Prospecting
- Obtaining the initial sales call (setting the appointment)
- Conducting the sales dialogue
  — Becoming acquainted
  — Asking questions and probing for prospect's needs
  — Listening to what prospect says and doesn't say
  — Presenting benefits of product/service features to match prospect's needs
  — Overcoming objections
  — Further probing if necessary to determine needs
  — Closing the sale
- Follow-up
  — To continue sales dialogue if prospect did not buy
  — To say thank you for order
  — To assure client this was the correct thing to do
  — To look for opportunities to upsell or cross-sell
  — To ask for leads and testimonials
  — To ask for another appointment or ask for another sale when client is again ready to purchase

Although sales training is most effective when customized, there are general factors that contribute to the success or failure of a salesperson. These should be considered when developing a sales training program.

Six factors have been determined to contribute to sales failure. Each is relevant to salespeople within the hospitality industry.[42]

1. Poor listening skills[43]
2. Failure to concentrate on top priorities
3. Lack of sufficient effort
4. Inability to determine customer needs
5. Lack of planning for sales presentations
6. Inadequate product/service knowledge

The president of a hospitality marketing group has been critical of the type of sales training used within the hotel industry and stated, "Professional selling skills that were developed 20 to 25 years ago to promote small consumer products are still being taught to salespeople today.

But the hotel business doesn't fit into the neat little box that's necessary for those skills to have a chance."[44] This executive suggested that a hotel training program should concentrate on the following:

- The customer's frame of reference. Understanding the customer's perspective and reasons for buying.
- Realization that adults are change resistant: listening, watching, and studying opportunities to change adult behavior through fulfillment of actual needs.
- Marketing-based selling, not traditional sales approach selling.
- Concentrate on incremental improvements over time to the skills and knowledge of the sales force, rather than dependence on an intensive seminar.
- Find ways to assist learning through motivation.
- Using trainers who understand the industry.

Sales training is the primary but not sole responsibility of the sales manager. It has been suggested that hotel sales managers should spend 50% of their time selling, 30% supervising and training staff, and the remaining percent with paperwork, meetings, and reviewing marketing plans.[45] Given the importance of an effective and professional sales force, others must assume some level of training responsibility.

Upper management, particularly the general manager and vice-president of sales/marketing, has a critical role. The authority and respect afforded upper management enables these individuals to establish and maintain a desired attitude in regard to policies, procedures, and planning. Members of upper management often assist in training by presenting an overview of the company and its history, culture, and norms. This sends a clear message to the sales force and helps to establish an effective learning attitude.

Sales managers often invite individuals from other departments, such as the chef or reservations manager, to attend sales meetings for the purpose of discussing product improvements. It is also important for salespeople to experience the company's service. Salespeople for a cruise line cannot effectively sell the excitement of sailing if they have never left dry land.

The hospitality industry has historically offered free or low-cost "fam trips" (familiarization trips) to travel agents and wholesalers. This may be considered as training of sales intermediaries. Other benefits, such as free flight privileges and expense accounts to entertain guests in the company's lounge and restaurants, also enhance product knowledge. These *perks* are often viewed with suspicion by employees and managers from other departments. It is essential that they be used judiciously. Sales managers have a responsibility to see that these necessary perks are not abused by members of their sales force.

Training Materials and Outside Training Assistance

Formal training may sometimes be necessary in which technical details must be memorized. The use of interactive video for this kind of training has proved effective. Some fast-food chains now use such systems to help train operational employees.

Videos, manuals, and books have a role provided they are carefully selected and viewed as additional learning tools, rather than the sole means for training. These must be carefully selected. Many sales managers err in purchasing an expensive training system of tapes, videos, and programmed learning from an outside vendor. Later these may be found to be too generic in content.

Organizations such as the Hotel/Motel Educational Association, the National Restaurant Association, universities such as Cornell University, and training institutes such as polytechnics offer materials specifically designed for the hospitality industry.

Universities are now forging strategic relationships with companies and trade associations to train management and staff on an ongoing basis. A group of hospitality authors and researchers believes that "The main training partnership in the next century will be manifested by a closer alignment between university Hotel/Restaurant Management programs and business partners. This alignment will plug into organizational needs, meaning fewer off-the-shelf programs."[46]

Preparatory training is enhanced by skills learned in the workplace. Ultimately, all training is perfected on the job. Some managers continue to believe that effective training consists solely of learning from one's trials and errors while selling. What is overlooked is that this is costly. For many individuals, this sink-or-swim system is extremely threatening and creates unnecessary turnover and morale problems.

As the new salesperson learns through experience, it is critical for the sales manager to monitor progress and offer encouragement and suggestions for improving areas of weakness. Effective sales managers are effective teachers. Individuals who do not enjoy teaching or coaching may find that their own management careers are limited.

All teachers dread a moment of truth. That is the time in which grades must be given. Granting A's is pleasurable and easy, but placing an F on someone's record requires soul searching. The same is true for a sales manager who must eventually come to the conclusion that no amount of training will create a professional salesperson of certain individuals.

Once this decision has been reached after serious study and thought, the sales manager has no alternative other than to promptly release the salesperson. Those who rescind this decision in face of emotion-laden pleas for a second chance only postpone the inevitable.

MANAGING THE SALES FORCE

Volumes of books and articles have been written about managing a professional sales force. The research and study dedicated to this subject clearly indicate that successful sales management is not the result of following a formula.

Successful sales managers cannot be described by a narrow profile. Successful sales managers come in all sizes, shapes, colors, and backgrounds. Perhaps, if a universal truth exists, it is that long-run successful sales managers exhibit a strong affinity for their subordinates, are willing to continuously learn, and must be reasonably bright. Even these conclusions sometimes seem to be disputed by observing some sales managers who meet objectives and please upper management yet seem weak in virtually every skill and talent normally accorded to successful sales managers.

The fact is that market conditions often have an inordinate influence over a sales manager's failure or success. An economic climate in which guests are begging for hotel rooms versus 3 years of deep economic recession with a surplus of hotel rooms can produce very different results. Sales managers, despite their skills or lack thereof, may look weak or triumphant.

Hospitality sales management is neither a precise science nor a formula-based work procedure. Nevertheless, there are functions or processes that have historically been associated with the management of a professional sales force. These should never be confused with the formula-based system of some selling areas, such as that employed by door-to-door vendors or telephone solicitors. Successful long-run hospitality sales requires a far more professional outlook and approach.

Selecting Sales Strategies

Sales successes within the hospitality industry are not the result of a hit-and-run sales mentality. Success depends on the development of excellent long-run relationships with clients or accounts. The 80/20 rule prevails within the hospitality industry. A bed and breakfast, a highway motel, or a discount airline may find no relevance, but major hotels and major airlines know well the phenomenon. This concept says that a majority of a firm's business comes from a minority of its customers. These are commonly referred to as key, national, or major accounts. Certain corporate clients and travel intermediaries, such as travel agents, generally serve as key accounts. These companies provide large numbers of customers.

Based on the concept of key customers, there are six general sales strategies that must be recognized by members of the hospitality industry.

1. *Prevent erosion of key accounts.* It does little good to attract new customers if key customers are lost. Companies operating on this kind of treadmill inevitably have higher than average sales-force turnover and experience employee morale problems. Determine reasons why key customers leave and initiate corrective steps. Initiate and carefully manage programs that treat key customers as royalty. A single sales/service person may be assigned to work with only a handful of key accounts. Unless these accounts are provided highly personal service, the risk of loss to a competitor is great.

   The CEO of a large hotel chain reportedly once told franchisees that they should view their properties as buckets with holes in the bottom. From these holes escape large numbers of customers. The message was that franchises must place even greater efforts into sales to attract new customers. Some who attended this meeting reported that the message had a depressing affect on the audience, who viewed themselves on a treadmill that regularly increased in speed. This was undoubtedly not the desired effect of the analogy.

Instead, the message should have been, each of us has holes in our respective buckets, but it is our responsibility to close or lessen the size of these holes so that we retain more of our customers.

2. *Grow key accounts.* Key accounts usually offer more sales potential than is currently realized. Key accounts may split their businesses between several provider companies. A hotel property or a hotel chain seldom obtains all or even a majority of a company's business. There is increasing evidence that companies are willing to reduce the number of hotel providers and to give more of their business to a few hotels if these companies meet their requirements for service and price.

Sometimes the sales force of a hotel becomes enamored with what appears to be a sales opportunity gold mine. Unfortunately, when this happens, traditional customers and traditional marketing channels that have consistently produced for the hotel are momentarily forgotten. This is the old and familiar phenomenon of "the grass is always greener on the other side of the fence."

In the summer of 1994, the sales department of many U.S. hotels thought they had discovered a "sure fire" client that would fill their hotel rooms. Organizers of the World Cup (soccer) convinced hotels to reserve large quantities of rooms for thousands of anticipated fans. Some luxury hotels blocked off up to 1000 room nights a week only to find that demand did not materialize, thus requiring them to release 50% to 80% of the reserved rooms.

Hyatt international sales vice-president, Craig Parsons, later described previous demand predictions as ludicrous. "We lost a lot of rooms that will not be resold because they have been out of the inventory too long," said Parsons. "Its the busy summer season and we did not need to have these rooms out of inventory because we could have sold them anyway."[47]

In addition to negating probable sales, Hyatt may have also infuriated good customers who were unable to book reservations and probably selected another hotel. It is possible that some of the guests may be difficult to recapture, particularly if they liked the competitor's hotel.

3. *Grow selected marginal accounts.* Selected marginal accounts can become key accounts if given sufficient time and a consistent level of service. They are currently marginal accounts for a variety of reasons, such as the following:

   - Experimenting or sampling your product or service. If they like it, they might provide substantially more business.
   - Have received poor service in the past and therefore use your services only when necessary.
   - Account manager changes have resulted in splitting the business between various hospitality firms.

- Comfortable with your service but competitors have acquired the bulk of their business through better follow-up.

4. *Eliminate selected marginal accounts.* Unfortunately, some accounts result in net losses for a hospitality company. These *negative yield* customers should be identified and eliminated whenever possible. It may be difficult to eliminate these customers due to an inability to identify them when the order or reservation is placed. A professional sales force has the responsibility to remove these customers from their list of prospects or active accounts and refrain from future sales calls or sales promotions directed to them.

5. *Retain selected marginal accounts but provide lower-cost sales support.* Many accounts represent infrequent purchases or low-yield business. These accounts cannot bear the cost of personalized sales calls or expensive promotions. A common method of dealing with these accounts is to assign them to an inside sales force. These salespeople don't make field calls, but instead interact with customers through telephone, telemarketing, catalogues, direct mail, and fax machines.

6. *Obtain new business from selected prospects.* The process of obtaining new accounts is costly and time consuming. Experienced salespeople know that it often requires five or more sales calls to obtain the business of a prospect. The cost of making a single sales call may be several hundred dollars when all costs are considered, such as travel expenses, salary, and benefits to the salesperson. The high cost of obtaining a new customer dictates that this individual must have the potential to significantly contribute to profits. It is inefficient and nonproductive to pursue sales prospects who have little or no likelihood of ever providing significant returns to the company.

Sales-force Tactics: Principles of Personal Selling

We turn now to the purpose of a sales force—to sell. Personal selling is an ancient art. Effective salespersons have more than instinct. They are trained in tactics to achieve sales success. Selling today is a profession that involves mastering and applying a set of principles.

Today's companies spend hundreds of millions of dollars each year to train their salespeople in the art of selling. All the sales training approaches try to convert a salesperson from being a passive order taker to an active order getter. Order takers operate on the following assumptions: Customers know their needs; they resent attempts at influence, and they prefer courteous and self-effacing salespersons.

In training salespeople to be order getting, there are two basic approaches, a sales-oriented approach and a customer-oriented approach. The first trains the salesperson in high-pressure selling techniques, such as those used in selling encyclopedias or automobiles. The techniques include exaggerating the product's merits, criticizing competitive products, using a slick presentation, selling yourself, and offering some price concession to get the order on the spot. This form of selling assumes that customers are not likely to buy except under pressure, that they are influenced by a slick presentation and ingratiating manners, and that they will not be sorry after signing the order or, if they are, it doesn't matter.

The other approach trains salespeople in customer problem solving. The salesperson learns how to listen and question in order to identify customer needs and come up with good product solutions. Presentation skills are made secondary to customer-need analysis skills. The approach assumes that customers have latent needs that constitute company opportunities, that they appreciate constructive suggestions, and that they will be loyal to sales representatives who have their long-term interests at heart. The problem solver is a much more congruent concept for the salesperson under the marketing concept than the hard seller or order taker.

We will briefly examine eight major aspects of personal selling. These are prospecting and qualifying, preapproach, approach, presentation and demonstration, negotiation, overcoming objections, closing, and follow-up/maintenance.

Prospecting and Qualifying

The first step in the selling process is to identify prospects. Although the company will try to supply leads, sales representatives need skill in developing their own. Leads can be developed in the following ways:

- Through call-ins
- Having a booth at appropriate travel or trade shows
- Participating in international travel missions
- Asking current customers for the names of prospects
- Cultivating other referral sources, such as suppliers, dealers, non-competing sales representatives, bankers, and trade association executives
- Through leads generated by the chain
- Joining organizations to which prospects belong
- Engaging in speaking and writing activities that will draw attention
- Examining data sources (newspapers, directories) in search of names
- Using the telephone and mail to find leads
- Dropping in unannounced on various offices (cold canvassing)
- Conducting a sales blitz

Sales representatives need skill in screening out poor leads. Prospects can be qualified by examining their financial ability, volume of business, special requirements, location, and likelihood of continuous business. The salesperson might phone or write to prospects before deciding whether to visit them. Leads can be categorized as hot leads, warm leads, and cool leads.

Preapproach

The salesperson needs to learn as much as possible about the prospect company (what it needs, who is involved in the purchase decision) and its buyers (their personal characteristics and buying styles). The salesperson should set call objectives, which might be to qualify the prospect or gather information or make an immediate sale. Another task is to decide on the best approach, which might be a personal visit, a phone call, or a letter. The best timing should be thought out because many prospects are busy at certain times. Finally, the salesperson should plan an overall sales strategy for the account.

Approach

The salesperson should know how to greet the buyer to get the relationship off to a good start. This involves the salesperson's appearance, the opening lines, and the follow-up remarks. The opening line should be positive, for example, "Mr. Smith, I am Alice Jones from the ABC Hotel Company. My company and I appreciate your willingness to see me. I will do my best to make this visit profitable and worthwhile for you and your company." This might be followed by key questions and active listening to understand the buyer and his or her needs.

Advertising helps to create awareness; the approach is easier if the prospect thinks favorably of your company. Courtesy of Opryland Hotel.

Presentation and Demonstration

The salesperson now tells the product "story" to the buyer, following the AIDA formula of gaining attention, holding interest, arousing desire, and obtaining action. The salesperson emphasizes throughout customer benefits, bringing in product features as evidence of these benefits. A benefit is any advantage, such as lower cost, less work, or more profit for the buyer. A feature is a product characteristic, such as weight or size. A common selling mistake is to dwell on product features (a product orientation) instead of customer benefits (a market orientation).

Companies have developed three different styles of sales presentation. The oldest is the canned approach, which is memorized sales talk covering the main points. It is based on stimulus/response thinking; that is, the buyer is passive and can be moved to purchase by the use of the right stimulus words, pictures, terms, and actions. Canned presentations are used primarily in door-to-door and telephone selling. The formulated approach is also based on stimulus/response thinking, but identifies early the buyer's needs and buying style and then uses a formulated approach to this type of buyer. The salesperson initially draws the buyer into the discussion in a way that reveals the buyer's needs and attitudes. Then the salesperson moves into a formulated presentation that shows how the product will satisfy the buyer's needs. It is not canned but follows a general plan.

The need/satisfaction approach starts with a search for the customer's real needs by encouraging the customer to do most of the talking. This approach calls for good listening and problem-solving skills. The salesperson takes on the role of a knowledgeable business consultant hoping to help the customer save money or make more money.

Sales presentations can be improved with demonstration aids such as booklets, flip charts, slides, movies, and audio- and videocassettes. During the demonstration, the salesperson can draw on five influence strategies.[48]

- **Legitimacy.** The salesperson emphasizes the reputation and experience of his or her company.
- **Expertise.** The salesperson shows deep knowledge of the buyer's situation and company's products, doing this without being overly "smart."
- **Referent power.** The salesperson builds on any shared characteristics, interests, and acquaintances.
- **Ingratiation.** The salesperson provides personal favors (a free lunch, promotional gratuities) to strengthen affiliation and reciprocity feelings.
- **Impression.** The salesperson manages to convey favorable personal impressions.

Negotiation

Much of business-to-business selling involves negotiating skills. The two parties need to reach agreement on the price and other terms of sale. Salespersons need to win the order without making deep concessions that will hurt profitability.

Although price is the most frequently negotiated issue, other issues include quality of goods and service offered; purchase volume; and responsibility for financing, risk taking, and promotion. The number of negotiation issues is virtually unlimited.

Unfortunately, far too many hotel salespeople rely almost exclusively on price as their negotiating tool. Even worse, they often begin negotiating from an already discounted price, rather than from rack rates. Negotiations should always begin with rack rates and price concessions should be given only when absolutely essential. Numerous bargaining tools exist, such as upgrades, complimentary tickets for the ski lift or golf courses, first-class coffee breaks instead of coffee and soft drinks, airport pickup, and use of hotel services such as the fitness center. A hotel sales force might package these amenities into bundles of services and give them names such as the President's Package, the Connoisseur's Package, and the Executive Package.

Sales-force members should be taught to negotiate using services or bundled services as the primary negotiating tool rather than price.

The possible difference in service package negotiations versus price negotiation is shown in Table 19-2. It is easy to see that the hotel benefits by offering a package of services rather than a price discount at all levels other than a 10% discount. Sales-force members must understand the economic value of these kinds of trade-offs before they enter into the negotiation process.

Table 19-2

Hotel Negotiation Cost Comparison: Offering a Service Package versus Price

	50 GUESTS AT 3 NIGHTS EACH	
	COST/GUEST	TOTAL COST
President's Package		
Airport pickup and delivery limousine service	$15	$ 750
Bottle of champagne in room	$20	$1000
Technician to take care of AV during the meeting	2 1/2 days at $50/hour × 20 hours	$1000
		$2750
PRICE DISCOUNTS	TOTAL REVENUE POTENTIAL	
Rack Rate ($150/night; 50 guests at 3 nights each)	$22,500	
	REVENUE LOST	
10%	$ 2,250	
20%	4,500	
30%	6,750	
40%	9,000	
50%	11,250	

Bargaining or negotiation, which we will use interchangeably, has the following features:

- At least two parties are involved.
- The parties have a conflict of interest with respect to one or more issues.
- The parties are at least temporarily joined together in a special kind of voluntary relationship.
- Activity in the relationship concerns the division or exchange of one or more specific resources and/or the resolution of one or more intangible issues among the parties or among those they represent.
- The activity usually involves the presentation of demands or proposals by one party and evaluation of these by the other, followed by concessions and counter-proposals.[49]

Marketers who find themselves in bargaining situations need certain traits and skills to be effective. The most important traits are preparation and planning skill, knowledge of subject matter being negotiated, ability to think clearly and rapidly under pressure and uncertainty, ability to express thoughts verbally, listening skill, judgment and general intelligence, integrity, ability to persuade others, and patience. These will help the marketer in knowing when to negotiate and how to negotiate.[50]

When to Negotiate Consider the following circumstances in which negotiation in the hospitality industry is an appropriate procedure for concluding a sale:

1. When many factors bear not only on price, but also on quality and service.
2. When business risks cannot be accurately predetermined.[51]

Negotiation is appropriate whenever a zone of agreement exists.[52] A zone of agreement exists when there are simultaneously overlapping acceptable outcomes for the parties.

Formulating a Bargaining Strategy Bargaining involves preparing a strategic plan before bargaining begins and making good tactical decisions during the bargaining sessions. A bargaining strategy can be defined as a commitment to an overall approach that has a good chance of achieving the negotiator's objectives. For example, some negotiators pursue a hard strategy with opponents, while others maintain that a soft strategy yields more favorable results.

The sales force of a hotel or resort is in a position to use negotiating skills nearly every day of their professional lives. Their negotiation process can be enhanced by understanding the negotiating strengths and weaknesses of the client, as shown in Table 19-3.

Bargaining Tactics during Negotiations Negotiators use a variety of tactics when bargaining. Bargaining tactics can be defined as maneuvers to be made at specific points in the bargaining process. Threats, bluffs, last-chance offers, hard initial offers, and other tactics occur in bargaining.

Table 19-3

Examples of Hotel Customer's Negotiating Strengths and Weaknesses

STRENGTHS	WEAKNESSES
1. Provide many guests.	1. Provide few guests.
2. Come in low or shoulder seasons.	2. Come in prime season.
3. Stay low-occupancy nights.	3. Stay high-occupancy nights.
4. Bring quality guests.	4. Bring undesirable guests.
5. Provide cross-purchase potential.	5. Provide little or no cross-sale potential.
6. Purchase upscale rooms.	6. Purchase lowest-priced rooms.

Fisher and Ury have offered advice that is consistent with their strategy of principles negotiation. Their first piece of tactical advice concerns what should be done if the other party is more powerful. By identifying your alternatives if a settlement is not reached, it sets a standard against which any offer can be measured. It protects you from being pressured into accepting unfavorable terms from a more powerful opponent.[53]

Another tactic comes into play when the opposing party insists on arguing his or her position instead of his or her interests and attacks your proposals or person. While the tendency is to push back hard when pushed, the better tactic is to deflect the attack from the person and direct it against the problem. Look at the interests that motivated the opposing party's position and invent options that can satisfy both parties' interests. Invite the opposing party's criticism and advice ("If you were in my position, what would you do?").

Another set of bargaining tactics is responses to opposition tactics that are intended to deceive, distort, or otherwise influence the bargaining to their own advantage. What tactic should be used when the other side uses a threat, or a take-it-or-leave-it tactic or seats the other party on the side of the table with the sun in his eyes? A negotiator should recognize the tactic, raise the issue explicitly, and question the tactic's legitimacy and desirability—in other words, negotiate over it. Negotiating the use of the tactic follows the same principled negotiation procedure: Question the tactic, ask why the tactic is being used, or suggest alternative courses of action to pursue. If this fails, resort to your best alternative to a negotiated agreement (BATNA) and terminate the negotiation until the other side ceases to employ these tactics. Meeting these tactics by defending principles is more productive than counterattacking with tricky tactics.

Overcoming Objections

Customers almost always pose objections during the presentation or when asked for the order. Their resistance can be psychological or logical. Psychological resistance includes resistance to interference, preference for established hotel or airline, apathy, reluctance to giving up something, unpleasant associations about the other person, predetermined ideas, dislike of making decisions, and neurotic attitude toward money. Logical resistance might consist of objections to the price or certain product or company characteristics. To handle these objections, the salesperson maintains a positive approach, asks the buyer to clarify the objection, denies the validity of the objection, or turns the objection into a reason for buying. The salesperson needs training in the broader skills of negotiation, of which handling objections is a part.

Closing

Now the salesperson attempts to close the sale. Some salespeople do not get to this stage or do not do it well. They lack confidence or feel uncomfortable about asking for the order or do not recognize the right psychological moment to close the sale. Salespersons need to know how to recognize closing signals from the buyer, including physical actions, statements or comments, and questions. Salespersons can use one of several closing techniques. They can ask for the order, recapitulate the points of agreement, offer to help the secretary write up the order, ask whether the buyers want A or B, get the buyer to make minor choices such as on color or size, or indicate what the buyer will lose if the order is not placed now. The salesperson might offer the buyer specific inducements to close, such as a special price.

A basic problem mentioned over and over by hotel sales managers is that some members of the sales force do not ask for the order. They may follow all the other steps to perfection but for some reason seem incapable of *asking for the order.*

Follow-up/Maintenance

This last step is necessary if the salesperson wants to ensure customer satisfaction and repeat business. Immediately after closing, the salesperson should complete any necessary details on delivery time, purchase terms, and other matters. Follow-up or foul-up is a slogan of most successful salespeople. The salesperson should develop an account maintenance plan to make sure that the customer is not forgotten or lost.

Motivating a Professional Sales Force

Some sales representatives will put forth their best effort without any special coaching from management. To them, selling is the most fascinating job in the world. They are ambitious and self-starters. But the majority of sales representatives require encouragement and special incentives to work at their best level. This is especially true of field selling, for the following reasons:

- **Nature of the job.** The selling job is one of frequent frustration. Sales representatives usually work alone, their hours are irregular, and they are often away from home. They confront aggressive, competing sales representatives; they have an inferior status relative to the buyer; they often do not have the authority to do what is necessary to win an account; they lose large orders that they have worked hard to obtain.

- **Human nature.** Most people operate below capacity in the absence of special incentives, such as financial gain or social recognition.
- **Personal problems.** Sales representatives are occasionally preoccupied with personal problems, such as sickness in the family, marital discord, or debt.

A basic model of motivating sales representatives follows:[54]

Motivation ⟶ Effort ⟶ Performance ⟶ Rewards ⟶ Satisfaction

This model implies the following:

1. Sales managers must be able to convince salespeople that they can sell more by working harder or by being trained to work smarter.
2. Sales managers must be able to convince salespeople that the rewards for better performance are worth the extra effort.

Sales-force Compensation

To attract and retain sales representatives, the company has to develop an attractive compensation package. Sales representatives would like income regularity, extra reward for an above-average performance, and fair payment for experience and longevity. On the other hand, management would like to achieve control, economy, and simplicity. Management objectives, such as economy, will conflict with sales representatives' objectives, such as financial security.

Management must determine the level and components of an effective compensation plan. The level of compensation must bear some relation to the going market price for the type of sales job and required abilities. If the market price for salespeople is well defined, the individual firm has little choice but to pay the going rate. The market price for salespeople, however, is seldom well defined. For one thing, sales compensation plans differ in the importance of fixed and variable salary elements, fringe benefits, and expense allowances. And data on the average take-home pay of competitors' sales representatives can be misleading because of significant variations in the average seniority and ability levels of the competitors' sales forces. Published data on industry sales-force compensation levels are infrequent and generally lack sufficient detail.

The company must next determine the components of compensation: a fixed amount, a variable amount, expenses, and fringe benefits. The fixed amount, which might be salary or a drawing account, is intended to satisfy the sales representatives' need for income stability. The variable amount, which might be commissions, bonus, or profit sharing, is intended to stimulate and reward greater effort. Expense allowances enable the sales representatives to meet the expenses involved in travel, lodging, dining, and entertainment. And fringe benefits, such as paid vacation, sickness or accident benefits, pensions, and life insurance, are intended to provide security and job satisfaction.

Fixed and variable compensations give rise to three basic types of sales-force compensation plans: straight salary, straight commissions, and combination salary and commission.

Many companies in the hospitality industry suffer from high sales-force turnover. A variety of reasons has been given to explain this situation, such as burnout. A survey of college graduates preparing to enter the hospitality industry ranked salary as number 10 among variables relating to what they wanted in a job.[55] A different study of young managers who left hospitality careers demonstrated that money was indeed important. Pay-related issues were the second most common reason for leaving, following long hours and inconvenient scheduling as the primary reason. One respondent wrote, "I had poor pay, high stress, low praise and recognition, and worked 75 to 80 hours a week, all for the chance to be a GM in 10 or 15 years with the same job characteristics."[56]

The importance of monetary rewards to a hospitality sales force must not be minimized. These individuals are expected to maintain a large fashionable wardrobe, to work long hours, experience stress, and often give up family experiences for the sake of their career. Under these circumstances, monetary reward becomes very important.

Hospitality managers should evaluate high sales-force turnover from the standpoint of multicosts, such as constant recruiting and training, plus intangible opportunity costs. The cost of finding ways to elevate monetary compensation for valuable sales-force members may then seem less unattractive.

Supplementary Motivators

Companies use additional motivators to stimulate sales-force effort. Periodic sales meetings provide a social occasion, a break from routine, a chance to meet and talk with "company brass," and a chance to air feelings and to identify with a larger group. Sales meetings are an important communication and motivational tool.[57] They can also be used for training in subjects such as how to make effective presentations.[58] Thus the sales meeting can and should assume increased importance to the sales force.

Companies also sponsor sales contests to spur the sales force to a special selling effort above what would normally be expected. The contest should present a reasonable opportunity for enough salespeople to win. If only a few salespersons can win or almost everyone can win, it will fail to spur additional effort. The sales contest period should not be announced in advance or else some salespersons will defer some sales to the beginning of the period; also, some may pad their sales during the period with customer promises to buy that do not materialize after the contest period ends.

Sales managers of hotels and resorts sometimes offer vacations at sister properties for winners of a sales contest. When the winners visit a sister property, they are introduced to the sales department and often learn new techniques. In turn, this information is transmitted to others when the winners return and give a report in the next sales meeting.

Evaluation and Control of a Professional Sales Force

We have been describing the feed-forward aspects of the sales supervision—how management communicates what the sales representatives should be doing and motivates them to do it. But good feed-forward requires good feedback. And good feedback means getting regular information from sales representatives to evaluate their performance.

Sales Quotas

Many companies set sales quotas prescribing what their sales representatives should sell during the year and by product. Compensation is often tied to the degree of quota fulfillment. Sales quotas are developed from the annual marketing plan. The company first prepares a sales forecast. This forecast becomes the basis for planning production, work-force size, and financial requirements. Then management establishes sales quotas for its regions and territories, which typically add up to more than the sales forecast. Sales quotas are often set higher than the sales forecast in order to stretch sales managers and salespeople to perform at their best level.

Each area sales manager divides the area's quota among the area's sales representatives. There are three schools of thought on quota setting. The high-quota school sets quotas that are higher than what most sales representatives will achieve but that are attainable. Its adherents believe that high quotas spur extra effort. The modest-quota school sets quotas that a majority of the sales force can achieve. Its adherents feel that the sales force will accept the quotas as fair, attain them, and gain confidence. The variable-quota school thinks that individual differences among sales representatives warrant high quotas for some and modest quotas for others.

Developing Norms for Salespeople

New sales representatives should be given more than a territory, a compensation package, and training—they need supervision. Supervision is the fate of everyone who works for someone else. It is the expression of the employers' natural and continuous interest in the activities of their agents. Through supervision, employers hope to direct and motivate the sales force to do a better job.

Companies vary in how closely they direct their sales representatives. Sales representatives who are paid mostly on commission generally receive less supervision. Those who are salaried and must cover definite accounts are likely to receive substantial supervision.

The number of calls that an average salesperson makes during a day has been decreasing. The downward trend is due to the increased use of technology, such as phone and fax machines, the increased reliance on automatic ordering systems, and the drop-in cold calls owing to better market research information for pinpointing prospects. It is also due to difficulties in reaching prospects due to traffic congestion, busy prospect schedules, and other complexities of contemporary business.

Companies often decide on how many calls to make a year on particular-sized accounts. Most companies classify customers into A, B, and C accounts, reflecting the sales volume, profit potential, and growth potential of the account. A accounts might receive nine calls a year; B, six calls; and C, three calls. The call norms depend on competitive call norms and expected account profitability.

Regardless of how a sales force is structured, individual salespeople must classify their customer base. A salesperson responsible for channel intermediaries, such as tour operators and travel agents, quickly learns that not all are capable of producing the same sales volume/profit. This is equally true for a salesperson who has responsibility for the conference/meeting segment and to some degree even for the individual responsible for national accounts.

Omni International Hotels emphasizes account planning with its sales force. The management of Dunfey Hotels Corporation, which became Omni International, believed that it is critical to understand the marketplace and to classify accounts as to their potential for Omni (Dunfey). President Jon Canas told a Harvard professor in a taped interview that not all prospects may be contacted in a particular year since they do not qualify as the best target customers. However, it is important to know the second- and third-tier prospects so that they can be contacted if a slowdown occurs within the top targeted groups.[59] Canas believed that this system was appropriate for all members of the hotel/resort industry.

Companies often specify how much time their sales force should spend prospecting for new accounts. Companies set up prospecting standards for a number of reasons. If left alone, many sales representatives will spend most of their time with current customers. Current customers are better-known quantities. Sales representatives can depend on them for some business, whereas a prospect might never deliver any business. Unless sales representatives are rewarded for opening new accounts, they might avoid new-account development.

Using Sales Time Efficiently

Sales representatives need to know how to use their time efficiently. One tool is the annual call schedule showing which customers and prospects to call on in which months and which activities to carry out.

Another tool is time-and-duty analysis. The sales representative spends time in the following ways:

- **Travel.** In some jobs, travel time amounts to over 50% of total time.
- **Food and breaks.** Some portion of the sales force's workday is spent in eating and taking breaks.
- **Waiting.** Waiting consists of time spent in the outer office of the buyer. This is dead time unless the sales representative uses it to plan or to fill out reports.
- **Selling.** Selling is the time spent with the buyer in person or on the phone. It breaks down into *social talk* and *selling talk*.
- **Administration.** This consists of the time spent in report writing and billing, attending sales meetings, and talking to others in the

company about production, delivery, billing, sales performance, and other matters.

Actual face-to-face selling time can amount to as little as 25% of total working time.[60] If it could be raised from 25% to 30%, this would be a 20% improvement. Companies are constantly seeking ways to improve sales-force productivity. Their methods take the form of training sales representatives in the use of "phone power," simplifying record-keeping forms, and using the computer to develop call and routing plans and to supply customer and competitive information.

Other Control Techniques

Management obtains information about its sales representatives in several ways. One important source is sales reports. Additional information comes through personal observation, customers' letters and complaints, customer surveys, and conversations with other sales representatives.

Sales reports are divided between activity plans and writeups of activity results. The best example of the former is the salesperson's work plan, which sales representatives submit a week or month in advance. The plan describes intended calls and routing. This report leads the sales force to plan and schedule their activities, informs management of their whereabouts, and provides a basis for comparing their plans and accomplishments. Sales representatives can be evaluated on their ability to "plan their work and work their plan."

Many hospitality companies require their sales representatives to develop an annual territory marketing plan in which they outline their program for developing new accounts and increasing business from existing accounts. The type of report casts sales representatives into the role of market managers and profit centers.

Sales representatives write up their completed activities on call reports. Call reports inform sales management of the salesperson's activities, indicate the status of specific customer accounts, and provide useful information for subsequent calls. Sales representatives also submit expense reports, new business reports, lost business reports, and reports on local business and economic conditions.

These reports provide raw data from which sales managers can extract key indicators of sales performance. The key indicators are (1) average number of sales calls per salesperson per day, (2) average sales call time per contact, (3) average revenue per sales call, (4) average cost per sales call, (5) entertainment cost per sales call, (6) percentage of orders per hundred sales calls, (7) number of new customers per period, (8) number of lost customers per period, and (9) sales-force cost as a percentage of total sales. These indicators answer several useful questions. Are sales representatives making too few calls per day? Are they spending too much time per call? Are they spending too much on entertainment? Are they closing enough orders per hundred calls? Are they producing enough new customers and holding on to the old customers?

Formal Evaluation of Performance. The sales force's reports along with other observations supply the raw materials for evaluating members of the sales force. Formal evaluation procedures lead to at least three benefits. First, management has to communicate their standards for judging sales performance. Second, management needs to gather comprehensive information about each salesperson. And, third, sales representatives know that they will have to sit down one morning with the sales manager and explain their performance or failure to achieve certain goals.

Salesperson-to-Salesperson Comparisons. One type of evaluation is to compare and rank the sales performance of a company's sales representatives. Such comparisons, however, can be misleading. Relative sales performance is meaningful only if there are no variations in territory market potential, workload, competition, company promotional effort, and so forth. Furthermore, current sales are not the only success indicator. Management should also be interested in how much each sales representative contributes to current net profits.

Customer Satisfaction Evaluation. A salesperson might be very effective in producing sales but not rate high with customers. An increasing number of companies are measuring customer satisfaction not only with their product and customer-support service but with their salespeople. The customers' opinion of the salesperson, product, and service can be measured by mail questionnaires or telephone calls. Company salespeople who score high on satisfying their customers can be given special recognition, awards, or bonuses.

Qualitative Evaluation of Sales Representatives

Evaluations can also assess the salesperson's knowledge of the company, products, customers, competitors, territory, and responsibilities. Personality characteristics can be rated, such as general manner, appearance, speech, and temperament. The sales manager can also review any problems in motivation or compliance. The sales manager can check that the sales representative knows and observes company policies. Each company must develop its own evaluation procedure. Whatever procedure is chosen, it must be fair to the salesperson and the company. If members of a sales force feel that they are being judged against incorrect norms, they will quickly become dissatisfied and may leave the company.

Hospitality sales is a profession and must be treated as such. It is very much to the advantage of any hospitality company to develop a professional, loyal, and contented sales force. Measurement of a salesperson's value and contribution must not be left to the last minute or to inappropriate standards and measures. No aspects of sales management is more important than developing and using the correct appraisal system for members of a professional sales force.

Chapter Review

I.   Sales Positions in the Hospitality Industry

1) Deliverer. The salesperson's job is predominantly to deliver the product.

2) Order taker. The salesperson is predominantly an inside order taker.

3) Missionary. The salesperson is not expected or permitted to take an order but is called only to build goodwill or to educate the actual or potential user.

4) **Technician.** The major emphasis is placed on technical knowledge.

5) **Demand creator.** Positions that demand the creative sales of tangible products or of intangibles.

II.   **Sales-force Objectives**

1)   **Setting Objectives**

a) **Prospecting:** Sales representatives find and cultivate new customers.

b) **Targeting:** Sales representatives decide how to allocate their scarce time among prospects and customers.

c) **Communicating:** Sales representatives communicate information about the company's products and services.

d) **Selling:** Sales representatives know the art of salesmanship: approaching, presenting, answering objections, and closing sales.

e) **Servicing:** Sales representatives provide various services to the customers: consulting on their problems, rendering technical assistance, arranging financing, and expediting delivery.

f) **Information gathering:** Sales representatives conduct market research and intelligence work and fill in a call report.

g) **Allocating:** sales representatives decide on which customers to allocate scarce products to.

2)   **Establishing and Meeting Objectives.** Sales volume, sales volume by selected segments, sales volume and price/margin mix.

3)   **Meeting Objectives—Control.** Quotas, call reports, weekly sales meetings, automated sales information systems.

4)   **Meeting Objectives—Motivation.** Peer recognition, frequent meeting and seminars, contests and special awards, extend horizons.

III. **Sales-force Strategy**

1)   **Ways That Sales Representatives Work with Customers**

a) **Sales representatives to buyer:** a sales representative discusses issues with a prospect or customer in person or over the phone.

b) **Sales representative to buyer group:** A sales representative gets to know as many members of the buyer group as possible.

c) **Sales team to buyer group:** A company sales team works closely with the members of the customer's buying group.

d) **Conference selling:** The sales representative brings company resource people to discuss a major problem or opportunity.

e) **Seminar selling:** A company team conducts an educational seminar for the customer company about state-of-the-art development.

2)   **Six Sales Strategies**

a) **Prevent erosion of key accounts**

b) **Grow key accounts**

c) **Grow selected marginal accounts**

d) **Eliminate selected marginal accounts**

e) **Retain selected marginal accounts,** but provide lower-cost sales support

f) **Obtain new business from selected prospects**

IV.   **Sales-force Structure**

1)   **Territorial-structured Sales Force.** Each sales representative is

assigned an exclusive territory in which to represent the company's full line.

> ***a) Territorial size:*** Territories are designed to provide either equal sales potential or equal workload.
>
> ***b) Territorial shape:*** Territories are formed by combining smaller units until they add up to a territory of a given sales potential or workload.

2) Product-structured Sales Force. Company structures its sales force along product lines due to the importance of sales representatives knowing their products.

3) Market-structured Sales Force. Company structures its sales force based on market segments.

V.   Determining Sales-force Size

1) Customers are grouped into size classes according to their annual sales volume.

2) The desired call frequencies are established for each class.

3) The number of accounts in each size class is multiplied by the corresponding call frequency to arrive at the total workload for the country in sales call per year.

4) The average number of calls a sales representative can make per year is determined.

5) The number of sales representatives needed is determined by dividing the total annual calls required by the average annual calls made by a sales representative.

VI.   Sales-force Compensation. Three basic types of sales-force compensation plans: straight salary, straight commission, and combination salary and commission.

VII. Managing the Sales Force

1) Recruiting and Selecting Sales Representatives. The effective salesperson has two basic qualities: empathy, the ability to feel as the customer does; ego drive, a strong personal need to make the sales.

2) When to Recruit. Three methods: recruit and train salespeople in a batch process; recruit only as needed for replacement and growth; always recruit.

3) Training. Three types of training: product/service training; policies, procedures, and planning training; sales techniques training.

4) Directing Sales Representatives. Developing norms for customer calls; developing norms for prospect calls; using sales time effectively (travel, food and break, waiting, selling, administration).

5) Motivating Sales Representatives

> ***a)*** Basic model:
>
> motivation ⟶ effort ⟶ performance ⟶ rewards ⟶ satisfaction.
>
> ***b)*** Sales quotas and supplementary motivator.

6) Evaluating Sales Representatives. Formal evaluation of performance: sales-to-salesperson comparisons; current-to-past sales comparisons; customer satisfaction evaluation; qualitative evaluation of sales representatives.

VIII. The Sales Process. prospecting and qualifying, preapproach, approach, presentation and demonstration, overcoming objections, closing, and **follow-up and maintenance.**

IX.   Negotiation. The art of arriving at transaction terms that satisfy both parties.

    1)   Features of Negotiation

        a) At least two parties are involved.

        b) The parties have a conflict of interest with respect to one or more issues.

        c) The parties are at least temporarily joined together in a special kind of voluntary relationship.

        d) Activity in the relationship concerns the division or exchange of one or more specific resources and/or the resolution of one or more intangible issues among the parties or among those they represent.

        e) The activity usually involves the presentation of demands or proposals by one party and evaluation of these by the other, followed by concessions and counterproposals.

    2)   When to Negotiate

        a) When many factors bear not only on price, but also on quality and service.

        b) When business risks cannot be accurately predetermined.

    3)   Bargaining Tactics during Negotiations

        a) BATNA—best alternative to a negotiated agreement.

        b) Focusing on problem, inventing options that satisfy both parties and inviting the opposing party's criticism and advice.

        c) Meeting tactics by defending principles other than counterattacking with tricky tactics.

X.   Relationship Marketing. The art of creating a closer working relationship and interdependence between the people in two organizations.

    1)   Team Sales. The purpose is to accomplish objectives through the synergism of two or more people that would be impossible or unduly costly through individual sales efforts.

    2)   Strategic Alliances. Alliances are relationships between independent parties that agree to cooperate but still retain separate identities.

    3)   Reasons Strategic Alliances Are Necessary. Globalization, complicated customer needs, large customers with multilocations, the need for technology, highly interdependent vendor/buyer relationship, intensified competition, and low profitability within the hospitality industry.

DISCUSSION QUESTIONS

1. Why should companies be concerned about key or national accounts?

2. What are the most common methods of structuring a sales force?

3. Discuss the importance of establishing sales objectives and the various kinds of sales-force objectives common to the hospitality industry.

4. What types of sales training are commonly employed?

5. Discuss the process of negotiation and how it can be effectively used by sales-force members.

KEY TERMS

Applicant rating procedure   A procedure used by companies to rank prospective members of the sales force.

Closing   The process of getting the order signed.

Control systems   Communications systems between management and members of the sales force to help assure that objectives are met.

Eighty/twenty rule   A majority of a company's business often comes from a minority of its accounts.

Experiential training   Learning on the job.

First-line sales force   Members of the sales force who interface with the customer, whether in the field or over the phone.

Ingratiation   Favors extended by a salesperson with the hope of reciprocity.

Key accounts   The most important accounts by sales volume/margin.

Legitamacy   The process of proving that a salesperson and the product are honest and reliable.

Market-structured sales force   A sales force structured according to customer groupings.

Missionary salesperson   Individuals who are expected to build goodwill, set up displays, but not take orders.

National account   Major accounts. Often synonymous with key accounts.

Negotiation   Verbal interaction between the client and the salesperson relative to the selling process.

Product-structured sales force   A sales force structured along product lines.

Prospecting   The process of searching for new accounts.

Qualifying   The process of determining the sales potential and probability of obtaining and closing an account.

Referent power   Shared characteristics a salesperson builds on.

Sales blitz   A concentrated burst of sales activity within a specific area by a group of salespeople, such as many persons in one territory.

Sales quotas   Quantitative sales achievement marks in terms of units, dollars, and profitability, or all three.

Strategic alliances   Partnerships between a seller and buyer.

Supplementary motivators   Motivators other than base salary and commission, such as sales contests.

Team sales   Multiperson involvement in the sales process.

Territory-structured sales force   A sales force structured according to geography.

Travel mission   Goodwill selling by a company as part of a broader group, such as an association establishing information booths at a travel show.

REFERENCES

1. BILL PRIMAVERA, "Introducing the First Lady of American Restaurants," Primavera Public Relations, Inc., 2718 Hickory Street, Yorktown Heights, NY 10598.

2. JEFFREY A. TANNENBAUM, "Franchises Takes Complaints against Pearle to FTC," A New Newsletter, *Wall Street Journal* (February 16, 1994).

3. ROBIN LEE ALLEN, "Ruth Fertel: Tireless Entrepreneur," *Nation's Restaurant News* (September 21, 1992), p. 81.

4. JOHN DE MERS, "Rare Ruth," *USAir Magazine* (February 1990), p. 78.

5. Adapted from Robert N. McMurry, "The Mystique of Super-Salesmanship," *Harvard Business Review* (March–April 1961), p. 114. Also see WILLIAM C. MONCRIEF III, "Selling Activity and Sales Position Taxonomies for Industrial Salesforces," *Journal of* *Marketing Research* (August 1986), pp. 261–270.

6. JOHN W. VERITZ, "Taking a Laptop on a Call," *Business Week* (October 25, 1993), p. 124.

7. EVERETT MARTIN, "Its Jerry Hale on the Line," 145, no. 15, *Sales and Marketing Management* (December 1993), p. 74.

8. SUSAN HANCOCK, "How to Generate Leads for High Ticket Items," *Potentials in Marketing*, Ziff Communications Company, Lakewood Publications, Inc., 1994, Vol. 27, no. 5, p. 52.

9. DONNA J. OWENS, "To Offset Their Seasonality, Canada's Resorts Should Stretch Their Seasons by Appealing to Multiple Market Segments," 35, no. 5, *Cornell Hotel and Restaurant Administration Quarterly* (October 1994), p. 29.

10. Ibid., p. 30.

11. LISA C. WEISS, "Days Inns of America: To Give 1400 General Managers, One Year Membership to Hospitality Sales and Marketing Associations International," *Business Travel News* (November 8, 1993), p. 10.

12. HOWARD FEIERTAG, "Database Marketing Proves Helpful in Group Sales," *Hotel and Motel Management* (March 8, 1993), p. 14.

13. OWENS, "To Offset Their Seasonality," p. 29.

14. WILLIAM J. QUAIN AND STEPHEN M. LEBRUTO, "Second-chance Selling," *Cornell Hotel and Restaurant Administration Quarterly*, 35, no 5 (October 1994), p. 81.

15. PETER RAINSFORD, "Selecting and Monitoring Hotel Management Companies," *Cornell Hotel and Restaurant Administration Quarterly*, 35, no. 2 (April 1994), p. 34.

16. MICHAEL P. SIM AND BURRITT M. CHASE, "Enhancing Resort Profitability with Membership Programs," *Cornell Hotel and Restaurant Administration Quarterly*, 34, no. 8 (August 1993), pp. 59–62.

17. EDDYSTONE C. NEBEL III, DENNY RUTHERFORD, AND JEFFREY D. SCHAFFER, "Reengineering the Hotel Organization," *Cornell Hotel and Restaurant Administration Quarterly*, 35, no 5 (October 1994), pp. 88–95.

18. *The Cruise Industry: An Overview*, Cruise Lines Association, 500 5th Avenue, Suite 1407, New York, NY 10110, July 1994, p. 31.

19. CHRISTOPHER SCHULZ, "Hotel and Travel Agents: The New Partnership," *Cornell Hotel and Restaurant Administration Quarterly*, 35, no. 2 (April 1994), p. 45.

20. AL GLANZBERG AND GLENN WITHIAM, "Andre Tatibouet: Maximizing Asset Value," *Cornell Hotel and Restaurant Administration Quarterly*, 35, no. 2 (April 1994), p. 26.

21. TAKETOSH YAMAZAKI, "Tokyo Hotel Construction Push Roger On," *Tokyo Business Today*, 59, no. 3 (March 1991), pp. 50–51.

22. WILLIAM A. KAVEN AND MYRTLE ALLARDYCE, "Dalmahoy's Strategy for Success," *Cornell Hotel and Restaurant Administration Quarterly*," 35, no. 6 (December 1994), p. 86–89.

23. SHERYL E. KIMES AND DOUGLAS C. LORD, "Wholesalers and Caribbean Resort Hotels," *Cornell Hotel and Restaurant Administration Quarterly*, 35, no. 5 (October 1994), p. 75.

24. PHILLIP R. MOGLE, "Planner under Siege," *Successful Meetings* (September 1990), p. 76.

25. ROBERT A. MEYER, "Understanding Telemarketing for Hotels," *Cornell Hotel and Restaurant Administration Quarterly*, 28, no. 2 (August 1987), p. 26.

26. BARBARA JEAN ROSS, "Training: Key to Effective Reservations," *Cornell Hotel and Restaurant Administration Quarterly*, 31, no. 3 (November 1990), pp. 71–79.

27. Ibid. p. 79.

28. TIMOTHY TROY, "Windsor Winning with Tried and True Formula," *Hotel and Motel Management*, 208 (November 22, 1993), p. 4.

29. "Intel to Handle Reservations for Omni," *Business Travel News* (November 22, 1993), p. 15.

30. GINA O'BRIEN, "Where the Action Is," *Travel Agent* (November 22, 1993), p. 26.

31. See NEIL RACKHAM, *SPIN Selling* (New York: McGraw-Hill, 1988); and FRANK V. CESPEDES, STEPHEN X. DOYLE AND ROBERT J. FREEDMAN, "Teamwork for Today's Selling," *Harvard Business Review* (March–April 1989), pp. 44–54, 58.

32. "Resorts' Makeup Means Sweet Smell of Success for Long-term Client," *Cornell Hotel and Restaurant Administration Quarterly*, 35, no. 3 (June 1994), p. 9.

33. S. DEV CHEKITAN AND SAUL KLEIN, "Strategic Alliances in the Hotel Industry," *Cornell Hotel and Restaurant Administration Quarterly*, 34, no. 1 (February 1993), p. 43.

34. BILL GILLETTE, "HFS Carlson Strikes Strategic Alliance," *Hotel and Motel Marketing*, 208, no. 2 (February 1, 1993), pp. 1, 26.

35. BILL GILLETTE, "Hostmark Making It's Mark," *Hotel and Motel Management*, 207, no 1 (January 13, 1992), pp. 3, 34.

36. GEORGE H. LUCAS, JR., A. PARASURAMAN, ROBERT A. DAVIS, AND BEN M. ENIS, "An Empirical Study of Salesforce Turnover," *Journal of Marketing* (July 1987), pp. 34–59.

37. See CHARLES GARFIELD, *Peak Performers: The New Heroes of American Business* (New York: Avon Books 1986); "What Makes a Supersalesperson?" *Sales and Marketing Management* (August 23, 1984), p. 86; "What Makes a Top Performer?" *Sales and Marketing Management* (May 1989); and TIMOTHY J. TROW, "The Secret of a Good Hire: Profiling," *Sales and Marketing Management* (May 1990), pp. 44–55.

38. DAVID MOYER AND HERBERT A. GREENBERG, "What Makes a Good Salesman," *Harvard Business Review* (July–August 1964), pp. 119–125.

39. Classified Post, *South China Morning Post*, 49, no. 193 (July 14, 1993), p. 3.

40. REG A. MADISON, *Selection, Training, and Retention: LIMRA's Market Facts*, Vol. 10, Issue 5 (September–October 1991), pp. 22–25.

41. JAMES M. COMER AND , ALAN J. DUBINSKY, *Managing the Successful Sales Force* (Lexington, Mass.: Lexington Books, 1985), pp. 5–25.

42. THOMAS N. INGRAM, CHARLES H. J. SCHUEPHER, AND DON HUTSON, "Why Salespeople Fail," *Industrial Marketing Management*, 21, no. 3 (August 1992), pp. 225–230.

43. JUDI BROWNELL, "Listening: The Toughest Management Skills," *Cornell Hotel and Restaurant Administration*

Quarterly, 27, no 4. (February 1987), pp. 64–71.

44. Harley Mayersohn, "That Dog Won't Hunt: Why What You've Always Done Won't Work Anymore," *Cornell Hotel and Restaurant Administration Quarterly*, 35, no. 5 (October 1994), p. 82.

45. Howard Friertag, "Sales Directors Build Productivity and Profitability," *Hotel and Motel Management*, 207, no. 19 (November 2, 1992), p. 14.

46. Florence Berger, Mark D. Fulford, and Michelle Krazmien, "Human Resource Management in the 21st Century: Predicting Partnerships for Profit," *Hospitality Research Journal*, 17, no. 1 (1993), pp. 90–91.

47. "U.S. Hoteliers Fail to Net Enough World Cup Trade," *Travel Trade Gazette*, U.K. and Ireland (June 1, 1994), p. 32.

48. Neil Rackman, *SPIN Selling* .

49. Jeffrey Z. Rubin and Bert R. Brown, *The Social Psychology of Bargaining and Negotiation* (New York: Academic Press, 1975), p. 18.

50. For additional reading, see Howard Raiffa, *The Art and Science of Negotiation* (Cambridge, Mass.: Harvard University Press, 1982); Samuel B. Bacharach and Edward J. Lawler, *Bargaining Power, Tactics, and Outcome* (San Francisco: Jossey-Bass, 1981); Herb Cohen, *You Can Negotiate Anything* (New York: Bantam Books, 1980); and Gerald I. Nierenberg, *The Art of Negotiating* (New York: Pocket Books, 1984).

51. Lamar Lee and Donald W. Dobler, *Purchasing and Materials Management* (New York: McGraw-Hill, 1977), pp. 146–147.

52. This discussion of zone of agreement is fully developed in Raiffa, *Art and Science of Negotiation*.

53. Roger Fisher and William Ury, *Getting to Yes: Negotiating Agreement without Giving in* (Boston: Houghton Mifflin, 1981).

54. See Gilber A. Churchill Jr., Neil A. Ford, and Orville C. Walker Jr., *Sales Force Management: Planning, Implementation, and Control* (Homewood, Ill.: Irwin, 1985).

55. See Ken W. McCleary and Pamela A. Weaver, "The Job Offer: What Today's Graduates Want," *Cornell Hotel and Restaurant Administration Quarterly*, 28, no. 4 (February 1988), pp. 28–31.

56. David V. Pavesic and Robert A. Brymer, "Job Satisfaction: What's Happening to Young Managers," *Cornell Hotel and Restaurant Administration Quarterly*, 30, no. 4 (February 1990), pp. 90–96.

57. Richard Cavalier, *Sales Meetings That Work* (Homewood, Ill: Dow-Jones, Irwin, 1983).

58. See Joyce I. Nies and Richard F. Tas, "How to Add Visual Impact to Your Presentations," *Cornell Hotel and Restaurant Administration Quarterly*, 32, no. 1 (May 1991), pp. 46–51.

59. "Dunfey Hotels Corporation: An Interview with Jon Canas, President," Harvard Business School, Publishing Division, Boston, MA 02163-1098, video, case number 9-883-502.

60. "Are Salespeople Gaining More Selling Time," *Sales and Marketing Management*, (July 1986), p. 29.

Destination Marketing

*T*he Greater Milwaukee Convention and Visitors Bureau (GMCVB) want-ed to produce a brochure with 20 reasons to visit Milwaukee, targeted at travel writers. Mary Denis, the bureau's tourism director, stated, "Originally we envisioned some type of four-color brochure."[1] The audience for the brochure was later expanded to include the group market: meeting planners, association executives, and tour operators.

    The advertising and public relations firm of Sprecher/Barrett/Bertalot and Company was given the task of creating the promotional piece. As it developed, John Sprecher was worried because the promotional piece did not have a theme. The day before the campaign was to be presented to the GMCVB, Sprecher was driving to a golf tournament sponsored by the GMCVB. He popped a CD of The BoDeans, a nationally known musical group from Milwaukee, into the car's CD player. While he was listening to the CD, he came up with the idea of packaging the promotion as a CD, a CD of Milwaukee's own BoDeans. Sprecher had previously talked to the group about doing a television commercial for Milwaukee. Although the television commercial was never pro-duced, he remembered that the group was eager to help their hometown. He called the group's manager and asked if they would be willing to help on this promotion. The BoDeans and their record company, Slash Records, responded by donating a never before released single to the GMCVB.

The result was "20 Spins on Milwaukee." The front cover of the CD unfolded into a brochure that had 20 different spins on things to do in Milwaukee. The following are examples of the spins:

Now You Can Spell Us Milwalkee. *A little bit of San Antonio come to Milwaukee in the romantic, glimmering new $10 million Riverwalk. Meandering along the peaceful Milwaukee River through the very heart of downtown, Riverwalk leads you to shops, dining, entertainment, and fun.*

Open 365 Days a Year. *Milwaukee is a city that plays, weather or not. Come summer, along comes Summerfest—the world's greatest music festival—attracting over 1 million partiers to the city's beautiful lakefront. And in winter? Well, nothing's cooler than Milwaukee's Winterfest, a city-wide, 10 day frolic of snow sculpting, ice skating, and warm camaraderie.*

Would You Like Water with That? *In Chicago, it's Rush Street. But in Milwaukee, the rush is on to downtown's Water Street, a magnificent mile of pubs, eateries, sports bars, live music, and good times. Just one block form the Milwaukee River and Riverwalk, Water Street rocks and rollicks every night with wall-to-wall friendlies.*

Bill Hanbury, president and CEO of GMCVB, described the CD as an excellent way to promote Milwaukee. "Milwaukee is experiencing a renaissance, and we've finally found the perfect vehicle to convey the exciting things that are happening."[2] Dawn Poker, director of sales for the GMCVB, said that one unanticipated benefit of the promotion was that it repositioned Milwaukee from a sleepy mid-western town to a vibrant city. The innovativeness of the CD as a promotion had a halo effect—people now think of Milwaukee as an innovative city.

Tourist destinations are products. They need to be positioned and promoted just as other products do. John Sprecher feels that agencies and convention and tourist bureaus are often too familiar with a city that they are trying to promote. He advises that they step back and gain a fresh perspective on the destination that they are about to promote by taking a tour of the city, a tour that would be given to a visiting travel writer or meeting planner.

The chapter opens with a discussion of the importance of tourism to the world's economy. This is followed by a discussion of the benefits of tourism to local economies.

Next the chapter discusses **tourism strategies and investments**. This is followed by a section on the **segmenting and monitoring of the tourist market**. Next we discuss the importance of **communicating with the tourist market**. This involves creating and maintaining the proper image and communicating to the market about the area's tourist attractions. The chapter ends with a discussion on **organizing and managing tourism**.

The word *tourism* has many definitions. We will use the British Tourist Authority's definition of tourism: "a stay of one or more nights away from home for holidays, visits to friends or relatives, business conferences or any other purpose except such things as boarding education or semipermanent employment."[3] This book uses the words tourism and travel interchangeably.

In discussing tourism, we need to address the following questions:

- How important can tourism be to a destination's economy?
- What kinds of strategies and investments must destination planners make to be competitive in the tourist industry?
- How can the tourist market be segmented and monitored for shifting trends, lifestyles, needs, and preferences?
- What kinds of messages and media are effective in developing and maintaining a destination's desired image?
- How should a visitor destination's marketing organization be managed?

In 1990, Cunard Lines celebrated the 150th anniversary of its first passenger ship service across the Atlantic. Cunard's transatlantic line was the first such service offered in 1840; virtually hundreds of competitors existed by 1920, and by 1990 Cunard was the last Atlantic passenger ship service left. In the interim, the world of travel had been revolutionized. The world had become a global community opening places unimaginable decades earlier: the wonders of Antarctica, the secrets of the Himalayas, the rain forests of the Amazon, the beauty of Tahiti, the Great Wall of China, the dramatic Victoria Falls, the origin of the Nile, and the wilds of Scottish islands. Travel has become a global business whose expanding market now leaves no place untouched.

According to the World Tourism Organization (WTO) of the United Nations, more than 500 million tourists traveled internationally in 1993, spending over $300 billion (excluding transportation). Tourism accounts for 8% of total world exports, more than 31% of international trade in services, and more than 100 million jobs worldwide. It employs more people than any single industrial sector and has infrastructure (lodging, transportation, and restaurants) investment conservatively estimated to exceed $3 trillion.[4]

Travel now affects every continent, country, and city. The economy is influenced either by people traveling elsewhere (import spending in other places) or travel service exports (expenditures by nonresidents in that place). Visitor destinations must decide how much travel service business they want to capture, because travel is today's fastest-growing business and is expected to become the world's largest industry in the next century. Yet, as an industry, it is subject to cycles, fashions, and intense competition.

THE GLOBALIZATION OF THE TOURIST INDUSTRY

IMPORTANCE OF TOURISM TO A DESTINATION'S ECONOMY

The Tourism Destination

Tourists travel to destinations. Destinations are places with some form of actual or perceived boundary, such as the physical boundary of an island, political boundaries, or even market-created boundaries such as those of a travel wholesaler who defines a South Pacific tour solely as Australia and New Zealand. Central America consists of seven nations, but few if any national tourist offices or tour planners view it that way. A commonly packaged tour of Central America includes only two or three nations, such as Costa Rica, Guatemala, and Panama. Others are excluded for reasons of political instability or deficient infrastructure.

Although Australia and New Zealand are often packaged together for the North American visitor, Australia has worked hard for many years to make it a single destination, rather than share the limited vacation time of Americans and Canadians. In turn, destinations within Australia, such as the state of Western Australia or cities such as Perth or Adelaide, feel that they must develop a distinct destination reputation to avoid being left out or used only as overnight stopovers.

The desire to become a recognized destination presents a difficult marketing challenge. Within eastern North Carolina, the town of New Bern has several interesting visitor attractions and events. The remainder of the county offers considerably less, yet visitor promotion funds are collected from a county-wide hotel bed tax. Political pressure has forced tourism officials to promote Craven County as a destination, rather than the town of New Bern. The promotion of a relatively unfamiliar town poses sufficient problems, but the promotion of a county greatly intensifies the challenge.

Macro destinations such as the United States contain thousands of micro destinations, including regions, states, cities, towns, and even visitor destinations within a town. It is not unusual to find tourists who view their Hawaiian destination as the Kahala Hilton or the Hilton Hawaiian Village in Honolulu and may rarely if ever venture outside the perimeter of these destination resorts. Thousands of visitors fly to Orlando and proceed directly to Disney World, where most or all of their vacation is spent. These tourists do not view Florida or Orlando as their destinations, but rather Disney World.

Benefits of Tourism

Tourism's most visible benefit is direct employment in hotels, restaurants, retail establishments, and transportation. A second but less visible benefit consists of support industries and professions (such as yield management consultants, university tourism professors, and others), many of which pay considerably more than the visible employment opportunities such as restaurant personnel. The third benefit of tourism is the multiplier effect as tourist expenditures are recycled through the local economy. Governments use economic impact models to estimate overall employment gains in goods and services consumption resulting from tourism multipliers. Tourism's fourth benefit is state and local revenues derived from taxes on tourism.

Tourism helps shift the tax burden to nonresidents. For example, tourism accounts for more than half of Bermuda's foreign exchange and tax revenues. Bermuda's $20 per head embarkation fee is one of the highest in

Islands in The South Pacific, such as Bora Bora, count on tourism to bring in much needed foreign currency. Courtesy of Club Med.

the world, as are its import taxes on durables from cars to refrigerators. It is one of the few developed countries without an income tax. New York's cumulative bed tax on hotel rooms raises more than $300 million in annual revenues. Dallas, Los Angeles, and Houston all have bed taxes in excess of 12%. Hawaii derives nearly 40% of its total state and county taxes from tourism. Taxation of travelers has become a popular, often hidden, tax, jumping by an estimated $2.5 billion in the United States alone in 1991 due to airline ticket taxes, hotel taxes, and other user fees.[5]

Critics of such taxation contend that these schemes are taxation without representation and eventually lead to careless government spending or spending that has little relevance to promoting tourism and enhancing the travel experience. Hospitality and travel managers must make sure that bed taxes and other tourist-related taxes go back into promoting tourism and developing the infrastructure to support tourism.

Tourism also yields a fifth benefit: It stimulates exports of place-made products. Estimates of visitor spending on gifts, clothing, and souvenirs are in the range of 15% to 20% of total expenditures. The degree to which these products are made or assembled in a destination affects the economic impact on the local economy.

Destinations, however, may not uniformly welcome tourists. Due to location, climate, limited resources, size, and cultural heritage, some places have few economic choices other than to participate in tourism. Some engage in tourism with mixed emotions and, at times, ambivalence. For instance, Bali is concerned that tourism is destroying its culture as farmland becomes resorts and new jobs unravel family values. "Bali and tourism is not a marriage of love," observed a Bali tourism official, clearly focusing on the dilemma of cultural breakdown and an economy booming from the receipts of 500,000 tourists a year.[6] Londoners need, but are not enthusiastic about, the Arab tourist influx. Many European capitals experience a mass summer exodus of residents to avoid incoming summer tourists.

Some people and businesses benefit from tourism; others may not. While a destination's economy may be better off from tourism, residents sometimes feel that losses in quality of life, convenience, and cultural and social values are not worth the economic benefits. Marketing Highlight 20-1 describes the debate about tourism in San Francisco.

Management of the Tourist Destination

Destinations that fail to maintain the necessary infrastructure or build inappropriate infrastructure run significant risks. Italy's Adriatic Sea coast has been devastated by the adverse publicity associated with the growth of brown algae that made bathing nearly impossible. Growing pollution levels at the Grand Canyon and overcrowding in Yosemite Valley may significantly diminish the attractiveness of these great national parks. Some of East Africa's renowned game parks are being turned into dust bowls by tourists ferried around in four-wheel-drive vehicles.

A destination's attractiveness can be diminished by violence, political instability, natural catastrophe, adverse environmental factors, and overcrowding. Greece's national treasure, the formerly white marble Parthenon in Athens, stands as a pollution-stained symbol of environmental neglect. Thailand's beautiful beach resorts and temples have been severely damaged by pollution and poor sanitation. The Indian government's plans to create a "Visit India Year" were undermined not only by sectarian and caste violence, but also plane crashes. Western countries, including the United States and Japan, declared India to be an unsafe destination.

A theory offered by futurist August St. John argues that a resort destination will experience a life cycle similar to the product life cycle and eventually go into decline, or the destruction stage as St. John calls it.[7] Tourism managers must manage their products and make sure that during the growth stage the foundation is built for an infrastructure that will support future tourism demands. In some cases, sustaining tourism in the mature stage may mean limiting the amount of tourists to a number that the infrastructure can handle. Tourist development must balance the temptation to maximize tourist dollars with preservation of the natural tourist attractions and the quality of life for local residents. This is often a difficult task (see Marketing Highlight 20-2 on page 640). Those tourist destinations that do not manage their product may have a short life. Those tourist destinations that build solid infrastructures can look for increased business by expanding from a seasonal product to a multiseasonal product or by expanding the geographical base of their product. For example, Aspen, Colorado, expanded from winter skiing to summer recreation, education, and culture. Quebec promotes summer–fall tourism and its winter carnival and skiing. West Virginia is popular in the summer–fall season, but also aggressively promotes the spring and winter season.

Stratford, Canada's Shakespeare Festival began as a small regional event and became a North American event for the United States and Canada. Most musical and cultural festivals in Europe followed the same pattern, such as Salzburg, Edinburgh, and Spoleto. Europe's Festival of Arts

Marketing Highlight 20-1

Lifting the Fog

Can a city place too much emphasis on tourism and hospitality industries? Are there risks? That's the question being debated in San Francisco these days, a city in which one of eight dollars in its economy comes from visitors' spending and where tourism employs more city residents than any other business.

Among the issues of public concern are how much the visitor industry actually generates for the city's economy. California's Department of Commerce estimates that San Francisco had 32,500 visitor-derived workers earning $47 million in 1986 and $78 million in visitor-generated local tax revenues, while the city's Convention Bureau estimates are double that. For the city's 3000 eating establishments and 25,000 hotel rooms, worries abound about the growth of low-paying, nonunion wages and workers. As important as the tourism and convention business is to San Francisco's economy, crit-

ics are equally concerned about the city's loss of financial service, corporate relocation to the suburbs, and the relative decline of shipping and other industrial-era businesses.

San Francisco must decide among three broad alternatives: (1) pursue tourism even more aggressively because its physical and historical beauty provides it with a competitive advantage in this industry; (2) hold tourism to its present level and invest in building other industries more aggressively; and (3) build tourism and other industries in a balanced way. The decision is not easy because of the conflicting interests of different voting blocks.

Sources: Louis Trager, "Trouble in Touristland," *San Francisco Examiner*, July 30, 1989, p. D1; and Carla Marinucci, "What Becomes a Legend Most," *San Francisco Examiner*, July 30, 1989, pp. D1–4.

---

provides a selection among 50 musical festivals from Norway to Spain, with several dozen dance competitions, major summer art exhibits, and theater from London's West End to Berlin's Festival Weeks. The entire European continent, including Eastern Europe, has exploded in summer-place competition for tourists.

Tourist competition is fierce amid a growing and constantly changing tourist market. In addition to strong tourist destinations, declining places upgrade and make new investments and new places appear. Leavenworth, Washington, an old logging and mining town, experienced revival when it transformed itself into a Bavarian village. Winterset, Iowa, John Wayne's birthplace, is now visited by tourists. Seymour, Wisconsin, lays claim to being home of the first hamburger, hosting August Hamburger Days. Seymour organizers cooked the world's largest hamburger, weighing 5520 pounds.

Countless examples exist of places rediscovering their past, capitalizing on the birthplace of a famous person, an event, a battle, or other "hidden gems." Places rely on various monikers for identification: Sheboygan, Wisconsin, as City of Cheese, Choirs, Children, and Churches; Crystal City, Texas, as the Spinach Capital of the World; Lexington, Kentucky, as the Athens of the West; New Haven, Connecticut, as the City of Elms. Many places still bear nicknames of their economic heritage: Hartford, Connecticut,

TOURISM STRATEGIES AND INVESTMENTS

Marketing Highlight 20-2

"Stop the Brutal Marketing"

Bumper stickers in the resort town of Steamboat Springs, Colorado, publicly proclaim dissatisfaction with tourism promotion. "Stop the Brutal Marketing of Steamboat" may be seen on local autos and pick-up trucks. Many are driven by employees of the visitor industry. A restaurant hostess, a beer truck driver, an art gallery assistant manager, and a convenience store clerk represent Steamboat's protesting citizens whose livelihood is directly derived from visitors.

Throughout the Rocky Mountain states, citizens are in revolt against the tourist industry. Colorado residents may vote that public funds should no longer be earmarked for tourism promotion. Advertising and promotion of Steamboat are supported by roughly $600,000 of tax-generated revenue. These funds and the marketing staff and programs that they support are clearly at risk.

"Greedy tourism developers brought us a bitter lemon but tell us it is a sweet plum. What is so sweet about $6.00 per hour waiter and bed-making jobs in a community where a home is unaffordable, our streets are crowded with vehicles, and the term professional career opportunity often means a night manager in a roadside motel, renamed a resort hotel?"

Summit County, Colorado, one and a half hours away, is home to resorts such as Breckenridge. It is also a parking lot for a large and ever-growing complex of factory outlet stores at the base of some of the most majestic scenery in the nation. That's what many in Steamboat fear. Residents of Steamboat Springs and other resort communities point to visitor surveys in which respondents state that they are searching for a refreshing mountain experience. When asked what this means, visitors reply that they want to see clear streams, fresh air, uncluttered mountain views, and mountain meadows filled with Hereford cows, not houseware stores. Once constructed, those houseware, clothing, and luggage outlets produce much more revenue than is possible from Herefords. Consequently, their numbers grow as the Herefords decline.

Opponents of tourism promotion point to the growth of specialty manufacturing in Colorado cities such as Durango. Steamboat Springs is home to TIC, a national construction company with sales of nearly one-half billion dollars per year. Many feel that the funds currently used to promote tourism could better be utilized to encourage and develop new enterprises that might one day become other TICs.

An expanding tourism base inevitably places a heavy burden on infrastructure, available land, and air quality. Opponents worry that dependency on an expanded visitor industry places a community at risk of economic cycles similar to those of cities, which previously depended on steel, rubber, or chemicals.

Quality versus quantity is a phrase often heard in the Rocky Mountains. "We're not opposed to the visitor industry, but we see no need for uncontrolled mass tourism," say the opponents. Why must the visitor industry set objectives of ever increasing numbers of tourists, hotel occupancy, automobiles, or mountain bike riders? Are we really better off with crowded streets and sidewalks, or was the previous balance between ranching, mining, and tourism a better model? Couldn't the industry improve the quality of its existing product, charge higher rates, and attract a higher-class visitor, or must we forever measure success by head count?"

How can the visitor industry sustain itself if industry workers cannot find affordable lodging in the town and must drive an hour or more over an icy mountain pass? Why should quality visitors continue to select this destination if they must stand in line and receive uncaring, depersonalized service by disenfranchised employees?

Hospitality industry executives and tourism marketers, however, disagree. "We are witnessing the pack mentality of suicidal lemmings. Tourism promotion brought this community year-round employment and annual increases in sales tax receipts accompanied by help wanted signs."

as Insurance City; Holyoke, Massachusetts, as Paper City; Westfield, New York, as Buggy Whip City; and Paterson, New Jersey, as Silk City. These destinations are not likely to become international tourist destinations, but they can be effective tourist products in the regional tourism market.

With the current U.S. trend toward shorter but more frequent vacations, many places within 200 miles or so of major metropolitan areas have found new opportunities to access the tourist market. Local tourism and convention bureaus tout the theme, "Stay Close to Home." The Louisiana Office of Tourism spent $6 million to market a summer travel bargain program to a 500-mile market.

Newer destinations are also appearing. The 1970s ushered in an era of theme parks led by Disneyland (Anaheim, 1961) and Walt Disney World (Orlando, 1972). More than 100 theme parks have since opened in the United States, some in cities, but most near major interstate highways accessible to several markets. Many have failed, did not meet expectations, or priced themselves out of family budgets. Given Walt Disney Company's success, many places have sought replication on a smaller scale. Tokyo's Disneyland has been a success, and a $4.4 billion Disneyland opened 20 miles outside of Paris in 1992. This new Euro Disneyland spreads over 5000 acres and is one-fifth the size of Paris. Some French critics have complained that Disney characters will pollute the nation's cultural ambience, but most anticipate eventual success and look forward to a future European EPCOT Center.

Investment in Tourist Attractions

To attract tourists, destinations must respond to the travel basics of cost, convenience, and timeliness. Tourists, like other consumers, weigh costs against the benefits of specific destinations—and investment of time, effort, and resources against a reasonable return in education, experience, fun, relaxation, and memories. Convenience takes on various meanings in travel decisions: time involved in travel from airport to lodging, language barriers, cleanliness and sanitary concerns, access to interests (beaches, attractions, amenities), and special needs (elderly, disabled, children, dietary, medical care, fax and communication, auto rental). Timeliness embraces factors that introduce risk to travel such as civil disturbances, political instability, currency fluctuations, safety, and sanitary conditions.

Places are increasingly developing events as a vital component in attracting tourists. Small or rural places typically initiate an event such as a festival to establish their identity. Urban newspapers and suburban weeklies often publish a listing of events, festivals, and celebrations occurring within a day's driving distance. State and local tourism offices do the same, making sure that travel agents, restaurants, hotels, airports, and train and bus stations have event-based calendars for posting. Nearly every European country now has a 900 number that you can call in the United States to get a listing of forthcoming events. Major U.S. cities have summer programs of scheduled events and some, such as Milwaukee, have well-established year-round events. Milwaukee's June–September lakefront festivals (Festa Italiana, German Fest, Afro Fest, Polish Fest, and others) attract tourists regionally and nationally.

Tourism investment ranges from relatively low cost market entry for festivals or events to multimillion dollar infrastructure costs of stadiums, transit systems, airports, and convention centers. Regardless of the cost, urban renewal planners seek to build tourism into the heart of their city's revitalization. Boston's Quincy Market, New York's Lincoln Center, and San Francisco's Fisherman's Wharf are examples. The ability to concentrate attractions, facilities, and services in a convenient, accessible location is essential to create a strong destination pull.

In centrally planned economies (Eastern Europe and developing countries), governments control, plan, and direct tourist development. Tourism is necessary to earn hard currencies for trade and development and serves national purposes. Tourist expansion is highly dependent on public investments, which have proved to be woefully inadequate without private investment and market mechanisms to respond to changing consumer needs and wants. These nations now promote private investment through joint ventures, foreign ownership, and time sharing for individual investors. The new Mexican Riviera (Puerto Vallarta, Cancun, Ixtapa) is an example of public–private combinations of successful tourism investments where state investment in infrastructure works with private investment in tourist amenities, from hotels, restaurants, and golf courses to shopping areas.

Destination tourism in the United States increasingly builds on public–private partnerships or joint development in planning, financing, and implementation. Public authority is required to clear, develop, and write down land costs and make infrastructure investments. The destination must often subsidize or provide tax incentives for private investment in hotels, convention centers, transit, and parking. Restoration is often carried out by nonprofit development corporations from the National Historic Trust to the U.S. Park Service, with private investment promoted through various tax incentives. From airlines to hotels, the tourist industry provides dedicated tax revenues from fuel, leases, bed taxes, and sales taxes to support a long-term bonus for capital construction of tourist-related infrastructure and other public improvements. Such steps made it possible for New York City to add the Southport Sea Museum, Javits Convention Center, and Ellis Island Immigration Museum to its tourist attraction portfolio.

Destinations must make more than financial or hospitality investments to attract tourists. Places find that they must expand public services, specifically public safety, traffic and crowd control, emergency health, sanitation, and street cleaning. They also must promote tourism internally to their own citizens and businesses—retailers, travel agencies, restaurants, financial institutions, public and private transit, lodging, police, and public servants. They must invest in recruiting training, licensing, and monitoring tourist-related businesses and employees. Singapore's cab drivers are known for their professional training and service, which include English language exams, safety programs, and location skills. Some places invest little in that area, even though airport cabs and public transit may be the first encounter points that visitors have with a place and can be critical to tourist satisfaction.

SEGMENTING AND MONITORING THE TOURIST MARKET

The decision to spend one's disposable income on travel versus new furniture, a boat or other purchase alternatives involves important psychological

Table 20-1

Psychological Determinants of Demand

Prestige   A level of prestige has always been attached to travelers, particularly long-distance travelers. Marco Polo gained historical fame through travel, as did the heroes of Greek and Roman mythology, such as Ulysses. Travel to Aspen, the Riviera, Switzerland, and many other destinations provides the traveler with a level of prestige, if only in the mind of the traveler.

Escape   The desire to momentarily escape from the day-to-day rhythm of one's life is a basic human need. Travel marketers have long recognized this need, as reflected by glamorous advertisements in which the word escape is often mentioned.

Sexual opportunity   This has both a positive and an ugly side. Travel has long been viewed as a means to meet attractive people. This has been part of the heritage of transatlantic ocean travel, the Orient Express, and riverboat travel. Unfortunately, the existence of sex tours to certain Oriental nations and the preponderance of houses of prostitution in some destination areas provide examples of a darker side.

Education   Travel in and of itself has historically been viewed as broadening. Many deeper psychological reasons for travel are masked by the rationale that educational benefits outweigh the cost, risks, and stress.

Social interaction   The opportunity to meet and interact with people previously unknown is a powerful motivator. Destination resorts and cruise lines commonly appeal to this need.

Family bonding   Family reunions have become an important market segment for many in the travel industry. In an era of intense pressure on the family, such as two careers, there is a strong need to refocus priorities and bond as a family. Unfortunately, the types of vacations selected by families do not always lead to bonding. If adults participate all day in activities such as diving, skiing, or golf, young children may be relegated to organized kids programs and experience little bonding with parents.

Relaxation   Observers of human and animal conduct sometimes state that the human being is either alone or among a limited number of species that continue to play into adulthood. Destination resorts and cruise ships best exemplify need fulfillment for play. It is small wonder that cruise line travel has become a "destination" in direct competition with land-bound places.

Self-discovery   For many, travel offers the opportunity to "find oneself." Witness the action of many people following a dramatic event in their lives, such as a divorce or the death of a family member. Throughout recorded history, people have sought self-discovery by "visiting the mountain," "finding solace in the desert," and "losing oneself." Many cultures, including so-called primitive ones, have encouraged or even forced their youth to travel alone to find self-discovery.[8] Youth hotels throughout the world serve a group of travelers, many of whom are seeking self-discovery. Temporary employment opportunities at resorts are often filled by those taking time off to learn more about who they are and wish to be. The concept of "holistic vacations" has been developed for individuals seeking self-discovery.[9]

determinants. Table 20-1 lists some of the major psychological determinants of demand for tourism. These determinants can be used as segmentation variables. Demographics and lifestyles are also important segmentation variables.

The growing percentage of retired Americans has vastly expanded the tourism business. An increasing percentage of two-career couples has resulted in a trend toward shorter, more frequent vacations. Longer vacations (10 or more nights) have been declining for years, while shorter vacations (3 nights including weekends) have become increasingly popular. Hotels and airlines have accommodated these trends with low-cost weekend excursion packages. Business travel now includes mixed business and leisure. To capture the trend toward shorter vacations within driving distance of home, new local and regional tourist attractions have been growing, as have family-oriented resorts.

Foreign visitor travel has become an increasingly important segment of the North American travel industry. Since the decline of the U.S. and Canadian dollars, foreign tourism has grown each year. British Isles visitors seek out New York and Florida, while Continental visitors have a strong fascination for the U.S. West, particularly California. Hawaii's tourist market consists of 66% from the mainland and 20% from Japan. Hawaii targets Japan because of its high GNP and spending and because 50% of all Japanese visitors to the U.S. mainland spend part of the trip in Hawaii. The Japanese repeat market outspends U.S. mainland visitors by a 4 to 1 margin, $586 per day versus $119 per day.

Accommodating changing life-styles and needs is a dynamic challenge for the tourism industry in light of demographic trends and income shifts. The high-living baby boomers of yesterday are today's older baby boomers. Where baby boomers once opted for status destinations and elaborate accommodations, older baby boomers now opt for all-inclusive resorts and package tours that promise comfort, consistency, and cost effectiveness. Indeed, some see travelers in the 1990s returning to the 1950s style vacation that their parents enjoyed. These "new traditionalists" look for bargains, up-front costs, flexibility, and convenience.

Tourism planners must consider how many tourists are desired, which segments to attract, and how to balance tourism with other industries. Choices will be constrained by the destinations' climate, natural topography, resources, history, culture, and facilities. Like other enterprises, tourist marketers must know the actual and potential customers and their needs and wants, determine which target markets to serve, and decide on appropriate products, services, and programs.

Not every tourist is interested in a particular destination. A destination would waste its money trying to attract everyone who travels. Instead of a shotgun approach, destinations must take a rifle approach and sharply define target markets.

Identifying Target Markets

A destination can identify its natural target markets in two ways. One is to collect information about its current visitors. Where do they come from? Why do they come? What are their demographic characteristics? How satisfied are they? How many are repeat visitors? How much do they spend? By examining these and other questions, planners can determine which visitors should be targeted.

The second approach is to audit the destination's attractions and select segments that might logically have an interest in them. We cannot assume that current visitors reflect all the potentially interested groups. For example, if Kenya promoted only safaris, it would miss groups interested in native culture, flora, or bird species.

Tourist segments are attracted by different features. The local tourist board or council could benefit by asking questions keyed to segmentation variables. These variables—attractions sought, market areas or locations, customer characteristics, and/or benefits sought—can help to define the best segments to target.

After a place identifies its natural target markets, tourism planners should conduct research to determine where these tourists are found. Which countries contain a large number of citizens who have the means and motivation to enjoy the particular place? For example, Aruba attracts mainly sun and fun tourists. The United States, Canada, and certain European countries are good sources. Eastern Europeans are ruled out because they lack the purchasing power. Australians are ruled out because they have their own nearby sun and fun destinations, even though "Aussies" are frequent travelers.

This analysis can uncover many or few natural target markets. If many are identified, the relative potential profit from each should be evaluated. The potential profit of a target tourist segment is the difference between the amount that the tourist segment is likely to spend and the cost of attracting and serving this segment. The promotional cost depends on the budget. The serving cost depends on the infrastructure requirements. Ultimately, potential tourist segments should be ranked and selected in order of their profitability.

If the analysis identifies too few natural tourist segments, investments may be needed in infrastructure and visitor attractions. Visitor industry investments consist of infrastructure improvements (hotels, transportation, and the like) and attractions that can potentially attract new types of tourists. The payoff from these investments may come only some years later, but this lag is often necessary if the destination is to become an active participant in an increasingly competitive marketplace.

Consider Ireland, which continues to attract many tourists, not only ethnic Irish from North America, but also many Europeans. The Irish Tourist Board recently observed that many young European tourists visited the Emerald Isle to enjoy its natural, unspoiled beauty as backpackers and campers, but spent little. A serious question for Ireland was whether its tourism scorecard should be based on the number of tourists attracted (the prevailing standard) or their spending level. A consensus emerged that Ireland should try to attract a relatively small market of high-income tourists who stay longer, spend more, and are culturally and environmentally compatible.

Toward this end, the Irish Tourist Board now touts not only Ireland's mountains, water, and ancient buildings, but also its literary giants, such as Oscar Wilde, George Bernard Shaw, and James Joyce. The Board wants to attract high-income, culture-seeking tourists to Dublin, where the Irish sparkling speech and wit can be experienced. The Irish are also ready to improve Dublin's hotel and restaurant facilities as an act of investment marketing.

Whatever tourist segment a destination seeks, it needs to be very specific. A ski area attracts skiers. Natural reefs attract snorkelers and divers.

This advertisement targets families living in cities in south and central Florida.
Courtesy of Robinson, Yesawich & Pepperdine, Inc.

Arts and crafts attract the art crowd, and gambling attracts gaming tourists. Yet, even with such givens, potential visitors must be segmented by additional characteristics. Sun Valley, Aspen, Vail, and Alta appeal to upper-income and professional skiers, and Keystone, Winter Park, Cooper Mountain, and Telluride attract the family market. Tahoe and Squaw Valley draw the skiing–gaming markets. Monte Carlo appeals to an international gaming segment, while Deauville, France, promotes a more regional gaming market near Paris.

Classification of Visitor Segments

Several classifications have been used to describe different visitor destination segments. The most commonly used classifications are based on whether the tourist travels with a group or independently. The common terms are the group inclusive tour (GIT) for group travel and IT—the *independent traveler*. National tourism offices, international airlines, and others involved in international travel frequently use these designations.

Here are some classifications describing tourists by their degree of institutionalization and their impact on the destinations.[10]

Organized mass tourist. This corresponds to the GIT. These people have little or no influence over their travel experience other than to purchase one package or another. They commonly travel in a group, view the destination through the windows of a tour bus, and remain in preselected hotels. Shopping in the local market often provides their only contact with the native population.

Individual mass tourist. These people are similar to the previous category but have somewhat more control over their itinerary. For instance, they may rent an auto to visit attractions.

Explorer. These people fall in the IT classification. They plan their own itineraries and make their own reservations, although they may use a travel agent. They tend to be very sociable people who enjoy interacting with individuals at the destination.

Drifters. These are the backpacker crowd who will seldom if ever be found in a traditional hotel. They may stay at youth hotels with friends or camp out. They tend to mix with lower socioeconomic native groups and are commonly found riding third-class rail or bus. Most tend to be young.

Another well-known tourist classification system is known as Plog's categorization.[11] (See Figure 20-1.) These designations are similar to the previously mentioned groups, but range from psychocentric to allocentric. Plog observed that destinations are first discovered by allocentrics (backpackers or explorers). As the natives discover the economic benefits of tourism, services and infrastructure are developed. When this occurs, allocentrics are turned off and find another unspoiled destination. The nature of visitors now changes, with each new group somewhat less adventurous than the previous, perhaps older, and certainly more demanding of creature comforts and service. Finally, a destination becomes so familiar that the least adventurous group of psychocentrics finds it acceptable.

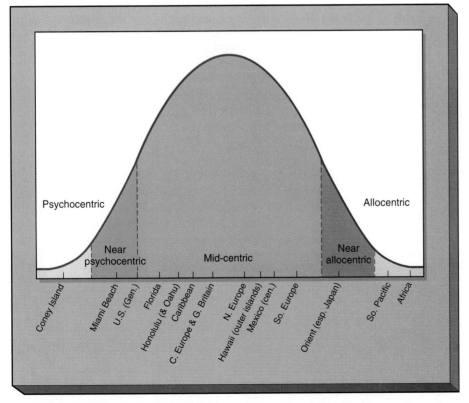

Figure 20-1
Plog's categorization of destinations, the height of the curve indicates the number of travelers in each category. Reprinted by permission of Elsevier Science, "Why Destinations Rise and Fall in Popularity," by Stanley C. Plog, *Cornell Hotel and Restaurant Administration,* vol. 14, no. 4, p. 58, ©1974 by Cornell University.

Monitoring the Tourist Markets

Tourist markets are dynamic, and a marketing information system is part of any well-run tourist organization. Destinations need to closely monitor the relative popularity of their various attractions by determining the number and type of tourists attracted to each. The popularity of the Metropolitan Museum of Art, Big Ben, or the Colosseum can suddenly or gradually change. Marketing information systems help to identify and predict environmental trends that are responsible for these changes. Information should be collected on the changes in the wants of existing markets, emerging markets, and potential target markets. For example, in the mid-1990s the Japanese yen appreciated relative to Western currencies. Australia, a popular destination for the Japanese, now became even more of a value because of the increased purchasing power of the Japanese tourist. The state of Queensland increased its marketing efforts toward the Japanese to take advantage of the favorable currency exchange.

The Las Vegas Convention and Visitors Authority (LVCVA) conducts an annual tourist profile. Information for this profile is collected through customer surveys on an ongoing basis. Survey results indicate that the majority of visitors spend less than 4 hours a day gambling. The visitors are coming for entertainment and the nongaming amenities of the megaresorts. This information has helped to attract a number of new restaurants, such as Spago, Wolfgang Puck's, Cafe Coyote, Planet Hollywood, and The Dive. Las Vegas is quickly developing a reputation as a restaurant town. This further enhances its image as a diverse destination, rather than just a gaming venue.

One job of a tourist organization is to increase the accessibility of a destination. The LVCVA uses information from its survey to identify emerging markets that can support direct airline flights. Armed with current travel patterns and projected travel patterns based on their surveys, the LVCVA makes presentations to airlines, trying to convince them to start new routes, which will be profitable for the airlines and provide another region of the country with direct air service to Las Vegas. The accessibility of Las Vegas by frequent and relatively inexpensive airfare is in part responsible for it being one of the top convention centers in the United States. This did not happen by accident; it happened as a result of efforts by the LVCVA.

The Wales Tourist Bureau used market research to identify a target market for the Swansea Marina. Using research, it identified persons in the West Midlands of England who had a similar socioeconmic profile to their existing users. These potential customers were reached through well-targeted advertising campaigns. The small size of the potential market for the Swansea Marina means that mass communication media would not be cost effective. Rather than waste advertising dollars covering a broad market, information from the Wales Tourist Bureau was used to effectively target the market for the marina.[12]

Tourist organizations need information to stay competitive. Tourist products must change to meet the needs of the changing market. Emerging markets must be identified and served. New markets that can be served by the existing tourist product must be identified. Tourist organizations trying to accomplish these tasks without good information are at a disadvantage.

Competition for Visitors Involves Image Making

Place images are heavily influenced by pictorial creations of the destination in movies or television, by music, and in some cases by popular entertainers and celebrities. Ireland exploits the John Wayne–Maureen O'Hara *Quiet Man* film as a successful image of the Irish, while Austria still relies on *The Sound of Music* image of its country's beauty and people. Burned to the ground by Civil War General William Sherman's army, Atlanta has revived its *Gone with the Wind* image by its selection as the site for the 1996 Olympics. The Olympics is billed as the city's second renaissance, the other being in 1864 after its wartime destruction. Australia's booming tourist business used actor Paul Hogan of the hit film *Crocodile Dundee* to dramatize the country's humor, adventure, and ruggedness. Australia also used Olivia Newton-John and Mel Gibson in ad campaigns, and Manchester featured the Beatles. Wales utilized Richard Burton, and Chicago touts Michael Jordan. South Dakota enjoyed a surge in tourism following the movie *Dances with Wolves*.

Television also affects destination attractiveness. The pub site for the television hit "Cheers" became an overnight tourist bonanza in Boston, while the Public Broadcasting System serialization of English dramas opened Britain to American audiences. Late in 1990, the PBS 11-hour series "The Civil War" also sparked record sales of Civil War reading material and memorabilia. The benefit for Virginia, where more than 60% of the war was fought over 4 years, was a record-breaking surge in tourism.

Changing an image, however, is more difficult. Las Vegas, for example, was once seen as a vice capital known for sex and gambling. Gambling still accounts for a sizable 60% of the local economy, but consider these facts: Las Vegas is (1) a family-oriented tourist mecca for sports, entertainment, recreation, and performing arts; (2) a university town with one of the fastest growing, most prestigious universities in the West; and (3) a high-tech regional service center. Greater Las Vegas has become the fastest-growing region in the country. The choices Las Vegas makes in selecting a mix of communication messages and channels will largely determine its emerging identity.

State media investment on attracting tourists has grown rapidly in recent years. States such as Texas and Alaska have more than quadrupled their tourism media budgets. Nations and states invade and advertise in each other's markets. For instance, Illinois targets New York, California, Texas, and Japan. It produces multilingual travel guides, videotapes, and radio segments.

Destinations have formed partnerships with travel, recreational, and communication businesses on joint marketing efforts. They advertise in national magazines and travel publications and do vertical marketing with business-travel promotions to link the growing business-leisure segment of the traveling public, and they target travel agencies. Many states have located welcome centers along major interstate highways that include unstaffed two-way video systems to answer questions from a central location or otherwise assist travelers. States also target their own residents with brochures, maps, and a calendar of events.

Finally, effective destination imaging requires a congruence between advertising and the place. Glossy photographs of sunsets, beaches, buildings, and events need to have some relationship to what tourists actually experience; otherwise destinations run the risk of losing tourist goodwill and generating bad word of mouth. Travel agents are extremely responsive to feedback from customers.

Developing Packages of Attractions and Amenities

An effective way of communicating with potential travelers is by offering packages. Tourist organizations, cities, and states must develop a package of attractions and amenities in the hope of becoming a chosen destination. Travelers make comparisons about the relative advantages and disadvantages of competing destinations. Destinations must provide easy access to attractions by bus, boats, carriages, and planes. They need to distribute brochures, audiotapes, and videotapes to travel agents and individual prospects. City bus companies might prepare half-day, full-day, and evening tours to highlight the place's major attractions. Concentrating attractions, services, and facilities in a small area creates excitement, adventure, and crowds.

Destinations constantly discover hidden assets that have vast tourist potential. Illinois, for example, has more public and semipublic golf courses per population than any other state except Florida. It now promotes golf tours. One successful buyer has been Japanese tourist agencies, who have packaged a golf and Chicago shopping tour. Pennsylvania has reclaimed old coal mining areas with championship golf courses, expanding its recreational facilities to promote tourism.

A destination may promote one, a few, or many of its attractions. Chicago's marketing theme—"Chicago's Got It"—featured pictures of its famous architecture, lakefront, symphony, world's tallest building, financial exchanges, and Wrigley Field (home of the Chicago Cubs) to suggest that the city had everything: business, culture, entertainment, recreation, and sports. In contrast, San Francisco played off its well-developed image as seductive and mysterious: a photo of a foggy, softly lit Golden Gate Bridge with the copy, "In the Beginning, God Created Heaved and Earth. San Francisco Took a Little Longer."

Attractions alone do not attract visitors. Most places seek to deepen the travel experience by providing greater value and making the experience more significant and rewarding. Such appeals are couched in history, culture, and people. New York City is a case in point. About one in four of the city's visitors is a foreign tourist. Consequently, city officials must make New York "foreign friendly" by creating tours that emphasize nationality interests, designing brochures in a variety of languages, and providing hassle-free currency exchanges. To provide that value-added dimension and friendship, these tour packages try to deepen cultural bonds and ties between the United States and the foreign visitors.

Competition among destinations extends to restaurants, facilities, sports, cultural amenities, and entertainment. Which place has the most four-star hotels, best culinary fare, most museums and theaters, best wine and drink, best chefs, or best native, cultural, or ethnic flair? Campaigns are carried out in specialty publications. Testimonials and rankings are found in travel brochures, advertising, and travel guides.

Making a destination tourist friendly is the task of a central tourist agency, which may be public, quasi-public, nonprofit, or private. These agencies are referred to as National Tourist Organizations or NTOs (see Marketing Highlight 20-3). Outside the United States, this agency is often run by the central government, state, or province, together with local government officials. The European Travel Commission, a 24 nation group bent on luring U.S. visitors to Europe, coordinates promotional activity in the United States.

Some cities divide responsibilities for promoting tourist and hospitality business; the former is largely public supported and the latter is supported by the travel–tourist business. In smaller communities, tourist–travel activities generally fall under a local chamber of commerce and private support. Local chambers of commerce have become aggressive promoters of bed-and-breakfast lodgings in private homes.

BARBADOS
Your vacation is part of our heritage.

Codrington College, theological seat of learning in the parish of St. John.

There are two main religions in Barbados. The other is Anglican.

Chattel houses are architecturally unique to Barbados and among the earliest dwellings.

Morgan Lewis sugar mill, the only surviving sugar windmill in the Caribbean.

*S*ince 1627, when English settlers first set foot on Barbados, this island, the most socially and politically stable country in the western world, has perfected the art of hospitality.

Barbados offers more cultural pursuits per square mile than any other Caribbean island. You can step back to the days when sugar was king and see the great plantation houses. Or relax amid the floral serenity of our botanical gardens with their rare collections of tropical plants. Or visit one of the only three remaining Jacobean houses this side of the Atlantic.

Or, if our beaches beckon too strongly, you can always immerse yourself in the entire history of Barbados, all under one roof. At the Barbados museum.

Make your next vacation the best it can be. Call your travel agent. Or, for information and brochures, call: USA 1-800-221-9831. Canada 1-800-268-9122.

*B*ARBADOS
THE BEST IT CAN BE

Marketing Highlight 20-3

National Tourism Organizations: How They Work

Countries and states usually have government or quasi-government agencies that market destination tourism. On the national level these are referred to as National Tourism Organizations, or NTOs. An NTO has two marketing tasks: (1) the NTO can formulate and develop the tourist product or products of the destination, and (2) it can promote them in appropriate markets. It can base its approach to development and promotion on market research and thus achieve a close match between the products and the markets. In doing this, the tourist organization is acting on behalf of the whole destination and is complementary to the development and promotion activities of individual tourist providers.[13]

The NTO is responsible for the following functions.[14]

Flow of research data. The NTO coordinates tourism research for the area. Information on origin of visitors, length of stay, type of accommodation used, and expenditures on different tourism products are collected and disseminated to members of the organization. This information helps the NTO to evaluate trends and develop marketing strategy. It also provides valuable information to hospitality and travel businesses.

Representation in markets. The NTO often has offices in major markets. These promote the country within the market. The promotion comes in the form of advertising with response mechanisms, such as advertisements in travel magazines featuring a toll-free number to call for additional information. Respondents receive a tour manual. The offices also answer questions from prospective visitors and facilitate the development of distribution linkages. They also serve as important sources of information about trends in the market.

Organization of workshops and trade shows. The NTO facilitates the interaction of tourism with members of the distribution channels, such as travel agents and wholesalers. In addition to developing workshops, the NTO purchases space at major travel shows and invites travel industry members to participate in the booth, either by displaying material or having a physical presence. This saves the member the cost of purchasing an individual booth.

Familiarization trips. The NTO develops familiarization trips for key members of the distribution channel and travel writers.

Participation in joint marketing schemes. Some NTOs provide cooperative advertising support to help members promote to selected markets. The British Tourist Authority, for example, helps to support British Airways advertising in the United States. It is hoped that these advertisements will develop additional tourists for Britain, thus helping the British hospitality and travel industry.

Support for new or small businesses. NTOs may provide support for new products and small businesses that are important to the overall tourism of the area. For example, rural tourism, regional festivals, and bed and breakfast accommodations are often promoted by NTOs.

Consumer assistance and protection. NTOs assist the consumer by providing product information. For example, in some countries there are classification schemes for lodging accommodations. These are designed to educate travelers concerning types of available lodging. Sometimes NTOs influence the design of lodging brochures and menus appropriate for a particular market segment.

General education. NTOs conduct conferences and courses to educate travel industry providers from their nation to understand the needs of foreign markets.

Like other organizations, NTOs must develop a mission statement, develop goals and develop a strategy. The following guidelines were developed to assist in formulating a mission statement.[15]

1. The past experiences in the region with regard to tourism must be considered, including the salient characteristics and history of the region, the regional tourism organization(s), and the tourism business units.

2. The regional tourism organization must be prepared to adapt the region's mission in response to the characteristics of the regional tourism environment. For example, there is increasing concern for the protection of the ecological environment. This should be incorporated into a regional mission statement.

3. The region's tourism resources make certain missions possible and others not. Northern Canada, for example, is unlikely to become the surfing mecca of North America.

4. The preferences of the region's major tourism publics, such as regional tourism organizations, tourism business units, local governments, and community organizations, must be considered. A successful mission statement will attempt to incorporate the priorities and expectations of the major publics in the region.

5. The mission must be based on the region's distinctive competencies. A concerted effort must be made to concentrate on the region's strengths. If, for example, a region's major tourism resource is its cultural heritage, then this should receive primary emphasis in the mission statement.

Goals provide direction to the organization. The following are typical tourism goals.[16]

- **Economic.** To optimize the contribution of tourism and recreation to economic prosperity, full employment, and regional economic development.

- **Consumer.** To make the opportunity for and the benefits of travel and recreation universally acceptable to residents and visitors. To contribute to the personal growth and education of the population and encourage their appreciation of the geography, history, and ethnic diversity of the region.

- **Environmental and natural resources.** To protect and preserve the historic and cultural foundations of the region as a living part of community life and development and to ensure future generations an opportunity to enjoy the rich heritage of the region. To ensure the compatibility of tourism, recreational, and activity policies with other regional and national interests in energy development and conservation, environmental protection, and judicious use of natural resources.

- **Government operations.** To harmonize to the maximum extent possible all government-related activities supporting tourism and recreation; to support the needs of the general public and the public and private sectors of industries involved with tourism and recreation; and to take a leadership role with all those concerned with tourism, recreation, and cultural heritage conservation. The underlying objective of regional strategy formulation is to translate current conditions in the region into desired situations. For example, a region with the goal of increasing the economic benefits of tourism to a specific subregion may select a strategy to increase visitation to that area. A region that is highly dependent on one specific geographic market for its demand may adopt a strategy of diversification.[17]

Tourist organizations differ significantly in their budget, revenue sources, and marketing programs. In general, chambers of commerce are critical for tourist boosterism by cooperating with the tourist–travel industry in developing products and directing bookings, marketing, and total place promotion. They are tourist industry advocates, negotiators, and key connection makers with public officials and agencies. In nearly all cases, these agencies believe that they are underfunded relative to their tasks.

It is important for all tourism businesses and agencies to work together to promote the destination and to ensure that visitors expectations are met. State tourist organizations should work with national organizations and local organizations. Hotel and airlines help with fam trips sponsored by tourist organizations. Local business provides managers who make sales calls on behalf of the destination at regional, national, and international conferences. Promoting a destination is a team effort.

Chapter Review

I.   Globalization of the Tourist Industry

1) Over a half-billion tourists. According to the World Tourism Organization (WTO) of the United Nations, more than 500 million tourists traveled internationally in 1993, spending over $300 billion (excluding transportation).

2) Tourism employs more people than any single industrial sector. Tourism accounts for 8% of total world exports, more than 31% of international trade in services, and more than 100 million jobs worldwide.

II.   Importance of Tourism to a Destination's Economy

1) Tourism Destination

a) **Destinations** are places with some form of actual or perceived boundary.

b) **Macro destinations** such as the United States contain thousands of micro destinations, including regions, states, cities, towns, and even visitor destinations within a town.

2) Benefits of Tourism

a) **Employment**

b) **Support industries and professions**

c) **The multiplier effect** as tourism expenditures are recycled through the economy.

d) **Source of state and local taxes**

e) **Stimulates exports of place-made products**

3) Management of the Tourism Destination

a) **Destinations must maintain the infrastructure:** Destinations that fail to maintain the necessary infrastructure or build inappropriate infrastructure run significant risks.

b) **A destination's attractiveness can be affected by the environ-**

ment: A destination's attractiveness can be diminished by violence, political instability, natural catastrophe, adverse environmental factors, and overcrowding.

c) **The preservation of natural attractions must be managed:** Tourist development must balance the temptation to maximize tourist dollars with preservation of the natural tourist attractions and the quality of life for local residents.

III. **Tourism Strategies and Investments**

    1) **Tourism Competition Is Strong**

        a) **New and upgraded destinations are constantly appearing.**

        b) **Destinations are rediscovering their past,** looking for a tourism hook.

        c) **Stay Close to Home.** Local tourism and convention bureaus are trying to get the locals to visit their own region.

    2) **Investment in Tourist Attractions**

        a) **Destinations must respond to the travel basics of cost, convenience, and timeliness.**

        b) **Events are being developed as a way of attracting tourists.**

        c) **Urban renewal is being designed with the tourist in mind.**

        d) **A combination of public and private investment is being used to develop major tourism developments.**

IV. **Segmenting and Monitoring the Tourist Market.** Tourism planners must consider how many tourists are desired, which segments to attract, and how to balance tourism with other industries.

    1) **Identifying Target Markets**

        a) **Collect information about its current visitors**

        b) **Audit the destination's attractions** and select segments that might logically have an interest in them.

    2) **Classification of Visitor Segments**

        a) **Group inclusive tour (GIT)**

        b) **Independent Traveler IT (formerly FIT)**

    3) **Monitoring Tourist Markets.** Tourist markets are dynamic and a marketing information system is part of any well-run tourist organization.

V. **Communicating with the Tourist Market**

    1) **Competition for visitors requires image making.**

    2) **Developing packages of attractions and amenities** is an effective way of communicating with potential travelers.

        a) **Attractions alone do not attract visitors.** Most places seek to deepen the travel experience by providing greater value and making the experience more significant and rewarding.

        b) **Competition among destinations** extends to restaurants, facilities, sports, cultural amenities, and entertainment.

VI. **Organizing and Managing Tourism Marketing.** Making a destination tourist friendly is the task of a central tourist agency, which may be public, quasi-public, nonprofit, or private. These agencies are referred to as National Tourist Organizations (NTOs).

DISCUSSION QUESTIONS

1. How does a tourism destination determine what to promote and to whom it should be promoted?

2. What benefits does tourism bring to your area?

3. Decribe an event (festival, concert, play, etc.) in your area that draws tourists. Is this event effectively promoted; if yes, why, if no, how could it be improved?

4. Choose one of the psychological determinants

of demand listed in Table 20-1 and describe a tourism product that is based on the determinant you have chosen.

5. Choose what you believe to be a good tourism promotion for a city, region, state, or country and tell why you think it is a good promotion. In your critique discuss the media used, target audience, and benefits the destination offers.

KEY TERMS

Allocentrics   Persons with a need for new experiences, such as backpackers and explorers.

Destinations   Places with some form of actual or perceived boundary, such as the physical boundary of an island, political boundaries, or even market-created boundaries.

GIT   Group inclusive tour.

Infrastructure   Hotels, roads, airports, water systems, utility systems, transportation and other systems needed to support tourism.

IT   (formerly referred to as FIT) An independent traveler.

Macro destinations   Destinations that contain thousands of micro destinations, including regions, states, cities, towns, and even visitor destinations within a town.

Multiplier effect   Tourist expenditures that are recycled through the local economy, being spent and respent.

NTO   National tourism office; a national government or quasi-government agency that markets destination tourism.

Psychocentric   Persons who do not desire change when they travel. They like nonthreatening places and to stay in familiar surroundings.

Tourism   A stay of one or more nights away from home for holidays, visits to friends or relatives, business conferences, or any other purpose, except such things as boarding education or semipermanent employment.[18]

REFERENCES

1. "Milwaukee CVB Goes on the Record with New Promotion," *USAE*, 14, no. 5 (January 31, 1995), p.1.

2. Ibid.

3. CHRIS RYAN, "The Determinants of Demand for Tourism," Chapter 2 in *Recreational Tourism: A Social Science Perspective*, London: Routledge, 1991, p. 5.

4. World Tourism Organization, *Yearbook of Tourism Statistics*. Madrid, Spain: 1994, pp. 2–4.

5. JONATHAN DAHL, "It Seems that Nothing Is Certain Except Taxes—and More Taxes," *Wall Street Journal* March 4, 1991, p. B1.

6. SUSAN CAREY, "Tourist Spots Developing 'Green' Images," *Wall Street Journal*, May 10, 1991, p. A7.

7. ANDREW NEMETHY, "Resorts Go Up and Down," *Snow County* (November 1990), p. 31–32.

8. J. CROMPTON "Motivations for Pleasure Vacations," *Annals of Tourism Research*, 6, (1974), pp. 408–424; A. MATHIESON AND G. WALL, *Tourism, Economics, Physical and Social Impacts*. Harlow, Essex, England: Longmans, 1982.

9. PETER HAWES, Holistic Vacations, *Hemisphere*, (March 1995), pp. 85–87.

10. E. COHEN, "Towards a Sociology of International Tourism," *Social Research*, 39, no. 1, (1972), pp. 164–182.

11. STANLEY C. PLOG, "Why Destinations Rise and Fall in Popularity," *Cornell Hotel and Restaurant Quarterly*, 14, no. 4 (February 1984), pp. 55–59.

12. RICHARD PRENTICE, "Market Targeting," in *Tourism Marketing and Management Handbook*, Stephen F. Witt and Luiz Moutinho, eds., Englewood Cliffs, N. J.: Prentice Hall, 1989, pp. 247–252.

13. CHRIS RYAN, "The Determinants of Demand for Tourism," Chapter 2 in *Recreational Tourism: A Social Science Perspective*, London: Routledge, 1991, p. 5.

14. A. J. BURKHART AND S. MEDLIK, *Tourism: Past, Present, and Future*, London: Heinemann, 1981, p. 256.

15. T. C. VICTOR, MIDDLETON, *Marketing in Travel and Tourism*, Oxford, England: Butterworth-Heinemann: 1994.

16. ERNIE HEATH AND GEOFFREY WALL, *Marketing Tourism Destination*, New York: John Wiley & Sons: 1992, p. 65.

17. R. C. MILLS AND A. M. MORRISON, 1985. *The Tourism System: An Introductory Text*. Englewood Cliffs, N.J.: Prentice Hall, p. 248.

18 ERNIE HEATH AND GEOFFREY WALL, *Marketing Tourism Destination*, New York: John Wiley & Sons, 1991, p. 74.

Next Year's Marketing Plan

21

*T*he Promus Companies, Inc., located in Memphis, Tennessee, is the
parent company of Promus Hotels and Harrah's Casinos. The hotel
brands, which the company owns and franchises, include Embassy Suites,
Hampton Inn, Hampton Inn and Suites, and Homewood Suites. Harrah's
operates casinos in every major land-based market, as well as numerous
riverboat and Native American reservation properties.

Lee Witherow joined the Promus Companies in June 1991, recruited
into its President's Associates Program, after graduating from Wake Forest
University with a master's in business administration degree. The
President's Associate Program was developed at Promus to attract high-
potential MBAs to ensure quality executive-level talent.

After a short stint at Embassy Suites corporate headquarters in
Memphis, Witherow served as the interim general manager for the
Embassy Suites hotel in Charlotte, North Carolina, and then in Kansas
City, Missouri. In fall 1991, Witherow was assigned as the general manager
of the Embassy Suites/Dallas Park Central property in Dallas, Texas. His
charge was to convert this former Park Suites Hotel to the Embassy Suites
flag. The hotel was performing under the market in penetration, average
daily rate (ADR), and occupancy. When Witherow was assigned to this
property, Embassy Suites president Clyde Culp called the property "our
company's biggest challenge and one of our most difficult hotels."

Upon arrival in Dallas, Witherow discovered a hotel that relied on two
major clients for more than 42% of the property's occupancy; therein lay
much of the hotel's average daily rate (ADR) problems. As a result,

Witherow developed a plan to replace a substantial amount of the current business with fewer rate-sensitive clients. Over the next two and one-half years, the hotel's occupancy grew by approximately 9% and the ADR increased by approximately $19. The net result was an increase in revenue in excess of $2 million.

Witherow attributes much of the success experienced in Dallas to two factors: (1) Embassy Suites' 100% satisfaction guarantee, which states, "If you are not happy, we don't expect you to pay"; and (2) working with a hand-picked staff to ensure that each guest was happy 100% of the time.

With respect to the hotel's sales and marketing effort, the team took a two-pronged approach: they worked to build occupancy, at the same time replacing lower-paying customers with business that would help achieve the ADR goals.

To ensure that the sales and marketing teams realized the importance of their jobs, during the first year Witherow often spent 15 to 20 hours per week making calls with the team. This approach not only helped the team, but also helped Witherow to get to know his clients through relationship marketing.

At Embassy Suites, standard operating procedure requires the general manager to have his or her office in the lobby of the hotel. This not only provided Witherow with the opportunity to build relationships with his customers, but provided his staff with direct access to the general manager. Simply put, happy employees make for happy and 100% satisfied guests.

Also adding to the success of the property, each month the Dallas hotel held an all-employee luncheon. During the meal, employees received awards and recognition, including a quarterly bonus based on the hotel's performance. Equally important, employees were informed of the hotel's financial performance, guest service ratings, and future goals. During this meeting, each department was informed of the role it would play in attaining these goals and what standards the department's employees would be measured against.

In August 1994, Witherow was promoted to vice-president and general manager of the Harrah's Casino in Vicksburg, Mississippi. Witherow was the first employee of Promus Hotels to move from the hotel side of the business to Harrah's as a general manager of a casino and hotel.

Casino gaming in Mississippi started out with a bang but, due to the state's policy of not restricting gaming licenses, competition quickly intensified. For example, the Vicksburg market had revenues of approximately $15 million per month in February 1994 with only two riverboats in operation. By June 1994, Vicksburg had four riverboats and still only $15 million in monthly revenue. All the casinos were experiencing erosion of margins and intense rivalry.

Witherow's assignment in Vicksburg was simple: achieve superior market penetration, raise customer service scores, and restore operating margins. Once again Lee found himself engaged in the development of a commonsense marketing plan to guide the company in a highly competitive market.

Chapter 21 provides a description of how to develop a marketing plan.

We start with **the purpose of a marketing plan**, and the contents of an **executive summary**. Then we move to a discussion of **the corporate connection** and **environmental analysis** and **forecasting** which includes **competitive analysis, market trends, market potential**, and **marketing research**.

After establishing this background, we discuss **segmentation** and **targeting** and **next year's objectives and quotas**. These lead to: **action plans: strategies** and **tactics**. A discussion follows of **resources needed** to **support strategies and meet objectives** and **marketing control**. The chapter concludes with tips concerning **presenting and selling the plan** and a brief discussion of **preparing for the future**.

Success in the marketplace is not guaranteed by understanding marketing concepts and strategies. Successful marketing requires planning and careful execution. It is easy to become so involved in the day-to-day problems of running a marketing department that little or no time is devoted to planning. When this occurs, the marketing department is probably operating without direction and is being reactive rather than proactive. Even experienced managers sometimes fail to see that this is occurring until it is too late. This may be one of the root causes for high turnover within hospitality, marketing, and sales departments.

Purpose of a Marketing Plan

A marketing plan serves several purposes within any hospitality company.

- Provides a roadmap for all marketing activities of the firm for the next year.
- Ensures that marketing activities are in agreement with the corporate strategic plan.
- Forces marketing managers to objectively review and think through all steps in the marketing process.
- Assists in the budgeting process to match resources with marketing objectives.
- Creates a process to monitor actual against expected results.

The development of a marketing plan is a rigorous process and cannot be accomplished in a few hours. Instead, it is best to set aside one or more days to develop next year's plan. Many marketing managers find it best to leave the office along with their staff and all necessary data while writing the plan. Constant interruptions that occur in the office are detrimental to the planning process.

To be effective, a new marketing plan must be written each year. Marketing plans written for periods longer than a year are generally not effective. At the same time, the annual marketing plan must be written against a longer-term strategic marketing plan that states what the company hopes to achieve, say, 3 to 5 years down the road.

Many managers believe that the process of writing a plan is invaluable, because it forces those writing it to question, think, and strategize. A plan should be developed with the input and assistance of key members of the marketing department. The discussion and thought process required to produce a plan is stimulating and very helpful in team building. It is also an excellent training device for younger staff members who wish to be managers.

A marketing plan should contain the following sections:

    I. Executive summary
   II. Corporate connection
  III. Environmental analysis and forecasting
  IV. Segmentation and targeting
   V. Next year's objectives and quotas
  VI. Action plans: strategies and tactics
 VII. Resources needed to support strategies and meet objectives
VIII. Marketing control
  IX. Presenting and selling the plan
   X. Preparing for the future

We will examine the role played by each section of the marketing plan.

SECTION I: EXECUTIVE SUMMARY

The executive summary and a few charts or graphs from the body of the plan may be the only parts ever read by top management. Consequently, it is of great importance to carefully write this section with top management in mind.

A few tips may assist in writing the executive summary.

- Write it for top executives.
- Limit the number of pages to between two to four.
- Use short sentences and short paragraphs. Avoid using words that are unlikely to be understood.
- Organize the summary as follows: Describe next year's objectives in quantitative terms; briefly describe marketing strategies to meet goals and objectives, including a description of target markets; describe expected results by quarter; identify the dollar costs necessary, as well as key resources needed.

- Read and reread the executive summary several times. Never write it once and then place it in the plan. Modify and change the summary until it flows well, is easily read, and conveys the central message of the marketing plan.

Relationship to Other Plans

A marketing plan is not a stand-alone tool. Instead, it must support other plans, such as the firm's strategic plan. Whenever possible, the marketing manager should participate in or provide input to the development of a strategic plan. If this is not practical, it remains imperative to understand the contents of the strategic plan prior to development of next year's marketing plan.

A marketing plan supports the company's strategic plan in several ways. Next year's marketing strategies and tactics must support strategic decisions such as the following:

- Corporate goals with respect to profit, growth, and so on
- Desired market share
- Positioning of the company or of its product lines
- Vertical or horizontal integration
- Strategic alliances
- Product line breadth and depth

Marketing-related Plans

In large organizations, marketing-related plans are sometimes developed by individuals who do not report to marketing. This is usually the result of (1) originally establishing these departments independent of marketing, (2) political maneuvering in which a nonmarketing executive desired control of these areas, and (3) failure by top management to understand the need to unify marketing-related activities.

Marketing-related areas in which plans may be written independently of marketing include the following:

Sales
Advertising and promotion
Public relations and publicity
Marketing research
Pricing
Customer service

If these plans are developed independently of a marketing plan with no consideration as to how they tie together, the result is often chaotic, counterproductive, and a source for continuous infighting among marketing-related areas.

When the organizational design of a company fails to place major marketing activities under the marketing umbrella, the task of writing and implementing a marketing plan is made more complex. Under these conditions, it behooves the marketing manager to invite the managers of other marketing-related areas to participate in the marketing plan development process. This action should then be reciprocated.

The activities of marketing and many other departments within a company are closely intertwined. Operations and finance are two areas that affect and in turn are affected by marketing. If guest experiences are diminished because of problem areas in operations, marketing will be adversely affected. Likewise, if financial projections are unrealistic for certain months or for various product lines, marketing will be called to task.

It is unrealistic to expect perfect harmony between marketing and other departments. It is by no means unrealistic to suggest that relations can usually be greatly improved and that a critical place to begin is by interchanging data, suggestions, and other assistance when department plans are being developed.

Corporate Direction

A good marketing plan begins with the fact that the only purpose of marketing is to support the enterprise. It is good politics and good sense to begin next year's plan by recognizing and restating these corporate elements. Let top management know that these helped to guide the development of next year's plan:

> Mission statement
> Corporate philosophy
> Corporate goals

SECTION III: ENVIRONMENTAL ANALYSIS AND FORECASTING

Hospitality companies are highly sensitive to changes in their social, political, and economic environments. A manufacturer of food or toiletries may not immediately feel the impact of these changes, but airlines, hotels, auto rental firms, and cruise lines witness an instant reaction.

The day the Gulf War was declared, hospitality firms felt the impact. Pleasure travel instantly evaporated as fear of possible terrorism gripped Americans. Unfortunately, some companies responded without clearly thinking. Several hotel chains quickly offered substantial discounts to guests. This did nothing to increase demand, but instead simply gave discounts to individuals who had to travel for business and would have paid a higher rate. A marketing plan is not a political or economic treatise, and hospitality marketers are not expected to be experts in these fields. They are expected to be aware of major environmental factors likely to affect the industry and the company, to consider their possible impact on marketing, and to respond quickly and intelligently to new events and trends.

Major Environmental Factors

Hospitality organizations need to anticipate the influence of these broad environmental factors on their business.

Social. Consider the possible impact of major social factors, such as crime, AIDS, and changing demographics. These factors will vary in their intensity and their geographical incidence. Social factors relevant to Los Angeles, or Sydney, Australia, may have little relevance to Rapid City, South Dakota.

Social conditions sometimes change rapidly to the benefit of alert marketers. The hotel market within India had long been considered as uninteresting by many hotel chains. In the 1990s, India's social and economic structure suddenly became conducive to mid-priced hotel development.[1]

In 1994, India had only 2000 international standard mid-priced hotel rooms in a nation of 900 million people, compared to 3.5 million mid-priced rooms in the United States. The sudden emergence of a potentially gigantic market attracted many chains, including Holiday Inn Worldwide, Choice Hotels, Carlson Hospitality Group (Radisson), Southern Pacific Hotels (Australia), and Oberoi Group of Hotels (India).

A U.S. hotel executive observed that "It's much easier to do a hotel here than in China. We have more entrepreneurial freedom and business security."

Political. Legislation affecting taxation, pension benefits, and casino gambling are only a few examples of political decisions likely to directly affect marketing. International politics is increasingly important to corporate hospitality marketing plans. The opening of Vietnam to investors and tourists after years of being off limits provides risk as well as potential rewards for the hospitality industry.[2]

Economic. Changes in economic variables such as employment, income, savings, and interest rates should be recognized. The hospitality industry, especially the lodging and cruising sectors, are highly sensitive to business-cycle movements.

An assessment of major environmental factors should assist planners to modify strategies and possibly consider new market segments. It may also prevent rash changes in tactics, such as the pricing example during the Gulf War.

Competitive Analysis

It is common practice for hospitality companies to conduct a competitive analysis. In some cases, this analysis deals primarily with the observable physical properties of a competitor. For example,

OUR HOTEL	THEIR HOTEL
500 Rooms	600 Rooms
1 Ballroom	2 Ballrooms
Executive center	No executive center

An analysis solely of physical differences usually misses major competitive advantages or disadvantages. It is doubtful that most guests know or care about the room count of competitive hotels. They do recognize differences in service level, cleanliness, staff knowledge, and the responsiveness of the sales departments. A competitive analysis must extend beyond inventory comparisons. True competitive advantages are factors that are recognized by guests and influence their purchase decisions. A creative and alert marketing manager will recognize competitive variables that are truly of importance to the customers and are controllable. Such a manager will develop strategies and tactics to improve areas of weakness and enhance already strong points.

Based strictly on a comparison of physical attributes, many hospitality firms should not exist. Bed and Breakfast establishments are usually old homes without a swimming pool and may have shared bathrooms; yet they fill a competitive niche. Hertz and Avis may compete head to head with clean, late-model cars, but Rent-a-Wreck auto rental company successfully offers automobiles that many people would be ashamed to be seen driving.

The single best way to conduct a competitive analysis is to involve members of the marketingsales department, such as the sales force. These individuals often have difficulty discussing environmental variables such as interest rates, but they can talk knowledgeably for hours about the competition and guest preferences.

Market Trends

Market trends are a reflection of environmental and competitive variables. Market trend information for the hospitality industry is often available from outside organizations free of change. Common sources include chambers of commerce, visitors bureaus, universities, government agencies, banks, trade associations, and commercial organizations such as CPA firms or consultants who publish information for publicity purposes.

Useful market trend information for writing a hospitality marketing plan includes the following:

> *Visitor trends:*   Origination areas, stop-over sites, visitor demographics, spending habits, length of stay, etc.
>
> *Competitive trends:*   Numbers, location, type of products offered (for example, all-suite hotels), occupancy levels, average rates, etc.
>
> *Related industry trends:*   Members of the hospitality industry are interdependent upon airline flights, convention center bookings, new airport construction, and new highways. It is important to study trends for supporting or related industries.

Caterers of in-flight meals were dramatically affected by the trend among U.S. airlines to eliminate or reduce onboard meal service. Companies such as Dobbs International Services, who provided full-course meals, had to find new markets and new products. Caterair International Corporation diversified into the repair of airplane audio headsets, and Sky Chefs explored the private-label business and food preparation for prisons, schools, and hospitals. Randall C. Boyd, senior vice-president marketing and customer service for Sky Chefs said, "We are good sandwich makers, salad makers, and pasta makers. Whether a prisoner or a college student is eating our sandwich, we don't care."[3]

Select only those trends that are useful in developing the plan. It is of no value to fill a plan with pages of information that have little or no direct relevancy.

Market Potential

Estimates of market potential often seem to be ignored by those who write hospitality marketing plans. Marketing managers in hotels sometimes feel that the concept has no application to them. "We view all travelers as potential guests" is a frequently heard comment. Others reply that the concept is theoretical for the hospitality industry and applies primarily to consumer packaged goods.

These opinions are incorrect! While it is true that measurement of true market potential is impossible, estimates can and should be made. The hospitality industry is notorious for ignoring or misinterpreting market potential estimates, thus leading to overbuilding, overcapacity, price cutting, and frantic advertising and promotion in an attempt to fill rooms or fill seats.

Market potential should be viewed as the total available demand for a hospitality product within a particular geographic market at a given price. It is important not to mix different hospitality products into an estimate of market potential.

It is common to hear individuals speak of the market for hotel rooms in a region as x number of room nights. For purposes of writing a marketing plan, such figures are interesting but do not indicate market potential for your products. Most markets consist of a mix of hotel properties, ranging from luxury to budget, with specialty lodging such as all-suites, condominium hotels, B&B, and others.

Each type of property faces its own peculiar market potential, except for times when a special event fills every bed in town. Estimates of market potential normally begin by examining the market for all hotels, but should then shift to specific markets for your hotel and directly competitive properties. To be precise, market potential estimates should be shown as demand estimates at various price points; however, this is generally unnecessary for most marketing plans. The average marketing manager for a property such as a hotel finds it impossible to make good quantitative estimates of market potential in room nights or dollars. These individuals lack marketing research support and most were not trained in quantitative analysis. Therefore, market potential estimates are often expressed in "guesstimates", such as the market seems to be growing or declining by about 5% a year.

Warning! Even though precise estimates may be beyond the abilities of many hospitality marketing managers, it is essential to go through the thought process of examining market potential. Never assume that market potential is static or that it is unimportant to marketing success.

By engaging in the process of trying to guesstimate or estimate market potential, those who develop marketing plans will become aware of potentially important market conditions and can then appropriately adjust marketing strategies. Remember, the process of developing a marketing plan is not a precise discipline such as engineering or chemistry. The exercise of writing a plan is usually as important to marketing success as the plan itself.

Marketing Research

The need for marketing intelligence is ongoing. Much of the information acquired by marketing research in a current calendar or fiscal year will serve as the basis for developing next year's marketing plan. Marketing research needs vary considerably by type and size of hospitality company. Companies such as Hertz or Hilton Hotels have corporate marketing research departments. An individual hotel property or car rental location may have need for additional marketing information. In these cases, the individual property or location is generally responsible for acquiring these data.

Marketing research needs can usually be divided into macro and micro market information. Macro market information includes but is not restricted to

- Industry trends
- Social-economic-political trends
- Competitive information
- Industry-wide customer data

Micro market information includes but is not restricted to

- Guest information
- Product/service information
- New product analysis and testing
- Intermediary buyer data
- Pricing studies
- Key account information
- Advertising/promotion effectiveness

One of the promising areas of marketing research has been called *yield marketing* by executives from two advertising agencies serving the hospitality industry. These advertising executives envision a linking of customer responses with a hotel's advertising and promotional efforts. This will be accomplished by linking sales, marketing, and reservations systems with property management systems through the use of small but powerful computers. This would enable a hotel to accurately and quickly measure and anticipate the effectiveness and efficiency of marketing investments.[4]

It is imperative that marketing managers keep abreast of developments such as this and provide an appropriate marketing research budget to include advancing technology. Marketing research too often is reactionary rather than proactive. Studies are conducted when a problem occurs or when competitors unexpectedly offer new products.

An example of a possible need for advertising research was offered by an advertisement by Hotel Sofitel in the June 9, 1994, *Wall Street Journal*. This ad showed two smiling Caucasian men with one extending papers to another in front of the concierge desk. The ad's headline read, "They didn't name a type of service after the French for nothing." The copy went on to say, "At Sofitel, our 'French service' is more a way of life than a particular action. The little things that make all the difference. So when you stay with us, you're taken care of. Your requests, even those that may seem beyond what you'd expect to be fulfilled, will be honored by our concierge."

While this particular advertisement addresses the issue of customer service in a positive way, one has to wonder how it might have been received by American readers.

- *French Service.* Do Americans view French service as good or do they view it as haughty and uncaring? Comments by American visitors to France often lead one to think of French service as poor. French food is widely admired by Americans, but is French service?
- *Two Males.* What is the market target profile for Sofitel Hotels in the United States? Is it predominately middle-age white males as seemed to be depicted in the ad, or is it women or non-Caucasians?

Sofitel's ad agency or ad department should conduct research using focus groups or some other methodology prior to running the ad. If so, the results should be positive.

Advertising research is often the responsibility of the ad agency, but in some cases it may be the responsibility of the property or corporate advertising or marketing. Adequate budget provisions must be made to include research of this nature.

Marketing, advertising, and sales managers need a continuous flow of reliable information. This occurs only when planned. A description of marketing research that is essential for the coming year must be a part of a marketing plan.

Segmentation Analysis

The heart of any marketing plan is careful analysis of available market segments and the selection of appropriate target markets. Not all market segments are appropriate for a hospitality company. The selection of segments is the result of (1) understanding who the company is and what it wishes to be and (2) studying available segments and determining if they fit the capabilities and desires of the company to obtain and secure them.

A common mistake within the hospitality industry is the selection of inappropriate segments. Marketing managers commonly err by allowing or encouraging the acquisition of low-yield segments in an effort to maintain occupancy. At the opposite extreme, companies sometimes feel they are serving "low-class" customers and attempt to attract quite different segments. If this is done in the absence of genuine product/service changes, the chances for success are slim to nonexistent.

In the case of a hotel, "A marketing plan tells you who is using your hotel, who might be using your hotel and where you can look to expand your business."[5] The Los Angeles Biltmore Hotel, which opened in 1923, had been the center of Los Angeles society for many years, but the property began to deteriorate in the 1960s. In 1984, the property was sold and the new owners faced the task of restoring life to the hotel. One of the first discoveries by the new owners was that the Biltmore's marketing plan was confused. Some people believed the hotel catered only to groups and tours, while others felt the hotel did not want their business and catered only to commercial and transient guests. The guest mix was found to be 28% commercial, 40% groups, and 32% leisure. The new management decided that a more appropriate mix was 40% commercial, 50% groups, and 10% leisure. With this directive in mind, the hotel was able to establish a new marketing plan that included repositioning the hotel, changing food and beverage operations, and changing prices.[6]

SECTION IV: SEGMENTATION AND TARGETING

When developing a marketing plan, marketers must look to both internal and external data sources for information concerning market segments.

ANALYSIS OF INTERNAL DATA	ANALYSIS OF EXTERNAL DATA
Guest registrations	Published industry information
Credit card receipts	Marketing research
Customer surveys	Guesstimates after talking with competitors,
Business card analysis	vendors, and others in the industry
(Generally placed in a box to qualify	
for a drawing, such as a free lunch)	

Targeting

No area of the marketing plan surpasses the selection of target markets in importance. If inappropriate markets are selected, marketing resources will be wasted. A high level of expenditures for advertising or sales promotion cannot compensate for misdirected marketing effort.

Target markets are selected from the list of available segments. These include segments currently served by the company and newly recognized markets. The selection of target markets is a primary responsibility of marketing management. This requires careful consideration of the variables already discussed in the development of the marketing plan. Far too many marketing managers in the hospitality industry simply select last year's target markets. While it is normally true that the majority of target markets will remain the same, new ones appear and the order of importance can change between years.

Many Asian and Australian hotel managers have discovered that their key segments in terms of spending and room nights are no longer American or European guests. Guests from Asian nations have surpassed in importance those from western nations.

An influx of international guests caught many U.S. hotel managers by surprise. Many were unprepared for the special needs of foreign visitors, such as cuisine and limited English language capabilities.

Women travelers no longer represent a fringe market for hospitality marketers. They represent a solid and growing percentage of travelers, with projections that they will constitute 50% of the market by the year 2000.[7]

A study of gender-based lodging preferences showed that "there were several significant differences between male and female business travelers in their hotel selection and use criteria."[8] For instance, women considered security facilities, room service, and low price to be more important, while men were more concerned about the availability of a fax machine and suite rooms with separate bed and office spaces.

Marketing planners need to stay abreast of such preferences, relay them to other departments within the hotel, and utilize this information in the selection of market segments.

Choosing target markets and developing a marketing mix for those markets is an important part of any marketing plan. This ad targets meeting planners. Courtesy of Robinson, Yesawich, and Pepperdine, Inc.

Objectives

The establishment of objectives provides direction for the rest of the marketing plan. The purpose of marketing strategies and tactics is to support objectives. The marketing budget must be sufficient to ensure adequate resources to achieve objectives and to meet timetables that describe the time period in which expected sales results will occur.

Occasionally, there is confusion as to what constitutes an objective. Statements such as "To be the best in our industry" or "To provide excellent guest service" are accepted as objectives. This is always an error since these types of statements are slogans or mottos. They are not objectives! Objectives are

- Quantitative: Expressed in monetary terms (dollars, pesos)
  Expressed in unit measurements such as room nights, passenger miles, number of cars to rent, or occupancy
- Time specific (1 year, 6 months)
- Profit/margin specific, such as an average margin of 22%

Table 21-1

Examples of Objectives Common to the Hotel Industry

OBJECTIVES:	AVERAGE OCCUPANCY	AVERAGE ROOM RATE

Subobjectives:	Occupancy per period of time
	Seasonal: prime, shoulder, trough
	    Monthly
	    Weekly
	    Daily
	    Weekend
	    Mid-week
		Average rate per period of time and by type of room

	TYPES OF SLEEPNG ROOMS	BY TIME
	Suites Pool side Regular room	Seasonal Monthly Weekly Daily Weekend

	Occupancy by type of
	sleeping room:
	    Suites
	    Pool side
	    Cabaña
	    Cottage
	    Regular sleeping rooms
	Occupancy per type of function room:
	    Ballroom
	    Seminar room
	    Executive conference room
		Note: Yield objectives are used by many members of the hospitality industry, such as hotels, rental cars, cruise lines, airlines, and passenger rail.

OBJECTIVES:	ANNUAL SALES BY:	ANNUAL SALES BY: UNITS DOLLARS

	Time period
	    Seasonal
	    Monthly
	    Weekly
	    Daily
	    Weekend
	Department
	    Group sales
	    Incentive sales
	Sales Territory
	    Eastern US	

	Western US
	Salesperson
	    Joe
	    Sally
	    June
	    Fred	

The process of establishing objectives is not an easy task and should not be accomplished by simply adding x percent to last year's objectives.

Objectives should be established after carefully considering the areas already discussed.

- Corporate goals
- Corporate resources
- Environmental factors
- Competition
- Market trends
- Market potential
- Available market segments and possible target markets

To ensure profitability and remain competitive in today's marketplace, it has become necessary to establish several subobjectives. For instance, a 1000-room hotel will undoubtedly have two broad objectives: average occupancy and average room rate. By themselves, these objectives do not serve as sufficient guides for developing marketing strategies. A set of sub-objectives is needed, as shown in Table 21-1.

Other subobjectives may also be established by the marketing department. Again, these should support corporate goals and next year's primary objectives. They should never stand alone as objectives, unrelated to the primary function of the marketing department.

Each marketing support area needs to be guided by a set of subobjectives. This includes areas such as advertising, promotion, public relations, marketing research, and, of course, sales.

Establishing measurable quantitative objectives for these areas is not an easy task, but, increasingly, top management is requiring that such be done. Advertising and promotion are areas in which measurement of results is particularly difficult. Management would like to know what the dollar return was for advertising or how much market share or occupancy increased as a result of advertising/promotion. With few exceptions, such as direct advertising, current measurement techniques do not permit accurate measurements of this type. Consequently, measurable objectives for advertising such as share of mind and awareness level are commonly used.

Quotas

No word creates more fear within the sales/marketing department than quotas. Yet, without quotas, the probability of accomplishing objectives is slim at best. To be effective, quotas must be

- Based on next year's objectives
- Individualized
- Realistic and obtainable
- Broken down to small units, such as each salesperson's quota per week

- Understandable and measurable, for example quota = $10,000 sales for product line x in week 5. An example of a quota that is not understandable or measurable is "to obtain 10% increase of market share early in the year."

Communicating the Plan

A sophisticated and brilliantly developed plan is of no use if it is not understood, believed, or used. "A marketing plan should not be just a call to action or a benchmark by which to judge the efficiency and effectiveness of decisions. The plan should also serve as a method for communicating marketing strategy to those people whose duty it is to implement or authorize the company's marketing strategies."[9] Several groups may serve as an audience for a marketing plan.

Top Management

This group must be convinced that the plan will accomplish the stated goals and objectives. Top management demonstrates acceptance or denial by their level of monetary support.

Marketing managers should strive for more than budgeting support. If top management "buys in" and demonstrates visible support, morale within the marketing department will increase and other departments will be willing to lend support. To the contrary, the company grapevine quickly knows if marketing is only weakly supported by top management. Support from others will be weak at best if there is a perception that management is not solidly behind marketing.

Board of Directors or Group of Investors

Occasionally, a board of directors or an investor's group may ask to be apprised of next year's marketing plan. This group generally does not seek details but instead wants to know

- Does the plan support corporate goals?
- What are the dollars and unit objectives?
- What are the major strategies to achieve these objectives?
- What is the cost?
- When can we expect to see results?

Subordinates

Members of the marketing and sales departments must understand and support the marketing plan. It is important to develop a group mentality that the marketing plan for next year is a realistic and important road map. Unfortunately, far too many individuals in hospitality companies believe that the development of a marketing plan is a waste of time since no one will ever pay it any heed.

Vendors

It is important to transmit some aspects of the marketing plan to selected vendors. This is particularly true as strategic alliances develop. Vendors such as advertising agencies, marketing research firms, computer software providers, public relations firms, consultants, and others need to know and understand the marketing plan. It may be advisable to include these individuals in the plan's development.

Other Departments

Other departments, such as housekeeping, front desk, customer service, and maintenance, will be affected by next year's plan. They have a right to know key elements of the plan.

It is common for marketing managers to be asked to briefly outline the marketing plan and answer questions in a monthly manager's meeting. If a forum such as this does not exist, marketing managers should initiate a review of next year's marketing plan with other department heads after obtaining clearance from the general manager or president.

Marketing strategies are designed as the vehicle to achieve marketing objectives. In turn, marketing tactics are tools that support strategies. Far too often, strategies and tactics have little relationship to objectives. This is always an error and is commonly the result of the following:

SECTION VI: ACTION PLANS: STRATEGIES AND TACTICS

- Desire to maintain status quo. Strategies and tactics do not change because they are perceived to be working even though solid proof of their effectiveness seldom exists.
- Lazy, incompetent, or unsure management. These individuals do not wish to risk their positions through new strategies and tactics.
- Failure to engage in marketing planning or to view the processes as being serious and meaningful to decision making.
- Undue heavy influence of outside vendors, such as advertising agencies, who do not wish to change direction or try new media.
- Failure to understand the relationship between objectives, strategies, and tactics.
- Myopic thinking that things are going well and one does not fix something that is not broken. Unfortunately, in the fast-paced, competitive hospitality industry, by the time the product is demonstrably broken, it is beyond repair.

Marketing strategies and tactics employ advertising and promotion, sales and distribution, pricing and product. Each must be custom designed to meet the specific needs of a company. It is unwise to follow ratios or industry averages concerning expenditures for advertising, new product development, or other strategy areas. Many managers have made the mistake of believing that if they expend at the same ratio as other firms in the industry they are following a responsible direction. Nothing could be further from the truth.

Strategies and tactics must always be custom made to fit the needs and culture of a company and to allow it to meet or exceed objectives. A study was conducted of marketing strategies and tactics employed by restaurants. It was found that many restaurants employ weak strategies, including following the leader, rather than developing individualized, unique strategies and tactics. The authors concluded that "Firms that seem to exhibit no strategy cannot expect to enjoy long-run successful performance. They may enjoy excellent returns for a number of years, but at some point their lack of strategy will cause the business to fail. When they begin to experience the consequences of this lack of strategic direction, it may well be too late to mount an effective alternative, especially if they operate a larger number of units."[10]

Sales Strategies

The sales force must develop and use sales strategies to support objectives. Examples of sales strategies follow:

1. Prevent erosion of key accounts
2. Grow key accounts
3. Grow selected marginal accounts
4. Eliminate selected marginal accounts
5. Retain selected marginal accounts but provide lower-cost sales support
6. Obtain new business from selected prospects

A description of sales strategies should start with these six general strategies and indicate how the sales department is going to implement each. Each general strategy is supported by specific sales tactics, such as the following:

Outside the Company

- Sales blitz of all or targeted accounts and projects
- Telephone, direct mail, and personal sales calls to selected decision makers and decision influencers
- Trade booths at selected travel shows
- Sales calls and working with travel intermediaries: tour wholesalers, travel agencies, incentive houses, international sales reps, others
- Luncheon for key customers, prospects, or decision influencers
- Travel missions and other tactics

Inside the Company

- Training of sales staff
- Involvement and support of nonsales personnel
- Motivational and control programs
- Involvement and support of management

The selection of appropriate channels of distribution is basic to the development of successful sales strategies. Hospitality companies must be ever alert to changing distribution channels and the need for change.

Traditionally, the bed and breakfast (B&B) lodging sector has depended on a direct sales and reservation system between the guest and the B&B operator. Glenn and Sally Priest of Vashon Island, off the coast of Seattle, have demonstrated that a new distribution system is possible for B&Bs. Glenn is president of the Vashon Island Bed & Breakfast Association and also owner of the Sweetbriar B&B. Having previously served as sales manager for a computer software and services company, Glenn put his knowledge to work by developing an 800 number reservations service for the association and a PC guest database.[11] Telecommuting has arrived in an industry sector previously viewed as somewhat old-fashioned.

Advertising and Promotion Strategies

Advertising and promotion strategies should be established by individuals within the company responsible for these strategies, such as the director of advertising, the sales manager, or the marketing manager. It is critical for this individual or these individuals to work with supporting groups such as an advertising agency, sales promotion firm, specialty advertising agencies, and consultants directly involved in the establishment and performance of advertising and promotion strategies.

It is inadvisable to give outside firms sole authority for deriving and implementing these strategies. History has shown that when this occurs the supporting group, such as an advertising agency, may produce brilliant copy and illustrations placed in well-respected media, only to find that the company totally fails to meet objectives. The reason is that outside groups may not view objectives the same way as the client. Many advertising agencies have won distinguished honors for ads that did little or nothing to increase sales or market share for the client. Outside professionals correctly view their client as the company or the company's management, not the end consumer. Unfortunately, this view leads to pleasing the managers who hired them, rather than achieving corporate or marketing objectives. Theoretically, corporate and marketing objectives and those of the manager should by synchronized. In fact, there is often a wide gap between the two. In some cases, outside professionals disdain client corporate or marketing objectives and view these as a detriment or obstacle to the creative process. The ideal is for corporate managers responsible for advertising/promotion to work as a team with selected outside professionals to derive strategies and tactics that satisfy objectives in a timely and cost-effective manner.

When this is accomplished, the team will develop an advertising/promotion mix of vehicles that includes tactics selected to achieve objectives, not simply to provide commissions, make life easy for the professionals, or produce a bland program that probably won't be criticized by management, but may accomplish little.

Those responsible for advertising/promotion strategies have the following responsibilities:

- Select a blend or mix of media that may include commissionable mass media, direct mail, trade shows, billboards, specialty advertising, and much more.

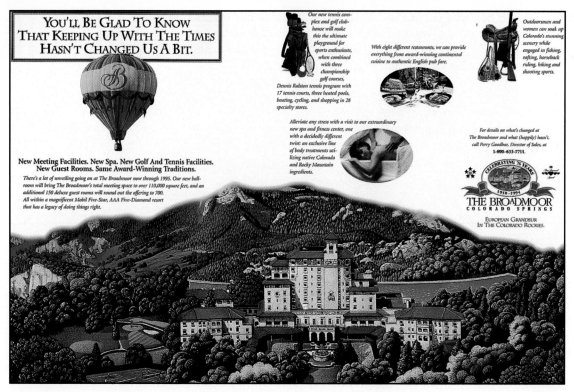

The Broadmoor's marketing plan included advertising to communicate the renovations and additions to the resort. Courtesy of Robinson, Yesawich and Pepperdine, Inc.

- Select or approve the message. This includes graphics, color, size, copy, and other format decisions.
- Design a media schedule showing when each medium including noncommissionable media, will be employed.
- Design a schedule of events, such as public relations events.
- Carefully transmit this information to management.
- Supervise the development and implementation of advertising/promotion programs, with particular care given to timetables and budget constraints.
- Assume responsibility for the outcome. Increasingly, top management is requiring those in charge of advertising/promotion to prove effectiveness and to stand behind results.

Unfortunately, despite decades of marketing teaching and thousands of articles on the subject, many managers in the hospitality industry continue to equate marketing with advertising. They fail to realize that advertising is simply one part of marketing. The authors of the restaurant strategy study referred to earlier concluded that "Many firms (restaurants) have attempted to hold market share by increasing advertising expenditures. Advertising alone will not ensure success."[12]

Another area of the advertising/promotion mix that needs consideration in a marketing plan is cooperative advertising/promotion. This requires teamwork and a place in the budget. For example, in the case of a resort, cooperative opportunities exist between

Resort and resort community (e.g., all resorts, restaurants, and attractions at Myrtle Beach)

Resort and tourism promotion groups (e.g., State Tourism Department or local chamber of commerce)

Resort and suppliers (e.g., Citrus Board or Columbia Coffee)

Resort and transportation companies (e.g., airlines, motorcoach, cruise lines)

Resort and sister hotels or resorts

An example of cooperative advertising/promotion opportunities is offered by hotels in Mexico. After an examination of the brochures of 10 hotel chains in Mexico, it was found that most made minimal or no reference to other Mexican hotels operated by the chain. Club Med made good use of this marketing tool. Club Med not only had a Mexican brochure for all their properties, but even had a special supplemental brochure for Club Med properties near prestigious archaeological sites.[13]

Pricing Strategy

Many hospitality plans devote little attention to pricing. Such plans commonly list rack rates and indicate that there will be differences in shoulder and trough seasons, but say little else about pricing. This is an error and is one of the primary reasons that many hospitality companies have removed pricing responsibility from marketing and assigned it to other departments, such as revenue management or yield management.

Pricing remains a function of marketing. If marketing managers do not maintain control of this area, they must interface with internal pricing departments. Marketing and sales departments will continuously be in conflict with pricing if pricing strategies are not understood and considered in marketing and sales plans.

For instance, sales has responsibility for working with intermediaries such as tour wholesalers and key customers. Both of these customers will ask for price discounts. Commitments for large blocks of rooms, airlines seats, autos, or ship berths will inevitably create problems with revenue or yield management departments. Marketing and sales plans cannot be effective if they are developed without sales forecasts and revenue projections by major market segments. If forecasts and revenue projections are made without the input of the revenue or yield management departments, conflict will occur.

Review again the objectives and subobjectives presented in Table 21-1. These call for average room rate objectives for each product class by season of the year. Using the concepts and practices of yield management, pricing objectives may be considerably enhanced to include weekly objectives and objectives by subsegments. Marriott Hotels uses a strategy known as *rational pricing*. This calls for "fencing" or placing restrictions on customer segments selected due to their perceived level of price elasticity. Fencing restrictions will immediately affect marketing and sales plans. Marketing managers are also advised to work with the reservations department during the planning process. Reservations often have considerable latitude to adjust prices and may account for a significant percentage of sales.

Pricing objectives and strategies affect every facet of marketing and sales. Sales promotions and advertising must support pricing decisions. The selection of appropriate target markets and the emphasis to be given each again depends on pricing.

Marketing and sales managers who view themselves at war with pricing managers are probably doomed to eventual failure. Top management in many hospitality companies has begun to realize that a 10% upward adjustment in rates can produce favorable profit results in excess of cost cutting or traditional marketing and sales strategies to increase the number of guests.

Pricing strategies are of great importance to chain restaurants and need to be constantly reviewed. As an example, food-service quality is the predominant influence on guest ratings for family, steak house, and casual dining restaurants. Family-price appeal enhances a guest's rating for a family restaurant chain, but not necessarily for a steak house or casual dining chain.[14]

A marketer who has gained experience in a family restaurant chain might make erroneous pricing decisions when hired by a steak house or casual dining chain. Despite the fact that restaurant chains may seem alike, different pricing strategies may need to be developed for each.

Product Strategies

Marketing has an important role to play in the improvement of existing products and the development of new ones. In some hospitality firms, marketing is expected to be heavily involved in the process; in others, marketing assumes only an advisory role; and, sadly, in others marketing is excluded from the process.

Hospitality products are rapidly changing. Las Vegas has been transformed from an adults-only playground to a destination resort for families in competition with Disney. Observers of the resort industry have concluded that "the traditional resort may no longer exist, or it may be just the core of a far more varied travel experience."[15]

Marketing professionals can exert considerable input and strategic direction when planning basic product changes as dramatic as those occurring within the resort industry. Marketing can also help to greatly enhance revenue from product changes as additions to the current product line. Hundreds or thousands of new product opportunities exist within most hospitality companies. The Alexis Park Resort in Las Vegas invented a "Cocktail Cruises," which is essentially a motorized cart driven by an employee who offers poolside guests drinks without moving.[16] The Opryland Hotel in Nashville uses a similar concept to sell hotel logo souvenir merchandise. "Whenever there is more to be sold than your customers are buying, profit potential is not being realized. Revenue boosting opportunities abound for the creative operator who is willing to offer facilities, services, and events that will attract customers and to train customer-contact employees to stimulate add-on sales and sales upgrades."[17]

The process of making product line changes requires the input and advice of many individuals and departments. Marketing may identify a need, such as the "neighborhood bakery" concept, for use in fast-food chains, but this new product concept directly affects production, finance, and human resources. When McDonald's, Burger King and Wendy's experimented with fresh biscuits or croissants, they discovered that these products prepared from scratch or frozen dough required additional working space, equipment, and employee training.[18]

Marketing plans must be written with available or likely available resources in mind. A common error in writing a marketing plan is to develop strategies that are probably highly workable but for which there is insufficient support. Another error is to assume that top management will not provide additional support regardless of the brilliance of the plan. Marketing plans can and must be sold to top management. A balance between mythical "pie-in-the-sky" plans and total acquiescence to perceived inflexibility of management is needed in any solid marketing plan.

**SECTION VII:
RESOURCES
NEEDED TO
SUPPORT
STRATEGIES
AND MEET
OBJECTIVES**

Personnel

Generally, the most costly and difficult resource needed to ensure success with marketing/sales strategies is personnel. Management commonly views the addition of personnel as unnecessary, impractical or unwise given current budgetary restrictions.

Obviously, there are times when the addition of salespeople, secretaries, analysts, and others is absolutely essential. Be prepared to justify this request and remember that many individuals, particularly salespeople, are not instantly productive. Training and recruiting costs must be considered with this resource request, as well as the time required by members of management to interview and work with these people.

The influence of the corporate culture cannot be overlooked in this process. Imagine a company such as the Ritz Carlton with the philosophy "We are ladies and gentlemen serving ladies and gentlemen." Fulfillment of this pledge with appropriate new personnel is demanding and may be time consuming.[19]

Ski resorts in Colorado initiated a drug testing program for all new hires, including seasonal personnel. This policy created extra time and expense because many potential employees failed this test and could not be considered for employment.

A marketing plan may need to specify the type of individuals required for a position if this is not described elsewhere, such as in company policies and procedures. Some hospitality companies operate under the philosophy that "We are always hiring excellent people." Marketing managers must plan personnel needs ahead for seasonal cost differences, such as a month with heavy trade show expenses or several weeks when brochures will be mailed to key customers and prospects. Budgets should reflect careful planning of resource use, such as temporary help on a week-by-week basis. A carefully constructed budget is simply a reflection of a well-thought-out marketing plan.

Equipment and Space

The acquisition of equipment such as PCs, fax machines, car phones, and audiovisual equipment may be viewed as necessary or helpful to achieve marketing objectives.

Space may also be a problem, particularly if new personnel are hired. Requests for additional space, such as a regional office or a storage area, are sometimes incorporated into the marketing plan.

Other Monetary Support

Monetary support not accounted for by salary, wages, and benefits must be carefully considered and included. This includes travel expenses, motivational costs, such as a trip to Las Vegas, and other monetary needs.

Research, Consulting, and Training

Hospitality companies often have need for outside professionals to assist with marketing research, such as focus groups; training, such as sales training; or consulting to provide objective outside appraisals and advice.

Miscellaneous Costs

This area should not be a source of slush funds. Many expenses, such as subscriptions to professional books and journals, may be included here.

Budgets

In larger organizations, corporate policies and procedures may direct marketing managers as to categories of expenses and items that may be included. Marketing managers of smaller companies may need to develop their own list and to use it each year as a guide to ensure that all essential resources are included.

Budgets should be established to reflect projected costs on a weekly, monthly, quarterly, and annual basis. This is not simply to make life easier for the finance/accounting area personnel next year.

SECTION VIII: MARKETING CONTROL

This discussion of marketing control presupposes that the sales plan is part of the marketing plan. This is not always the case; some hospitality organizations separate the two functions.

The essentials for writing a sales plan follow the same general procedure as those described for a marketing plan. A sales plan will not have need for all aspects of a marketing plan such as advertising or marketing research since these may be furnished by support departments. A sales plan will pay particular attention to the sales force and its objectives, and strategies to ensure that sales quotas are met and possibly exceeded.

Sales Objectives

Sales objectives must be established for each sales area, division, region, salesperson, and time period. The broad sales objectives previously discussed serve as the basis for establishing individual objectives. The sum of all sales objectives or quotas for members of the sales force must equal or exceed annual objectives.

One method of establishing annual sales objectives for the company is to begin with sales planning among members of the sales force. Each member should be expected to develop a list of all sales accounts currently served by that person, plus prospects for the coming year. From this, an estimate of potential sales by account and prospect will provide a means of forecasting next year's sales.

Management, beginning with the sales manager and ending with the general manager or other member of top management, then has the responsibility for critically examining these forecasts. Management seldom accepts the forecasts of the sales force without amending them, usually upward. This is known as bottom-up, top-down planning.

Management will amend sales-force forecasts for the following reasons:

1. Sales-force members often wish to protect themselves and give lower sales estimates than are actually possible.
2. The company has certain sales objectives that it expects based on the needs of the company.
3. Management may have access to marketing research information not available to the sales force.
4. Management may have a history of dealing with the sales force and realizes that forecasts are generally too high or too low by $X\%$.
5. Management may be willing to provide the marketing/sales department with additional resources that are unknown to members of the sales force.

A typical hotel sales forecast for a salesperson is shown in Table 21-2 on page 684.

Sales managers have the responsibility to work closely with their salespeople to ensure that sales forecasts are accurate. They must then provide a composite sales forecast for their department and present it to management.

Sales Forecast and Quotas

Eventually, all members of the sales force must be presented with sales quotas. Annual sales quotas should then be broken down into monthly and quarterly sales. Many sales managers and experienced salespeople break monthly quotas into weekly figures.

Sales managers have the responsibility for working with their salespeople to ensure that quotas are met or surpassed. It is important to continually evaluate sales results and develop corrective tactics if it appears that actual sales will not meet forecasts or quotas. Sales managers and salespeople who wait several months before evaluating actual sales against forecasts usually find it is too late to take corrective action.

Expenditures against Budget

It is also important for marketing/sales managers to continually monitor actual expenditures against budgeted figures. This too must be done on a regular basis.

Table 21-2

Example of a Sales Forecast for a Hotel Salesperson

SALESPERSON: JANET CHIN	SALES CURRENT YEAR			SALES ROJECTED NEXT YEAR		
MAJOR COMMERCIAL ACCOUNTS (KEY ACCOUNTS)	ROOM NIGHTS	REVENUE	AVG. RATE	ROOM NIGHTS	REVENUE	AVG. RATE
1.						
2.						
3.						
4.						
Other commercial accounts						
1.						
2.						
3.						
4.						
Major intermediary accounts						
1.						
2.						
3.						
4.						
Other intermediary accounts						
1.						
2.						
3.						
4.						
Airline accounts						
1.						
2.						
3.						
4.						
Other accounts						
1.						
2.						
3.						
4						
Prospects for next year						
1.						
2.						
3.						
4.						
Total accounts/prospects	Totals current year			Totals projected next year		

Periodic Evaluation of All Marketing Objectives

The role of marketing and sales managers is sometimes compared to an adult baby-sitter. A frequent comment made by individuals in these positions is that they spend a great deal of time simply making sure that individuals under their direction perform tasks in a timely fashion. There is much truth in this comment because a critical role of marketing/sales managers is to ensure that all objectives are met or exceeded on time.

Managers responsible for functions such as advertising, promotions, and marketing research have a responsibility to ensure that all tasks are performed on time. If a summer rates brochure is printed 3 weeks after the due date, chances are very good that the sales force may miss the opportunity to send or deliver this advertising medium to prospects and key accounts during the time that they make travel decisions. In turn, the sales force may fail to make summer sales quotas. All marketing/sales tasks are important. If this is not true, the task and the position should be eliminated.

Marketing Activity Timetable

One method commonly used by marketing/sales managers to ensure that tasks are completed on time is the use of a marketing activity timetable. This simple device lists major activities, the dates they must be completed, the individual responsible, and a space for checking whether the task has been accomplished.

Readjustments to Marketing Plan

Humans are incapable of devising a perfect marketing plan. Market conditions change, disasters occur, and many other reasons create a need to refine marketing plans. Generally, refinements should be made in the area of tactics, budgets, and timing of events, rather than in major objectives or strategies. Changes in tactics normally do not require top management approval and are viewed as the normal responsibility of marketing/sales managers.

Changes in major objectives such as annual sales volume and in major strategies always require approval by top management. Marketing/sales managers are advised to refrain from considering changes in major objectives and strategies. Top management will almost certainly view the necessity for change as a reflection of poor management by marketing/sales managers unless the cause was a disaster, such as a major fire in a hotel.

Never assume that a marketing plan is so logical that it will sell itself. A marketing plan must be sold to many individuals. These include the following:

- *Members of marketing/sales department.* Many individuals within the marketing/sales areas do not believe in planning. They view the process of developing, writing, defending, and using a written plan to be a waste of time. Comments are frequently heard such as "If management would just let us do our job and quit all this planning, the company would do better." This common sentiment may

SECTION IX: PRESENTING AND SELLING THE PLAN

exist due to poor experience with prior planning, fear of the process, or genuine ignorance about the benefits. Marketing/sales managers need the support of subordinates in the planning process. It is best to sell the benefits of the process, rather than to force acquiescence.

- *Vendors/ad agencies and others.* Outside organizations, such as advertising and marketing research agencies, need to be involved in the planning process. They must be made aware that their participation in the marketing planning process is an expected part of their responsibilities as team members.

- *Top management.* Top management must approve the annual marketing plan. It is seldom sufficient to write a lengthy plan, send it through company mail to top management, and expect an enthusiastic endorsement. Marketing/sales managers must sell the plan to members of management through meetings, such as a friendly luncheon and formalized presentations. Key members of the staff may be expected to participate in formal presentations. These appearances should always be treated with the same careful planning and professionalism that would be expected if a sales presentation were made to a key prospect for $2 million worth of business. Use professional presentation materials when appropriate, such as 35mm slides, computerized presentations, overheads, and bound copies of the annual plan. Prepare selected charts, graphs, and tables that are easy to understand and quickly reinforce key points.

SECTION X: PREPARING FOR THE FUTURE

The process of marketing planning is a continuum. The task is never ending. Marketing/sales managers must always be planning. In reality, the development of next year's marketing plan begins the day this year's plan is approved.

Data Collection and Analysis

Marketing plan development depends on the availability of reliable information. This task can always be improved. The process of data collection and analysis from internal and external sources continues each day. Marketing/sales managers must always be alert for methods to improve the process.

Marketing Planning as a Tool for Growth

A good marketing plan will assist your company and department to prosper and grow. What is not so obvious to many is that a good plan will also enable individuals to prosper and grow. This occurs in several ways.

- The participatory planning process allows individuals to understand the management process.
- Individuals learn to become team players during the process.

- Individuals learn to establish objectives and set timetables to ensure that they are met.
- The process of establishing realistic strategies and tactics to meet objectives is learned.
- Individuals who approach the planning process with a receptive mind and employ the marketing plan will usually find it enhances their professional career.

Many hospitality companies, such as Omni International Hotels, have developed a planning culture in which there is a respect for marketing planning as a positive process. This is a reflection of a corporate culture and top management support. Changes in top management sometimes mean that support for marketing planning will decrease or in some instances planning will be discouraged. A strong corporate culture that emphasizes and encourages planning within all levels of the company will be rewarded. Sometimes management becomes discouraged by the process, particularly when market conditions worsen as a new competitor threatens market share. It is at times like this that a corporate culture of planning provides stability and assurance of purpose and direction.

An example of the need for planning in poor economic times, rather than resorting to reactive "just-do-something" tactics, is offered by the California Country Club of Los Angeles. This club, like many others in Southern California, had a waiting list of potential members until 1993. By March of that year, the waiting list had changed to one of people wanting to leave the club.

Instead of panicking and grasping for an immediate marketing cure-all, the management of CCC pursued a process of market planning, starting with an analysis of the market and competitors. The planning process allowed CCC to recognize marketing opportunities, such as pricing strategies, including the elimination of golf-only fees. The need for a customer-directed policy of "Just Say Yes" was also discovered and implemented. These and other changes represented a complete turnover from previous policies and procedures, thus allowing the club to increase market share and revenue.[20]

A study of the process used by hotels to develop marketing plans has shown that "The most important features in the development of a marketing plan appear to be management participation and commitment at all levels, sufficient time for development, specific training in developing a marketing plan and tying incentives to the achievement of goals and objectives."[21]

In good times or bad, consistency in marketing planning pays good dividends for any hospitality company and its employees.[22]

Chapter Review

I. **Purpose of a Marketing Plan**
    1) Serves as a road map for all marketing activities of the firm for the next year.
    2) Ensures that marketing activities are in agreement with the corporate strategic plan.

3) Forces marketing managers to objectively review and think through all steps in the marketing process.

4) Assists in the budgeting process to match resources with marketing objectives.

II.   Tips for Writing the Executive Summary

1) Write it for top executives.

2) Limit the number of pages to between two to four.

3) Use short sentences and short paragraphs.

4) Organize the summary as follows: Describe next year's objectives in quantitative terms; briefly describe marketing strategies to meet goals and objectives; identify the dollar costs necessary as well as key resources needed.

5) Read and reread before final submit.

III. Corporate Connection

1) Relationships to Other Plans

  a) Corporate goals: profit, growth, and others

  b) Desired market share

  c) Positioning of the enterprise or of product lines

  d) Vertical or horizontal integration

  e) Strategic alliances

  f) Product-line breadth and depth

2) Marketing-related Plans also Include

  a) Sales

  b) Advertising and promotion

  c) Marketing research

  d) Pricing

  e) Customer service

3) Corporate Direction

  a) Mission statement

  b) Corporate philosophy

  c) Corporate goals

IV. Environmental Analysis

1) Analyze Major Environmental Factors

2) Competitive Analysis

  a) List the major existing competitors confronting your firm next year.

  b) List new competitors.

  c) Describe the major competitive strengths and weaknesses of each competitor.

3) Marketing Trends. Visitor trends, competitive trends, related industry trends.

4) Market Potential

  a) Market potential should be viewed as the total available demand for a firm's product within a particular geographic market at a given price. It is important not to mix different products into an estimate of market potential.

  b) Provide an estimate or guesstimate of market potential for each major product line in monetary terms such as dollars and in units such as room nights or passengers.

5) **Marketing Research**

   a) *Macro market information:* Industry trends, social-economic-political trends, competitive information, industry-wide customer data.

   b) *Micro market information:* Guest information, product/service information, new product analysis and testing, intermediary buyer data, pricing studies, key account information, and advertising/promotion effectiveness.

6) **Desired Action**

   a) List and describe the types of macro and micro marketing information needed on a continuing basis.

   b) List and describe types of marketing research needed on a one-time basis next year.

V. Segmentation and Targeting. The selection of segments is the result of

   1) Understanding who the company is and what it wishes to be.

   2) Studying available segments and determining if they fit the capabilities and desires of the company to obtain and secure them.

VI. Action: Segmentation and Targeting

   1) List and describe each market segment available for next year in as much demographic and psychographic detail as is available and practical for use in developing marketing strategies and tactics.

   2) Rank these segments in order of descending importance as target markets.

   3) Continue this process for different product lines that require individualized marketing support such as conference and ballroom facilities.

VII. Next Year's Objectives and Quotas

   1) Objectives

   ***a)* Quantitative objectives** are expressed in monetary terms, expressed in unit measurements, time-specific and profit/margin specific.

   ***b)* Other objectives:** Corporate goals, corporate resources, environmental factors, competitions, market trends, market potential, and available market segments and possible target markets.

   ***c)* Actions:**

   i) List primary marketing/sales objectives for next year.

   ii) List subobjective for next year.

   iii) Break down objective by quarter, month, and week.

   iv) List other specific subobjectives by marketing support area such as advertising/promotion objectives.

   2) Quotas

   ***a)* Based on next year's objectives**

   ***b)* Individualized**

   ***c)* Realistic and obtainable**

   ***d)* Broken down to small units,** such as each salesperson's quota per week

   ***e)* Understandable/measurable**

   3) Action Quotas. Break down and list quotas for sales departments, sales territories, all sales intermediaries, each sales intermediary, and each salesperson.

VIII. Action Plans: Strategies and Tactics

1) **Sales Strategies**
   a) **Prevent erosion of key accounts**
   b) **Grow key accounts**
   c) **Grow selected marginal accounts**
   d) **Eliminate selected marginal accounts**
   e) **Retain selected marginal accounts,** but provide lower-cost sales support
   f) **Obtain new business** from selected prospects

2) **Actions: Sales**
   a) **List the six major sales strategies and indicate how these will be accomplished in the coming year.**
   b) **List and describe all tactics that support major sales strategies.**

3) **Advertising/Promotion Strategies**
   a) **Select a blend or mix of media.**
   b) **Select or approve the message.**
   c) **Design a media schedule** showing when each media, including noncommissionable media will be employed.
   d) **Design a schedule of events.**
   e) **Carefully transmit this information to management.**
   f) **Supervise the development and implementation of advertising/promotion programs,** with particular care given to timetables and budget constraints.
   g) **Assure responsibility for the outcome.**

4) **Action: Advertising/Promotion**
   a) **Develop advertising/promotion strategies to meet marketing/sales objectives.**
   b) **Develop an advertising/promotion mix of appropriate media.**
   c) **Develop messages appropriate for the selected media to reach designed objectives.**
   d) **Develop a media and event schedule.**

5) **Pricing Strategy**
   a) **Carefully review pricing objective with departments** responsible for pricing planning and implementation.
   b) **Refine pricing objectives** to reflect sales and revenue forecasts.
   c) **Describe pricing strategies** to be used throughout the year.
   d) Make certain that **price, sales, promotion/advertising objectives are synchronized** and working in support of corporate objectives.

6) **Product Strategies**
   a) **Describe the involvement of the marketing department in major strategic product development.**
   b) **Describe the role of marketing in new-product acquisition or product development.**
   c) **Describe ongoing or planned product development programs for which marketing has responsibility.**

IX. Resources Needed to Support Strategies and Meet Objectives

1) Study and then list the **need for new marketing/sales personnel**, including temporary help during the next year.

2) Study and list the **type and amount of equipment and space** that will be needed to support marketing/sales.

3) Study and list the amount of **monetary support** needed next year.

4) Study and list the amount and type of **other costs** necessary next year.

5) Study and list the amount of **outside research, consulting, and training** assistance needed.

6) Prepare a marketing budget for approval by top management.

X. Marketing Control

1) Sales-force members often wish to **protect themselves and give lower sales estimates** than are actually possible.

2) The **company has certain sales objectives it expects** based on the needs of the company.

3) Management may have access to marketing research information not viewed by the sales force.

4) Management may have a history of dealing with the sales force and realizes that **forecasts are generally too high or too low** by x%.

5) Management may be willing to provide the marketing/sales department with **additional resources**.

XI. Presenting and Selling the Plan

1) Members of **marketing/sales departments**

2) Vendor/ad agencies and others.

3) Top management

XII. Preparing for the Future

1) The **participatory planning process** allows individuals to understand the management process.

2) Individuals learn to become **team players** during the process.

3) Individuals learn to **establish objectives** and set timetables to ensure that they are met.

4) Learning the process of **establishing realistic strategies and tactics** to meet objectives.

5) Individuals who approach the planning process with a **receptive mind** and employ the marketing plan will usually find that it enhances their professional career.

DISCUSSION QUESTIONS

1. What is the purpose of a marketing plan?
2. What is the relevancy of environmental factors to an annual marketing plan?
3. Why is the determination of market potential so important?
4. How should market segments and targets be described in a marketing plan?
5. Should marketing objectives be described in quantitative terms? Why or why not?
6. What is the relationship, if any, between marketing strategies and marketing objectives?
7. Is marketing control really necessary in a marketing plan or is it an optional managerial exercise?

KEY TERMS

Competitive analysis An analysis of the primary strengths and weaknesses, objectives, strategies, and other information relative to competitors.

Environmental factors Social, political, and economic factors that affect a firm and its marketing program.

Executive summary A short summary of the marketing plan to quickly inform top executives.

Market potential The total estimated dollars or unit value of a defined market for a defined product, including competitive products.

Market trends External trends of many types that are likely to affect the marketing in which a corporation operates.

Marketing objectives Quantitative and time-specific accomplishment measurements as to what is expected of a marketing program.

Quotas Quantitative and time-specific accomplishment measurements established for members of a sales force.

Segmentation analysis The process of examining various submarkets and selecting those most appropriate for a company.

Timetable Specific dates to accomplish strategies and tactics.

REFERENCES

1. MIRIAN JORDAN, "In India Demand for Mid-priced Hotels Soars and Companies are Charging in," *Wall Street Journal* (January 4, 1995), p. A8.

2. PERRY J. S. HOBSON, HENRY C. S. VINCENT, AND KYE-SUNG CHON, "Vietnam's Tourism Industry: Can It Be Kept Afloat?", *Cornell Hotel and Restaurant Administration Quarterly*, 35, no. 5 (October 1994), pp. 42–49.

3. RICHARD GIBSON, "Flight Caterers Widen Horizons beyond Airlines," *Wall Street Journal* (January 16, 1995), pp. B1, B8.

4. PETER WARREN AND NEIL W. OSTERGREN, "Marketing Your Hotel, Challenger of the 90's," *Cornell Hotel and Restaurant Administration Quarterly*, 31, no. 1 (May 1990), p. 58.

5. CARL K. LINK, "Developing a Market Plan: Lessons from the Inn at Plum Creek," *Cornell Hotel and Restaurant Administration Quarterly*, 34, no. 5 (October 1993), p. 35.

6. L. K. PREVETTE AND JOSEPH GIUDICE, "Anatomy of a Turnaround: The Los Angeles Biltmore," *Cornell Hotel and Restaurant Administration Quarterly*, 30, no. 3 (November 1989), p. 32.

7. C. STONES, "Marketing Women Are 36% of Stays in Key Markets," *Hotel and Restaurants International*, 22, no. 10 (October, 1988), pg. 84.

8. KEN W. MCCLEARY AND PAMELA A. WEAVER, "Gender-based Differences in Business Travelers' Lodging Preferences," *Cornell Hotel and Restaurant Administration Quarterly*, 35, no. 2 (April 1994), p. 51.

9. FRANCIS BUTTLE, "The Marketing-strategy Worksheet: A Practical Tool," *Cornell Hotel and Restaurant Administration Quarterly*, 33, no. 3 (June 1992), p. 57.

10. JOSEPH J. WEST AND MICHAEL D. OLSEN, "Grand Strategy: Making Your Restaurant a Winner," *Cornell Hotel and Restaurant Administration Quarterly* 31, no. 2 (August 1990), p. 77.

11. JEFFREY YOUNG, "Vashon Statement," *Forbes*, 153 (February 28, 1994), pp. 110–111.

12. JOSEPH J. WEST AND MICHAEL D. OLSEN, "Grand Strategy: Making Your Restaurant a Winner," *Cornell Hotel and Restaurant Administration Quarterly*, 31, no. 2 (August 1990), p. 77.

13. HANAM AYALA, "Mexican Resorts: A Blueprint with an Expiration Date," *Cornell Hotel and Restaurant Administration Quarterly*, 34, no. 3 (June 1993), p. 40.

14. MICHAEL S. MORGAN, "Benefit Dimensions of a Midscale Restaurant Chain," *Cornell Hotel and Restaurant Administration Quarterly*, 34, no. 2 (April 1993), pp. 44–45.

15. WILLIAM P. WHELIHAN, III AND CHAN KYE-SUNG, "Resort Marketing Trends of the 1990's" *Cornell Hotel and Restaurant Administration Quarterly*, 32, no. 2 (August 1991), p. 59.

16. CARL K. LINK, "Internal Merchandising: Creating Revenue Opportunities," *Cornell Hotel and Restaurant Administration Quarterly*, 30, no. 3 (November 1989), p. 56.

17. Ibid., p. 57.

18. REGINA ROBICHALLD AND MAHMOOD A. KHAN, "Responding to Market Changes: The Fast Food Experience," *Cornell Hotel and Restaurant Administration Quarterly*, 29, no. 3 (November, 1988), p. 47.

19. WILLIAM E. KENT, "Putting up the Ritz: Using Culture to Open a Hotel," *Cornell Hotel and Restaurant*

Administration Quarterly, 31, no. 3 (November 1990), pp. 16–24.

20. Jeffrey L. Pellissier, "Remarketing: One Club's Response to a Changing Market," *Cornell Hotel and Restaurant Administration Quarterly*, 34, no. 4 (August 1993), pp. 53–58.

21. S. Dev Chekitan, "Marketing Practices at Hotel Chains," *Cornell Hotel and Restaurant Administration Quarterly*, 31, no. 3 (November 1990), pp. 54–63.

22. For more on developing a marketing plan, see James C. Makens, *The Marketing Plan Workbook*, (Englewood Cliffs, N.J.: Prentice Hall, Inc., 1985) and James C. Makens, *Hotel Sales and Marketing Planbook*, (Pfafftown, N.C.: Marion-Clarence Publishing House, 1990).

Index